Pro Business Applications with Silverlight 5

Chris Anderson

Pro Business Applications with Silverlight 5

ISBN 978-1-4302-3500-2

ISBN 978-1-4302-3501-9 (eBook)

President and Publisher: Paul Manning
Lead Editor: Jonathan Hassell
Developmental Editor: Richard Carey
Technical Reviewers: Tony Champion, Ashish Ghoda
Editorial Board: Steve Anglin, Mark Beckner, Ewan Buckingham, Gary Cornell, Morgan Ertel, Jonathan Gennick, Jonathan Hassell, Robert Hutchinson, Michelle Lowman, James Markham, Matthew Moodie, Jeff Olson, Jeffrey Pepper, Douglas Pundick, Ben Renow-Clarke, Dominic Shakeshaft, Gwenan Spearing, Matt Wade, Tom Welsh
Coordinating Editors: Brent Dubi, Adam Heath
Copy Editors: Heather Lang, Vanessa Moore
Compositor: Mary Sudul
Indexer: SPi Global
Cover Designer: Anna Ishchenko

Distributed to the book trade worldwide by Springer Science+Business Media New York, 233 Spring Street, 6th Floor, New York, NY 10013. Phone 1-800-SPRINGER, fax (201) 348-4505, e-mail orders-ny@springer-sbm.com, or visit www.springeronline.com.

For information on translations, please e-mail rights@apress.com, or visit www.apress.com.

Apress and friends of ED books may be purchased in bulk for academic, corporate, or promotional use. eBook versions and licenses are also available for most titles. For more information, reference our Special Bulk Sales–eBook Licensing web page at www.apress.com/bulk-sales.

Any source code or other supplementary materials referenced by the author in this text is available to readers at www.apress.com. For detailed information about how to locate your book's source code, go to http://www.apress.com/source-code/.

For Olga. Thank you for being so patient with me during this long arduous process, and keeping me sane through it all. I'm looking forward to being able to spend a lot more time with you now.

—Chris

Contents at a Glance

Contents

About the Author

 **Chris Anderson** has been a professional developer for over 12 years, specializing in building desktop, web, and mobile business applications using Microsoft technologies for industries as wide ranging as accounting, property valuation, mining, the fresh produce industry, logistics, field services, sales, construction, and software development tools. He holds a Bachelor of Engineering in Computer Systems with a Diploma in Engineering Practice from the University of Technology, Sydney.

Chris is currently the Developer UX Architect at expanz (http://www.expanz.com). Currently specializing in Silverlight and WPF, Chris has spoken on this topic at conferences such as Code Camp Australia, TechEd Australia, Silverlight Code Camp Australia, REMIX Australia, and numerous Sydney Silverlight Designer and Developer Network (SDDN) meetings. Chris maintains a blog at http://chrisa.wordpress.com, and can be found on Twitter at http://twitter.com/christhecoder.

About the Technical Reviewers

 **Tony Champion** is a software architect with over 15 years of experience developing with Microsoft technologies. As the president of Champion DS and its lead software architect, he remains active in the latest trends and technologies. He is currently focused on the entire XAML stack from Silverlight to Windows Phone 7 and Windows RT.

Tony is a Microsoft Silverlight MVP and recipient of the Microsoft Community Contributor award. He is a director of the North Houston .NET Users Group and gives technical presentations across the country. Tony maintains several open source projects, participates on multiple forums, can be found on Twitter at `http://twitter.com/tonychampion` and has a blog at `http://tonychampion.net`.

When he is not in front of his computer, Tony spends his time at his home just outside of Houston, TX, with his wife and their 3 children.

Awarded with British Computer Society (BCS) Fellowship, **Ashish Ghoda** is founder and president of Technology Opinion LLC, a unique collaborative venture striving for strategic excellence by providing partnerships with different organizations and the IT community. He is also the director at a Big Four accounting firm.

As an accomplished author he authored 4 books and as a technical reviewer he reviewed 5 books on Microsoft platform. He also teaches at NJIT and UMUC.

Acknowledgments

I'd like to start by thanking the members of the Apress team whom I worked closely with throughout the writing process, for their guidance and encouragement. I'd like to thank Jonathan Hassell, and in particular Brent Dubi who kept me upbeat as I worked through the dead of night by randomly sending me songs to listen to while I worked. My great thanks also go to my technical editor Tony Champion, who came on board rather late in the process, but expertly picked up numerous issues I had missed, and made some great suggestions.

I would like to thank Greg Harris (www.GregMHarris.com) who donated his time to review several chapters, and provided me with extensive feedback. His feedback with the previous edition was a huge help, and once again he volunteered his time to reviewing several chapters - his contributions have been invaluable. I would also like to thank Peter Gfader who allowed me to pick his brain on duplex communication strategies.

My thanks go to all the Silverlight bloggers who provided solutions to difficult problems. I've credited you in the text when you've provided information that helped me along my way. I also would like to thank the readers of the previous edition who provided feedback such that I could improve this edition, including Ben Hayat, Josh Sommers, and Marc Tempkin.

Finally, on a personal note, I'd really like to thank my girlfriend Olga. She has been very patient with me as I worked feverously on this book, with not much time for anything else. She kept me sane when it all started to get too much, and I feel really blessed to have her in my life.

Introduction

Silverlight is a web-based platform from Microsoft that can be used to build Rich Internet Applications (RIAs). Of the many new possibilities it enables, one of its key focuses is as a platform for building business applications. Community support for the technology has been overwhelmingly positive, and Microsoft has gone on to use it within a number of other products such as LightSwitch, Windows Azure (in its portal), and Microsoft Lync, as well as offering it as means of developing Windows Phone 7 applications.

If you've previously developed Windows Presentation Framework (WPF) applications, you'll already have a good foundation for developing Silverlight applications. If you have only been exposed to Windows Forms and ASP.NET development, Silverlight development will no doubt be a brave new world—one with a steep learning curve, but ultimately, the benefits make the initial effort worthwhile. However, with this book to help you through your journey, you should find a lot of pain taken out of the learning curve; this book will guide you in the right direction while you build your first business application in Silverlight.

Who This Book Is For

This book covers not just Silverlight as a technology but also the important concepts in designing and developing business applications. From structuring your application to actually implementing features, it covers the complete development life span for a business application in Silverlight.

To follow along with this book, you should know your way around Visual Studio well, have a reasonable degree of familiarity with C# and its features (such as generics and LINQ, although experience with a similar language such as Visual Basic or Java may suffice), be comfortable with designing and querying databases, and have a good understanding of object-oriented design (OOD). Some prior business application development experience (or understanding of what building a business application entails) is an advantage but isn't absolutely necessary, as I will discuss the reasoning behind many of the concepts unique to business application development as needed. However, you may need to refer to alternative sources for more information when the concepts are particularly complex and detailed. For example, a good understanding of design patterns (such as those described in the influential book *Design Patterns*, by the authors typically referred to as the Gang of Four [Addison-Wesley, 1994]) is important when designing business applications, but complete coverage of these in the context of designing Silverlight applications is really a whole book in its own right.

About This Book

This is not a book simply about Silverlight as a technology, and it isn't about covering Silverlight from end to end. Silverlight features such as streaming video, Deep Zoom, 3D graphics, animations, sounds, and others that are not generally core requirements in business applications will not be covered. This book specifically targets the needs of those designing and developing business applications using Silverlight as a development platform. That said, you may be well versed in the process of business application design and merely be interested in how to apply your knowledge to developing business applications in Silverlight—this book caters to you too. You may even pick up a few new design tidbits as you go!

You may have noticed that many books, web articles, and presentations take a rather simplistic view when discussing building business applications in Silverlight, and these techniques rarely hold up to scrutiny in real-world projects. Instead of just giving you all the pieces and leaving you to fit them together yourself, this book is designed to act as your guide when creating your own business application, leading you through the difficult problems you will encounter and providing one or more solutions for each problem. Business applications involve more than simply retrieving some data and displaying it on the screen—this book will allow you to peer into all the nooks and crevices that represent good business and application design practices.

This book is designed to be read from start to end rather than simply being a reference guide. It will lead you through the process of creating an end-to-end Silverlight business application. Note that some of the Silverlight-specific lessons in early chapters are not designed to be put into immediate use, as they won't necessarily reflect all the recommended development practices in real-world projects, but are provided merely as a means of easing you into the world of Silverlight development.

■ **Note** For example, the Model-View-ViewModel (MVVM) design pattern commonly used in Silverlight and WPF business application development is not covered until the second half of this book. You will generally want to use this pattern in your applications, but the early chapters forgo this pattern in their examples, as implementing it requires a wide array of Silverlight knowledge that you will not have gained as yet. Despite its later position in this book, incorporating this design pattern into your project should not be an afterthought. Therefore, this book should not be considered a step-by-step guide, but an all-encompassing guide to all the concepts important to building business applications in Silverlight.

After completing this book, you will have gained the knowledge that you need for designing robust business applications and how to implement these techniques with a Silverlight-based project. While it would be impossible to cover each and every concept that could be employed when designing and developing business applications, this book will cover those that are the most important for developing a well-structured business application.

Unfortunately, exploring the complete myriad of scenarios that you may encounter in your application requirements simply isn't possible, nor is it possible to cover every possible solution to a problem. For example, due to the wide array of means for a Silverlight application to communicate with a server, covering them all and doing them justice would be impossible. For this reason, I chose to cover one technology in depth. For most end-to-end business applications in Silverlight (which is the primary focus of this book), RIA Services is your best option for handling communication between the Silverlight client and the server; therefore, this book will primarily focus on using that technology as the framework for this task.

■ **Note** If you decide RIA Services is not suitable for your needs, don't despair—the functionality covered in this book is not solely dependent on RIA Services, and there will still be large amounts of information useful to your project. We will take a brief look at creating and consuming plain WCF too.

You won't need to use every concept taught in this book in your own applications, because at times, some concepts may be excessive (depending on the size and type of project you are working on) or inappropriate. These concepts will be noted with the scenarios that they are most suitable for to help you make an informed choice.

Introducing Silverlight

Microsoft has a number of different platforms for building applications, with Silverlight being the newest addition to the family. Let's take a look at what Silverlight is and how it fits into the big picture of software development platforms.

What Is Silverlight?

It's important at this stage to establish exactly what Silverlight is and what it isn't. Silverlight is a Rich Internet Applications (RIA) platform. RIAs could be considered a cross between desktop applications and web applications. They run within the user's web browser (with some exceptions) and use a browser plug-in to run the application within a (mostly) sandboxed environment. Silverlight bridges the gap between web applications (which can be deployed easily and run on multiple platforms) and applications that are native to the host operating system (applications that are considered to be rich). RIAs are not a new concept, although not all have been a success for various reasons. Adobe Flash is a notable exception, having achieved huge popularity over the last decade.

You will find a number of parallels between Silverlight and Adobe Flash. Both run as browser plug-ins, providing a platform for self-contained applications running on the client (as opposed to being dependent on a server controlling the application). Of course, there are numerous differences between the two technologies, but if you take a look at the space in which Silverlight is competing, Adobe Flash (combined with Adobe Flex) is without doubt Silverlight's biggest competitor.

In the .NET world, Silverlight's closest relative would be Windows Presentation Framework (WPF). Both use Extensible Application Markup Language (XAML) to define their user interfaces, and Silverlight essentially started as a web-deployed subset of WPF. If you are familiar with WPF, you will be able to write Silverlight applications reasonably easily (and vice versa), despite a number of features in each that are not available in the other (although they are becoming more aligned with each of their releases).

Market Penetration and Reach

Silverlight is installed on approximately 60–70% (depending on your data source) of Internet connected devices (see www.statowl.com and www.riastats.com, two sources falling in that range). At the time of this writing (prior to Silverlight 5's release), most of these installs are Silverlight 4. In comparison, the nearest competitor to Silverlight, Adobe Flash, has an almost ubiquitous market penetration (over 95% of Internet-connected devices, according to the same sources), but the market penetration of the much younger Silverlight is still reasonably high and growing.

One of the biggest concerns regarding Silverlight's (and any RIA's) reach is its penetration on mobile devices (such as phones and tablets). The emergence of the iPad and its ensuing popularity has many businesses looking toward developing applications that can also run on the iPad. However, Apple has steadfastly refused to allow the Adobe Flash runtime environment on iPads and iPhones (to much controversy), and Silverlight unfortunately suffers the same fate (preventing these technology's reach to these devices). Even Windows Phone 7, whose applications are generally built using Silverlight, cannot run Silverlight applications delivered via the browser (it only runs Silverlight applications specifically compiled for the phone). Apple promotes HTML5 as their answer for rich web applications over plug-ins, and we'll discuss the topic of HTML5 vs. plug-ins later in this chapter.

For in-house business applications, the issue of Silverlight's market penetration on desktop PCs is of little concern, as the Silverlight runtime can be incorporated into an organization's standard operating environment (SOE) and deployed automatically to all the machines throughout that organization. However, for public-facing applications, you should be aware that not all client machines will have the Silverlight runtime installed. Deploying both the Silverlight runtime and your application effectively to users is detailed in Chapter 17.

Focus

Silverlight's initial focus was toward media applications (directly targeting Adobe Flash's biggest market)—particularly in the area of video, vector graphics, and animations. From version 3, it turned its focus heavily toward business applications and is arguably the most powerful of the competing RIA platforms in this respect. With advanced support for data binding, a rich set of standard and third-party controls, and the RIA Services framework, it has also become a viable platform for many business applications. Having matured in support for both media and business applications, Silverlight 5 has started focusing on improving its graphics and gaming capabilities.

Compatibility

The Silverlight browser plug-in works with all major browsers (Internet Explorer 6+, Firefox 3+, Chrome 4+, Safari 3+), and across the two most popular operating systems—Microsoft Windows and Apple Mac OS (Intel x86–based machines only). The Moonlight project (by the team from Novell working on Mono, a cross-platform, open source implementation of the .NET Framework) can be used to run Silverlight applications on Linux, but unfortunately, its releases lag behind the Microsoft releases. Silverlight 2 compatibility was reached with Moonlight 2, and a preview of Moonlight 4 (compatible with Silverlight 4) was released in early 2011. However, with the sale of Novell to AttachMate, the future of Moonlight and the Mono project is still uncertain at the time of this writing.

Windows Phone 7

The Windows Phone 7 operating system has a Silverlight-based user interface, meaning that most applications for it are written in Silverlight. Applications need to be written specifically to run under this operating system, because it doesn't run standard Silverlight applications (i.e., you can't browse to an application in the web browser and run it). Much of the code is identical between "desktop" and mobile Silverlight. However, applications written for the phone are essentially Silverlight 3 based (the Mango release due late in 2011 will be Silverlight 4 based), resulting in the phone version lagging somewhat behind the desktop version. Despite this, you should be able to port much of the same code you write for your business applications targeting Silverlight 5 to a Windows Phone 7 version. This opens many exciting new possibilities for sharing a large portion of your code base (and development knowledge) between both your standard and mobile applications.

The Silverlight Runtime

The Silverlight runtime is a 6.6MB download (small by today's standards) including a subset of the .NET Framework and a full implementation of the Common Language Runtime (CLR) engine. Packaging these frameworks has the huge advantage of enabling you to write code in any .NET language, including (but not limited to) C# and Visual Basic—meaning that you can develop applications in exactly the same language that you are used to working with. Application code is compiled into assemblies, which (along with XAML files and other resources) are combined into a XAP file. This file can then be downloaded to the client and executed within the plug-in.

■ **Note** Silverlight applications cannot make use of assemblies that target the full .NET Framework, but assemblies targeting Silverlight can be used in applications that target the full .NET Framework.

Out-of-Browser (OOB) Experiences

Although Silverlight applications are generally run from within a browser, from version 3 of Silverlight onward, they can be run outside of the browser as if they were standard Windows or Macintosh applications. An icon can be placed on the desktop and/or the Start menu to open the application, and the application can automatically update itself when a new version is available on the server.

Sandboxing

Silverlight was initially designed as a completely sandboxed platform (that is, it had no permissions to interact with anything outside its container), making running any Silverlight application very safe, without the worry of whether the application would do something untoward to a user's machine. However, as Silverlight became more and more popular, developers started wanting to do more things with it than were possible within its sandboxed nature. Silverlight 4 introduced the ability for OOB applications to be installed with elevated trust permissions. This enabled the application additional access to the host machine and opened up a new range of possibilities to Silverlight applications (but only when the application is being run in OOB mode). This included access to the Component Object Model (COM), which, being a Windows-only feature, somewhat broke the truly cross-platform nature of Silverlight but enabled developers to access many Windows features and integrate more tightly with other applications and the operating system. Silverlight 5 takes this OOB experience to another level by enabling applications requiring elevated trust to be run inside (not just outside) the browser and to allow access to the low-level platform invocation service calls (known as P/Invoke) so native Windows code can be called from Silverlight.

Tracing the Evolution of Silverlight

Silverlight has matured rapidly since its release. Let's take a look at how it has evolved over that time.

Before there was Silverlight, there was WPF. Introduced with version 3 of the .NET Framework, WPF targeted the rich client market, pioneered the use of XAML to define user interfaces, and demonstrated the new possibilities that XAML could enable. WPF applications could be deployed via a web browser (as XAML browser application, better known as an XBAP), but they required the full .NET Framework to be installed and could be run only under Windows. This is where Silverlight stepped in.

Silverlight 1: September 2007

Microsoft started working on a project called WPF Everywhere (WPF/E), which was essentially designed to be a web-deployed subset of WPF that had its own runtime and ran within a browser plug-in. It used XAML to define the user interface and required you to write code in JavaScript. It had little in the way of controls and was predominantly focused on media-type applications (video, animations, and vector graphics). WPF/E became Silverlight 1.

Silverlight 2: October 2008

With Silverlight 2, developers really started to become interested in Silverlight. It now had the CLR, a subset of the .NET Framework, and a decent set of standard controls, enabling developers to start writing RIAs without needing to learn a new language.

Silverlight 3: July 2009

Silverlight 3 focused on developing business applications. It included richer data binding support, the DataForm control, validation controls, and the ability to run Silverlight applications OOB. In addition, although it was in beta, Microsoft simultaneously released a new framework called RIA Services, which provided a powerful and structured means for Silverlight applications to communicate with servers and pass data between them—making business applications easier to develop in Silverlight.

Silverlight 4: April 2010

Whereas Silverlight 3 immediately made creating business applications viable in Silverlight, Silverlight 4 smoothed many of the rough edges. It introduced printing capabilities (resolving a big complaint by business application developers of a missing feature), implicit styling (making theming your application a lot easier), webcam and microphone support, elevated trust when running outside the browser, COM access, toast notifications, additional data binding capabilities, and more.

Silverlight 5: Late 2011

With its fourth version, Silverlight had really matured as a business application platform. Thus Silverlight 5 has moved on and turns its attention toward graphics and gaming capabilities, including introducing a 3D graphics API. It did include, however, quite a number of new features useful for business application developers, such as support for vector printing, custom markup extensions, implicit data templates, elevated trust inside the browser, multiple windows when running outside the browser, and the ability to set breakpoints on bindings in XAML.

What Can Silverlight Bring to Your Business Application?

You could develop your business applications on numerous platforms, so you may be wondering why you should develop in Silverlight. The biggest benefits are undoubtedly the following:

- The deployment model is easy—applications are delivered over the Web via a browser.
- There's no need for the full .NET Framework, just a small runtime.
- Applications can be written in your favorite .NET language (C#, Visual Basic, etc.).
- Applications can be run on multiple platforms (namely both Windows and Mac).
- It's faster to develop and richer than HTML–based applications.

Combined, these benefits have created a platform that many developers hope can solve the various problems that they face every day. However, many more benefits can be gained by using Silverlight over other technologies.

If you are used to developing HTML–based applications (for example, using ASP.NET), you'll gain the following benefits:

- You are no doubt used to having your applications render differently between browsers and operating systems. The big advantage of an RIA like Silverlight is that it renders in *exactly the same way* in each browser and operating system. This saves a lot of time testing and solving cross-browser issues.

- Silverlight applications are richer than HTML applications and (arguably) faster to develop.

- Because Silverlight is a rich client, users don't have to deal with constant postbacks to the server, and the applications feel more responsive to the user.

- With the CLR and a subset of the .NET Framework running on the client, you don't need to write in JavaScript, and you can reuse code from other projects in your Silverlight application.

- Applications can be run offline.

- Applications can be detached and run like standard applications.

- The tooling for Silverlight development (i.e., Visual Studio and Expression Blend) is very good (arguably some of the best development tooling available for any platform), enabling you to create rich applications very easily.

If you are used to developing rich client applications (such as with Windows Forms), you'll gain the following benefits:

- Silverlight's use of XAML to define user interfaces enables you to create unique and flexible user interfaces that have extensive support for data binding, vector graphics, and animations.

- RIA Services makes designing applications that communicate with a server clean and easy.

- You will be able to share code with Windows Phone 7 and WPF applications.

- Users can be set up with both the Silverlight runtime and your application with ease in a matter of minutes.

As you can see, Silverlight brings a lot to the table, and this book intends to demonstrate how it can lead to brilliant business applications. However, Silverlight is not always the best choice in some scenarios—let's take a look at those now.

Deciding When to Use Silverlight

Choose the technologies you use wisely; don't just choose a technology because it's "cool" or for the sake of it—you need to justify your choice and ensure that the platform will meet the needs of the business and that the business is obtaining a reasonable return on investment (ROI). As with any technology, Silverlight is not the perfect platform for all development projects. It has strengths and weaknesses that need to be weighed, evaluated, and considered in relation to the problem domain before you commit yourself (and your business!) to that technology. You need to select the most appropriate platform to suit the requirements of the project, focusing in particular on the reach and the richness that your application requires.

Comparing to HTML-Based Applications

In comparison to HTML-based applications, a big issue is Silverlight's reach. HTML-based applications can be run almost everywhere. Desktop PCs (including Linux) and Internet-capable mobile devices all display HTML (although not identically at times), meaning that the reach of these applications is almost 100 percent. For machines that *can* run Silverlight (Windows, Mac OS, and to an extent Linux), the user is required to install a plug-in, which isn't always possible on locked-down machines in corporate or government settings (without getting the IT department involved). In addition, many businesses are requesting that their applications run on an iPad or Android-based tablet—neither of which can run Silverlight applications. This issue of reach is one of the key reasons for the current push toward HTML5 applications, rather than applications that require a browser plug-in like Silverlight.

Comparing to Rich Desktop Applications

In comparison to rich desktop applications, Silverlight applications have restricted functionality and features. Only a subset of the .NET Framework is available to Silverlight applications (although it is a fairly reasonable subset), and the capabilities and features of the controls are somewhat limited too, so you will find that some things tend to be more difficult (or impossible) to do in mobile Silverlight than in its desktop counterpart. For example, Silverlight was designed as a sandboxed platform, not for integrating with other applications, the underlying operating system, or hardware devices. That said, the elevated trust features introduced in Silverlight 4 (and enhanced in Silverlight 5) enable you to get around many of these limitations. The downsides are that elevated trust features are not always available, and the user will either have to install your application or specifically permit elevated trust inside the browser to enable them. In addition, elevated trust features such as access to COM and P/Invoke calls are only available on Windows, which starts to limit the cross platform nature of your applications. If you need to integrate deeply with the host operating system, often a rich desktop application platform (such as WPF) might be more suitable for your needs.

These are the primary considerations you will have to take into account before choosing Silverlight as a platform. Determine the current and potential future requirements of your application, identify any features that conflict with Silverlight's limitations, and then decide whether Silverlight is really the best-suited platform for your needs.

Comparing to Other Microsoft Platforms

Let's compare Silverlight with the other core platforms Microsoft provides and identify the primary pros and cons of each.

WPF

The following considerations apply when comparing Silverlight and WPF:

- Shared features

    - Both use XAML for defining user interfaces (with Silverlight essentially a subset of WPF).

    - Both can be deployed via a browser as sandboxed applications.

- Pros of choosing WPF

    - WPF has minimal restrictions, and it is not sandboxed (unless deployed via a browser as an XBAP without full trust turned on).

    - WPF has the power of the full .NET Framework behind it.

- Cons of choosing WPF

    - WPF requires the full .NET Framework to be installed on the machine.

    - WPF is limited to running on Windows only.

    - WPF does not have the hype and support from the community and Microsoft that Silverlight has.

Windows Forms

Here's how Windows Forms measures up against Silverlight

- Shared feature

    - Both can be downloaded via a browser (although Windows Forms applications cannot be run within the browser like Silverlight applications) and update themselves automatically when a new version is available (using click-once with Windows Forms applications).

- Pros

    - Windows Forms has minimal restrictions and is not sandboxed.

    - It has the power of the full .NET Framework behind it.

    - It is very easy to develop (no need to understand XAML).

    - It is mature, having been around since the inception of the .NET Framework.

    - No graphical skills are required to design user interfaces with the standard style of Windows applications.

- Cons

    - It requires the full .NET Framework to be installed on the machine.

    - It is limited to running on Windows only.

    - It is an aging platform with waning support.

    - Data binding capabilities aren't as rich.

    - User interfaces aren't as flexible and don't have the same styling capabilities.

ASP.NET

ASP.NET and Silverlight compare as follows:

- Shared feature
    - Both ASP.NET and Silverlight are available via a web browser (for Silverlight applications, the Silverlight plug-in must be installed first).

- Pros
    - ASP.NET runs on almost all Internet-connected devices.
    - It does not require a plug-in to be installed, just a web browser.
    - It has the power of the full .NET Framework behind it (on the server side only).
    - It is mature, having been around since the inception of the .NET Framework.

- Cons
    - It requires the full .NET Framework to be installed on a Windows server running IIS (although the Mono project provides a potential alternative, enabling ASP.NET applications to run on Linux servers).
    - Client-side code must be written in JavaScript, requiring developers to learn that language.
    - It is completely sandboxed and does not permit integration with the host operating system.
    - It can render differently between browsers, requiring a lot of testing.
    - Data binding capabilities aren't as rich.
    - It isn't as rich or responsive (although Ajax and jQuery can help).
    - It cannot run with elevated trust to integrate with other software on the users' machines or hardware.

Comparing to Adobe Flash/Flex

With Adobe Flash/Flex being Silverlight's biggest competitor, it's worth comparing the two (at a high level).

- Similar features
    - Both are RIA platforms deployed via a web browser.
    - Both can run applications outside of the browser (Silverlight with no additional requirements, Flash with Adobe Air).
    - Both use XML–based markup languages to define their user interfaces.

- Pros:
    - The Flash runtime is installed on almost all Internet-capable PCs.

- The core Flash runtime is a smaller download (3MB vs. 9MB), although running outside the browser requires the Adobe Air runtime (which is 12MB).

- Cons:

  - Code must be written using ActionScript, a JavaScript derivative that is not as capable or popular as managed code languages (e.g., there's no equivalent to LINQ and generics) and is specific to Flash/Flex (i.e., code can't be reused with other applications).

  - It requires an additional download to run applications outside the browser (Adobe Air), and applications must be packaged separately to run in this runtime (whereas the same Silverlight application will run both within and outside the browser).

Comparing to HTML5

HTML5 is often seen as one of the biggest alternatives to Silverlight when building business applications these days, despite not even being ratified as a standard yet. HTML5's greatest strength will be its reach, and of course, when choosing a development platform, ideally you'd like your applications to be run by as many people and on as many devices as possible. However, as a general rule, the wider a platform's reach, the less rich it becomes (and the more restrictions are placed on it, preventing interaction with the host operating system and limiting its possibilities). For example, WPF is a very rich platform and is not restricted from interacting with the host operating system. However, it will only run on computers running Windows. On the other hand, HTML 4 has a very broad reach, with most (if not all) Internet-connected devices available today capable of rendering HTML 4. However, HTML 4–based applications are not generally considered rich, and they operate within a sandbox and thus have very limited interaction with the host operating system.

HTML5 will enable rich web applications to be developed without the use of plug-ins, but these applications will still operate within a sandbox. In addition, different browsers tend to render HTML slightly differently and have differing levels of support for various HTML features. Many people are still using older browsers (such as Internet Explorer 6, a well known offender for not following HTML standards and rendering websites differently to other browsers), and although users may be able to load your application, there's no guarantee that their browser will have the features your application uses or that it will render your application in the same way that you designed it (unless you test your application in every possible browser). Thus the broad reach of HTML applications can actually have a negative impact on your development, increasing the amount of development time and testing required. A big push is being made by browser makers to support the HTML5 standard exactly, so any HTML5 application should render in these browsers and behave in exactly the same way. How long it will be until the browsers support the entire standard (once ratified) and users upgrade their browser to one of these is yet to be seen.

■ **Note** You can detect HTML5 features in browsers by using a JavaScript library such as Modernizr and implement a fallback when using a feature not supported by the browser. However, this adds additional complexity and testing to your development, and you don't need to deal with such issues when using Silverlight.

In addition to its expected future reach, another of HTML5's strengths will be the development community that has started to spring up around it and will continue to grow. Silverlight's development community is one of its greatest strengths, but the number of HTML5 developers will no doubt outstrip Silverlight developers over the coming years as HTML5 gains traction.

Here are the pros for choosing HTML5 over Silverlight:

- HTML5 applications will have a far greater reach than Silverlight applications in the future, running on both desktop and mobile devices.

- HTML5 applications don't require a plug-in to run (though they do require a modern browser).

HTML5 has many shortcomings in comparison to Silverlight. The HTML5 standard is still not fully implemented by the major browsers, and more importantly, it's not even a standard yet; it still has not been ratified by the World Wide Web Consortium (W3C). Parts of the specification are still a work in progress, and completion and ratification of the standard are not expected for quite some time. Also, despite the future expected reach of HTML5 applications, Silverlight applications currently have a far greater reach than HTML5 applications (i.e., the Silverlight plug-in is currently far more widespread than browsers supporting HTML5).

Cons for choosing HTML5 include the following:

- HTML currently has a limited and fractured reach.

- The tooling for HTML5 is currently very immature, reducing developer productivity.

- You'll be living somewhat on the bleeding edge, until a larger development community grows (for support) and more open source projects pop up to make various common tasks easier.

- HTML5 applications are confined to a sandbox (i.e., unable to interact with the host operating system) limiting the possibilities of your application.

- You'll need to perform much more testing on your applications to ensure that they behave correctly in all browsers and on devices (i.e. write once, test everywhere).

- The automatic reach of HTML5 to devices means that you'll need to design your application to support multiple form factors for them to be useable on those devices, including phone, tablet, and PC form factors.

- HTML5 will be a "lowest common denominator" technology, where only features that will work everywhere that it's supported can exist in its feature set. This is an inherent tradeoff to enable its intended extensive reach.

Here are some of the key reasons you might like to use Silverlight over HTML5:

- Silverlight applications render and behave exactly the same way regardless of the browser they're run in (minimizing the amount of testing that you need to do before running your application in multiple environments).

- Silverlight applications can run in older browsers (such as Internet Explorer 6), an especially important issue when your applications need to run in corporate environments that have standardized on a browser that doesn't support HTML5.

- Silverlight code is compiled and can be obfuscated, helping to protect your intellectual property.

- Silverlight will continue to be updated with new features regularly, whereas the HTML standards are very slow to evolve.

- You can leverage your existing .NET coding skills and use your favorite .NET language when programming the front end of your application.

- The language you use in your front end can be the same as the language you use on the server.

- Although Silverlight generally operates in a sandbox (by default), it has the ability to break out of that sandbox and interact with the host operating system.

- The tooling for Silverlight development and debugging (primarily Visual Studio and Expression Blend) is very mature, which leads to greater developer productivity.

In conclusion, if you're choosing between Silverlight and HTML5 for your business application, you'll have to weigh many factors. One technology is not better than the other, and you'll most likely ultimately end up making a tradeoff between the richness and the reach of your application. HTML5 is often promoted as a solution to all the world's development problems, but as you can see from the points in this section, this is clearly not the case. You need to make sure that you choose the right platform for the project at hand, and Silverlight still has the upper hand in many scenarios.

▨ **Note** Take a look at the excellent white paper by Colin Eberhardt, detailing his comparison of Flex, Silverlight, and HTML5. You can get it at `www.scottlogic.co.uk/blog/colin/2011/05/flex-silverlight-html5-time-to-decide/`.

Introducing Business Applications

Business applications—sometimes also referred to as line-of-business (LOB) applications—are core applications critical to the running of a business. Businesses the world over rely on software to function, much of which has been custom developed to capture and support the unique processes and needs of the businesses—without this software, they would not be able to function effectively, if at all.

Business applications tend to have the following key features in common:

- The ability to access and maintain data in a central data store

- Client/server communication

- A workflow providing a structured means of entering/modifying data

- A user interface providing an efficient means of entering/modifying data

- Business rules

- Data validation rules

- The ability to obtain information from the system (via reports)

- Authentication and authorization of users

Each of these facets of business applications will be investigated in this book, with information on how to implement each in Silverlight to produce a complete end-to-end business application.

Summary

Microsoft has positioned Silverlight primarily as a platform for developing business applications, and the platform has become one of the best around for doing so, despite some strong competition. It evolved very quickly during its early life, but now that it has matured as a platform, the pace of releases has slowed somewhat. It provides an excellent balance between richness and reach, enabling you to develop rich applications that can run on both the Windows and Mac operating systems. Let's now get started learning how to build business applications in Silverlight.

Getting Started with Silverlight

To start developing with Silverlight, you need to set up your machine with a number of applications and tools. This chapter will walk you through that setup. Then, we'll take a look at the Silverlight project templates available to you, create a Silverlight application using one of these templates, and explore its structure.

Collecting the Required Tools

The best place to find all the tools you need to get started with Silverlight is the Microsoft Web Platform Installer 3.0 which you can download here: www.microsoft.com/web/downloads/platform.aspx. The Web PI (for short) is a free tool that enables you to easily download and install components of the Microsoft Web Platform. You will find the tools that you require for Silverlight development in the Tools category on the Web Platform tab. Alternatively, you can visit the Get Started page on the official Silverlight web site, at http://silverlight.net/GetStarted, which has links to the required downloads.

The following subsections give a breakdown of the various tools required (or recommended) for Silverlight development and what each does.

■ **Note** The following sections give you a starting point for what you should have installed to begin developing Silverlight applications; however, these are not all the tools you'll eventually need—additional tools will be introduced as required throughout this book.

Visual Studio

Theoretically, you don't need an integrated development environment (IDE) to develop Silverlight applications; that scenario is only for the most hardcore developers. The Professional edition (or higher) of Visual Studio 2010 is your best option by far as an IDE for Silverlight development, as it has no limitations to constrain you. However, for those of you on a budget, Visual Web Developer 2010 Express (containing a subset of Visual Studio functionality and available for free) provides an alternative IDE for building Silverlight applications. For the sake of simplicity, any instructions throughout this book will refer to the action to be taken in the professional edition of Visual Studio 2010.

■ **Note** Visual Studio 2008 does not support Silverlight 4 or 5 development—you will need to upgrade to Visual Studio 2010 if you haven't done so already.

Expression Blend 5 and SketchFlow

Expression Blend could be described as an IDE for designing XAML user interfaces and animations, although its capabilities have been extended from version 3 onward to also include the ability to edit code. You could technically build an entire Silverlight application using only Expression Blend, but the tool is not designed to be used as such, and Visual Studio is much better suited for this purpose (Expression Blend is designed to be used primarily for designing and building user interfaces, rather than for writing code).

Expression Blend is targeted toward designers (user interface, user experience, and graphic designers), rather than developers, with a focus on helping support and enhance the developer/designer workflow. This book is primarily focused on a developer audience; therefore, we'll spend most of our time in Visual Studio when designing user interfaces. Designing user interfaces is much easier in Visual Studio 2010 than it was in Visual Studio 2008, which essentially had no user interface designer. However, it is not as feature rich or powerful as what you'll find in Expression Blend (particularly when it comes to creating animations). If you're serious about creating nontrivial user interfaces, Expression Blend will be a very useful tool in your arsenal.

SketchFlow is a prototyping tool within Expression Blend and is great to use as part of the user experience design process. With it, you can map out the flow of your screens and their layouts, and it can actually generate a Silverlight (or WPF) project for you.

Expression Blend is not a free tool—it must be purchased as a stand-alone product or as a part of Expression Studio. A 60-day trial is available from the Microsoft web site if you want to try out the tools before committing your hard-earned money. Expression Design (also a part of Expression Studio) can also be a useful tool to have (as a vector drawing program), but neither tool is essential for Silverlight development.

■ **Note** Both Visual Studio and Expression Studio are included in the MSDN Premium and the Expression Professional subscriptions (the Expression Professional subscription is a new type of MSDN subscription specifically targeting designers and web developers), which you may find to be the most cost-effective means of obtaining these tools. These subscriptions also include licenses for Office, Windows, and various other Microsoft software products.. Startup software businesses less than three years old can take advantage of the Microsoft BizSpark program, which provides you an MSDN subscription (with all these tools) and numerous other benefits for $100 when you *leave* the program—a fantastic way to get the tools for no initial investment. Details and eligibility requirements can be found at www.microsoft.com/bizspark.

Silverlight 5 Tools

Visual Studio 2010 comes with support for Silverlight 3 out of the box, and Visual Studio 2010 Service Pack 1 adds Silverlight 4 support, but you will need to install the Silverlight 5 Tools in order to develop applications targeting Silverlight 5. The Silverlight 5 Tools download includes the Silverlight 5 SDK, the Silverlight 5 developer runtime, WCF RIA Services, and support for Silverlight 5 in Visual Studio. Once these tools are installed, you will find new project templates available in Visual Studio for creating Silverlight applications.

WCF RIA Services

WCF RIA Services provides a prescriptive pattern and framework for creating end-to-end Silverlight applications. The WCF RIA Services code generator projects your business object model on the server onto your Silverlight application along with shared business logic, and it provides the infrastructure that enables methods on the server to be called by your Silverlight application. We'll take a thorough look at WCF RIA Services in Chapters 4 and 5. This is now included as a part of the Silverlight 5 Tools installer, but you can install an associated toolkit containing additional features (most of which are still under development) if you wish.

Silverlight Toolkit

The Silverlight Toolkit is a free and open source project hosted on CodePlex, developed and maintained by Microsoft. This is an ongoing project that adds greatly to the available controls that you can use in your Silverlight project. The Silverlight 5 SDK contains only basic user interface controls (TextBox, Button, Canvas, Grid, and so on), so the Silverlight Toolkit provides a raft of more advanced controls, such as TreeView, Calendar, and Charting, among many others.

Blacklight is a similar open source project hosted on CodePlex, but unlike the Silverlight Toolkit it is a community-run project and does not attempt to overlap with the controls available in the Silverlight Toolkit. It's not listed on the Silverlight.net Get Started page, but you can get it here: www.codeplex.com/blacklight.

SQL Server 2008 R2 Express Edition

Business applications (as described in the introduction) are data-centric applications—hence they (almost always) interact with some sort of database. Silverlight applications can't read or write to a remote database directly—you need to provide a set of services to expose the data from the server to client applications. This means you aren't limited to a set number of supported databases—using Silverlight has no bearing on which database you can use. As long as you can communicate with the database in a standard .NET application, you can provide a way to allow your Silverlight application to communicate with it. For the purposes of this book, we'll be using SQL Server 2008 R2 Express Edition as our database of choice, because it's free and reasonably full featured. In most business settings, you would probably want to use the full SQL Server 2008 R2 product; the code provided in this book will work that edition without any changes. Earlier versions of SQL Server would be acceptable too. You can download SQL Server 2008 R2 Express Edition at www.microsoft.com/express/sql/download. Ensure (at a minimum) that you choose the Runtime with Management Tools option.

Silverlight Spy (and .NET Reflector)

Silverlight Spy is not a mandatory tool to obtain, but it's certainly recommended because it is extremely handy when debugging your Silverlight application. Silverlight Spy, created by Koen Zwikstra of First Floor Software, allows you to inspect the internals of a Silverlight application (including its file structure, XAML visual tree, and styles), monitor its memory and processor usage, and monitor its network connector (among many other features). It also integrates with .NET Reflector (a tool from Red Gate Software) to decompile the assemblies within the XAP file and view their code. From a debugging perspective, this tool is invaluable. Early versions of Silverlight Spy were free, but with its version 3 release, it became a commercial product with a price attached. A free edition with a limited number of features was later released (with integration with .NET Reflector being one of the features not included). .NET Reflector was a free tool (with a separate commerical version available), until version 7 was released in March 2011. At this point, Red Gate decided to pull the free version, leaving only the commercial one. Other free decompilers have popped up, but only Silverlight Spy integrates with .NET Reflector (at the time of this writing). Because both tools can save you a lot of time, and with their purchase prices being quite reasonable, they are both worthwhile tools to purchase.

You can download and purchase Silverlight Spy at http://silverlightspy.com/silverlightspy and .NET Reflector at www.red-gate.com/products/reflector.

Working with the Silverlight Project Templates

Once you have installed the Silverlight 5 Tools, you will find a number of project templates have been added to Visual Studio's New Project dialog under the Silverlight category (as shown in Figure 1-1).

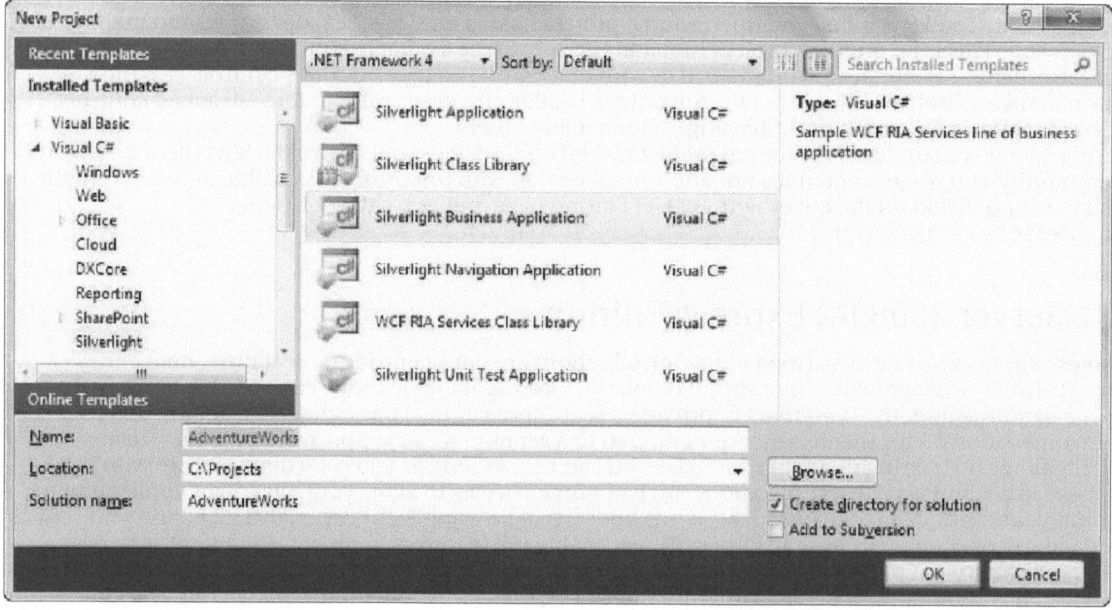

Figure 1-1. The New Project window

Let's take a look at when and how you would use each of these project templates.

Silverlight Application

Silverlight Application is a basic project template for Silverlight projects; it simply includes a single blank view for the user interface. Back in Silverlight 2, this was the only project template available to create a Silverlight application, and it didn't provide much to get you started (it was just a blank slate). This project template might still be useful when creating widgets, games, banners, advertisements, and video players, for example—where an initial project infrastructure isn't particularly required. For business applications, on the other hand, you will find the Silverlight Navigation Application or Silverlight Business Application project templates that were introduced with Silverlight 3 a much better starting point.

Silverlight Navigation Application

Silverlight 3 introduced a navigation framework that essentially provides an application framework for Silverlight applications. This project template implements the navigation framework and provides a good starting point for building applications that contain multiple views. We'll take a look at the features of the navigation framework in Chapter 3.

Silverlight Business Application

The Silverlight Business Application template is similar to the Silverlight Navigation Application template, but with a number of additional features. It automatically assumes you want a web application project and links the Silverlight project and the web application project with WCF RIA Services. It includes login/registration screens and some built-in authentication functionality. In addition, all strings are stored in resource files so that the application can be easily localized and support different languages. This will be the template you will usually base your business applications on.

■ **Note**   If you don't see the Silverlight Business Application project template in the New Project dialog, ensure that you have selected version 4 of the .NET Framework in the framework selection drop-down.

Silverlight Class Library

A Silverlight Class Library project is essentially the same as a standard class library project but is marked for use in Silverlight projects (because Silverlight has its own version of the .NET Framework). You might use this project template if you were creating a custom control library, reusable code library, or business logic library, for example.

■ **Note**   Silverlight projects *cannot* reference assemblies targeting the full .NET Framework. However, projects targeting the full .NET Framework *can* reference Silverlight assemblies. Therefore, if you need to share a class library assembly between both types of projects, your best option is to create a Silverlight class library. Alternatively, you could create two projects (one for each project type) and link the files between them—a technique that may be useful if you have additional functionality not supported by Silverlight that you want to add to the class library targeting the full .NET Framework.

WCF RIA Services Class Library

The default scenario for WCF RIA Services assumes that you will create your business objects to be shared between the server and the client within your web project, and these will be replicated within your Silverlight project. However, this scenario doesn't create an ideal separate "middle tier" where your business objects are contained within a separate assembly that can then be reused between applications. This is where the WCF RIA Services Class Library project template comes in. When you use this template, it creates not one but two separate projects (one for the server and the other for the client) that are linked. Also, the automatic business object replication is done between these two projects rather than your Silverlight and web projects, providing much more flexibility and enabling a much better structure for your solution. This will be discussed further in Chapter 4.

■ **Note** As with the Silverlight Business Application template, the WCF RIA Services Class Library template will not appear in your project templates if you do not have version 4 of the .NET Framework selected in the framework selection drop-down.

Silverlight Unit Test Application

The Silverlight Unit Test Application project template is installed with the Silverlight Toolkit. This creates a project that you can use to unit test your Silverlight application with the Silverlight Unit Test Framework.

⚙ Workshop: Creating a Silverlight Project

Let's create a Silverlight project, using the Silverlight Business Application project template.

1. In Visual Studio, select File ➤ New ➤ Project.

2. Select the Silverlight subcategory from under the Visual C# category, in the Installed Templates tree (see Figure 1-2).

3. Select Silverlight Business Application from the list of project templates.

4. Give the project a name. We will be using AdventureWorks, because later workshops in this book will build on this one and connect to Microsoft's AdventureWorks sample database.

5. Click OK.

Clicking OK will create a solution containing two projects: AdventureWorks (a Silverlight application) and AdventureWorks.Web (a web application). The web application hosts both the Silverlight application and any associated services that might serve data to it, and it is set as the start up project for the solution.

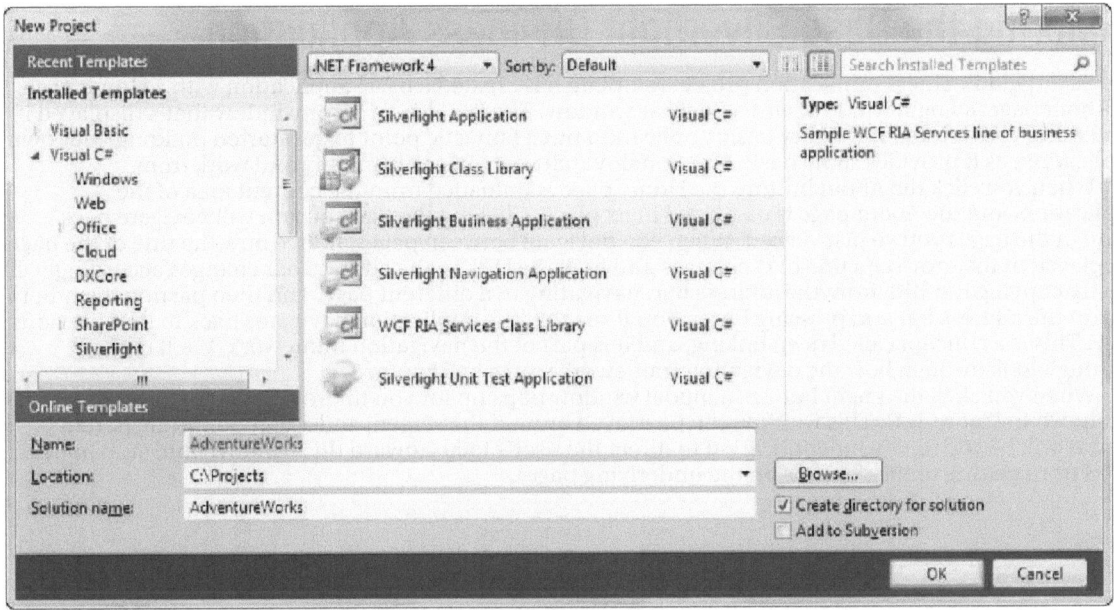

Figure 1-2. The New Project dialog in Visual Studio

■ **Note** Silverlight applications don't need to be hosted in an associated web application. When a Silverlight application is the startup project in a solution, a HTML page will be automatically generated to host it, and it will run in the browser using a local file URL. However, if you're exposing services to the Silverlight application (and most business applications do), an associated web application to host both them and the Silverlight application will usually be necessary.

You can now compile and run the project without making any changes to it. As Figure 1-3 shows, you get a reasonable starting point for your application.

Figure 1-3. User interface created by the Silverlight Business Application project template

Let's now explore the content of this application and its underlying structure.

Exploring the Base Silverlight Business Application

The Silverlight Business Application project template has created a basic application with a Home page, an About page, a Login window, and a Register window. There's also an Error window that's displayed if something goes wrong. It is a very basic application but a fantastic point to get started building your own application, as it provides some basic functionality that you can easily modify and work from.

When you click the About button, the Home page is unloaded from the content area of the application, and the About page is displayed in its place. Clicking the Back button will navigate back through the pages you've just viewed. When you navigate between pages, notice how the title of the page (displayed in the browser's title bar) changes and how the URL in the address bar changes accordingly. If you try copying the URL from the address bar, navigating to a different page, and then pasting the other URL in the address bar and pressing Enter, you'll see that the application navigates back to that previous page. This is a concept called deep linking, and it is part of the navigation framework. We'll take a thorough look through how the navigation framework works in Chapter 3.

When you click the Login button, a modal window pops up for you to provide your login credentials (as shown in Figure 1-4). This window can be moved around the screen, and a dark semitransparent overlay will be added to your application to direct the user's focus toward this window (and stop mouse clicks from getting to the controls on the underlying page).

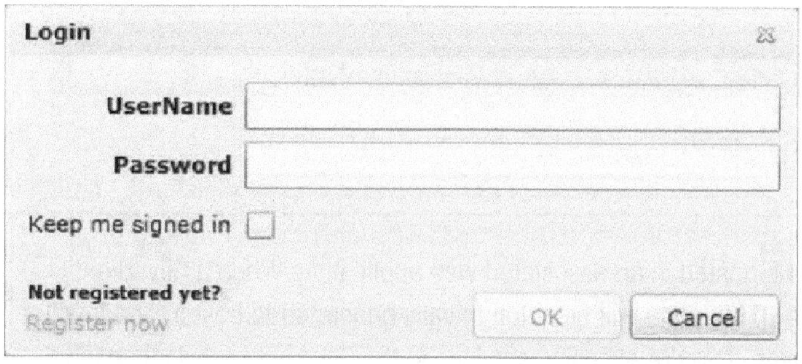

Figure 1-4. The Login window

Clicking the Register Now link in this window will display a window allowing you to register yourself as a new user (see Figure 1-5). This is an example of the DataForm control in action, which is very useful for creating forms for data entry in Silverlight that include data validation (discussed further in Chapter 7).

If you put your mouse cursor over the little information symbol next to the password box, a tooltip will appear providing information about the type of validation that is applied to that field. Try entering a password that doesn't conform to the password strength rules or entering an invalid e-mail address. See how the field validates the data entered and notifies you if the validation fails? The label for that field turns red, and a red border (with a red triangle at the top right) will appear around the text box. If you put your mouse over the red triangle or move the focus to the field, a tooltip will appear indicating what validation rule was broken.

Register yourself as a user. When you do so, a SQL Server database will be created on the server with the ASP.NET membership tables, views, and so on, and attach to it as a user instance. You'll find the database file in the App_Data folder in the web application project (you might need to click Show All Files to see it because it might not have been added to the project).

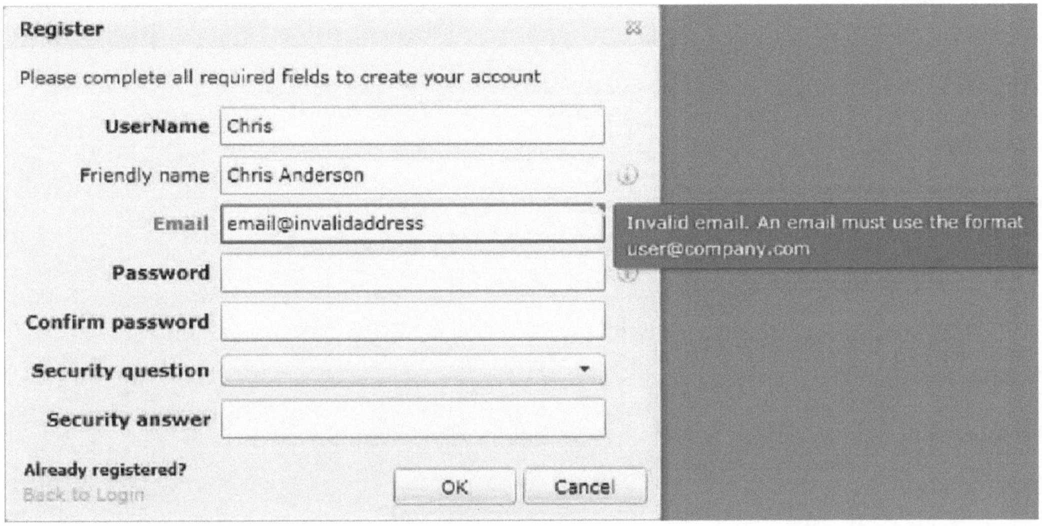

Figure 1-5. The Register window with validation errors

■ **Note** In Chapter 8, we'll configure the application to store user data in the AdventureWorks database instead.

While it's creating the user on the server, a little window will pop up (as shown in Figure 1-6) with an animation to show that the application is doing something (a type of wait indicator). This is an example of the BusyIndicator control, which you can use to notify users that something is happening and that they need to wait for it to complete.

Once the new user has been created, the user interface of the application changes to hide the Login button and show a Logout button instead, along with a welcome message displaying the friendly name of the logged-in user (for example, "Welcome Chris Anderson").

In summary, you can see that the default project template provides us with a business application–like user interface framework (with styling), some sample pages, and some security functionality. As you can see, this is pretty solid base on which to build your business application in Silverlight.

Figure 1-6. The BusyIndicator control

■ **Note** By default, the process of debugging the web project will use the Visual Studio Development Server (code named Cassini) to act as a host for the web site, but you can change this to run under IIS (or IIS Express) by opening the Web tab in the project properties and changing the settings as required.

Exploring the Initial Silverlight Project Structure

Going back to our solution structure in Visual Studio, let's now see what it took to get this amount of application functionality and explore a Silverlight project. Figure 1-7 shows the structure of the default solution in the Solution Explorer window created from the Silverlight Business Application project template.

As you can see, the project template has created a sizeable solution structure, containing two projects—a Silverlight project and a Web Application project. Note that the web project is the startup project in the solution—*not* the Silverlight application (this was touched on earlier). The web page hosting our application is requested by the client, which the browser reads, then downloads and runs the Silverlight application. The Silverlight project is linked to the web project in the solution to support this process. Because the client needs to download the application from the web site, the compiled Silverlight application must be available for download from an accessible location within the site. By default, this location is the ClientBin folder. If you expand this folder (after the solution has been compiled for the first time), you'll find the Silverlight application (a XAP file). XAP files are discussed later in this chapter.

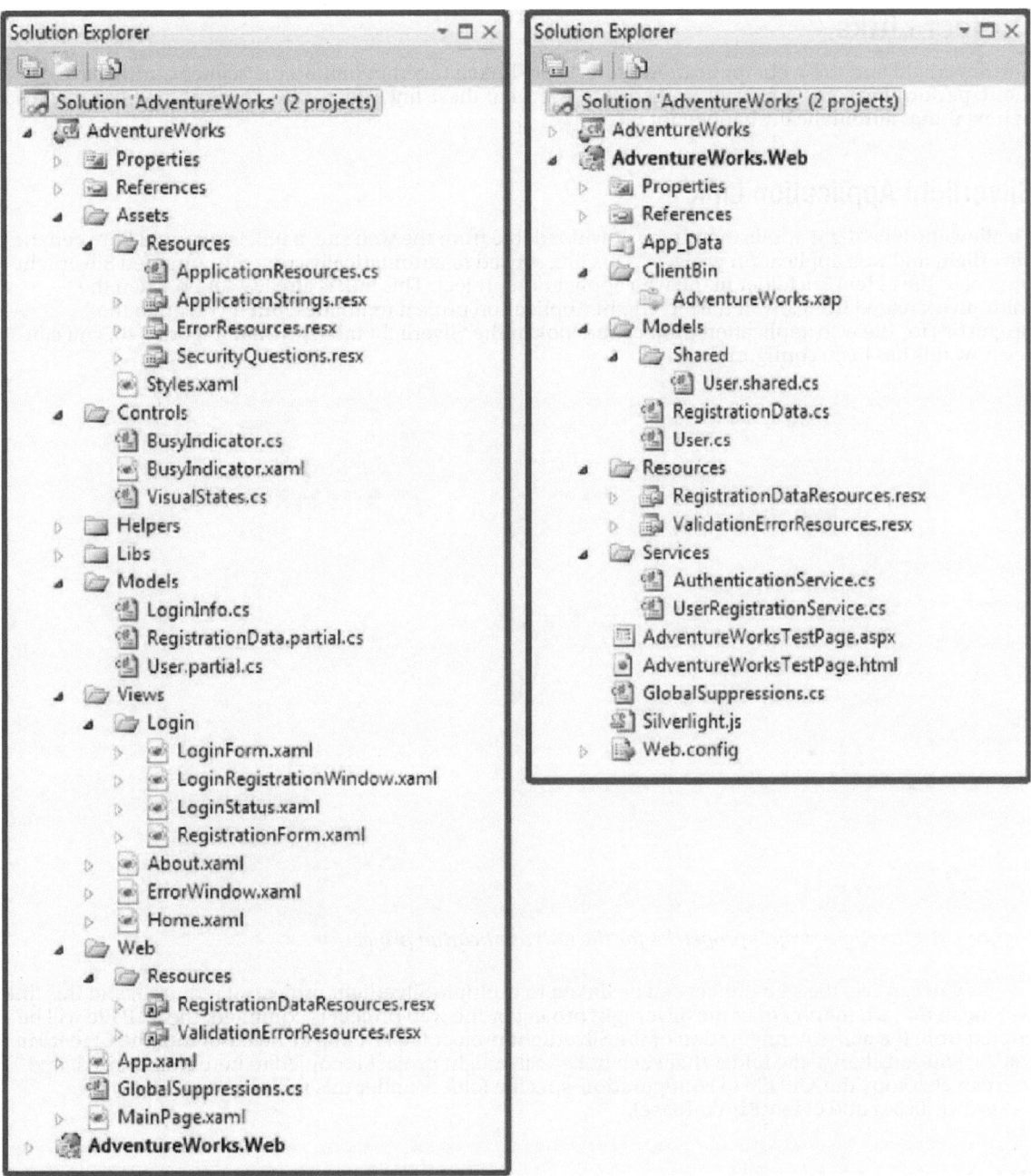

Figure 1-7. The initial Silverlight Business Application project structure (client/server)

Project Links

The Silverlight and the Web Application projects are linked together behind the scenes during development, performing some magic for us. Let's explore what these links do, to take some of the mystique away of how things automatically happen for us.

Silverlight Application Link

To allow the Silverlight application to be downloadable from the web site, a link is required between the Silverlight and web application projects. This link is used to automatically copy the compiled Silverlight project to the `ClientBin` folder in the web application project. This link is already set up when the solution is created from any of the Silverlight Application project templates, but if you open the properties for the web application project and look at the Silverlight tab (shown in Figure 1-8), you can see how this has been configured.

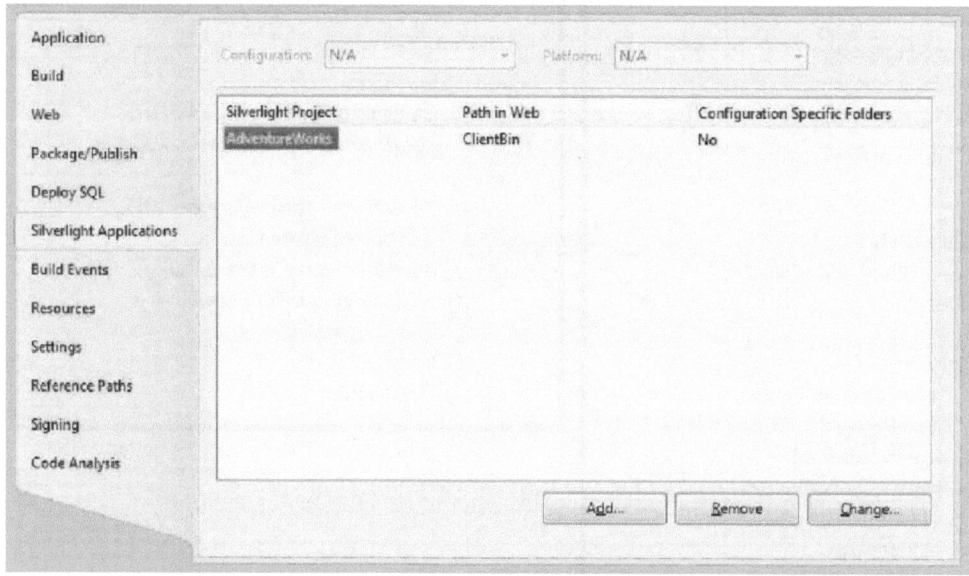

Figure 1-8. *Silverlight project properties for the web application project*

As you can see, the web project can be linked to multiple Silverlight projects if required, and this link will mean that whenever *either* the Silverlight project or the web project is compiled, the XAP file will be copied from the active configuration of the Silverlight project (i.e., Debug or Release) into the `ClientBin` folder. You can change the folder that each linked Silverlight project is copied to here if so desired, and you can also copy the XAP file to configuration-specific folders under this folder (e.g., `ClientBin\Debug` and `ClientBin\Release`).

RIA Services Link

RIA Services (discussed in Chapters 4 and 5) generates code in the Silverlight project to facilitate communication with the services you define in the web application project. If you click the Show All

Files button for the Silverlight project in Solution Explorer, you will see a hidden folder called Generated_Code. This folder contains all the code that WCF RIA Services automatically generates to communicate with the services defined in your Web project (as illustrated in Figure 1-9).

Figure 1-9. The Generated_Code hidden folder

For the code generator to know which project to generate code into, a link is required between the Silverlight project and the web application project. Open the properties for your Silverlight project, and take a look at the Silverlight tab (shown in Figure 1-10).

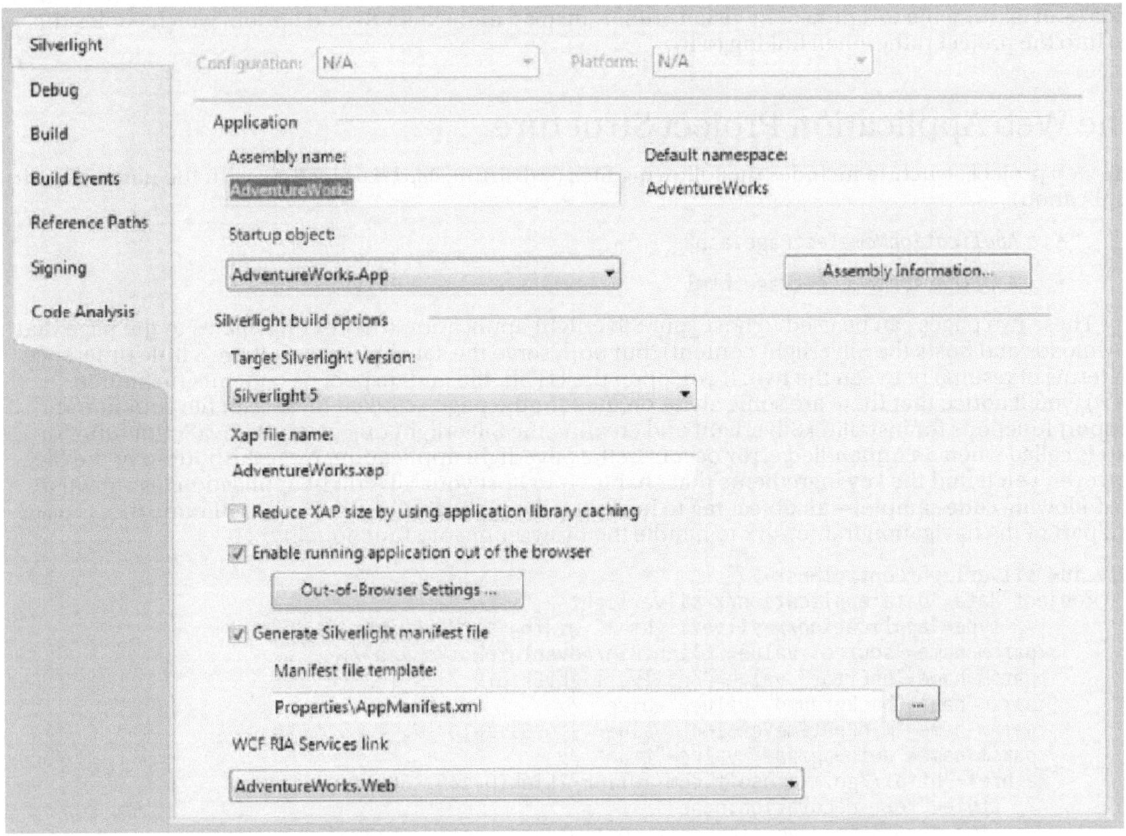

Figure 1-10. Silverlight project properties for the Silverlight project

At the bottom is the WCF RIA Services link field and a drop-down box to select the project to generate corresponding WCF RIA Services client-side code from; this defaults to the Web project in the solution. When services are defined in the linked project, corresponding code will be generated in the Silverlight project to interface with them. Again, this will all be described further in Chapter 4.

■ **Note** Never modify any of the generated code, as these changes will be overwritten the next time the project is compiled.

Linked Resource Files

There are also some linked resource files between the web application project and the Silverlight project. The link enables the resource files, which are used to store localized strings such as validation error messages, to be maintained in one location and shared between the two projects. These are simple file links. A file link acts as a shortcut to a file. File links are created by selecting the Add As Link option when adding an existing file to a project in Visual Studio (instead of the default Add option, which copies the file into the project rather than linking to it).

The Web Application Project Structure

The web project structure includes the following files (substitute *ApplicationName* with the name of your application):

- *ApplicationName*TestPage.aspx
- *ApplicationName*TestPage.html

These two pages can be used to host your Silverlight application (the user navigates to the page that downloads and hosts the Silverlight content), but both serve the same purpose—there's little difference (in terms of results) between the two. If you open the HTML file and inspect its contents (in Source view), you'll notice that there are some styles defined for the page, a linked JavaScript file containing support functions for installing Silverlight and creating the Silverlight object, and a JavaScript function that is called when an unhandled error occurs in the Silverlight application. Near the bottom of the file, however, you'll find the key ingredients that enables it to host your Silverlight application (as shown in the following code sample)—an object tag to host the Silverlight application, and an IFrame that is used as a part of the navigation framework to handle the browser history functionality:

```
<div id="silverlightControlHost">
    <object data="data:application/x-silverlight-2,"
            type="application/x-silverlight-2" width="100%" height="100%">
        <param name="source" value="ClientBin/AdventureWorks.xap"/>
        <param name="onError" value="onSilverlightError" />
        <param name="background" value="white" />
        <param name="minRuntimeVersion" value="5.0.61118.0" />
        <param name="autoUpgrade" value="true" />
        <a href="http://go.microsoft.com/fwlink/?LinkID=149156&v=5.0.61118.0"
            style="text-decoration:none">
            <img src="http://go.microsoft.com/fwlink/?LinkId=161376"
                alt="Get Microsoft Silverlight" style="border-style:none"/>
        </a>
    </object>
```

```
<iframe id="_sl_historyFrame"
        style="visibility:hidden;height:0px;width:0px;border:0px">
</iframe>
</div>
```

The `object` tag loads the Silverlight runtime and passes it the URL for your Silverlight application to run (among various other parameters). If the Silverlight runtime isn't installed on the client machine, an image will be displayed instead, pointing the users to where they can download the runtime. This will be discussed further in Chapter 17.

The `Models` folder (shown in Figure 1-11) contains a couple of files containing data transfer object (DTO) classes (`User` and `RegistrationData`) that will be used to pass data between the server and the client. The `Shared` subfolder in the `Models` folder contains a file (`User.shared.cs`) containing code to be shared between the server and the client (for which WCF RIA Services will generate corresponding code in the Silverlight project). Sharing code in this manner will be discussed in Chapter 4.

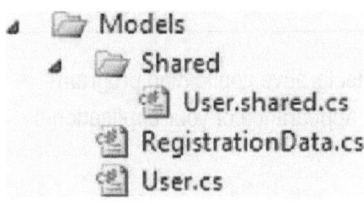

Figure 1-11. The Models folder

The `Resources` folder (shown in Figure 1-12) contains resource files (`RegistrationDataResources.resx` and `ValidationErrorResources.resx`) that are used to define strings used for localizing the application. As described earlier, these files are defined in this project and shared with the Silverlight project as linked files.

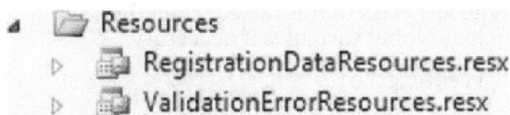

Figure 1-12. The Resources folder

The `Services` folder (shown in Figure 1-13) contains files for two domain service classes (`AuthenticationService` and `UserRegistrationService`) that are used to implement the server-side security functions for the application. These classes expose data and operations to the client using the WCF RIA Services framework. Again, this will be discussed further in Chapter 4.

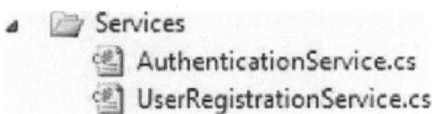

Figure 1-13. The Services folder

The `GlobalSuppressions.cs` file is a project suppression file that defines which messages should be suppressed when using the Code Analysis feature of Visual Studio and should not appear in the violation list. The easy way to add violations to this file is to right-click the message in the Error List window, select the Suppress Message(s) menu item, and select the In Project Suppression File item from its submenu. Note that the Silverlight project also contains a GlobalSuppressions.cs file.

The Silverlight.js file contains various JavaScript functions to help install the Silverlight runtime on the client (if it isn't already installed), and help instantiate a Silverlight object in an HTML or ASPX page. Because this file has been "minified" to reduce its size when downloading, it is more or less unreadable, but in any case, you should have no reason to modify it and should leave it as is. If you do want to read or modify it, you can format it to be more readable using an online tool such as the Online Javascript Beautifier (http://jsbeautifier.org).

The Silverlight Application Project Structure

Let's move on to the structure of the Silverlight application. You'll notice that most of the files are actually XAML files—many of which have a corresponding code-behind file (having a .xaml.cs extension).

■ **Note**   XAML files are XML-based files that are defined as "markup files for declarative application programming." One of the primary functions of XAML files is to define the structure and appearance of your application's user interface. We'll cover XAML in depth in Chapter 2.

In the root of the application there are two XAML files: App.xaml and MainPage.xaml. These are two very core files in a Silverlight project, and each has a vastly different purpose.

App.xaml can contain the resources (such as styles) available globally in your application (in the XAML file) and handles applicationwide events (in the App.xaml.cs code-behind file). The App class inherits from Application and is set as the startup object for the application. You could say this class effectively represents the application itself. There is a Startup event (and an Application_Startup event handler already defined, as shown in the following code snippet) on the App class that is raised when the application starts; this class allows you to initialize things such as global variables if necessary.

```
private void Application_Startup(object sender, StartupEventArgs e)
{
    // This will enable you to bind controls in XAML to
    // WebContext.Current properties.
    this.Resources.Add("WebContext", WebContext.Current);

    // This will automatically authenticate a user when using Windows
    // authentication or when the user chose "Keep me signed in" on a previous
    // login attempt.
    WebContext.Current.Authentication.LoadUser(Application_UserLoaded, null);

    // Show some UI to the user while LoadUser is in progress.
    this.InitializeRootVisual();
}
```

As you can see, the Application_Startup event handler calls the InitializeRootVisual method (shown following), which configures the root node of the Silverlight application's visual tree. This configuration is discussed in Chapter 2 but in summary, represents the hierarchy of objects forming the user interface.

```
protected virtual void InitializeRootVisual()
{
    AdventureWorks.Controls.BusyIndicator busyIndicator =
        new AdventureWorks.Controls.BusyIndicator();
    busyIndicator.Content = new MainPage();
    busyIndicator.HorizontalContentAlignment = HorizontalAlignment.Stretch;
    busyIndicator.VerticalContentAlignment = VerticalAlignment.Stretch;

    this.RootVisual = busyIndicator;
}
```

The InitializeRootVisual method assigns the BusyIndicator control as the root node (resulting in it always remaining in the visual tree) and sets the control to disable its content while it's active. Its content is assigned a new instance of the MainPage object, which really forms the basis of our user interface. The MainPage object is defined in MainPage.xaml and could be considered the master page for the application—that is, a page that hosts content pages (also called views).

■ **Note** You might recognize this concept of master/content pages if you've done some ASP.NET development previously.

If you now take a look at the content of the MainPage.xaml file, you will find a Frame control that's used to host the views and the surroundings to this content area (such as the application header and menu). Because this page has been designed to be highly configurable through theme files, its XAML may appear to be a bit disorganized, but disregard that for now. The views to be displayed within the Frame control are located within the Views folder (shown in Figure 1-14)—with the sample views Home.xaml and About.xaml already defined for you.

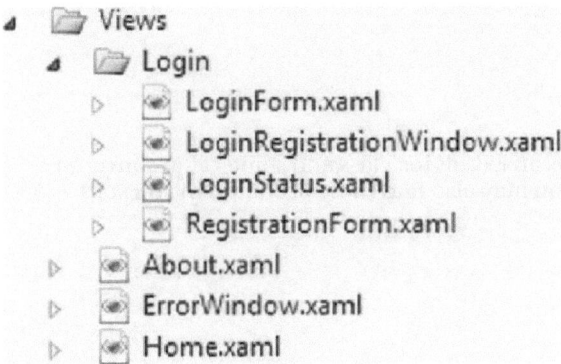

Figure 1-14. The Views folder

In the Views folder, you will also find the ErrorWindow.xaml file, which inherits from the ChildWindow class (to provide modal pop-up window behavior) and can be used to display any errors that occur to the user. For an example of using this class, take a look at the Application_UnhandledExceptions event handler in the App class, which uses it to display any error messages in the application that have not been caught by a try...catch block.

The Login subfolder of the Views folder contains a number of controls relating to the user login and registration functionality already implemented in the application by the project template.

The Assets folder (shown in Figure 1-15) contains a number of files containing project assets (resources and dictionaries). The Styles.xaml file in the Assets folder is a resource dictionary containing the styles for the application theme, defining the visual appearance of the application. This resource dictionary is merged into App.xaml, making the styles available globally in the application. You could consider this file to be similar in concept to a Cascading Style Sheets (CSS) file in ASP.NET projects (or any HTML web site). A number of alternative application themes are available for download that you can drop into your project (overwriting the current Styles.xaml file) to instantly transform the visual appearance of the application. Customizing the application styles is detailed in Chapter 9. The Assets folder also has a Resources subfolder, containing resource files defining various strings used throughout the application (for localization purposes).

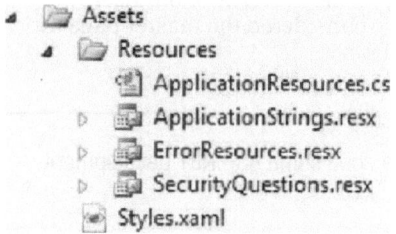

Figure 1-15. *The Assets folder*

The Controls folder (shown in Figure 1-16) contains the source for the BusyIndicator custom control (the BusyIndicator.xaml, BusyIndicator.cs, and VisualStates.cs files), which is used to indicate to the user that something is happening behind the scenes.

Figure 1-16. *The Controls folder*

The Helpers folder (shown in Figure 1-17) contains an Extension class and some value converter classes that are used throughout the default project. You may also find these useful when you start adding your own functionality to the project.

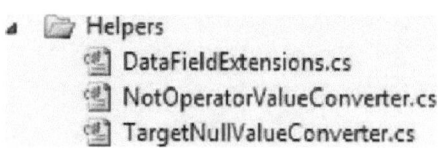

Figure 1-17. *The Helpers folder*

The Libs folder (shown in Figure 1-18) contains a DLL that is referenced by the project but is not a part of the official Silverlight assemblies. System.Windows.Controls.Data.DataForm.Toolkit.dll is an assembly from the Silverlight Toolkit that provides the DataForm control (illustrated in Figure 1-5).

Figure 1-18. *The Libs folder*

The Models folder (shown in Figure 1-19) contains three files: LoginInfo.cs, RegistrationData. partial.cs, and User.partial.cs. The latter two classes extend the partial classes generated by the WCF RIA Services code generator (adding additional client-side functionality and properties), while the LoginInfo.cs file contains the LoginInfo class that the DataForm control in the login window can bind to (particularly to add metadata to the properties, dictating how the corresponding data entry fields will be displayed in the form).

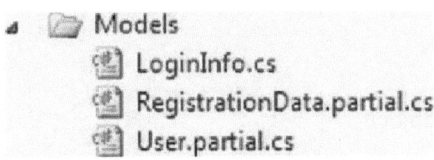

Figure 1-19. *The Models folder*

The Web folder doesn't contain any files, but it does have a subfolder called Resources (shown in Figure 1-20), which links to the two resource files defined in the web application project. This enables the localization strings within these files to be maintained in one location but used by both projects.

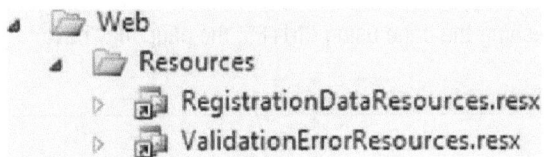

Figure 1-20. *The Web folder*

Recommended Project Template Modifications

As you've seen, you get quite a reasonable starting point for a business application in Silverlight, but you'll probably want to make a few changes to the default template before you get started developing.

As described previously, the following files can be found in the web application project in your solution:

- *ApplicationName*TestPage.aspx

- *ApplicationName*TestPage.html

These two pages do much the same thing—there's little difference (in terms of results) between the two, so you only really need one of them. ASPX pages need to be processed on the server by ASP.NET, so unless you want to do some processing in the code-behind of the page (such as checking security credentials), you can simply use the HTML page instead. You can then delete the one you don't need. On the remaining page, right-click its entry in Solution Explorer, and select Set as Start Page from the context menu to ensure it is automatically loaded in the browser when the project is run.

When you run the Silverlight project, you might expect the Silverlight application to have the focus, but actually, the web page has the focus. Therefore, if the starting page in your application has a text box with the focus explicitly set to it when the page is loaded, you will see some strange behavior. The text box may not have focus automatically, or it might have focus but not show the blinking caret. We can resolve this issue by adding a little bit of JavaScript code to the web page.

Open the HTML page to inspect its contents (in Source view). Add the following code directly below the onSilverlightError JavaScript function at the top of the page:

```
function appLoad(sender, args)
{
    var xamlObject = document.getElementById('silverlightControl');

    if (xamlObject != null)
        xamlObject.focus();
}
```

Add this property to the Silverlight object tag:

```
id="silverlightControl"
```

And add the following line to the properties of the Silverlight object:

```
<param name="onLoad" value="appLoad" />
```

Run the project again, and you will find that the text box now correctly has the focus. You can see the caret blinking, and typing (without clicking the application first) will populate the text box with the typed characters.

■ **Note** If the change doesn't seem to have worked, try refreshing the page using Ctrl+F5; the page may have been cached and not updated with the changes made.

At this stage, you might want to also add the following property to the Silverlight object:

```
<param name="Windowless" value="True" />
```

The purpose of this will be discussed in Chapter 15, where it is necessary in order to overlay the application with an IFrame to display reports. There are performance impacts to setting this property to True, but as most business applications aren't graphicly intensive, this should not be too much of an issue. You are now ready to start working on your Silverlight project.

In the Silverlight project, open the ApplicationStrings.resx file (under the Assets\Resources folder). Find the ApplicationName resource, and change its value to the name of your application. This name will appear in the header of the application when you run it.

Understanding XAP Files

When you compile a Silverlight project, it is all combined into a single file with a .xap extension. This file contains the assemblies and any other content files associated with the project, which are bundled together and compressed using the ZIP file format. You can prove this by simply changing the file extension from .xap to .zip and unzipping the file to inspect its contents. The XAP file can then be hosted on a web server, enabling it to be downloaded and run by client computers.

■ **Note** Some compression utilities (such as 7-Zip) add items to the context menu in Windows Explorer, which you can use to open the archive without needing to change the XAP file's extension. Alternatively, you can associate the .xap file extension with a compression utility, enabling you to simply double-click the .xap file in Windows Explorer to inspect its contents.

The easiest (and most feature-rich) way to inspect a XAP file, is to simply load it into Silverlight Spy (shown in Figure 1-21) and inspect it that way.

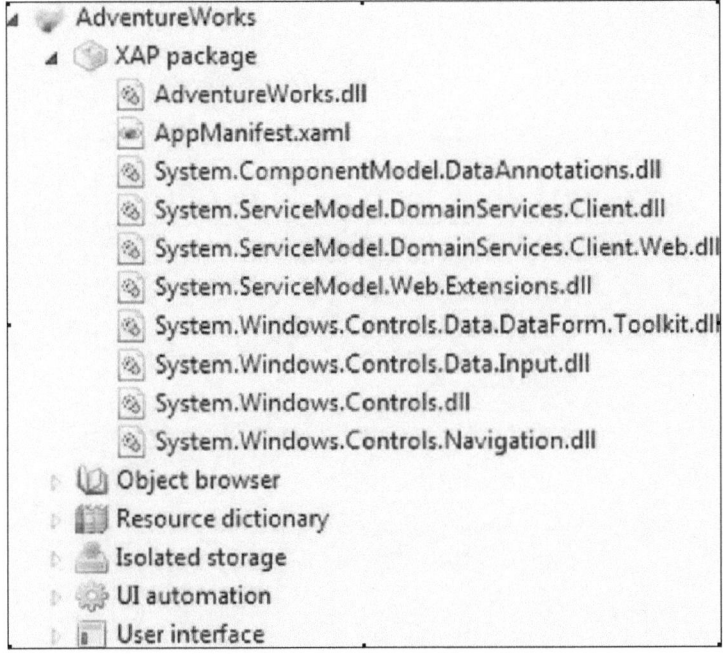

Figure 1-21. Silverlight Spy project view explorer

Summary

You're set up and ready to start developing Silverlight applications. You should now understand how a Silverlight solution is structured, what features have already been implemented in the Silverlight Business Application project template to get you started, and how the Silverlight and web projects are connected. In the next chapter, we'll take a look at the features and syntax of XAML and how that language helps you design and build a user interface for your application.

C H A P T E R 2

An Introduction to XAML

Extensible Application Markup Language (XAML—pronounced *zammel*) is an XML-based declarative markup language used to represent a hierarchy of objects.

In Silverlight, XAML is primarily used to define the layout and contents of user interfaces. The use of XAML for defining user interfaces is not a Silverlight-specific concept, however. It actually has its origins in Windows Presentation Foundation (WPF); Silverlight emerged essentially as a subset of WPF designed for use on the Web (hence its early name of WPF/E, or WPF Everywhere, before being christened with the catchier "Silverlight").

Despite being used to define user interfaces in Silverlight and WPF, this is not XAML's sole purpose. XAML was designed to simply represent a hierarchy of objects, giving it a rather broad scope in which it can be used. Silverlight also uses XAML to define resource dictionaries, animations, and the application root. In fact, XAML has gone on to be used in multiple Microsoft technologies, including Windows Workflow Foundation (WF)—used to define process workflows—and the XML Paper Specification (XPS)—used to define an electronic paper format. In this chapter, we will focus specifically on Silverlight's use of XAML and the XAML extensions that Silverlight implements.

HyperText Markup Language (HTML) is a form of markup language that you are almost certainly familiar with and have possibly used to define user interfaces for web-based applications. HTML was designed as a markup language for structuring documents for display within a web browser but was soon being coerced into doing things it was never designed to do (including formatting documents and positioning document elements to form application user interfaces). Scalable Vector Graphics (SVG) is another markup language that you may be familiar with; it's used to define vector graphics.

XML was designed to provide a standardized yet extensible framework for designing new markup languages that could be used for an almost infinite number of purposes (SVG being one of those languages). XAML builds on this XML framework and takes the capabilities of a markup language much further than ever before—primarily by combining the features found in both the HTML and SVG formats (and much more) into a single powerful markup language definition. As a result, XAML is a powerful, flexible, and extensible means of defining a hierarchy of objects that can serve an array of purposes, and hence these benefits can be harnessed by Silverlight.

Overcoming XAML's Steep Learning Curve

Unfortunately, despite all XAML's benefits, learning, understanding, and becoming productive in XAML is likely to be your greatest hurdle when attempting to develop your first Silverlight applications. Things will seem harder than they should be and will invariably lead to initial frustration with the technology. The problem is that (as a general rule) the more flexible something is, the more complex it is to understand and use. XAML unfortunately suffers from this same pitfall. As a result, you will be faced with a steep learning curve. XAML introduces new concepts to the way to define and design user interfaces and requires you to invest in a new way of thinking in how you do so.

Some examples of the types of issues you are likely to face when getting up to speed with XAML include the following:

- Things may seem harder than you initially think should be. For example, no property on the Button control lets you display an image on the button. This is because XAML has enabled a more flexible method to display custom content in buttons (an example of this can be found in the "Content Element Syntax" section of this chapter).

- XAML introduces many new concepts that may not have been part of previous technologies you've worked with. For example, concepts such as attached properties, markup extensions, styles, and data templates will likely be new to you.

- Properties you are used to finding on controls in previous technologies you've worked with may not exist in Silverlight controls or will have different names from what you might expect. For example, the Button control has no Text property in Silverlight. Neither does it (or any other control) have properties that can be used to position it within the user interface. Some of these differences will be raised throughout this chapter.

Despite the challenges of learning XAML, it is worth the effort to work through them, and the reason XAML is structured the way it is will make sense in the end, enabling you to start harnessing its power.

Why Learn XAML?

You may be wondering why you need to understand and write XAML, as Expression Blend has always been available to act as a XAML designer for building user interfaces that can take away most of the need to write XAML itself. In addition, Visual Studio 2010 now contains a drag-and-drop XAML designer too, although it's not quite as fully featured as Expression Blend's. It's important to remember that Silverlight as a technology revolves around its XAML core. Understanding the fundamental concepts of XAML is akin to learning how to count—you need to learn how to count before you can get a grasp on algebra. Therefore, your primary concern when learning Silverlight is to understand the underlying concepts of XAML, even if you don't initially completely learn its syntax.

In the early days, there wasn't a drag and drop designer surface in Visual Studio for Silverlight developers, which made it necessary to either write the XAML by hand or use Expression Blend. However, now that there is a XAML designer for Silverlight developers in Visual Studio 2010, you could probably get away with not learning the XAML syntax for a while and solely use that or the Expression Blend designer to design your user interfaces. You will, however, need to learn and understand the underlying concepts for structuring user interfaces in XAML in order to develop them effectively.

If you've ever worked on an ASP.NET project, you probably have resorted to modifying the HTML directly instead of using the HTML designer, and you will unfortunately face this same issue with XAML at times. Therefore, it's best to avoid having a complete reliance on the drag-and-drop designers. XAML may look confusing at first, but with a good understanding of the concepts and some help from IntelliSense, you will find that the syntax, becomes very easy to read and write.

Most of this chapter is designed to help you understand the concepts, structure, and syntax of XAML, but it is also interspersed with practical examples to demonstrate the concepts and put them into perspective.

Understanding XAML Syntax, Document Structure, and Features

XAML files are easily spotted by their `.xaml` extension and often have a corresponding code-behind file (`.xaml.cs`). In this section, we'll take a look at the structure of these XAML files, the XAML syntax, and the most important features of XAML.

■ **Note**   An easy way to understand XAML is to inspect existing XAML files and compare the XAML to the output in the designer. Enabling split mode (that is, XAML and designer in the same view), a feature available in both Expression Blend and Visual Studio 2010, is the ideal means for doing so, because this allows you to make a change in one and immediately see the result in the other.

Core XAML Syntax

XAML is based on XML, and thus inherits numerous concepts from it—the two most important being elements and attributes. Therefore, if you're familiar with XML, you'll already be familiar with the basic syntax of XAML.

Each element in a XAML file maps to a .NET class, which will often be a control. In most cases, an element will consist of both an opening and a closing tag. An opening tag consists of a less-than angle bracket (`<`), followed by the class name, and closed with a greater-than angle bracket (`>`). The closing tag is similar; however, the `<` is followed by a forward slash (`/`). For example, to insert a button into your XAML, you can use the following syntax:

```
<Button></Button>
```

Because the button in this example does not have any content (that is, nothing between the opening and closing tags), you may choose to use the shorter form, where the closing tag is omitted, but the `>` is preceded by a `/`, as demonstrated here:

```
<Button />
```

When you reference a control in XAML, you no doubt will want to assign values to its properties. There are a number of ways to do this in XAML, as will be described later in the "Assigning Property Values to Controls" section, but here, we'll specifically look at the attribute syntax for doing so. Each attribute on the XML element maps to a property or event on the referenced control.

Attributes are specified within the opening tag of an element. The control name should be followed by a whitespace character (space or new line), after which you can start assigning values to attributes. The syntax for an attribute is the name of the property you wish to assign a value to, followed by an equal sign (`=`), followed by the value surrounded by double quotes (`"`). For example, you can assign some text (`Hello`) to the `Content` property of the `Button` control in the previous example using attribute syntax like so:

```
<Button Content="Hello" />
```

While the standard character to surround the value of the attribute is the double quote (`"`), you can exchange it with a single quote (`'`) if necessary. You might want to do this, for example, if you wanted to actually include a double quote as a part of the value, in which case any double quote character between the single quotes will be considered a part of the value and ignored as being a XAML markup token character.

■ **Note**   Element and attribute names are case sensitive.

Creating an Object Hierarchy

When you create a XAML file, you are essentially defining a hierarchy of objects—also known as an object graph or object tree. A XAML file can have only a single root-level node, and elements are nested within each other to define the layout and content of the user interface. Most of the objects in the object tree in Silverlight will be controls.

■ **Note**   The topmost object in the application's object hierarchy is called the root visual, and a reference to this object can be obtained in code using the RootVisual property of the Application object.

Let's inspect the structure of a simple XAML file. Say we've added a new file named SimpleXAMLFile.xaml to the AdventureWorks project (created in Chapter 1), using the Silverlight User Control item template. This will generate the following XAML file:

```
<UserControl x:Class="AdventureWorks.SimpleXAMLFile"
    xmlns="http://schemas.microsoft.com/winfx/2006/xaml/presentation"
    xmlns:x="http://schemas.microsoft.com/winfx/2006/xaml"
    xmlns:d="http://schemas.microsoft.com/expression/blend/2008"
    xmlns:mc="http://schemas.openxmlformats.org/markup-compatibility/2006"
    mc:Ignorable="d"
    d:DesignHeight="300" d:DesignWidth="400">

    <Grid x:Name="LayoutRoot" Background="White">

    </Grid>
</UserControl>
```

Unfortunately, despite being a simple XAML file, it still incorporates a range of XAML concepts that we aren't quite ready to cover yet, including some namespace prefix declarations (the attributes starting with xmlns:) and some attached properties, such as the d:DesignHeight and d:DesignWidth properties, which differ from standard properties such as the Background property on the Grid element. Let's ignore these for the time being, strip this XAML right back to just its structure, and focus on that:

```
<UserControl>
    <Grid>
    </Grid>
</UserControl>
```

Here, you have UserControl as your root element, with a Grid control element as its content. You could read this as, "The user control contains a grid control." You cannot add any more elements to the UserControl element, because the UserControl control accepts only a single child element. However, the Grid control *does* accept multiple child elements.

■ **Note** A nice way of visualizing and navigating the object hierarchy (especially when your XAML file is complex) is using the Document Outline tool window in Visual Studio (View ▶ Other Windows ▶ Document Outline).

This is a very simple object hierarchy, and a long way from defining anything useful; however, we'll keep adding to this basic structure throughout this chapter to define a very simple user interface.

■ **Note** The object hierarchy is often referred to as the *visual tree*. You can traverse the objects in the visual tree in code using the VisualTreeHelper class, found in the System.Windows.Media namespace. It exposes methods to get the children of a XAML object (GetChild and GetChildrenCount), the parent of a XAML object (GetParent), and all the objects within a given area on the screen around an object (FindElementsInHostCoordinates).

Defining Namespaces

Before we stripped the XAML file introduced earlier back to its core structure, you may have noticed that the opening tag of the root element contained a number of attributes that start with xmlns:. Let's take another look at that element:

```
<UserControl x:Class="AdventureWorks.SimpleXAMLFile"
    xmlns="http://schemas.microsoft.com/winfx/2006/xaml/presentation"
    xmlns:x="http://schemas.microsoft.com/winfx/2006/xaml"
    xmlns:d="http://schemas.microsoft.com/expression/blend/2008"
    xmlns:mc="http://schemas.openxmlformats.org/markup-compatibility/2006"
    mc:Ignorable="d"
    d:DesignHeight="300" d:DesignWidth="400">
```

A number of namespace prefixes are defined on this root node (in bold), each declared using xmlns, the XML attribute used for declaring namespace prefixes. XAML namespace prefix declarations are conceptually similar to adding using statements at the top of a class in C#, but with a few notable differences. To use controls in your XAML file, the CLR namespace that they are defined in must be declared in the root element and assigned a prefix that is unique within the XAML file. This prefix will be used when referencing a control in order to remove any ambiguity as to which control you are referring to.

■ **Note** Although namespace prefixes are generally declared in the root element in the XAML file, they can actually be declared at any level (that is, in any element) in a XAML file and be referenced anywhere below that element in the hierarchy. However, it is generally standard practice to define them all on the root element of the XAML file.

Prefixes are a type of alias, reducing the verbosity of XAML by letting you qualify a control with the prefix you have defined, rather than with its whole namespace. The prefix is defined immediately following the colon after xmlns.

Note that the first namespace declared on the root element in the example isn't actually assigned a prefix:

```
xmlns="http://schemas.microsoft.com/winfx/2006/xaml/presentation"
```

This is because it is defining the default namespace (the Silverlight namespace) for the file, enabling Silverlight controls to be used throughout the file without the need to qualify their names with a namespace prefix. However, the second namespace reference does define a prefix (x—used to reference the XAML namespace):

```
xmlns:x="http://schemas.microsoft.com/winfx/2006/xaml"
```

■ **Note** Unfortunately, these default namespace declarations aren't the best examples to use, as none of them directly reference CLR namespaces and assemblies, as will the namespaces you generally declare. Instead, they map to URIs—known as consolidated namespaces. Consolidated namespaces combine multiple namespace declarations into one declaration, enabling you to declare a single URI namespace instead of needing to reference multiple namespaces. However, you don't need to worry about this concept—leave these declarations as they are, and simply add additional declarations as required following them. If you do want to consolidate a number of namespaces, you can use the XmlnsDefinition attribute, which will be described in Chapter 10. Another consolidated namespace that isn't referenced by default, but that you may find useful, is the SDK consolidated namespace—it brings all the namespaces in the Silverlight SDK together, so that instead of defining prefixes for all these namespaces in your XAML file, you can simply define just the one namespace prefix (sdk) instead to reference all the controls in the SDK:

```
xmlns:sdk="http://schemas.microsoft.com/winfx/2006/xaml/presentation/sdk"
```

When you declare a namespace prefix, it will almost always begin with clr-namespace:; referencing a CLR namespace and the assembly that contains it. Prefixes can be anything of your choosing, but it is best to make them short, yet meaningful. For example, in the following declaration we are declaring a prefix for the System.Windows.Controls namespace in the System.Windows.Controls.Data assembly, which we'll name data:

```
xmlns:data="clr-namespace:System.Windows.Controls;assembly=System.Windows.Controls.Data"
```

Once you've declared a namespace prefix, you can use controls within that namespace like so:

```
<data:DataGrid></data:DataGrid>
```

> **Note** IntelliSense in Visual Studio 2010 is very helpful when both declaring namespaces and referencing controls in those namespaces. After you enter a namespace prefix and press = (e.g., `xmlns:data=`), IntelliSense will display a list of all the namespaces and their corresponding assemblies referenced in the project. You can then select a namespace from the list and press Tab to insert the namespace and assembly name into the declaration. When using the designer, dropping a control from the toolbox onto the design surface, from a namespace that is not currently declared, will automatically declare its namespace and assign a default namespace prefix. When using a control, starting the open tag of the element with (`<`) will display a list of the namespace prefixes defined in the file, along with the controls from the default namespace. After you select or type the namespace prefix, IntelliSense will display a list of the controls in the mapped namespace for you to choose from. The XAML syntax for declaring namespaces and using controls from those namespaces may initially look intimidating, but IntelliSense makes writing this XAML completely effortless.

Assigning Property Values to Controls

After inserting a control element into a XAML file, you will in most cases want to set some property values on that control (e.g., the background color of a text box). You can of course use the Properties window in both Visual Studio and Expression Blend to do so (in most cases), but let's look at the different methods of assigning property values to controls in XAML. The method you use will depend on the nature of the property and the value you are assigning to it. The reasons you might use each method will be explained, along with its corresponding syntax.

Attribute Syntax

The simplest way to assign values to properties in XAML is to set them inline, using attribute syntax. This syntax is used when the property has a primitive type, such as string, integer, Boolean, and so on, or when the property's type has an associated type converter that can accept a string and convert it to that type. Regardless of the type of the property, all values should be enclosed within single or, preferably, double quotes. The following example demonstrates assigning the Content property of a Button control using attribute syntax:

```
<Button Content="Hello" />
```

Content Element Syntax

Some controls define a property whose content (that is, the XAML between its beginning and end tags) will be assigned to the property's value. This is known as content element syntax, and the control defines this content property by decorating its class with the ContentProperty attribute. A further discussion of how this behavior is achieved will be covered in Chapter 12. There's no clear way of determining which property, if any, is assigned the content of the control, but you will find it in the MSDN documentation for the control. As a general rule, however, most properties defined as content properties are named Content because this property is provided by the ContentControl base class that most controls accepting custom content derive from. The following example has exactly the same output as the previous example. However, it uses content element syntax to assign the value to the Content property, because the Content property is designated as a content property on the Button control:

```
<Button>Hello</Button>
```

■ **Note** No quotes are required around the value when using content element syntax.

You may wonder at this point why there are two methods to achieve exactly the same outcome. The reason is that rather than just simple values, many content properties accept complex values that can't be assigned using attribute syntax. (The value would be treated as plain text if you were to try.) Instead, using content element syntax, the Content property of the Button control can accept any XAML object hierarchy that will be displayed as the content of the button. You may have noticed that unlike the Button control in Windows Forms, there doesn't appear to be an Image property on the Silverlight Button control. This may initially make you think the Button control in Silverlight is very limited in its capabilities, but you would be mistaken, because this is where the Content property demonstrates the flexibility of XAML. Because the Content property will accept XAML elements as values, you can specify some XAML to display both an image and some text as the content of the button, as the following example demonstrates:

```
<Button Width="80" Height="35">
    <StackPanel Orientation="Horizontal">
        <Image Source="accept.png" Width="16" Height="16" />
        <TextBlock Margin="7,0,0,0" Text="OK" />
    </StackPanel>
</Button>
```

Here, we are using a StackPanel (discussed later in this chapter) containing both an Image control and a TextBlock control to achieve the result shown in Figure 2-1. Although using the StackPanel may initially appear to require more work than achieving the same outcome in Windows Forms, it does enable you to easily lay out the content of the button in whatever form you choose, rather than how the control chooses to implement the layout, and demonstrates the incredible flexibility of Silverlight and XAML. Using this method you could have any Silverlight control in the content of the Button, such as a ComboBox or even a DataGrid—practicality issues aside!

Figure 2-1. A Button control with custom content

■ **Note** Unless the content property is a collection, the content you assign to it can consist only of a single control XAML element, although that element can have child elements as required. Otherwise, you will get the error, "The property *XXX* is set more than once." If the property is a collection, you can assign multiple elements, as detailed shortly, using collection syntax.

Property Element Syntax

What if you want to assign a complex value to a property that isn't defined as a content property on a control? This is still possible using property element syntax. Property element syntax requires you to create a new element between the control element's opening and closing tags, of the form `<control.property>`. The dot in the element's name indicates to the XAML parser that this is a property element rather than an object element.

In this example, we'll assign the same value to the Content property of the button as we did in the previous example, but this time, we'll assign the property value using property element syntax, with the property element highlighted in bold:

```
<Button Width="80" Height="35">
    <Button.Content>
        <StackPanel Orientation="Horizontal">
            <Image Source="accept.png" Width="16" Height="16" />
            <TextBlock Margin="7,0,0,0" Text="OK" />
        </StackPanel>
    </Button.Content>
</Button>
```

You will find yourself often using property element syntax to assign resources to a control's Resources property (as will be discussed later in this chapter in the "Working with Resources and Resource Dictionaries" section), or basically any control property that accepts a complex value that can be defined in XAML. However, if that property is designated as a content property, like the Content property in the preceding example, it's standard to simply use the content element syntax instead and omit the property element's tags.

Collection Syntax

As stated earlier, properties that can accept XAML content can be assigned only a single control (although that element can have its own child elements), unless the property is a collection type. If the property is a collection type, you can use collection syntax to assign multiple items (generally, controls) to that collection, with each top-level element defined in the value being added as an item to the collection. The Items property on the ComboBox control is an example of where collection syntax can be used, as it is a collection that maintains all the items in the combo box. Because the Items property is designated as the content property for the ComboBox control, we can simply use content element syntax to assign the controls to the Items property. This method is equally applicable using property element syntax.

```
<ComboBox>
    <ComboBoxItem Content="First item" />
    <ComboBoxItem Content="Second item" />
    <ComboBoxItem Content="Third item" />
    <ComboBoxItem Content="Fourth item" />
</ComboBox>
```

■ **Note** You can also assign values to multiple properties on a control, maintain these in a central location as a resource, and assign them to multiple controls using styles. These will be discussed later in this chapter in the "Styles" section.

Attached Properties

Attached properties are special types of properties that are assigned a value on a control, but the properties actually belong to another control, usually higher up in the hierarchy. In essence, controls can register particular properties as attached properties, which can then be used by *any* control. This may seem a rather confusing concept initially; therefore, the best way to demonstrate this concept is by an example.

Say you have a control whose position in the user interface is being controlled by a parent control—for example, a Button control that is contained within a Canvas control. No positioning properties are defined on the Button control, as the type of layout control the button is contained within determines how it is positioned and what positioning properties it requires (the "Layout Controls" section later in this chapter discusses this topic further). The Canvas control needs to know where to position the Button control on its surface, so it needs to expose two properties, Left and Top, as attached properties, which can be used by the Button control to allow the Canvas to position the button accordingly. You may like to consider it as the Button control *inheriting* the Left and Top properties from the Canvas control.

To use these Canvas properties on the Button control, you need to include the name of the control that the properties belong to, using property element syntax. The following example demonstrates the Button control assigning values to the Left and Top properties that it inherited from the parent Canvas control:

```
<Canvas>
    <Button Canvas.Left="30" Canvas.Top="15" />
</Canvas>
```

■ **Note** The values of attached properties actually belong to the control that you are setting them on. In this case, despite the Left and Top properties belonging to the Canvas control, the values themselves belong to the Button control.

The ToolTipService control is used to provide tooltip functionality to controls and uses attached properties to do so. However, unlike the previous example, where the control defining the attached properties exists higher up in the control hierarchy from the control that the attached property values are being applied to, ToolTipService demonstrates that this does not necessarily have to be the case. As previously mentioned, attached properties can be used by any control, and not necessarily via inheritance.

In this example we are using the ToolTipService.ToolTip attached property to assign a tooltip to a Button control:

```
<Button ToolTipService.ToolTip="This is an example tooltip" />
```

■ **Note** Attached properties require a special technique to be used if you want to set their values in your code-behind. This will be covered in Chapter 11.

XAML Namespace Properties

The namespace assigned to the x: prefix, found in almost every XAML file, maps to the XAML namespace. This namespace contains a number of important attached properties that you will make extensive use of in your XAML files. Let's take a look at the most important properties in this namespace, and the scenarios in which you might use them.

x:Class

Looking at the first line of the root element in this XAML file, you will notice that it assigns a value to the x:Class attribute:

```
<UserControl x:Class="AdventureWorks.SimpleXAMLFile" ... />
```

This property is used to associate this XAML file with its corresponding code-behind class. As this property is automatically configured when you create a new XAML file in Visual Studio, you will rarely need to worry about it—just be aware of its importance.

x:Name

You will need to give controls names to interact with them in the code-behind or bind to them in XAML using ElementName binding, which will be discussed in Chapter 11. Most controls will have a Name property that you can use to assign the control a name:

```
<TextBox Name="UserNameTextBox" />
```

For those that don't have this property, you can use the x:Name attached property from the XAML namespace instead, like so:

```
<TextBox x:Name="UserNameTextBox" />
```

It doesn't matter which method you use, because they both serve exactly the same purpose. However, good standard to stick to is to use the Name property where it has been implemented and use x:Name only where it hasn't. Alternatively, you can choose to standardize on x:Name, which is applicable to every control.

Regardless of which you choose, a member variable will be automatically created for the control once you have given it a name, in the hidden code-generated designer class, which you can use to refer to that control in code.

■ **Note** At times, the member variable will not be created in the hidden code-generated designer class until you compile the application.

---

x:Key

Instead of a name, resources are assigned a unique key using this property, which controls can use to reference that resource. See the "Working with Resources and Resource Dictionaries" section later in this chapter for more information.

x:ClassModifier and x:FieldModifier

By default, the backing class to your XAML file will be have a scope of `public`, and surprisingly, the corresponding backing fields for any controls that you give a name to will have their scope set to `internal`. The `x:ClassModifier` and `x:FieldModifier` properties enable you to explicitly set these access levels in the XAML: the `x:ClassModifier` property is used to specify the class's scope, and the `x:FieldModifier` property to set the scope for controls. For example, the following XAML uses this property to set the button's scope to `private`, preventing it from being accessed from outside the XAML file's backing class:

```
<Button x:Name="OKButton" x:FieldModifier="private" Content="OK" />
```

■ **Note** If you change the access level of the class using the `x:ClassModifier` property, you will need to manually update the scope for your code-behind class accordingly; otherwise, you will receive a compilation error stating that partial declarations of the class have conflicting accessibility modifiers (that is, "the scope of the automatically generated partial designer class for the XAML file does not match that of the code-behind partial class").

Design-Time Properties

The Expression Blend 2008 namespace contains some attached properties that can be used to improve the design-time experience when developing Silverlight applications. The values for these attached properties will then be ignored at runtime.

Take another look at the root element of the simple XAML file that we have been using:

```
<UserControl x:Class="AdventureWorks.SimpleXAMLFile"
    xmlns="http://schemas.microsoft.com/winfx/2006/xaml/presentation"
    xmlns:x="http://schemas.microsoft.com/winfx/2006/xaml"
    xmlns:d="http://schemas.microsoft.com/expression/blend/2008"
    xmlns:mc="http://schemas.openxmlformats.org/markup-compatibility/2006"
    mc:Ignorable="d"
    d:DesignHeight="300" d:DesignWidth="400">
```

In bold are two attached properties, `DesignHeight` and `DesignWidth`, from the Expression Blend 2008 namespace (assigned a prefix of `d`), and another attached property, `Ignorable`, from the Markup Compatibility namespace (assigned a prefix of `mc`).

Try removing the `DesignHeight` and `DesignWidth` properties from the element, including their values. You will find that the design surface in the designer has shrunk to the size of its contents—which means shrinking away to nothing because there's currently no content in the user control. You could set the `Height` and `Width` properties of the UserControl instead, which will work but will also affect how the user control will be rendered at runtime, where you may want it to expand to fill the browser window area. Therefore, the `DesignHeight` and `DesignWidth` properties can be very useful for sizing your design surface at design time, while still allowing the user control to behave as required at runtime.

If you were to look in the Expression Blend 2008 namespace, you would also find that there are other design-time data-related properties, including `DataContext`, `DesignData`, and `DesignSource`, in addition to the `DesignInstance` and `DesignData` markup extensions. It can often be useful to specify the structure of the data that you will be binding to and populate your design surface with sample data in order to see how it might look at runtime. This is a concept often referred to as blendability. This concept will be explained in detail in Chapter 10.

In order for these design-time properties to be ignored at runtime, the mc:Ignorable attached property is used, from the Markup Compatibility namespace, to tell the XAML parser to ignore the namespace declaration d and any references to it. If you remove this property and attempt to compile your Silverlight application, you will find that the compilation fails, stating the following:

```
XAML Namespace http://schemas.microsoft.com/expression/blend/2008 is not resolved
```

Markup Extensions

Often, you have scenarios where you want to set the value of a control's property, but this value is not known at design time or should be determined at runtime. A typical example of this would be when you want to display data that has been retrieved from the server—a problem that the concept of data binding was designed to solve.

To support these types of scenarios and specify them in XAML, including but not limited to enabling data binding, is the concept of markup extensions. A markup extension is essentially a class containing some logic that is evaluated at runtime. The resulting value is then assigned to the control's property that the markup extension was applied to. When used in XAML, markup extensions are denoted by the curly brackets surrounding them. The brackets indicate to the XAML parser that what is inside them is a markup extension, and therefore the value to be assigned to the control's property needs to be evaluated by the markup extension. Common markup extensions include

- StaticResource: Used to assign a resource as the value of the property (discussed later in this chapter in the "Working with Resources and Resource Dictionaries" section).

- Binding: Used to specify a data binding expression (discussed later in this chapter in the "Data Binding" section).

- TemplateBinding: Used in custom control templates to assign a value from a property exposed by the control (discussed further in Chapter 12).

- RelativeSource: Used to bind the value of a property to that of another control relative to it in the object hierarchy (discussed further in Chapter 11).

- x:Null: Used to assign a null value to a property.

The simplest use of a markup extension is to use x:Null to assign a null value to a property, as demonstrated here:

```
<TextBox Background="{x:Null}" />
```

Markup extensions can have properties whose values can be assigned following the markup extension name (within curly brackets). For example, here, we are using the Binding markup extension and assigning ListPrice as the value of its Path property:

```
<TextBox Text="{Binding Path=ListPrice}" />
```

■ **Note** Notice the lack of double quotes around the property value. Since the entire value of the property (the markup extension) is surrounded by quotes, to use quotes within this value would result in invalid markup, and your application would fail to compile. Therefore, you must omit the double quotes from around the value, or use single quotes (') instead, which would be required if the value contains a comma.

Some markup extensions have specified a default property, enabling you to specify a value for that property without explicitly identifying the property. For example, since the `Path` property of the `Binding` markup extension is its default property, we can instead write the same expression like so:

```
<TextBox Text="{Binding ListPrice}" />
```

Note that the properties of a markup extension, in turn, can be assigned a markup extension value. Here, we are assigning a `StaticResource` markup extension to the `Converter` property of the `Binding` markup extension:

```
<TextBox Text="{Binding ListPrice, Converter={StaticResource CurrencyConverter}}" />
```

■ **Note**   To support markup extensions, a new concept had to be introduced on the code side of things, with special types of properties called dependency properties. These will be discussed later in this chapter, but it's important to note that all properties to which you want to assign a markup extension *must* be dependency properties. This should not be too much of an issue, however, because most of the important properties on the standard Silverlight controls are already registered as such.

A new feature in Silverlight 5 is the ability to write your own markup extensions. Writing custom markup extensions will be covered in Chapter 10.

■ **Note**   On occasion, you may have a scenario where you want to assign a literal value to a property in XAML whose first character is an open curly bracket. However, the XAML parser will attempt to process this as a markup extension, and a runtime error will occur. This error is especially likely when specifying tokens in a URI mapping with the navigation framework (covered in the next chapter), as these also use curly brackets as identifiers. To work around this issue, you can use an escape sequence, which is an open bracket immediately followed by a closing bracket ({}), after which the rest of the value will be treated as a literal. For example, to assign a value of {page} to the `Uri` property of a `UriMapping` element in XAML, you would need to preface the value with {}, like so:

```
<navigation:UriMapping Uri="{}{page}" MappedUri="/Views/{page}.xaml" />
```

Namescopes

XAML namescopes are not a concept you will likely need to worry about much, as they are handled automatically by the XAML parser behind the scenes. However, they are worth mentioning, as they important in how named controls are managed in XAML.

If you were to create two controls in a view, assign them the same name (for example, `ItemText`), and then attempt to compile your application, you would get the following compile error:

```
The type 'XXX' already contains a definition for 'ItemText'
```

The designer would also state the following:

```
Name 'ItemText' alread exists in the current name scope.
```

This makes perfect sense, because when you name a control, the compiler creates a variable in the code-behind that you can use to reference that control in your code. If you had multiple controls with the same name in your view, Silverlight wouldn't know which of these controls you were actually referring to.

However, ensuring that all control names added to the object hierarchy are unique is simply impossible. For example, let's say you have a control that is made up of a number of elements. If one of the elements making up the control had a name, using the control multiple times in a single view would result in the named element being added to the object hierarchy multiple times. Thus, multiple controls with the same name would exist in the object hierarchy, colliding with one another. To permit this scenario without creating collisions, Silverlight segments the object hierarchy into namescopes at given intervals. Control names within each namescope still need to be unique, but controls in different namescopes can have the same name.

Your application will have a default namescope, created with the root visual, and other namescopes will be automatically created by the XAML parser where required. Examples of instances where a new namescope may be created include when you load in XAML from an external source, such as when you use XAMLReader.Load, when you use a UserControl, and when you use a template (DataTemplate, ControlTemplate, and so on).

Templates will be discussed later in this chapter, but let's look at a simple example of where new namescopes are created due to the use of a template. Say you have a ListBox control with a number of items, and you want to customize the appearance of each item by assigning a template to them. This template may have various controls within it. For example, it may have an Image control and a Text-Block control, like so:

```
<ListBox Name="FolderList">
    <ListBox.ItemTemplate>
        <DataTemplate>
            <StackPanel Orientation="Horizontal">
                <Image Source="folder.png" />
                <TextBlock Name="ItemText" Text="{Binding}" />
            </StackPanel>
        </DataTemplate>
    </ListBox.ItemTemplate>
</ListBox>
```

In the preceding XAML, the TextBlock in the template is assigned a name of ItemText. However, once the template is applied to multiple list items, there will be multiple text blocks having the name ItemText in the object hierarchy. Therefore, the XAML parser will create a new namescope each time the template is applied to a list item, and the controls created from that template will live in that, preventing the control names from colliding with one another in the same namescope used by the view.

There are two instances in which you are likely to find the effects of namescopes. When you use the FindName method on a control to find an element with a given name below that control in the object hierarchy, it will search for that name only within the current namescope. Therefore, searching in the view containing the ListBox in the previous example for an element named ItemText, like so

```
object namedElement = this.FindName("ItemText");
```

will not find the TextBlock control, because any instances of it will be in a different namescope.

In addition, it's possible to bind the property of a control to that of another named control, using ElementName binding, but you can bind only to other controls that exist in the same namescope.

■ **Note** Any named control that forms a part of a template, such as the `ItemText` TextBox in the recent ListBox item template example, will not have a variable created for it in the code-behind. This is because the control may be created multiple times in the view, and the Silverlight runtime wouldn't know which instance you are referring to.

Controls

Controls are the fundamental building blocks of user interfaces in XAML. Silverlight comes with an extensive set of core controls, quite similar what's available in Windows Forms (and WPF). Where controls are missing, such as the TreeView control, you may find that these additional controls are available in the Silverlight Toolkit project (created and maintained by Microsoft) on the CodePlex web site.

In this section, we'll specifically look at a subset of these core controls used to lay out controls on the user interface surface, which we'll call layout controls. We'll also look at some of the naming differences between control properties in Windows Forms and Silverlight. Then, we'll take a look at specifying event handlers that can handle an event in the code-behind when it is raised by the given control. However, let's first look at the base control classes in Silverlight that all controls derive from.

Base Control Classes

While you will never use these directly, it's worth taking a cursory look at the `DependencyObject`, `UIElement`, `FrameworkElement`, `Control`, and `ContentControl` base control classes that other controls derive from. The inheritance hierarchy of these controls is shown in Figure 2-2.

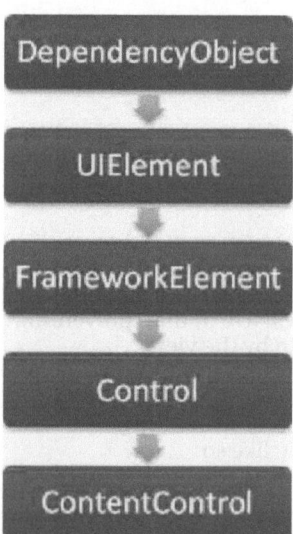

Figure 2-2. *Inheritance hierarchy of the base control classes*

DependencyObject

One of the concepts for supporting special features required by XAML is the *dependency property*. Dependency properties are special types of properties on XAML controls that are defined in a different way from normal CLR properties, and they support additional features. Possibly the most important feature dependency properties support is the ability to accept an expression that must be resolved as its value at runtime. This feature enables markup expressions to be assigned to the property in XAML, enabling data binding and so forth, as the values of markup extensions need to be determined at runtime. Dependency properties also enable the concept of attached properties.

In order for dependency properties to be supported on an object, that object must be a dependency object (that is, inherit from the DependencyObject class). Dependency properties register themselves with the dependency object, and the dependency object then maintains the value for each of these dependency properties and provides helper methods for setting/getting these values. All XAML controls derive from DependencyObject, although, as a general rule, indirectly via the Control or ContentControl class.

■ **Note** Whether or not an object is a dependency object or a property is a dependency property are generally not issues you will need to worry about, at least until you try to create your own user/custom controls. A more complete discussion of dependency properties and how to create them will be covered in Chapter 12.

UIElement

The UIElement class derives from DependencyObject and adds functionality for handling user input (keyboard, mouse, and stylus) and control focus. It also adds the base layout functionality for controls.

FrameworkElement

The FrameworkElement class derives from UIElement and adds additional layout functionality to that provided by UIElement, along with object lifetime events (primarily the Loaded event) and support for data binding, via the GetBindingExpression and SetBinding methods.

Control

The Control class derives from FrameworkElement and is the class that most XAML controls inherit from. It adds functionality used to define the appearance of the control, most importantly by defining the Template property.

ContentControl

The ContentControl class inherits from Control and adds functionality to help derived controls define a content area in their control template, using the ContentPresenter control, into which custom content can be inserted by using the Content property that it defines. For example, the Button control inherits from this control indirectly via the ButtonBase class, enabling the content of the button to be customized, such as by displaying an image next to the text in the button, as demonstrated earlier in this chapter in the "Content Element Syntax" section.

Creating content controls will be detailed in Chapter 12.

Layout Controls

When you start experimenting with Silverlight, you'll find that none of the controls have properties to enable you to specify how they should be positioned on the design surface. In Windows Forms, positioning controls was as easy as assigning values to a control's Left and Top properties; however, these are nowhere to be found on Silverlight controls. How exactly can you then position controls on a Silverlight surface? The solution to this problem comes in the form of layout controls.

Layout controls are invisible container controls (controls designed specifically to act as a container for other controls) that handle the positioning of their children. So that controls can specify how they should be laid out, layout controls have attached properties that they can use when required. There are a number of layout controls in Silverlight—each with its own logic and behavior for positioning the controls that they contain. These layout controls can be mixed and matched as required (that is, nested within one another) to achieve the layout you are after.

Using layout controls means that, instead of designing your views using the fixed positioning of controls that you may be used to, you can design very flexible layouts that can automatically adjust to various conditions, such as browser/window resizing and so forth—all controlled by the layout controls that you use.

Out of the box, Silverlight provides three layout controls for positioning controls in a view—the Canvas, Grid, and StackPanel controls. These all inherit from the Panel class, which provides the base layout functionality to which they add their own specific layout functionality. The Silverlight Toolkit also includes some additional layout controls that you may find useful. Let's take a look at each of these now.

Canvas

The Canvas layout control enables you to position controls on its surface using fixed coordinates. With this control, you can easily position controls but doesn't lead to particularly flexible layouts. It can be useful in some circumstances, however. Using it is quite simple. Here, we define a Canvas control and place a TextBlock control within it (see Figure 2-3):

```
<Canvas Width="300" Height="150" Background="Gainsboro">
    <TextBlock Text="Hello" />
</Canvas>
```

Figure 2-3. *A TextBlock control within a Canvas control, with no positioning*

The problem here is that the TextBlock will be positioned in the upper-left corner of the Canvas, as you can see in Figure 2-3, and it has no properties enabling it to specify the coordinates where it should be positioned. Because the properties that would be required to position it depend on the type of layout control that it is contained within, the TextBlock control doesn't have any positioning properties defined on it. Instead, the Canvas provides these properties to the TextBlock as attached properties, enabling the

TextBlock to specify where it should be positioned within the Canvas. For this purpose, the Canvas control provides two attached properties: Left and Top. It can then use those values when given the task of positioning all the controls that it contains.

The following XAML demonstrates assigning values to the Left and Top attached properties provided by the Canvas control values on our TextBlock control, enabling the Canvas control to position the TextBlock control on its surface accordingly. You can see the result in Figure 2-4.

```
<Canvas Width="300" Height="150" Background="Gainsboro">
    <TextBlock Text="Hello" Canvas.Left="100" Canvas.Top="50" />
</Canvas>
```

Figure 2-4. *A TextBlock control positioned within a Canvas control*

Grid

The most commonly used layout control in Silverlight is the Grid control. Unlike when using the Canvas control, you do not specify the location of controls within a Grid using absolute coordinates. Instead, you divide up the grid into rows and columns (forming cells) that you can place controls into. Rows and columns can have a fixed height and width, automatically size to fit their contents, expand to fill all the remaining available space, and be sized relative to the size of other rows/columns. This allows for very flexible control layouts, and thus the Grid control is generally preferred over the Canvas control for laying out controls.

When you create a new UserControl or Page in your project, you will find that it already has a Grid control, named LayoutRoot, in place but with no rows or columns defined:

```
<Grid x:Name="LayoutRoot" Background="White">

</Grid>
```

The first thing you will need to do is divide it up into rows and columns. You can do so using the RowDefinitions and ColumnDefinitions properties of the Grid control. These are collections, to which you need to add RowDefinition and ColumnDefinition objects, using a combination of property element syntax and collection syntax in XAML. For example, this 300 × 150–pixel grid is divided into two columns and three rows:

```
<Grid x:Name="LayoutRoot" Background="White" Width="300" Height="150">
    <Grid.ColumnDefinitions>
        <ColumnDefinition />
        <ColumnDefinition />
    </Grid.ColumnDefinitions>
```

```
    <Grid.RowDefinitions>
        <RowDefinition />
        <RowDefinition />
        <RowDefinition />
    </Grid.RowDefinitions>
</Grid>
```

Figure 2-5 shows a Grid control (in the Visual Studio designer) defined using this XAML.

Figure 2-5. *A Grid control in the Visual Studio Designer, with two columns and three rows defined*

■ **Note**   The XAML designer in Visual Studio makes the task of defining a Grid control quite easy, so you don't have to write all the XAML-defining rows and columns by hand. When a Grid control is selected, a light-blue margin will appear at the top left of the Grid. Clicking in one of these margins will create a row/column at that position.

Weighted Proportion Sizing

When no column widths and row heights are explicitly set, they will have a default value of an asterisk (*), which is used to specify a weighted proportion. Weighted proportions enable you to have columns or rows whose width and height are relative to one another. Any fixed or automatically sized columns or rows are allocated their requested space in the Grid, after which columns/rows with weighted proportions divide up the remaining available space according to their weights. Essentially, each column/row takes a percentage of this remaining space.

Looking at the columns in the preceding example, each column will have its default width of *. This will result in them dividing their sizes up evenly, with each column taking 50 percent of the width of the Grid. To make the first column take twice the space assigned to the second column, you can prefix the asterisk in the value of the width property with a multiplier. For example, when the columns are defined like so:

```
<Grid.ColumnDefinitions>
    <ColumnDefinition Width="2*" />
    <ColumnDefinition Width="*" />
</Grid.ColumnDefinitions>
```

the first column will take 66.67 percent of the Grid's width, and the second column will take 33.33 percent, as shown in Figure 2-6. As the Grid is 300 pixels wide, the first column will be 200 pixels wide, and the second column will be 100 pixels wide.

Figure 2-6. A Grid control in the Visual Studio Designer, demonstrating weighted proportions

---

■ **Note** A width of * is the same as 1*.

If the Grid control doesn't have a width/height specified, it will expand to fill the space available to it. As its size is changed, such as when the browser/window is resized, its columns and rows will also resize themselves accordingly. This enables you to design a layout that will automatically resize itself to fill the space available to it, resulting in a very flexible user interface layout that will adjust accordingly to whatever size is allocated to it.

Fixed-Width Sizing

You can give a column or row a fixed width/height by assigning it a numeric value (in pixels). For example, the first column in the following example will have a width of 200 pixels, and the second column will have a width of 100 pixels:

```
<Grid.ColumnDefinitions>
    <ColumnDefinition Width="200" />
    <ColumnDefinition Width="100" />
</Grid.ColumnDefinitions>
```

Figure 2-7 shows a Grid control using these column definitions.

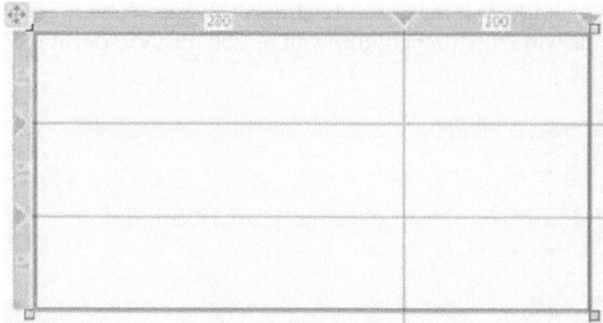

Figure 2-7. *A Grid control in the Visual Studio Designer, demonstrating fixed width proportions*

■ **Note** If you simply set the width of the second column to *, the remaining width of the Grid will be filled after the 200 pixels have been assigned to the first column. If the width of the Grid is 300 pixels, the second column will be 100 pixels wide. If the width of the Grid is 500 pixels, the second column will be 300 pixels wide.

Automatic Sizing

At times, you may not know what width or height a column or row should be, but you want it to automatically expand to the size of its contents. To do this, set the column or row's Width/Height property to Auto.

```
<Grid Width="300" Height="150">
    <Grid.ColumnDefinitions>
        <ColumnDefinition Width="Auto" />
        <ColumnDefinition Width="Auto" />
    </Grid.ColumnDefinitions>

    <Grid.RowDefinitions>
        <RowDefinition />
        <RowDefinition />
        <RowDefinition />
    </Grid.RowDefinitions>

    <Button Width="50" Grid.Column="0" Grid.Row="0" Margin="5" />
    <Button Width="100" Grid.Column="0" Grid.Row="1" Margin="5" />
    <Button Width="75" Grid.Column="0" Grid.Row="2" Margin="5" />

    <Button Width="120" Grid.Column="1" Grid.Row="0" Margin="5" />
</Grid>
```

As Figure 2-8 shows, the Grid's columns automatically size to fit the largest of their contents, plus their associated margin (ways to position controls within Grid cells are discussed in the next section).

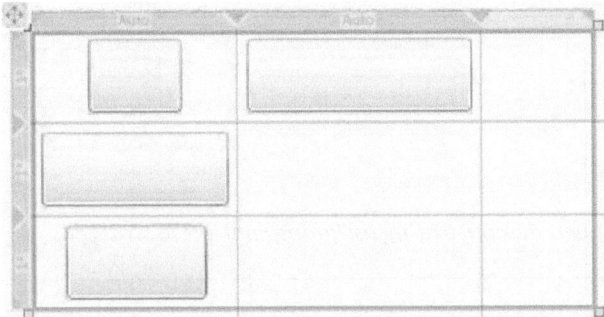

Figure 2-8. *A Grid control in the Visual Studio Designer, demonstrating automatic sizing*

■ **Note** Note that each Button control was assigned a 5-pixel margin. This inserts some space between the controls and their containing cells, which you can see in Figure 2-8.

Assigning Controls to Grid Cells

Once you've defined the rows and columns in your Grid, you can start assigning controls to its cells. As with the Canvas control, the Grid control provides attached properties that your controls can use to tell the Grid which row and column it should be positioned within. These attached properties are Row and Column. These properties specify an index in the RowDefinitions and ColumnDefinitions properties, and thus are zero-based—that is, to put a control in the first row in the Grid, set its Grid.Row attached property to 0. If you want a control to span across more than one row or column in the grid, you can use the Grid's RowSpan and ColumnSpan for this purpose.

The following example demonstrates three controls being positioned within the Grid, which is shown in Figure 2-9. The TextBlock control is being placed in the first column of the first row, while the TextBox control is being placed in the second column of the first row. The Button control is being placed in the first column of the second row but will span both columns in the Grid:

```
<Grid Width="300" Height="85">
    <Grid.ColumnDefinitions>
        <ColumnDefinition />
        <ColumnDefinition Width="2*" />
    </Grid.ColumnDefinitions>
    <Grid.RowDefinitions>
        <RowDefinition Height="35" />
        <RowDefinition />
    </Grid.RowDefinitions>

    <TextBlock Grid.Column="0" Grid.Row="0" Text="Name:"
            VerticalAlignment="Center" />
    <TextBox Grid.Column="1" Grid.Row="0" Margin="0,5" />
    <Button Grid.Column="0" Grid.Row="1" Grid.ColumnSpan="2" Margin="0,5"
            Content="OK" />
</Grid>
```

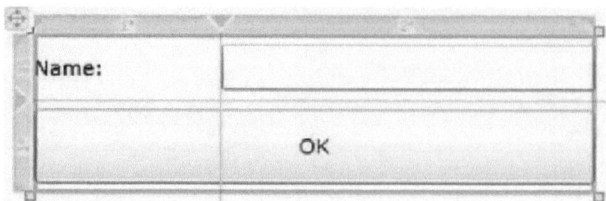

Figure 2-9. *A Grid control in the Visual Studio Designer, demonstrating assigning controls to Grid cells*

> ■ **Note**   When you drop a control from the toolbox into a grid cell, a margin will be applied to the control to position it within that cell. To remove this margin easily, right-click the control, and select Reset Layout ▸ Margin from the menu. Otherwise, you can simply remove it from the XAML defining that control.

StackPanel

The StackPanel control is used for stacking controls one after another, either horizontally or vertically, which you specify via a control's Orientation property. For example, you could put a TextBlock control and a TextBox control within a StackPanel whose Orientation property was set to Horizontal, and this will position the TextBox next to the TextBlock, as shown in Figure 2-10:

```
<StackPanel Orientation="Horizontal">
    <TextBlock Text="Name: " />
    <TextBox Width="155" />
</StackPanel>
```

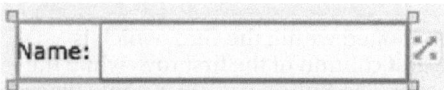

Figure 2-10. *A StackPanel control in the Visual Studio Designer, demonstrating horizontal orientation of controls*

Alternatively, you could set the StackPanel's Orientation property to Vertical, and this will position the TextBox immediately below the TextBlock, as shown in Figure 2-11:

```
<StackPanel Orientation="Vertical">
    <TextBlock Text="Name: " />
    <TextBox Width="155" />
</StackPanel>
```

Figure 2-11. *A StackPanel control in the Visual Studio Designer, demonstrating vertical orientation of controls*

Silverlight Toolkit Layout Controls

The Silverlight Toolkit contains some additional layout controls that you may find useful. In the System.Windows.Controls.Toolkit.dll assembly, you will find the WrapPanel and DockPanel layout controls.

■ **Note** Note that the toolkit namespace prefix needs to be declared in the XAML for these code samples to work. To do so, add the following to the root node in your XAML file:

```
xmlns:toolkit="http://schemas.microsoft.com/winfx/2006/xaml/presentation/toolkit"
```

Wrap Panel

The WrapPanel is much like the StackPanel, when stacking controls horizontally, but once the controls within it hit the right edge of the WrapPanel, new items will wrap and start being displayed on the next line. You might use this, for example, when you have thumbnails of photos and want to lay them out in much the same way as Windows Explorer does.

The following code demonstrates using this control, positioning Button controls within its area.

```
<toolkit:WrapPanel Width="200" Height="200" Background="WhiteSmoke">
    <Button Content="1" Width="50" Height="50" Margin="5" />
    <Button Content="2" Width="50" Height="50" Margin="5" />
    <Button Content="3" Width="50" Height="50" Margin="5" />
    <Button Content="4" Width="50" Height="50" Margin="5" />
    <Button Content="5" Width="50" Height="50" Margin="5" />
    <Button Content="6" Width="50" Height="50" Margin="5" />
    <Button Content="7" Width="50" Height="50" Margin="5" />
</toolkit:WrapPanel>
```

This will produce the output shown in Figure 2-12.

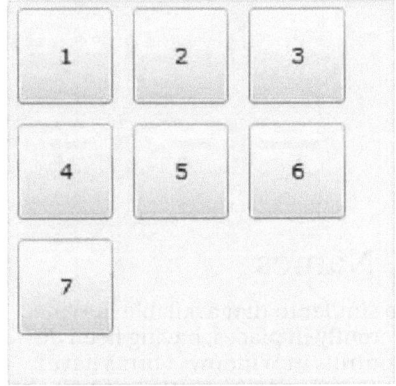

Figure 2-12. *A WrapPanel control in the Visual Studio designer, demonstrating horizontal wrapping*

As you can see, the Button controls are stacked horizontally and wrapped onto the next "line" once a control will fall outside the WrapPanel control's area. You can alternatively stack the controls vertically by setting the WrapPanel control's Orientation property to Vertical.

Dock Panel

The DockPanel enables you to dock the controls contained within it to one of its edges or fill the remaining space. If you miss the ability to dock controls from Windows Forms, this will provide you the same ability in Silverlight.

To dock a control to a position in the DockPanel control, use the Dock attached property that it provides, as demonstrated in the following code:

```
<toolkit:DockPanel Width="400" Height="300"
    <Button Height="80" toolkit:DockPanel.Dock="Top" Content="Dock Top" Margin="2" />
    <Button Width="80" toolkit:DockPanel.Dock="Left" Content="Dock Left" Margin="2" />
    <Button Width="80" toolkit:DockPanel.Dock="Right" Content="Dock Right" Margin="2" />
    <Button Height="80" toolkit:DockPanel.Dock="Bottom" Content="Dock Bottom" Margin="2" />
    <Button Content="Fill" Margin="2" />
</toolkit:DockPanel>
```

As you can see, each button docks itself to an edge, except the final button which will fill the remainder of the space left, as shown in Figure 2-13.

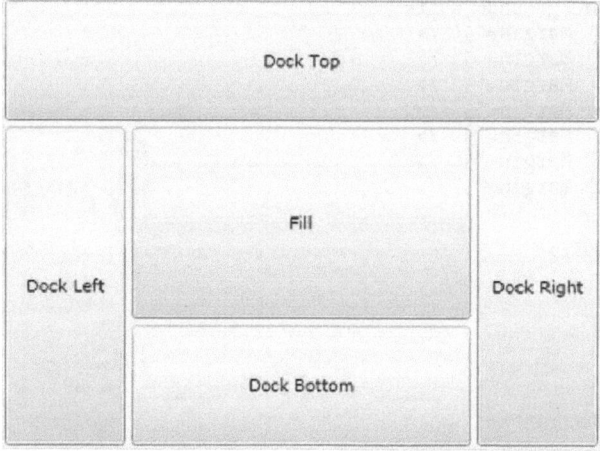

Figure 2-13. *A DockPanel control in the Visual Studio designer*

XAML vs. Windows Forms Controls' Property Names

You will find that, despite the core control set in Silverlight being quite similar to that available in Windows Forms, Silverlight's controls are actually implemented quite differently in places, having been developed from the ground up. In particular, some of the properties of controls in Windows Forms have different names in Silverlight. For example, most Boolean properties are prefixed with Is (IsEnabled, IsTabStop, IsHitTestVisible, and so on) in XAML. Also worth noting is that the Visibility property, which was named Visible in Windows Forms and used to show or hide controls, is now an enumeration with two possible values: Visible or Collapsed. This may seem rather strange and confusing at first, and in terms of Silverlight development it probably is! The reason for this is purely for compatibility with WPF, which supports an additional value of Hidden, which, in WPF, hides the control like Collapsed does but unlike Collapsed still consumes space in the layout. However, since Silverlight doesn't support that value, we are left with an enumeration with just Visible or Collapsed as its possible values.

Assigning Event Handlers

Controls have the ability to raise events that the code-behind can handle to respond to something that has happened to the control, such as a Button control raising a Click event in response to being clicked. Assigning an event handler to a control in XAML is a case of simply using attribute syntax, the same way you assign a value to a property on the control, to assign the name of the event handler in the code-behind that should be called when the event is raised. For example, assigning an event handler called OKButton_Click to the Click event on a Button control is achieved like so:

```
<Button Name="OKButton" Content="OK" Click="OKButton_Click" />
```

■ **Note** As a general rule (though not mandatory), the name of event handler methods are of the form ControlName_EventName.

Assigning Event Handlers in XAML in Visual Studio

In Visual Studio, typing in the event name and pressing the equal sign will give you a list of event handler methods in the code-behind to choose from (that match the required method signature), and it will also give you the following option: <New Event Handler>. Clicking this, or simply pressing Tab, will automatically generate a name for the event handler, assigning it to the event in XAML and automatically creating the corresponding event handler method in the code-behind.

However, if you choose to type in the name of the event handler, you will find that the event handler will not be automatically created in the code-behind. In this case, the easiest way to create the event handler is to right-click the name of the event handler in the XAML, and select the Navigate to Event Handler option from the context menu. This will open up the code-behind class and create the event handler method for you.

This option can also be useful if you've deleted the event handler in the code-behind and want to re-create it. It's also particularly useful when you simply want to navigate to an event handler in the code-behind for a given control in XAML.

■ **Note** Many controls define a default event, enabling you to simply double-click the control in Visual Studio's designer to automatically assign an event handler to that event on the control and create the event handler method in the code-behind. For example, double-clicking a Button control will create a Click event handler in the code-behind and assign that method to the Button's Click event in the XAML. You can also use the Events view of the Properties window to create event handlers without resorting to writing the XAML yourself.

Assigning Event Handlers in XAML in Expression Blend

Unfortunately, working with events is not so straightforward in Expression Blend. Events don't appear in Expression Blend's IntelliSense; you can't double-click a control to have it generate and assign the event handler for the default event of the control, nor can you right-click an event handler name in XAML and navigate to it in the code-behind. The only way to automatically create an event handler for a control in the code-behind and assign it to the control is to use the Events view in the Properties window.

Routed vs. Direct Events

Silverlight supports a special type of event called a routed event. Routed events are passed up the object hierarchy (which is known as "bubbling" the event), and the event is raised on each control until an event handler marks the event as handled or the root visual is reached. Although most events are *direct* events (that is, the event handler is called only on the control that raised the event), many user interaction–related events are routed events, such as mouse/key input events and focus events, and these will bubble up the object hierarchy until they are handled.

■ **Note**   Unlike WPF, Silverlight does not support any tunneling of events (where the event is raised on controls from the root visual object down to the event source).

Assigning Event Handlers in Code

Event handlers can be assigned to control events in the code-behind as per C#'s standard language syntax, for example:

```
this.Loaded += MainPage_Loaded;
```

Be particularly aware, however, that adding an event handler to a control can result in the control not being garbage collected once it is no longer required, hence leading to memory leaks. This is because the control will still have a reference to it via the event handler, and thus the garbage collector will assume the control is still required and not clean it up.

For example, say you add a button to a view and add a Click event handler to it, and then remove the button from the view. A reference to the button will still exist by way of the event handler, preventing it from being garbage-collected, for example:

```
// Add the button and handle its Click event
Button button = new Button();
button.Click += button_Click;
LayoutRoot.Children.Add(button);

// Now remove the button and clear the variable reference
LayoutRoot.Children.Remove(button);
button = null;
```

Even though, at the completion of this code, the button no longer exists in the object hierarchy and there is no variable referencing it any longer, it still will not be garbage collected because there is still a subscription to the Click event being maintained. This situation will result in a memory leak. Although the impact of this example is small, if you did it many times or with bigger objects that consume more memory, the memory usage of your application could grow over time to potentially unacceptable levels. To avoid such a scenario, when you have a long-lived object with an event handler to a short(er)-lived one, remember to always remove that event handler once the control is no longer required:

```
button.Click -= button_Click;
```

■ **Note** Another solution is to use a weak event listener that subscribes to the event without maintaining a strong reference, allowing the control to be cleaned up when there are no other references to the control. The Silverlight Toolkit contains a `WeakEventListener` class that you could use for this purpose if you wish.

⚙ Workshop: Creating a Simple User Interface

Now that we've gone through most of XAML's important concepts, let's put them together to create a simple XAML user interface. For this example, we'll create a simple application where you enter some information about yourself (first and last name), which will then be displayed in a message box when you click a button. We'll be using a form containing two text boxes with corresponding labels, a combo box, and a button, all laid out using a Grid control. When in the designer, it should look similar to Figure 2-14.

Figure 2-14. *A simple user interface layout*

1. Create a new project named Chapter02Workshop using the Silverlight Application project template.

2. Open the `MainPage.xaml` file in this new project. You'll find the following XAML:

```xml
<UserControl x:Class="Chapter02Workshop.MainPage"
    xmlns="http://schemas.microsoft.com/winfx/2006/xaml/presentation"
    xmlns:x="http://schemas.microsoft.com/winfx/2006/xaml"
    xmlns:d="http://schemas.microsoft.com/expression/blend/2008"
    xmlns:mc="http://schemas.openxmlformats.org/markup-compatibility/2006"
    mc:Ignorable="d"
    d:DesignHeight="300" d:DesignWidth="400">

    <Grid x:Name="LayoutRoot" Background="White">

    </Grid>
</UserControl>
```

3. Note the Grid named LayoutRoot. We will use this to lay out our controls by configuring the rows and columns (three rows and two columns). This will be used to lay out the controls in your view:

```
<Grid x:Name="LayoutRoot">
    <Grid.ColumnDefinitions>
        <ColumnDefinition Width="80" />
        <ColumnDefinition Width="190" />
    </Grid.ColumnDefinitions>
    <Grid.RowDefinitions>
        <RowDefinition Height="Auto" />
        <RowDefinition Height="Auto" />
        <RowDefinition Height="Auto" />
    </Grid.RowDefinitions>
</Grid>
```

4. We can now define our controls within this Grid. Add two TextBlock controls, one displaying the text "First Name:" and the other displaying "Last Name:". Adding these gives you two TextBox controls for entering the data into and a Button control displaying OK as its content to the Grid's content area.

```
<Grid x:Name="LayoutRoot">
    <Grid.ColumnDefinitions>
        <ColumnDefinition Width="80" />
        <ColumnDefinition Width="190" />
    </Grid.ColumnDefinitions>
    <Grid.RowDefinitions>
        <RowDefinition Height="Auto" />
        <RowDefinition Height="Auto" />
        <RowDefinition Height="Auto" />
    </Grid.RowDefinitions>

    <TextBlock Text="First Name:" />
    <TextBox />
    <TextBlock Text="Last Name:" />
    <TextBox />
    <Button Content="OK" />
</Grid>
```

5. All of these controls will be overlapping each other in the Grid's top-left cell. We now need to assign each control to a specific row/column in the Grid using the Grid's Row and Column attached properties:

```
<TextBlock Grid.Column="0" Grid.Row="0" Text="First Name:" />
<TextBox Grid.Column="1" Grid.Row="0" />
<TextBlock Grid.Column="0" Grid.Row="1" Text="Last Name:" />
<TextBox Grid.Column="1" Grid.Row="1" />
<Button Grid.Column="1" Grid.Row="2" Content="OK" />
```

6. Give each user input control a name so that we can reference them in the code-behind:

```
<TextBlock Grid.Column="0" Grid.Row="0" Text="First Name:" />
<TextBox Grid.Column="1" Grid.Row="0" Name="firstNameTextBox" />
<TextBlock Grid.Column="0" Grid.Row="1" Text="Last Name:" />
<TextBox Grid.Column="1" Grid.Row="1" Name="lastNameTextBox" />
<Button Grid.Column="1" Grid.Row="2" Name="OKButton" Content="OK" />
```

7. To complete the layout, add some margins to the controls, align the TextBlock controls so that they are centered vertically in their Grid cells, give the button a width, and align it horizontally to the right:

```
<TextBlock Grid.Column="0" Grid.Row="0" Margin="3" Text="First Name:"
        VerticalAlignment="Center" />
<TextBox Grid.Column="1" Grid.Row="0" Margin="3" Name="firstNameTextBox" />
<TextBlock Grid.Column="0" Grid.Row="1" Margin="3" Text="Last Name:"
        VerticalAlignment="Center" />
<TextBox Grid.Column="1" Grid.Row="1" Margin="3" Name="lastNameTextBox" />
<Button Grid.Column="1" Grid.Row="2" Margin="3" Name="OKButton" Content="OK"
        Width="100" HorizontalAlignment="Right" />
```

■ **Note** If you're typing this XAML out by hand, you will find that Visual Studio's IntelliSense is a big help, making it quite quick and easy to write. However, this project is available online for you to download if required.

8. Now, add an event handler for the Click event to the Button control. As the Click event is the default event for the Button, the easy way to create the event handler in the code-behind and wire up the control to it in the XAML is to simply double-click the button in the designer. Alternatively, you can set the Click attribute on the Button element to the name of the event handler in the code-behind:

```
<Button Grid.Column="1" Grid.Row="2" Margin="3" Name="OKButton" Content="OK"
        Width="100" HorizontalAlignment="Right" Click="OKButton_Click" />
```

9. The XAML defining the user interface is now complete. The complete XAML for the page you should now have follows:

```
<UserControl x:Class="Chapter02Workshop.MainPage"
    xmlns="http://schemas.microsoft.com/winfx/2006/xaml/presentation"
    xmlns:x="http://schemas.microsoft.com/winfx/2006/xaml"
    xmlns:d="http://schemas.microsoft.com/expression/blend/2008"
    xmlns:mc="http://schemas.openxmlformats.org/markup-compatibility/2006"
    mc:Ignorable="d">

    <Grid x:Name="LayoutRoot">
        <Grid.ColumnDefinitions>
            <ColumnDefinition Width="80" />
            <ColumnDefinition Width="190" />
        </Grid.ColumnDefinitions>
        <Grid.RowDefinitions>
            <RowDefinition Height="Auto" />
            <RowDefinition Height="Auto" />
            <RowDefinition Height="Auto" />
        </Grid.RowDefinitions>

        <TextBlock Grid.Column="0" Grid.Row="0" Margin="3" Text="First Name:"
                VerticalAlignment="Center" />
        <TextBox Grid.Column="1" Grid.Row="0" Margin="3" Name="firstNameTextBox" />
```

```
        <TextBlock Grid.Column="0" Grid.Row="1" Margin="3" Text="Last Name:"
                   VerticalAlignment="Center" />
        <TextBox Grid.Column="1" Grid.Row="1" Margin="3" Name="lastNameTextBox" />
        <Button Grid.Column="1" Grid.Row="2" Margin="3" Name="OKButton" Content="OK"
                Width="100" HorizontalAlignment="Right" Click="OKButton_Click" />
    </Grid>
</UserControl>
```

10. Now, we move to the code-behind for the XAML page (in `MainPage.xaml.cs`). We need to handle the button click and display a message box containing the text that the user entered in the text boxes. Add the following code to the event handler in the code-behind, to obtain the values from the controls and display them in a message box:

```
private void OKButton_Click(object sender, RoutedEventArgs e)
{
    MessageBox.Show("Hello " + firstNameTextBox.Text + " " + lastNameTextBox.Text);
}
```

And now you're finished with your very first XAML user interface! Run the application, and try it out. As another exercise, try building the same user interface with Visual Studio 2010's designer using a drag-and-drop approach.

Working with Resources and Resource Dictionaries

Resources are essentially reusable objects and values, somewhat similar in concept to constants in code Resources are ideal for when you want to define a commonly used value once and use it multiple times in your XAML. The advantage of defining a value as a resource is that when you want to change that value, the change can be made in just one place, and it will be automatically applied to all the controls that reference it—making your application much easier customize and maintain.

For example, let's say you have multiple controls that all use the same color as their background:

```
<TextBox Background="LemonChiffon" />
<ComboBox Background="LemonChiffon" />
<CheckBox Background="LemonChiffon" />
```

If you were to change your mind as to what color the control backgrounds should be, you would have to update each control's `Background` property individually. To avoid this issue, you'd ideally define the value as a constant, and have each control reference that constant instead. Resources enable you to do this.

Defining and Referencing Resources

Resources can be defined in the `Resources` property of any control in the object hierarchy. Each resource is assigned a key that can be used to reference it, using the `x:Key` attached property from the XAML namespace, discussed earlier in this chapter. The resource is then available for use by any controls further down the object hierarchy, by referencing it with the key you provided.

■ **Note** The control you define a resource on cannot actually reference that resource. Only controls lower than the control in the object hierarchy on which a resource is defined will have access to that resource.

For example, if you wanted to define a resource available for use by any control within a UserControl, you could define it in its UserControl.Resources. Or if you wanted it to be available projectwide, you could define it in the Application.Resources property on the Application element (in App.xaml). For example, here, we'll create a SolidColorBrush resource in the resources of a UserControl to define a color that can be assigned to control properties throughout that XAML file:

```
<UserControl.Resources>
    <SolidColorBrush x:Key="ControlBackgroundColor" Color="LemonChiffon" />
</UserControl.Resources>
```

Once you have defined a resource, you can assign it to control properties in XAML using the StaticResource markup extension and referencing the resource by its key:

```
<TextBox Background="{StaticResource ControlBackgroundColor}" />
```

■ **Note** It is perfectly legal to define more than one resource with the same key at different levels of the object hierarchy. This enables you to redefine a resource and assign an alternative value to it that had previously been defined higher up in the object hierarchy. For example, you could define the ControlBackgroundColor resource at the application level, and then define another resource with a key of ControlBackgroundColor at the UserControl level but with a different value. Any controls in the UserControl that references the ControlBackgroundColor resource will use the value defined at the UserControl level. When a resource is referenced, the runtime traverses the object hierarchy starting at that control and working upward, until it finds a control that defines a resource with a matching key. It will use the first resource with a matching key that it finds.

Resource Dictionaries

Silverlight also supports defining resources in a resource dictionary. A resource dictionary is a separate XAML file whose root node is ResourceDictionary and that defines a collection of resources that you can then merge into the resources of a control.

■ **Note** You can easily create a new resource dictionary file using the Silverlight Resource Dictionary item template from the Add New Item dialog in Visual Studio or Expression Blend.

As shown earlier, you define resources in a resource dictionary in exactly the same way as in the resources of a control:

```
<ResourceDictionary
    xmlns="http://schemas.microsoft.com/winfx/2006/xaml/presentation"
    xmlns:x="http://schemas.microsoft.com/winfx/2006/xaml">

    <SolidColorBrush x:Key=" ControlBackgroundColor" Color="LemonChiffon" />
</ResourceDictionary>
```

Once you have defined your resource dictionary, you will need to merge it into the resources of a control, enabling those resources to be used by the controls lower in the object hierarchy. The best example of a resource dictionary is the Styles.xaml file in the Silverlight Business Application project template (in the Assets folder). It's merged into the application's resources by adding a ResourceDictionary element to the Resources property, using property element syntax, and adding the resource dictionary file to its MergedDictionaries property:

```
<Application.Resources>
    <ResourceDictionary>
        <ResourceDictionary.MergedDictionaries>
            <ResourceDictionary Source="Assets/Styles.xaml"/>
        </ResourceDictionary.MergedDictionaries>
    </ResourceDictionary>
</Application.Resources>
```

One of the advantages of defining the style resources in a resource dictionary is that you can simply drop a different Styles.xaml file into the Assets folder, with the same resources defined but with different values, to change the theme of your application by overwriting the existing one. The next time you run your Silverlight application, it will be completely restyled according to the resources in the new Styles.xaml file.

■ **Note** Even strings can be defined as resources, which can be very useful to help you localize your application. You can define the strings used in your application in resource dictionaries (one resource dictionary per language) and reference those, rather than hard-coding the strings into your user interface XAML files. You can then merge the appropriate resource dictionary, based on which language the application should use, into your application's resources.

Applying Styles

Let's say that you have multiple TextBox controls in your application that have a common set of property values, which often will specify the formatting applied to the control, like so:

```
<TextBox Background="LemonChiffon" Foreground="Brown" FontWeight="Bold" />
```

Instead of applying these same common property values on each control individually, ideally you would define the property values once in a group, as a resource, and then point the controls that you want to use those values to that resource.

■ **Note** If you've worked on some web-based projects previously, you might like to think of styles as a type of CSS for XAML.

The difference between the resource value method discussed earlier (where you could define a property value as a resource and reuse it) and styles is that the value stored as a resource was only a single value, whereas styles allow you to group a common set of property values and apply them all to a control in one hit. A disadvantage of styles, though, is that the value stored as a resource can be applied to any property of any control, whereas a style must specify what control it applies to and can be applied only to that control.

By removing the need to set property values on each control as they are used, styles enable you to simplify your XAML, make your XAML more maintainable by allowing you to make changes in one place (on the style), have those changes automatically flow through to all the controls that reference that style, and enable you to maintain consistency across the look of all you controls.

Let's now look at how you define and use styles.

Defining a Style Resource

Styles are defined as resources. To use a style, you must define it as a resource on a control somewhere higher up in the object hierarchy. Let's say the values of the Background, Foreground, and FontWeight properties on the TextBox in our previous example are used by multiple text boxes in our application. We can define these property values in a style, like so:

```
<UserControl.Resources>
    <Style TargetType="TextBox" x:Key="TextBoxStyle">
        <Setter Property="Background" Value="LemonChiffon" />
        <Setter Property="Foreground" Value="Brown" />
        <Setter Property="FontWeight" Value="Bold" />
    </Style>
</UserControl.Resources>
```

This style has been defined on the Resource property of the UserControl, using property element syntax, as discussed earlier in this chapter. Note that the type of control that the style can be applied to is specified using the TargetType property of the style (this is mandatory). We also assign the style resource a key using x:Key—the controls we want to apply it to can reference it by this key. Then, it's a case of creating a Setter element for each property you want to define a value for, providing it the name of the property and its corresponding value.

Applying the Style to a Control

You can then apply this style to each control that should use it using the StaticResource markup extension and the resource key assigned to the style:

```
<TextBox Style="{StaticResource TextBoxStyle}" />
```

This example *explicitly* applies the style to the control by assigning the style resource to its Style property, but Silverlight 4 introduced the ability to *implicitly* apply a style to controls instead. Implicit styling enables you to create a style and have it automatically applied to all controls matching the style's TargetType. Using an implicit style makes adding a theme to your application a lot easier and reduces the verbosity of your XAML. The downside is that implicit styling doesn't allow you to selectively apply the style to given controls matching the TargetType. Implicit styles are identical to explicit styles, except you omit the resource key when defining the style resource. This style will then be automatically used by all controls matching the style's TargetType (those lower in the object hierarchy than the style resource definition), without their Style properties needing to be set.

■ **Note** Explicit and implicit styles will be discussed in detail in Chapter 9.

Introducing Templates

Templates enable you to completely customize the way a control or part of a control looks and are arguably one of XAML's most powerful features. Whereas styles enable you to define a group of property values that can be applied to a control or part of a control, templates enable you to completely redefine the XAML that forms its appearance. Because XAML enables a clear separation between look and behavior, maintaining only a contract between the two, as long as you fulfill the needs of the contract you can modify the control to look however you desire. These templates can be stored as resources and reused by multiple controls. There are two key types of templates in Silverlight: control templates and data templates.

A control template enables you to completely redefine the XAML for a control, hence completely changing its appearance. For example, you may want to customize a Button control to be round, instead of its default rectangular shape. You can define the XAML that accomplishes this alternative appearance as a control template and then apply this template to any Button controls that you want to look that way. Control templates are covered further in Chapters 9 and 12.

A data template enables you to define a custom way in which data should be displayed in a control. For example, you may want to customize the appearance of each item in a ComboBox control. Let's say the ComboBox is displaying a list of countries, but you also want to display the country's flag next to its name. To achieve this result, you can specify alternate XAML that the control will use to display each item as a data template. Data templates are covered further in Chapters 6, 7, and 10.

Data Binding

Data binding provides a way of connecting your user interface to a source of data, such as an object in your application. This is an elegant means of displaying data in your user interface and enabling the user to update the data and have those changes automatically pushed back into the bound object.

Rather than pushing data into the user interface from the code-behind, XAML's powerful data binding capabilities enable the user interface to pull data in from the appropriate source and populate itself as required.

Silverlight supports a very rich and flexible data binding model, and this data binding model is one of Silverlight's key strengths and one you will find extremely useful when building business applications. In Silverlight, you can bind to objects, resources, and even properties on other controls. As long as a property is a dependency property (dependency properties are a special type of property, discussed in Chapter 12), you can bind it to almost anything. Data binding is implemented using the Binding markup extension.

A data binding requires a source and a target. The source is usually a property on an object, and the target is usually a property on a control. When bound together, the property on the control will be assigned the value of the property on the object.

Figure 2-15 provides a visual interpretation of a binding, connecting the FirstName property of a class named Person (source) to the Text property of a TextBox control (target).

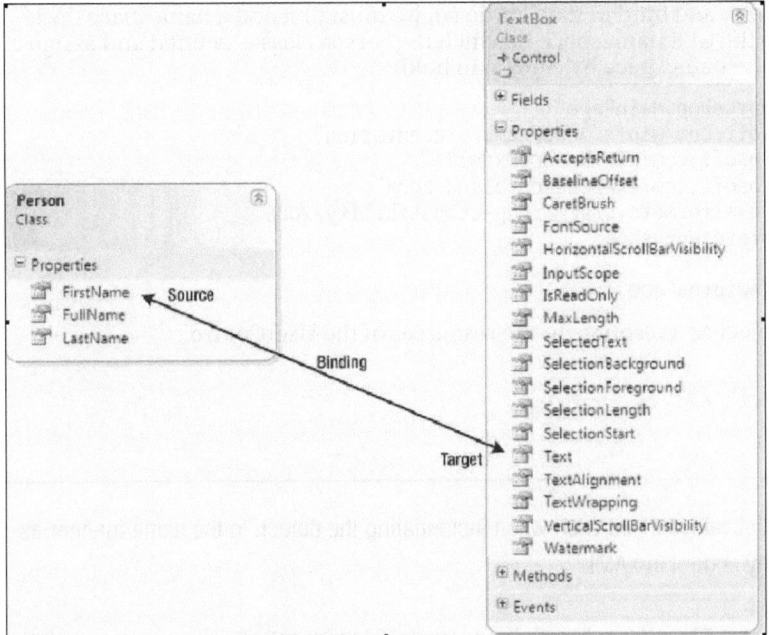

Figure 2-15. *Visual interpretation of a binding*

There are a number of ways to set the source of a data binding. Let's look at those now.

Setting the Source of a Binding

As previously mentioned, you bind a property of a control to a property on an object in XAML using the Binding markup extension. Recall from earlier in this chapter that a markup extension is just a class containing some logic, which is evaluated at runtime and returns a value as a result. When used in XAML, markup extensions are denoted by the curly brackets surrounding them. Before we get into how we specify what source that a binding should use, let's actually set up that source.

Say we have a class called Person in our project, containing the properties FirstName and LastName, matching the fields in our user interface created earlier:

```
public class Person
{
    public string FirstName { get; set; }
    public string LastName { get; set; }

    public string FullName
    {
        get { return FirstName + " " + LastName; }
    }
}
```

This class has to be instantiated as an object, and its properties should be assigned some values before it is consumed by a binding. We could push a Person object into the user interface via some code-behind or use a data source control to obtain it, but for this example, we'll take a XAML-only approach, and instantiate the object as a resource and bind to that. To do so, we must first add a namespace declaration to our XAML file to reference the CLR namespace in which the Person class is defined and assign a prefix that we can use to reference the namespace by (shown in bold):

```
<UserControl x:Class="Chapter02Workshop.MainPage"
    xmlns="http://schemas.microsoft.com/winfx/2006/xaml/presentation"
    xmlns:x="http://schemas.microsoft.com/winfx/2006/xaml"
    xmlns:d="http://schemas.microsoft.com/expression/blend/2008"
    xmlns:mc="http://schemas.openxmlformats.org/markup-compatibility/2006"
    xmlns:my="clr-namespace:Chapter02Workshop"
    mc:Ignorable="d"
    d:DesignHeight="300" d:DesignWidth="400" >
```

Then, we can instantiate the object as a resource in the resources of the UserControl:

```
<UserControl.Resources>
    <my:Person x:Key="personObject" />
</UserControl.Resources>
```

■ **Note**   You can assign the object initial values if you wish when instantiating the object, in the same manner as you would assign property values on any control in XAML:

```
<UserControl.Resources>
    <my:Person x:Key="personObject" FirstName="Chris" LastName="Anderson" />
</UserControl.Resources>
```

Now, we have an object that our bindings can use as a data source. Let's say we have a TextBox control and want to bind its Text property (the target) to the FirstName property on this object (the source). There are two things that we need to set as part of this binding: the object we should use as the data source and the property on that object it should get the value from. The Binding markup extension has a Source property and a Path property, so we can point these properties to the object resource and property name respectively, like so:

```
<TextBox Text="{Binding Source={StaticResource personObject}, Path=FirstName}" />
```

One problem with this syntax is that you often have many bindings on a control that use the same data source, and specifying the data source on every binding leads to messy and unmaintainable XAML. The solution to this is to assign the data source to the control's DataContext property. You can omit setting the Source property on the bindings, and the bindings on this control will then use the value assigned to the DataContext property as their data source, unless a binding specifies otherwise.

```
<TextBox DataContext="{StaticResource personObject}" Text="{Binding Path=FirstName}" />
```

However, you often have many controls whose bindings share the same data source, and assigning the same data source to the DataContext property on each control still leads to messy and unmaintainable XAML. Fortunately, when you assign a value to the DataContext property on a control, the value will also be inherited down the object hierarchy. This means that any controls below that control will also have the object assigned to their DataContext properties. Let's say all the controls that you wished to bind to the object were in a Grid control. You could, therefore, simply assign the object to the Grid's DataContext property, and all controls within it would inherit its value for their own data context, without requiring you to assign their DataContext properties individually:

```xaml
<Grid DataContext="{StaticResource personObject}">
    <TextBox Grid.Column="1" Grid.Row="0" Margin="3" Text="{Binding Path=FirstName}" />
    <TextBox Grid.Column="1" Grid.Row="1" Margin="3" Text="{Binding Path=LastName}" />
</Grid>
```

■ **Note**   You may be familiar with data source controls such as the BindingSource control in Windows Forms or the ObjectDataSource control in ASP.NET. These data sources often have the role of obtaining the data to be displayed in the user interface (handling the pulling process), which controls in the view can then bind to. No data source control is included in the standard control library in Silverlight. However, Chapter 5 covers the Domain-DataSource control, which is a part of RIA Services, and discusses data source control type behavior.

 Workshop: Binding to an Object

For this example, we'll use the simple user interface created earlier in the previous workshop and walk through instantiating an object (in XAML), using that object as the data source of any bindings on the TextBox controls. We'll then bind the Text property on the TextBox controls to it, which will display the object's property values and enable them to be updated by the user.

1.   Add a new class to your project, named Person. Add the following code to it:

```csharp
namespace Chapter02Workshop
{
    public class Person
    {
        public string FirstName { get; set; }
        public string LastName { get; set; }

        public string FullName
        {
            get { return FirstName + " " + LastName; }
        }
    }
}
```

2.   In the MainPage.xaml file we created in the previous example, add a person-Object resource to your project that references the Person class just created, setting some default values for its properties. You should have the following XAML:

```xaml
<UserControl x:Class="Chapter02Workshop.MainPage"
    xmlns="http://schemas.microsoft.com/winfx/2006/xaml/presentation"
    xmlns:x="http://schemas.microsoft.com/winfx/2006/xaml"
    xmlns:d="http://schemas.microsoft.com/expression/blend/2008"
    xmlns:mc="http://schemas.openxmlformats.org/markup-compatibility/2006"
    xmlns:my="clr-namespace:Chapter02Workshop"
    mc:Ignorable="d"
    d:DesignHeight="300" d:DesignWidth="400" >
```

```
<UserControl.Resources>
    <my:Person x:Key="personObject" />
</UserControl.Resources>

<Grid x:Name="LayoutRoot">
    <Grid.ColumnDefinitions>
        <ColumnDefinition Width="80" />
        <ColumnDefinition Width="190" />
    </Grid.ColumnDefinitions>

    <Grid.RowDefinitions>
        <RowDefinition Height="Auto" />
        <RowDefinition Height="Auto" />
        <RowDefinition Height="Auto" />
    </Grid.RowDefinitions>

    <TextBlock Grid.Column="0" Grid.Row="0" Margin="3" Text="First Name:"
            VerticalAlignment="Center" />
    <TextBox Grid.Column="1" Grid.Row="0" Margin="3" Name="firstNameTextBox" />
    <TextBlock Grid.Column="0" Grid.Row="1" Margin="3" Text="Last Name:"
            VerticalAlignment="Center" />
    <TextBox Grid.Column="1" Grid.Row="1" Margin="3" Name="lastNameTextBox" />
    <Button Grid.Column="1" Grid.Row="2" Margin="3" Name="OKButton" Content="OK"
            Width="100" HorizontalAlignment="Right" />
</Grid>
</UserControl>
```

3. Find the opening tag of the Grid control (named LayoutRoot), and assign the personObject resource to its DataContext property:

```
<Grid x:Name="LayoutRoot" DataContext="{StaticResource personObject}">
```

4. The final step is to bind the controls to this data by writing a data binding expression, using the Binding markup expression. Here, we want to associate the FirstName property of the person object with the Text property of the TextBox to show the person's first name; we're using the Path property of the Binding markup expression and the LastName property of the person object with the Text property of the TextBox to show the person's last name:

```
<TextBox Grid.Column="1" Grid.Row="0" Margin="3"
        Name="firstNameTextBox" Text="{Binding FirstName, Mode=TwoWay}" />

<TextBox Grid.Column="1" Grid.Row="1" Margin="3"
        Name="lastNameTextBox" Text="{Binding LastName, Mode=TwoWay}" />
```

■ **Note** The default property of the `Binding` markup expression is the `Path` property, enabling you to specify a value for the `Path` property without needing to explicitly specify which property you are assigning it to in the binding expression. This means that

```
Text="{Binding Path=FirstName, Mode=TwoWay}"
```

can instead be written as

```
Text="{Binding FirstName, Mode=TwoWay}"
```

You may have noted that we are explicitly setting the `Mode` property on the binding expression. The binding mode specifies the direction of the data flow. There are three different binding modes:

- `OneTime`: This option enables the target to obtain a value from the source object, after which the binding is discarded, until a new object is assigned to the data context. Changes to the source object will *not* be propagated back to the target property, and changes to the target property's value in the user interface will *not* be propagated back to the source object. Use this option when the source object is guaranteed not to change.

- `OneWay`: This option enables the target to obtain a value from the source object and be notified when that source value is updated so that the target can update itself with the new value. Changes to the source object *will* be propagated back to the target property, but changes to the target property's value in the user interface will *not* be propagated back to the source object. Use this option when the source object may change, but the value cannot be changed in the user interface, such as when binding to a TextBlock control.

- `TwoWay`: This option enables the target to obtain a value from the source object, be notified when that source value is updated so that it can update itself with the new value, and update that value with changes made to the target. Changes to the source object *will* be propagated back to the target property, and changes to the target property's value in the user interface *will* be propagated back to the source object. Use this option when any changes made to the target in the user interface, such as the Text property of the TextBox control, should update the source object accordingly.

By default, data binding expressions use the `OneWay` mode. Since changes made to the data in the user interface are not saved back to the source object with `OneWay` mode, it is therefore particularly necessary for data input controls to explicitly specify `TwoWay` mode on their binding expressions.

■ **Note** In order for changes made to a data-bound property in the code-behind to be propagated to the user interface, you will need to implement the INotifyPropertyChanged interface on your class and call the PropertyChanged event in the property's setter. Changes to the values of automatically implemented properties will not notify the user interface that they have been updated because, unfortunately, they do not support the INotifyPropertyChanged interface, and hence any changes to them will not be reflected on the screen. However, dependency properties *do* automatically notify any controls bound to them when their value changes. Further discussion of this topic and examples of implementing the INotifyPropertyChanged interface can be found in Chapter 7.

Any changes made in the text boxes in the user interface will update the properties on the source object that they're bound to automatically. You can prove this by updating the values in the text boxes and then displaying the corresponding property values from the bound object in a message box:

```
private void OKButton_Click(object sender, RoutedEventArgs e)
{
    Person person = LayoutRoot.DataContext as Person;
    MessageBox.Show("Hello " + person.FullName);
}
```

■ **Note** You can use many advanced options when binding, such as converting the data in the source object to something different before assigning it to the target (and vice versa) with a value converter, which is particularly useful for converting the data from one type to another, and specifying how invalid data exceptions are handled. These more advanced data binding concepts are covered in Chapter 11.

Binding to a Collection

You will find that binding a control to a collection is a slightly different scenario than binding to a single object. Controls that expect a collection to bind to (for example, DataGrid, ComboBox, and ListBox) have a different property, often named ItemsSource, that the items to be displayed in that control will be populated from; they don't obtain the collection from the DataContext property.

For example, say you have a class representing a collection of Person objects:

```
public class People : List<Person>
{
    public People()
    {
        this.Add(new Person() { FirstName = "Homer", LastName = "Simpson" });
        this.Add(new Person() { FirstName = "Marge", LastName = "Simpson" });
        this.Add(new Person() { FirstName = "Bart", LastName = "Simpson" });
        this.Add(new Person() { FirstName = "Lisa", LastName = "Simpson" });
        this.Add(new Person() { FirstName = "Maggie", LastName = "Simpson" });
    }
}
```

and you instantiate this class as a resource in XAML:

```
<UserControl.Resources>
    <my:People x:Key="peopleCollection" />
</UserControl.Resources>
```

You can bind this resource to the ItemsSource property of a ListBox control and set its DisplayMemberPath property to the name of the property on the Person object whose value will be displayed for each item in the list:

```
<ListBox ItemsSource="{StaticResource peopleCollection}" DisplayMemberPath="FullName" />
```

The ListBox control takes this collection, and it creates a corresponding ListBoxItem object for each Person object in the People collection, which it adds to its Items collection. The most interesting part of this is that the DataContext property of each ListBoxItem is automatically assigned its corresponding Person object from the collection. This allows you to identify the source object for a particular ListBoxItem—when it is selected, for example—and enables you to template each item and bind to properties on that object.

■ **Note** Visual Studio 2010 provides a very good data binding expression builder from the Properties window, which can be very helpful when learning how to write data binding expressions. Visual Studio 2010 also has a great way to easily create forms, complete with bindings, from an object. Simply add your object as a new data source to the Data Sources tool window, select the type of controls the object and each of its properties should use, and drag it from the Data Sources tool window onto your design surface. You can then change the generated form as you see fit.

Designing User Experiences

Although I can't go into too much depth here about designing user experiences, it's worth touching on the concept anyway, because it's something you will often hear about when XAML-based technologies are being discussed.

Traditionally, developers have an inherent focus on function over form when it comes to designing applications—that is, ensuring that they work as per the specifications rather than focusing on how they look and behave. However, there is a big push nowadays for producing applications that are not only functional but also a pleasure for the user to use—software that works the way that the user works, rather than making the user work the way that it works. From the wish to achieve this outcome, the process of user experience (often referred to as UX) design emerged.

Contrary to popular belief, designing user experiences is not about designing the look of the application (which is the role of a graphic designer) but instead designing the behavior of the application. The outcome of this process should be a user interface that is tailored to the needs of the users and how they interact with the application. Hence, the user experience design process may or may not be the role of graphic designers, depending on their skill set. (User experience design is a whole skill in itself, not necessarily related to the ability to create visually pleasing user interfaces.) Instead, UX design has given rise to the specialized role of the user experience designer, whose responsibility is to design the user interface from a user-centric perspective.

The concept of user experience design is regularly used in conjunction Silverlight and WPF development because these technologies leverage the power of XAML for designing user interfaces. XAML is the key technology that enables the design of unique and customized user experiences in Silverlight.

Because of the incredible flexibility provided by XAML to intricately customize the look and behavior of your application, unique user experiences, and unique user interfaces, can emerge.

Because the controls are highly customizable, you are no longer locked into only the functionality and appearance—including the limitations—that a control provides out of the box. Hence, you have a lot of power to bend the user interface to your requirements.

In particular, there is a big debate over the overuse of the DataGrid control in business applications. The DataGrid control is generally used as a quick, easy, all-purpose control; however, this is often at the expense of the user's experience. Every time you use it, you should ask yourself whether you should really be using that control and reinforcing the old paradigm, to the possible detriment of the user, or instead see whether there is a way to achieve a better interaction with the user for that feature.

User experience design should be done before you actually start development on the application, as the outcome of the user experience design will have a big impact on the core design. SketchFlow, a part of Expression Blend, provides a lot of support for the user experience design process and provides a basis from which you can build a fully functional application.

Enhancing the Designer/Developer Workflow

The designer/developer workflow is another topic that is beyond the scope of this book, but it's worth noting that XAML is the key enabler in providing a clear separation of concerns between the user interface and the code, and hence a reasonably clear separation between the roles of the designer and those of the developer. Generally, the designer will be focused on the look and behavior of the user interface, while the developer will be focused on writing the code that services the needs of the user interface.

The clear separation of these roles enabled by XAML reduces the friction between the designer and the developer, enabling a designer to work in Expression Blend on a feature for the user interface at the same time the developer is working in Visual Studio on the code aspects of the corresponding feature, without clashing.

Designing XAML User Interfaces from a Different Perspective

XAML brings many benefits to developing user interfaces, but requires you to take a different approach to laying out the controls on the page and interacting with the code-behind. If you primarily develop Windows Forms applications, you are probably used to simply dropping controls on a form and pushing data into them from the code-behind. Essentially, you are probably used to the code-behind controlling the user interface, with the user interface functioning in a subservient role.

While this structure is still possible in Silverlight, the power of XAML enables the user interface to take the controlling role, with the code-behind (or a ViewModel, which is a part of the Model-View-ViewModel [MVVM] design pattern) merely supporting it. This requires a mental leap, because your user interface should now pull the data into itself—a concept enabled by XAML's advanced data binding capabilities.

This new perspective for designing and structuring an application requires a new supporting pattern, and this comes in the form of the new MVVM design pattern. The primary reasons you'd want to use this design pattern are to help maintain a clean separation between the designer and developer components of a project and to design a more testable application than was previously possible. We'll cover this pattern in depth in Chapter 13, but in the meantime, to keep the number of new concepts being demonstrated at any one time to a minimum, we'll discuss the more familiar and easier approach of simply using the code-behind to support and control the user interface.

Summary

As you've seen through this chapter, there is a lot to learn about XAML, and yet this is just an introduction covering XAML's core features! Chapter 10 will cover many more advanced features of XAML, but this chapter should have given you enough to get started developing user interfaces in Silverlight, and you will use many of the concepts covered here in the following chapters.

The power and flexibility of XAML, unfortunately, results in a steep learning curve that even experienced and productive developers in other technologies will need to climb. This will take some time and possibly lead to some frustration and will require patience and a willingness to learn. Expect to be less productive as a developer than normal while you get up to speed. However, once you do so, you will really start to appreciate the benefits and new possibilities that the use of XAML provides. You will also be able to transfer many of these new skills to WPF development, which shares most of Silverlight's XAML concepts, and to Windows Phone 7 development, whose applications are mostly developed using Silverlight, as it gains in popularity as a technology for developing rich desktop applications.

The best way to learn XAML is probably to start with dragging controls from the toolbox onto the designer, setting properties in the Properties window, and observing the XAML that the designer produces. The designer, however, won't always be there for you, and you may find that you have to resort to writing XAML by hand at times. Therefore, a complete reliance on letting the designer write the XAML for you is probably unwise. Inspecting existing XAML files created by other developers or designers and cross-referencing the XAML in them with what's been discussed in this chapter is another method that might help you get up to speed.

In the end, you may choose to use the designer for most tasks and let it produce the XAML, but it's important to at least understand the underlying concepts of XAML and have some familiarity with its syntax. If you choose to hand write XAML, or find yourself needing to do so, you will find that once you understand the syntax, the IntelliSense in both Visual Studio 2010 and Expression Blend make writing XAML a breeze.

CHAPTER 3

The Navigation Framework

One of the issues in the early versions of Silverlight was that when you created a new Silverlight project, you were essentially given a blank slate—with no existing user interface structure or framework to help you get started. This created quite a barrier for creating business applications in Silverlight, which typically contain complex user interfaces with numerous views that the user must navigate between. Therefore, to attempt to create a business application of any size in Silverlight 2, you had to start by creating a user interface framework.

Note When you create a new project using the Silverlight Application project template, you get exactly the user interface structure that was available in Silverlight 2.

Silverlight 3 introduced the navigation framework to act as the foundation and structure for your application's user interface, which helped this problem significantly. It provides a user interface framework for creating single document interface (SDI) applications, in which only a single screen of information (that is, content) is presented to the user at a time, but users are able to navigate between multiple screens (which will be referred to as "views").

Two project templates were added in Silverlight 3 (the Silverlight Navigation Application and Silverlight Business Application project templates discussed in Chapter 1), which already implement the navigation framework and help you get started building an application.

In this chapter, we'll take a look at how you make use of the navigation framework in your applications—but let's first discuss the various types of application navigation patterns and where the navigation framework fits into these.

Getting Started with the Navigation Framework

A typical business application consists of a number of views, which act as content to be displayed within an outer shell. This shell generally includes ways of navigating around the application (along with headers, footers, etc.). The project created in Chapter 1 using the Silverlight Business Application project template is a good example of this. If you haven't done so already, create a new project using this template now. In this project, you will have a shell and two views (Home and About). When you compile and run this project, you will get the user interface shown in Figure 3-1.

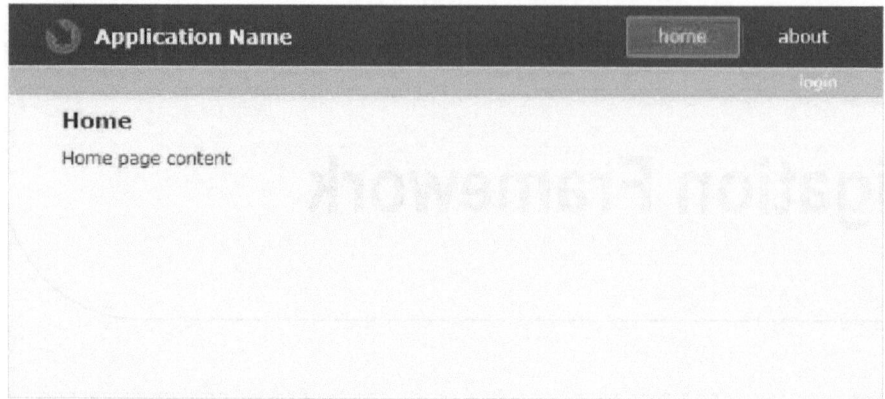

Figure 3-1. The default user interface created with the Silverlight Business Application project template

When you click the "home" and "about" buttons in the header, the view that is displayed in the body of the application's user interface will change accordingly. If you use the browser's navigation functions (i.e., the Back and Forward buttons), you can navigate through the navigation history in your application in much the same way as if it were a web site. The navigation framework provides all this functionality for you.

Looking now at the project structure (as shown in Figure 3-2) and how it relates to what you see on the screen, the MainPage.xaml file acts as the application shell, while the Home.xaml and About.xaml files in the Views folder are the individual views that are displayed as content within the shell.

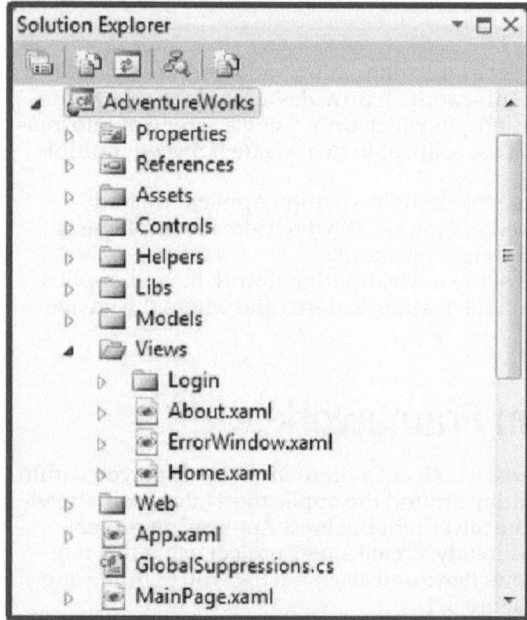

Figure 3-2. The project structure

■ **Note** Windows Presentation Foundation (WPF) also has a navigation framework, and the structure of the navigation framework in Silverlight was designed to be closely aligned with its WPF counterpart.

Exploring the Components of the Navigation Framework

The two core components of the navigation framework are the Frame control and the Page class. There are also two other helper objects that enable you to navigate between views and get information about a navigation operation—the NavigationService class and the NavigationContext class. Let's take a look at each of these components and what roles they play in the navigation framework.

The Frame Control

The Frame control is a host container for views. Therefore, it is normally used in a master page that provides the outer shell of the application and hosts the views as content. When provided with a URI specifying the view to load and display, it will pass that URI through a converter to obtain a path to the view that it can then navigate to.

The Frame control also provides browser journal (history) integration and handles navigation events raised by the browser, such as clicking the Back and Forward buttons, entering new URIs via the address bar, and so on.

In the project you created from the Silverlight Business Application project template, the MainPage.xaml file, acting as the application shell, contains a Frame control, enabling it to host the views.

The Page Class

Views must inherit from the Page class, which enables them to be hosted in a Frame control.

■ **Note** There's somewhat of an inconsistency in the use of terminology within the navigation framework (pages vs. views), which should be clarified to avoid confusion. In the Model-View-ViewModel (MVVM) design pattern discussed in Chapter 13, I refer to each of these "content" pages as a "view." In the default Silverlight Business Application project template these views reside in the Views folder, which makes perfect sense. However, the views inherit from the Page class, and you use the Silverlight Page item template when adding a new view to your project. The term "page" tends to conjure up the image of a web page, which is not really a valid comparison. From its name, you might also expect the MainPage class to inherit from Page, but it actually inherits from UserControl. Ideally, the Page class would have been named View instead, which would have solved this inconsistency. However, this would put it out of alignment with WPF's navigation framework. If this bothers you, you might consider creating a class called View that inherits from Page, which you can use in Page's place. Generally, it's also a good idea to suffix the name of each view with View—for example, HomeView, AboutView, and so forth. Throughout this book, when I mention the term "view," it will generally be in reference to one of these XAML files that inherits from Page.

In the project you created from the Silverlight Business Application project template, you will find that the Home.xaml and About.xaml files in the Views folder both inherit from the Page class.

You can create additional views by using the Silverlight Page item template when adding a new item to your project.

■ **Note** On each view, ensure that you set the Title property, which is inherited from the Page class, to the name of that view. The value of this property will be displayed in the browser's title bar and in the history when the view has been navigated to.

The NavigationService Object

Each Frame control instance creates a NavigationService object that is shared with the views it hosts, accessible via a property on the Page class each view inherits from. This NavigationService object is used to maintain an independence between the views and their host (the Frame control) and contains the methods that enable you to programmatically navigate around the application.

The NavigationContext Object

The NavigationContext object contains information about the navigation operation that led to the current view being displayed, which amounts to the query string appended to the URI.

You define the layout/structure of your user interface (outer shell) in the MainPage class, and this generally provides the means to navigate between the views. The MainPage class inherits from UserControl, and each view inherits from the Page class, which is a part of the navigation framework. By inheriting from the Page class, the views can be hosted within a Frame control and can handle the various navigation events provided by the navigation framework.

Navigating Between Views

To load and display a view in a Frame control, you need to navigate to it. Navigation operations can be initiated either by code; by a control, such as the HyperlinkButton control; by property bindings, or from the browser via the user clicking the Back and Forward buttons or changing the URI in the address bar. How you invoke a navigation operation depends on from where you are attempting to initiate the navigation. In this section we'll take a look at the various ways that you can initiate a navigation operation in your application, but let's first look at how you specify a view to load and display using a URI.

Using View URIs

In much the same way that a URL can be used to specify the location of a web page to retrieve from a server, you can specify the location of a view to load and display in your application using a URI.

■ **Note** A URL (uniform resource locator) is a type of URI (uniform resource identifier)—a URL is a subset of a URI, as is a URN (uniform resource name). There is a lot of confusion as to the difference between the terms and when to use them. "URI" is the more generic term and thus is generally the safest to use. More information on the differences can be found in the following Wikipedia article:

http://en.wikipedia.org/wiki/Uniform_Resource_Identifier.

This URI will specify the path to the view in your project. For example, in the project you created from the Silverlight Business Application project template, the Home.xaml file would have a URI of /Views/Home.xaml. If you look again at Figure 3-2, you will see that the Home.xaml view can be found in the Views folder, which you can see is represented in the URI. You can therefore load and display this view by navigating to this URI.

To pass data to a view in the URI, you can append query string parameters to it, in much the same way that you might append query string parameters to the URL to a web page. You can even perform fragment navigation (these will be discussed later in this chapter).

Before attempting to load a view from a URI, the Frame control will run it through a URI mapper. A URI mapper takes in a URI and converts it to the path of the view in your application that it corresponds to, using a custom mapping scheme that you can define. This means that when navigating to a view, instead of having to specify the full path of the view to navigate to, you can simply navigate to a custom URI representing that view, and the URI mapper will translate it to the actual path for the Frame control to navigate to. For example, you can define that the "/Home" URI maps to the view found at "/Views/Home.xaml". Configuring URI mapping will be discussed in detail later in this chapter.

■ **Note** It's even possible to navigate to a view in another assembly referenced by your project. The path to the view needs to be of the form "/[assembly];component/[viewpath]". For example, if the Home.xaml view existed in the Views folder of a referenced assembly named MyViews.dll, the path to navigate to it would be "/MyViews;component/Views/Home.xaml".

Navigating using the Frame Control

When you are trying to navigate to a view and display it within a Frame control, you can simply use the navigation methods on the Frame control:

- Navigate
- GoBack
- GoForward
- StopLoading
- Refresh

The Navigate method navigates to a view, taking the URI of the view as a parameter. For example, the following code instructs a Frame (named ContentFrame) to navigate to the Home.xaml view in the project's Views folder:

```
ContentFrame.Navigate(new Uri("/Views/Home.xaml", UriKind.Relative));
```

■ **Note** We are explicitly specifying that a relative URI is being passed in via the UriKind parameter. Although the Uri class has a constructor where only the URI needs to be passed in, it will assume it is an absolute URI instead of a relative URI, and an exception will be raised.

The GoBack and GoForward methods are fairly self-explanatory. They simply mimic the user clicking on the browser's Back and Forward buttons.

The StopLoading method is rarely used when using the Navigation Framework out of the box but can be useful when you implement a custom content loader (discussed later in this chapter) that undertakes a task asynchronously before loading a view that you want to cancel. This will raise the NavigationStopped event on the Frame control.

The Refresh method reloads the current view. Navigating to the URI of the currently loaded view using the Navigate method doesn't actually reload that view, but you can force a reload using this method.

Navigating using the NavigationService Object

The previous example is fine when you are initiating the navigation from the page hosting the Frame control. However, you also might attempt to initiate a navigation operation in code from within a view itself, where you don't have a reference to the Frame control. In this case, the current view is closed, and the view being navigated to is displayed in its place. This is where the NavigationService object, provided by the inherited Page class via a property, comes in. It has the methods that you can use to request a navigation operation on the Frame control hosting the view. It contains the same navigation methods that you will find on the Frame control, and thus is used in the same way:

```
NavigationService.Navigate(new Uri("/Home", UriKind.Relative));
```

Using a HyperlinkButton Control

Another way to initiate a navigation operation is to use the HyperlinkButton control. The HyperlinkButton control contains built-in functionality to request a Frame to navigate to a given view. Here is some sample XAML to define a HyperlinkButton element to navigate to the Home view:

```
<HyperlinkButton Name="HomeLink" NavigateUri="/Home"
                 TargetName="ContentFrame" Content="home" />
```

In this example we are doing the following:

- Giving the element a name (Name)

- Providing the URI to navigate to (NavigateUri)

- Specifying the name of the Frame to navigate within (TargetName)

- Setting the hyperlink's text to be displayed on the screen (Content)

If you have only one Frame on the page, you can leave the TargetName property blank. If you are using the HyperlinkButton control within a view, you can leave the TargetName property blank in that case too.

> ■ **Note** The HyperlinkButton control can also be used to navigate to standard HTML web pages, although these won't be displayed within a Frame control, and attempts to do so will raise an exception. To navigate to a web page, set the `TargetName` property to `_blank`, which will open the link in a new browser window, or set it to `_self` to open it in the current browser window/tab—closing your Silverlight application.

Using the Source Property of the Frame Control

The Frame control has a `Source` property to which you can assign a URI for the Frame control to navigate to and display. This is most useful when you want to bind to a data source containing the URI of the view to be displayed. However, the `Source` property expects a value of type `Uri`, so if you wish to bind it to a string, you will need to use a `ValueConverter` to convert the value to a type of `Uri`.

User-Initiated Navigation

One of the features of the navigation framework is that the current view's URI is appended to the application's URL in the browser's address bar as a bookmark. The user can enter or modify this bookmark manually and have the application navigate to the view that they specify. The Frame control will note this, parse the URI in the bookmark by using a URI mapping scheme and then load the corresponding XAML view within the Frame. This is a concept known as deep linking, which will be discussed in more detail later in this chapter.

Passing Data Between Views

In standard web development, HTML pages are essentially stateless—that is, when the server processes each page request, it is not aware of the requests that came before it. Session variables, cookies, and ASP.NET's view state are workarounds to this issue that simulate statefulness as you navigate through a web site. To pass data to another page in a request, you would usually pass this as query string parameters appended to the end of the URL of the page that accepts the data. Alternatively, you may post complex state data containing state information, such as view state, back to the server to be processed.

By existing entirely on the client side, Silverlight applications aren't subject to this problem of statelessness and are inherently stateful, in the same way as a rich desktop application is stateful. The state of the application is maintained as the user navigates between the views. However, it would not be particularly good design to maintain state information belonging to a small set of views at a global level simply as a means of passing state data between them. Since each view using the navigation framework has an associated URI, the navigation framework follows the standard URI pattern and enables you to include query strings in them, which you can harness to pass data between the views.

Passing Data Using Query String Parameters

Query string parameters enable you to pass simple data types (strings, integers, and so on) from one view to another as you navigate between them. For example, you might want to pass the ID of a selected product from a view displaying a list of products to the view displaying the details of that product.

The query string parameters are appended to the end of the bookmark in the URI when navigating to a view that will consume them. The format that these normally take is:

```
/Views/ProductDetailsView.xaml?ProductID=879
```

In this example, we are passing the `ProductDetailsView` view a query string containing a parameter named `ProductID` and with a value of 879. Note that a question mark, which indicates the start of the query string, is appended to the URI, followed by the parameter name and its value, separated by an equal sign.

You can pass multiple parameters to a view, separating each with an ampersand (&). The following example demonstrates passing the `ProductDetailsView` view both a `ProductID` and a `SupplierID`:

```
/Views/ProductDetailsView.xaml?ProductID=879&SupplierID=437
```

Depending on your URI mapping scheme, the query string parameters don't need to take this extended form (`ParameterName=Value`). Instead, we could use a much friendlier URI in place of the one from the first example, such as:

```
ProductDetails/879
```

This URI will be mapped and parsed internally in the application using the specified URI mapping scheme to convert it to its standard form. How this is achieved will be discussed later in this chapter when we cover URI mapping.

Reading Query String Parameters

When a view needs to read the parameters passed to it in its query string, it can use the `QueryString` property on the view's `NavigationContext` object. This is an indexed collection, where the index is the name of the property you wish to retrieve the value for, for example:

```
object productID = NavigationContext.QueryString["ProductID"];
```

One of the problems with this code is that it returns an object that you will need to cast to the required type. However, if that parameter wasn't provided in the query string, a null value will be returned, and there's no guarantee that it will be of the correct type (requiring additional code to check for this before attempting to convert it).

Parsing query string parameters each time you use them makes for messy code that is hard to read and maintain. This process generally requires you to do the following:

- Ensure the parameter exists.
- Check that the value is of the correct type.
- Convert the value from a string to the required type.

The best way to handle this parsing process is to require that all expected query string parameters have a corresponding strongly typed property (getter only) in the view's code-behind and return the value as the correct type. If a required parameter has not been passed in or is malformed—that is, cannot be converted to the required type or contains an invalid value—it should return a default value or throw an exception. Wrapping the retrieval of a query string parameter in a property this way makes for much cleaner and more maintainable code. For example, the following code is used to handle access to the `ProductID` parameter within a view. As you can see, it checks to see whether the value has been passed in and then parses out the value as an integer and returns it. Whenever you need the value of the `ProductID` query parameter, you can now simply get it from the `ParamProductID` property.

```
private int ParamProductID
{
    get
    {
        int paramValue = 0;
        const string paramName = "ProductID";
```

```
        if (NavigationContext.QueryString.ContainsKey(paramName))
            int.TryParse(NavigationContext.QueryString[paramName], out paramValue);

        return paramValue;
    }
}
```

Passing Complex Data Types Between Views

As you've seen, simple data types can be passed easily between views using query string parameters. However, what if you wanted to pass some more complex data types, such as objects? Say, for example, you wanted to pass the entire product object to the product details view instead of just its ID. You might be able to serialize the product object to a string and pass that as a parameter in the query string, but this idea is exceedingly messy and open to exceeding the maximum length of an acceptable URL, which depends on the browser—but the general recommendation is that it should not exceed approximately 2,000 characters, and the usual advice for user-friendliness is to keep it short. Of course, we could create an application-wide cache to store objects in and retrieve them from, but this design isn't particularly nice or robust.

Unfortunately, the Silverlight navigation framework has no built-in means to post or pass complex data types between views, without resorting to storing them globally in an application-wide cache before navigating away from a view and then retrieving and removing them from the cache when the destination view has loaded. Ideally, an additional parameter to the NavigationService.Navigate method would take an object to which you could attach your state-based values and then pass directly to the view being navigated to, but sadly, this is not the case. The navigation framework is a part of the Silverlight Toolkit, enabling you to add the behavior yourself if you were so inclined. However, modifying a framework like this—where the change cannot be submitted back to the original project, because Microsoft maintains the Silverlight Toolkit project and is the only contributor—is not generally good practice. It makes your implementation nonstandard, preventing you from easily updating to new releases in your project. In Chapter 13, we'll discuss the MVVM pattern, which provides an alternative solution to global variables by maintaining the state in a ViewModel and making it accessible to multiple views.

■ **Note** You should be wary when using the object serialization method of passing complex data between views in a query string parameter. Users may potentially alter the query string in the browser's address bar (or exclude it altogether). They also may potentially bookmark a view with data in the query string and come back to it later, when the data may no longer be valid. Checks should be made to ensure that expected data is available and valid, and situations in which it's not should be handled.

Working with Deep Links

If your Frame control has its JournalOwnership property configured accordingly, you will find that the URI used to navigate to the currently displayed view is appended to the application's host page URL in the address bar. For example, in the link shown in Figure 3-3, notice the hash character (#) indicating the start of the bookmark, followed by ProductDetails. The URI mapping scheme will translate this and load the ProductDetails view.

Figure 3-3. *A sample URL containing a deep link*

This is known as a deep link. Deep linking support is an important feature of the navigation framework, enabling URI-based navigation in your application. While every page in a web site has a URL that enables you to directly navigate and link to it, traditionally, the URL for RIA applications could only point to the entry point of the application. The users would then need to navigate to where they wanted to go within the application from the entry point. Now, with deep linking support, you can provide a URI containing the location of a view deep within your application and have the application automatically navigate there when it is loaded. This deep link can include query string parameters, enabling you, for example, to deep link to a view and display the details of a specific product.

Benefits of deep linking include the following:

- The user can bookmark a location within your application and come back to it later without needing to navigate through the application to get to it.

- The user can send a link to another user, pinpointing a location within the application.

- Deep linking enables the user to go backward and forward, using the browser's Back and Forward buttons, through the navigation history.

Enabling Friendly URIs with URI Mapping

As discussed earlier in this chapter, it's possible to set up a mapping scheme to automatically transform the URI that has been navigated to (visible to the user in the browser's address bar) into a form that the navigation framework can act on, which typically contains the path to the view to navigate to and any query string parameters to pass to it. For example, the mapping could transform the following URI

```
ProductDetails/879
```

to its actual representation internally:

```
/Views/ProductDetailsView.xaml?ProductID=879
```

The feature of the navigation framework that makes this automatic transformation possible is the URI mapper, which is assigned to the Frame control's UriMapper property. When a navigation operation takes place in your application, the Frame control will first parse and transform the given deep link via its URI mapper. It will then use this result to determine what view to load and the query string to pass to it. You will be familiar with the concept of URI mapping if you've worked on an ASP.NET MVC project before, as this mapping is quite similar to the URL routing functionality available there—although in this case we are rewriting only the deep link—not the entire URL, as with ASP.NET MVC URL routing.

■ **Note** Setting up URI mappings in your project is by no means essential, but one advantage of doing so is that it enables you to hide the internal structure of your project, with a side benefit of allowing you to change this internal structure without affecting the links to the views. It can make the URIs less complex and much more readable to end users.

Take a look at the definition of the Frame control in `MainPage.xaml` as generated by the Silverlight Business Application project template, and note the following `UriMapper` property value definition:

```
<navigation:Frame.UriMapper>
    <uriMapper:UriMapper>
        <uriMapper:UriMapping Uri="" MappedUri="/Views/Home.xaml"/>
        <uriMapper:UriMapping Uri="/{pageName}" MappedUri="/Views/{pageName}.xaml"/>
    </uriMapper:UriMapper>
</navigation:Frame.UriMapper>
```

This mapping is used to transform the given URI to the path of its corresponding view, which the Frame control can then navigate to. Note the use of {pageName} in the second route in both the `Uri` and `MappedUri` properties. This parameter token is used to create generic mapping routes. When the format of a URI maps to a route template that contains a token, the corresponding wildcard part of the match will be used to replace the instances of the token in the mapped URI.

To create a token, you simply need to define a name of your own choosing, surround it with curly brackets, and insert it into the appropriate locations in both the URI route template (`Uri` property) and the mapped URI (`MappedUri` property), like so:

```
<uriMapper:UriMapping Uri="/{pageName}" MappedUri="/Views/{pageName}View.xaml"/>
```

So, if a URI with the value /About is passed into the mapper, it matches the preceding route template and map to /Views/AboutView.xaml. This process also comes in handy when mapping query string parameters. For example, to map the following URI from:

```
ProductDetails/879
```

to

```
Views/ProductDetailsView.xaml?ProductID=879
```

we could use the following route template:

```
<navigation:UriMapping Uri="ProductDetails/{id}"
            MappedUri="/Views/ProductDetailsPage.xaml?ProductID={id}" />
```

How does the URI mapper determine whether the given URI maps to a given template? It would be simple if the mapper just checked string equality, but the support for parameter tokens means that it must do pattern matching using regular expressions behind the scenes. The mapper matches the passed-in URI to the constant (that is, nontokenized) parts of the route template, with wildcards in place of the tokens. When a match is found, the value of the tokens is obtained from the wildcard parts in the match.

It is entirely possible that a given URI matches more than one mapping template defined in the scheme. In this case, the first URI mapper that can successfully map the given URI will win, so you need to take care when ordering your routes. Take, for example, the following generic mapping route:

```
<uriMapper:UriMapping Uri="/{pageName}" MappedUri="/Views/{pageName}View.xaml"/>
```

Perhaps you want the deep link to read /AboutUs but the actual XAML view this corresponds to is in the Views folder and named AboutView.xaml. If this deep link were transformed by the preceding route, it would attempt to look for a view called AboutUsView.xaml, which doesn't exist. In this case, to retain the preceding route but still handle this scenario, you would have to ensure that you place the route defining this specific case *above* the generic mapping, like so:

```
<uriMapper:UriMapping Uri="/AboutUs" MappedUri="/Views/AboutView.xaml"/>
<uriMapper:UriMapping Uri="/{pageName}" MappedUri="/Views/{pageName}View.xaml"/>
```

In summary, you should ensure that the concrete route mappings are placed above the generic (tokenized) mappings. Therefore, the order in which you define the route mappings is important; they should be ordered from least generic to most generic. Using the preceding mapping scheme, when the /AboutUs deep link is navigated to, it will be matched to the first route and immediately directed to the AboutView.xaml file as required.

■ **Note** The project won't compile if you try to define a mapping that starts with a tokenized parameter (for example, Uri="{pageName}"). If you start with an open curly bracket, the XAML parser will think you are specifying a markup extension as the value. As described in Chapter 2, in the "Markup Extensions" section, to have this value treated as a literal, you'll need to add open and closed curly brackets with nothing between them before your token, like so: Uri="{}{pageName}".

When a URI is passed in that cannot find a route to map to, the mapping process will fail. When this occurs, the NavigationFailed event will be raised on the Frame control, which you can handle accordingly. The default project template will display an error window when this occurs, but you can change this—for example, to navigate to a different view instead.

You may not want your URI mappings defined directly on the Frame control, because they are in the default project template output or even in the XAML file hosting the Frame control. If so, you can define your mapping scheme as a resource in the App.xaml file or a stand-alone resource dictionary instead and reference it as you would any other resource—using the StaticResource markup extension:

UriMapper="{StaticResource uriMapperKey}"

■ **Note** If you find that you need complex or custom mapping logic that can't be implemented easily using the standard UriMapper URI mapping class, you can write your own mapping class. Create a new class, inherit from UriMapperBase, and override the MapUri method, which will handle the mapping logic. Then, after you've written your logic, you can reference this class as your URI mapper rather than the standard one.

Integrating with the Browser History

In addition to the view changing, you may notice the following when you navigate between views in your application:

- The URI in the address bar changes.
- The status of the browser history buttons is updated.
- The browser's title bar is changed to display the title of the view.

These changes occur because the navigation framework integrates with the browser's journal, which maintains the browser's history. When each view is navigated to in your application, it will be added to the browser's journal, which enables you to navigate through views you have previously visited, using the browser's Back and Forward buttons as if the views were standard HTML web pages.

How the browser maintains these navigation events in its history depends on which browser the user is using. For example, Internet Explorer's history only displays a single entry for the web page hosting the Silverlight application, while Firefox displays each view within the Silverlight application in its history.

■ **Note** In Chapter 16, we'll discuss having the application run outside the browser. In that situation, the browser Back and Forward buttons are not available, nor is the address bar (since it's not running within a browser). However, a navigation journal is still maintained within the application, and if it's important for the users to have the ability to navigate backward and forward through their navigation history, you can detect whether the application is running outside of the browser (checking the value of the App.Current.IsRunningOutOfBrowser property) and display your own Back and Forward buttons to provide this functionality via the GoBack and GoForward methods. You will want to make use of the CanGoBack and CanGoForward properties to check whether each operation is valid before attempting it, because an exception will be raised if the operation cannot be performed.

Generally, you would only have one Frame control in a XAML file, but you can actually host more than one Frame if you wish, and views can also host other "subviews" in a Frame. However, only the top-level Frame can integrate with the browser's journal.

You can use the JournalOwnership property on the Frame control to control whether or not the Frame control integrates with the browser's journal. Valid values for this property include:

- Automatic: This will choose the correct option based on whether a higher-level frame is already using the browser's journal. This is the default value.

- UsesParentJournal: The Frame control will integrate with the browser's journal, as previously described.

- OwnsJournal: With this option, the Frame can still navigate between pages, but moving backward and forward through the history must be done via code. Frames that don't integrate with the browser's journal will not respond to deep links entered into the browser's address bar, and the URI displayed in it will not change as pages are navigated between in that Frame. If the Frame needs to track the history of loaded views, it will need to track them itself.

■ **Note** An example scenario where you might use multiple Frame controls in a view might be where you have a dashboard containing multiple content sections and each content section allows the user to navigate between subviews when drilling down on data.

Handling Navigation Events

When navigation operations take place, you need to know what's happening so you can respond accordingly. The Frame control raises events that you can handle in the MainPage class (the class that hosts the Frame control), while within a view you can choose to either handle the events on the NavigationService object or simply override the navigation methods on the view itself (which are inherited from the Page class).

Frame Events

The Frame control provides the following events that enable you to respond to navigation operations and their current statuses:

- Navigating
- Navigated
- NavigationStopped
- NavigationFailed
- FragmentNavigation

The Navigating event is raised before a navigation operation actually takes place, while the Navigated event is raised after the operation is complete. If you want to stop the navigation operation from actually taking place, you can set the value of e.Cancel to true in the Navigating event handler.

The NavigationStopped event is raised when the StopLoading method on the Frame control or the NavigationService object is called. The NavigationFailed event is raised if the application navigated to an invalid deep link—that is, one that couldn't be mapped to a view by the URI mapper—or the user manually entered an invalid deep link as part of the URI in the browser's address bar.

The FragmentNavigation event is raised instead of the Navigating/Navigated events in a couple of different scenarios. If you start a navigation operation for the view that is currently active in the Frame and you are passing in the same parameters that were passed to the view previously, the FragmentNavigation event is raised. The view is not reloaded. An example of this is clicking the Home button to navigate to the Home view while you are already there. This event might be useful when you need to know that a navigation operation has taken place but the view was not reloaded. This event would also be raised if you were to start a navigation operation and have appended a fragment to the end of the URI to navigate to. For example, you might try this navigation operation:

```
ContentFrame.Navigate(new Uri("ProductDetails/879#StockLevels", UriKind.Relative));
```

Note the # used to indicate the start of the fragment. This syntax might be initially confusing, as the start of the deep link in the resulting URI, which points to the view, is indicated by the same symbol (#). However, you will find that the resulting URI is as follows:

```
ProductDetails/879$StockLevels
```

As you can see, the # is converted to a $, which now indicates the start of the fragment. The purpose of having a fragment in a URI will depend on your needs, but you can easily access its value via the e.Fragment property, which is passed in as a parameter to the FragmentNavigation event handler.

A scenario where you might want to hook into the navigation events on the Frame control might be when you have a toolbar on the Frame host page that needs to know when the active view has been changed in the Frame so that it can highlight the appropriate toolbar button. You can implement this requirement by handling the Navigated event on the Frame control. You can actually find this exact scenario already implemented for you in the default Silverlight Navigation Application project template. The MainPage class handles the Navigated event and changes the styles on the buttons according to whether its corresponding view is currently open. Note also that it handles the NavigationFailed event and displays an error message window if that event is raised.

View Events

There are two methods of responding to a navigation operation within a view. The first is to add an event handler to an event on the NavigationService object (obtained by the NavigationService property on the view), like so:

```
NavigationService.Navigating += NavigationService_Navigating;
```

The same events that were available on the Frame control are available on the NavigationService object.

■ **Note** You cannot add event handlers for the NavigationService's events in the view's constructor, as the NavigationService object will be null at that point and will result in a NullReferenceException being thrown. You should add any event handlers in the view's Loaded event handler instead.

Alternatively, you can override any of the following virtual methods in the view's class, inherited from the Page class, that you want to respond to:

- OnNavigatedTo
- OnNavigatingFrom
- OnNavigatedFrom
- OnFragmentNavigation

Note that there are no overridable methods corresponding to the NavigatingTo, NavigationStopped, or NavigationFailed events on the NavigationService object, but there are two new "events" that we can handle: OnNavigatingFrom and OnNavigatedFrom. One use for overriding the OnNavigatingFrom method is to check whether the current data form is dirty (that is, has unsaved changes) and ask the user whether the changes should be saved before moving away from the view. The navigation operation can be cancelled from within this method by setting the value of e.Cancel to true.

■ **Note** The NavigatedTo event is raised *before* the Loaded event on the view.

Caching Views

When you navigate away from a view, by default, all references to the view are removed, and the view will be cleaned up the next time the garbage collector runs. However, this is not ideal if you need to retain the state of the view, such as when the user has entered unsaved data and is navigating away temporarily, or the view has been populated with data that would need to be retrieved again and repopulated.

You can, however, change this default behavior to cache the view and maintain its state by setting the NavigationCacheMode property on the view appropriately. NavigationCacheMode is a property of the Page class, which you can set in XAML. There are three options:

- `Disabled`: This will result in the view being destroyed once it has been navigated away from and re-created when it's navigated back to. This is the default value.

- `Enabled`: This means that the view will be added to a cache (maintained by the Frame that hosts it) when it is navigated away from. When the user navigates to the view again, this previous instance will be used instead of a new instance being created.

- `Required`: Because caching views can be quite memory intensive, the cache stores only a given number of views, configurable by the `CacheSize` property on the Frame control, after which it removes the oldest entries to be cleaned up by the garbage collector. However, this is not ideal behavior in all scenarios, as you may want to have more control over whether the view can be removed from the cache. To stop a view from automatically being removed from the cache, set the `NavigationCacheMode` property of the view to `Required`, instead of `Enabled`. This will result in it remaining in the cache indefinitely, regardless of the size of the cache.

If you want to retain a view so that data doesn't have to be loaded repeatedly, a value of `Enabled` would be quite satisfactory. However, if you are retaining unsaved data that you don't want to lose, `Required` would be a better option in this scenario.

To force a view to be removed from the cache once it is no longer required to be cached, simply set its `NavigationCacheMode` property to `Disabled` in your code. When it's navigated away from, it will be removed from the cache. The next time it is navigated to, a new instance of it will be created, and it will go back to using its default value for `NavigationCacheMode`.

■ **Note** When the view has been retrieved from the cache, rather surprisingly both the `Load` and `NavigatedTo` events for the view are still raised when it is navigated to, and there is no property that indicates whether it was retrieved from the cache or that it had previously been loaded. If you have code to populate the view in these events, it would defeat the purpose of caching the view if you were to just populate the view again. The best method to work around this omission is to have a class-level private Boolean variable called `isContentLoaded` with a default value of `false` that you can set to `true` once the view has been populated. You can then check this variable the next time one of these events is raised.

⚙ Workshop: Practicing with Views and Navigation

In this section, you'll create a new view and add a link to it in the menu (part 1). You will then create another view that you pass data to as a query string parameter (part 2). Finally, you will map a custom URI, demonstrating how you can make the URI "friendlier" in the address bar (part 3).

Part 1: Creating a New View

In this first exercise, let's create a new view and add a link to it.

1. Open the AdventureWorks solution you created in Chapter 1.

2. Add a new item to the Views folder in your project called `ProductListView.xaml`, using the Silverlight Page item template.

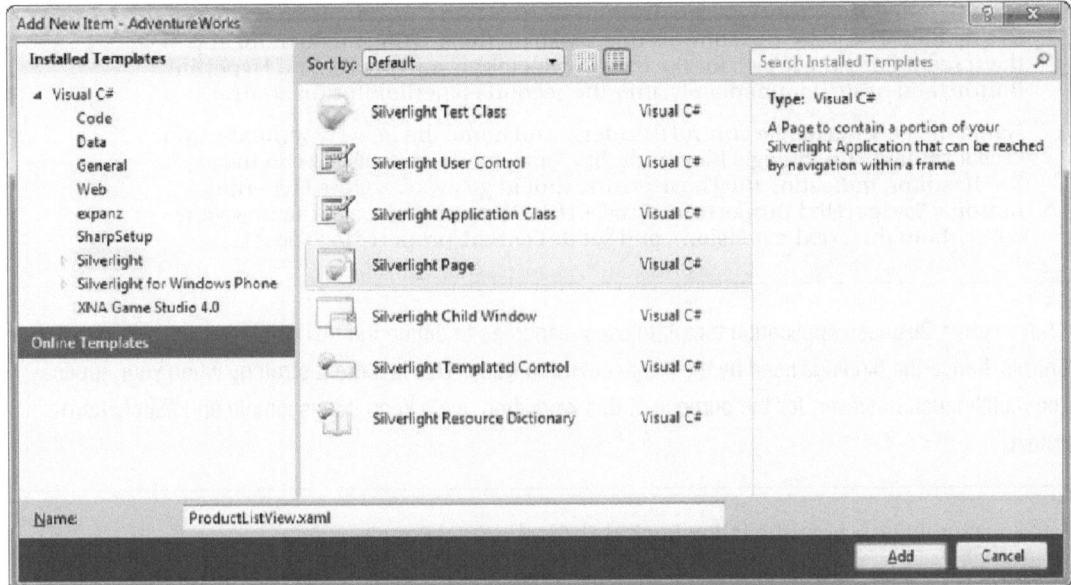

Figure 3-4. Adding a new view to the project

3. Visual Studio will open this view in the designer. You will note that it has no content as yet. We'll modify this view to actually display a list of products in Chapter 6, but in the meantime, you might want to put a control on it just so you know it's successfully loaded when you navigate to it later in this workshop. You might also like to change the default value of the root element's Title property from "ProductListView Page" to "Product List".

4. Let's now add a link to this view to the navigation menu at the top of the screen. Open MainPage.xaml, and search for a StackPanel control named LinksStackPanel:

```
<StackPanel x:Name="LinksStackPanel"
            Style="{StaticResource LinksStackPanelStyle}">

    <HyperlinkButton x:Name="Link1" Style="{StaticResource LinkStyle}"
                     NavigateUri="/Home" TargetName="ContentFrame"
                     Content="{Binding Path=Strings.HomePageTitle,
                               Source={StaticResource ApplicationResources}}"/>

    <Rectangle x:Name="Divider1" Style="{StaticResource DividerStyle}"/>

    <HyperlinkButton x:Name="Link2" Style="{StaticResource LinkStyle}"
                     NavigateUri="/About" TargetName="ContentFrame"
                     Content="{Binding Path=Strings.AboutPageTitle,
                               Source={StaticResource ApplicationResources}}"/>
</StackPanel>
```

5. Note that there are two HyperlinkButton controls and a Rectangle control used as a divider. These are the controls that make up the existing menu at the top of the screen. Copy the XAML for the existing Rectangle and the second Hyperlink Button, and paste it immediately after the second HyperlinkButton control.

6. Name the new Rectangle control Divider2, and name the new HyperlinkButton ProductsLink. The squiggly blue underline both these controls have in the XAML editor, indicating they have errors, should go away. Set the Hyperlink-Button's NavigateUri property to /ProductListView (the name of the new view, but without the .xaml extension), and set its Content property to Products.

■ **Note** Silverlight's Business Application template uses resources to define the text displayed by the Hyperlink-Button controls, hence the bindings used by their Content properties. This is a great strategy when your application is to be multilingual. However, for the purpose of this workshop, we'll keep things simple and simply hard-code their text.

---

7. You should now have the following XAML for the StackPanel:

```
<StackPanel x:Name="LinksStackPanel"
            Style="{StaticResource LinksStackPanelStyle}">

    <HyperlinkButton x:Name="Link1" Style="{StaticResource LinkStyle}"
                     NavigateUri="/Home" TargetName="ContentFrame"
                     Content="{Binding Path=Strings.HomePageTitle,
                               Source={StaticResource ApplicationResources}}"/>

    <Rectangle x:Name="Divider1" Style="{StaticResource DividerStyle}"/>

    <HyperlinkButton x:Name="Link2" Style="{StaticResource LinkStyle}"
                     NavigateUri="/About" TargetName="ContentFrame"
                     Content="{Binding Path=Strings.AboutPageTitle,
                               Source={StaticResource ApplicationResources}}"/>

    <Rectangle x:Name="Divider2" Style="{StaticResource DividerStyle}"/>

    <HyperlinkButton x:Name="ProductsLink" Style="{StaticResource LinkStyle}"
                     NavigateUri="/ProductListView" TargetName="ContentFrame"
                     Content="Products"/>
</StackPanel>
```

8. Run your application now. You should see your new menu item appear in the menu, as shown in Figure 3-5, and clicking it should display your new view.

Figure 3-5. *The new Products button we've added to the menu*

Part 2: Passing Data Between Views

Let's add a view that we'll pass some data to using a query string parameter, and I'll demonstrate accessing the value from that view.

1. Add a new item to the Views folder in your project named ProductDetailsView.xaml, using the Silverlight Page item template (as demonstrated in part 1).

2. Add a TextBlock control to this view (as content of the LayoutRoot Grid), named DisplayValueTextBlock:

```
<Grid x:Name="LayoutRoot">
    <TextBlock Name="DisplayValueTextBlock" Width="100" Height="25" />
</Grid>
```

3. We want to pass some data to this view from the ProductListView view and display that in the DisplayValueTextBlock TextBlock control. Go back to the ProductListView view, and add the following content in bold to the LayoutRoot Grid control in that view:

```
<Grid x:Name="LayoutRoot">
    <StackPanel Height="25" Orientation="Horizontal" Width="155">
        <TextBox Name="ValueField" Width="100" />
        <Button Width="50" Content="Go" Margin="5,0,0,0" />
    </StackPanel>
</Grid>
```

4. Double-click the button. This will add an event handler in your code-behind and switch to the code editor.

5. In this event handler, we'll navigate to the ProductDetailsView view in code and pass it the text entered into the ValueField text box in its query string, as a parameter named Value. We'll use the NavigationService property, inherited from the Page class, for this purpose. Add this code to the event handler:

```
Uri uri = new Uri("/ProductDetailsView?Value=" + ValueField.Text, UriKind.Relative);
NavigationService.Navigate(uri);
```

6. Let's now access this value in the ProductDetailsView view. Add the following property, simplifying safe access to the Value query string parameter, to its code-behind:

```
private string ParamValue
{
    get
    {
        string paramValue = "";
        const string paramName = "Value";

        if (NavigationContext.QueryString.ContainsKey(paramName))
            paramValue = NavigationContext.QueryString[paramName];

        return paramValue;
    }
}
```

7. Now, we can get the query string parameter value from this property and display it in the TextBlock we previously added to the view. Add this line to the override of the view's OnNavigatedTo method. You'll find this method is already defined in the view's code-behind.

```
DisplayValueTextBlock.Text = ParamValue;
```

8. You can now run your application. Go the ProductListView view, via the menu, and enter some text in the text box. When you click the button, the ProductDetailsView view is navigated to and displays the value that you entered in the text box in the previous page.

Part 3: Mapping a URI

Instead of navigating to this (somewhat ungainly) URI:

```
/ProductDetailsView?Value=SomeValue
```

Let's create a custom URI mapping, so we can navigate to the following URI instead:

```
/ProductDetails/SomeValue
```

So far, we've been making use of one of the default mappings, which has allowed us to exclude the Views/ and the .xaml portions of a view's name when navigating to it. Let's take things to the next level and create our own mapping.

1. Find the Frame control in MainPage.xaml, and then find its UriMapper property:

```
<navigation:Frame.UriMapper>
    <uriMapper:UriMapper>
        <uriMapper:UriMapping Uri="" MappedUri="/Views/Home.xaml"/>
        <uriMapper:UriMapping Uri="/{pageName}" MappedUri="/Views/{pageName}.xaml"/>
    </uriMapper:UriMapper>
</navigation:Frame.UriMapper>
```

2. Add a new entry to the mappings. We want this to take precedence over the mapping we were using, so it should be the *second* mapping in the list. In order to achieve our desired result, we want to take the mapping we've been currently using:

```
<uriMapper:UriMapping Uri="/{pageName}" MappedUri="/Views/{pageName}.xaml"/>
```

and extend it to omit the View part of the view's name and to define a token to automatically assign the "second part" of the URI as the value of the Value query string parameter, like so:

```
<uriMapper:UriMapping Uri="/{pageName}/{value}"
                      MappedUri="/Views/{pageName}.xaml?Value={value}"/>
```

3. Open the code-behind for the ProductListView.xaml view. In the Button control's event handler, change the line defining the URI to make use of our new mapping:

```
Uri uri = new Uri("/ProductDetailsView/ " + ValueField.Text, UriKind.Relative);
```

4. Now, run your application. When you click the button that navigates to the `ProductDetailsView` view, the navigation should still work correctly and the value entered into the `ProductListView` view should still appear. As a further exercise, take a look at the URI in the browser's address bar, and modify the `Value` part of the URI. You will find that the `ProductDetailsView` view displays the value you entered in the address bar.

Applying Visual Transition Effects

Using a visual transition effect when navigating from one view to another can provide a nice touch to your application and can help add some "wow" factor that will impress your client and the users, a step toward securing their acceptance of the new application. By default, Silverlight's navigation framework doesn't incorporate any transitions when navigating between views—it simply removes the current view from the Frame and displays a new one in its place. However, a nice alternative might be to slide the current view out to the left and bring the new view to be displayed in from the right, or fade out the current view as a new one fades in. The options are boundless, limited only by your skills in designing animations in XAML. The focus of this book isn't on animations in XAML, so we won't delve too deeply into the process of creating transition effects, but we will take a quick overview of how view transitions can be implemented within the navigation framework. When designing animations, however, consider Expression Blend your best friend—it will make the process of designing the transition much easier.

▪ **Note** Just a word of warning—in small quantities animations can improve the look of your application, but they can just as easily detract from your application and make it look amateurish. It's a fine line, and it's better to underuse animations than overuse them. Animations should be simple and fast to effectively add a professional feel to your application, and they should be used sparsely and not attempt to attract the user's attention. In this situation, less is more. What can amuse the first time can soon get old, especially if it slows the user down from the task at hand.

The easiest way to implement transitions is to make use of the `TransitioningContentControl`, which is a part of the Silverlight Toolkit. You can include this, along with an animation for the transition, as a part of the control template for the Frame control in `MainPage.xaml`. Here are the steps to do this:

5. Create a copy of the Frame control's default control template. Performing this task manually is a difficult process, requiring you to use a tool like RedGate's Reflector or some other decompilation tool to extract the default template from the `System.Windows.Controls.Navigation.dll` assembly, paste it into your project, and set it as the template for your Frame control. Expression Blend makes this process much easier, as it takes care of those steps for you. Open your AdventureWorks project in Expression Blend, and open the `MainPage.xaml` view in the designer. Right-click the Frame control, and select Edit Template ➤ Create Copy from the context menu. Give it a key—for example, `TransitioningContentControlTemplate`—and define it in the `Styles.xaml` resource dictionary, as shown in Figure 3-6.

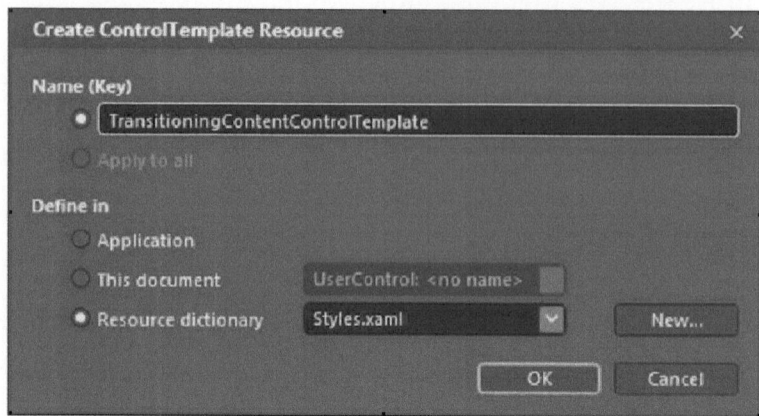

Figure 3-6. Creating a copy of the Frame control's default template

6. Back in Visual Studio, add a reference to the
   `System.Windows.Controls.Layout.Toolkit.dll` assembly to your project.

7. Open `Styles.xaml`, and find the `TransitioningContentControlTemplate` control
   template that Expression Blend created for you:

```
<ControlTemplate x:Key="TransitioningContentControlTemplate"
                 TargetType="navigation:Frame">
    <Border Background="{TemplateBinding Background}"
            BorderBrush="{TemplateBinding BorderBrush}"
            BorderThickness="{TemplateBinding BorderThickness}"
            HorizontalAlignment="{TemplateBinding HorizontalContentAlignment}"
            VerticalAlignment="{TemplateBinding VerticalContentAlignment}">
            <ContentPresenter
                    Content="{TemplateBinding Content}"
                    Cursor="{TemplateBinding Cursor}"
                    Margin="{TemplateBinding Padding}"
                    HorizontalAlignment="{TemplateBinding HorizontalContentAlignment}"
                    VerticalAlignment="{TemplateBinding VerticalContentAlignment}"/>
    </Border>
</ControlTemplate>
```

8. At the top of `Styles.xaml`, declare a prefix for the Silverlight Toolkit's layout
   controls namespace. (This should be on one line.)

```
xmlns:layout="clr-
namespace:System.Windows.Controls;assembly=System.Windows.Controls.Layout.Toolkit"
```

9. Change the `ContentPresenter` reference in the control template to
   `TransitioningContentControl`, using the namespace prefix you defined in the
   previous step. Keep the other properties as they were defined for the
   `ContentPresenter` on the `TransitioningContentControl`.

```
<layout:TransitioningContentControl
        Content="{TemplateBinding Content}"
        Cursor="{TemplateBinding Cursor}"
        Margin="{TemplateBinding Padding}"
```

```
HorizontalAlignment="{TemplateBinding HorizontalContentAlignment}"
VerticalAlignment="{TemplateBinding VerticalContentAlignment}"/>
```

10. As it is now, the transitioning will work without any further changes, using
    a default transition of fading the old view out and the new one in. To use
    your own transition, you will need to set the Style property for the
    TransitioningContentControl control to use a new style that you will create for
    it. This style will contain a control template for the TransitioningContentControl
    control that defines the animation to use when navigating from one view to
    another.

■ **Note** Some example transition animations can be found in the sample code for this chapter.

Creating Custom Content Loaders

Out of the box, the navigation framework simply loads XAML files from your project or from a referenced
assembly into a Frame control. However, perhaps you want to add some custom logic to this process,
such as dynamically downloading XAPs from the server or checking that the users are authorized to access the view they've navigated to. Silverlight 4 introduced the concept of content loaders into the navigation framework. A custom content loader enables you to add your own logic to the process of loading
content into a Frame control.

The navigation framework comes with a default content loader named PageResourceContentLoader,
but it only allows you to load views existing in the current XAP file. However, perhaps you'd rather dynamically download XAPs from the server on demand and load views from them instead. This would enable you to split your application up into smaller chunks and download these chunks only when the user
needs them, reducing both bandwidth and the load time of your application. This is particularly useful
when your application is large and users only tend to use a small portion of it.

When a navigation event takes place, the navigation framework follows this process:

- The Frame control's UriMapper performs its URI mapping (as normal).

- The NavigationService passes the content loader the both current view's URI and
  the mapped URI, and the content loader asynchronously handles the loading of
  the content.

- Once the content loader has loaded the content for display, it notifies the
  NavigationService that it is ready. The NavigationService then calls the content
  loader's EndLoad method, which returns the content to be displayed in the Frame
  control, usually a view inheriting the Page class, as part of its result.

Put simply, the content loader is passed in a URI, and it returns the content to be displayed.

To create your own custom content loader, you need to create a class that implements the
INavigationContentLoader interface (implementing its BeginLoad, CanLoad, EndLoad, and CancelLoad
methods) with the required logic and point the Frame control's ContentLoader property to it.

Going deep into implementing content loaders is beyond the scope of this book, but David Poll has
some excellent articles covering the use of content loaders to dynamically download XAP files and loading views from them, as well as performing authentication and authorization when a view has been navigated to. You can find these articles at his blog here: http://www.davidpoll.com/tag/
contentloader/. Jeff Prosise also has an excellent article on implementing a content loader that dynamically downloads content, using a different method than David's, at http://www.wintellect.com/
CS/blogs/jprosise/archive/2010/06/27/dynamic-page-loading-in-silverlight-navigation-apps.aspx.

■ **Note** We'll look at making use of a custom content loader in Chapter 17 when we discuss breaking down your application into modules and dynamically downloading them when they are required.

Working with Alternative User Interface Frameworks

The navigation framework isn't the only user interface framework available for Silverlight (although it is the only one with support out of the box). Other alternatives that you may wish to consider include the following:

- *Prism*: This open source framework is for creating modular applications and corresponding guidance dictating patterns and practices for doing so. You can download it at http://compositewpf.codeplex.com.

- *nRoute Framework*: This open source framework created and maintained by Rishi Oberoi describes itself as a "composite application framework for creating MVVM-style applications in Silverlight, WPF, and Windows Phone 7." You can download it at http://nroute.codeplex.com.

- *Silverlight.FX*: This open source framework created and maintained by Nikhil Kothari describes itself as a "light-weight application framework for building Rich Internet Applications with Silverlight." You can download it at http://projects.nikhilk.net/SilverlightFX.

- *Caliburn*: This open source framework created and maintained by Rob Eisenberg describes itself as a "client framework for WPF and Silverlight." You can download it at http://caliburn.codeplex.com.

- *ClientUI Framework*: This commercial framework from Intersoft Solutions describes itself as a "next-generation user interface library for the client platform." You can find out more at www.clientui.com.

- *FloatingWindow control*: This control developed by Jevgenij Pankov provides a nice framework for implementing a multiple document interface (MDI) style application. You can download it at http://jevgenijpankov.heliocode.com/articles/FloatingWindow.aspx.

Summary

In this chapter, you learned how to use the navigation framework as the structural foundation of your application's user interface. As the Silverlight Business Application project template uses this by default, as soon as you've created the project, you will have something that you can compile and run and that you can use as a solid basis from which to build your application.

CHAPTER 4

Exposing Data from the Server

By their very nature, business applications are highly data-centric applications. Therefore, one of the primary concerns you will have when designing your Silverlight business application is how you will expose data from the server, and then consume that data in your application.

For example, a typical Silverlight business application will want to request data from the server, make changes to it, and then pass any changes back to the server to be stored.

There are numerous means to achieve this workflow in Silverlight, but it can often be difficult to determine the best and most appropriate technology to use. Ultimately, WCF RIA Services is generally the best solution to implement this functionality and, thus, is the primary technology that we will focus on throughout this book. We will, however, also briefly discuss some of the alternative means and technologies for exposing data from the server, should you find that RIA Services does not suit your needs.

When working with data in a Silverlight application, there are two key parts you need to take care of: exposing the data from the server, and consuming it in your application. In this chapter, we'll be focusing solely on how to expose data from the server; we'll cover consuming that data in your Silverlight application in the following chapter.

Why Expose Data from the Server via Services

If you're used to writing applications that communicate directly with a database (such as SQL Server), you might be surprised to find that there is no object in Silverlight to enable you to do so (SqlConnection, OdbcConnection, etc.). This is because Silverlight is a client platform, designed to be run from within a browser anywhere in the world, and so it does not make sense for it to be able to access databases directly because databases are generally hidden behind a firewall. The purpose of a service is to provide an interface for exposing data publicly from the server, acting as a conduit between the data in the database and external applications.

In addition to exposing data from the server, services also enable you to do the following:

- Specify the types of operations that can be performed on the data

- Execute logic as a part of these operations

- Implement security, deciding what data can be exposed to whom, and who can perform what operations on the data

.NET applications typically use Windows Communication Foundation (WCF) Services to implement these services. WCF RIA Services is a layer on top of WCF, providing enhanced functionality and structure for consuming data in your Silverlight applications. Although this chapter will primarily focus on RIA Services, it's worth taking a look at its underlying WCF foundation first. Before we do that, we need a source of data to expose from the server, so let's set up a database and make it available to our AdventureWorks.Web project.

Creating a Data Access Layer Using the Entity Framework

As this book is focused on Silverlight as a technology, we won't be going into too much depth on database-related concepts such as database terminology and principles, creating and managing databases in SQL Server Management Studio, or methods of accessing data, such as ORMs, the Entity Framework, LINQ to SQL, ADO.NET, and so on. These are considered prerequisite knowledge for this book, so we'll focus on how to actually expose the data publicly via a domain service, and then focus on how to consume it in a Silverlight application in the next chapter.

■ **Note** If you're not familiar with the Entity Framework, which we'll be using throughout this book, you can find more information and videos on using it here: http://msdn.microsoft.com/en-us/data/videos.aspx.

Configuring the Database

Throughout this book you'll be creating a business application in Silverlight for a fictional bicycle sales chain called Adventure Works Cycles. The application will enable employees to manage the various aspects of the business, including product inventory, sales, and purchasing. For this, we'll be using SQL Server 2008 as our database server (the free Express version installed with Visual Studio will be sufficient), and the database that will be supporting this scenario will be the AdventureWorks OLTP sample SQL Server database from Microsoft, which you can download from http://msftdbprodsamples.codeplex.com. Choose the AdventureWorks 2008R2 SR1 release. We're using the AdventureWorks database because it is an example of a typical business database with a suitably complex structure, and is also well populated with sample data.

■ **Note** The AdventureWorks database comes with an installer that includes a number of other databases. The only database that you need to install is the AdventureWorks OLTP database. Ensure that you select the check box next to this database in the installer so that it will actually be created as a database in the selected SQL Server instance. Otherwise, the database installer script will be installed, but not executed.

About the Entity Framework

In order to retrieve and persist data to the database, we'll be using the Entity Framework as our data access layer. The Entity Framework is an object-relational mapper (ORM) that enables you to create a conceptual object model, known as an entity model, and map it to the database schema—for example, tables, views, and stored procedures. You can query this object model in code using *LINQ to Entities.* LINQ is specifically designed for querying an entity model.

The Entity Framework takes care of translating the LINQ to Entities queries to SQL queries in the database, and returns the data as the objects, known as *entities*, that you've defined in your model. Essentially, the Entity Framework makes working with database data in code a much more pleasant and robust experience, as it enables you to work with the data as objects and collections instead of as rows and tables, and to write strongly typed queries against the entity model.

The Entity Framework was subject to some controversy at its initial release, including a "vote of no confidence" petition signed by many prominent members in the developer community. However, it has undergone numerous improvements since then (with the .NET Framework version 4) to counter the issues that were raised with the first version, and it is working its way toward becoming a robust yet easy-to-use ORM.

One of the benefits of using the Entity Framework for this project is that RIA Services has been designed to work very smoothly in conjunction with it, enabling services with the standard CRUD (Create, Read, Update, Delete) operations to be created very easily for given entities.

However, the Entity Framework is by no means the only data access technology supported by RIA Services. It also has support for LINQ to SQL models, which can be found in the WCF RIA Services Toolkit (discussed in the "WCF RIA Services Toolkit" section, later in the chapter), and in fact it can work with any data source, although doing so involves a degree of additional work when creating a domain service. So if you have an existing data access layer to access your database, or you want to use a different ORM, such as nHibernate, RIA Services can also support these scenarios.

In fact, employing the built-in support for exposing entities directly from your Entity Framework model could in some ways be considered bad practice. While taking advantage of this support to expose given entities to the client makes creating and maintaining services incredibly easy, the entities are essentially a model of your data layer, and ideally these entities should not be exposed to the presentation layer. Whether you pass entities or plain-old CLR objects (referred to as POCOs, but also known as presentation model types in RIA Services) of your own design back and forth is a decision you will have to make, dependent on many factors. Using entities will make development much faster, but will also be less flexible than using custom presentation model types. RIA Services works just as well using presentation model types as it does with entities, despite more work being involved in initially creating the domain services. Therefore, the best practice would be to use presentation model types as the data transfer mechanism, which can be populated with data from your entity model. That said, we will take a look at both of these methods, beginning with directly exposing entities because they provide the easiest and fastest means to get started.

⚙ Workshop: Creating an Entity Model

After you've installed the database, you can create your entity model. This is a very straightforward process, which the Entity Data Model Wizard will guide you through.

1. Add a new item to your Web Application project, select the ADO.NET Entity Data Model item template (from under the Data category), and name it AdventureWorksModel.edmx.

2. In the first step of the wizard that appears, select the "Generate from database" option, and press the Next button.

3. Create a connection to the database, pointing it to the AdventureWorks database you previously installed. Ensure the "Save entity connection settings in Web.Config as:" check box is selected, and name the setting "AdventureWorks-Entities". Press the Next button.

4. The tables, views, and stored procedures from the database will be loaded into a tree. Select the "Tables" item to include all the tables in the database in your entity model. Ensure that the "Pluralize or singularize generated object names" and the "Include foreign key columns in the model" check boxes are selected. Also ensure that the model namespace is "AdventureWorksModel". Press the Finish button.

The entity model will now be generated, and displayed in the entity model designer.

WCF Services

You will no doubt be familiar with WCF if you have ever written an application (using another .NET technology, such as WPF, ASP.NET, etc.) that consumes data from a server. Let's take a look at how you can create and consume WCF Services in your Silverlight application.

A Short Overview of WCF

Microsoft introduced WCF as part of version 3.0 of the .NET Framework. WCF is a unified communication layer, designed to bring a wide array of messaging technologies, such as Web services and remoting, together in one technology-agnostic model. WCF enables you to write the messaging features for an application against this model, and then specify the actual technology to be used, referred to as *bindings*, through configuration files. In other words, you can write the communication functionality for your application without worrying about what technology it will use and how that communication will take place, and without tying your application to a specific messaging technology.

The WCF model is broken into three components: the service's *address*, its *bindings*, and its *contract*, with a clear separation maintained between each. You define the contract—that is, the functionality to be exposed by your service—and then you can configure the address and the bindings that the service supports to form a service *endpoint*.

If you've built and consumed WCF Services previously with other .NET technologies, you'll be able to use your existing knowledge when working with WCF Services in Silverlight. However, there are just a few slight differences and limitations that you'll need to be aware of. Let's look at those differences and limitations now.

The Silverlight-Enabled WCF Service Item Template

It's possible to consume existing WCF Services in Silverlight, assuming they are configured to use a binding (i.e., messaging technology) supported by Silverlight. Silverlight has a limited number of bindings that it supports, and the binding used by many WCF Services by default (wsHttpBinding) is one of those *not* supported by Silverlight. Therefore, you will need to configure a binding supported by Silverlight for the WCF service on the server before it can be consumed by a Silverlight application. The bindings supported by Silverlight applications are detailed in the next section.

When creating a new WCF service, there is an item template that you can use to create a WCF service that can be consumed by a Silverlight application "out of the box." When you add a new item to your project, you will find an item template named "Silverlight-enabled WCF Service" under the Silverlight category. This item template creates a WCF service that automatically implements a binding supported by Silverlight, so it's the best method of getting a WCF service up and running that can be consumed by a Silverlight application. Let's say you add a new WCF service using the Silverlight-enabled WCF Service item template to your AdventureWorks.Web project, named ProductService.svc. If you now open up the web.config file in the project, you will see that a new custom binding has been defined:

```
<customBinding>
    <binding name="AdventureWorks.Web.ProductService.customBinding0">
        <binaryMessageEncoding />
        <httpTransport />
    </binding>
</customBinding>
```

An endpoint has been configured for the service that uses this binding:

```
<services>
    <service name="AdventureWorks.Web.ProductService">
        <endpoint address="" binding="customBinding"
```

```
                bindingConfiguration=
                        "AdventureWorks.Web.ProductService.customBinding0"
                contract="AdventureWorks.Web.ProductService" />
        <endpoint address="mex" binding="mexHttpBinding"
                contract="IMetadataExchange" />
    </service>
</services>
```

As you can see, a custom binding is defined that binary-encodes the messages before sending them over an HTTP connection. The reason that we need to define a custom binding is because none of the bindings supported by Silverlight implement binary encoding of messages. By binary-encoding messages (instead of sending them as plain text), you have much smaller messages passed between the server and the client. Therefore, it's worth creating a custom binding in order to be able to use just that feature.

■ **Note** WCF RIA Services are also automatically configured to use a custom binding that binary-encodes messages, in much the same way.

If you now look at the code for the service that the item template generated for you, you will find the following code:

```
using System;
using System.Linq;
using System.Runtime.Serialization;
using System.ServiceModel;
using System.ServiceModel.Activation;

namespace AdventureWorks.Web
{
    [ServiceContract(Namespace = "")]
    [SilverlightFaultBehavior]
    [AspNetCompatibilityRequirements(RequirementsMode =
                            AspNetCompatibilityRequirementsMode.Allowed)]
    public class ProductService
    {
        [OperationContract]
        public void DoWork()
        {
            // Add your operation implementation here.
            return;
        }

        // Add more operations here and mark them with [OperationContract].
    }
}
```

The SilverlightFaultBehavior attribute applied to the service's class is particularly worth noting. When an error is thrown in a WCF service, this exception will normally be returned and raised on the client. However, Silverlight applications don't exhibit this behavior because they use the browser's networking stack (by default), and this stack can only return the 200 and 404 HTTP status codes to plug-ins. WCF Services return exceptions using the 500 HTTP status code (Internal Server Error) and, consequently, are not passed through to the Silverlight application. Instead, the browser will pass this to the Silverlight plug-in as HTTP status code 404, which represents the Not Found error. Hence, your server may throw an exception—for example, a concurrency exception—but your Silverlight application will throw a 404 Not Found exception in response. Of course, this error is incredibly misleading in this context, and can create quite some confusion. Once you understand why this happens, you'll still want to know on the client what exception occurred on the server so that you can notify the user or handle it accordingly.

■ **Note** This behavior does not apply when using the client networking stack. We'll discuss the browser versus the client networking stacks in Chapter 5.

The `SilverlightFaultBehavior` attribute changes this behavior by implementing a custom endpoint behavior that inspects all outgoing messages looking for faults—that is, the result of exceptions being raised. When a fault is found, it simply changes the HTTP status code to 200 (OK) so that the response makes it through the browser's networking stack and to the Silverlight plug-in.

The client will now know that an exception was thrown on the server, but it still won't know what exception was thrown, because, for security reasons, exception details are not returned to the client by default. You can change this behavior, though, by changing the `IncludeExceptionDetailInFaults` attribute in the `web.config` file to `true`. The details of any exception thrown by the server will now make their way to the client.

It's also worth noting the `AspNetCompatibilityRequirements` attribute applied to the service's class. If you have ASP.NET compatibility enabled for your Web project, enabled by setting the `aspNetCompatibilityMode` property of the `serviceHostingEnvironment` element in the `web.config` file to `true`, you must decorate your service class with this attribute, and set its `RequirementsMode` property to either `Allowed` or `Required`. Otherwise, you will receive an error when you try to create a service reference in your Silverlight project for this service.

As you can see, the Silverlight-enabled WCF Service item template makes generating a WCF service suitable for consumption by a Silverlight application much easier.

Supported Bindings

As previously mentioned, the biggest limitation to consuming WCF Services in Silverlight is that not all bindings (messaging technologies) supported by WCF in the full .NET Framework are supported by Silverlight applications. Therefore, you must ensure that the WCF service that you wish to consume is actually configured to use a binding that Silverlight supports. Silverlight supports the following bindings:

- `basicHttpBinding`: Uses the XML-based SOAP 1.1 protocol when communicating with the server. This is the protocol used by the older-style ASMX Web services, and sends messages in clear text over HTTP.

- `pollingDuplexHttpBinding`: Enables the server to push messages to the client, in addition to simply handling client requests. As its name suggests, this binding works over HTTP, with the client using HTTP long-polling the server (behind the scenes), waiting for it to send it a message. This is useful when you want the server to send notifications to the clients, although the TCP binding is now a better performing choice to implement this type of behavior.

- `netTcpBinding`: Used for similar purposes as `pollingDuplexHttpBinding`; however, instead of working over HTTP, it uses the net.tcp protocol. The performance of this binding is much better than `pollingDuplexHttpBinding` (primarily because there is no polling of the server); however, it is better suited to intranet scenarios, as it uses ports other than HTTP port 80 (although it's restricted by Silverlight to ports 4502 to 4534), which are often blocked by firewalls. Issues that you might face when using this binding include the fact that you cannot use transport-level security (it's not supported by Silverlight with the net.tcp protocol), there are a number of features you need to configure on your machine to support net.tcp communication, and you need to expose a socket policy file on port 943 in order to permit TCP connections from Silverlight applications.

- `customBinding`: Enables you to tailor a binding to suit your requirements where a standard binding matching these requirements does not exist. Defining a custom binding enables you to customize the configuration of the various layers forming the binding, which includes the encoding of the messages (such as clear text, binary, etc.) and the transport over which they will be transferred (such as HTTP, HTTPS, TCP, etc.).

■ **Note** The `wsHttpBinding` often used by the default endpoints configured by Visual Studio for WCF Services is not supported in Silverlight. Therefore, you will need to explicitly define an additional endpoint or modify the existing configuration of an endpoint that implements a binding supported by Silverlight. If you are creating the WCF service yourself, use the Silverlight-enabled WCF Service item template instead of the standard WCF Service item template, which will be configured in a manner friendly to being consumed by a Silverlight application, using a binding supported by Silverlight, and allowing the service to run in ASP.NET compatibility mode.

Sharing Code and Business Objects Between the Server and Client

One of the great features of RIA Services is the ability to share code, business objects, and business logic between the server and the client. However, it does this via code generation, generating code into the client project, corresponding to the code written in the server project, which some developers don't like and, hence, prefer to use plain WCF Services instead. There is, however, a little-known method for sharing code between the server and client project when using plain WCF Services, using a class library project containing the common code. The trick is to put the classes and shared code in a Silverlight Class Library project, and then add a reference to this assembly to both your Silverlight and Web projects. Specifically create this project as a Silverlight class library, rather than one targeting the full .NET Framework, because you can add a reference only to an assembly targeting the Silverlight runtime to a Silverlight project; however, projects targeting the full .NET Framework can reference assemblies that target the Silverlight runtime. Now you have any code and business objects that you include in this assembly shared between both the client and the server.

■ **Note** You can alternatively use the Portable Library Tools instead of a Silverlight class library. Class libraries created using these tools can be run on a variety of .NET-based platforms (.NET 4.0, Silverlight, Windows Phone 7) without the need to recompile your project. You can get the Portable Library Tools here: `http://visualstudiogallery.msdn.microsoft.com/b0e0b5e9-e138-410b-ad10-00cb3caf4981/`.

Note that this still leaves you the task of manually populating your business objects after data has been retrieved from the server. This leads to trick number two: when you create your WCF service in the server project, expose data using the business objects from this shared class library. Usually, adding a service reference to a project creates a proxy containing objects with the structure matching the objects being exposed by the service. It then populates these proxy objects with data returned from the server, and accepts objects of these types only when sending data back to the server. However, you can configure your service reference to populate the types defined in one or more given assemblies, instead of populating the proxy objects. After selecting the service you want to add a reference to, in the Add Service Reference dialog, click the Advanced button to open the Service Reference Settings dialog. Ensure that the "Reuse types in referenced assemblies" check box is selected. You can then select specific assemblies for it to use, or have it search for matching types in all the assemblies referenced by the project. This means that it will automatically populate objects from the shared assembly when you request data from the server, and accept objects of those types when you pass data back to the server, thus saving you the need to copy the data between the service's proxy objects and the business objects from your shared assembly when communicating with the WCF service.

⚙ Workshop: Creating a WCF Service

In this workshop, we'll create a WCF service that exposes a collection of Product entities from our Entity Framework model.

1. Add a new item to the AdventureWorks.Web project, named ProductService.svc, using the Silverlight-enabled Web Service item template.

2. Remove the DoWork operation that was created by the item template, as the template created it for demonstration purposes only. You should be left with the following code in the file:

```
using System;
using System.Linq;
using System.Runtime.Serialization;
using System.ServiceModel;
using System.ServiceModel.Activation;

namespace AdventureWorks.Web
{
    [ServiceContract(Namespace = "")]
    [SilverlightFaultBehavior]
    [AspNetCompatibilityRequirements(RequirementsMode =
                        AspNetCompatibilityRequirementsMode.Allowed)]
    public class ProductService
    {

    }
}
```

3. Add a using statement to the top of the file for the System.Collections.Generic namespace.

```
using System.Collections.Generic;
```

4. It's not essential to do so, but it's recommended that you set a namespace for the service contract, by setting the Namespace property of the ServiceContract attribute applied to the class. This will be used to help maintain the uniqueness of your service's contract.

```
[ServiceContract(Namespace = "http://www.apress.com")]
```

5. Create a method named GetProducts, with a return type of IEnumerable<Product>. Decorate this method with the OperationContract attribute so that it will be exposed as a service operation.

```
[OperationContract]
public IEnumerable<Product> GetProducts()
{

}
```

6. In this method, we need to get a collection of Product entities from our Entity Framework model, and return them as the method's result.

```
[OperationContract]
public IEnumerable<Product> GetProducts()
{
    AdventureWorksEntities context = new AdventureWorksEntities();
    context.ContextOptions.LazyLoadingEnabled = false;
    return context.Products;
}
```

■ **Note** Notice how we're setting the LazyLoadingEnabled property of the entity model's context to false. If we didn't do this, as the Product entities are being serialized, the serializer would attempt to also serialize the related data for each Product entity (and their related data, and so on), resulting in numerous queries to the database and ultimately the operation call timing out. Turning off lazy loading will prevent related data from being "lazily loaded" from the database, and return only the Product entities (and any data that has been explicitly loaded).

7. The full code for your service should now be as follows, and is ready for consumption by a Silverlight application. We'll look and how you do so in Chapter 5.

```
using System;
using System.Linq;
using System.Runtime.Serialization;
using System.ServiceModel;
using System.ServiceModel.Activation;
using System.Data.Objects;
using System.Collections.Generic;

namespace AdventureWorks.Web
{
    [ServiceContract(Namespace = "http://wwww.apress.com")]
    [SilverlightFaultBehavior]
    [AspNetCompatibilityRequirements(RequirementsMode =
                            AspNetCompatibilityRequirementsMode.Allowed)]
```

```
public class ProductService
{
    [OperationContract]
    public IEnumerable<Product> GetProducts()
    {
        AdventureWorksEntities context = new AdventureWorksEntities();
        context.ContextOptions.LazyLoadingEnabled = false;
        return context.Products;
    }
}
```

WCF RIA Services

Although you can consume WCF Services in Silverlight, you will probably find that creating and maintaining your services becomes somewhat of a chore. The drawbacks of creating and consuming WCF Services include the following:

- A lot of repetitive boilerplate code is required to implement CRUD-style operations.

- Services become more complex when you add support for filtering/sorting/grouping/paging.

- You will constantly need to update your service references in your client whenever the contract on the server changes.

- You will need to write and maintain logic, such as validation and business rules, on both the server and the client. This duplicated code requires additional effort to write, test, and maintain, and the code can easily get out of sync between the tiers.

To try to combat these problems and simplify access to data in Silverlight applications, Microsoft introduced WCF RIA Services, commonly referred to just as RIA Services, primarily designed for use when developing end-to-end Silverlight applications, but with support for additional presentation technologies such as JavaScript now being added. Let's take a deep dive into how you can expose data from the server via WCF RIA Services.

What Is WCF RIA Services?

RIA Services is a layer on top of WCF that provides a prescriptive pattern and framework that you can use when building data-driven Silverlight applications that consume data from a server. Another way of saying that is that RIA Services is a framework that helps you expose data from a server, consume it in your Silverlight application, and share business/validation logic between the two.

RIA Services can be described as follows:

- Partly a data-centric design pattern for structuring your application.

- Partly a framework that provides advanced data management, authentication/authorization management, and querying features.

- Partly a code generator that generates code in one project based on the code written in another project so that common code to be used in multiple tiers can be written in one place.

RIA Services piggybacks on top of WCF Services, which provides the communication mechanism between the middle tier and the presentation tier, as illustrated in Figure 4-1.

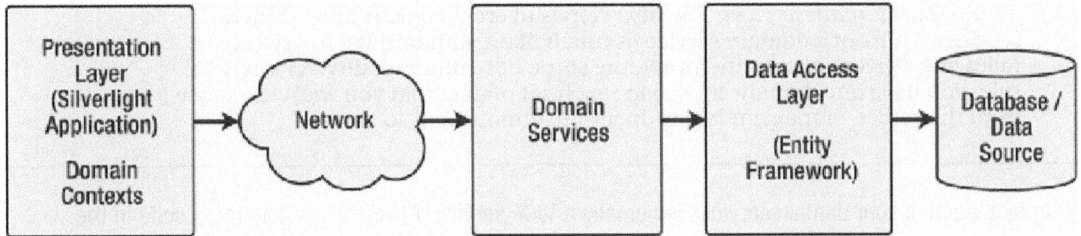

Figure 4-1. Communications mechanism between middle tier and presentation tier

The focus of the RIA Services pattern is very much directed toward the middle tier. It's not tied to a specific data access technology, although it integrates particularly well with both the Entity Framework and LINQ to SQL, the latter requiring the WCF RIA Services Toolkit to be installed, as discussed in the "WCF RIA Services Toolkit" section, later in this chapter. It isn't designed to be tied to a specific presentation technology, although the focus is currently primarily on Silverlight, with limited support for other presentation technologies such as JavaScript, WPF, and Windows Forms.

RIA Services is an end-to-end technology; therefore, you need to have control over both the server and the client tiers of the application in order to use it effectively. If you need to access existing services without routing the requests through the server, or if you need to use services being developed by a separate team, RIA Services might not be suitable for your project.

The framework portion of RIA Services provides a host of functionality, right out of the box, that vastly simplifies building an application. Features include the following:

- A data source control that can be used in XAML to communicate with a service.

- Tracking of changes made to data on the client, and processing these changes on the server.

- The ability to write a LINQ query on the client, and have that query executed on the server.

- An out-of-the-box working authentication service.

An Overview of How to Use WCF RIA Services

Following is a brief overview of the process of working with RIA Services. Let's get familiar with the process, before drilling down into the details.

1. *Link your Silverlight and Web projects:* RIA Services requires you to follow a pattern in structuring your application. First, your server (Web) project and your client (Silverlight) project must be linked so that the RIA Services build task/code generator can generate code in the client project to enable it to interact with the server. This means that your client and server projects must exist in the same solution.

■ **Note** There is support to have your entities and metadata classes in a separate project from your server project, using the WCF RIA Services Class Library project template discussed in the "Encapsulating Logic in a Separate WCF RIA Services Class Library" section later in this chapter.

---

2. *Create your domain services:* The next step is to create one or more domain services. Think of a domain service as much like a standard WCF service, but following a given pattern and providing some base functionality. As a general rule, you have one domain service for each set of data that you want to expose from the server—for example, products, customers, and so on.

■ **Note** In fact, each of your domain services is actually a WCF service. RIA Services generates code in the client project to automatically communicate with the domain service, meaning that you don't have to worry about adding service references to your domain services. However, because domain services are standard WCF Services, you can add them as service references to your projects if you wish (including Windows Forms, WPF, and ASP.NET projects).

---

3. *Create domain operations on your domain services:* On your domain service you create domain operations, which will typically expose data to the client and accept changes following the create, read, update, and delete (CRUD) pattern. For example, a domain service exposing product data will usually provide domain operations such as GetProducts, InsertProduct, UpdateProduct, and DeleteProduct.

4. *Decorate your entities with validation logic and other attributes:* The entities being exposed by a domain service can be decorated with attributes (such as data validation rules), either directly or by applying the attributes to associated classes (known as metadata classes).

5. *Specify code to be shared between the server and the client:* You can share code between the server and the client projects by simply placing the code to be shared in one or more files with the .shared.cs extension.

6. *Consume the domain services in the client project:* The RIA Services build task automatically generates code in the client project that enables it to interact with the domain services on the server. It creates a *domain context* for each domain service, and proxy classes for each of the entities exposed by the domain service. You can then use the domain contexts to request data from the server, work with it, and submit any changes back to the server.

We will cover consuming data in your Silverlight project in Chapter 5.

How the WCF RIA Services Code Generator Works

RIA Services requires the server and the client projects to be within the same solution and linked together. One contains services that expose data (acting as a server), and the other communicates with the services and consumes the data (acting as a client).

When a domain service is created in the server project, the RIA Services build task in Visual Studio generates corresponding code in the client project (that is, a code generation process) that simplifies the process of interacting and communicating with the service. It also generates corresponding proxy data object classes, which are generally referred to as *entities*, in the client project for any entities that are exposed by the service; applies attributes, such as those that denote validation logic on the entities and their properties; and copies code marked as shared code from the server project into the client.

■ **Note** This code generation is generally referred to as *projection*, because code is projected from the server project onto the client project.

Let's investigate what is happening under the covers when you link the two projects via RIA Services. For this, we'll use the solution that we created back in Chapter 1 (also used in Chapter 3). This solution was created using the Silverlight Business Application project template, and is already configured to use RIA Services, with the two projects in the solution already linked with a RIA Services link.

Start by toggling the Show All Files option (the second button from the left in the Solution Explorer window's toolbar) to "on" for the Silverlight project. There is a Generated_Code folder, as shown in Figure 4-2, into which code is generated by the RIA Services build task when the Silverlight project is compiled. This code enables you to access all the operations, data, and logic from the Silverlight project that has been exposed on the server via RIA Services.

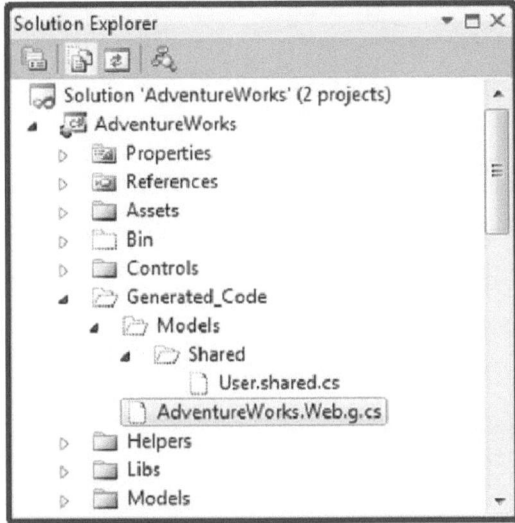

Figure 4-2. The Silverlight project structure, showing the hidden Generated_Code folder

---

■ **Note** You can have a look at the code that has been generated for the client, but don't change anything because any changes you make will be overwritten when the Silverlight project is next compiled (which regenerates the code in this folder). The generated classes are partial classes, which enables you to extend them on the client with client-only logic, should you find the need. We will take a closer look at this generated code in the "Inspecting the Generated Code in the Silverlight Project" section of Chapter 5.

The code generator is intelligent enough to ascertain the nature of operations on the services. The logic it uses is discussed in the "Domain Operations" section, later in this chapter.

You can govern how entity classes are generated in the client project (what properties are included or excluded) by decorating the entity's properties with attributes, also known as *data annotations*. How you do this is discussed in the "Decorating Entities" section, later in this chapter.

Code that should be shared between the server and the client (copied from the server project into the client project by the RIA Services build task) must be placed into files that have the .shared.cs extension, so that the build task knows to copy these files from the server project to the client project. Sharing code is discussed in the "Sharing Code and Logic Across Tiers" section, later in this chapter.

Creating the RIA Services Link

The AdventureWorks project we created in Chapter 1 using the Silverlight Business Application project template is set up to use RIA Services by default, and already provides some basic functionality using RIA Services. Therefore, we will continue working from that base and the minor modifications we made in Chapter 1 and Chapter 3. Figure 4-3 displays the structure of the Web project in this solution.

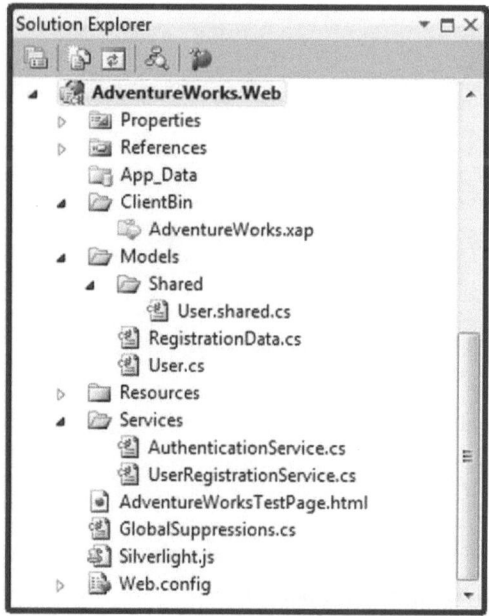

Figure 4-3. The structure of the Web Application project

Note from Figure 4-3 that there is a Services folder and a Models folder in the project. The Services folder already contains two domain services (AuthenticationService and UserRegistrationService) for providing authentication and user registration operations to the client (these will be discussed further in Chapter 8). The Models folder contains two data classes (User and RegistrationData) that are passed between the server and the client. You will also find a Shared folder under the Models folder, which has a file called User.shared.cs that contains code to be shared between the server and the client projects.

As demonstrated in Chapter 1, the Silverlight and Web projects are linked together. The purpose of this link is to copy the compiled XAP file generated by your Silverlight application to a location under the Web project when the project/solution is compiled. However, RIA Services requires another link to be created between the projects. The purpose of this link is to configure what project contains the domain services that the Silverlight application will be consuming data from. This will enable the RIA Services build task to generate the required code to communicate with those services in your Silverlight project accordingly.

Whereas the project link to copy the Silverlight application's XAP file into the Web project was configured in the Web project's project properties, the RIA Services link is configured in the project properties of the Silverlight project, as shown in Figure 4-4.

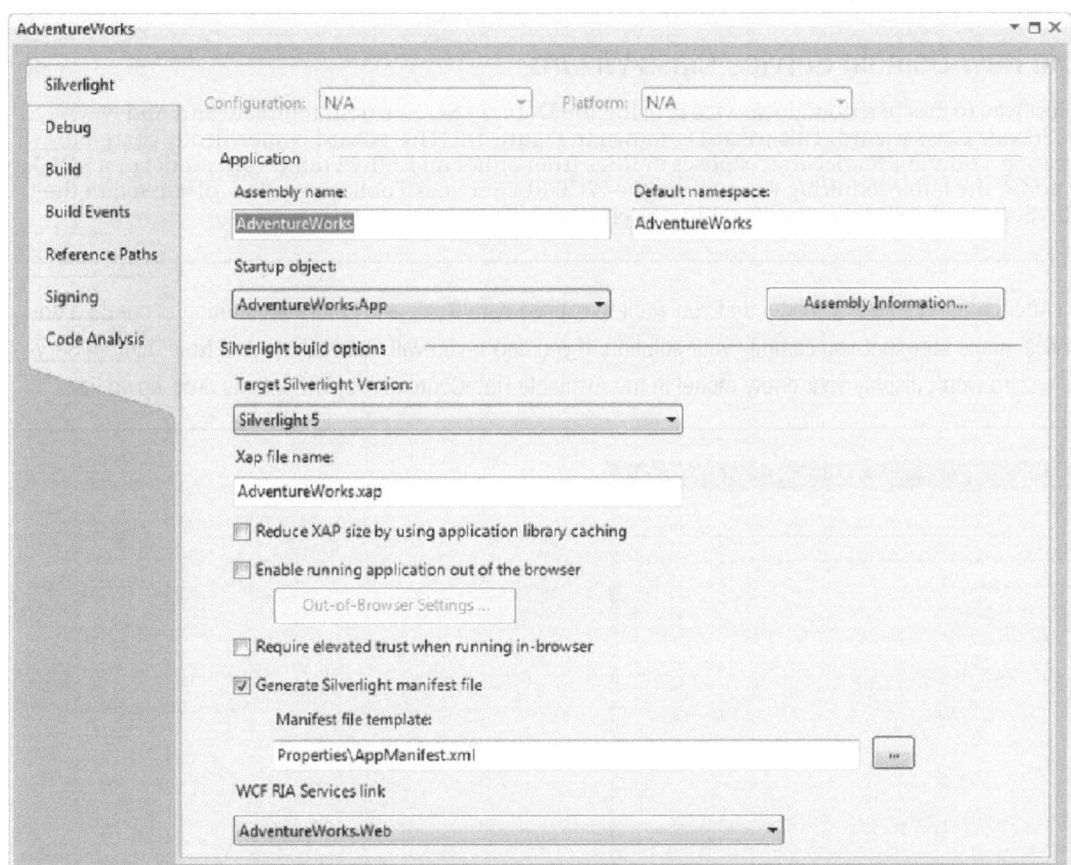

Figure 4-4. *The project properties for the Silverlight project, with the WCF RIA Services link configuration at the bottom*

This link will already be set up by using the Business Application project template; however, if you have an existing Silverlight project or Web application that you want to use RIA Services with, you can manually link the projects together using this property.

Now you are ready to start creating some domain services. The example you'll work through in this chapter demonstrates some of the key concepts of the RIA Services pattern. Your aim will be to expose data and operations from the server, and make them accessible from the client. In doing so, you will also be sharing some validation logic and code between the server and the client, which will be executed on both the server and the client. First, however, you need to set up a data source/layer from which you will expose data to the client.

Domain Services

After you have created a RIA Services link between your Silverlight and Web projects and configured a data source on the server, your next task is to expose some data and operations from the server, which you will consume in your Silverlight client in subsequent chapters of this book. You will achieve this through the use of a domain service. A domain service typically consists of basic CRUD operations, and any other custom operations you wish to be callable from the client.

The Add New Domain Service Class Wizard

The easiest way to create a domain service is using the Domain Service item template and Add New Domain Service Class wizard. This wizard is shown in Figure 4-5. This wizard is specifically geared toward creating a domain service that exposes entities from either an Entity Framework model or a LINQ to SQL model, the latter requiring you to have the WCF RIA Services Toolkit installed (discussed in the "WCF RIA Services Toolkit" section, later in this chapter).

■ **Note**   After creating an entity model that you want to expose data from, and before attempting to create a domain service, make sure that you compile your solution. If you don't, you will find that the Add New Domain Service Class wizard won't display your entity model in the Available DataContexts/ObjectContexts drop-down list.

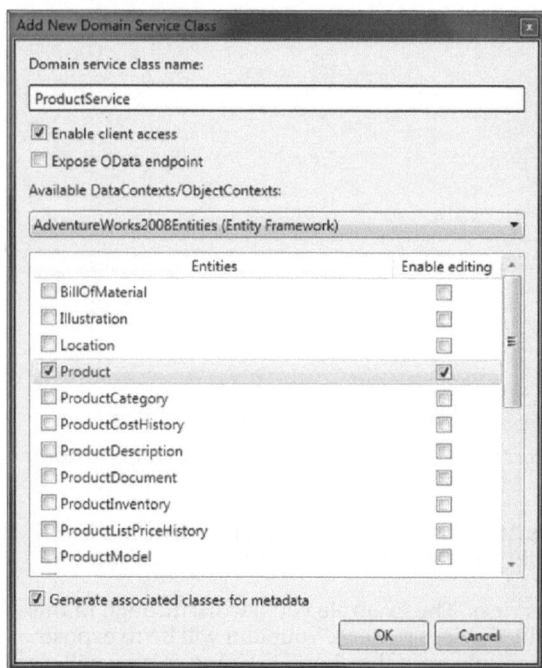

Figure 4-5. The Add New Domain Service Class wizard dialog

Let's now take a look at each element of this dialog and what it does.

Available DataContexts/ObjectContexts

The "Available DataContexts/ObjectContexts" drop-down list enables you to select an Entity Framework model or LINQ to SQL model whose entities will populate the entity list. If your model doesn't appear in the list, close the wizard, compile your project, and try again. The project must be compiled after the model is created and before this wizard is run in order for the entities to appear in the list.

If you want to expose presentation model (POCO) types instead of Entity Framework or LINQ to SQL entities, you will need to select the <empty domain service class> option from the Available Data-Contexts/ObjectContexts drop-down list, and implement the domain operations to expose these types yourself.

The Entity List

The entity list enables you to select the entities that you want to expose via this domain service. A domain operation will be created in the domain service for each selected entity, and this operation will return a collection of the corresponding entity to the client. If you want to also be able to modify an entity from the client, select the "Enable editing" option next to it. For each entity marked as editable, the wizard will create insert, update, and delete domain operations for that entity on the domain service.

■ **Note** As a general rule, each domain service will only expose a single set of data, such as product data or customer data, rather than all the data you want to expose to the client application from your database.

Enabling Client Access

Make sure that the "Enable client access" check box is checked before moving on from this dialog. This will decorate the domain service class with the EnableClientAccess attribute, which will indicate to the RIA Services code generator that it should generate code in the Silverlight project to enable it to consume this domain service.

Exposing an OData Endpoint

The "Expose OData endpoint" check box enables your domain service to expose data using the Open Data (OData) protocol. OData is a set of extensions for the ATOM protocol to standardize the creation of HTTP-based data services, somewhat similar to REST data services—returning the data as an ATOM feed and providing CRUD operations on the data. While this is a new protocol, it has Microsoft backing, and Microsoft is integrating support for OData into a number of its products, such as SharePoint and Power-Pivot. Selecting this check box will enable your domain service to be consumed by products supporting this OData protocol.

Generating Associated Classes for Metadata

The "Generate associated classes for metadata" check box creates a metadata class for each entity selected in the entity list. Metadata classes will be covered in the "Decorating Entities" section later in this chapter, but in summary, they enable you to decorate the properties on your entities with attributes, such as data validation attributes, without the need to modify the entities themselves. Entities are generated code, created by the Entity Framework modeler, and modifying generated code is not a good idea. Doing so would prevent you from regenerating the code again at a later stage—if you did regenerate the code after manually altering it, then you would lose the changes you had made.

Metadata classes provide the solution to this problem. Each entity can have a corresponding metadata class, with each property on the entity having a corresponding field in the metadata class. You can then decorate the fields in the metadata class with attributes that RIA Services will map to the entity and use at design time when generating the corresponding entity on the client, and at runtime when persisting entities passed from the client to the database to revalidate the data.

The Add New Domain Service Class wizard can generate these metadata classes for you for the entities you have selected from the list. These will go into a .metadata.cs file—for example, the ProductService domain service will have a corresponding ProductService.metadata.cs file created, containing metadata classes for all the entities that the ProductService domain service exposes.

It's not essential that you generate metadata classes for the entities that you expose from your domain service. However, if you choose not to create them when creating the domain service, and then decide you wish to use them at a later time, you will need to either create them manually or create another temporary domain service for the entities, from which you can get the generated metadata classes and then delete the domain service.

Creating a Domain Service Using Snippets

Another way of easily creating a domain service is to use Visual Studio's snippets feature. Colin Blair has created some snippets to help you create a domain service without using the Add New Domain Service Class wizard, and made them available as part of the RIA Services Contrib project that he maintains and which is detailed in the "The WCF RIA Services Contrib Project" section, later in this chapter. You can find more information about these snippets on his blog at www.riaservicesblog.net/Blog/2011/06/default.aspx.

 ## Workshop: Creating an Entity Model

Let's work through the process of exposing a Product entity from the entity model.

1. Compile your Web project after creating your entity model (from the workshop titled "Creating an Entity Model").

2. Add a domain service to the Services folder in your Web (server) project, using the Domain Service item template, which you'll find under the Web category. We will be using this service to serve up product data, so call it ProductService.cs. This will initiate the Add New Domain Service Class wizard shown in Figure 4-5.

3. Select your AdventureWorks entity model from the Available DataContexts/ObjectContexts drop-down list. This will display each entity in your entity model in the list.

4. Select the Product entity and its corresponding Enable editing check box.

5. Ensure that the Enable client access check box is selected.

6. Ensure that the Generate associated classes for metadata check box is selected.

7. Click the OK button.

This will then create the domain service, and a ProductService.metadata.cs file containing the metadata class for the Product entity in your Web project. Your Silverlight application will now actually be able to get/query a collection of products, and insert/update/delete products via the domain service that has been created for you by the wizard.

Domain Operations

Domain operations are methods on a domain service that can be invoked from a client. These operations will typically be CRUD operations, but you can also have invoke operations and custom operations. The Add New Domain Service Class wizard creates the domain operations on the domain service required to enable CRUD functionality on entities for you, but it's well worth understanding how these domain operations work.

In order for the RIA Services code generator to ascertain what type of operation a given method is, so that it can correctly generate the corresponding code in the client project, it uses a convention-based approach (by default). The conventions prescribe how the operation methods should be named and what pattern their signature should follow.

Alternatively, you can decorate the operation's method with an attribute that identifies what type of operation it is. The naming/signature conventions and alternative attribute decorations for each operation will be included in this section's discussion.

■ **Note** Some people prefer to decorate their operations, even when they follow the naming/signature convention, in order to explicitly define what type of operation is being represented.

Let's now take a look at each of the various types of domain operations that you might have in a domain service.

Query Operations

A query operation enables you to expose data to a client. This data may be either a collection of entities/objects or a single entity/object. Let's first look at the naming/signature convention used for query operations, and then we'll look at each of these cases separately.

Naming/Signature Convention

A query operation has no convention for its naming, and can accept any or no parameters. For it to be implicitly identified by the RIA Services code generator as a query operation, however, it must return an IQueryable<T>, IEnumerable<T>, or an entity. Otherwise, decorate the method with the Query attribute.

■ **Note** You can configure the query operation to cache the results in order to save calls back to the server from the client or calls to the database, depending on how you configure the caching. Data caching is ideal when you have data that rarely or never changes. To utilize output caching, decorate the query operation with the OutputCache attribute, and configure the caching behavior by specifying values for its constructor parameters. These parameters include where the data should be cached (most commonly either on the server and/or the client), and how long the data should be cached (in seconds). Note that client-side caching requires the browser to honor the cache header of the response, which they don't always do. More information on the OutputCache attribute can be found on Matthew Charles' blog at http://blogs.msdn.com/b/digital_ruminations/archive/2011/01/05/ria-services-output-caching.aspx.

Returning a Collection of Entities

In the `ProductService` class we created in the previous workshop, you will find a query operation that returns a collection of `Product` entities to the client, as follows:

```
public IQueryable<Product> GetProducts()
{
    return this.ObjectContext.Products;
}
```

The `GetProducts` operation returns an expression, via an `IQueryable<T>` interface type, that when executed by a LINQ provider will return a collection of the `Product` entity. Throughout this book, the LINQ provider we are using is LINQ to Entities for querying an Entity Framework model, although any LINQ provider can be used. Although you could return an actual collection from the query operation, such as a `List<T>`, returning an `IQueryable<T>` expression provides numerous benefits, and enables one of the most powerful features that RIA Services provides.

By returning an expression that hasn't been executed against the LINQ provider as yet, you enable RIA Services to add additional query criteria to the expression, which it can then execute, and can subsequently return the results to the client. As you will see in Chapter 5, the client can specify filtering, sorting, and paging criteria as a LINQ query when calling a query operation on the server. Let's say that the client wants all the products whose name starts with "A" and provides the LINQ query to do so when calling the `GetProducts` domain operation. This LINQ query will then be serialized and sent to the server when the request is made, and this query will be appended to the existing LINQ to Entities query before it is executed and the results are returned to the client. This provides a neat, easy, and elegant way of passing criteria from the client to the server, and having them included in the query to the database.

Query operations can accept parameters as part of their signature, which you can use as an alternative means to pass filters and other criteria to the query operation. For example, the following query operation accepts a string that it will use to filter the results and which must be provided when calling the operation from the client:

```
public IQueryable<Product> GetProducts(string nameFilter)
{
    return this.ObjectContext.Products.Where(p =>
                                    p.Name.StartsWith(nameFilter));
}
```

Returning a Single Entity

In addition to returning a collection of entities, you will often want to add a domain operation that returns a single entity matching the key you pass through to it as a parameter. This will support the drill down–type scenario that will be covered in Chapter 7. To demonstrate this, we'll add a new domain operation to the `ProductService` domain service called `GetProduct`, which will return the `Product` entity with the matching `ProductID` passed through to it as a parameter:

```
public Product GetProduct(int productID)
{
    return ObjectContext.Products
        .Where(p => p.ProductID == productID)
        .FirstOrDefault();
}
```

> **Note** GetProduct, which returns a single Product entity, is very similar in name to the default GetProducts domain operation, which returns a collection of Product entities. It's best not to have such similarly named operations on your domain service because it will cause confusion and lead to mistakes being made on both the server and the client. Therefore, it's best to rename the GetProducts domain operation to something such as GetProductCollection or GetProductList.

Insert/Update/Delete Operations

When a client application submits a *changeset* to the server, RIA Services will call the appropriate insert/update/delete operation for each entity in the changeset, based on the action specified for that entity in the changeset. These operations cannot be called explicitly from the client.

Naming/Signature Convention

The insert/update/delete operations must accept a single entity as their parameter, upon which it will perform the corresponding operation, with no additional parameters, and not return a value. When naming the methods, note the following:

- *Insert* operation method names must start with Insert, Create, or Add. Otherwise, you will need to apply the Insert attribute to the method. For example:

  ```
  public void InsertProduct(Product product)
  ```

- *Update* operation method names must start with Update, Change, or Modify. Otherwise, you will need to apply the Update attribute to the method. For example:

  ```
  public void UpdateProduct(Product currentProduct)
  ```

- *Delete* operation method names must start with Delete or Remove. Otherwise, you will need to apply the Delete attribute to the method. For example:

  ```
  public void DeleteProduct(Product product)
  ```

Understanding the Domain Service Life Cycle for Insert/Update/Delete Operations

Let's take a quick look at how a domain service works and the various phases in its life cycle when changes are submitted to the server. The core interaction that a client has with a domain service is to retrieve a collection of entities or a single entity from the domain service, and return any of these entities that have been modified (or additional entities that have been inserted into the collection) back to the server as a *changeset*.

When a client submits a changeset to a domain service, the domain service's Submit method is called, initiating the start of the domain service's life cycle. The domain service will work through the following phases in order:

- The *authorize changeset* phase essentially verifies that the user passing through the changeset is actually authorized to execute the operations in that changeset. It checks that each operation to be called from that changeset is permitted according to the security-related rules defined on each of these operations in the domain service, by decorating the operations with security rule attributes. Configuring security rules on domain operations is covered in Chapter 8.

- The *validate changeset* phase performs server-side validation of the entities being passed through in the changeset according to the validation rules applied to each object and its properties, by decorating them with validation rule attributes, within the changeset. Although the objects and their properties are validated on the client side, the domain service validates them again according to the validation rules to verify that someone didn't circumvent the validation rules on the client, as is proper practice. Configuring validation rules on objects and their properties is covered later in this chapter.

- Once the changeset has been fully authorized and validated, the *execute changeset* phase can begin. This phase enumerates through each entry in the changeset and calls the specified domain operation—that is, the insert, update, delete, or custom operation on the domain service—passing in the given entity to perform that operation upon.

- The final phase in the domain service's life cycle is the *persist changeset* phase. When you are using a data access layer that maintains its own changesets, such as the Entity Framework or LINQ to SQL, the final task is to persist that changeset to the database. For example, when using an Entity Framework model as your data access layer, this phase would be used to call the SubmitChanges method on the data context and complete the transaction. If changes are immediately committed to the database in the domain operations, then this phase will usually be ignored.

Each of these phases is automatically performed by the domain service; however, there is a corresponding method on the domain service that you can override and hook into if you need to provide some custom behavior in addition to what is provided by the base domain service class. These methods are

- AuthorizeChangeSet

- ValidateChangeSet

- ExecuteChangeSet

- PersistChangeSet

You can also override the Submit method, which encompasses each of these phases, in order to hook into that, too. While in a phase, the logic for that phase will be run over every object in the changeset. If an exception is thrown on any of these objects during any of these phases, the entire changeset submission will be cancelled.

Example Insert/Update/Delete Operations

If you have enabled editing on the Product entity in the Add New Domain Service Class wizard, you will find that insert, update, and delete operations have been created and implemented for you in the ProductService domain service.

The following code performs an insert operation:

```
public void InsertProduct(Product product)
{
    if (product.EntityState != EntityState.Added)
    {
        if (product.EntityState != EntityState.Detached)
        {
            this.ObjectContext.ObjectStateManager.ChangeObjectState(product,
                                                EntityState.Added);
        }
        else
```

```
        {
            this.ObjectContext.AddToProducts(product);
        }
    }
}
```

The following code performs an update operation:

```
public void UpdateProduct(Product currentProduct)
{
    if (currentProduct.EntityState == EntityState.Detached)
    {
        this.ObjectContext.Products.AttachAsModified(currentProduct,
                        this.ChangeSet.GetOriginal(currentProduct));
    }
}
```

The following code performs a delete operation:

```
public void DeleteProduct(Product product)
{
    if (product.EntityState == EntityState.Detached)
    {
        this.ObjectContext.Attach(product);
    }
    this.ObjectContext.DeleteObject(product);
}
```

Invoke Operations

An invoke operation is a nonspecific domain operation, and behaves the same way as a service operation in a standard WCF service. As a general rule, invoke operations don't return or act upon entities. They either initiate an action on the server—for example, requesting the server to send an e-mail—or request data from the server, which returns a simple value or data for which changeset tracking is not required—for example, requesting the current currency exchange rate.

Like query operations, invoke operations are methods that the client application can call directly. These operations are called immediately, unlike custom operations, which are queued and only called when a changeset is submitted to the server.

Naming/Signature Convention

Invoke operations do not need to adhere to any naming or method signature convention, and essentially any operation in a domain service that does not fall into any of the other operation categories via its name or method signature is considered by RIA Services to be an invoke operation. To explicitly define a method as an invoke operation, apply the Invoke attribute to the method.

An Example Invoke Operation

The following code is an example of an invoke operation:

```
public decimal GetExchangeRate(string fromCurrency, string toCurrency)
{
    return ExchangeRates.GetRate(fromCurrency, toCurrency);
}
```

Custom Operations

Custom operations perform an action on an entity. For example, you might have an operation that discontinues a product, with all the logic to do so to be performed on the server. However, whereas an invoke operation is called immediately from the client, custom operations have their execution on the server deferred until the client submits a changeset to the server and are treated in the same way as insert/update/delete operations.

When a custom operation is generated in the client project, it will be created as a method on the entity that it acts upon. In addition, it will also be created as a method on the domain context associated with the domain service.

■ **Note** Custom operations are called *after* any insert or update operations are called on the server. If a custom operation is called on an entity that is later deleted and before the changes are submitted to the server, the custom operation will not be called and will be discarded when the changes are submitted.

Naming/Signature Convention

Custom operations do not having a naming convention; however, they must not return a value, and they must accept an entity as their first parameter. (Any number of additional parameters is permitted.) There is no specific attribute for identifying a custom operation, but instead you should use the Update attribute and set its UsingCustomMethod property to true.

An Example Custom Operation

The following code is an example of a custom operation:

```
public void DiscontinueProduct(Product product)
{
    // Logic to discontinue the product...
}
```

Decorating Entities

Decorating entities is the process of applying attributes to entity classes and properties to convey a certain intention. There are three primary reasons why you would want to decorate your entities with RIA Services attributes and data annotations. They are as follows:

- So you can control how the entity is created on the client (i.e., the properties from the server entity class that will be created on the client entity), and hence what data is passed over the wire

- To apply validation rules to the entity and its properties, validating what values are acceptable

- To apply miscellaneous data annotations, such as whether the property is a key that uniquely identifies the entity, whether the property should be used for concurrency checks, to display options for how the property should be presented on the client, and so on

You can decorate entities with the required attributes directly or via metadata classes.

■ **Note** If you have used the ASP.NET Dynamic Data scaffolding framework, you will be quite familiar with these attributes, as RIA Services uses the same attributes (defined in the `System.ComponentModel.DataAnnotations` namespace).

Metadata Classes

As previously described, metadata classes enable you to decorate your entity with attributes without actually modifying the entity class itself, which is useful when you code-generate your entities and a re-generation re-creates the entity class. A metadata class is associated with an entity using an attribute on the entity class. In order to not have to modify the entity class to apply this attribute, the usual method is to create a partial class for the entity and apply the attribute to it instead.

Open up the `ProductService.metadata.cs` metadata class that was created for the `Product` entity (from your Entity Framework model) to see how it is structured. This file contains a partial class that extends the `Product` entity. This is merely so the `MetadataType` attribute can be applied to the `Product` entity, designating its corresponding metadata class (`Product.ProductMetadata`). This provides the link between the entity class and the metadata class, which is used by RIA Services to associate the two together.

```
[MetadataTypeAttribute(typeof(Product.ProductMetadata))]
public partial class Product
{
    internal sealed class ProductMetadata
    {
        // Field definitions (removed for the purposes of brevity)
    }
}
```

■ **Note** It's not essential to use a nested class as your metadata class; you can actually use a class anywhere that can be referenced, but by default the metadata classes created by RIA Services are created as nested classes. You can then treat the metadata class as if it were the actual entity class, and decorate it with the required attributes.

The metadata class that was created by the Add New Domain Service Class wizard contains a public field representing each property on the associated entity, which you can decorate with attributes as required. Let's look at the various types of attributes you might like to decorate these properties (and the class itself) with.

Controlling Client Entity Generation

You might not necessarily want the entity that is created in the client project by the RIA Services code generation to be exactly the same as the entity that is in your entity model. For example, the entity might consist of properties that shouldn't be transferred to the client and/or made accessible to it, such as password properties, images, calculated properties, credit card numbers, and so on. Let's look at customizing what's generated on the client-side entity and what data is transferred to the client from the server.

Properties Included/Excluded in Generated Client Entity by Default

By default, all public properties on an entity that return simple types (such as `string`, `int`, and `bool`), or a small predefined group of complex types (such as byte arrays), will be automatically created as properties on the client entity unless they have the `Exclude` attribute applied. However, this means that other complex values, such as an entity collection associated with each requested entity being returned (i.e., entities associated with the associated entities via a foreign key relationship), will not be transferred to the client when the entity is transferred, and the collection property providing the association will not be created on the client's corresponding entity.

For example, take the following random subset of properties from the `Product` entity:

```
public string ProductLine { get; set; }
public EntityCollection<ProductInventory> ProductInventory;
public ProductModel ProductModel { get; set; }
public Nullable<int> ProductModelID { get; set; }
```

By default, when the RIA Services code generator creates the `Product` entity on the client, it will only create properties for the `ProductLine` and `ProductModelID` properties because they return "simple" types, whereas the `ProductInventories` and `ProductModel` properties return "complex" types.

Including/Excluding Properties

Although properties are automatically included or excluded on the client entity based upon their return types, you can explicitly specify that a given property is created on the client by decorating it with the `Include` attribute, or not created by decorating it with the `Exclude` attribute, both found in the `System.ServiceModel.DomainServices.Server` namespace.

For example, we can change the default generation behavior by specifying that the `ProductModelID` property should not be included as part of the client entity, and that the `ProductModel` and `ProductInventories` properties should, by decorating them (in the entity's metadata class) with the `Include/Exclude` attributes like so:

```
public string ProductLine { get; set; }

[Include]
public EntityCollection<ProductInventory> ProductInventories;

[Include]
public ProductModel ProductModel { get; set; }

[Exclude]
public Nullable<int> ProductModelID { get; set; }
```

■ **Note** Despite the `ProductModel` and `ProductInventories` properties being created on the client-side entity now, their value will always be null. You also need to request the `ProductModel` and `ProductInventory` properties in the LINQ to Entities query, as described in the next section.

Including Data for Associated Entities

As just noted, the `ProductModel` and `ProductInventories` properties are null by default when the `Product` entity or a collection of `Product` entities is requested from the server. You've seen how to ensure that corresponding properties are created on the client-side entity using the `Include` attribute, but now you need to ensure that they are populated with data, because the following default query will *not* do so:

```
public IQueryable<Product> GetProducts()
{
    return ObjectContext.Products;
}
```

You will need to explicitly request (using LINQ to Entities) that the data for the `ProductModel` and `ProductInventories` properties on each `Product` entity are retrieved from the database, using the `Include` method in the query, like so:

```
public IQueryable<Product> GetProducts()
{
    return ObjectContext.Products.Include("ProductModel")
                                 .Include("ProductInventories");
}
```

■ **Note** Here, we are chaining `Include` methods, and you can do this for as many associated entities that you want returned with the query.

Enabling Associated Entities to Be Editable

Although the `ProductModel` entity and `ProductInventories` collection are now populated with data for the `Product` entity on the client, you will not be able to edit their data without specifically adding support to enable this in the domain service. That is, you won't be able to change the description of the product model, or add/update/delete entities in the `ProductInventories` collection. In practice, there's no need for the description of the product model to be updatable on the client, but you might like to be able to maintain the product inventory. So we'll focus on this scenario only.

Currently, if you were to attempt to instantiate a `ProductInventory` entity on the client, the following exception would be thrown:

```
This EntitySet of Type 'AdventureWorks.Web.ProductInventory' does not support the 'Add' operation.
```

And if you were to attempt to change the value of a property on an existing `ProductInventory` entity in the collection, the following exception would be thrown:

```
This EntitySet of Type 'AdventureWorks.Web.ProductInventory' does not support the 'Edit' operation.
```

To make the `ProductInventories` collection editable and prevent these exceptions, you will need to create the insert/update/delete operations for the `ProductInventory` entity on the `ProductService` domain service, like so:

```
public void InsertProductInventory(ProductInventory productInventory)
{
    if ((productInventory.EntityState != EntityState.Detached))
    {
```

```
            this.ObjectContext.ObjectStateManager
                .ChangeObjectState(productInventory, EntityState.Added);
        }
        else
        {
            this.ObjectContext.ProductInventories.AddObject(productInventory);
        }
    }

    public void UpdateProductInventory(ProductInventory currentProductInventory)
    {
        this.ObjectContext.ProductInventories
            .AttachAsModified(currentProductInventory,
                              this.ChangeSet.GetOriginal(currentProductInventory));
    }

    public void DeleteProductInventory(ProductInventory productInventory)
    {
        if ((productInventory.EntityState != EntityState.Detached))
        {
            this.ObjectContext.ObjectStateManager
                .ChangeObjectState(productInventory, EntityState.Deleted);
        }
        else
        {
            this.ObjectContext.ProductInventories.Attach(productInventory);
            this.ObjectContext.ProductInventories.DeleteObject(productInventory);
        }
    }
}
```

Validation

One of the important problems that RIA Services tries to resolve is where validation logic needs to be written and executed on both the server and the client. Not only is it a duplication of code and effort to write the same logic in both places, but this logic can easily get out of sync with a change being made in one place but not the other. It's important to execute the validation logic in both places because you want to have a responsive user interface, without waiting for the server to tell the user that something is invalid, but you also want to validate the data on the server because there is no guarantee that the data came from your own client application and that its rules weren't circumvented. By enabling you to define your validation logic on your entities on the server, and automatically applying the same validation attributes when it generates the corresponding entities in the client project, RIA Services overcomes this problem. Your validation logic only needs to be written and maintained in a single location, and is kept synchronized by the code generation of the entities in the client project.

Predefined Validation Attributes

You can apply a number of basic validation rules to your properties via attributes (from the System.ComponentModel.DataAnnotations namespace), including the following:

- The Required attribute enables you to specify that the property must have a value (non-null). It also enforces, by default, that a string must not be empty, although the AllowEmptyStrings named property allows you to disable this behavior.

- The Range attribute lets you specify the minimum and maximum values permissible for the property.

- The StringLength attribute allows you to set a minimum and maximum number of characters permissible for a string property. The default constructor accepts a maximum length, with a default minimum length of 0 characters, and you can also specify the minimum length using the MinimumLength named property.

- The RegularExpression attribute enables you to validate the value of the property with a regular expression. For example, you might want to validate that an e-mail address conforms to a valid e-mail address format using one of the many commonly used regular expressions for that purpose, of which many aren't perfect but are considered acceptable.

Examples of these rules are shown in the following code:

```
[Required]
[StringLength(50)]
[RegularExpression(@"(?<user>[^@]+)@(?<host>.+)")]
public string EmailAddress;

[Range(0, 150)]
public int Age;
```

Custom Property Validation Attributes

Of course, these are only basic validation rules, so what if you need a validation rule that isn't included in the ones provided? In that case, you can write your own. However, in writing the code for a validation rule, you will need it to be available on the client too. Luckily, RIA Services helps because it contains code-sharing functionality (between the server and the client), where code written on the server can be duplicated on the client by the RIA Services code generator. This feature is covered later in this chapter, but in the meantime, let's take a look at what's required to write a validation rule.

You have two ways of creating your own validation rule. One way uses the CustomValidation attribute to decorate the property or class to be validated, to which you can pass a type (class name) and the name of the method in the class that does the validation. This method isn't ideal, because it requires you to pass the method name as a string, which is likely to cause problems when refactoring.

A better and much neater way is to create your own custom validation attribute. You do so by creating a class that inherits from the ValidationAttribute class (found in the System.ComponentModel.DataAnnotations namespace), and overriding the IsValid method. The value of the property to be validated will be passed in as a parameter to this method, along with a validation context—which contains information about the property being validated, the entity instance that the property belongs to, and so on. This method must return either a result of ValidationResult.Success, if the validation rule is passed, or an instance of the ValidationResult class to which you've passed an error message as the constructor parameter value. Let's create a custom validation attribute now.

 Workshop: Creating a Custom Property Validation Attribute

Let's create a simple validation attribute that ensures the value of the Class property is restricted to a small set of predefined values. The valid values for this property are validated in a database using check constraints; however, ideally, we'd like to validate the property value before it gets to this stage.

1. Create a new folder in your Web project, named ValidationRules.

2. Add a new class to the ValidationRules folder, named
   ProductClassValidationAttribute.shared.cs. The ".shared" part of the file
   name is important, as the RIA Services code generator needs to know that this
   code should be copied into the Silverlight project. We'll discuss sharing
   code/logic between the server and the client later in this chapter.

```
using System;
using System.Collections.Generic;
using System.Linq;
using System.Web;

namespace AdventureWorks.Web.ValidationRules
{
    public class ProductClassValidationAttribute
    {
    }
}
```

3. Remove the using statement for the System.Web namespace, as Silverlight does
   not have this namespace, and this code will be copied to the Silverlight project
   by the RIA Services code generator.

4. Add a using statement to the top of the class for the
   System.ComponentModel.DataAnnotations namespace.

```
using System.ComponentModel.DataAnnotations;
```

5. Make the class inherit from ValidationAttribute.

```
public class ProductClassValidationAttribute : ValidationAttribute
{
}
```

6. Override the IsValid method from the base class. Note that there are two
   IsValid methods that you can override in the Web project, but Silverlight only
   supports overriding the method that takes in a ValidationContext parameter,
   so you must override that one. This code is copied to the Silverlight project by
   the RIA Services code generator.

```
public class ProductClassValidationAttribute : ValidationAttribute
{
    protected override ValidationResult IsValid(object value,
                                    ValidationContext validationContext)
    {
        return base.IsValid(value, validationContext);
    }
}
```

7. You can now write your validation logic in this method, and return either
   ValidationResult.Success, if the validation rule is passed, or an instance of the
   ValidationResult class to which you've passed an error message as the con-
   structor parameter value. Add the code below (in bold) to the IsValid method.

```
using System;
using System.ComponentModel.DataAnnotations;
using System.Linq;
```

```
namespace AdventureWorks.Web.ValidationRules
{
    public class ProductClassValidationAttribute : ValidationAttribute
    {
        protected override ValidationResult IsValid(object value,
                                            ValidationContext validationContext)
        {
            bool isValid = true;

            if (value != null)
            {
                string productClass = value.ToString();

                string[] validClasses = new string[] { "H", "M", "L", "" };
                isValid = validClasses.Contains(productClass.ToUpper());
            }

            return isValid ? ValidationResult.Success : new ValidationResult(
                                            "The class is invalid");
        }
    }
}
```

8. The custom validation attribute is now complete. You can now apply the at-
    tribute to the property or properties to be validated using this rule. Add a using
    statement to the top of the metadata class for the Product entity, pointing to
    the AdventureWorks.Web.ValidationRules namespace. Now find the Class
    property in that class and decorate it with the attribute, like so:

```
[ProductClassValidation]
public string Class;
```

■ **Note** By convention, all attributes should have "Attribute" appended to their name. However, you don't need to
specify this suffix when using the attribute. For example, although the name of our custom validation attribute
class is ProductClassValidationAttribute, we do not need to specify this suffix when we decorate properties
with it, as just demonstrated.

Custom Class Validation Attributes

Sometimes, a validation rule involves two or more properties on an entity. For example, you might want
to validate that the finish date property's value is later than the start date property's value. In this scenario, you don't want the validation rule to run as soon as you modify one of the properties, because it
will prove frustrating to users to raise a validation error when they make a change to one, but have yet to
make a change to the other.

To solve this problem, you can create a custom validation rule and apply it to the entity as a whole,
rather than at the individual property level. Specifying a validation rule at the entity level validates the
entity when it is saved or navigating to another one. When the validation rule is run, the entire entity is

passed into the value parameter. You can then cast this to the type of entity you expect it to be applied to, and access its properties to perform the validation.

 ## Workshop: Creating a Custom Class Validation Attribute

Creating a validation rule to validate an entity is done in much the same way as creating the ProductClassValidation attribute. Let's create a custom validation rule for ensuring that the sell finish date on a Product entity is later than the sell start date.

1. Follow steps 2 to 6 from the previous workshop, but name the file SellDatesValidationAttribute.shared.cs instead.

2. Add the following code (in bold) to the attribute's IsValid method. Note how we cast the value parameter that was passed in to a Product entity type, and use its property values to perform the validation rule.

```
using System;
using System.Linq;
using System.ComponentModel.DataAnnotations;

namespace AdventureWorks.Web.ValidationRules
{
    public class SellDatesValidationAttribute : ValidationAttribute
    {
        protected override ValidationResult IsValid(object value,
                                        ValidationContext validationContext)
        {
            Product product = value as Product;
            return product.SellEndDate == null ||
                product.SellEndDate > product.SellStartDate ?
                    ValidationResult.Success : new ValidationResult(
                "The sell end date must be greater than the sell start date");
        }
    }
}
```

Presentation

Decorating your entities, which are essentially middle-tier components, with information for the presentation tier is somewhat controversial—it can make creating forms in your application very easy, by using the drag-and-drop features in Visual Studio 2010, but it blurs the line between the middle tier and the presentation tier. Ideally, the middle tier should know nothing about how the presentation tier will display the data. Despite your feelings on this issue, some attributes are available that enable you to provide presentation information on your entities—whether you use these attributes or enforce a strict separation of concerns is up to you.

The primary attribute used for this purpose is the Display attribute. The DataForm control from the Silverlight Toolkit uses this attribute, if available, when it is automatically creating a data entry form from an entity, and the DataGrid control uses it when creating a data grid with automatically generated columns. The Display attribute has a number of properties that suggest to the presentation tier how the property should be displayed. Some of these properties control the following:

- Whether a column should be created in a DataGrid control, and a field created in a DataForm control for this property (AutoGenerateField)

- A "friendly" name for the property that will be used as the label of a corresponding field/column in a DataForm or DataGrid control (Name/ShortName)

- A description for the property that will be displayed in a DataForm control as a tool-tip when the user moves the mouse cursor over an information icon next to the field (Description)

- The order in relation to the other properties in which a property will be displayed in a DataForm or DataGrid control (Order)

- What grouping the field for this property should be displayed under in a DataForm control (GroupName)

The following code shows an example of the Display attribute being applied to the ProductID and Name properties on the Product entity. With these attributes applied, when the Product entity is bound to a DataForm control, a field will not be created for the ProductID property, the label for the Name field will be "Product Name:", and the description for the Name field will display "The name of the product."

```
[Display(AutoGenerateField = false)]
public int ProductID { get; set; }

[Display(Name = "Product Name:", Description = "The name of the product.")]
public string Name { get; set; }
```

Miscellaneous Data Annotations

A number of important miscellaneous data annotations don't fit into either of the previous annotation type categories, but are used to control how RIA Services manages the entity, or to provide information to the presentation tier on how this entity should be displayed.

Some of the more important data annotations used by RIA Services are as follows:

- The Key attribute is used to specify that a property or multiple properties on an entity uniquely identifies that entity (i.e., represents a primary key).

- The Editable attribute is used to specify whether a property should be editable or not. By default, properties are editable, but you can decorate a property with this attribute, passing a value of false to its allowEdit constructor parameter to specify that the value of the property should not be able to be altered. Any attempt to do so will raise an exception on the client. You would typically apply this to the property that contains the entity key.

- The ConcurrencyCheck attribute is used to specify that a property should be used when performing concurrency checks back on the server before updating or deleting the entity in the database. The original value of the property, as retrieved from the server, will be passed back to the server when performing an update/delete operation so that it can be used in the concurrency check. Identifying and handling concurrency violations is discussed later in the chapter, in the "Handling Data Concurrency Violations" section.

- The RoundtripOriginal attribute is used to specify that the original value of the property, as retrieved from the server, will be passed back to the server when performing an update/delete operation.

- The `Timestamp` attribute is used to specify that the property is a binary number (not a date/time) that is being used to version the entity, and is often used in concurrency checks. The original values of properties with this attribute will, like those with the `ConcurrencyCheck` or `RoundtripOriginal` attributes, be passed back to the server when performing an update/delete operation.

- The `Association` attribute is used to provide an association between a parent entity and its child—for example, the `Product` entity and the `ProductModel` entity are associated, joining on their respective `ProductModelID` properties. Entities from your Entity Framework model will already have the parent/child associations configured, but you might need to use this attribute when returning presentation models from a domain operation. The `Association` attribute's constructor takes as its parameters a name for the association (of your own choosing), and the property names that link the parent and the child together. We'll look at an example of using this attribute when we discuss presentation model types later in this chapter.

- You can configure your entity association as a compositional hierarchy by decorating the property representing that association with the `Composition` attribute. This will cause the parent entity to be marked as updated when one of its children's entities is modified, and will send all the children entities, regardless of whether they have been modified, back to the server when performing an update—effectively treating both the parent and child entities as a single unit. You can then handle updates of the children in the parent entity's update operation rather than requiring them to have their own update operations. For example, you could apply the `Composition` attribute to the `ProductInventories` property on the `Product` entity. This means that all the `ProductInventory` entities associated with a `Product` entity will be passed back to the server when the `Product` entity is modified on the client and changes are submitted, regardless of whether they have been modified. You will then need to persist the `ProductInventory` entities to the database in the `Product` entity's update domain operation.

- When your entities are a part of an inheritance hierarchy, and you want to return various derived types of a base entity type from a domain operation, you can decorate the base entity with the `KnownType` attribute (from the `System.Runtime.Serialization` namespace) to associate it with these derived types, and use this as the type in your domain operations. For example, say you have an entity named `Person`, which acts as the base for `Employee` and `Customer` entities. You can decorate the `Person` entity with the `KnownType` attribute, passing it the `Employee` and `Customer` types, but have your domain operations only reference the `Person` entity (although they can return/accept the derived types). Going into this in depth is beyond the scope of this book, but you can find more information in this MSDN article: http://msdn.microsoft.com/en-us/library/ee707366(v=vs.91).aspx.

Presentation Model Types

The examples so far have passed entities from an Entity Framework model on the server to the client. Sometimes, however, this practice will not suit your needs. For example:

- You might not be using an Entity Framework (or LINQ to SQL) model in your application.

- You don't want to share data access layer objects with your presentation layer, instead wishing to maintain a clean separation of concerns.

- The entities in your model just don't match one-to-one what is required to be displayed in the presentation tier. That is, the data to be displayed needs to be aggregated from multiple entities.

- You want summarized/totaled data.

- You need to denormalize the data so that it's suitable for display to the user.

Fortunately, RIA Services is not limited to just transferring entities from an entity model. You can solve these issues by creating custom objects to be passed between the server and the client instead of entities. You can populate these objects on the server from your data access layer, and then, if these objects are editable, manually persist the changeset returned from the client back to the data access layer. You may think of these objects in traditional terms where they might be called data transfer objects (DTOs) or POCO types. Generally, when using them with RIA Services, they are termed *presentation model* types.

■ **Note** Once upon a time, a common practice was to return data from Web services in DataSets. Despite being a "heavy" way of exposing data, many developers liked to use DataSets for their simplicity and ability to modify the data structure being returned without needing to update references to the services exposing them. However, time has shown that the use of DataSets is a source of numerous problems in projects, and their use is now considered bad practice. Thus, many developers have turned to exposing data using lightweight, strongly typed DTOs instead. If no other reason compels you to stop using DataSets, the fact that Silverlight has no support for DataSets puts the final nail in their coffin. Therefore, don't try to expose DataSets from your domain service in an attempt to return an untyped object whose structure you can modify at will. Neither RIA Services nor Silverlight has any support for DataSets—consider them finally dead!

The process of exposing presentation model types from a domain service involves the following steps:

- Create a class with the properties required to be sent to the client.

- Create a domain service class that inherits from `DomainService`.

- Manually implement the get/query domain operations that expose the presentation model type.

- Manually implement the insert/update/delete operations if the presentation model type should be editable.

Let's take a look at how to implement a domain service that passes a presentation model type between the server and the client.

⚙ Workshop: Creating the Presentation Model Class

In this series of workshops, we'll expose a presentation model class from a domain service, which can be used to populate a product summary list in your Silverlight application. (We'll use this domain service in the workshops in Chapter 6.) The data to populate this presentation model class will be sourced from multiple entities in your entity model, demonstrating a scenario in which you would commonly expose presentation model types instead of entities. For the purpose of demonstration, we'll then enable the client application to edit this data and update the database with the changes accordingly.

Take note of the following when creating a presentation model class:

- At least one property must be decorated with the Key attribute, indicating that the value of the property uniquely identifies the object. Otherwise, you will receive a compilation error, because the changeset manager on the client cannot manage the changes without it.

- You can decorate this class and its properties with the various attributes described in the "Decorating Entities" section of this chapter. If you don't want to or cannot decorate the class and its properties with attributes directly, you can create a corresponding metadata class, as previously described, and apply the attributes in that manner.

- RIA Services does not require your presentation model class to be defined in the Web project or even in a WCF RIA Services Class Library project, described later in this chapter. For example, you may have the objects you want to expose from your domain service in a referenced assembly for which you don't have the code, and this is possible because RIA Services simply reflects over the given object and generates the code it requires accordingly in the client project—no source required.

In this first workshop, we'll create a presentation model class containing the properties that should be transferred between the client and the server, including the following:

- A key property that will be used to drill down on the record

- Various properties from the product record (name, number, etc.)

- A thumbnail image of the product, which is obtained from a different entity in the entity model on the server than the core Product entity, hence demonstrating combining data from multiple entities into a single object

- The total quantity of that product available from all the inventory locations, demonstrating summarizing/totaling related data

- The denormalized descriptions of the product's category, subcategory, and model, which are each stored in their own table, and referred to by a foreign key on the Product entity

The steps required to create this class are as follows:

1. Create a new class under the Models folder in your Web project, named ProductSummary.

2. Add the following properties to the class:

```
public int       ID                { get; set; }
public string    Name              { get; set; }
public string    Number            { get; set; }
public decimal   ListPrice         { get; set; }
public byte[]    ThumbnailPhoto    { get; set; }
public int?      QuantityAvailable { get; set; }
public string    Category          { get; set; }
public string    Subcategory       { get; set; }
public string    Model             { get; set; }
public bool      MakeFlag          { get; set; }
public DateTime  ModifiedDate      { get; set; }
```

3. Add a using statement for the `System.ComponentModel.DataAnnotations` namespace to the top of the file.

```
using System.ComponentModel.DataAnnotations;
```

4. Decorate the ID property with the Key attribute. Also decorate the ID property with the Editable attribute, passing it's constructor a value of false. This will prevent the client application from changing its value.

```
[Key]
[Editable(false)]
public int ID { get; set; }
```

5. Here is the complete code you should now have for the class:

```
using System;
using System.ComponentModel.DataAnnotations;

namespace AdventureWorks.Web.Models
{
    public class ProductSummary
    {
        [Key]
        [Editable(false)]
        public int       ID                { get; set; }
        public string    Name              { get; set; }
        public string    Number            { get; set; }
        public decimal   ListPrice         { get; set; }
        public byte[]    ThumbnailPhoto    { get; set; }
        public int?      QuantityAvailable { get; set; }
        public string    Category          { get; set; }
        public string    Subcategory       { get; set; }
        public string    Model             { get; set; }
        public bool      MakeFlag          { get; set; }
        public DateTime  ModifiedDate      { get; set; }
    }
}
```

⚙ Workshop: Populating and Exposing Your Presentation Model Types

In this workshop, we'll create a domain service containing a domain operation that exposes a collection of ProductSummary objects. Unfortunately, the Add New Domain Service Class wizard only generates the CRUD operations in your domain service when you are using entities from the Entity Framework or objects from a LINQ to SQL model—it doesn't allow you to select objects of other types, because the CRUD logic for these objects does not necessarily follow a specific model. Therefore, we must create the domain service ourselves from scratch. Let's do this now.

1. Add a new item to the Services folder in your Web project named
   ProductSummaryService, using the Domain Service Class item template. Since
   our data will be sourced from an entity model, select your AdventureWorks-
   Entities entity model as the object context. Don't select any entities from the
   entity list, however; simply click OK. This creates an empty domain service to
   which we can add the required domain operations.

```
namespace AdventureWorks.Web.Services
{
    using System;
    using System.Collections.Generic;
    using System.ComponentModel;
    using System.ComponentModel.DataAnnotations;
    using System.Data;
    using System.Linq;
    using System.ServiceModel.DomainServices.EntityFramework;
    using System.ServiceModel.DomainServices.Hosting;
    using System.ServiceModel.DomainServices.Server;
    using AdventureWorks.Web;


    // Implements application logic using the AdventureWorksEntities context.
    // TODO: Add your app logic to these methods or in additional methods.
    // TODO: Wire up authentication (Windows/ASP.NET Forms) and uncomment the
    // following to disable anonymous access.
    // Also consider adding roles to restrict access as appropriate.
    // [RequiresAuthentication]
    [EnableClientAccess()]
    public class ProductSummaryService :
                        LinqToEntitiesDomainService<AdventureWorksEntities>
    {

    }
}
```

■ **Note** If the data to populate your presentation model class comes from an Entity Framework or LINQ to SQL
model, select that model from the Available DataContexts/ObjectContexts drop-down in the wizard dialog, as we
did here. If the data is being sourced from elsewhere, select <empty domain service class> instead. When you do
this, the domain service inherits from DomainService, instead of the generic LinqToEntitiesDomainService
class that the previous domain services (that served up entities from the Entity Framework model) inherited from.

2. Add a using statement to the AdventureWorks.Web.Models namespace—that is,
   the location of the ProductSummary class that we are exposing from this domain
   service.

3. Now we need to add the query operation to the domain service. Because the
   data is coming from a query to the Entity Framework model, we can still take
   advantage of the benefits of returning an IQueryable expression by projecting
   data from the Entity Framework model onto a collection of the presentation

model objects, and returning this query from the operation. Therefore, the client can specify any additional sorting/filtering/grouping/paging that it requires, and have that query run on the server. The following code returns an IQueryable expression that populates a collection of ProductSummary objects with data from the entity model:

```
public IQueryable<ProductSummary> GetProductSummaryList()
{
    return from p in this.ObjectContext.Products
           select new ProductSummary()
           {
               ID = p.ProductID,
               Name = p.Name,
               Number = p.ProductNumber,
               ListPrice = p.ListPrice,
               ThumbnailPhoto = p.ProductProductPhotoes.FirstOrDefault().
                                                ProductPhoto.ThumbNailPhoto,
               QuantityAvailable = p.ProductInventories
                                    .Sum(pi => pi.Quantity),
               Category = p.ProductSubcategory.ProductCategory.Name,
               Subcategory = p.ProductSubcategory.Name,
               Model = p.ProductModel.Name,
               MakeFlag = p.MakeFlag,
               ModifiedDate = p.ModifiedDate
           };
}
```

■ **Note** Keep in mind that we're returning an image from the database in the ThumbnailPhoto property of the ProductSummary object. Returning an image from the database for each item to display in a summary list results in increased network and bandwidth usage, so it's recommended to return images only if they add value to your application, and make sure that they are small, preferably less than 2 KB each.

When executed, this expression will populate and return a collection of our presentation model object (ProductSummary) to the client.

⚙ Workshop: Making Your Presentation Model Types Editable

You can also implement insert, update, and delete domain operations for your presentation model types. In this workshop, we'll implement these operations for our ProductSummary presentation model type, although in reality, it's unlikely you'd want the ProductSummary object to be editable, as we'll only be using it for displaying a list of products to the user.

■ **Note** To keep things simple, we'll only support making the Name, Number, and ListPrice properties of the ProductSummary class editable.

1. Let's start by adding stubs for the insert, update, and delete domain operation methods to the `ProductSummaryService` class, using the method signature convention, as described earlier in this chapter, which will allow RIA Services to recognize them as such:

```
public void InsertProductSummary(ProductSummary productSummary)
{

}

public void UpdateProductSummary(ProductSummary productSummary)
{

}

public void DeleteProductSummary(ProductSummary productSummary)
{

}
```

■ **Note** Be aware that each domain operation method takes in a `ProductSummary` object.

---

2. We can now implement these operations. The `Insert` operation involves creating a new `Product` entity instance, setting its property values from the `ProductSummary` object passed into the method, and adding it to the collection of products in the entity model.

```
public void InsertProductSummary(ProductSummary productSummary)
{
    Product product = new Product();
    product.Name = productSummary.Name;
    product.ProductNumber = productSummary.Number;
    product.ListPrice = productSummary.ListPrice;
    product.ModifiedDate = DateTime.Now;

    // Need to set default values for these properties,
    // otherwise the save will fail
    product.SellStartDate = DateTime.Now;
    product.SafetyStockLevel = 1;
    product.ReorderPoint = 1;

    this.ObjectContext.Products.AddObject(product);
}
```

3. The `Update` operation involves getting the stored version of the given product, and updating its property values.

```
public void UpdateProductSummary(ProductSummary productSummary)
{
    Product product = this.ObjectContext.Products
```

```
        .Where(p => p.ProductID == productSummary.ID)
        .First();

    product.Name = productSummary.Name;
    product.ProductNumber = productSummary.Number;
    product.ListPrice = productSummary.ListPrice;
    product.ModifiedDate = DateTime.Now;
}
```

4. The Delete operation involves creating a Product entity with the given ID, attaching it to the object context, and telling the entity model to delete this entity.

```
public void DeleteProductSummary(ProductSummary productSummary)
{
    Product product = new Product();
    product.ProductID = productSummary.ID;
    product.ModifiedDate = productSummary.ModifiedDate;
    this.ObjectContext.AttachTo("Products", product);
    this.ObjectContext.DeleteObject(product);
}
```

■ **Note** We're also setting the ModifiedDate property value on the new Product entity. Although doing so is not required now, it will be required when we use this field to maintain concurrency checks later in this chapter.

⚙ Workshop: Returning Auto-Generated Property Values Back to the Client

When inserting (and sometimes updating) data on the server, you will generally want to return values that have been generated on the server back to the client, such as a primary key value generated by the database when inserting a row, or a timestamp value being used for row versioning in the database. You can do this using the Associate method on the domain service's ChangeSet object. Pass this method the presentation model object, the entity that was updated, and a callback method. After the database has been updated, the callback method will be called, at which point you can update the presentation model object as required from the entity.

This workshop will demonstrate updating the ProductSummary object with the ProductID and ModifiedDate assigned to the Product entity when inserting a new record into the database.

1. Add the following callback method to the ProductSummaryService class. This method will update the ProductID and ModifiedDate properties on the ProductSummary object, and return these values to the client:

```
private void UpdateProductSummaryValues(ProductSummary productSummary,
                                        Product product)
{
    productSummary.ID = product.ProductID;
    productSummary.ModifiedDate = product.ModifiedDate;
}
```

2. Now call the Associate method of the ChangeSet object, telling it to call the callback method after the Product entity has been persisted to the database.

133

```
public void InsertProduct(ProductSummary productSummary)
{
    Product product = new Product();
    product.Name = productSummary.Name;
    product.ProductNumber = productSummary.Number;
    product.ListPrice = productSummary.ListPrice;
    product.ModifiedDate = DateTime.Now;

    // Need to set default values for these properties,
    // otherwise the save will fail.
    product.SellStartDate = DateTime.Now;
    product.SafetyStockLevel = 1;
    product.ReorderPoint = 1;

    this.ObjectContext.Products.AddObject(product);
    this.ObjectContext.SaveChanges();

    ChangeSet.Associate(productSummary, product, UpdateProductSummaryValues);
}
```

Enabling Related Data to Be Editable

If your presentation model object contains a property exposing a collection of another object that you want to be passed to the client, as discussed earlier in the "Controlling Client Entity Generation" section of this chapter, you must explicitly specify that the property should be generated on the client by decorating it with the Include attribute. For example, you might want to expose the collection of product inventory objects associated with each product object, with the ProductSummary object containing a property representing a collection of related ProductInventoryPM objects, like so:

```
[Include]
public IEnumerable<ProductInventoryPM> ProductInventory { get; set; }
```

If the objects in the ProductInventory collection are to be editable, you will need to add corresponding insert/update/delete operations to the domain service for the object type, as demonstrated in the previous section. However, when you attempt to compile the project, you will find that you receive a compile error stating that you have an invalid Include specification. This is because you need to provide an association between the child object (ProductInventoryPM) and its parent (ProductSummary) by decorating the property that exposes the collection on the parent with the Association attribute. The Association attribute takes as its parameters a name for the association (of your own choosing) and the property names that link the parent and the child together. The following example demonstrates implementing a property that provides an association between the ProductSummary and ProductInventoryPM objects:

```
[Include]
[Association("ProductPM_ProductInventory", "ProductID", "ProductID")]
public IEnumerable<ProductInventoryPM> ProductInventory { get; set; }
```

■ **Note** Entity models automatically have this Association attribute applied, indicating associations between entities, but you need to apply it manually for presentation model types.

Sharing Code and Logic Across Tiers

At times, you might want to share custom code between the middle tier and the presentation tier. For example, you might want to share custom validation logic and some types of business logic between the server and the client. RIA Services enables code to be written in the Web project, and the RIA Services code generator will copy specially marked code files from this project into the client project, effectively enabling the code to be maintained in one place, but used on both the server and the client.

Shared Code Files

There are many reasons why you'd want to share code between the server and the client. However, you'd generally use this method when you want to extend an entity, using a partial class, to add additional methods and computed properties; or you might want to share completely new classes, such as custom validation attribute classes, as discussed earlier in the "Validation" section of this chapter.

The RIA Services code generator enables code to be shared between the server and client projects by automatically copying any files in the server project with a `.shared.cs` extension into the client project (untouched). Therefore, you can write the code in one place (the server) and know that the client will be updated accordingly. Of course, because the shared code will be running on both platforms, you should ensure that the code you write will successfully run on both platforms, and that it doesn't use any platform-specific functions.

■ Note If the property or method you are sharing is required only on the client, shared code might not be the most appropriate means of extending the entity. In this case, you would be better off writing the partial class in the Silverlight project directly, extending the entity with the required functionality on the client only.

Workshop: Creating a Shared Code File

You've already created a shared code file back in the workshop where you created custom property and class validation attributes. Let's implement a slightly different scenario in this workshop, by extending the `Product` entity in order to add a calculated property named `ProfitMargin` to it. This property simply calculates the expected profit to be made on the product by subtracting the `StandardCost` from the `ListPrice`. By writing the code in a shared file, this property will be able to be used on both the server and the client.

1. Create a new class in the `Models\Shared` folder of your Web project, named `Product.shared.cs`.

```
using System;
using System.Collections.Generic;
using System.Linq;
using System.Web;

namespace AdventureWorks.Web.Models.Shared
{
    public class Product
    {
    }
}
```

2. Remove the using statements from the top of the file. We don't need the first three, and the fourth will prevent the Silverlight project from compiling because that namespace doesn't exist in the Silverlight runtime.

3. We need to extend the Product entity from our entity model using partial classes. Therefore, you need to change the namespace of the class to the same namespace and name of your entity, and make it a partial class.

```
namespace AdventureWorks.Web
{
    public partial class Product
    {
    }
}
```

4. Add the following code to implement the ProfitMargin property:

```
namespace AdventureWorks.Web
{
    public partial class Product
    {
        public decimal ProfitMargin
        {
            get { return ListPrice - StandardCost; }
        }
    }
}
```

This file will automatically be copied to the Silverlight project and, thus, extend the Product entity accordingly in both the server and client projects.

Encapsulating Logic in a Separate WCF RIA Services Class Library

By default, when using RIA Services, your Silverlight project is linked directly to your Web project, which is what the examples so far have demonstrated. You are defining your business objects and business logic in your Web project, and this is being copied directly into your Silverlight project. However, from a design perspective, this is possibly not an ideal structure for your solution, depending on the nature and scale of your Web application, because this tightly couples both your Silverlight project and your business objects/logic to your Web project and limits their reusability.

It is possible, however, to move the business logic out of the Web project and into a separate class library, using the WCF RIA Services Class Library project template. Unfortunately, the process to do so is not particularly straightforward, but let's first look at the structure that using RIA Services class libraries gives us.

WCF RIA Services Class Libraries

The WCF RIA Services Class Library project template was designed to be added to an existing Silverlight project solution rather than to provide a full solution template. When you add a new project to your solution using this template, it will actually add two projects to your solution, one with .Web appended to the name you specified. Both get placed into a solution folder that the project template creates, as shown in Figure 4-6. These two projects will share a RIA Services link, meaning that you can now remove the link directly between the Web project and the Silverlight project, removing the tight coupling between the two. Now you can move your domain services, entity model, metadata classes, presentation model classes, and shared code into the .Web class library, and RIA Services will generate the corresponding code into the Silverlight class library, in the same way it previously did into the Silverlight application.

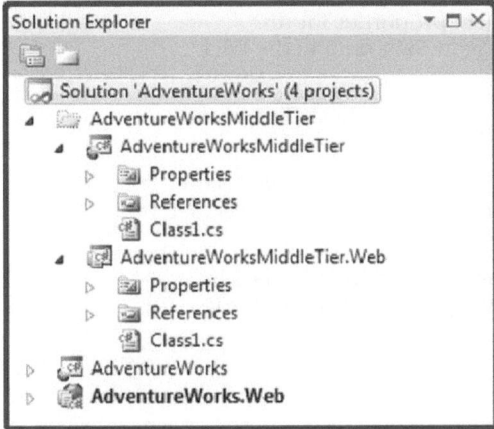

Figure 4-6. The structure of the RIA Services Class Library projects

Now it *should* simply be a case of adding a reference to the .Web class library to your Web project, and adding a reference to the other class library to your Silverlight project. Unfortunately, however, this will most likely not be the case. If you are using the authentication features of RIA Services (which will be discussed in Chapter 8), you will find that by putting the AuthenticationService in the class library, the WebContext object will not be generated by RIA Services in the Silverlight application, which is required to access the authentication service. You can work around this problem, however, by manually implementing the WebContext class and setting the AuthenticationContext when the application starts.

⚙ Workshop: Using WCF RIA Services Class Libraries

In this workshop, we're going to implement RIA Services class libraries in our solution, and move the business logic from our Web project into these libraries. The Web project will then be used purely for serving up the XAP file to the client.

■ **Note** Future workshops in this book will assume that your solution has *not* separated out the business logic into RIA Services class libraries, as shown here.

---

1. Add a new project to the solution named `AdventureWorksMiddleTier`, using the WCF RIA Services Class Library project template. Two projects will actually be created in your solution, one for the server and one for the client, as shown in Figure 4-6. The client project will automatically have a RIA Services link to the server project.

2. Remove the existing RIA Services link between the `AdventureWorks` and the `AdventureWorks.Web` projects, by opening the project properties for the `AdventureWorks`project, and selecting the `<No Project Set>` item in the WCF RIA Services link drop-down field.

3. Each class library project has a file named `Class1.cs`. Delete these files, as they are not required.

4. Open the project properties page for the `AdventureWorksMiddleTier.Web` class library, and change its default namespace from `AdventureWorksMiddleTier.Web` to `AdventureWorks.Web`.

5. Open the project properties page for the `AdventureWorksMiddleTier` class library, and change its default namespace from `AdventureWorksMiddleTier` to `AdventureWorks`.

■ **Note** Changing the default namespaces for these class library projects saves you the need to update all the `using` statements in files that you move between the projects. If you prefer to leave these namespaces as is, you will simply need to update the `using` statements in the files from `AdventureWorks.*` to `AdventureWorks-MiddleTier.*`.

---

6. Now move all your domain services, entity model, resources, metadata classes, presentation model classes, and shared code from the `AdventureWorks.Web` project into the `AdventureWorksMiddleTier.Web` class library. You can do this by dragging the files/folders between the projects, holding down the Shift key while you do so (holding down the Shift key will move the files/folders instead of copying them).

7. Add references to the following assemblies in the `AdventureWorksMiddleTier.Web` class library:

   - `System.ComponentModel.DataAnnotations`
   - `System.ServiceModel.DomainServices.EntityFramework`
   - `System.ServiceModel.DomainServices.Server`
   - `System.ServiceModel.DomainServices.Hosting`
   - `System.Web`
   - `System.Web.ApplicationServices`

   You can also remove these assembly references from your `AdventureWorks.Web` project if you wish.

8. Confirm that you can now successfully build the
   `AdventureWorksMiddleTier.Web` project.

9. Create a folder named `Models` in the `AdventureWorksMiddleTier` project. Move
   the `RegistrationData.partial.cs` and `User.partial.cs` files from the `Models`
   folder in the Silverlight project into this new folder.

10. A number of properties and methods in the `RegistrationData.partial.cs`
    class need to have their access modifier changed from `internal` to
    `public`: `PasswordAccessor`, `PasswordConfirmationAccessor`, `CurrentOperation`,
    and `UserNameEntered`. To prevent these properties from being generated as
    data entry fields in the registration screen in the Silverlight application,
    decorate them with the `Display` attribute, setting its `AutoGenerateField` prop-
    erty to `false`. For example:

```
[Display(AutoGenerateField = false)]
public Func<string> PasswordAccessor { get; set; }
```

11. You'll note that the linked `.resx` files in the `Web\Resources` folder in the Silver-
    light project now have icons indicating they can no longer be found because
    we moved the source files from the `AdventureWorks.Web` project to the
    `AdventureWorksMiddleTier.Web` project. Delete the `Web` folder and its contents;
    we'll re-create this structure in the `AdventureWorksMiddleTier` class library
    project.

12. Create a folder named `Web` in the `AdventureWorksMiddleTier` project, and a
    folder named `Resources` under the new `Web` folder.

13. Right-click on the Resources folder in the `AdventureWorksMiddleTier` project,
    and select Add ➤ Existing Item… from the context menu. Navigate to the
    Resources folder under the `AdventureWorksMiddleTier.Web` project's folder.
    Select all the files in this folder. We want to add a link to these files. You can do
    this by clicking on the drop-down icon on the Add button, and selecting Add
    As Link from the menu.

14. Confirm that you can now successfully build the `AdventureWorksMiddleTier`
    project.

15. Add a reference to the `AdventureWorksMiddleTier.Web` class library to your
    `AdventureWorks.Web` project, and add a reference to the
    `AdventureWorksMiddleTier` class library to your `AdventureWorks` project.

16. Create a new class in the `AdventureWorks` project named `WebContext` with the
    following content:

```
using System.ServiceModel.DomainServices.Client.ApplicationServices;
using AdventureWorks.Web;

namespace AdventureWorks
{
    public sealed partial class WebContext : WebContextBase
    {
        partial void OnCreated();

        public WebContext()
        {
            this.OnCreated();
```

```
        }

        public new static WebContext Current
        {
            get
            {
                return ((WebContext)(WebContextBase.Current));
            }
        }

        public new User User
        {
            get
            {
                return ((User)(base.User));
            }
        }
    }
}
```

17. The final step is to set the authentication context when the application starts. Open the App.xaml.cs file in the AdventureWorks project. Add the following line of code in bold to the Application_Startup method:

```
private void Application_Startup(object sender, StartupEventArgs e)
{
    ((WebAuthenticationService)WebContext.Current.Authentication)
            .DomainContext = new AdventureWorks.Web.AuthenticationContext();

    this.Resources.Add("WebContext", WebContext.Current);
    WebContext.Current.Authentication
                    .LoadUser(this.Application_UserLoaded, null);

    this.InitializeRootVisual();
}
```

18. We're finally done! Your solution should now compile and run successfully.

Handling Errors

When errors occur on the server, it's useful to log them—for example, write them to the event log, the database, or a text file—to help track down the problem that led to the exception. Often, you might also wish to perform some other tasks when an error occurs, such as sending an e-mail notification to the system administrator. You could handle this in each domain operation, but that would mean repetitive exception-handling code in each operation. An easy way to handle errors at a domain service level with RIA Services is to simply override the domain service's OnError method, like so:

```
protected override void OnError(DomainServiceErrorInfo errorInfo)
{
    // Log exception here.
}
```

This method will be called each time an exception is thrown anywhere in the domain service. You can then log the error, and add in any additional error-handling logic you want. Useful information that you should include with any logged error includes the following:

- When the error occurred (i.e., the date and time)

- Who encountered the error (if the user is logged in)

- Where the error occurred (i.e., the method)

- The error message

- A stack trace

- Any associated data—such as the current changeset, which can be obtained simply using the ChangeSet property on the domain service—that could help identify the cause of the issue

You will find most of these as properties on the errorInfo object. To test your error logging and simulate something going awry in your domain service, you can simply throw an exception in one of the domain operations, which will then call your OnError override method, enabling you to log the error.

■ **Note** You can choose whether to directly propagate these exceptions to the client, or sanitize them first to avoid exposing the potentially sensitive details of the inner workings of your service and the stack trace to the client. The steps to configuring your Web project to sanitize the exceptions are detailed in Chapter 8.

Handling Data Concurrency Violations

When you have multiple users updating data in your application, you are sure to eventually be faced with data concurrency violations. Say you have two users who retrieve an entity representing the same product in the database at roughly the same time, such that the Product entity returned to both is identical. If both of those users decide to update that product, however, then you face a conundrum. If one user were to submit their changes, followed later by the other user, the first user's changes would be overwritten by the second user's changes, leading to the first user's updates being lost, and creating potential data integrity issues in your database.

This scenario is what is known as a *concurrency violation*. Ideally, you want the second user to be informed that the product has changed on the server, since they retrieve the data when they attempt their update, and to be able to respond to that situation accordingly, which may differ from application to application, or even based upon the particular data being modified.

■ **Note** Although concurrency violations are rare, you must cater for them accordingly in your code. Otherwise, you will find people complaining that the system is "losing data," with no idea why.

Methods of Identifying Concurrency Violations

To appropriately handle this type of scenario, you will need to create and design a strategy to identify, handle, and resolve these concurrency violations, on both the server and the client. RIA Services uses optimistic concurrency (i.e., the record in the database isn't locked from being updated by other users after being retrieved), so you will need to design your strategy within these boundaries. Optimistic concurrency violations are generally identified by comparing given properties on the original version of an entity, before it had been modified on the client, with those on the stored version of the entity as it currently exists in the database, immediately before persisting data to the database. Therefore, concurrency checks generally involve the following three versions of the entity:

- The *original* version containing the state of the entity as originally retrieved from the server

- The *current* version, which generally consists of updates made on the client to the original version of the entity, and is now being sent back to the server to be committed to the database

- The *stored* version, which can be currently found in the database prior to being updated

A common strategy to identify concurrency violations is to have a column on your database table that is updated whenever the row is changed. Common column types for this purpose include the following:

- A timestamp/rowversion column

- A uniqueidentifier (i.e., GUID) column

- A datetime column

When performing an update operation on an entity, RIA Services will retrieve the entity as it is currently stored in the database, and compare the original value of the given concurrency check property (sent back from the client) with its stored value as found in the database. If the values are different, then a concurrency violation has been identified. The reason why the value of this property has changed since it was retrieved from the database is because another user has updated the entity since the original version had been retrieved from the server.

Alternatively, if you don't have a single property on the entity that you can use for concurrency checks, then you may compare a number of (or all) properties on the entity between its original version and the stored version, and raise a concurrency violation if any of the values are different. This method is far more cumbersome than the single-column method, although it does let you pick and choose which properties whose changes you don't want to be lost, while ignoring changes to others whose changes might be unimportant.

Implementing Concurrency Violation Checks

By default, RIA Services and the Entity Framework will simply update an entity without performing any concurrency checks. You will need to configure it to perform these checks before updating/deleting data in the database. This involves ensuring the following:

- You have a property on the entity whose original and stored versions can be compared to check for a concurrency violation.

- The original value of this property is returned by the client, along with the updated entity.

When the client sends an entity back to the server, it only sends it the updated (current) version of the entity. However, the original value of any properties decorated with the ConcurrencyCheck attribute, the TimeStamp attribute, or the RoundtripOriginal attribute *will* be sent back to the server when performing an update operation. You will generally apply the ConcurrencyCheck attribute to the property or properties that will be used as part of the concurrency check, which will ensure that you have its original value in addition to its current value returned from the client. This means you have the data required to perform the concurrency check, but RIA Services doesn't actually provide the logic to implement the concurrency checks itself. Instead, it leaves the task of identifying concurrency violations to the data access layer.

If you are using the Entity Framework as your data access layer (as we are in this book), you can simply configure the entities in your entity model to perform concurrency checks prior to an update, specifying which of the entity's properties will participate in the comparison check. In your entity model, select one of these properties on the entity, and from the Properties window change its Concurrency Mode property from None to Fixed. If you need to compare more than one property on the entity for a concurrency violation, then repeat this for each property that should participate in the comparison. A handy side-effect of doing this is that the property will automatically have the ConcurrencyCheck attribute applied to it behind the scenes, leaving nothing else to be done to implement concurrency checks for the entity.

Now, prior to any update of that entity, the stored version of the entity will be loaded from the database, and the stored value of each property in the concurrency check will be compared to its corresponding current value as returned from the client. A concurrency violation exception will be thrown if any of the values being compared are different.

■ **Note** The OnError method, as discussed earlier in the "Handling Errors" section of this chapter, is thrown when a concurrency violation has been identified. If you are logging errors, you will probably want to ignore the OptimisticConcurrencyException exception, as the errors do not indicate a failure in the system and, thus, are of little value being logged.

⚙ Workshop: Configuring an Entity Model to Check for Concurrency Violations

The Product entity contains a property called ModifiedDate, of type DateTime. We can use this property to perform concurrency checks, like so:

1. Open your AdventureWorksModel entity model.

2. Find the Product entity.

3. Select the ModifiedDate property, and set its Concurrency Mode property to Fixed (using the Properties tool window).

4. The ModifiedDate field on the Products table in the AdventureWorks database is not automatically updated by a database trigger when the record is updated. Therefore, we need to explicitly update this property when the Product entity is being added/updated. Find the update domain operation in the ProductService domain service created earlier.

```
public void UpdateProduct(Product currentProduct)
{
    this.ObjectContext.Products.AttachAsModified(currentProduct,
                        this.ChangeSet.GetOriginal(currentProduct));
}
```

5. Update the ModifiedDate property on the currentProduct entity that has been passed into the method as a parameter with the current date/time.

```
public void UpdateProduct(Product currentProduct)
{
```

```
currentProduct.ModifiedDate = DateTime.Now;

this.ObjectContext.Products.AttachAsModified(currentProduct,
                         this.ChangeSet.GetOriginal(currentProduct));
}
```

■ **Note** You should always set this value on the server, not the client side, as doing so on the client side would assign the client PC's date/time, which can vary greatly based upon the user's time zone or if they have the incorrect date/time set on their machine—potentially misrepresenting the actual time that the record was updated. The value you set here will be automatically passed back to the client.

The entity is now configured to perform concurrency checks when it's being updated.

Testing Your Solution

Assuming you have implemented functionality in your Silverlight application to retrieve and update Product entities, you can test it using two copies of your Silverlight application that are open at the same time in different browser windows. Retrieve a given Product entity from the server in one instance of the application, and retrieve exactly the same entity in the other. Make a change to the entity in one instance, and send it to the server to update the database with the change. Now make a change to the entity in the other instance and send the update to the server. Because you updated the entity in the first instance, the ModifiedDate property of that entity on the server will have changed from its original value that is being sent through with the update in the second instance. Therefore, when the Entity Framework compares these values and finds that they are different, it will throw a concurrency exception.

Implementing Concurrency Violation Checks for Presentation Model Types

As mentioned earlier, a little more work is required if you are exposing presentation model objects to the client instead of entities. In this case, you will need to specify which properties should have their original values sent back to the server when updating an object, and then perform the concurrency check logic yourself when updating the database.

The first step will be to decorate the properties on the presentation model object that will participate in the concurrency check (generally in the object's metadata class) with one of the attributes that ensure that the original value of that property will be sent back with any update of the object to the server (i.e., ConcurrencyCheck, TimeStamp, or RoundtripOriginal). For example:

```
[ConcurrencyCheck]
public DateTime ModifiedDate { get; set; }
```

You then need to compare the original value of this property with its stored value in the update operation of the domain service. However, you will find that only the updated version of the entity is passed into the operation as a parameter, whereas you also need the original version of this entity for your comparison. You can retrieve the original version of the object using the GetOriginal method of the ChangeSet object. Note that on this "original" object, only the properties specified to be round-tripped will have values.

```
var originalProduct = ChangeSet.GetOriginal<ProductSummary>(productSummary);
```

The next step depends on how you have implemented your data access layer. If your data access layer already performs concurrency checks, then no additional work is required. Otherwise, your update domain operation will need to manually retrieve the stored version of the entity from the database and compare the values of the properties between this and the original version to identify a concurrency violation. If one is found and you want to notify the client, you will need to get the ChangeSetEntry object for the object being updated, and assign values to its ConflictMembers, StoreEntity, and IsDeleteConflict properties. For example:

```
var originalProduct = ChangeSet.GetOriginal<ProductSummary>(productSummary);
ProductSummary storedProduct = GetProduct(productSummary.ProductID);

if (storedProduct.ModifiedDate != originalProduct.ModifiedDate)
{
    ChangeSetEntry entry =
        ChangeSet.ChangeSetEntries.Single(p => p.Entity == productSummary);

    List<string> conflicts = new List<string>();
    conflicts.Add("ModifiedDate");
    entry.ConflictMembers = conflicts;

    entry.IsDeleteConflict = false;
    entry.StoreEntity = storedProduct;
}
else
{
    // Save ProductSummary...
}
```

Resolving Conflicts in the Domain Service

In this sort of scenario, your domain service will inherit from LinqToEntitiesDomainService, which provides the ResolveConflicts method that you can override, which will be called when a concurrency conflict has occurred, and enable you to handle it using some custom logic on the server side if you wish. This method returns a Boolean value—if it returns false, the client will simply be notified of the conflicts. If your method returns true, the changeset will be resubmitted to the database once again (this will happen only once).

■ **Note** We'll discuss resolving concurrency conflicts on the client in Chapter 5.

Transactions

Transactions are often used when updating data in a database, such that if an update fails (if a concurrency violation is identified, for example), the updates made since the transaction was started will be rolled back, leaving the database in the same state as it was before the transaction started. The use of transactions ensures that the database doesn't get into an unknown or inconsistent state because some changes but not others have been written to the database, potentially compromising its integrity.

Often, you will want to encapsulate the changes being submitted to the database within a transaction, particularly when using a data access layer other than the Entity Framework or LINQ to SQL, because these both already automatically implement transactions when submitting changes. You can do so in a domain service by overriding the Submit method from the base class, and encapsulating the call to the Submit method in the base class in a transaction scope, as demonstrated here:

```
public override bool Submit(ChangeSet changeSet)
{
    bool result = false;

    TransactionOptions transactionOptions = new TransactionOptions();
    transactionOptions.IsolationLevel =
        System.Transactions.IsolationLevel.ReadCommitted;

    using (TransactionScope transaction = new TransactionScope(
                TransactionScopeOption.Required, transactionOptions))
    {
        result = base.Submit(changeSet);
        transaction.Complete();
    }

    return result;
}
```

■ **Note** You will need to add a reference to the System.Transactions assembly and a using statement to the System.Transactions namespace in your class in order to implement the preceding example.

WCF RIA Services Toolkit

The WCF RIA Services Toolkit consists of a number of out-of-band features that are not included in the core RIA Services framework. These typically are features that haven't quite reached the maturity required to be full-fledged members of the core RIA Services framework, but are updated frequently and made available for you to use while they gain maturity (albeit without any guarantees that they will work as required, or won't radically change and/or break your code with future updates). By making them available in the toolkit, Microsoft is able to garner feedback from developers and update them accordingly in a timely manner without needing to wait for a new release of the full framework. In turn, Microsoft is providing new features on a regular basis for you to use, much earlier than you would otherwise be able to.

At the time of writing, the following features can be found in the WCF RIA Services Toolkit:

- *LinqToSqlDomainService:* Unfortunately, there is currently no support for LINQ to SQL models out of the box in the RIA Services framework. However, to provide this support, you can find the LinqToSqlDomainService class in the toolkit, similar to the LinqToEntitiesDomainService in the framework, but for LINQ to SQL.

- *MVVM Support:* Provides a DomainCollectionView class that enables you to easily consume data from RIA Services and expose it from a view model. We'll discuss this class further in Chapter 5, and also Chapter 13 when we discuss the MVVM design pattern in depth.

- *T4 Templates:* Allows you to customize the code generated in the client project.

- *SOAP Endpoint:* Enables you to expose a SOAP endpoint for your domain services.

- *JSON Endpoint:* Enables you to expose a JSON endpoint for your domain services.

- *jQuery Support:* Provides a jQuery client that enables you to communicate with domain services from jQuery, with support for both querying data and submitting changes to the server.

- *Entity Framework Code-First Support:* Provides a DbDomainService class that your domain services can inherit from, enabling them to support the Entity Framework 4.1's code-first and DbContext features.

- *Windows Azure Table Storage:* Provides a TableDomainService class that your domain services can inherit from, enabling them to use Windows Azure table storage as the data layer.

- *ASP.NET DomainDataSource and DomainValidator Controls:* Provides a data source control that enables you to communicate with your domain services in an ASP.NET application or web site.

You can find a link to download the WCF RIA Services Toolkit on the WCF RIA Services page on the Silverlight web site, at www.silverlight.net/getstarted/riaservices. Alternatively, much of the toolkit is available as a series of NuGet packages, all prefixed with RIAServices.

The WCF RIA Services Contrib Project

The WCF RIA Services Contrib project is a collection of tools for RIA Services, contributed by the community, and coordinated by Colin Blair.

Contents of note include the following:

- Combo box extensions, with support for cascading combo boxes, asynchronous loading of items, and support for entity associations

- An alternative data validation framework to that provided by RIA Services

- Extension methods that add additional functionality to entities

- T4 templates to generate domain services, metadata, and localization for an entity model

- A tool to scaffold DbDomainServices for your Entity Framework Code-First model

You can get the WCF RIA Services Contrib project from http://riaservicescontrib.codeplex.com, or as NuGet packages (their names all starting with RiaServicesContrib). Blog posts and documentation for the project are available on Colin's blog at www.riaservicesblog.net/Blog/.

WCF Data Services

Although we won't go into it deeply here, it's worth mentioning the availability of WCF Data Services as an alternative to RIA Services. WCF Data Services (Data Services, for short) is another data-centric communication technology built on the WCF stack that exposes data to clients as JSON- or ATOM-serialized RESTful resources using the OData protocol. The OData protocol specifies how a client can query, navigate, and update data exposed by a service. Using this protocol, the client can communicate with the service in a RESTful manner by retrieving data using a standard HTTP GET call, using specially constructed URIs, and sending updates to the server using a standard HTTP POST call.

Data Services shares a number of similarities with RIA Services and, in a way, you could consider the two to be sibling technologies, at times both jostling for attention and attempting to outdo each other. Both are built on top of WCF and conform to a pattern to expose data to clients, but each has a somewhat different focus. For now, RIA Services primarily targets Silverlight clients, whereas Data Services is client agnostic. While RIA Services generates code in the client project in order for the client to communicate with the services (an aspect that concerns some developers who are against "magic" code generation that they have no control over), Data Services does not need a link to the client project, and no code generation is required. Instead, Data Services provides a client library (System.Data.Services.Client.dll) to help the client interact with the service.

In a similar manner to RIA Services, Data Services exposes queryable endpoints by returning IQueryable expressions from operations. By using the client library, you can write LINQ queries on the client against these endpoints and have them executed on the server. This was one of the most powerful features provided by RIA Services, and it's also available, with a slightly different implementation, in Data Services.

It can be difficult to identify whether you should use RIA Services or Data Services in your project, and how the two differ. However, you can break it down to the following:

- *RIA Services* has a rich model designed for the development of end-to-end Silverlight applications, with the server tightly linked with its client via the code generation process.

- *Data Services* is designed simply to expose data as RESTful resources in a standalone manner that a range of clients can consume, such as reporting tools that can consume data exposed over HTTP and serialized as either ATOM or JSON.

Note that RIA Services can also expose data as RESTful resources that can be consumed by a range of clients, by enabling OData or exposing a JSON endpoint using the functionality provided in the WCF RIA Services Toolkit. Also, together with its ability to share code and validation logic with the client, among the numerous other features it provides, you will find that RIA Services is generally the best solution when writing an end-to-end Silverlight application. However, if you want your service to support a wide variety of clients without having a tight relationship to your Silverlight project, Data Services is a viable alternative.

Duplex Communication (Pull + Push)

So far, we've discussed means of providing one-way ("simplex") communication with the client. The client makes a request to a service, and in return gets a response. However, sometimes you want to be able to provide two-way ("duplex") communication between the client and the server, in which the server can "push" messages to clients. The client establishes a connection with the server, which is kept alive, thus enabling the server to push messages to the client, and avoiding the need for the client to constantly poll the server for new data. This is particularly useful when you have continually changing data (such as a stock ticker), want to be able to send out notification messages to the clients, or are implementing a chat application, and you want the client to be notified of updates in "real-time."

Silverlight supports the following three technologies that enable communicating with the server in a duplex fashion:

- Sockets

- HTTP Polling Duplex

- net.tcp (a higher-level sockets implementation)

Each of these technologies has their own advantages and disadvantages, described as follows:

- *Sockets:* As sockets are a low-level means of communicating over a network, they require a lot more effort to implement than higher-level technologies. Unless you need such low-level control, you are usually better off using a higher-level technology like NET.TCP. Support for sockets in Silverlight can be found in the System.Net.Sockets namespace. Note that you are restricted to only using ports 4502 to 4534, unless you are running with elevated privileges. This means that sockets are best used in intranet applications, rather than public-facing applications, because the ports will possibly be blocked behind a firewall. In addition, traffic over sockets is not encrypted.

- *HTTP Polling Duplex:* This is a long polling mechanism that is a part of WCF. A connection is established with the server, and it polls the server for messages over this connection. One of the key benefits of HTTP polling duplex is that it communicates over port 80/443 (the HTTP/HTTPS ports), which firewalls do not typically block. It also supports encryption of the data when using SSL. However, its main disadvantage is its lack of performance and reduced scalability in comparison to net.tcp.

- *net.tcp:* This is a higher-level, sockets-type communication mechanism that is a part of WCF. It has much better performance over HTTP polling duplex, and is also much more scalable. The downside is that, like sockets, you are restricted to only using ports 4502 to 4534 unless you are running with elevated privileges, and traffic over this connection is not encrypted.

As you can see, it can be a hard decision to choose between HTTP polling duplex and net.tcp. A recommended approach is to actually implement both in your application. Your application can try to establish a connection using net.tcp over one of the supported ports. If this connection fails, likely due to a firewall blocking the communication between the client and the server, your application can then fall back to HTTP polling duplex and use that instead. So you get the performance benefit of using net.tcp if it's available, but have a fallback approach with HTTP polling duplex if it's not. One issue to be aware of when using this fallback approach, however, is that you will also need to implement two different authentication schemes, assuming that the user requires authentication—one for each technology.

■ **Note** Both sockets and net.tcp require the server to have a cross-domain policy file in place in order for Silverlight applications to be able to access them. Cross-domain policy files are discussed in Chapter 5.

Discussing these means of duplex communication in depth is beyond the scope of this book, but you can find an excellent series of articles written by Gill Gleeren, covering the implementation of each of these technologies, at the following locations on the SilverlightShow web site:

- Sockets: www.silverlightshow.net/items/The-duplex-story-looking-at-duplex-communication-in-Silverlight-4-Part-2-Using-Sockets.aspx

- HTTP Polling Duplex: www.silverlightshow.net/items/The-duplex-story-looking-at-duplex-communication-in-Silverlight-4-Part-1.aspx

- net.tcp: www.silverlightshow.net/items/The-duplex-story-looking-at-duplex-communication-in-Silverlight-4-Part-3-Using-Net.Tcp.aspx

Summary

This chapter showed you how to use WCF RIA Services to expose data and operations from the server to your client Silverlight application, and how to implement all the server-based requirements associated with doing so, such as handling errors, identifying and handling concurrency violations, and sharing code across tiers. You now have a `ProductService` domain service that exposes product data from the server and enables the product data to be maintained—that is, products can be inserted, updated, and deleted. The next chapter will show you how to consume this data in order to create a functional Silverlight application.

CHAPTER 5

Consuming Data from the Server

In Chapter 4, we looked at exposing data from the server, briefly using plain WCF Services and then RIA Services in more depth. It's now time to switch to the client side and look at consuming data from these services. In this chapter, we'll briefly look at how you can access data exposed by a WCF Service, before moving on to how you consume data using RIA Services—including querying data and submitting any changes back to the server.

Communicating Asynchronously

The first thing you need to be aware of when attempting any server communication in Silverlight is that it *must* be performed asynchronously. The Silverlight team made the decision to not support synchronous communication in order to avoid service/HTTP/socket calls blocking the Silverlight application's user interface (and in turn, the browser, as Silverlight runs in the browser's user interface thread) while waiting for a response. Regularly hanging the browser would not make Silverlight a good plug-in citizen. Therefore, you will need to become accustomed to asynchronous programming. This typically involves making a call to the server, and waiting for an event to be raised indicating that the call is complete. The call will be performed on a background thread and return immediately, preventing the user interface from being blocked while the call is made.

Developers tend to prefer making synchronous calls when calling web services, and the like, despite the fact that it blocks the user interface while it waits for the results to be returned (resulting in a poor user experience). If you're a developer used to writing only synchronous code, asynchronous programming will require you to think a little differently in how you structure the flow of your code. However, it will no doubt make you a better developer as a result.

■ **Note** As a general rule, if an asynchronous call raises an event when it completes, the event will usually be raised on the user interface thread. However, if it uses an asynchronous callback delegate (taking an AsyncCallback object as a parameter instead), the callback method will be executed on a background thread. The problem with the callback method executing on a background thread is that you can update the user interface only from the user interface thread. Therefore, if you want to update the user interface from a callback method, you will need to invoke the code that performs the update on the user interface thread, using the BeginInvoke method of the Dispatcher object for the view you're updating. Otherwise, you will encounter cross-thread synchronization issues, which result in an exception being thrown. To avoid this complexity, if a Completed event is available, update the user interface from it instead.

Throughout this chapter, you'll see how you can effectively perform asynchronous calls. RIA Services provides some patterns that make asynchronous programming much simpler, and we'll also touch on using inline (anonymous) methods to handle events, which you might prefer over creating a dedicated event handler method.

Consuming Data from the Server Using WCF Services

Although this chapter primarily focuses on consuming data with RIA Services, it's worth briefly looking first at how you can consume data using plain old WCF Services.

⚙ Workshop: Querying Data Exposed by a WCF Service

In Chapter 4, we created a WCF Service that returned a collection of Product entities from an Entity Framework model. You can consume data from a WCF Service in Silverlight in essentially the same way as you would in a Windows Forms or WPF application; you're just forced into using the asynchronous methods when using Silverlight, as the synchronous methods are not available.

■ **Note** For each operation in your WCF Service (for example, GetProducts), the service reference proxy generator will generate a corresponding method (the operation's name, suffixed with Async; for example, GetProductsAsync) on the service reference proxy class that will begin the call to the server. A corresponding event will also be created (with the operation's name, suffixed with Completed; for example, GetProductsCompleted), that will be raised when the call to the server completes.

There are a number of ways you can connect to a WCF service. You can use the ChannelFactory class, or you can create a class that inherits from the generic System.ServiceModel.ClientBase class. However, the easiest way is to use a service reference proxy, which is the method we'll use in this workshop. We'll call the GetProducts method on the WCF Service we created in Chapter 4, and display the results in a DataGrid control.

1. Using the AdventureWorks solution we've been working with in previous chapters, right-click the Silverlight project in Visual Studio's Solution Explorer tool window, and select Add Service Reference… from the context menu.

2. Click the Discover button to automatically search for any WCF Services in your solution. The ProductService.svc service you created in Chapter 4 should appear in the list, as shown in Figure 5-1.

3. You need to provide a namespace for all the classes that the service reference generator creates for you. Enter Services into the Namespace text box at the bottom of the window. Click OK. This will generate the service reference proxy for you, which you can see if you expand the Service References folder that has been added to your project.

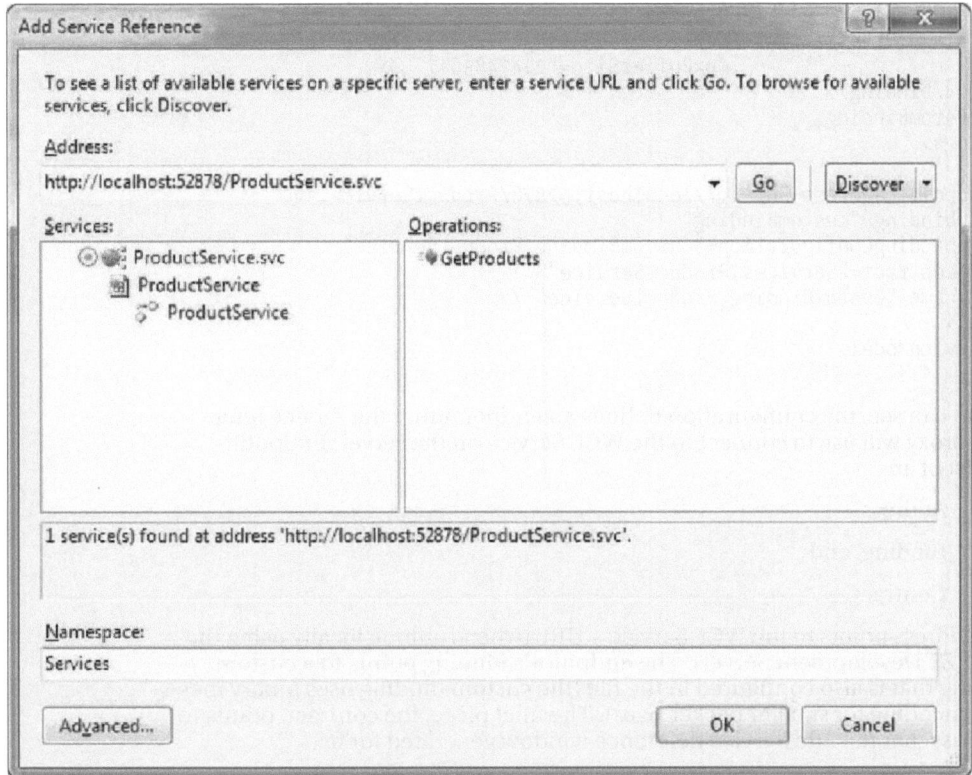

Figure 5-1. Visual Studio's Add Service Reference window

■ **Note** You might recall from Chapter 4 that Silverlight does not support all the WCF bindings available with the full .NET Framework. If you attempt to add a reference to a service that has no endpoint using a binding supported by Silverlight, the service reference will still be added to your project, but a warning will appear in the Error List window stating that the endpoint is not compatible with Silverlight. Your project will compile, but attempting to make a call to the service will result in an InvalidOperationException exception.

You'll note that a file named ServiceReferences.ClientConfig has been added to your project. As its name suggests, this file contains the configuration of the service references in your project.

```
<configuration>
    <system.serviceModel>
        <bindings>
            <customBinding>
                <binding name="CustomBinding_ProductService">
```

```
                    <binaryMessageEncoding />
                    <httpTransport maxReceivedMessageSize="2147483647"
                                   maxBufferSize="2147483647" />
                </binding>
            </customBinding>
        </bindings>
        <client>
            <endpoint address="http://localhost:52878/ProductService.svc"
                binding="customBinding"
                bindingConfiguration="CustomBinding_ProductService"
                contract="Services.ProductService"
                name="CustomBinding_ProductService" />
        </client>
    </system.serviceModel>
</configuration>
```

As you can see, the configuration defines an endpoint that the service reference proxy will use to connect to the WCF Service on the server. Endpoints consist of an

- Address,

- Binding, and

- Contract.

The address points to the WCF Service's URL (when running locally using the ASP.NET Development Server). The endpoint's binding points to a custom binding that is also configured in the file (the custom binding uses binary message encoding for smaller packet sizes). The final piece, the contract, points to the class that the Add Service Reference window generated for us.

4. Add a reference to your project to the `System.Windows.Controls.Data.dll` assembly. This assembly contains the `DataGrid` control. An alternative way to reference this assembly is to simply drag the `DataGrid` control from the toolbox onto a view's design surface.

5. Add a new view to the Views folder in your application, named `WCFServiceTestView.xaml`, using the Silverlight Page item template. Add a `DataGrid` control to this view, and name it `productDataGrid`. You should have the following XAML:

```
<navigation:Page x:Class="AdventureWorks.Views.WCFServiceTestView"
    xmlns="http://schemas.microsoft.com/winfx/2006/xaml/presentation"
    xmlns:x="http://schemas.microsoft.com/winfx/2006/xaml"
    xmlns:d="http://schemas.microsoft.com/expression/blend/2008"
    xmlns:mc="http://schemas.openxmlformats.org/markup-compatibility/2006"
    xmlns:sdk="http://schemas.microsoft.com/winfx/2006/xaml/presentation/sdk"
    mc:Ignorable="d"
    xmlns:navigation="clr-namespace:System.Windows.Controls; ↵
                        assembly=System.Windows.Controls.Navigation"
    d:DesignWidth="640" d:DesignHeight="480"
    Title="WCFServiceTestView Page">

    <Grid x:Name="LayoutRoot">
        <sdk:DataGrid Name="productDataGrid" />
```

```
    </Grid>
</navigation:Page>
```

6. Open the code-behind for the view (WCFServiceTestView.xaml.cs). Add the following using statement to the top of the file:

```
using AdventureWorks.Services;
```

7. In the constructor, you can now instantiate the service reference proxy class, wire up an event handler to its GetProductsCompleted event, and call its GetProductsAsync method, as follows:

```
public WCFServiceTestView()
{
    InitializeComponent();

    ProductServiceClient service = new ProductServiceClient();
    service.GetProductsCompleted += service_GetProductsCompleted;
    service.GetProductsAsync();
}
```

In the completed event handler, you can then check if an error occurred; if not, you can assign the result to the DataGrid control's ItemSource property (which will display the results in the DataGrid):

```
private void service_GetProductsCompleted(object sender,
                                    GetProductsCompletedEventArgs e)
{
    if (e.Error == null)
    {
        productDataGrid.ItemsSource = e.Result;
    }
    else
    {
        MessageBox.Show(e.Error.Message);
    }
}
```

Alternatively, instead of wiring up the event handler for the GetProductsCompleted event in the constructor, you can "inline" the call completed logic using an anonymous method, like so:

```
public WCFServiceTestView()
{
    InitializeComponent();

    ProductServiceClient service = new ProductServiceClient();

    service.GetProductsCompleted += (sender, e) =>
        {
            if (e.Error == null && !e.Cancelled)
            {
                productDataGrid.ItemsSource = e.Result;
            }
            else
            {
```

```
                    MessageBox.Show(e.Error.Message);
              }
        };

    service.GetProductsAsync();
}
```

8. You can now run your application and navigate to this view. (You might want to add a menu item that points to it, as described in Chapter 3, or alternatively simply use #/WCFServiceTestView as the "bookmark" portion of the URL in your browser's address bar.) The DataGrid control will be populated with the data returned by the WCF Service.

■ **Note** You can configure the URL for the WCF Service in the ServiceReferences.ClientConfig file, but sometimes you need to specify the correct URL at runtime. The constructor for the service reference proxy class has several overloads, some of which accept an endpoint address, to which you can pass the URL. Often, you will want to point to the service at the site of origin for the Silverlight application (i.e., the site from which the Silverlight application was downloaded). You can ascertain this URL using the Source property of the Application.Current.Host object.

Common Pitfalls

There are a few pitfalls to be aware of when calling WCF Services in Silverlight. As RIA Services are built upon WCF, these issues also apply to it as well.

Maximum Message Size

The WCF Service on the server has a limit to the maximum message size it will return as a response, and the Silverlight client also has a maximum message size that it will accept. Although the default maximum message size accepted by the Silverlight client is configured at an impossibly large 2 GB, the service in the Web project has a default maximum message size of 64 KB. Attempting to return a response larger than this from your service (common when returning large lists of data) will result in an exception being thrown. You can modify this limit by customizing your binding properties in the Web project's Web.config file, setting an alternative maximum message size (in bytes). That said, it's probably better to design your server/client communication to transfer smaller messages where possible. Unless the user requires all that data at the one time, you would be better aiming to minimize data traffic, and hence the time that the user is left waiting for a response from the server, sending only the data back to the client that the user requires at that time. For example, when displaying a list of data to the user, request the data in pages rather than as a single unit.

ASP.NET Session State

Despite Silverlight enforcing that server calls must be performed asynchronously, if you have ASP.NET session state turned on in your Web project, you will find that calls are executed on the server sequentially, resulting in the calls appearing slower than expected.

You can tell if ASP.NET session state is turned on by using a tool such as Fiddler (which you can download from www.fiddler2.com) to intercept the responses from the server. If a cookie with the name ASP.NET_SessionId appears in the header, then ASP.NET session state is turned on. Generally, ASP.NET session state will be turned on automatically when you add a Global.asax file to your project.

This behavior occurs only when using the browser networking stack, which is the default when the application is running inside the browser. To work around this behavior, you can either stop using ASP.NET session state or simply use the client networking stack instead (discussed in the section "Choosing a Networking Stack," later in this chapter).

Consuming Data from the Server Using RIA Services

In Chapter 4, we primarily focused on how you can expose data from the server using RIA Services. Let's now look at how you can consume this data in your Silverlight application. The RIA Services code generator has generated code in the Silverlight project that enables you to communicate with the domain services in your Web project. In this section, we'll look at this generated code, and how it helps us consume data from the server.

Inspecting the Generated Code in the Silverlight Project

We briefly discussed how the RIA Services code generator works in Chapter 4. Now that it's time to make use of it, let's inspect it a little closer. As you may recall, RIA Services automatically generates code in a hidden folder (named Generated_Code) under the Silverlight project that enables your Silverlight application to communicate with the domain services in your Web project. You can view the code generated in this folder (as shown in Figure 5-2) by selecting the Silverlight project in Solution Explorer and toggling the Show All Files button to "on," using the second button from the left in the Solution Explorer window's toolbar.

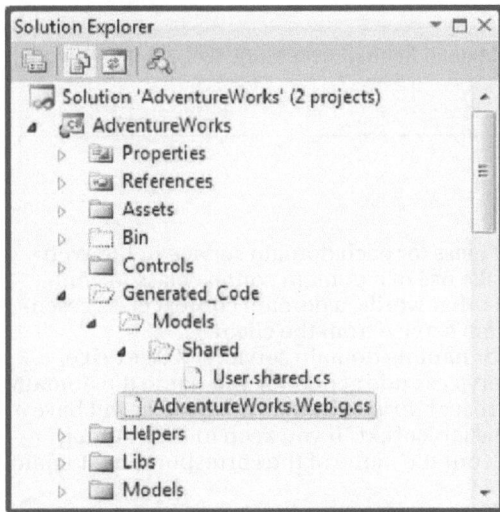

Figure 5-2. The Silverlight project structure, showing the hidden Generated_Code folder

As you can see, there are a couple of files under the Generated_Code folder. There's a "core" generated class, named AdventureWorks.Web.g.cs (the selected file), containing most of the generated code, which we'll delve into further shortly. The rest of the files are the files in your Web project that you marked as being shared (i.e., gave a .shared.cs extension to). These shared files are simply copied from your Web project, and are organized in the same folder hierarchy that you have in your Web project.

■ **Note** Inspecting the code generation files can also be useful when attempting to identify code generation problems. When debugging, you can also step into these files and set breakpoints to help identify issues. Just be sure not to modify these generated files, because any changes you make will be overwritten by the RIA Services code generator the next time it updates that file. If you want to add additional functionality to a generated class, create a separate file defining a partial class and extend the class in that manner.

Let's focus in on the AdventureWorks.Web.g.cs file. The name of this file is based upon the name of your Web project, using the format [webprojectname].g.cs. Because our Web project's name is AdventureWorks.Web, this file is named AdventureWorks.Web.g.cs. If you open this file, you will find that it consists of a number of classes. You should be aware of the following key classes:

- Domain context classes
- Model classes
- The WebContext class

Let's look at each of these categories further.

■ **Note** All classes in this file are partial classes, allowing you to extend them, if necessary, without modifying the generated code.

Domain Context Classes

The RIA Services code generator generates a domain context class for each domain service in the Web project. The code you write in your Silverlight project can make use of a domain context class to communicate its corresponding domain service on the server. In other words, a domain context class essentially acts as a proxy to facilitate communication with a domain service from the client.

Assuming you follow the standard naming convention for naming domain services (XXXService, where XXX can be anything of your own choosing), the RIA Services code generator will name the domain context XXXContext. For example, a domain service named ProductService in the Web project will have a corresponding domain context created in this file named ProductContext. If you keep to this naming scheme for your domain services, you should be able to work out the name of the corresponding domain context class very easily.

The domain context class also has methods corresponding to each query, invoke, and custom operation defined on the domain service. These methods allow you to call the corresponding methods on the domain service from the client.

We'll look at how you work with the domain context classes shortly.

■ **Note** The insert/update/delete operations do not have corresponding methods created on the domain context, because they are never explicitly called from the client. Instead, as changes are made to an entity collection that's returned from a query operation, the domain context will maintain a changeset, consisting of the actions performed on the entities in the collection. When the SubmitChanges method is called on the domain context, RIA Services will send the changeset to the server and call the corresponding insert/update/delete operations on the domain service, as required.

Entity/Model Classes

Each entity (or presentation model class) exposed by a domain service will have a corresponding class created in this file. Any attributes applied to the class in the Web project (via its corresponding metadata class) will be applied directly to this generated client-side class.

The WebContext Class

The WebContext class is instantiated when your Silverlight application is started, and this instance is kept alive for the lifetime of the application as an "application extension service." If you look at the code in the App.xaml.cs file in your AdventureWorks project, you'll find that an instance of this class is created when the application starts, and is added to the application's ApplicationLifetimeObjects collection. This keeps the instance alive as long as the application is alive. You can get a reference to this instance using the class's static Current property.

The purpose of this class is to act as the "context" for the application, maintaining the current user object, and providing access to an instance of the AuthenticationContext class. You can extend this class with a partial class if you'd like it to maintain any other data for you.

Customizing the Generated Code

As you've seen, RIA Services generates a lot of code for you. This code will suit most purposes, and the generated classes are extensible via partial classes, but sometimes you want more control over the code that is generated for you. You should *never* modify the generated code, as it will be overwritten the next time you compile your Web project. The RIA Services team has provided two methods to customize the generated code, however. You can replace the client proxy generator either with a T4 text template, or with a class that implements the IDomainServiceClientCodeGenerator interface. Your T4 template/client code generator class can then take the place of the standard RIA Services code generator, and generate the code itself.

This topic is beyond the scope of this book, but you can find more information on Varun Puranik's blog (http://varunpuranik.wordpress.com) or this blog post by Willem Meints:
http://blogs.infosupport.com/using-t4-to-change-the-way-ria-services-work/

■ **Note** You need the RIA Services Toolkit (discussed in Chapter 4) installed in order to have the tools to create a custom client code generator class/T4 template.

Consuming Data Declaratively in XAML via the DomainDataSource Control

RIA Services gives you the option of consuming data declaratively in XAML, where you can simply bind to the data via RIA Services' DomainDataSource control, or alternatively you can request the data in code using a domain context object. Let's start consuming data by looking at how the XAML-based method works.

The DomainDataSource Control

Declaratively wiring up your user interface to data from the server is a quick and easy way to consume data in your application. The key component that enables this XAML-based approach is the DomainDataSource control. The DomainDataSource control is a part of the RIA Services framework, and provides a bridge that enables you to declaratively interact with a domain context in XAML. You configure it by pointing it to a domain context, and telling it which method to call to request the data. The controls in your view can then bind to its Data property, from which the data retrieved from the server will be exposed. This method makes it very easy to consume data in your application without having to write any code.

Here is the XAML for a fairly standard use of a DomainDataSource control, which requests data from a domain service named ProductService:

```
<riaControls:DomainDataSource Name="productDomainDataSource"
                    AutoLoad="True"
                    QueryName="GetProductsQuery"
                    LoadedData="productDomainDataSource_LoadedData">
    <riaControls:DomainDataSource.DomainContext>
        <my:ProductContext />
    </riaControls:DomainDataSource.DomainContext>
</riaControls:DomainDataSource>
```

To support this XAML, a namespace prefix for the DomainDataSource control (riaControls) and for the ProductContext object (my) will also be declared in the root element of your XAML file, as follows:

```
xmlns:riaControls=
    "clr-namespace:System.Windows.Controls;  ↵
                assembly=System.Windows.Controls.DomainServices"
xmlns:my="clr-namespace:AdventureWorks.Web.Services;assembly=AdventureWorks"
```

Let's take a quick walkthrough of the important aspects of this XAML:

- You need to set the Name property of the DomainDataSource control. The controls in your view that will display the data retrieved from the server will need to use ElementName binding to bind to this control (ElementName binding enables the property of one control to be bound to the property of another control). For those bindings to find this DomainDataSource control, it needs to have a name.

■ **Note** ElementName binding is discussed in more detail in Chapter 11. You'll also see it in action in the following workshop.

- The `AutoLoad` property is set to `True`, meaning that the call to the server will be made as soon as the view is loaded.

- The `QueryName` property is set to the name of the method on the domain context that corresponds to the query domain operation that you want to call on the domain service. The operation on the domain service we want to call is named `GetProducts`, which has a corresponding method named `GetProductsQuery` on the domain context. We'll discuss this convention further shortly, when we discuss consuming data via code.

- An event handler is assigned to handle the `LoadedData` event. The event handler contains code to display a message box if an error occurs while attempting to retrieve the data. It's not mandatory that you handle the `LoadedData` event, but it is recommended, as otherwise an exception will be thrown. This will be discussed further in the section "Handling Load Errors," later in this chapter.

- The `DomainContext` property is pointed to the domain context class that will handle obtaining the entity collection from the server. Because the domain service was named `ProductService`, the corresponding domain context in the Silverlight project will be named `ProductContext`.

These are the core requirements for configuring a `DomainDataSource` control, and after these properties are configured, your user interface controls can consume the data retrieved from the server by binding their `DataContext` or `ItemsSource` property to its `Data` property (using `ElementName` binding).

⚙ Workshop: Querying Data in XAML

In this workshop, we'll consume data from the `ProductService` domain service that we created in Chapter 4, and display the results in a `DataGrid` control—all without writing any code. Although you could drag and drop a `DomainDataSource` control from the toolbox (or write the XAML by hand) and configure it manually, the easiest way to set up and configure one is to enlist the Data Sources window to help you. This is the method that we'll use in this workshop.

1. Open the view named `ProductList.xaml` (created in Chapter 3), and delete any controls that you previously placed on the view.

2. Open the Data Sources tool window (Data ➤ Show Data Sources). Note that a data source has already been created for each domain context created by RIA Services in the Silverlight project, with the entities that they expose beneath them, as shown in Figure 5-3.

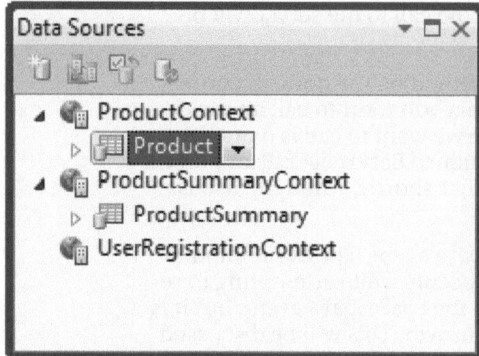

Figure 5-3. The Data Sources window

■ **Note** The icon next to the entity in the Data Sources window will indicate the type of control that will be created when the entity is dragged and dropped onto the design surface. You can change the type of control created by selecting the entity, clicking the drop-down button that appears (shown in Figure 5-3), and selecting an alternative control type or layout format from the menu.

---

3. Drag the entity (in this case the Product entity) from the Data Sources window and drop it onto the design surface. This will create a DomainDataSource control for you, which is already configured to retrieve a collection of Product entities from the server. A DataGrid control has also been created, with its ItemsSource property bound to the Data property of the DomainDataSource control using ElementName binding.

```
<riaControls:DomainDataSource AutoLoad="True"
              d:DesignData="{d:DesignInstance my:Product, CreateList=true}"
              LoadedData="productDomainDataSource_LoadedData"
              Name="productDomainDataSource" QueryName="GetProductsQuery"
              Height="0" Width="0">
    <riaControls:DomainDataSource.DomainContext>
        <my:ProductContext />
    </riaControls:DomainDataSource.DomainContext>
</riaControls:DomainDataSource>

<sdk:DataGrid AutoGenerateColumns="False" Height="200"
      HorizontalAlignment="Left"
      ItemsSource="{Binding ElementName=productDomainDataSource, Path=Data}"
      Margin="185,53,0,0" Name="productDataGrid" Width="400"
      RowDetailsVisibilityMode="VisibleWhenSelected" VerticalAlignment="Top">
    <sdk:DataGrid.Columns>
        <sdk:DataGridTextColumn x:Name="classColumn"
                                Binding="{Binding Path=Class}"
                                Header="Class" Width="SizeToHeader" />
```

```
        <sdk:DataGridTextColumn x:Name="colorColumn"
                                Binding="{Binding Path=Color}"
                                Header="Color" Width="SizeToHeader" />
        <!-- Additional columns removed for brevity-->
    </sdk:DataGrid.Columns>
</sdk:DataGrid>
```

■ **Note** We didn't need to select in the Data Sources window the method that should be used on the domain context. Instead, the Data Sources window was able to infer the correct one, because usually there will be only one query domain operation on a domain service that returns the selected entity. However, if you do happen to have two or more query domain operations on a domain service that return the entity (or collection of entities) that you want to bind to, you can select which domain operation you want to be called by selecting the entity in the Data Sources window, clicking the drop-down button, and selecting the required domain operation from the menu.

---

4. Run the application and navigate to the `ProductListView.xaml` view, using the menu button that you added for it in Chapter 3. The `DataGrid` control will be populated with all `Product` objects returned from the server.

Consuming Data in Code via the Domain Context Class

Whereas a XAML-based approach using the `DomainDataSource` control is a nice, easy way of populating a view with data from the server, often you will want to have more control over this process—especially if you're using the MVVM design pattern. Therefore, let's take a look at how you can request data from the server via code.

Mapping Domain Context Methods to Domain Service Operations

The query/invoke/custom operations on the domain service have corresponding methods on the domain context object that can be used to call them. These methods have the same name as the corresponding operation on the domain service, but are suffixed with `Query`. For example, the `GetProducts` operation on our `ProductService` domain service will have a corresponding method on the domain context named `GetProductsQuery`, as shown in Figure 5-4.

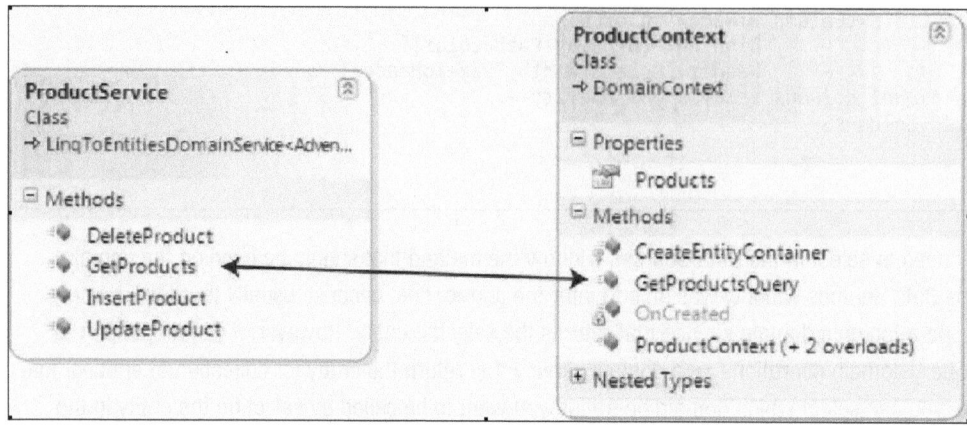

Figure 5-4. The domain service class and the corresponding domain context class, side-by-side

Requesting Data from the Server via Code

A number of steps are required when requesting data from the server via code. Calling the GetProductsQuery method on the domain context doesn't actually initiate the request to the server. Instead, it returns an EntityQuery object that represents the domain service query.

```
ProductContext context = new ProductContext();
EntityQuery<Product> qry = context.GetProductsQuery();
```

The concept of obtaining an EntityQuery object in order to query the server probably seems a little strange, but it makes more sense when you realize that sometimes you want to refine the query in order to have the data filtered/sorted/paged on the server before it is returned to the client. We will look at how you can do this in the "Manipulating Summary List's Contents" section of Chapter 6, but for now we'll just focus on requesting the full raw set of results from the database.

After you have an EntityQuery object, you can then pass it to the Load method on the domain context, which initiates the request for the data, like so:

```
LoadOperation<Product> operation = context.Load(qry);
```

Note that the Load method doesn't actually return you the data. Instead, it returns a LoadOperation object that contains an Entities property consisting of a collection of the requested objects; however, this collection will currently be empty. As with calling standard WCF Services in Silverlight, all calls to domain services using the RIA Services framework are asynchronous; therefore, the Load method will not wait for the data to be returned before returning control back to your code.

Now that the request for data has been made to the server, we need to wait for and then do something with the results. There are two ways you can go about this:

- The LoadOperation object returned by the data context's Load method has a Completed event, which it raises when the data has been retrieved from the server. The event args parameter e passed into the event handler has an Entities property, from which you can access the results.

- The LoadOperation object itself has an Entities property. This collection will initially be empty due to the asynchronous nature of the call, but will be automatically populated after the data is retrieved from the server. This allows you to immediately assign the collection to the DataContext or ItemsSource property of a control after the Load method has returned, and the control will update itself automatically when the collection is populated. This is possible because the collection implements the INotifyCollectionChanged interface, which contains an event named CollectionChanged. This event is used to notify listeners when items are added to or removed from the collection. Because Silverlight controls listen for the CollectionChanged event on collections that implement the INotifyCollectionChanged interface, they'll know to update themselves accordingly when the results have returned from the server, without the added complexity of handling the LoadOperation object's Completed event. We'll discuss this behavior further in Chapter 6 when we cover the ObservableCollection<T> type.

■ **Note** The second method, using the Entities property on the LoadOperation object, is a much simpler and neater implementation for populating a ListBox or DataGrid control with results from the server. However, it is still recommended that you handle the LoadOperation object's Completed event, as per the first method, so you can identify whether an error occurred during the request, and handle it accordingly.

Putting all these steps together, we can display the results in a DataGrid control named productDataGrid with just the following code:

```
ProductContext context = new ProductContext();
EntityQuery<Product> qry = context.GetProductsQuery();
LoadOperation<Product> operation = context.Load(qry);
productDataGrid.ItemsSource = operation.Entities;
```

■ **Note** This code will return *all* the products from the server, and display them in the DataGrid control. We'll look at how you can add filtering, sorting, and paging criteria shortly.

⚙ Workshop: Querying Data in Code

In this workshop, we'll implement the steps described in the previous section, to populate a DataGrid control with Product entities from the server.

1. Delete the DomainDataSource control and DataGrid control from the ProductListView.xaml view that you created in the previous workshop, so we essentially start with a blank view again.

2. Add a DataGrid control to your view, and name it productDataGrid.

```
<sdk:DataGrid Name="productDataGrid" />
```

3. Open the code-behind file for the view (ProductListView.xaml.cs). Add the following using statements to the top of the class:

```
using System.ServiceModel.DomainServices.Client;
using AdventureWorks.Web;
using AdventureWorks.Web.Services;
```

4. In the constructor for the class, we now want to request data from the server, and assign the results to the `DataGrid` control's `ItemsSource` property as follows:

```
public ProductListView()
{
    InitializeComponent();

    ProductContext context = new ProductContext();
    EntityQuery<Product> qry = context.GetProductsQuery();
    LoadOperation<Product> loadOperation = context.Load(qry);
    productDataGrid.ItemsSource = loadOperation.Entities;
}
```

5. Run the application and navigate to the `ProductListView.xaml` view, using the menu button that you added for it in Chapter 3. The `DataGrid` control will be populated with all `Product` entities returned from the server.

■ **Note** The preceding code does not handle any errors that could occur when making the request. We'll look at this shortly in the section "Handling Load Errors."

Choosing the Right Approach

With two approaches available to choose from (XAML-based or code-based), you might be wondering how to decide which approach you should use. Data source controls provide a quick-and-easy means to populate your user interface with data. Being a declarative data-pull mechanism, a data source control doesn't require you to write any code. Also, as was demonstrated, the Data Sources tool window in Visual Studio makes configuring a view to display data from the server even easier. The XAML-based approach is often used in presentations for this very reason; however, in practical applications, this approach has its drawbacks.

The biggest concerns come from a design/architectural perspective. The use of data source controls leads to a tightly coupled application, where you are mixing the user interface definition and data access logic. Any form of tight coupling in software is generally considered bad practice, and something to be avoided in your design. Data source controls also lead to a loss of control over the process of retrieving/saving data, and also make any issues you have in communicating with the server difficult to debug.

The XAML-based approach is also not compatible with the MVVM design pattern popularly used in Silverlight applications (discussed further in Chapter 13). Therefore, if you are following this design pattern, using the `DomainDataSource` control isn't really applicable in any case.

In summary, the XAML-based approach is quick and easy—great for prototyping applications—but the code-based approach, especially when used in conjunction with the MVVM design pattern, leads to better application design.

Specifying Query Criteria

Passing additional clauses to the server to be appended to the database query is generally a messy process to implement with standard WCF Services. Often, you need to add additional parameters to the query operations to accept the clauses, and then manually append these clauses to the main query to be run before returning the results to the client.

RIA Services has a powerful solution to this problem. As you saw in Chapter 4, collections of entities can be exposed from a domain operation as an `IQueryable<T>`. When returning an `IQueryable<T>` expression (specifically a LINQ to Entities query), the power of the RIA Services framework is demonstrated in that you are able to write a LINQ query on the client specifying how you want the resulting entity collection filtered, sorted, and paged. RIA Services serializes this LINQ query and sends it to the server, where it is appended to the query expression returned from the query operation before it is executed. This enables the collection to be filtered/sorted/paged on the server without requiring the entire collection to be sent back to the client first, minimizing the required data traffic, and without the need for providing specific support for handling query criteria in the domain services.

■ **Note** The ability to specify additional query clauses from the client does not allow the client to circumvent any filters you might have applied at the server on your query—for example, if you've applied a Where clause to filter out data that the user does not have permission to access. This feature *does not* open you up to SQL injection type attacks in any way.

From the client side, the DomainDataSource control contains the functionality to enable each of the data manipulation actions listed earlier to be applied to any data that it is configured to consume. You achieve this by defining *descriptors* on the DomainDataSource for these actions. You may define these actions either declaratively at design time (in XAML) or at runtime (in code). This makes performing those actions easy when using a XAML-based approach to consuming data.

■ **Note** In Chapter 6, we'll look at how you can use the FilterDescriptors, SortDescriptors, and GroupDescriptors properties of the DomainDataSource control, along with the DataPager control to filter, sort, group, and page data in a declarative manner in XAML. For now, we'll focus on the code-based approach for applying criteria to a query operation on the client side using LINQ queries, when querying data from the server. Some familiarity with LINQ is assumed.

When using the code-based approach, you can add clauses to a query domain operation call using LINQ query operators. Let's take a look at what query operators are available for you to use, and how you can use these query operators when querying data from the server.

Client-Side Query Operators

In the previous workshop, "Querying Data in Code," we simply requested the entire collection of entities that the domain operation could return. However, the EntityQueryable class provides you with a number of query operator extension methods. These methods enable you to append clauses to an EntityQuery object that will then be run on the server. The methods it provides include the following:

- OrderBy: Orders the results, with the records sorted by the given property in ascending order.

- OrderByDescending: Orders the results, with the records sorted by the given property in descending order.

- Select: Does nothing; only empty selections are accepted.

- Skip: Generally used when paging data to skip a given number of records before "taking" a given number.

- Take: Generally used to limit the maximum number of records to be returned, or when paging data to return a given number of records after skipping a given number.

- ThenBy: Adds an additional clause to order the records, with the records sorted by the given property in ascending order.

- ThenByDescending: Adds an additional clause to order the records, with the records sorted by the given property in descending order.

- Where: Used to filter the data being returned based upon given criteria.

■ **Note** The EntityQueryable class does not provide a GroupBy method. Grouping in the context of returning data to display is actually a type of data sorting, so you would use the OrderBy and ThenBy methods instead to "group" the data.

 ## Workshop: Specifying Query Criteria Using Lambda Expressions

Following on from the previous workshop, "Querying Data in Code," let's add a simple Where clause to the query to request only the out-of-stock products from the server.

1. Add a using statement for the System.ServiceModel.DomainServices.Client namespace.

```
using System.ServiceModel.DomainServices.Client;
```

■ **Note** Without the using statement, you won't see the query operator methods on the EntityQuery object.

2. After you've retrieved the EntityQuery object from the domain context, apply the Where clause to it before passing it to the domain context's Load method, like so:

```
ProductContext context = new ProductContext();
EntityQuery<Product> qry = context.GetProductsQuery();
qry = qry.Where(p => p.SellStartDate <= DateTime.Now);
LoadOperation<Product> loadOperation = context.Load(qry);
productDataGrid.ItemsSource = loadOperation.Entities;
```

■ **Note** Various combinations of these clauses can be appended one after the other in a fluent manner using the standard query operators and lambda expressions to achieve the results that you require. For example, you can both filter and order the results, like so:

```
qry = qry.Where(p => p.QuantityAvailable == 0).OrderBy(p => p.Name);
```

Now when you run this query from the client, the clauses you added will be automatically applied to the query on the server and included in the SQL query to the database that returns the results.

Specifying Query Criteria Using a Declarative Query Expression

LINQ provides two syntaxes for querying data: lambda expressions, as demonstrated in the previous workshop, and declarative query expressions. Some people prefer lambda expressions for their terseness, whereas others prefer the SQL-like declarative query expression syntax for its readability and similarity to SQL syntax. Throughout this book, we'll use lambda expressions in examples, but it's worth noting that you can also use declarative query expression syntax. Here is an example of using declarative query expression syntax to retrieve only the out-of-stock products from the server (as per the previous workshop):

```
ProductContext context = new ProductContext();
EntityQuery<Product> qry = from p in context.GetProductsQuery()
                           where p.SellStartDate <= DateTime.Now
                           select p;
LoadOperation<Product> loadOperation = context.Load(qry);
productDataGrid.ItemsSource = loadOperation.Entities;
```

■ **Note** You can easily prove that your clauses have been applied to the database query on the server (and see the query that was generated) using SQL Profiler. Simply monitor SQL queries against your database and make a request for data (with additional clauses applied) from the client—the resulting SQL statement will be displayed in the profiler. If you don't have the full version of SQL Server, you can use a free tool with similar functionality to the SQL Profiler called SQL Server Express Profiler, created by AnjLab. You can download this tool from `http://sites.google.com/site/sqlprofiler`.

Explicitly Specifying a Domain Service Host

Note that we haven't had to explicitly specify the URI to the domain service when we consume data from the server. Fortunately, in the standard scenario, in which the site of origin for the Silverlight application also hosts the domain services, this is already taken care of for you. The domain context assumes that you will be communicating with a domain service from the site of origin (the web site that the Silverlight application is hosted on), and automatically determines the correct address of the domain service to communicate with. This means that you don't need to worry about manually reconfiguring the domain service addresses each time you deploy the application to a different host—the client will always look to the server from which it was obtained for the services.

However, it is possible to override this behavior by explicitly specifying an alternate URI to locate the services. If you have a scenario in which the application should communicate with domain services located on a different host from where your application was downloaded, you can specify the address of the corresponding domain service by passing in the new URI as a constructor parameter when instantiating the domain context, like so:

```
Uri uri =
    new Uri("http://localhost/AdventureWorks-Web-Services-ProductService.svc",
            UriKind.Absolute);
ProductContext context = new ProductContext(uri);
```

Note the format of the path to the service. Our `ProductService` domain service is located in the `Services` folder under the `AdventureWorks.Web` application. RIA Services generates a URI for each domain service in the project, enabling clients to use domain services as if they were standard WCF Services. You can also use this URI to point a domain context to a particular domain service. RIA Services doesn't actually create an actual `.svc` file, but it does listen for and handle requests for that URI. The URI will be located in the root of the application, and have a format of `[ApplicationName]-[Folder]-[DomainServiceName].svc`. Certain characters such as periods and slashes will be replaced by hyphens, as you'll note in the example.

■ **Note** If you're having trouble determining the name of the `.svc` file, search for "[DomainServiceName].svc" (e.g., `ProductService.svc`) in the `.g.cs` file that the RIA Services code generator created for you under the hidden Generated_Code file in the Silverlight project. You will find its full name there.

Assuming that any cross-domain issues have been taken care of with a client access policy file on that server (discussed later in this chapter in the section "Cross-Domain Access Policies"), the domain context will communicate with the domain service at the specified URI instead.

■ **Note** Unfortunately, specifying a domain service address is possible only with the code-based approach; this option is not available when using the `DomainDataSource` control.

Handling Load Errors

Because of the asynchronous nature of calls to the server in Silverlight, handling errors that are raised when a call to the server fails is a somewhat different process than you might be used to. For example, if you are using the code-based approach to consuming the data, you will find that putting `try/catch` blocks around a call to the server are of little use, as those calls immediately return control back to your code while the call happens on a background thread. Therefore, any errors that are raised on the server or in communicating with the server will not be caught by these exception handlers.

To actually catch these errors, you need to handle the event that is normally raised when the server communication is complete. When using the XAML-based approach, you will need to handle the

DomainDataSource control's LoadedData event; when using the code-based approach, you will need to handle the LoadOperation's Completed event.

As mentioned earlier, if you drag and drop an entity from the Data Sources window onto the design surface, the DomainDataSource control that is created will already handle the LoadedData event and check for whether an exception occurred, as follows:

```
private void productDomainDataSource_LoadedData(object sender,
                                                LoadedDataEventArgs e)
{
    if (e.HasError)
    {
        System.Windows.MessageBox.Show(e.Error.ToString(), "Load Error",
                                 System.Windows.MessageBoxButton.OK);
        e.MarkErrorAsHandled();
    }
}
```

■ **Note** Simply dropping a DomainDataSource control from the toolbox will not automatically create an event handler to handle its LoadedData event. Using the method of dropping an entity from the Data Sources window onto the design surface is the only way to do so.

If you are using the code-based approach, handling the LoadOperation's Completed event is very similar to handling the DomainDataSource's LoadedData event, except you need to cast the sender parameter to a generic LoadOperation object, like so:

```
private void loadOperation_Completed(object sender, EventArgs e)
{
    LoadOperation<Product> op = sender as LoadOperation<Product>;

    if (op.HasError)
    {
        System.Windows.MessageBox.Show(op.Error.ToString(), "Load Error",
                                 System.Windows.MessageBoxButton.OK);
        op.MarkErrorAsHandled();
    }
}
```

Note how we are calling the MarkErrorAsHandled method in both the DomainDataSource control's LoadedData event handler and the LoadOperation object's Completed event handler. If you don't call this method, the domain context will throw the exception, which will become an unhandled exception. Unhandled exceptions are caught by the Application_UnhandledException event handler method in the App class and handled there, showing a pop-up error window displaying the details of the error, to prevent your application from crashing. However, best practice is to prevent exceptions reaching this event handler where possible.

You can check the exception to find out what type of exception occurred and handle it accordingly. The exception is returned simply as an Exception type, but you can cast it to a DomainOperationException to get more useful information about it. Of most interest is the Status property that it exposes. This will tell you what type of exception occurred, using the OperationErrorStatus enumeration, so that you can handle it accordingly. The following values in this enumeration are of most interest when loading data:

- ServerError: An exception was raised on the server, or the application could not reach the server.

- Unauthorized: The user does not have permission to perform the operation. Restricting access to domain operations based upon the user's role is discussed in Chapter 8.

Therefore, you can check this value to determine the category of the error, and handle it accordingly. The following example demonstrates a structure for handling the errors in the LoadedData event handler of the DomainDataSource control. (Change e to the instance of the LoadOperation if using the domain context method.)

```
if (e.HasError)
{
    DomainOperationException error = e.Error as DomainOperationException;

    switch (error.Status)
    {
        case OperationErrorStatus.ServerError:
            // Handle server errors
            break;
        case OperationErrorStatus.Unauthorized:
            // Handle unauthorized domain operation access
            break;
    }
}
```

■ **Note** If you are using the code-based approach but don't want an exception to be thrown when an error occurs, use one of the overloads of the domain context's Load method that accepts the throwOnError parameter, and set it to false.

You can test your exception handler by throwing an exception in your query domain operation on the domain context. For example, add the following code to the domain operation method, before returning the query results, to see the effect of that exception in your Silverlight application:

```
throw new Exception("Test exception handling exception!");
```

Submitting Changes to the Server Using RIA Services

You've now seen how to query data from the server, but it's rare that a business application only displays data. As a general rule, the user will also want to edit, add, and delete data within the Silverlight application. RIA Services helps you by tracking the changes made to a collection of entities, and sending only the entities that have changed to the server when the user wants to save their changes. In this section, we'll look at how RIA Services implements change tracking and how you can send submit changes back to the server.

Change Tracking

When you query a collection of entities from the server via RIA Services, changes made to that collection (add/edit/delete) will automatically be tracked by the instance of the domain context that was used to retrieve the data (as a changeset). Therefore, when you submit the collection back to the server, only the entities in the collection that were changed will be sent, reducing the amount of data traffic sent from the client to the server, and ensuring that unchanged entities will not raise concurrency conflicts.

■ **Note** It is essential that you retain the instance of the domain context object that was used to retrieve the data from the server, and use that same instance to submit the changes back to the server. The domain context is in charge of change tracking, so if you copy your entities into another collection, for example, the domain context will no longer be able to track what entities have changed.

If you wanted to find out what entities have changed from the client side, you can get an `EntityChangeSet` object for a domain context, containing separate collections for the added entities, modified entities, and the removed entities. The following code demonstrates getting the changeset from a domain context named `productDomainContext`:

```
EntityChangeSet changeset = productDomainContext.EntityContainer.GetChanges();
```

⚙ Workshop: Submitting Changes via the DomainDataSource Control

Submitting changes to data retrieved using a `DomainDataSource` control is simply a case of calling the `DomainDataSource` control's `SubmitChanges` method. You can call this method in the code-behind, but the easy way is to bind to the `SubmitChangesCommand` command on the `DomainDataSource` control. We won't look at commands until Chapter 11, but in summary they provide a means for you to bind to logic (as opposed to data). We can bind a Button control's `Command` property to the `SubmitChangesCommand` property on the `DomainDataSource` control, and the `DomainDataSource` control will submit the changes to the server when the button is clicked.

■ **Note** As discussed in Chapter 4, there are no insert/update/delete domain operations created on the domain context. Instead, you simply call the `SubmitChanges` method on the domain context, which passes the changeset back to the server. RIA Services will then automatically handle calling the appropriate insert/update/delete domain operations on your domain service, plus any custom operations that were called.

In the "Querying Data in XAML" workshop earlier in this chapter, you used the Data Sources window to create a `DomainDataSource` control that would request a collection of `Product` entities from the server, and display the results in a `DataGrid` control. Let's now continue that workshop and enable the user to save the changes that they make to the data in the `DataGrid`.

1. Add a Button control to your view.

```
<Button Content="Save Changes" Width="100" Height="30" />
```

2. Now bind the Button control's Command property to the DomainDataSource control's SubmitChangesCommand property.

```
<Button Content="Save Changes" Width="100" Height="30"
        Command="{Binding SubmitChangesCommand,
                      ElementName=productDomainDataSource}" />
```

Now if you make some changes to the data in the DataGrid and then click the button, the changes will be submitted to the server and persisted to the database.

■ **Note**   You will find that the button is enabled only when changes have been made to the data.

Workshop: Submitting Changes via a Domain Context

The domain context has a SubmitChanges method, which passes the changeset associated with the domain context back to the server.

In the "Querying Data in Code" workshop earlier in this chapter, you requested data from the server via code. Let's now continue that workshop and enable the user to save the changes that they make to the data in the DataGrid.

1. Add a Button control to your view, whose Click event is handled in the code-behind.

```
<Button Content="Save Changes" Click="SaveChangesButton_Click"
        Width="100" Height="30" />
```

2. We now need to call the data context's SubmitChanges method. Remember that, as mentioned earlier, you need to call the SubmitChanges method of the instance of the data context that was used to retrieve the data. So we need to modify our code from the previous workshop slightly, in order to store the instance of the domain context object as a member variable that we can reference in the Button control's Click event (changes in bold).

```
private ProductContext _context = null;

public ProductListView()
{
    InitializeComponent();

    _context = new ProductContext();
    EntityQuery<Product> qry = _context.GetProductsQuery();
    LoadOperation<Product> operation = _context.Load(qry);
    productDataGrid.ItemsSource = operation.Entities;
}
```

3. In the Button control's Click event handler method, you can now call the data context's SubmitChanges method, as follows:

```
private void SaveChangesButton_Click(object sender,
                                      System.Windows.RoutedEventArgs e)
{
    SubmitOperation submitOperation = _context.SubmitChanges();
}
```

Handling Submit Errors

If any exceptions are thrown on the server when submitting data or if the client cannot reach the server at all, these will automatically be thrown as exceptions on the client. You can determine on the client whether any errors occurred when the changes were submitted, and prevent the exceptions from actually being thrown, by handling the SubmittedChanged event (if using a DomainDataSource control), or by handling the Completed event of a SubmitOperation object (if submitting via a domain context). You can then insert your own behavior for how errors should be handled. Both use a slightly different means of passing you the results of the operation, so we'll take a look at them separately.

Handling Errors with the DomainDataSource Control

The DomainDataSource control has a SubmittedChanges event that you can handle. The event handler method has a SubmittedChangesEventArgs object passed in as a parameter that enables you to check the results of the operation. This object has a HasError property whose value will be true when an exception is thrown on the server. You can get the error message that was thrown from the Error property, which is also on this object.

```
bool hasError = e.HasError;
Exception error = e.Error;
```

To prevent the exception being thrown on the client and consequently bubbling up to be caught by the event handler for the UnhandledException event on the App object (which you'll find in the App.xaml.cs file in your project), you can simply call the MarkErrorAsHandled method on the SubmittedChangesEventArgs object, like so:

```
e.MarkErrorAsHandled();
```

A sample event handler for the DomainDataSource control's SubmittedChanges event that shows the error message in a message box, and marks the exception as handled, is as follows:

```
private void productDomainDataSource_SubmittedChanges(object sender,
                                           SubmittedChangesEventArgs e)
{
    if (e.HasError)
    {
        MessageBox.Show(e.Error.Message);
        e.MarkErrorAsHandled();
    }
}
```

Handling Errors with a Domain Context

When you submit changes via a domain context, you need to handle the Completed event of the SubmitOperation object that's returned when you call the domain context's SubmitChanges method, as follows:

```
SubmitOperation submitOperation = _context.SubmitChanges();
submitOperation.Completed += submitOperation_Completed;
```

From there, you handle the exception similarly to how you did with the DomainDataSource control's SubmittedChanges event. Note, however, that the Completed event of the SubmitOperation object does not use the same SubmittedChangesEventArgs object as the DomainDataSource control's SubmittedChanges event did. Instead, it passes in the SubmitOperation object via the sender parameter, which you can get the results of the operation from when you cast it to a SubmitOperation. The SubmitOperation object also has a HasError property and an Error property to provide information as to anything that went wrong when submitting the changes, plus it has a MarkErrorAsHandled method that you can call to prevent an exception from being thrown.

```
private void submitOperation_Completed(object sender, System.EventArgs e)
{
    SubmitOperation submitOperation = sender as SubmitOperation;

    if (submitOperation.HasError)
    {
        MessageBox.Show(submitOperation.Error.Message);
        submitOperation.MarkErrorAsHandled();
    }
}
```

Determining the Type of Error

The exception is returned simply as an Exception type, but you can cast it to a DomainOperationException to get more useful information about the exception. Of most interest is the Status property that it exposes. This will tell you what type of exception occurred, using the OperationErrorStatus enumeration, so that you can handle it accordingly. The following values in this enumeration are of most interest:

- ServerError: An exception was raised on the server, or the application could not reach the server.

- ValidationFailed: The data sent to the server has failed the validation rules (which are rerun on the server).

- Conflicts: The data being updated/deleted has been changed on the server since it was originally retrieved, causing a concurrency violation. This is discussed in the next section, "Handling Concurrency Violations."

- Unauthorized: The user does not have permission to perform the operation. (Restricting access to domain operations based upon the user's role is discussed in Chapter 8.)

You can check this value to determine the category of the error and handle it accordingly. The following example demonstrates a structure for handling the errors in the Submitted event handler of the DomainDataSource control. (Change e to the instance of the SubmitOperation if using the domain context method.)

```
if (e.HasError)
{
    DomainOperationException error = e.Error as DomainOperationException;

    switch (error.Status)
    {
```

```
        case OperationErrorStatus.Conflicts:
            // Handle concurrency violations
            break;
        case OperationErrorStatus.ServerError:
            // Handle server errors
            break;
        case OperationErrorStatus.Unauthorized:
            // Handle unauthorized domain operation access
            break;
        case OperationErrorStatus.ValidationFailed:
            // Handle validation rule failures
            break;
        default:
            // Handle other possible statuses
            break;
    }
}
```

■ **Note** You can test your error handling by simply adding a line of code that throws an exception in your insert/update/delete operations in your domain service.

Handling Concurrency Violations

In Chapter 4, we looked at how to check for concurrency violations when performing update/delete operations. As shown in the previous section, you are notified of concurrency violations found on the server when you handle the Submitted/Completed event, depending on whether you are using a DomainDataSource control or the domain context directly, and can check for an exception representing a concurrency conflict in the results. This exception will be a DomainOperationException with a status of Conflicts.

If conflicts have been reported, you can find out which entities failed the concurrency check from the EntitiesInError property of the SubmittedChangesEventArgs/SubmitOperation object that was passed into the Submitted/Completed event. You can then compare the different versions of each of these entities (the current, original, and store versions) that you can get from the entity's EntityConflict property, and handle the conflict accordingly.

Options you have for handling a concurrency conflict include the following:

- Discard the user's update and get them to reenter the data (an easy solution, but not very user friendly).

- Simply overwrite the values on the server with the user's update in a last-update-wins strategy (potentially resulting in lost data).

- Display both the current version (the version that was sent to the server by the user) and the store version (the version in the database) to the user and get them to manually merge the changes.

- Attempt to automatically merge the changes programmatically.

The names of the properties that failed the concurrency checks are available from the PropertyNames property of the EntityConflict object.

The following example demonstrates a structure for automatically handling the conflicts after a submit operation has returned. (That is, add the following code to the Completed event handler of a SubmitOperation object, or the Submitted event handler of the DomainDataSource control.)

■ **Note** If you're handling the DomainDataSource control's Submitted event, change submitOperation to e in the following code.

```
if (submitOperation.HasError)
{
    DomainOperationException error =
                        submitOperation.Error as DomainOperationException;

    if (error.Status == OperationErrorStatus.Conflicts)
    {
        // Loop through the entities with concurrency violations
        foreach (Product product in submitOperation.EntitiesInError)
        {
            EntityConflict conflictinfo = product.EntityConflict;
            Product currentProduct = conflictinfo.CurrentEntity as Product;
            Product originalProduct = conflictinfo.OriginalEntity as Product;
            Product storeProduct = conflictinfo.StoreEntity as Product;

            // Handle any conflicts automatically (if you wish)
            // You can get the names of the properties whose value has changed
            // from the conflictinfo.PropertyNames property

            // Force the user's version to overwrite the server's version
            product.EntityConflict.Resolve();
        }
    }
}
```

After resolving the changes, remember to resubmit them back to the server.

■ **Note** Instead of handling the conflicts manually, you might like to take a look at using the generic method Sergey Klementiev created for handling concurrency errors via RIA Services, which allows users to decide whether to keep or discard their changes when conflicts are identified. He has blogged about this at http://sklementiev.blogspot.com/2010/03/wcf-ria-and-concurrency.html.

HTTP Requests

Despite being considerably more work, because you will have to parse the results yourself, another means of communicating with a server is through the use of standard HTTP requests. For example, you might wish to download an XML file from the server, or even consume RESTful services (a.k.a. WebHTTP services). You will also use HTTP requests to download files from a server (such as images).

Making an HTTP Request

There are two ways to make HTTP requests in Silverlight. Silverlight has both a WebClient and a WebRequest class that you can use for uploading and downloading data over HTTP to/from the server. WebRequest gives you finer control over the request; however, WebClient is the easiest to use for simple HTTP download tasks. It provides two means of downloading data (DownloadString and OpenRead), and two means of uploading data (UploadString and OpenWrite). DownloadString/UploadString simply downloads/uploads the data as a string, making communicating plain text easy, and OpenRead/OpenWrite uses a stream (best for binary data). For example, the following is all it takes to download a text file from the server and load the contents into a string variable:

```
private void StartDownload(string url)
{
    WebClient client = new WebClient();
    client.DownloadStringCompleted += client_DownloadStringCompleted;
    client.DownloadStringAsync(new Uri(url));
}

private void client_DownloadStringCompleted(object sender,
                                            DownloadStringCompletedEventArgs e)
{
    string result = e.Result;
    // Do something with the result
}
```

Choosing a Networking Stack

By default, Silverlight uses the browser's networking stack, when running inside the browser, which places some limits on what you can do when making HTTP requests from Silverlight. Limitations that the browser's networking stack imposes include the following:

- You can use only the GET and POST HTTP verbs. This limitation becomes particularly problematic when you want to access REST services, as they generally also require the use of the PUT and DELETE HTTP verbs.

- The browser will return only the 200 and 404 HTTP status codes returned from the server. This causes problems when the server returns a different HTTP status code, and your application needs to respond accordingly. For example, WCF Services returns a status code of 500 when an exception occurs on the server, but the browser's networking stack changes this to a 404 status code.

- You cannot access HTTP response headers.

To support out-of-browser (OOB) mode, the client networking stack was introduced in Silverlight 3, but you can also invoke this networking stack instead, while running inside the browser, to work around these limitations of the browser's networking stack.

■ **Note**   There are some downsides of using the client networking stack, such as the lack of content caching and authentication support.

To use the client networking stack, simply call the `RegisterPrefix` method on the `WebRequest` (or `HttpWebRequest`) class, passing in a prefix (which can be the scheme, or even a domain) to which future calls will use the given networking stack, and passing in the networking stack that those calls will use, with `ClientHttp` representing the client networking stack, like so:

```
WebRequest.RegisterPrefix("http://", WebRequestCreator.ClientHttp);
```

Cross-Domain Access Policies

By default, the Silverlight runtime limits your application to communicating with services that originate from the domain that the Silverlight application was downloaded from, known as the "site of origin." This restriction was put in place for security purposes to avoid denial-of-service (DoS), cross-site forgery, and various other attacks.

However, there are perfectly valid requirements for needing to communicate with servers other than the site of origin. For example, you might want to write an application in which your domain services exist in a different location from where the Silverlight application is downloaded, or write an application that communicates with external services such as Amazon's web services or the Twitter API. Alternatively, you might simply want to download a file from another web site. However, this is prevented by the Silverlight runtime, unless that site explicitly permits cross-domain access. To permit such access, Silverlight needs to provide a cross-domain policy file that Silverlight can download, permitting the application access to that domain.

■ **Note**   Silverlight applications that run in out-of-browser mode with elevated trust, as described in Chapter 16, do not have this restriction in place—they can communicate with any domain.

Silverlight respects both its own cross-domain policy file (`clientaccesspolicy.xml`) and Adobe Flash's (`crossdomain.xml`). It requests the Silverlight policy file from the server first, and if it's not found, it requests the Flash policy file. Silverlight looks for these files in the root of the domain (*not* the root of the application). If a valid policy file of either type is returned from the server, the web request made by the Silverlight application is permitted to proceed. However, if no cross-domain policy file is found, an exception, containing a `SecurityException` exception as its inner exception, is thrown.

■ **Note**   Obtaining the cross-domain policy is all done behind the scenes by the Silverlight runtime, and is required when the application attempts to communicate with a domain other than the site of origin. You can monitor this behavior using a web traffic–logging program, such as Fiddler, to view the server requests, looking for one of these files. You'll find that when your application attempts to access a resource not from the application's site of origin, it will attempt to download a file named `clientaccesspolicy.xml` from the root of that resource's

---

domain. If that file is not found (Fiddler will show the request in red), then it will attempt to download a file named crossdomain.xml from the same location. If that file also can't be found, then the Silverlight runtime will refuse your application access to that resource. If a policy file is found, then the Silverlight runtime will use the permissions that it contains to determine whether access should be granted or denied to that resource. After the Silverlight runtime has downloaded a valid cross-domain policy file for a given domain, it won't attempt to download it again for future requests to that domain during the current application session. Fiddler will show you all this happening, and is an extremely useful tool for debugging when you find that you're having trouble accessing resources on the Web.

Note that a connection to a service running in the same domain, but on a different port, is still considered a different domain and, thus, requires that domain to provide a cross-domain policy file to permit the application access. This is particularly pertinent if you are hosting your web service in a different ASP.NET project in your solution than the project serving up your Silverlight application, and you are debugging your project using the ASP.NET Development Server instead of IIS. Because all ASP.NET projects are running in their own instances of the ASP.NET Development Server, they are exposed from the localhost domain on a different port from each other. Therefore, the Silverlight runtime sees these as different domains, and requires the domain containing the web service to provide a cross-domain policy file. Otherwise, the Silverlight application downloaded from the other project will be refused access to the web service by the Silverlight runtime.

Implementing Cross-Domain Policies for HTTP-Based Communication

This scenario actually provides the easiest means to demonstrate the cross-domain restriction and test a cross-domain policy file. Add a new project using the ASP.NET Empty Web Application project template to your solution, and add a new WCF Service to this project using the Silverlight-enabled WCF Service item template. Reference this WCF Service from your Silverlight application and call the DoWork method it exposes. When you run the application and call that method, the call will fail with a CommunicationException exception. Now add a text file named clientaccesspolicy.xml to the root of this project, with the following content:

```xml
<?xml version="1.0" encoding="utf-8"?>
<access-policy>
  <cross-domain-access>
    <policy>
      <allow-from http-request-headers="*">
        <domain uri="*" />
      </allow-from>
      <grant-to>
        <resource path="/" include-subpaths="true" />
      </grant-to>
    </policy>
  </cross-domain-access>
</access-policy>
```

■ **Note** The policy shown in the preceding example implements totally unrestricted access to your domain by Silverlight clients. Of course, standard security restrictions still apply. Best practice is to open up access only to resources you actually want to make available to Silverlight client applications. MSDN has a comprehensive guide to the policy options available at `http://msdn.microsoft.com/en-us/library/cc645032.aspx`.

Now when you run the application, the service call will be successful. If it fails, try using Ctrl+F5 in the browser to refresh your application, as the policy file might have been cached by the browser.

Implementing Cross-Domain Policies for Socket-Based Communication

When communicating with a server via sockets, a cross-domain policy is required, whether or not you are attempting to communicate with the site of origin, because a different port is considered a different domain. You can explicitly configure the application to look for a cross-domain policy file hosted on port 80 (the HTTP port) in the root of that domain—that is, in exactly the same fashion as for standard web requests. However, if that server is not serving HTTP requests, another means is obviously required to obtain a cross-domain policy. The solution involves listening on port 943 and serving up the policy when it's requested by the client. A sample sockets policy file is provided as follows:

```
<?xml version="1.0" encoding="utf-8" ?>
<access-policy>
  <cross-domain-access>
    <policy>
      <allow-from>
        <domain uri="*"/>
      </allow-from>
      <grant-to>
        <socket-resource port="4502-4534" protocol="tcp"/>
      </grant-to>
    </policy>
  </cross-domain-access>
</access-policy>
```

Implementing Cross-Scheme Access Policies

Another scenario you should be aware of is one in which you have a cross-scheme communication. An example of this is when you want to deliver the application to the client over HTTP but have it communicate with the server securely over HTTPS. This also constitutes a cross-domain call and, thus, must be explicitly permitted by the server in its cross-domain policy file. Despite the `allow-from` node in the preceding policy file using a wildcard to accept callers from any domain, it doesn't actually permit callers using a different scheme to the service. You must explicitly specify the schemes that will be permitted access. To do so, replace the following line from the cross-domain policy file:

```
<domain uri="*" />
```

with the following two lines:

```
<domain uri="http://*" />
<domain uri="https://*" />
```

Summary

In this chapter, we focused on how you could consume data from the server using RIA Services. All communication with the server in Silverlight is asynchronous, which can make the process initially a little difficult for developers new to asynchronous programming. RIA Services provides two ways of consuming data in your application: a pure XAML declarative means using the `DomainDataSource` control, and a code-based means by interacting with a data context object directly. You learned how to add criteria when querying data from the server, and submit changes made to the data back to the server. In the following two chapters, we're going to build on the knowledge that you gained in this chapter, and focus on how you can effectively display this data to the user in your Silverlight application, thus enabling the user to drill down on the data and edit it, before submitting the changes back to the server.

CHAPTER 6

Implementing Summary Lists

Summary lists (see Figure 6-1) are designed to enable users to quickly locate and identify a record of a given type among the existing data in the system. After they have found the record, they can then drill down to the record to view it in detail and, potentially, edit it.

Instead of requiring the full record for each item in the list to be sent to the client, summary lists generally only request and display enough data from the server to enable the user to identify the record they wish to view/edit. After the user has selected the record, the application will go back to the server and retrieve the remaining data for that record, and any associated and supporting data, to populate a details screen or data entry form. This is a common strategy for working with data in business applications, which minimizes the amount of data being sent to the client from the server, and facilitates a drill-down approach for interacting with the detailed data.

In this chapter, we'll consume data from the ProductSummaryService domain service that we created back in Chapter 4, and populate a DataGrid or a ListBox with the list of ProductSummary entities that it returns. We'll then look at ways of filtering, sorting, grouping, and paging the data in the summary list, and enable the user to drill down on a particular item.

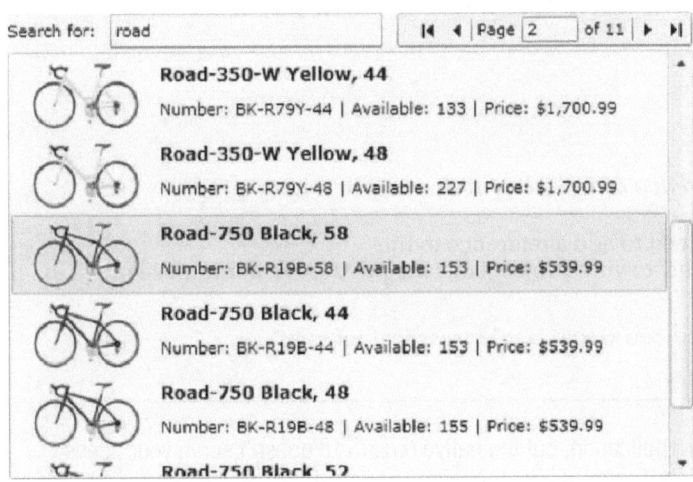

Figure 6-1. A summary list

Creating the Summary List

In Chapter 5 we looked at how you can consume data from the server. Now it's time to display that data to the user. The most commonly used controls for presenting a summary list to the user are the DataGrid control and the ListBox control, so we will investigate how to configure both these controls, and compare and contrast the two so you can determine the most appropriate control to use for your purposes.

Using the DataGrid Control

Configuring a DataGrid control essentially involves setting up the columns to be displayed. If you happen to have presentation layer information, using the Display attribute discussed in Chapter 4, in the metadata of the entity being displayed, then simply assigning the collection to the ItemsSource property of the DataGrid and setting the AutoGenerateColumns property to True (its default value) is all that is necessary. However, assuming that you don't have this metadata available (as having presentation layer information in the middle tier isn't generally recommended), you will need to manually configure the columns to be displayed. Let's look at how to produce the output shown in Figure 6-2 using a DataGrid control.

Name	Qty Available	Made In-House
Adjustable Race	1085	
All-Purpose Bike Stand	144	
AWC Logo Cap	288	
BB Ball Bearing	1352	☑
Bearing BallE	1109	
Bike Wash - Dissolver	36	
Blade	1361	☑
Cable Lock	252	
Chain	589	
Chain Stays	1629	☑
Chainring	1684	

Figure 6-2. *A simple summary list displayed in a DataGrid control*

To use the DataGrid control, you will need to add a reference to the System.Windows.Controls.Data.dll assembly to your project, and declare the sdk namespace prefix in your views, like so:

```
xmlns:sdk="http://schemas.microsoft.com/winfx/2006/xaml/presentation/sdk"
```

■ **Note** If you want to use a DataGrid in your application, but the native DataGrid doesn't serve your needs, there are a number of third-party DataGrid controls available that you could use instead, from vendors such as Telerik, ComponentOne, Infragistics, ComponentArt, DevExpress, and Syncfusion.

Populating a DataGrid Control with Data

The DataGrid control has an ItemsSource property that you can bind to a collection of objects, or directly assign a collection of objects. For example, you can bind the DataGrid control's ItemsSource property to the Data property of a DomainDataSource control using ElementName binding. ElementName binding is covered in Chapter 11, but in summary, it binds the value of one control's property to the value of another control's property. In the following XAML, the ItemsSource property of a DataGrid control is being bound to the Data property of a DomainDataSource control named productSummaryDDS:

```
<sdk:DataGrid Name="productsDataGrid"
              ItemsSource="{Binding ElementName=productSummaryDDS, Path=Data}" />
```

Alternatively, you can simply assign a collection to the control's ItemsSource property in the code-behind, where collection is a collection of objects to be displayed, like so:

```
productsDataGrid.ItemsSource = collection;
```

Configuring DataGrid Columns

Each column will need to be defined on the Columns property of the DataGrid. The following three different column types are available for the DataGrid control in Silverlight:

- DataGridTextColumn: This is the most commonly used column type in summary list scenarios. In read-only mode it shows the bound property value in a TextBlock, and in edit mode it shows it in a TextBox.

- DataGridCheckBoxColumn: This column type is used for showing Boolean value. It displays the bound property value in a CheckBox in both read-only and edit modes. (It simply disables it when it's in read-only mode.)

- DataGridTemplateColumn: This column type is for use when neither of the other two column types are appropriate. Essentially, you can configure this column to work the way you want by defining a cell template for the column (providing the CellTemplate property with a *data template*), and if you wish, an alternative cell-editing template (providing the CellEditingTemplate property with a data template). In other words, you can define two templates for a column—one for read-only scenarios, and one for editing scenarios. If only one of these templates is provided, it will be used in both scenarios. In these cell templates you can define the control(s) that you want displayed, and their layout if required, providing practically limitless possibilities for a cell's contents.

■ **Note** Data templates are defined and briefly described in Chapter 2. We'll discuss data templates further shortly, when we look at the ListBox control.

The following example XAML demonstrates a simple DataGrid configuration with three columns, each demonstrating one of the preceding column types. Each column has a binding to a property on the entity, and assigns the text to be displayed in the column header. Note that both a cell template and an edit template are being defined for the quantityAvailableColumn column—using a TextBlock control to display the data for read-only scenarios, and a NumericUpDown control to enable the value to be altered in edit mode.

```
<sdk:DataGrid AutoGenerateColumns="False">
    <sdk:DataGrid.Columns>
        <sdk:DataGridTextColumn Binding="{Binding Name}" Header="Name" />

        <sdk:DataGridTemplateColumn Header="Qty Available">
            <sdk:DataGridTemplateColumn.CellTemplate>
                <DataTemplate>
                    <TextBlock Text="{Binding QuantityAvailable}" />
                </DataTemplate>
            </sdk:DataGridTemplateColumn.CellTemplate>
            <sdk:DataGridTemplateColumn.CellEditingTemplate>
                <DataTemplate>
                    <TextBox
                        Text="{Binding QuantityAvailable, Mode=TwoWay}" />
                </DataTemplate>
            </sdk:DataGridTemplateColumn.CellEditingTemplate>
        </sdk:DataGridTemplateColumn>

        <sdk:DataGridCheckBoxColumn Binding="{Binding MakeFlag}"
                                    Header="Made In-House" />
    </sdk:DataGrid.Columns>
</sdk:DataGrid>
```

■ **Note**   When you bind a collection to the ItemsSource property of a DataGrid or ListBox control, the control will create a row/item for each item in the collection, and that row/item will have its DataContext property bound to the corresponding entity from the collection.

Creating Column Definitions the Easy Way

There is a trick that can save you time when manually configuring the columns of a DataGrid control. In Chapter 5 we looked at how you could drag an entity from the Data Sources window in Visual Studio onto a view, and a list or edit screen will be generated for you and wired up to a DomainDataSource control. Even if you have chosen not to use the DomainDataSource control to consume data in the view, you can still use this approach to generate a DataGrid control, with a column definition for each property on the entity created for you. You can then customize and reorganize/delete the columns that it defined for you to your heart's content, saving you from having to configure each of these manually. If you don't want to use the DomainDataSource control that was also created, simply delete it from the XAML, and delete the binding to it that was assigned to the ItemsSource property of the DataGrid control.

In addition, this approach can save you much time when you are using template columns to display/edit various properties on the entity, where the control to display/edit the value isn't available as a part of a standard DataGrid column—that is, DataGridTextColumn or DataGridCheckBoxColumn. For example, you might want a numeric property to be able to be edited using a NumericUpDown control instead of a standard TextBox control. Select the control that should be used to edit the data for a property in the Data Sources window from the drop-down menu that appears when the property is selected. If the control doesn't appear in the list, click the Customize menu item and select the control from the list of all available controls. Remember to also select the data type that the control should appear for! Selecting this control type for a property will automatically create a template column for that property in the DataGrid that is created, with a preconfigured cell template containing that control bound to the property.

■ **Note** Often, you will want the last column in the `DataGrid` to simply fill the remaining space, especially in summary list–type scenarios. You can achieve this by simply setting the `Width` property of the column to *.

Displaying an Image in a Column

We'd also like to display an image of each product against the corresponding item in the `DataGrid`. This is another scenario in which a template column can be used, with a bound `Image` control in the cell template. However, properties that expose images on your entity will, in most cases, be represented by a simple byte array (`byte[]`). Unfortunately, the `Image` control cannot accept a byte array, and cannot be bound to it. The `Image` control can accept a `BitmapImage`, so we need to find a way to convert the byte array to a `BitmapImage` so it can be bound. There are a number of ways to achieve this, including the following:

- Defining a partial class for your entity, and creating a property that converts and exposes the byte array as a `BitmapImage`, which you can bind to

- Creating your own `Image` control that can accept an image as a byte array

- Creating a value converter that can be used as a part of a binding to convert the bound value before it is applied to the property of the control

All of these are viable solutions, and have their own pros and cons. As a general rule, using a value converter is the better option. Value converters are a powerful feature of the binding mechanism in Silverlight, enabling the properties of two objects to be bound together, even if their types don't match. The value converter sits in the middle of the binding, translating the value of the source property and returning the result so that it can be applied to the destination property, and vice versa. You simply design a class that implements the `IValueConverter` interface, and insert the logic to translate one value to another—in this case, a byte array to a `BitmapImage`. Value converters are covered in full in Chapter 11, so we won't go into details here, but in summary, you can use a value converter to convert the byte array to a `BitmapImage`, which the `Image` control can understand, so that it can display a thumbnail image for the product.

■ **Note** When it comes to exposing images from the AdventureWorks database, unfortunately we hit a small hurdle. The images are stored in the database as GIFs—an image format not actually supported by Silverlight. Therefore, we need to either convert them to an image format Silverlight supports on the server before sending them to the client (such as PNG or JPG), or find a way to do so on the client. Converting images for each item on the server when the client requests a summary list would put an excessive load on the server and reduce the scalability of your application. Therefore, it would be better to leave that task to the clients. Luckily, there is a CodePlex project called ImageTools for Silverlight (`http://imagetools.codeplex.com`) that provides a GIF decoder that you can use. This library is used in the sample project by calling it in our value converter, used when binding the image property to an `Image` control in XAML, to convert the byte array returned from the server to a `BitmapImage`. The GIF decoder from the library is used to decode the byte array from the GIF format, which is then reencoded using the PNG encoder from the library to a `BitmapImage`, which can then be bound to an `Image` control. This conversion process can be performed in the value converter, which will read in the byte array, convert the image to a PNG, and then assign it to a BitmapImage, which it will then return. Since this is a rather obscure implementation detail, we won't go into details of the conversion process here. However, you'll find code that does this in the code accompanying this book, which is available from the Source Code/Download area of the Apress web site (www.apress.com).

The following code demonstrates defining a template column containing an Image control whose Source property is bound to the ThumbnailPhoto property of the ProductSummary object. Note how the Converter property of the binding is assigned a custom value converter called GifConverter, which is defined as a resource higher up in the object hierarchy. This is the converter being used to handle the translation of a GIF image in a byte array to a PNG image in a BitmapImage object.

```
<sdk:DataGridTemplateColumn>
    <sdk:DataGridTemplateColumn.CellTemplate>
        <DataTemplate>
            <Image Margin="2"
                    Source="{Binding ThumbnailPhoto,
                                Converter={StaticResource GifConverter}}" />
        </DataTemplate>
    </sdk:DataGridTemplateColumn.CellTemplate>
</sdk:DataGridTemplateColumn>
```

Creating Calculated Columns

You can use the same value converter technique to implement a calculated column. Bind the property to your whole object so that the whole object is passed into the value converter, and then you can calculate a value to display in that column from the property values on the object; for example, *total amount = quantity × price*, where *total amount* is the calculated value, and the *quantity* and *price* values are retrieved from the object. However, since this is business logic rather than user interface logic, you are probably best off defining a partial class for that object and creating a property that performs the calculation there instead, which can then be bound to.

Editing Data in the DataGrid

The DataGrid control is primarily designed for editing data, and thus, grid cells are in edit mode by default. However, you can disable the editing behavior to use the control more like a list by setting the IsReadOnly property of the DataGrid to True. We'll look at the DataGrid control's editing behavior in Chapter 7.

■ **Note** Being primarily designed for editing data, by default the DataGrid control uses a cell selection–type behavior, whereas in a summary list–type scenario, you really want the selection behavior to involve the full row. You'll find that when a cell is selected, the full row does have a selected appearance, but the cell has an additional (and quite prominent) selection square around it. There is no easy way to hide this, unfortunately, but you can use Silverlight's styling support to hide it yourself. This process involves applying a custom style to the CellStyle property of the DataGrid and retemplating the DataGridCell control to hide the rectangle (named "FocusVisual") that it incorporates. Retemplating a control using a control template is covered in Chapter 9.

Additional Built-In Behaviors

When you use the DataGrid, you get a lot of additional built-in features and behaviors "for free," which is one of the primary reasons that the DataGrid control has such a wide appeal to many developers. Some of these features are listed in the following subsections.

Sorting

Simply click the header of a column to sort the DataGrid by its values, and click it again to reverse the sorting. This feature is automatically turned on, but can be turned off by setting the CanUserSortColumns property of the DataGrid to False. It can also be toggled off/on selectively by setting the appropriate value to the CanUserSort property of a column.

Grouping

One of the most powerful features of Silverlight's DataGrid control is its ability to display grouped data. Most summary lists in business applications have the need to group data, and the DataGrid control has this ability built in. This feature alone makes Silverlight's DataGrid more powerful and functional than that available natively in any other Microsoft platform. Multiple levels of grouping can be displayed, meaning that you can group items by category and then by subcategory, for example.

■ **Note** Grouping cannot actually be configured directly on the DataGrid control itself. Instead, you must bind it to a collection view and configure the grouping on it. This is discussed further in the section "Workshop: Grouping the Summary List," later in this chapter.

Resizing of Columns

Users can increase or decrease the size of a column by clicking and dragging the right edge of the column header to the size they want. They can also double-click the right edge of the column header to make the column automatically size itself to a width at which all its content is visible. This feature is automatically turned on, but can be turned off by setting the CanUserResizeColumns property of the DataGrid to False. It can also be set on specific columns using their CanUserResize property.

Reordering of Columns

Users can rearrange the columns to their liking by dragging a column header to a new position. This feature is automatically turned on, but can be turned off by setting the CanUserReorderColumns property of the DataGrid to False. It can also be set on specific columns using their CanUserReorder property.

Displaying Additional Row Details

The DataGrid has a RowDetailsTemplate property that enables you to define a data template containing a layout of additional details you want to display about a row beneath the main row. For example, you might want to display only some of the details on the entity in the columns, and then display more details when the row is selected. You can even have quite a complex layout in which selecting a row displays another DataGrid below it showing a list of related items (e.g., the line items on an invoice). You can choose to have the row details displayed for each row automatically, display the details for a row only when it is selected, or only display them manually, via the RowDetailsVisibilityMode property on the DataGrid. We'll look at this feature further in the section "Displaying Details Using the DataGrid's Row Details," later in the chapter.

Validation Support

When the DataGrid is in edit mode, any validation rules you've defined in your entity's metadata will be run over the entered values, and a validation rule failure message will appear so the user knows what the problem is so that they can fix the issue. We'll look at implementing validation rules in Chapter 7.

Workshop: Configuring a DataGrid Control for Displaying a Summary List

In this workshop, we'll create a DataGrid control that displays columns for the following three properties when bound to a ProductSummary entity (which we created and exposed from the server in Chapter 4): Name, QuantityAvailable, and MakeFlag. This will demonstrate each of the three types of DataGrid columns: DataGridTextColumn, DataGridTemplateColumn, and DataGridCheckBoxColumn. For now, we'll merely define it, and look at approaches to populating it with data later, in the section "Populating a Summary List with Data." When it's populated with data, you will have a DataGrid control that looks the same as that shown in Figure 6-2.

1. In a previous workshop, we created a view named ProductListView.xaml. Delete this view, and re-create it so that you start afresh.

2. Add a reference to the System.Windows.Controls.Data.dll assembly to your project.

3. Define the sdk namespace prefix in the root element of this XAML file, as follows:

```
xmlns:sdk="http://schemas.microsoft.com/winfx/2006/xaml/presentation/sdk"
```

4. Now define the DataGrid control, like so:

```
<sdk:DataGrid AutoGenerateColumns="False">
    <sdk:DataGrid.Columns>
        <sdk:DataGridTextColumn Binding="{Binding Name}" Header="Name" />
```

```
            <sdk:DataGridTemplateColumn Header="Qty Available">
                <sdk:DataGridTemplateColumn.CellTemplate>
                    <DataTemplate>
                        <TextBlock Text="{Binding QuantityAvailable}" />
                    </DataTemplate>
                </sdk:DataGridTemplateColumn.CellTemplate>
            </sdk:DataGridTemplateColumn>

            <sdk:DataGridCheckBoxColumn Binding="{Binding MakeFlag}"
                                        Header="Made In-House" />
        </sdk:DataGrid.Columns>
</sdk:DataGrid>
```

5. To populate the DataGrid control with data, you will need to bind its ItemsSource property to a source of data. We'll look at how you do this shortly.

Using the ListBox Control

One of the big advantages of using a ListBox control over a DataGrid is its flexibility. By default, a ListBox simply displays a line of text for each item in the list, as shown in Figure 6-3.

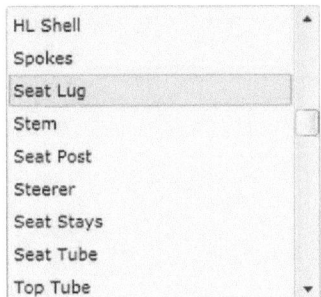

Figure 6-3. A ListBox control (with no customizations)

Despite this apparent simplicity, the ListBox control is actually quite a versatile control, with much more potential than you might initially assume. Let's take a look at the techniques you can use to customize the ListBox control to your needs.

Populating a ListBox Control with Data

Like the DataGrid control, the ListBox control has an ItemsSource property that you can bind to a collection of objects, or directly assign a collection of objects. You use this property in exactly the same manner as you do with the DataGrid control. For example, you can bind its ItemsSource property to the Data property of a DomainDataSource control, like so:

```
<ListBox Name="productsList"
         ItemsSource="{Binding ElementName=productSummaryDDS, Path=Data}" />
```

Or you can simply assign a collection to the control's ItemsSource property in the code-behind, where collection is a collection of objects to be displayed, like so:

```
productsList.ItemsSource = collection;
```

■ **Note** Unlike the DataGrid control, the ListBox control has an Items property, exposing a collection that you can explicitly add/remove items to in the code-behind, assuming the control's ItemsSource property is not bound to a collection. However, this is rarely used in Silverlight, as binding a collection to the control's ItemsSource property is the preferred approach for populating a ListBox control. As you'll learn shortly, the ListBox control automatically listens for the CollectionChanged event on bound collections that implement the INotifyCollectionChanged interface (such as the ObservableCollection<T> type). As items are added to or removed from the bound collection, the CollectionChanged event will be raised, and the ListBox control will automatically update itself accordingly.

Templating List Items

A data template enables you to define a custom way in which data should be displayed in a control. The ListBox control allows you to define a data template that will be applied to each item, enabling you to completely customize the appearance of items in the list. To do this, simply define a data template and assign it to the ItemTemplate property of the ListBox. For example, take the following data template:

```
<DataTemplate>
    <Grid Height="50">
        <Grid.ColumnDefinitions>
            <ColumnDefinition Width="100" />
            <ColumnDefinition />
        </Grid.ColumnDefinitions>
        <Grid.RowDefinitions>
            <RowDefinition />
            <RowDefinition />
        </Grid.RowDefinitions>

        <Image Margin="2"
               Source="{Binding ThumbnailPhoto,
                          Converter={StaticResource GifConverter}}"
               Grid.RowSpan="2" />
        <TextBlock Name="NameField" Text="{Binding Name}" Margin="2"
                   Grid.Row="0" Grid.Column="1" FontWeight="Bold" FontSize="12" />

        <StackPanel Orientation="Horizontal" Grid.Row="1" Grid.Column="1">
            <TextBlock Text="Number:" Margin="2"  />
            <TextBlock Text="{Binding Number}" Margin="2"  />
            <TextBlock Text="| Available:" Margin="2"  />
            <TextBlock Text="{Binding QuantityAvailable}" Margin="2"  />
            <TextBlock Text="| Price:" Margin="2"  />
            <TextBlock Text="{Binding ListPrice, StringFormat=C}" Margin="2" />
        </StackPanel>
    </Grid>
</DataTemplate>
```

Applying this data template to the ItemTemplate property of a ListBox, like so:

```
<ListBox ItemsSource="{Binding ElementName=productSummaryDDS, Path=Data}">
    <ListBox.ItemTemplate>
        <!-- Put data template XAML here -->
    </ListBox.ItemTemplate>
</ListBox>
```

results in the output shown in Figure 6-4.

Figure 6-4. *A ListBox control (with a custom item template)*

As you can see, this enables you to provide a very customized view of the data, that is both attractive and highlights the important details of each item.

Implicit Data Templates

Implicit data templates are a new feature in Silverlight 5. Previously, you could define only a single data template that would be applied to all items in the list. However, the source collection may consist of different object types, and you might want to display the items in the list differently, with each item using a data template according to the type of object it is bound to. Say, for example, that you have an ErrorLog collection, of type ObservableCollection<LogMessage>. (We'll introduce you to the ObservableCollection<T> type shortly, but it's essentially a standard collection type with some additional behavior added.) For this example, the LogMessage class will simply have a single property: Message, of type string. You also have three classes, each inheriting from LogMessage: ErrorLogMessage, WarningLogMessage, and InformationLogMessage. The ErrorLog collection is populated with instances of each of these classes, each representing a message added to the log; the type representing the severity of the message. When you populate a ListBox control with this collection, it would be nice for each item to use a custom template according to the object type that it's bound to. You might want to highlight the error message items with a red background so that they stand out, and have each item display an icon representing the severity of the message being represented. This behavior is easy to implement using implicit data templates. Essentially, you can define a separate data template for each type of object that will appear in the ErrorLog collection.

The following XAML demonstrates the scenario just detailed. Here, we have a ListBox control, which has three data templates defined as resources. Each data template has its DataType property set (in bold) to the type of object that it will be applied to. Unlike standard data templates, implicit data templates are not explicitly assigned to the ListBox control's ItemTemplate property. Instead, when the ListBox control is populated, it will automatically search for a DataTemplate resource within its scope for each item in the list. It will search for a DataTemplate resource whose DataType property corresponds to the type of object the item is being bound to. If it finds one, then it will apply that data template to the item.

```xml
<ListBox ItemsSource="{Binding ErrorLog}">
    <ListBox.Resources>
        <DataTemplate DataType="models:ErrorLogMessage">
            <Grid>
                <Grid.ColumnDefinitions>
                    <ColumnDefinition Width="35" />
                    <ColumnDefinition Width="*" />
                </Grid.ColumnDefinitions>

                <Image Source="/ImplicitDataTemplateSample;component/Images/Error.png"
                       Stretch="None" />
                <TextBlock Text="{Binding Message}" Grid.Column="1"
                           VerticalAlignment="Center" />
            </Grid>
        </DataTemplate>

        <DataTemplate DataType="models:WarningLogMessage">
            <Grid>
                <Grid.ColumnDefinitions>
                    <ColumnDefinition Width="35" />
                    <ColumnDefinition Width="*" />
                </Grid.ColumnDefinitions>

                <Image Source="/ImplicitDataTemplateSample;component/Images/Warning.png"
                       Stretch="None" />
                <TextBlock Text="{Binding Message}" Grid.Column="1"
                           VerticalAlignment="Center" />
            </Grid>
        </DataTemplate>

        <DataTemplate DataType="models:InformationLogMessage">
            <Grid>
                <Grid.ColumnDefinitions>
                    <ColumnDefinition Width="35" />
                    <ColumnDefinition Width="*" />
                </Grid.ColumnDefinitions>

                <Image Source="/ImplicitDataTemplateSample;component/Images/Information.png"
                       Stretch="None" />
                <TextBlock Text="{Binding Message}" Grid.Column="1"
                           VerticalAlignment="Center" />
            </Grid>
        </DataTemplate>
    </ListBox.Resources>
</ListBox>
```

■ **Note** In the preceding example, we define the data templates as resources on the ListBox control. Note, however, that they can be defined as resources further up the hierarchy instead if you wish (such as at the view, or even application level), making them available to all the ListBox controls or to any other controls that support data templating.

A sample application putting this example into action can be found in the code accompanying this book, available from the Source Code/Download area of the Apress web site (www.apress.com).

Customizing the Layout of the Items

Items don't have to appear vertically in a list when using the ListBox. For example, you may choose to have items appear in a horizontal layout instead, or implement a thumbnail for each item in the list (as you find in Windows Explorer), or even display items in the form of contact cards. You can achieve these effects by assigning a new items panel template to the ItemsPanel property of the ListBox. This property enables you to customize how the items are laid out in the ListBox.

Let's take a look at how to implement the contact card–type layout. For this scenario, we want the items to stack horizontally until they reach the right edge of the ListBox, at which point they should wrap around to the next line. This is a scenario that the WrapPanel control from the Silverlight Toolkit is ideally suited for, as it was designed specifically to achieve this effect. First, you declare the toolkit namespace prefix in the root element in your XAML file, like so:

```
xmlns:toolkit="http://schemas.microsoft.com/winfx/2006/xaml/presentation/toolkit"
```

Then, simply assign this to the ItemsPanelTemplate property of the ListBox's ItemsPanel property. For example, apply this template to the ItemsPanel property of the ListBox:

```
<ItemsPanelTemplate>
    <toolkit:WrapPanel />
</ItemsPanelTemplate>
```

Then, apply this data template to the ItemTemplate property:

```
<DataTemplate>
    <Grid Width="270" Margin="5">
        <Grid.ColumnDefinitions>
            <ColumnDefinition Width="100" />
            <ColumnDefinition />
        </Grid.ColumnDefinitions>
        <Grid.RowDefinitions>
            <RowDefinition Height="Auto" />
            <RowDefinition Height="Auto" />
            <RowDefinition Height="Auto" />
            <RowDefinition Height="Auto" />
            <RowDefinition Height="Auto" />
        </Grid.RowDefinitions>

        <Rectangle Stroke="Black" RadiusX="3" RadiusY="3"
                Grid.RowSpan="5" Grid.ColumnSpan="2">
            <Rectangle.Fill>
                <LinearGradientBrush StartPoint="0,0" EndPoint="0,1">
```

```
                    <GradientStop Color="White" Offset="0" />
                    <GradientStop Color="#6D6D6D" Offset="1" />
                </LinearGradientBrush>
            </Rectangle.Fill>
            <Rectangle.Effect>
                <DropShadowEffect ShadowDepth="2" />
            </Rectangle.Effect>
        </Rectangle>

        <Border BorderBrush="Black" Background="White" Margin="8" Height="70"
                VerticalAlignment="Top" CornerRadius="3" Grid.RowSpan="5">
            <Border.Effect>
                <DropShadowEffect ShadowDepth="2" />
            </Border.Effect>
            <Image Source="{Binding ThumbnailPhoto,
                                Converter={StaticResource GifConverter}}"
                VerticalAlignment="Center" HorizontalAlignment="Center" />
        </Border>

        <TextBlock Name="NameField" Text="{Binding Name}" Margin="2,8,2,2"
                Grid.Row="0" Grid.Column="1" FontWeight="Bold" FontSize="12" />

        <StackPanel Orientation="Horizontal" Grid.Row="1" Grid.Column="1">
            <TextBlock Text="Number:" Margin="2" />
            <TextBlock Text="{Binding Number}" Margin="2" />
        </StackPanel>

        <StackPanel Orientation="Horizontal" Grid.Row="2" Grid.Column="1">
            <TextBlock Text="Available:" Margin="2" />
            <TextBlock Text="{Binding QuantityAvailable}" Margin="2" />
        </StackPanel>

        <StackPanel Orientation="Horizontal" Grid.Row="3" Grid.Column="1">
            <TextBlock Text="Price:" Margin="2" />
            <TextBlock Text="{Binding ListPrice, StringFormat=C}" Margin="2" />
        </StackPanel>
    </Grid>
</DataTemplate>
```

Finally, setting the ScrollViewer.HorizontalScrollBarVisibility property on the ListBox to Disabled, disabling its horizontal scroll bar so that the items will wrap, results in the output shown in Figure 6-5.

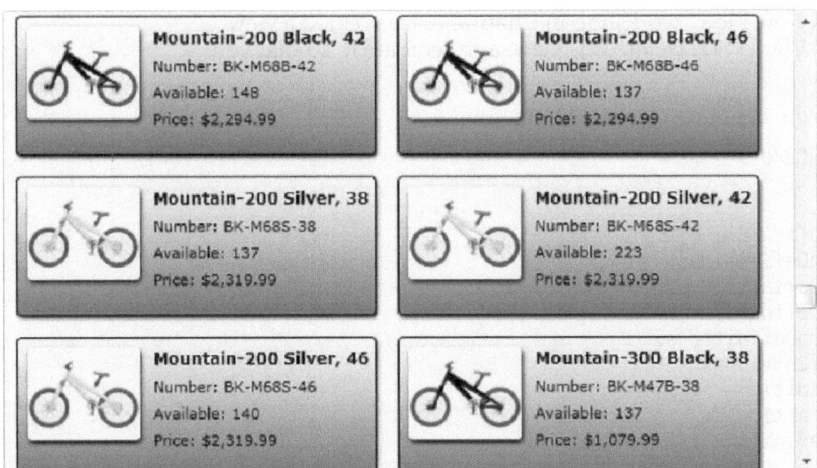

Figure 6-5. *A ListBox control (with a custom item panel and item template)*

Limitations of the ListBox Control

Despite all its flexibility, the ListBox control does have its limitations. One big issue comes when you want to group the items in the list. Unlike the DataGrid control, the ListBox unfortunately doesn't have any built-in grouping functionality. Data can be grouped within the ListBox; however, there is no support for displaying group headers. You could attempt to implement group headers yourself, but this would require quite a bit of code and could become a messy solution. If you require grouping in your summary list, you could potentially add some custom styling and behavior to the TreeView control, to make it look and behave like a list, as it is fundamentally designed to support hierarchical data, which grouped data could be considered to be. However, a fair amount of manual effort is still required to achieve the correct effect. Therefore, if you need to display grouped data beneath headers in your summary list, the DataGrid control might be your best option.

⚙ Workshop: Configuring a ListBox Control for Displaying a Summary List

In this workshop, we'll create a templated ListBox control that displays data for a ProductSummary entity, which we created and exposed from the server in Chapter 4. For now, we'll merely define it, and look at approaches to populating it with data later, in the section "Populating a Summary List with Data." When it's populated with data, you will have a ListBox control that looks the same as that shown in Figure 6-4.

▪ **Note** As mentioned earlier, the images returned from the server are in the GIF format, which Silverlight does not support. We can convert them to a usable format using a library to help us, but for the purpose of this workshop, we'll simply define an unbound placeholder Image control. The sample code for this chapter does, however, have a full implementation.

---

1. In a the "Creating a New View" workshop in Chapter 3, we created a view named `ProductListView.xaml`. Delete this view, and recreate it, so that you start afresh.

2. In this view, define the `ListBox` control, like so:

```
<ListBox Height="300" Width="480">
    <ListBox.ItemTemplate>
        <DataTemplate>
            <Grid Height="50">
                <Grid.ColumnDefinitions>
                    <ColumnDefinition Width="100" />
                    <ColumnDefinition />
                </Grid.ColumnDefinitions>
                <Grid.RowDefinitions>
                    <RowDefinition />
                    <RowDefinition />
                </Grid.RowDefinitions>

                <Image Margin="2" Grid.RowSpan="2" />
                <TextBlock Name="NameField" Text="{Binding Name}" Margin="2"
                           Grid.Row="0" Grid.Column="1" FontWeight="Bold" FontSize="12" />

                <StackPanel Orientation="Horizontal" Grid.Row="1" Grid.Column="1">
                    <TextBlock Text="Number:" Margin="2"  />
                    <TextBlock Text="{Binding Number}" Margin="2"  />
                    <TextBlock Text="| Available:" Margin="2"  />
                    <TextBlock Text="{Binding QuantityAvailable}" Margin="2"  />
                    <TextBlock Text="| Price:" Margin="2"  />
                    <TextBlock Text="{Binding ListPrice, StringFormat=C}" Margin="2" />
                </StackPanel>
            </Grid>
        </DataTemplate>
    </ListBox.ItemTemplate>
</ListBox>
```

   Note how the majority of this XAML is for the `ListBox` control's item template. When the `ListBox` control is populated, this item template will result in the output shown in Figure 6-4, but without the `Image` control displaying the image.

3. To populate the `ListBox` control with data, you will need to bind its `ItemsSource` property to a source of data. We'll look at how you do this shortly.

Choosing the Right Control

With these two controls in Silverlight suitable for displaying summary lists, you are left with the potentially difficult decision of which one you should use.

The `DataGrid` is a powerful and versatile control, revered by developers but detested by most user experience designers. Developers tend to like to use the `DataGrid`, as it provides a lot of functionality out of the box, with little work required to enable it. Hence, developers treat it like a "god" control that can do everything and make their lives easier. By simply binding a collection to the `DataGrid` control, you get display and editing behavior, sorting, header resizing, header reordering, multilevel grouping, data validation, and more—all with little or no work required on the part of the developer. However, because of this, it is sometimes overused and implemented in scenarios in which a ListBox would be a more appropriate choice, often at the expense of the application's user experience and user interface design.

■ **Note** Ease of implementation should not provide the basis for your decision on which control you should use. Your decision should solely be based upon what will provide the best experience for the user, and often you will find that the easiest-to-use control for the developer is not always the easiest to use or understand for the user. Keep this in mind when making your choice.

The manner in which the DataGrid has its columns spread out over its width (and beyond) is not always the most efficient way to display the data, especially when the columns extend beyond the width of the DataGrid, where horizontal scrolling would be required. It's important to design your user interface based upon the needs of the user—not simply using what a control provides you.

As a general rule, the DataGrid control is best suited to data entry scenarios; but again, select with care for use in these scenarios too. Generally, you would use the DataGrid, as opposed to something like the DataForm control, for data entry purposes when the user needs to enter the details for a number of records associated with a parent record. For example, the DataGrid is very useful for enabling users to enter line items in an invoice, because there are typically only a few fields required for each invoice line item. However, for general data entry purposes, laying out controls in a form might be more appropriate. (This topic is discussed further in Chapter 7.)

While the ListBox control is row driven by design, the DataGrid is primarily cell driven, which becomes an issue when using it to display a summary list. The purpose of a summary list is to locate and drill down on the data, and as a general rule, the user will use it to drill down upon the data at the row level (not the cell level). Therefore, cell selection behavior in this scenario can be somewhat confusing to the user. If you do use the DataGrid for displaying summary lists, it is recommended that you change the default cell style to remove the selection rectangle from around the selected cell. This way, the cell won't appear selected, but instead the whole row will, as it already exhibits highlighting behavior.

As discussed earlier, the DataGrid does have a big advantage over the ListBox when you need to implement grouping in a summary list, as the ListBox simply doesn't have that capability. (Implementing grouping in a DataGrid will be discussed later in this chapter in the section "Workshop: Grouping the Summary List.") One of the reasons why few developers tend to use the ListBox control is simply because they don't realize the possibilities opened by templating its items; or if they do, they think it's too much work. You might have to design a data template first to lay out any data to be displayed that involves more than one field.

Ultimately, the most appropriate control for displaying summary lists is the ListBox, even if it does require a little more work to lay out and to implement various behaviors that are built into the DataGrid. It's much more lightweight than the DataGrid, and it's very flexible when templated. The DataGrid does have its place, but should be used only when the user experience design calls for it.

Populating a Summary List with Data

As you've seen, you populate the DataGrid and ListBox controls in exactly the same manner as one another, by assigning/binding a collection or collection view to their ItemsSource properties.

Let's now look into this topic further, and investigate the type of data that these controls will accept. We'll introduce the ObservableCollection<T> type, and then introduce the concept of collection views that will allow us to manipulate the data displayed in the summary list without affecting the underlying collection. We'll then demonstrate how you can go about wiring these controls up to this data.

■ **Note** A key concept in Silverlight is that a view should "pull" data into itself, rather than have data "pushed" into it from the code-behind. Although Silverlight enables you to "push" data into a view, as a general rule and best practice, you should take the "pull" approach when populating a view with data, which is the sole approach that we'll take from now on. If you're used to "pushing" data into views, a common practice with technologies such as Windows Forms, this will require you to take a different mindset when you are designing your application, and can take a little getting used to. However, after you get the hang of it, you won't want to go back to your old ways.

The ObservableCollection<T> Type

Silverlight supports many of the common generic collection types you might be used to from the full .NET Framework, including List, Dictionary, LinkedList, Stack, and Queue. Other nongeneric collections, such as the ArrayList and Hashtable, aren't implemented in Silverlight, but you can find an appropriate alternative among the generic collections.

However, the most important collection type that you find yourself using in Silverlight is the ObservableCollection<T> collection. This is a generic collection type, unique to Silverlight and WPF, that implements the INotifyCollectionChanged interface, which exposes a CollectionChanged event—raised when items are added or removed from the collection.

This behavior is incredibly useful because Silverlight controls such as the ListBox, DataGrid, and ComboBox listen for this event when their ItemsSource property is bound to an ObservableCollection<T> collection, and automatically update themselves when the collection has changed. This means that you can update the collection in code, and the changes will be automatically propagated to the user interface. So when you add an item to the collection, it will be automatically added to the control's items, and when you remove an item from the collection, it will be automatically removed from the control's items. This means that you don't need to write code to update the control when an item is added to or removed from the collection, and the code that is modifying this collection doesn't actually need to know that the collection is even bound to a control! Therefore, the ObservableCollection<T> collection can help facilitate a clean separation of concerns between layers in your application, making it a key part of Silverlight's data binding ecosystem—particularly when you come to implement the MVVM (Model-View-ViewModel) design pattern, which we'll cover in Chapter 13.

Collection Views

Another important data binding concept related to collections is that of *collection views*. A collection view is a wrapper around a collection that allows the collection to be manipulated in the user interface, *without altering the underlying collection*. Think of it as a "view of a collection." Typical manipulations you might want to perform include filtering, sorting, grouping, and paging the collection's items. For example, you might want to bind a collection to a ListBox, and enable the user to dynamically filter the items displayed by entering some text into a TextBox. Instead of adding/removing items from the bound collection, you can wrap the collection in a collection view, bind the control to this collection view instead of directly to the collection, and then simply apply a filter to the collection view. The collection view will expose only the items from the underlying collection that conform to the filter, and thus, the bound control will only display these items.

Another key feature of collection views is their current record pointer, which tracks the current item in the collection, enabling multiple controls bound to the same collection view to be kept synchronized. Collection views expose a number of methods and properties that you can use to move this pointer and navigate through the items in the collection. We'll investigate this behavior further in Chapter 11, staying focused on the filtering/sorting/grouping/paging features of collection views in this chapter.

■ **Note**   Collection views all implement the `ICollectionView` interface. Some also implement the `IEditableCollectionView` interface, which allows the underlying collection to be edited via the collection view, and some also implement the `IPagedCollectionView` interface, which provides paging capabilities to the collection view.

Like the `ObservableCollection<T>` collection, collection views help facilitate a clean separation of concerns between layers in your application, and are particularly useful when you come to implement the MVVM design pattern, which we'll cover in Chapter 13.

■ **Note**   Some controls have built-in behavior that can manipulate the output of collection views. A good example of this is the `DataGrid` control. It allows you to sort its rows by clicking a column header, and it does this without modifying the source collection. It simply tells the collection view that wraps it how the items should be sorted. If the `DataGrid` control is bound directly to a collection, it internally wraps it in a collection view, and binds to that instead. Therefore, the `DataGrid` control can still manipulate the items without modifying the collection that it is bound to.

There are a number of different types of collection views in Silverlight, and the type you use will really depend on the given scenario. Let's take a look at the most common collection views that you will use, and the scenarios in which you might use them.

The ListCollectionView/EnumerableCollectionView Collection Views

The `ListCollectionView`/`EnumerableCollectionView` collection views can filter, sort, and group items in their underlying collection in memory. (Note that they don't support paging of the data.) You can't instantiate these collection views directly (their constructors are marked internal), but they can be instantiated with the help of the `CollectionViewSource` class.

The `CollectionViewSource` class acts as a collection view "proxy," which can be used to create a collection view, usually as a means to do so declaratively in XAML. Let's say you want to bind a control to a collection in XAML, but display a filtered/sorted/grouped "view" of that collection, without modifying the collection itself. Wrapping the collection in a collection view enables you to do this. The `CollectionViewSource` class provides a means of declaratively wrapping a collection in a collection view in XAML, which you can then bind to.

You define the `CollectionViewSource` as a resource, assign a collection to its `Source` property, and it will provide you a corresponding collection view from its `View` property as either a `ListCollectionView` or an `EnumerableCollectionView`, depending on the type of collection that is being wrapped, which you can then bind to. The `CollectionViewSource` class allows you to declaratively specify how the items from the collection should be filtered, grouped, and sorted (but not paged), via properties such as `Filter`, `GroupDescriptions`, and `SortDescriptions`.

■ **Note** You can also use the `CollectionViewSource` class to create a collection view in code. However, as a general rule, it is primarily used to create collection views declaratively in XAML.

Use the `ListCollectionView`/`EnumerableCollectionView` collection views when you encounter one of the following situations:

- You have all the data loaded client-side.
- You need to wrap a collection in a collection view declaratively in XAML.
- You don't need to page the data in the user interface.

The PagedCollectionView Collection View

Unlike the `ListCollectionView`/`EnumerableCollectionView` collection views, a `PagedCollectionView` can be instantiated directly, and also supports paging of the data. A `PagedCollectionView` is often used when you are following the MVVM design pattern, and the view model wants to have some control over the filtering/sorting/grouping/paging behavior of the collection view.

■ **Note** To use the `PagedCollectionView` collection view, your project needs a reference to the `System.Windows.Data.dll` assembly.

Use the `PagedCollectionView` collection view when you encounter one of the following situations:

- You have all the data loaded client-side (that is, server-side manipulation of data is not necessary).
- You'd like some control over how the items are filtered/sorted/grouped/paged in your view model class.
- You need to page the data in the user interface.

The DomainDataSourceView Collection View

The `DomainDataSourceView` collection view is exposed by the `DomainDataSource` control via its `DataView` property, and provides a view over the collection of entities requested from the server. You normally won't interact directly with this collection view, but it's worth knowing that it exists. You can't create an instance of a `DomainDataSourceView` object in your code; only the `DomainDataSource` control can create this collection view (the two are tightly coupled together). You can apply filtering, sorting, grouping, and paging criteria to a `DomainDataSource` control, and this collection view will display the data accordingly is performed on the server.

The DomainCollectionView Collection View

The `DomainCollectionView` collection view was introduced as part of the WCF RIA Services Toolkit to help make RIA Services more MVVM friendly. It essentially provides the same behavior as the `DomainDataSource` control (loading of data via RIA Services, and server-side filtering, sorting, and paging of data), but in a manner that allows for a cleaner separation of concerns between your view and the domain context, such that the view does not need to know anything about how the data is obtained.

■ **Note** To use the `DomainCollectionView` collection view, you need to have the WCF RIA Services Toolkit installed (discussed in Chapter 4, in the section "WCF RIA Services Toolkit"), and your project needs a reference to the `Microsoft.Windows.Data.DomainServices.dll` assembly.

Whereas the `CollectionViewSource` collection view proxy and `PagedCollectionView` collection view manipulate the data in memory on the client, the `DomainCollectionView` collection view is a little bit different in that it handles loading data from the server (via RIA Services), and actually manipulates the data on the server, in the same manner as the `DomainDataSource` control. This is particularly useful when you're paging the data, as the server will return only the data for the current page, saving a lot of network traffic between the server and the client if there are many records on the server. When the client changes the filtering/sorting/grouping of the collection, or wants a new page of data, the `DomainCollectionView` will request a new page of results from the server, and populates its source collection when the data is returned.

There are three key components involved when using the `DomainCollectionView`. There's the `DomainCollectionView` itself, the source collection that it wraps, and a "loader," which is the class that actually handles the communication with the server and updates the source collection. The `DomainCollectionView` acts as a bridge between the user interface and this loader. For example, say that the user interface wants a new page of data. The user interface will ask the `DomainCollectionView` for the new page, which will then ask the loader for the new page, which will request the page of data from the server. When the response is received from the server, the loader will populate the source collection with that data, which gets fed back to the user interface via the `DomainCollectionView`. The diagram in Figure 6-6 might help you understand the relationship between these components.

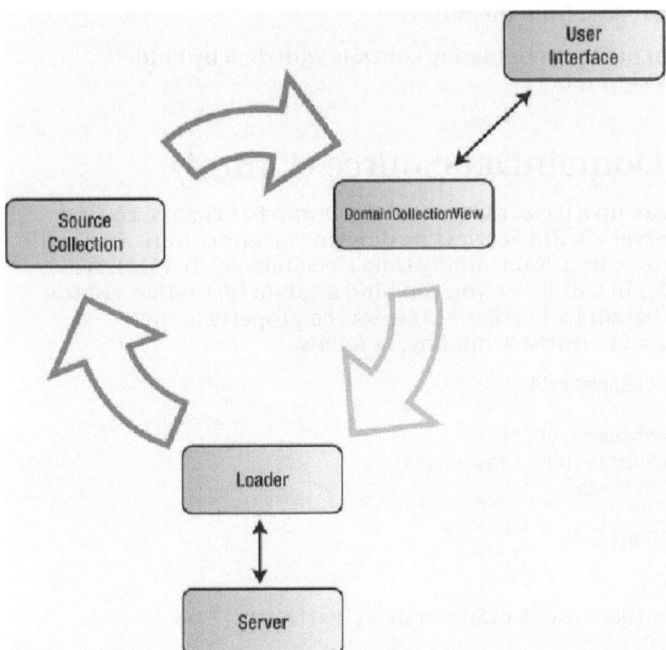

Figure 6-6. The relationship between the source collection, the loader, and the `DomainCollectionView`.

The WCF RIA Services Toolkit comes with a default loader implementation, named DomainCollectionViewLoader. This loader merely passes the work of loading the data back to you. It takes method delegates as parameters to its constructor and calls those methods when data needs to be loaded or has been loaded, so it isn't particularly intelligent.

■ **Note** You can create your own custom loader if you want a smarter, less generic loader than the DomainCollectionViewLoader. Kyle McClellan, from the RIA Services team, has information on how to do so on his blog here at http://blogs.msdn.com/b/kylemc/archive/2011/05/13/writing-a-custom-collectionviewloader-for-the-domaincollectionview-and-mvvm.aspx, but we'll stick with the default loader implementation for now.

As the class DomainCollectionViewLoader simply offloads the work of loading the data requested by the user interface back to you, it's up to you to write the logic to load the data from the domain context (demonstrated in Chapter 5). When creating the query to the server, you will need to apply the state of the DomainCollectionView—that is, the sorting/grouping criteria and current page number—to the query. To help you with this, the CollectionViewExtensions class, found in the WCF RIA Services Toolkit, contains some extension methods for the EntityQuery class that can apply the state of the collection view to the query for you. We'll look at how you do this in the DomainCollectionView approach section of the "Paging the Summary List" workshop.

Use the DomainCollectionView collection view when you encounter one of the following scenarios:

- You are using RIA Services to obtain data from the server.

- You're following the MVVM design pattern, populating controls with data by binding them to a data exposed from a view model.

Binding a Summary List to a DomainDataSource Control

In Chapter 5, you saw how you could easily wire up a DataGrid control to a DomainDataSource control and populate it with data exposed from the server via RIA Services by dragging an entity from the Data Sources tool window in Visual Studio. (See the section "Consuming Data Declaratively in XAML via the DomainDataSource Control" in Chapter 5.) In summary, you can bind a DataGrid/ListBox control to a DomainDataSource control by binding the DataGrid/ListBox's ItemsSource property to the DomainDataSource control's Data property using ElementName binding, as follows:

```
<riaControls:DomainDataSource Name="productSummaryDDS"
                    AutoLoad="True"
                    QueryName="GetProductSummaryList"
                    LoadedData="productSummaryDDS_LoadedData">
    <riaControls:DomainDataSource.DomainContext>
        <my:ProductSummaryContext />
    </riaControls:DomainDataSource.DomainContext>
</riaControls:DomainDataSource>

<sdk:DataGrid ItemsSource="{Binding ElementName=productSummaryDDS, Path=Data}" />
```

■ **Note** Populating a view with data from the server by binding controls to a DomainDataSource control is an easy way to prototype an application or get a simple application up and running quickly. However, when it comes to building robust applications, you are generally better off avoiding this approach and obtain data via the DomainCollectionView collection view instead.

Binding a Summary List to a View Model Class

As a best practice, each view will have a "view model" class that will expose data to it, which the view can bind to. This is a key concept in the MVVM design pattern, which will be discussed in depth in Chapter 13. In the meantime, you should still start getting familiar with coding in this manner now, even if you don't understand all the MVVM design pattern concepts yet.

The Basic Process

The process of creating a simple "view model" class and binding your view to it is really quite a straight-forward process. Let's say you have a view named ProductListView. Commonly, you'll have a corresponding view model class named ProductListViewModel, which will contain all or most of the logic for the ProductListView view. Most view logic should go into this class instead of being written in the code-behind. The view model class will expose data (via properties) and operations (generally via commands) to the view. An instance of the view model class can then be assigned to its DataContext property, enabling controls in the view to bind to its properties.

■ **Note** Generally, your view model class will inherit from a base view model class that provides logic commonly implemented by view model classes. However, for now we're keeping things simple; we'll look at creating a base view model class in Chapter 13.

⚙ Workshop: Creating and Binding to the View Model Class

Now that you understand the basic concept of binding a view to a view model, let's look at how you do this in practice.

1. In the DataGrid/ListBox workshops earlier in this chapter, we (re)created a view named ProductListView.xaml. If you haven't done one of these workshops, do so now, as we'll be using this view and the DataGrid/ListBox control that we configured to display our summary list.

2. Create a new class named ProductListViewModel in the same folder as the view (the Views folder).

```
namespace AdventureWorks.Views
{
    public class ProductListViewModel
    {
    }
}
```

3. Add the following using statements to the top of the class's file:

```
using System.Collections.Generic;
using AdventureWorks.Web.Services;
using AdventureWorks.Web.Models;
```

4. We want to expose a collection of ProductSummary entities (which we created and exposed from a domain service named ProductSummaryService in Chapter 4) from our view model, so add the following property to the class to do so:

```
public IEnumerable<ProductSummary> Products { get; set; }
```

5. We need to populate this collection with data from the server. For now, we'll use the ProductSummaryContext domain context to get the complete list of ProductSummary entities from the server. Create a constructor for the class that loads the data and assigns the results to the property, like so:

```
public ProductListViewModel()
{
    var context = new ProductSummaryContext();
    var qry = context.GetProductSummaryListQuery();
    var op = context.Load(qry);
    Products = op.Entities;
}
```

6. Your entire class should be as follows:

```
using System.Collections.Generic;
using AdventureWorks.Web.Services;
using AdventureWorks.Web.Models;

namespace AdventureWorks.Views
{
    public class ProductListViewModel
    {
        public IEnumerable<ProductSummary> Products { get; set; }

        public ProductListViewModel()
        {
            ProductSummaryContext context = new ProductSummaryContext();
            var qry = context.GetProductSummaryListQuery();
            var op = context.Load(qry);
            Products = op.Entities;
        }
    }
}
```

■ **Note** The preceding example demonstrates using RIA Services to access data from the server, but it is equally applicable to whatever approach you might be using. Simply populate the collection with data using your chosen approach.

7. Your view model class is now ready for use by the view. In the view's constructor (in the code-behind), create an instance of the view model class and assign it to the view's `DataContext` property, as follows:

```
public ProductListView()
{
    InitializeComponent();

    this.DataContext = new ProductListViewModel();
}
```

■ **Note** You can actually instantiate the `ProductListViewModel` class and assign it to the view's `DataContext` property declaratively in XAML. For now, however, we'll do this in the code-behind, as doing so in XAML adds some complexity, such as checks for design-time/runtime mode, and so on. We look at how you can instantiate an object and assign it to the view's `DataContext` property declaratively in XAML in Chapter 13.

---

8. We can now bind controls in our view to this view model. For example, we can bind the `ItemsSource` property of a `DataGrid` control to the `Products` property on the view model, like so:

```
<sdk:DataGrid ItemsSource="{Binding Products}" />
```

9. Run your application, and navigate to the `ProductListView.xaml` view. The summary list control will be populated with all the records from the server.

Wrapping the Collection in a Collection View

As you've seen, wrapping a collection in a collection view allows you to display a filtered, sorted, grouped, and paged "view" of the collection without actually modifying the collection. In the previous workshop, the summary list consumed the collection directly, but let's now wrap it in a collection view so we can manipulate the display of the collection in the view. We'll look at how you wrap a collection using each of the collection views detailed earlier. (See those definitions for when you should use each type of collection view.)

⚙ Workshop: Using the CollectionViewSource Class

As you previously saw, the `CollectionViewSource` collection view proxy allows you to wrap a collection in a collection view declaratively in XAML. Let's use it to wrap the `Products` collection exposed by our view model.

1. Add a resources element to the `ProductListView` view's root element, like so:

```
<navigation:Page.Resources>

</navigation:Page.Resources>
```

2. Define a CollectionViewSource resource for the view, named productCollectionView, and bind its Source property to the Products collection on our view model, as follows:

```
<navigation:Page.Resources>
    <CollectionViewSource x:Key="productCollectionView" Source="{Binding Products}" />
</navigation:Page.Resources>
```

3. Now bind the summary list's ItemsSource property to this resource, like this:

```
<sdk:DataGrid ItemsSource="{Binding Source={StaticResource productCollectionView}}" />
```

4. Now run your application. The summary list should be populated as normal. We'll look at how to filter, sort, and group this data using the collection view in later workshops.

■ **Note** You might have noted that the collection view is being exposed from the CollectionViewSource class's View property, but we're not explicitly binding to its View property. This is because the binding engine recognizes that it is binding to a CollectionViewSource, and assumes that it's not the CollectionViewSource itself that you want to bind to, so it automatically drills down to its View property and binds to that instead. The CollectionViewSource essentially becomes transparent when binding to it, such that you are binding to the collection view that it exposes, rather than the CollectionViewSource itself. You can turn off this View property drilling behavior for the CollectionViewSource by setting the BindsDirectlyToSource property on the property bindings to True.

Workshop: Wrapping Data in a PagedCollectionView

To wrap a collection in a PagedCollectionView, you will need to do so in code. Therefore, we'll need to wrap the collection in a PagedCollectionView inside our view model, and expose it as a property from the view model to which the summary list can bind. Let's use it to wrap the Products collection exposed by our view model.

1. Add a reference to the System.Windows.Data.dll assembly to your project.

2. Add the following using statement to the top of the ProductListViewModel class's file:

```
using System.Windows.Data;
```

3. Add a new property to the ProductListViewModel class, named ProductCollectionView, of type PagedCollectionView, like so:

```
public PagedCollectionView ProductCollectionView { get; set; }
```

4. Now wrap the collection in a PagedCollectionView in the view model's constructor, and assign the result to the ProductCollectionView property, as follows:

```
public ProductListViewModel()
{
    ProductSummaryContext context = new ProductSummaryContext();
    var qry = context.GetProductSummaryListQuery();
```

```
var op = context.Load(qry);
Products = op.Entities;

ProductCollectionView = new PagedCollectionView(Products);
}
```

5. In the ProductListView.xaml view, we can now bind the summary list's ItemsSource property to the ProductCollectionView property on the view model, like this:

```
<sdk:DataGrid ItemsSource="{Binding ProductCollectionView}" />
```

6. Now run your application. The summary list should be populated as normal. We'll look at how to filter, sort, group, and page this data using the collection view in later workshops.

⚙ Workshop: Obtaining Data via a DomainCollectionView

Like the PagedCollectionView, you will need to configure the DomainCollectionView in code. We'll do this inside our view model, and expose it as a property from the view model to which the summary list can bind. Let's use it to expose a collection of ProductSummary entities from the server from our view model.

1. Ensure that you have the WCF RIA Services Toolkit (discussed in Chapter 4) installed, and add a reference to the Microsoft.Windows.Data.DomainServices.dll to your Silverlight project.

2. Add the following using statements to the top of the ProductListViewModel class's file:

```
using System.ServiceModel.DomainServices.Client;
using Microsoft.Windows.Data.DomainServices;
```

3. Add a new property to the ProductListViewModel class, named ProductCollectionView, of type DomainCollectionView, like so:

```
public DomainCollectionView ProductCollectionView { get; set; }
```

4. Add the following field to your view model class:

```
private ProductSummaryContext _context = new ProductSummaryContext();
```

Since filtering/sorting/grouping/paging the data in the DomainCollectionView will each result in a request to the server, this will maintain a single instance of the domain context for use by each request.

5. Add the following two methods to your view model class:

```
private LoadOperation<ProductSummary> LoadProductSummaryList()
{
    EntityQuery<ProductSummary> query = _context.GetProductSummaryListQuery();
    return _context.Load(query);
}

private void OnLoadProductSummaryListCompleted(LoadOperation<ProductSummary> op)
{
    if (op.HasError)
    {
```

```
        // NOTE: You should add some logic for handling errors here, and mark
        //       the error as handled.
        // op.MarkErrorAsHandled();
    }
    else if (!op.IsCanceled)
    {
        ((EntityList<ProductSummary>)Products).Source = op.Entities;
    }
}
```

The LoadProductSummaryList method performs the request to the server (via the domain context) for data, and the OnLoadProductSummaryListCompleted method populates the source collection with the entities returned from the server. Note that the OnLoadProductSummaryListCompleted method should contain some logic for handling errors (as per the comment), but for the purpose of this workshop, we'll leave exceptions unhandled.

6. Clear the contents of the view model's constructor, and add the following code (in bold) to it:

```
public ProductListViewModel()
{
    Products = new EntityList<ProductSummary>(_context.ProductSummaries);

    var collectionViewLoader = new DomainCollectionViewLoader<ProductSummary>(
            LoadProductSummaryList, OnLoadProductSummaryListCompleted);

    ProductCollectionView =
        new DomainCollectionView<ProductSummary>(collectionViewLoader, Products);

    ProductCollectionView.Refresh();
}
```

The preceding code creates a new EntityList<ProductSummary> collection and sets its backing entity set to that exposed from the domain context. It then instantiates the loader object, passing it delegates to the load and load completed methods we created in the previous step. We then instantiate the DomainCollectionView object, passing its constructor the loader and the source collection, connecting the three together. Finally, we call the Refresh method on the DomainCollectionView, which will make it ask the loader to populate the source collection with data from the server.

7. In the ProductListView.xaml view, we can now bind the summary list's ItemsSource property to the ProductCollectionView property on the view model, like so:

```
<sdk:DataGrid ItemsSource="{Binding ProductCollectionView}" />
```

8. Now run your application. The summary list should be populated as normal. We'll look at how to filter, sort, group, and page this data using the collection view in later workshops.

Manipulating Summary List's Contents

Displaying a summary list is one thing, but it only partly fulfills the objective of helping the user find the record(s) that they are after. This is particularly relevant when the list contains many items, especially if they aren't sorted in such a manner to help the user in this task. Therefore, summary lists typically provide a number of data manipulation actions that the user can apply to the list in order to browse it more efficiently, including the following:

- Filtering
- Sorting
- Grouping
- Paging

In this section, we'll look at how you implement each of these data manipulation actions for each of the key scenarios we're addressing in this chapter—that is, when you are using the DomainDataSource control to consume data from the server, when you use the CollectionViewSource collection view proxy to wrap a client-side collection declaratively in XAML, when you wrap a client-side collection in a PagedCollectionView in code, and when you use the DomainCollectionView to consume data from the server via RIA Services in an MVVM-friendly manner.

■ **Note** The DomainDataSource/DomainCollectionView approaches detailed here request the data manipulation to be performed on the server, while the CollectionViewSource/PagedCollectionView approaches use a client-based means of manipulating the data. Performing the data manipulation on the server is extremely useful when you don't have or don't want the entire summary list returned to the client, such as when you want to page the list. When the client has only a subset of the full list, such as when paging is implemented, any filtering/sorting/grouping actually needs to be performed on the server so that the given action can be applied to the entire list, as it will often affect which records will appear in the current page.

⚙ Workshop: Filtering the Summary List

Let's enable the user to filter the summary list by product name, as shown in Figure 6-7. We'll implement this feature so that as the user types the text, the list will automatically filter the list's contents, displaying only the products whose name contains the text that the user has entered into the text box. As you can see in Figure 6-7, the user has searched for "chain," with the list displaying the five items whose name starts with "chain" as a result.

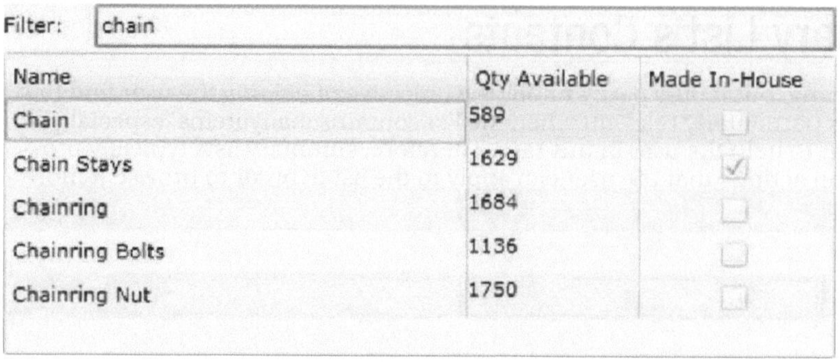

Figure 6-7. *A summary list with a filter*

1. Add a TextBox control to the view into which the user can enter some text to filter the list, and set its name to SearchTextBox, as follows:

```
<Grid>
    <Grid.RowDefinitions>
        <RowDefinition Height="30" />
        <RowDefinition Height="*" />
    </Grid.RowDefinitions>

    <Grid>
        <Grid.ColumnDefinitions>
            <ColumnDefinition Width="Auto" />
            <ColumnDefinition Width="*" />
        </Grid.ColumnDefinitions>

        <TextBlock Text="Filter: " VerticalAlignment="Center" />
        <TextBox Name="SearchTextBox" Grid.Column="1" Margin="0, 3" />
    </Grid>

    <sdk:DataGrid Name="productsDataGrid" Grid.Row="1" />
</Grid>
```

2. Now follow one of the approaches described in the following sections, using the approach that corresponds to your scenario, to actually filter the list to only those items that contain the text entered into this text box.

DomainDataSource Approach

The FilterDescriptors property on the DomainDataSource control enables you to add a new FilterDescriptor object specifying the property to filter the list by (PropertyPath), bind to the Text property of a TextBox containing the search text (Value), and provide an operator for how the comparison will be performed (Operator).

1. Add the following code (in bold) to the DomainDataSource control to filter the items to only those whose Name property contains the text entered into the text box named SearchTextBox, as follows:

```
<riaControls:DomainDataSource AutoLoad="True" Height="0" Width="0"
                              LoadedData="productSummaryDDS_LoadedData"
```

```
                         Name="productSummaryDDS"
                         QueryName="GetProductSummaryListQuery">
    <riaControls:DomainDataSource.DomainContext>
        <my:ProductSummaryContext />
    </riaControls:DomainDataSource.DomainContext>

    <riaControls:DomainDataSource.FilterDescriptors>
        <riaControls:FilterDescriptor PropertyPath="Name"
                        Operator="Contains"
                        Value="{Binding ElementName=SearchTextBox, Path=Text}" />
    </riaControls:DomainDataSource.FilterDescriptors>
</riaControls:DomainDataSource>
```

2. Now run your application. As you enter text into the search text box, the summary list will dynamically filter itself accordingly, with the filtering being performed on the server.

■ **Note** In the preceding example, we are using the `Contains` operator, so that the query will match on any part of the product name, with the user not needing to know the entire name of the product in order to get a match. This is great for the user but doesn't allow the database engine on the server to make use of the column index (if it has one) to perform the search, making the search much slower, and putting more strain on the database server. If you find that your database is struggling, you might be better off using the `StartsWith` operator instead, which will be able to use the index. However, this will return only products whose name starts with the given search text.

CollectionViewSource Approach

To filter the items in the collection created by the `CollectionViewSource` collection view proxy, you need to assign a handler to its `Filter` event, which will be called for each item in the source collection when the collection view is loaded or refreshed. Sadly, this means that you have to write code to filter items with a `CollectionViewSource`, despite its key benefit being that you can use it to wrap a collection in a collection view solely in XAML, without the need for code. Even more code needs to be written if you want to rerun the filter after the collection view has been created, such as in response to user input in the search text box we created earlier.

The filter works by calling the event handler for each item in the source collection, where you can have logic determining whether the item passes the filter or not. If it does, the `Accept` property on the `FilterEventArgs` object passed into the event handler should be set to true, or false if it does not.

Let's implement filtering using the `CollectionViewSource` now.

1. Earlier in this chapter, you defined a `CollectionViewSource` as a resource, and used it to wrap the `Products` collection on your view model class in a collection view. Assign an event handler to its `Filter` event, like so:

```
<navigation:Page.Resources>
    <CollectionViewSource x:Key="productCollectionView" Source="{Binding Products}"
                        Filter="productCollectionView_Filter" />
</navigation:Page.Resources>
```

2. In the code-behind for the view, define the corresponding event handler method, as follows:

```
private void productCollectionView_Filter(object sender, FilterEventArgs e)
{

}
```

3. Add the following using statement to the top of the view's code-behind file:

```
using System.Windows.Data;
using AdventureWorks.Web.Models;
```

4. We want to filter the collection view to those items whose Name property contains the text entered in the SearchTextBox text box. Therefore, add the following code to the event handler:

```
private void productCollectionView_Filter(object sender, FilterEventArgs e)
{
    e.Accepted = ((ProductSummary)e.Item).Name.IndexOf(SearchTextBox.Text,
                          StringComparison.InvariantCultureIgnoreCase) != -1;
}
```

5. We now need to refresh the collection view whenever the user changes the text in the SearchTextBox text box. Assign an event handler to its TextChanged event, like so:

```
<TextBox Name="SearchTextBox" Grid.Column="1" Margin="0, 3"
         TextChanged="SearchTextBox_TextChanged" />
```

6. In the code-behind for the view, define the corresponding event handler method, as follows:

```
private void SearchTextBox_TextChanged(object sender, TextChangedEventArgs e)
{

}
```

7. In this event handler, we need to get a reference to the CollectionViewSource resource, and call the Refresh method on the collection view exposed from its View property in order to rerun the filter, like so:

```
private void SearchTextBox_TextChanged(object sender, TextChangedEventArgs e)
{
    var cvs = this.Resources["productCollectionView"] as CollectionViewSource;
    cvs.View.Refresh();
}
```

8. Now run your application. As you enter text into the search text box, the summary list will dynamically filter itself accordingly.

PagedCollectionView Approach

To filter the items in a PagedCollectionView, you need to assign a callback method to its Filter property, which will be called for each item in the source collection when you call the Refresh method on the PagedCollectionView. An item will be passed into the method, and the method should return true if the item passes the filter, false if it does not. Alternatively, you can implement this same result by simply applying a lambda expression that returns a Boolean to the PagedCollectionView's Filter property, which tends to be a neater solution. This is what we'll do in this workshop.

You basically need configure the filter when you create the PagedCollectionView, and then call its Refresh method whenever you want the filter to be executed. In this workshop, we'll create a SearchText property on our view model class that the search text box in the user interface can bind to. We'll then configure a filter on the PagedCollectionView, right after it's instantiated, that will display only the items whose name contains the text assigned to the SearchText property, and when the SearchText property is changed, we'll refresh the PagedCollectionView to execute the filter so that the summary list will display only the items matching the filter.

1. Add the following code for the SearchText property to your view model class. (Note how it's calling the ProductCollectionView collection view's Refresh method when its value is changed to rerun the filter.)

```
private string _searchText = "";

public string SearchText
{
    get { return _searchText; }
    set
    {
        _searchText = value;
        ProductCollectionView.Refresh();
    }
}
```

2. In the view model class's constructor, specify the filter for the ProductCollectionView collection view immediately after it has been instantiated. In this code, we're filtering the items to just those whose Name property contains the text assigned to the SearchText property on the view model class, using a case-insensitive comparison, as follows:

```
ProductCollectionView = new PagedCollectionView(Products);
ProductCollectionView.Filter = item =>
    ((ProductSummary)item).Name.IndexOf(SearchText,
                                StringComparison.InvariantCultureIgnoreCase) != -1;
```

■ **Note** You have to cast the function argument (item) to the type of object contained in the collection, as the PagedCollectionView collection is not restricted to your object type (i.e., any type of object can be added to the collection), so the argument being passed in (item) is of type object, not ProductSummary.

---

3. In the ProductListView.xaml view, you can now bind the SearchTextBox text box to the SearchText property on our view model class. Note how we are setting the binding's Mode property to TwoWay so that when the user enters text into the text box, the SearchText property on the view model class will be updated accordingly. In addition, we're setting the binding's UpdateSourceTrigger property to PropertyChanged. The PropertyChanged option is new in Silverlight 5, and its effect is to update the bound property immediately whenever the text is

changed instead of only when the TextBox control loses focus. This results in a much nicer search experience for the user.

```
<TextBox Name="SearchTextBox" Grid.Column="1" Margin="0, 3"
         Text="{Binding SearchText, Mode=TwoWay, UpdateSourceTrigger=PropertyChanged}" />
```

4. Now run your application. As you enter text into the search text box, the summary list will dynamically filter itself accordingly.

DomainCollectionView Approach

Like the PagedCollectionView, the DomainCollectionView has a Filter property to which you can assign a callback method that implements filtering logic. However, this filters only the items on the client, whereas you will generally want to implement server-side filtering when using the DomainCollectionView, and have only the items satisfying the filter returned from the server. We can, however, apply a Where clause to the query that we pass to the server as part of the loader's logic.

Similar to the previous workshop for the PagedCollectionView, in this workshop, we'll create a SearchText property on our view model class that the search text box in the user interface can bind to. We'll then apply a Where clause to the query that's used to request data from the server, which will request only the items whose name contains the text assigned to the SearchText property from the server. When the SearchText property is changed, we'll refresh the DomainCollectionView to load the items matching the filter from the server, and display them in the summary list.

1. Add the following code for the SearchText property to your view model class. (Note how it's calling the ProductCollectionView collection view's Refresh method when its value is changed to rerun the filter.)

```
private string _searchText = "";

public string SearchText
{
    get { return _searchText; }
    set
    {
        _searchText = value;
        ProductCollectionView.Refresh();
    }
}
```

2. In the LoadProductSummaryList method in your view model class, add the Where clause to the query before passing it onto the domain context's Load method. The Where clause in this example filters the items to just those whose Name property contains the text assigned to the SearchText property on the view model class, using a case-insensitive comparison, like so:

```
private LoadOperation<ProductSummary> LoadProductSummaryList()
{
    EntityQuery<ProductSummary> query = _context.GetProductSummaryListQuery();
    query = query.Where(x => x.Name.Contains(_searchText));
    return _context.Load(query);
}
```

■ **Note** The previous two workshops used the string class's IndexOf method to perform the comparison, but in this workshop we're using the Contains method instead. This is because LINQ to Entities on the server cannot translate the IndexOf method to a SQL query expression. We didn't use the Contains method in the previous workshops, as it doesn't provide the means to perform a case-insensitive comparison in Silverlight. However, when the Contains method is translated to a LINQ to Entities expression, the expression is actually performed by the database as a case-insensitive comparison, which is exactly what we need.

3. In the ProductListView.xaml view, you can now bind the SearchTextBox text box to the SearchText property on our view model class. As detailed in the previous workshop for the PagedCollectionView, we are setting the binding's Mode property to TwoWay, and setting the binding's UpdateSourceTrigger property to PropertyChanged.

```
<TextBox Name="SearchTextBox" Grid.Column="1" Margin="0, 3"
    Text="{Binding SearchText, Mode=TwoWay, UpdateSourceTrigger=PropertyChanged}" />
```

4. Now run your application. As you enter text into the search text box, the summary list will dynamically filter itself accordingly, with the filtering being performed on the server.

⚙ Workshop: Sorting the Summary List

If you are using the DataGrid to display the summary list, you'll note that it contains its own action to enable the user to initiate a sorting action (i.e., clicking a column header). It also sorts its contents accordingly with no code required, including automatically refreshing its data from the server when bound to a DomainDataSource control or a DomainCollectionView, assuming you apply the state of the DomainCollectionView to the server query, as will be covered in the DomainCollectionView workshop shortly. If you are using a different control to display the data, you will need to implement your own mechanism to enable the user to specify how they want the list to be sorted. In this workshop, we'll look at how you can specify that the summary list should be sorted by the Name property on the ProductSummary entities. If you're using the DataGrid control to display the data, you'll also be able to change the sorting of the summary list at runtime by clicking on a column header.

DomainDataSource Approach

The SortDescriptors property on the DomainDataSource control enables you to add sort criteria by adding SortDescriptor objects to the collection, specifying the property to sort the list by (PropertyPath) and the direction to sort by (Direction).

1. Add the following code (in bold) to the DomainDataSource control to sort the entities by their Name property, in ascending order:

```
<riaControls:DomainDataSource AutoLoad="True" Height="0" Width="0"
                    LoadedData="productSummaryDDS_LoadedData"
                    Name="productSummaryDDS"
                    QueryName="GetProductSummaryListQuery">
```

```
<riaControls:DomainDataSource.DomainContext>
    <my:ProductSummaryContext />
</riaControls:DomainDataSource.DomainContext>

<riaControls:DomainDataSource.SortDescriptors>
    <riaControls:SortDescriptor PropertyPath="Name" Direction="Ascending" />
</riaControls:DomainDataSource.SortDescriptors>
</riaControls:DomainDataSource>
```

2. Now run your application. The products will be sorted by their name. Note that you can specify multiple sort descriptors by adding additional SortDescriptor objects to the DomainDataSource control's SortDescriptors property, as required.

■ **Note** If you bind a DataGrid to the DomainDataSource control, whenever the user clicks a column header in the DataGrid it will automatically update the sort descriptors on the DomainDataSource control to sort by that column and requery the server for the reordered list. It requires the server to be requeried because, if the results are paged, the results to be displayed in the page will likely be different than the current set of items. Therefore, the sort operation must be performed on the server against the entire set of results, before returning the new results for the current page.

CollectionViewSource Approach

The SortDescriptions property on the CollectionViewSource collection view proxy enables you to sort rows in the summary list. Simply add SortDescription objects to the collection, specifying the property to sort the items by (PropertyName) and the direction in which they should be sorted (Direction).

1. Add the following namespace prefix definition to the root element in the view's XAML file:

```
xmlns:scm="clr-namespace:System.ComponentModel;assembly=System.Windows"
```

2. Add the following code (in bold) to the CollectionViewSource resource to sort the entities by their Name property, in ascending order:

```
<CollectionViewSource x:Key="productCollectionView" Source="{Binding Products}">
    <CollectionViewSource.SortDescriptions>
        <scm:SortDescription PropertyName="Name" Direction="Ascending" />
    </CollectionViewSource.SortDescriptions>
</CollectionViewSource>
```

3. Now run your application. The products will be sorted by their name. Note that you can specify multiple sort descriptions by adding additional SortDescription objects to the CollectionViewSource's SortDescriptions property, as required.

PagedCollectionView Approach

To sort the items in a PagedCollectionView, simply instantiate a SortDescription object, passing it the property to sort the collection by and a sort direction, and then add it to the PagedCollectionView's SortDescriptions collection property.

1. Add the following using statement to the top of your view model class file:

```
using System.ComponentModel;
```

2. After instantiating the PagedCollectionView, use the following code (in bold) to sort the collection by the Name property of each item (in ascending order):

```
ProductCollectionView = new PagedCollectionView(Products);
SortDescription sortBy = new SortDescription("Name", ListSortDirection.Ascending);
ProductCollectionView.SortDescriptions.Add(sortBy);
```

3. Now run your application. The products will be sorted by their name. Note that you can specify multiple sort descriptions by adding additional SortDescription objects to the PagedCollectionView's SortDescriptions property, as required.

DomainCollectionView Approach

Sorting the items in a DomainCollectionView is performed in exactly the same manner as for the PagedCollectionView. Simply instantiate a SortDescription object, passing it the property to sort the collection by and a sort direction, and then add it to the DomainCollectionView's SortDescriptions collection property.

1. Add the following using statement to the top of your view model class file:

```
using System.ComponentModel;
```

2. After instantiating the DomainCollectionView, use the following code (in bold) to sort the collection by the Name property of each item (in ascending order):

```
ProductCollectionView =
    new DomainCollectionView<ProductSummary>(collectionViewLoader, Products);
SortDescription sortBy = new SortDescription("Name", ListSortDirection.Ascending);
ProductCollectionView.SortDescriptions.Add(sortBy);
```

3. Now run your application. The products will be sorted by their name. Note that you can specify multiple sort descriptions by adding additional SortDescription objects to the DomainCollectionView's SortDescriptions property, as required. As with the DomainDataSource control, if you bind a DataGrid to the DomainDataSource control, whenever the user clicks a column header in the DataGrid, the sort descriptors on the DomainCollectionView will be updated to sort by that column, and the DomainCollectionView will automatically ask the loader to requery the server for the reordered list.

■ **Note** The preceding operation performs the sorting of the items on the client. If you're paging the summary list on the server, you'll want the sorting to actually be performed on the server so that the correct set of sorted results are included in the page. See the `DomainCollectionView` approach section of the "Paging the Summary List" workshop later in this chapter, for how you implement this behavior.

⚙ Workshop: Grouping the Summary List

Grouping is a feature often required in business applications. It essentially enables you to group related data together and display that data under a heading in the list. Often, this extends beyond a single level of grouping to two or even more levels. As discussed earlier in this chapter, the `DataGrid` has built-in grouping functionality, as shown in Figure 6-8, but the `ListBox` has none at all. Data can be sorted in the `ListBox`, but not under headers separating record groups, so the `ListBox` isn't really applicable in this scenario. For the purpose of this workshop, we'll assume that you're using the `DataGrid` control to display the data. We'll group the product summary entities by their `Model` property.

Name	Qty Available	Made In-House
⊿ Model: ML Mountain Tire (1 item)		▲
ML Mountain Tire	669	☐
⊿ Model: ML Road Frame (5 items)		
ML Road Frame - Red, 44		☑
ML Road Frame - Red, 48		☑
ML Road Frame - Red, 52		☑
ML Road Frame - Red, 58		☑
ML Road Frame - Red, 60		☑
⊿ Model: ML Road Frame-W (5 items)		
ML Road Frame-W - Yellow, 40		☑
ML Road Frame-W - Yellow, 42		☑
ML Road Frame-W - Yellow, 44		☑

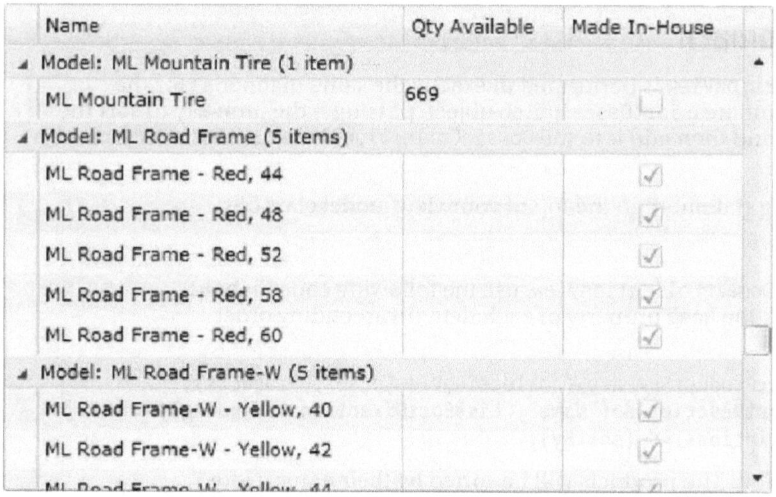

Figure 6-8. Grouped items in a DataGrid control

DomainDataSource Approach

The `GroupDescriptors` property on the `DomainDataSource` control enables you to add a new `GroupDescriptor` object specifying the property to group the list by (`PropertyPath`).

1. Add the following code (in bold) to the `DomainDataSource` control to group the entities by their `Model` property:

```
<riaControls:DomainDataSource AutoLoad="True" Height="0" Width="0"
                              LoadedData="productSummaryDS_LoadedData"
                              Name="productSummaryDDS"
```

```
                              QueryName="GetProductSummaryListQuery">
  <riaControls:DomainDataSource.DomainContext>
      <my:ProductSummaryContext />
  </riaControls:DomainDataSource.DomainContext>

  <riaControls:DomainDataSource.GroupDescriptors>
      <riaControls:GroupDescriptor PropertyPath="Model" />
  </riaControls:DomainDataSource.GroupDescriptors>
</riaControls:DomainDataSource>
```

2. Now run your application. The products will be grouped in the DataGrid by
    their model. Note that you can specify multiple sort descriptors by adding
    additional GroupDescriptor objects to the DomainDataSource control's
    GroupDescriptors property, as required.

CollectionViewSource Approach

The GroupDescriptions property on the CollectionViewSource collection view proxy enables you to
group rows in the summary list. Simply add PropertyGroupDescription objects to the collection, specifying the property to group the items by (PropertyName).

1. Add the following code (in bold) to the CollectionViewSource resource to
    group the entities by their Model property:

```
<CollectionViewSource x:Key="productCollectionView" Source="{Binding Products}">
    <CollectionViewSource.GroupDescriptions>
        <PropertyGroupDescription PropertyName="Model" />
    </CollectionViewSource.GroupDescriptions>
</CollectionViewSource>
```

2. Now run your application. The products will be grouped in the DataGrid by
    their model. Note that you can specify multiple group descriptions by adding
    additional GroupDescription objects to the CollectionViewSource's
    GroupDescriptions, property as required.

PagedCollectionView Approach

To group the items in a PagedCollectionView, simply instantiate a PropertyGroupDescription, passing it
the property to group the collection by, and then add it to the PagedCollectionView's GroupDescriptions
collection property.

1. Add the following using statement to the top of your view model class file:

```
using System.Windows.Data;
```

2. After instantiating the PagedCollectionView, use the following code (in bold) to
    sort the collection by the Name property of each item (in ascending order):

```
ProductCollectionView = new PagedCollectionView(Products);
PropertyGroupDescription groupBy = new PropertyGroupDescription("Model");
ProductCollectionView.GroupDescriptions.Add(groupBy);
```

3. Now run your application. The products will be grouped in the DataGrid by their model. Note that you can specify multiple group descriptions by adding additional PropertyGroupDescription objects to the PagedCollectionView's GroupDescriptions property, as required.

■ **Note** You can also supply a value converter as a parameter to the constructor of the PropertyGroupDescription object to convert the property value before it is grouped. This is particularly useful in scenarios where you want to group by a property that is a foreign key to data located elsewhere, such as in another collection. For example, say you want to group the products by category, but the product object only contains an ID representing the category, not its name. You could group it by ID, but the ID would appear in the group header instead of the category name. You would, generally, also want the groups sorted alphabetically by category name rather than category ID. This feature enables you to write a value converter that converts the category ID into a category name, assuming you have a collection of category names and their corresponding IDs on the client, and use the output value of this converter as the value to display as the item's group. Value converters are discussed in Chapter 11.

DomainCollectionView Approach

Grouping the items in a DomainCollectionView is performed in exactly the same manner as for the PagedCollectionView. Simply instantiate a PropertyGroupDescription object, passing it the property to group the collection by, and then add it to the DomainCollectionView's GroupDescriptions collection property.

1. Add the following using statement to the top of your view model class file:

```
using System.Windows.Data;
```

2. After instantiating the DomainCollectionView, use the following code (in bold) to group the collection by the Model property of each item in ascending order:

```
ProductCollectionView =
        new DomainCollectionView<ProductSummary>(collectionViewLoader, Products);
PropertyGroupDescription groupBy = new PropertyGroupDescription("Model");
ProductCollectionView.GroupDescriptions.Add(groupBy);
```

3. Now run your application. The products will be grouped in the DataGrid by their model. Note that you can specify multiple group descriptions by adding additional PropertyGroupDescription objects to the DomainCollectionView's GroupDescriptions property, as required.

■ **Note** The preceding operation performs the grouping of the items on the client. If you're paging the summary list on the server, you'll want the grouping to be performed on the server so that the correct set of results are included in the page. See the `DomainCollectionView` approach section of the "Paging the Summary List" workshop later in this chapter, for how you implement this behavior.

⚙ Workshop: Paging the Summary List

When you have hundreds or even thousands of records in the summary list, generally, you don't want to display the complete list to the user. Not only does it overwhelm and confuse the user, but it also consumes excessive memory. In addition, if the data needs to be retrieved from the server, loading the entire list will result in excess network traffic and will require the user to wait for all the data to be downloaded from the server before they can see it, slowing down your application, and making it less responsive. If you have or anticipate a large number of records in the list, paging the items will help solve these issues. Paging data displays only a small subset of the full list, and the user can navigate between pages as required. If the full list is located on the server, navigating between pages should query the server for the new page of data to display

To help implement paging in your user interface, Silverlight has a `DataPager` control, as shown in Figure 6-9, that keeps track of the current page number, and provides an interface to enable the user to navigate backward and forward through the pages. Declaring a `DataPager` control in XAML is as simple as the following:

```
<sdk:DataPager PageSize="30" Source="{Binding Products}" />
```

You simply set its page size to the number of items/rows to appear in each page, and bind its `Source` property to the collection to be paged. The control handles the rest. When bound to a collection view, the `DataPager` control will request each page of data from the collection view, which then handles the paging logic.

The `DataPager` control supports different display modes—with options such as a page number button for each page, first and last buttons plus page number buttons, first/previous/next/last buttons, and so on—which you can specify using its `DisplayMode` property. It also has an `IsTotalItemCountFixed` property that, if set to `True`, will stop the user from navigating beyond the calculated number of pages by disabling the Next button. If set to `false`, it will keep the Next button enabled even when the last page is reached, which is useful when the list could have an uncertain or rapidly changing size.

■ **Note** When querying the server for paged data, the data must be sorted, with an `OrderBy` clause in the query, in order to be paged. Otherwise, you will get an error message stating that "The method 'Skip' is only supported for sorted input in LINQ to Entities" when you attempt to load any pages after the first.

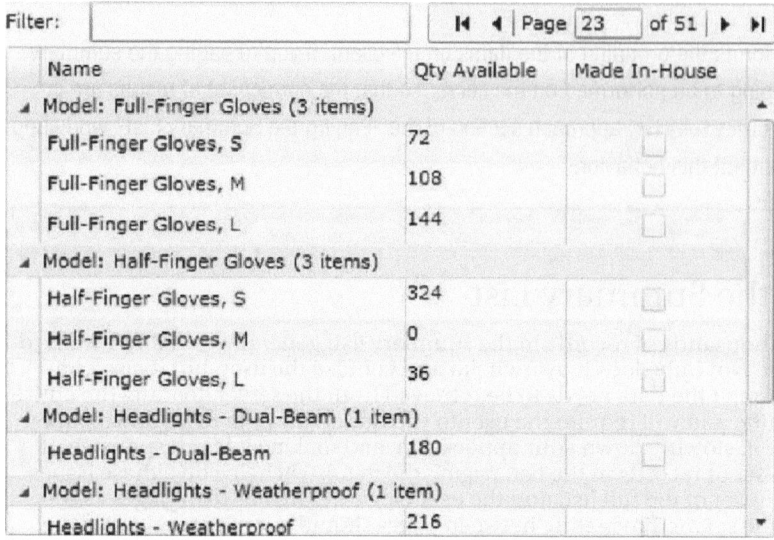

Figure 6-9. *A summary list with an associated DataPager control*

Let's add paging support to the summary list now.

1. Make sure you have the following namespace prefix declared in the root element in the view's XAML file. If not, add it now.

```
xmlns:sdk="http://schemas.microsoft.com/winfx/2006/xaml/presentation/sdk"
```

2. Add a DataPager control to your view, and set its page size to 30, like so:

```
<Grid>
    <Grid.RowDefinitions>
        <RowDefinition Height="30" />
        <RowDefinition Height="*" />
    </Grid.RowDefinitions>

    <Grid>
        <Grid.ColumnDefinitions>
            <ColumnDefinition Width="Auto" />
            <ColumnDefinition Width="*" />
            <ColumnDefinition Width="*" />
        </Grid.ColumnDefinitions>

        <TextBlock Text="Filter: " VerticalAlignment="Center" />
        <TextBox Name="SearchTextBox" Grid.Column="1" Margin="0, 3" />
        <sdk:DataPager PageSize="30" Grid.Column="2"
                       VerticalAlignment="Center" Margin="3,0,0,0" />
    </Grid>

    <sdk:DataGrid Name="productsDataGrid" Grid.Row="1" />
</Grid>
```

3. Now use one of the following methods, corresponding to your scenario, to bind the Source property on the DataPager control to the source collection that the summary list is bound to, which will actually perform the paging of the list:

    •   MoveToFirstPage

    •   MoveToLastPage

    •   MoveToNextPage

    •   MoveToPreviousPage

    •   MoveToPage

You can use these methods directly on the collection view to navigate between pages (without using the DataPager control) if you wish.

■ **Note**   Only collection views that implement the IPagedCollectionView interface, such as the PagedCollectionView, DomainDataSourceView, and DomainCollectionView, support paging of the source collection. This interface requires collection views to implement a PageSize and a PageIndex property, along with the preceding methods, to navigate between pages.

DomainDataSource Approach

The DomainDataSource integrates very nicely with the DataPager control to provide server-based paging to the summary list. In fact, you don't even configure paging on the DomainDataSource control itself; instead you simply bind the Source property of the DataPager control to the DomainDataSource control's Data property, and the DomainDataSource control will automatically implement the paging behavior accordingly.

1. Bind the DataPager control's Source property to the DomainDataSource control in exactly the same way that you bind the summary list's ItemsSource property to the DomainDataSource control, like so:

```
<sdk:DataPager PageSize="30"
               Source="{Binding Data, ElementName=productSummaryDDS}" />
```

2. Now run your application. Only 30 products will be requested from the server and displayed in the summary list. As you navigate between pages, a request will be made to the server for the new page of data. If the page has already been loaded, instead of going back to the server, the DomainDataSource control will return its cached copy of the page, saving an unnecessary request to the server.

■ **Note** The DataPager provides you with another feature when used with the DomainDataSource control: setting a different number of items to be retrieved from the server than what's actually displayed in the list. For example, if users are regularly navigating through pages, it can be useful to retrieve more data from the server in a single call than is displayed in a single page. For example, you might only want to display 20 items/rows to the user at a time, but load 5 pages worth (100 items/rows) to save the user from waiting for the server to return the data for each page as they navigate through the list. The (optional) LoadSize property on the DomainDataSource control enables you to set the number of items/rows that should be retrieved from the server at a time. The PageSize property will continue to define how many items/rows are presented to the user at the one time on the client, with the additional items/rows remaining cached in the background. The DomainDataSource control will then automatically go back to the server to retrieve the next set of results when the user attempts to view a page whose items have not been retrieved yet.

CollectionViewSource Approach

The collection views created by the CollectionViewSource collection view proxy do not implement the IPagedCollectionView interface and, hence, do not support paging of data. You will need to use a PagedCollectionView instead if your summary list needs to be paged.

PagedCollectionView Approach

Paging the items/rows in a PagedCollectionView requires no work on your part when using the DataPager control. Simply bind the DataPager control to the PagedCollectionView being used as the source for your summary list, and the DataPager will tell the PagedCollectionView what page of items should appear in the list.

1. Bind the DataPager control's Source property to the ProductCollectionView property on your view model class (in exactly the same way that you bind the summary list's ItemsSource property to the collection view), like so:

```
<sdk:DataPager PageSize="30"
               Source="{Binding ProductCollectionView}" />
```

2. Now run your application. Only 30 products from the source collection will be displayed in the summary list. As you navigate between pages, a new page of items will be displayed in the summary list.

DomainCollectionView Approach

When you're implementing paging using the DomainCollectionView, you need to tell the server what page of data you want. This state is stored in the DomainCollectionView and needs to be applied to the query that's passed to the server. You will also need to apply sorting criteria to the query (with some sorting required when paging data, as mentioned earlier), with the sorting state often specified on the DomainCollectionView too.

When the user navigates between pages using the DataPager control, it will refresh the collection view. This will result in a new query to the server. It's at this point that you need to apply the state of the DomainCollectionView to the query; that is, the current page number being requested, and the sorting criteria. The WCF RIA Services Toolkit makes doing so easy, by providing some extension methods for the EntityQuery class: SortBy, PageBy, and SortAndPageBy. (These extension methods are defined in the CollectionViewExtensions class.) Generally, you will use the SortAndPageBy extension method, so that's the approach that we'll use in this workshop.

■ **Note** Paging works by telling the server to ignore all the records that belong in the previous pages, and then to take the following number of records until the page size has been reached. Let's say you have 100 records in the database and a page size of 10 items. Getting the first page is easy: you simply tell the server to take the first 10 records and ignore the rest. When getting subsequent pages, however, you need to skip as many records as the page size multiplied by the page number, take the number of records up to your page size, and then ignore the rest. To implement this functionality, you need to tell the server to skip a given number of records by applying the Skip clause to the query, and then take a given number of records by applying the Take clause to the query. When using the DomainCollectionView, the SortAndPageBy extension method does all of this for you.

---

1. Bind the DataPager control's Source property to the ProductCollectionView property on your view model class in exactly the same way that you bind the summary list's ItemsSource property to the collection view, like so:

```
<sdk:DataPager PageSize="30"
               Source="{Binding ProductCollectionView}" />
```

2. In the LoadProductSummaryList method in your view model class, apply the collection view's state to the query using the SortAndPageBy extension method on the query before passing the query to the domain context's Load method, as follows:

```
private LoadOperation<ProductSummary> LoadProductSummaryList()
{
    EntityQuery<ProductSummary> query = _context.GetProductSummaryListQuery();
    query = query.SortAndPageBy(ProductCollectionView);
    return _context.Load(query);
}
```

3. To fully implement its paging behavior, the DataPager control needs to know how many items are in the full summary list. While not essential, this allows it to calculate how many pages of data there are, and enables the move to last page button. This requires the server to tell us how many records are in the complete list, but the server does not do this calculation by default because it requires a separate query to the database, resulting in overheads due to additional work being performed by the database server. You can explicitly tell the server to calculate the total number of records by setting the IncludeTotalCount property on the query object to true, like so:

```
private LoadOperation<ProductSummary> LoadProductSummaryList()
{
```

```
    EntityQuery<ProductSummary> query = _context.GetProductSummaryListQuery();
    query = query.SortAndPageBy(ProductCollectionView);
    query.IncludeTotalCount = true;
    return _context.Load(query);
}
```

4. When the response from the server is received, you need to assign this total record count to the DomainCollectionView by calling its SetTotalItemCount property, and passing in the value returned by the server (available from the TotalEntityCount property on the LoadOperation object), like this:

```
private void OnLoadProductSummaryListCompleted(LoadOperation<ProductSummary> op)
{
    if (op.HasError)
    {
        // NOTE: You should add some logic for handling errors here
        op.MarkErrorAsHandled();
    }
    else if (!op.IsCanceled)
    {
        ((EntityList<ProductSummary>)Products).Source = op.Entities;

        if (op.TotalEntityCount != -1)
            ProductCollectionView.SetTotalItemCount(op.TotalEntityCount);
    }
}
```

5. Make sure you have set at least one sort description on the DomainCollectionView. (See the DomainCollectionView approach section of the "Sorting the Summary List" workshop for how to do this.) Otherwise, you are likely to receive exceptions when you try to navigate between pages, as discussed earlier.

6. Currently, in the constructor for the view model class, you call the Refresh method on the DomainCollectionView to tell the loader to load the data from the server. Remove this line of code, and replace it with the following code:

```
using (ProductCollectionView.DeferRefresh())
{
    ProductCollectionView.PageSize = 30;
    ProductCollectionView.MoveToFirstPage();
}
```

This sets the page size, and sets the current page number for the DomainCollectionView. Both of these actions would normally each result in a call being made to the server for data. However, we want to make only a single call, which is where the DeferRefresh method on the collection view comes in handy. By wrapping the two lines of code in a using block that "uses" an object that the DeferRefresh method creates, the DomainCollectionView will prevent any calls to the loader while this object is alive. When the using block is exited, the object will be disposed, and call the object's Dispose method. The Dispose method calls the DomainCollectionView's Refresh method, loading the data from the server.

7. Now run your application. Only 30 products from the source collection will be displayed in the summary list. As you navigate between pages, a new page of items will be requested from the server and displayed in the summary list.

■ **Note** Sometimes, when using the DomainCollectionView, you'll want to build a complex query at a time where the query object hasn't even been created yet. The WCF RIA Services Toolkit comes to the rescue again, providing the QueryBuilder class to help you with this problem. The QueryBuilder class essentially allows queries to be built without knowing anything about the EntityQuery object. To define a query using the QueryBuilder class, instantiate a QueryBuilder object with the type of entity that the query will be applied to as its generic parameter (for example, var queryBuilder = new QueryBuilder<ProductSummary>();). You can then call LINQ methods on this object as required (for example, queryBuilder = queryBuilder.Where(x => x.Name.Contains("bike");). Finally, when you come to make a call to the server, you can apply the QueryBuilder object's state to the query using the QueryBuilder class's ApplyTo method (for example, query = queryBuilder.ApplyTo(query);).

Using the BusyIndicator Control

It's always a good idea to let the user know that the application is busy retrieving or submitting data. Usually, you can do this by providing an animation that runs while the communication is being completed. You can design your own animation or take advantage of the BusyIndicator control (a part of the Silverlight Toolkit), which provides a simple message and animation for you, as shown in Figure 6-10. This control (in source form) has already been included in your project by the Silverlight Business Application project template and is implemented in the user login and registration functions.

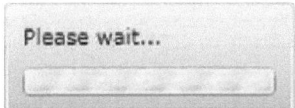

Figure 6-10. The BusyIndicator control

Displaying the BusyIndicator Control

The key property on the BusyIndicator control is the IsBusy property. Setting this to True will show the animation, and setting it to False will hide the animation. If you decide to take the XAML-based approach to consuming the data and use the DomainDataSource control in your view, you can simply bind the IsBusy property of the BusyIndicator control to the IsBusy property of the DomainDataSource control, which will be set to True when the DomainDataSource control is waiting for the server request to complete, using ElementName binding. When the property value is changed on the source control, the bound property's value will be changed accordingly. Here we want the IsBusy property of the BusyIndicator control to have the same value as the IsBusy property of the DomainDataSource control, so we bind the two control properties using the following binding syntax:

```
<controlsToolkit:BusyIndicator
    IsBusy="{Binding ElementName=productSummaryDDS, Path=IsBusy}" />
```

If you are taking an MVVM-based approach instead, you can create an IsBusy property on your view model class, and set it to true when you initiate the server request, and set it back to false in the LoadOperation's Completed event. You can then bind the IsBusy property of the BusyIndicator control to this IsBusy property on your view model class.

■ **Note** You can determine whether the DomainDataSource control is loading data or submitting changes by its IsLoadingData and IsSubmittingChanges properties, which you can use to alter the message displayed in the BusyIndicator control accordingly.

Customizing the BusyIndicator Control's Content

By default, the text reads "Please wait . . ." but you can change that to something more meaningful by assigning the text you want displayed to the BusyContent property, like so:

```
<controlsToolkit:BusyIndicator BusyContent="Retrieving products..." />
```

The BusyContent property is actually a content property, and can accept any control as its value, using the content element syntax, as discussed in Chapter 2. Therefore, this provides you with a simple means to customize the layout of the BusyIndicator control to your liking. For example, you might wish to add a button to cancel the communication, or add your own animation.

However, one thing may get in the way of you laying out the contents of the BusyIndicator control completely the way you want it: the animated bar. The animated bar is not affected by setting the content of the BusyContent property, and remains where it is. This bar is actually just a progress bar, and its style is exposed to you by the ProgressBarStyle property on the control. This means you can assign a style to modify its properties, including its Visibility property. Therefore, you can set its value to Collapsed and hide it completely if you so wish, as follows:

```
<controlsToolkit:BusyIndicator.ProgressBarStyle>
    <Style TargetType="ProgressBar">
        <Setter Property="Visibility" Value="Collapsed"/>
    </Style>
</controlsToolkit:BusyIndicator.ProgressBarStyle>
```

■ **Note** Rather than just modifying the content of the BusyIndicator control, you can completely change its look, including changing the gray gradient background, by assigning it a new control template. Control templates are covered in Chapter 9.

Modal Behavior

In addition to displaying an animation to let the user know something is happening, the `BusyIndicator` control can also be used to automatically disable an area of your user interface while the server communication is taking place. The `BusyIndicator` control inherits from `ContentControl` and, therefore, has a `Content` property that can contain other controls in the same way as the `Grid` or the `Canvas` controls can. These content controls and any other controls within the area consumed by the control will be disabled when the `IsBusy` property is set to `True`. It disables the controls by overlaying a semitransparent `Rectangle` control over its area so that they cannot be clicked. Note that if used in a `Grid`, the `BusyIndicator` control actually fills the area of its cell, and just shows the indicator in the middle. Hence, the overlay will fill the entire grid cell, overlaying any other controls within that same cell. You can modify the properties of this `Rectangle` control via the `OverlayStyle` property on the `BusyIndicator` control.

▓ **Note** Disabling user interface controls is not so important when retrieving data for summary lists, but it can be useful when you have a data entry form to stop the user from attempting to resubmit or alter the changes they've made while communicating with the server.

The DisplayAfter Property

To stop the `BusyIndicator` control from flashing on and off when a very short server call is made, or when multiple server calls are made in succession, you can control how long the control should be in the busy state before actually displaying the indicator to the user with the `DisplayAfter` property. By default it's set to 0.1 seconds, but you can change this, as required.

Drilling Down on a Record

Summary lists are generally used as a means to find and drill down on a record to get more details and/or edit the record. There are a number of approaches you can take to implement this type of behavior, including the following"

- Navigating to a details view
- Opening the details in a pop-up window
- Using the row details feature of the `DataGrid` to display the details
- Using a master/details view

Which approach you choose really depends on the workflow you are implementing. Each has its own pros and cons, and your choice will largely depend upon the user experience design for your application. In this section, we will take a look at each of these approaches and how to implement them.

Navigating to the Details View

One simple way of displaying the details of a given item is to simply create a details view, and navigate to it using the Navigation Framework. How you can initiate this behavior isn't particularly straightforward, however. You have probably implemented this type of behavior in the past by having the user double-click an item in the list, but there are no DoubleClick events in Silverlight. In fact, there's no RowClick event on the DataGrid either, nor is there an ItemClick event on the ListBox. So how can you enable the user to drill down on a record? Let's take a look at some approaches you might like to take.

■ **Note** If you still want to use a double-click behavior, you can implement it yourself using a behavior or a trigger. You can also find various double-click behaviors and triggers already created by other developers with a quick search on the Web. Behaviors are covered in Chapter 10.

If you are using a DataGrid, then you can use a template column and add a control such as a Button or HyperlinkButton to it that the user can click to navigate to the details view. Alternatively, if you are using a ListBox, then you can simply include one of these controls in your item template.

Unfortunately, the Navigation Framework doesn't allow you to pass complex objects between views. Therefore, in order to enable the details view to know which record it should load and display, you will need to pass a unique identifier to that view as a query string parameter. You could use the HyperlinkButton control, which can be configured to automatically navigate to the details view with no code required; however, it unfortunately does not have the ability to automatically include the unique identifier of the record as a parameter in the URI to navigate to the details view. Your options in this case are to either handle the HyperlinkButton's Click event in the code-behind and build the URI to navigate to manually prior to initiating the navigation, or to bind the NavigateUri property of the HyperlinkButton to the property representing the unique identifier on the bound object and use a value converter to build the full URI. The value converter approach is probably the most appropriate choice, especially if you are using the MVVM design pattern; however, it does not apply if you are using a Button control, because the Button control has no NavigateUri property. Therefore, we'll focus on the code-behind approach here instead, which you can use with either a HyperlinkButton control or a Button control.

The following XAML demonstrates the definition of a HyperlinkButton control, which can be added to the cell template of a DataGrid template column or to a ListBox item template, that displays the name of the product as its text, has a Click event handler, and binds the whole ProductSummary object to its Tag property, which it does by assigning {Binding} to its property value, as follows:

```
<HyperlinkButton Content="{Binding Name}" Tag="{Binding}"
                 Click="NameButton_Click" />
```

Now, in the Click event handler for the HyperlinkButton, we can get the HyperlinkButton that raised the event, which is passed into the event handler as the sender parameter, and then get the ProductSummary object corresponding to its summary list item/row from its Tag property. The structure of this URI will depend on how your URI mapping has been configured. (See Chapter 3 for more information on URI mapping.) The following example demonstrates building a URI that navigates to the product details view, and passes it the ID of the product to display, which it can obtain from the query string and retrieve the corresponding details from the server for.

```
private void NameButton_Click(object sender, System.Windows.RoutedEventArgs e)
{
    HyperlinkButton button = sender as HyperlinkButton;
    ProductSummary productSummary = button.Tag as ProductSummary;

    Uri detailsUri = new Uri("ProductDetails/" + productSummary.ID.ToString(),
                             UriKind.Relative);
    NavigationService.Navigate(detailsUri);
}
```

> **Note** You should also handle the KeyDown event of the control to capture the Enter key being pressed, and navigating to the details view corresponding to the selected item/row. This helps enable users to use the keyboard to navigate around the application instead of having to switch between using the keyboard and the mouse.

Opening Details in a Pop-Up Window

Silverlight has a neat class built in called ChildWindow that enables you to display a modal pop-up window with content that you define. This makes it perfect for use in scenarios in which you want the user to be able to select a record in a summary list and display the related details in a pop-up window.

To implement a child window, add a new item to your project and select the Silverlight Child Window item template from the dialog. This will create a new XAML file (and corresponding code-behind class) inheriting from the ChildWindow class. As shown in Figure 6-11, you have a nice window-type layout that you can style to suit your user interface design if necessary, already set up with OK/Cancel buttons, which you can add your own control layout to so that the user can view and edit the details of the selected record in the summary list.

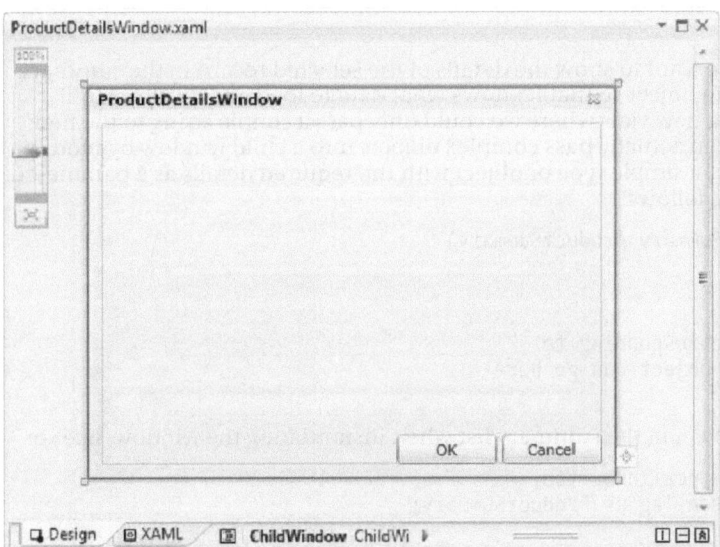

Figure 6-11. A ChildWindow in design mode

After you have defined the layout of the child window, you need to be able to display it when the user clicks a record in the summary list. Using the approaches described in the previous section, instead of navigating to a new view you can simply handle the Click event of the hyperlink or button defined for an item/row and display the child window. All that is required to display a child window is to instantiate the class and call the Show method, like so:

```
ProductDetailsWindow window = new ProductDetailsWindow();
window.Show();
```

■ **Note** While the child window is displayed modally, unlike displaying modal windows in Windows Forms or WPF, the method returns immediately, instead of waiting for the window to be closed. If you need to perform an action, such as updating the summary list, after the window is closed, you will need to handle either the Closing or Closed event of the child window and put your logic to do so in there.

The modality of the child window is provided by applying a semitransparent Rectangle control overlaying the application's user interface, positioning the child window control on top of this, and disabling the root visual. Therefore, any mouse clicks outside the child window will be ignored, effectively providing a modal behavior.

The source code for the ChildWindow class can be found in the Silverlight Toolkit, so you can modify this modal behavior by modifying the source code if you wish. With slight modifications to the code, you can enable multiple child windows to be displayed simultaneously. Microsoft Silverlight program manager Tim Heuer has actually already done this with a control called the FloatableWindow, which includes additional behavior such as the ability for it to be resized by the user. It is available on CodePlex at http://floatablewindow.codeplex.com.

However, in this scenario, where we want to show the details of the selected record in the summary list, we need to pass in an identifier or an object so that it knows what data to load and display. Unlike the previous approach to navigating to a new view where we could only pass a simple string to the new view to tell it which record to load, we can actually pass complex objects into a child window by modifying the constructor of the class to accept a simple type or object with the required details as a parameter. For example, change the constructor, as follows:

```
public ProductDetailsWindow(ProductSummary productSummary)
{
    InitializeComponent();

    // Logic to load product data corresponding to
    // the passed-in productSummary object can go here
}
```

You can now pass it the selected object in the summary list when instantiating the window, like so:

```
HyperlinkButton button = sender as HyperlinkButton;
ProductSummary productSummary = button.Tag as ProductSummary;

ProductDetailsWindow window = new ProductDetailsWindow(productSummary);
window.Show();
```

Figure 6-12 demonstrates displaying the details of a product in a child window.

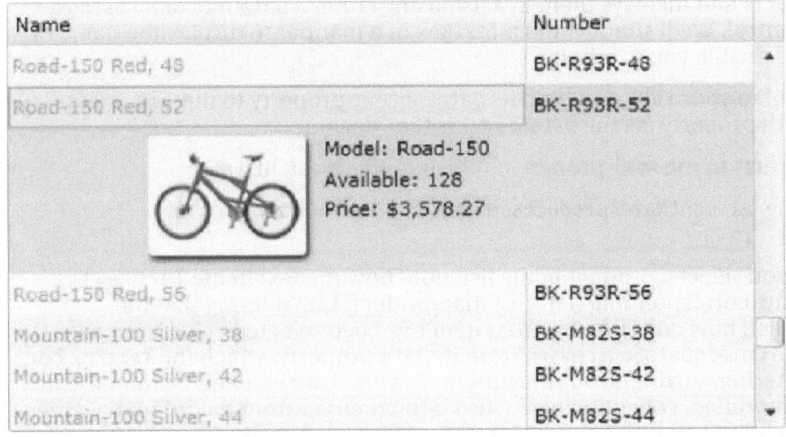

Product Details

Name:	Adjustable Race	List Price:	$0.00
Product Number:	AR-5381	Standard Cost:	$0.00
Model:	▼	Sell Start Date:	1/06/1998
Category:	▼	Sell End Date:	<d/MM/yyyy>
Subcategory:	▼	Discont. Date:	<d/MM/yyyy>
Product Line:		Safety Stock:	1000
Class:		Reorder Point:	750
Style:		Days To Man.:	0
Color:		Make:	☐
Size:	▼	Finished Goods:	☐
Weight:	▼		

OK   Cancel

Figure 6-12. Product details in a child window

Displaying Details Using the DataGrid's Row Details

The row details feature in the DataGrid enables you to display additional data related to a row in the DataGrid—useful when you only want to show limited details from the bound object in the main row, and display additional details in an area below it, as demonstrated in Figure 6-13. This is especially useful when you want to show additional details about a row without displaying those details in a pop-up window or navigating away from the summary list view.

Name	Number
Road-150 Red, 48	BK-R93R-48
Road-150 Red, 52	BK-R93R-52
Model: Road-150 Available: 128 Price: $3,578.27	
Road-150 Red, 56	BK-R93R-56
Mountain-100 Silver, 38	BK-M82S-38
Mountain-100 Silver, 42	BK-M82S-42
Mountain-100 Silver, 44	BK-M82S-44

Figure 6-13. Row details in a DataGrid control

This is achieved by assigning a data template defining the layout of the row details area to the RowDetailsTemplate property of the DataGrid. For example:

```
<sdk:DataGrid>
    <sdk:DataGrid.RowDetailsTemplate>
        <DataTemplate>
            <!-- Row details layout goes here -->
        </DataTemplate>
    </sdk:DataGrid.RowDetailsTemplate>
</sdk:DataGrid>
```

You can assign a value to the RowDetailsVisibilityMode property to specify whether the row details are displayed only when the row is selected (VisibleWhenSelected), displayed for every row in the DataGrid (Visible), or never displayed (Collapsed). You can use the RowDetailsVisibilityChanged event to handle when the row details are shown/hidden, enabling you to implement behaviors such as loading related data from the server into the row details when the row is selected and the row details section is displayed.

By default, if the DataGrid has columns extending beyond the width of the DataGrid, its horizontal scrolling functionality will also allow horizontal scrolling of the row details area. However, you can freeze the row details so that they remain fixed in position regardless of any horizontal scrolling motion by setting the AreRowDetailsFrozen property to True.

Implementing a Master/Details View

The master/details view is a relatively common user interface pattern in which the summary list (acting as the master) occupies one part of the view, and when the user selects an item from the list, the complete record (acting as the details) are displayed in another part of the view for editing. For example, you might have a list of products (i.e., the master), and when the user selects a product from this list, details of the selected product will be displayed in a data entry form in another part of the view, where they can be edited.

This is actually quite easy to implement, thanks to the synchronization behavior provided by collection views, with no code actually required. Let's say you are using a DomainDataSource control in your view that retrieves the list of products and displays them in a list, using either a DataGrid or a ListBox bound to the DomainDataSource control. We'll simply bind a TextBox in a manner to display the name of the selected product in the list and enable you to edit it.

1. Add a TextBlock control to your view and bind its DataContext property to the DomainDataSource's Data property (as the DataGrid/ListBox does).

2. Now bind its Text property to the Name property of the bound object, like so:

```
<TextBlock DataContext="{Binding ElementName=productSummaryDDS, Path=Data}"
           Text="{Binding Name}" />
```

Now run your project. When you select a product in the list, note how the text in the TextBlock automatically changes to display the corresponding name of that product. Considering that the TextBlock isn't even bound to the list, how does it know what item has been selected? This is because the DomainDataSource control returns a DomainDataSourceView from its Data property, which the TextBox control is binding to. In addition to filtering/sorting/grouping functions, which are enabled without the underlying collection needing to be modified, collection views also implement current record management functions, including properties such as CurrentItem and CurrentPosition, and methods such as MoveCurrentToNext and MoveCurrentToPosition. When a property on a control that accepts a value (rather than a collection) is bound to a collection view, the data binding engine will recognize that the binding source is a collection view and will assume that you don't actually want to bind to the collection view itself. It, therefore, drills down to the collection view's CurrentItem property and binds to the given property on that instead.

■ **Note** Optionally, you can use "{Binding CurrentItem.Name}" as the binding expression instead, with exactly the same results, but explicitly drilling down to the CurrentItem property on the collection view isn't necessary unless you have a property on the object you want to bind to that has the same name as a property on the collection view object, such as Count.

When you click on a new product in the list, the list will automatically update the CurrentItem property on the collection view that it's bound to and set it to that of the selected item. In other words, by default, list controls automatically synchronize the CurrentItem property of the collection view to which they are bound with their selected item. When the CurrentItem property of the collection view is changed, any other controls in the view that are bound to it will have their binding source changed accordingly. The effect of this behavior is that those controls will display the details of the currently selected item in the list, effectively providing a master/details type behavior that your application can leverage.

■ **Note** Although most of the time you will want this synchronization behavior, sometimes you might want to have more control over the process. You will find that some of these controls, such as the ListBox control, have an IsSynchronizedWithCurrentItem property whose default value is null. You can't actually set this property to true (it will throw an exception if you try), as it depends on whether or not the binding source is a collection view for whether synchronization with the current item is possible. If the binding source is a collection view, current item synchronization will automatically be turned on, although you can explicitly turn it *off* if you want by setting the property to false. If you do so, you can control what item is the current item in the collection view manually (in code), using the record navigation methods (such as MoveCurrentToNext and MoveCurrentToPosition).

Summary

You should now have the ability to create a summary list view, and the knowledge to choose the most appropriate approach to populate it with data. You've learned that the DataGrid control is an easy way to implement a summary list, but the ListBox control is often a better choice due to its flexibility. You've learned how a collection view can be used to wrap a collection, and manipulate the collection without modifying it. You've also learned about four key collection view types, and the scenarios that each is best suited to. Finally, you learned how the user can drill down on an item in a summary list to display/edit its details. In the next chapter, we'll look at how you can actually enable users to edit the details of a record and submit the changes back to the server.

CHAPTER 7

Building Data Entry Forms

Now that you've learned how to retrieve data from the server and display it in the form of a read-only list, you need to learn how to display the data in a form such that the user can modify it and submit the changes back to the server. This chapter will take you through creating a data entry form that enables the user to add, edit, and delete records from the system and submit the changes back to the server.

Creating the Data Entry User Interface

A typical data entry form consists of a number of editable fields—such as text boxes, drop-down lists, and check boxes, each with a corresponding label displaying the name of that field, and a tab order assigned such that users can tab between fields in a logical fashion. Ideally, the users should be able to enter data into the form and submit it without ever having to use the mouse (i.e., the process should be able to be completely keyboard driven), making the data entry process smoother and more efficient. As a developer, you likely will have created countless data entry forms in your career, so this will be a fairly familiar task for you. Let's take a look at how to create a data entry form that achieves these goals in Silverlight, and then move on to refine its functionality.

Laying Out the Data Entry Form

In the past, you may have been used to laying out data entry forms using fixed positioning, with each control assigned a Left and a Top value. Although you can do this in Silverlight by laying out the controls on a canvas, it's usually better to create a flexible layout using the Grid control and lay out the controls in the Grid control's cells. This helps you keep the controls aligned and enables you to have the controls dynamically resize according to the size of the application's window.

You can use a number of different methods to create a data entry form. Although you can manually lay out the form yourself, a couple of time-saving means are available to help you create a data entry form from the object that it will be bound to. Let's take a look at those now.

Using the Data Sources Window

As shown in Chapter 6, you can open the Data Sources tool window in Visual Studio and drag an entity from this window onto your design surface. A DataGrid will be created in the view, with a column defined for each property on the entity. You can make this process create a details view instead by selecting Details from the drop-down menu for the entity in the Data Sources window (as shown in Figure 7-1) before dragging it onto the design surface.

Data Sources
ProductContext
Product
DataGrid
ListBox
Details
[None]
Customize...
GetProductsQuery
Name
ProductID
ProductLine
ProductModelID

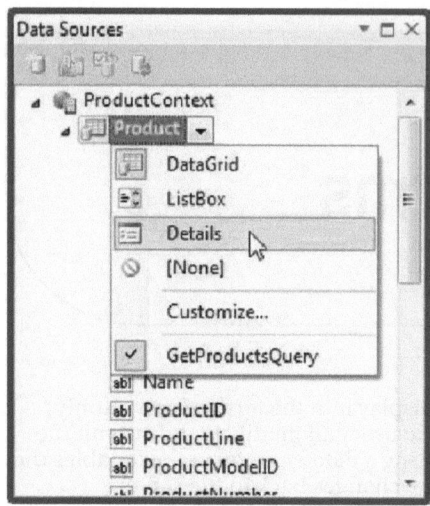

Figure 7-1. Selecting the control to generate for an entity

Now when you drag the entity onto the design surface, a field and corresponding label will be created for each property on the entity, laid out using a Grid control (as shown in Figure 7-2), with the field's binding to the source property already configured.

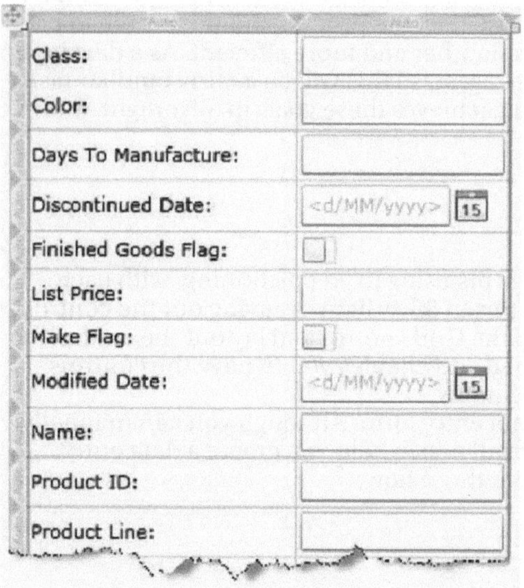

Class:
Color:
Days To Manufacture:
Discontinued Date:
<d/MM/yyyy>
15
Finished Goods Flag:
List Price:
Make Flag:
Modified Date:
<d/MM/yyyy>
15
Name:
Product ID:
Product Line:

Figure 7-2. Details form generated by the Data Sources window

The control created for each property on the entity will default to the one best suited to the property's type (e.g., TextBox for strings, CheckBox for Booleans, DatePicker for dates), but you can change the type of controls that will be generated by expanding the entity in the Data Sources window and selecting different control types for the properties that you want to change (as shown in Figure 7-3). The labels will contain the name of the property, with some spaces intelligently inserted into the name, followed by a colon.

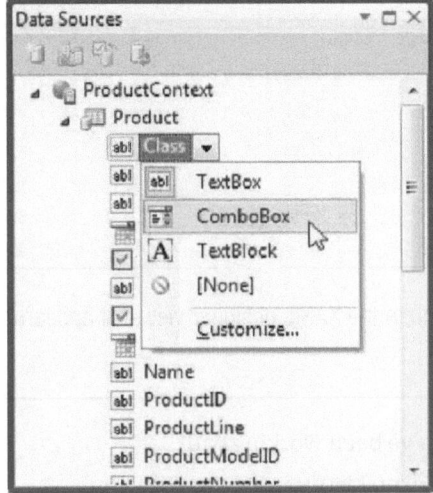

Figure 7-3. Selecting the control that will be generated for a property on the entity

---

■ **Note** Unfortunately, there is no way to order the properties of an entity in the Data Sources window before dragging it onto the view. This means that the fields will be created on the form in alphabetical order rather than the actual logical order that you want for them. Therefore, you will need to reorder the fields once they have been created in the form, assigning the fields to the actual grid row in which you want them to appear.

A DomainDataSource control will be automatically configured for you if one doesn't already exist in the view, and the DataContext property of the "container" Grid control will be bound to it and will be inherited and available to all the controls within the Grid.

This is an easy way of creating the fields required for a data entry form, but the lack of ability to order the data entry fields before dragging it onto the view does result in the need for quite a bit of additional work in arranging it to suit your needs.

Workshop: Using XAML Power Toys

Another method you can use to create a data entry form is to use the XAML Power Toys add-in for Visual Studio, created by Karl Shifflet, which you can get at http://karlshifflett.wordpress.com/xaml-power-toys. After you download and install this add-in, it will add a new submenu to your right-click context menus in the XAML and code editors, as shown in Figure 7-4.

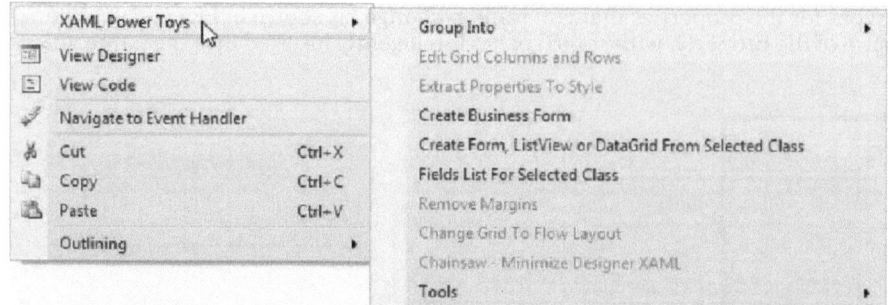

Figure 7-4. *The XAML Power Toys menu*

■ **Note** The context menu doesn't appear in the right-click context menu in the XAML designer view—it appears only in the XAML editor view.

---

1. Add a new view to the AdventureWorks project that you've been working with.

2. Right-click in the XAML editor, and select the "Create Form, ListView or DataGrid From Selected Class" menu item from the XAML Power Toys submenu.

3. From the dialog that appears, you need to select the object that you want to create the data entry form from (i.e., the object that the form will bind to). Select the Product class from under the AdventureWorks.Web namespace, and click the Next button. The screen shown in Figure 7-5 will be displayed.

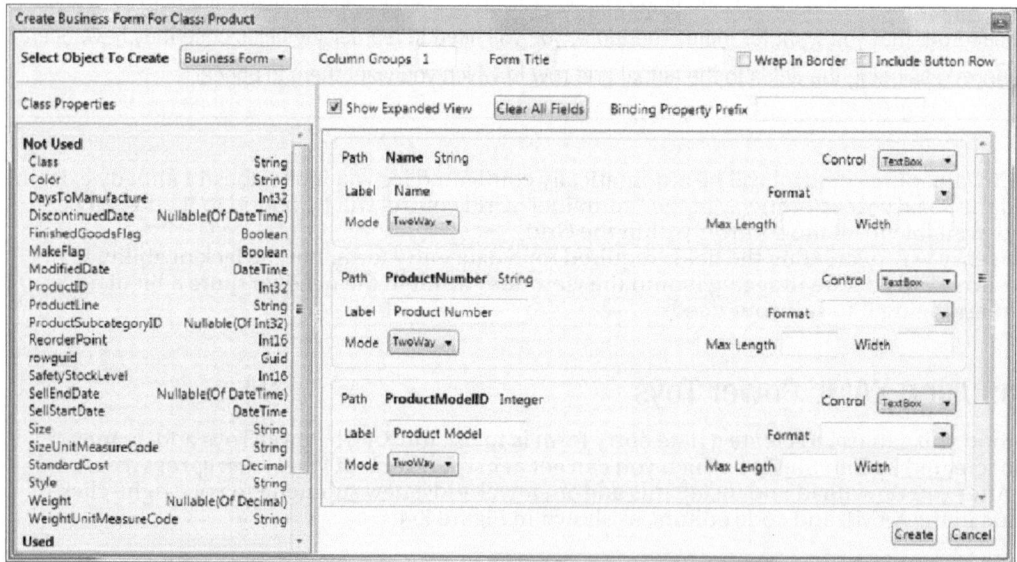

Figure 7-5. *The XAML Power Toys add-in's Create Business Form For Class dialog*

4. Ensure that the "Select Object To Create" drop-down box at the top left of the dialog is set to Business Form.

5. Now, drag and drop properties from the Class Properties section on the left side of the screen into the right side. You can then configure various properties for each field as required, including

- The type of control

- Its display format, maximum length, and width

- Its binding mode, which needs to be set to TwoWay so that the updated value can be propagated back to the bound object, as discussed in Chapter 2

- Its label

■ **Note** The tool helps you by automatically setting a default value for the label based on the property name. It intelligently splits the property name into separate words, inserting a space before each capital letter in the property name.

---

6. Reorder the fields if required, by simply clicking and dragging the item up and down to a new position in the list.

7. Once you've completed configuring your form, you can click the Create button.

8. Clicking the Create button doesn't actually insert anything into your XAML. Instead, the XAML that was generated has been copied to the clipboard and is ready for you to paste in the appropriate location in your XAML file. Place the cursor at the position in the XAML file to insert the form, and paste the contents of the clipboard to that location (press Ctrl+V). Your data entry form has now been created, and you can modify the XAML further as required.

■ **Note** You may have to declare various namespace prefixes used in the generated XAML—these are included when you paste the XAML into the XAML editor in commented-out form. You can then add them to your root element if they aren't already declared.

There are numerous other options that we won't go into here, but essentially, this method enables you a lot more control over the configuration of the data entry form before it's generated than the Data Sources window provides.

■ **Note** XAML Power Toys includes number of other features that you will probably find useful when working with XAML, in both Silverlight and WPF. The source code is also available for download, enabling you to make modifications, including adding features to help you create data entry forms faster.

Using the DataForm Control

In addition to the two methods shown previously, you can take another approach to creating a data entry form—using the DataForm control. The DataForm control is a part of the Silverlight Toolkit whose key feature is that it can dynamically create a data entry form at runtime from an object.

■ **Note** The DataForm control is designed to be bound to an object. For simple unbound data entry scenarios, such as a login window, it's best not to use the DataForm control—simply lay out standard controls within a Grid control instead.

Creating a DataForm Control with Automatically Generated Fields

The DataForm control makes is very easy to create data entry forms. You can simply drop a DataForm control onto the design surface, and either bind its CurrentItem property to an object for the user to edit or bind its ItemsSource property to a collection of objects for when you want the user to be able to edit multiple objects. The DataForm control will then dynamically generate a data entry form at runtime suitable for editing the object that it's currently bound to.

 Workshop: Adding the DataForm Control to a View

Let's create a DataForm control and bind it to a DomainDataSource control that will handle retrieving a collection of Product entities from the server.

1. Create a new view in the AdventureWorks project that you've been working with, and add a DomainDataSource control to it, configured to load product data from the server:

```
<riaControls:DomainDataSource AutoLoad="True" QueryName="GetProducts"
                              Name="productDomainDataSource"
                              Height="0" Width="0">
    <riaControls:DomainDataSource.DomainContext>
        <my:ProductContext />
    </riaControls:DomainDataSource.DomainContext>
</riaControls:DomainDataSource>
```

■ **Note** The riaControls namespace prefix should be defined in your view, like so:

```
xmlns:riaControls="clr-namespace:System.Windows.Controls;  ↵
    assembly=System.Windows.Controls.DomainServices"
```

---

2. Define the toolkit namespace prefix in the root element of the view:

```
xmlns:toolkit="http://schemas.microsoft.com/winfx/2006/xaml/presentation/toolkit"
```

Add a DataForm control to your view, set its Header property, and bind its ItemsSource:

```
<toolkit:DataForm Header="Product Data Entry"
        ItemsSource="{Binding ElementName=productDomainDataSource, Path=Data}" />
```

■ **Note** If you want to bind the DataForm control to a collection of objects, you bind the collection to the Data-Form control's ItemsSource property, as was demonstrated here. However, if you want to bind the DataForm to a single object, you need to bind that object to the DataForm control's CurrentItem property instead.

3. Now if you run your application, a data entry form similar to that shown in Figure 7-6 will be displayed.

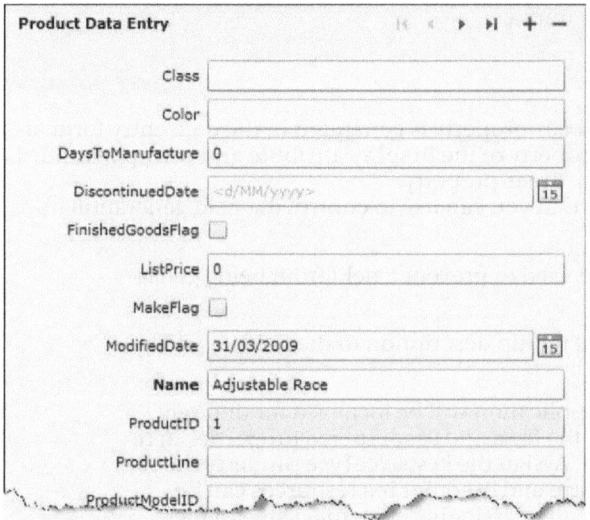

Figure 7-6. A DataForm control

■ **Note** This data entry form is generated at runtime, so none of these fields will appear at design time unless you bind the form to sample data, as discussed in Chapter 10. Alternatively, you can bind its CurrentItem property to an object using the design-time data properties discussed in Chapter 10. However, when doing so, you will not be able to simultaneously have a binding assigned to the DataForm control's ItemsSource property because that will result in an error.

Configuring the Layout of the Fields

You may have noticed from the DataForm created in the previous workshop that the output is not suitable for users as yet. Issues with the layout include

- There is no logical order to the fields. Instead, fields were created in alphabetical order by property name.

- The fields use the names of the properties that they're bound to as their labels, rather than something more meaningful for users.

- A field is being created for *all* the properties on the object.

- The fields aren't necessarily generated using the control that you want to be used for editing the property value.

You can have more control over the process and customize it to your needs however. In Chapter 4, you saw how to decorate the properties of your entities/objects with attributes—either directly or via metadata classes. You can use the Display attribute that was described to control the generation of the corresponding fields in the DataForm control, for example:

```
[Display(Name="Product Number:", Order=3)]
public string ProductNumber;
```

When the corresponding field for the ProductNumber property is generated in the data entry form, its label will have the text that is assigned to the Name property of the Display attribute and will appear third in the list of fields, based on the value assigned to the Order property.

Other useful properties of the Display attribute that you can use to control the field generation include the following:

- AutoGenerateField: This property can be used to prevent a field from being generated for the property.

- Description: This can be used to assign a tooltip description to the field, as will be described shortly.

- ResourceType: In scenarios where your application will be localized for different languages, you can define the values for the Name and Description properties in resource files instead of hard-coding them. Assign the ResourceType property the resources file's type, denoting where the Name and Description resources can be found for this entity property. Then instead of assigning an actual value to the Name and Description properties, you need to assign each the name of its corresponding string resources. For example, the following Display attribute specifies that the Name and Description property values should come from a resource file named ProductResources, and their values will come from resources in that file named ProductNumberLabel and ProductNumberDescription respectively:

```
[Display(ResourceType = typeof(ProductResources), Name="ProductNumberLabel",
        Description="ProductNumberDescription")]
public string ProductNumber;
```

■ **Note** When using resources in this manner, you will need to link the resource file in your web project to your Silverlight project so that the two projects share the same resources. The Silverlight Business Application project template generates projects with two resource files already shared between the two projects: `RegistrationDataResources.resx` and `ValidationErrorResources.resx`.

Miscellaneous Issues

Now, when the fields are generated at runtime in the DataForm, they will use this metadata and be laid out accordingly. However, there are some issues with generating the data entry form in this manner. The first is the still-limited control you have over how the data entry form is generated. For simple forms, this won't be too much of a problem; however, for more complex forms where you need to use other controls, such as ComboBox controls, assign custom properties to each field control, or have less of a structured layout (e.g., with multiple fields in a single row), then this method really isn't satisfactory. Some of these issues can be worked around by handling the DataForm control's `AutoGeneratingField` event, which is raised when each field is being created, enabling you to make changes to the field being generated.

■ **Note** See the LoginForm and RegistrationForm user controls in your project (created by the Silverlight Business Application project template) for examples of how you can customize the fields generated by the DataForm control while it's generating them.

The most important issue, however, is really conceptual. Decorating your entities/objects with presentation-related attributes violates the separation-of-concerns principle. How the data entry form is laid out is a presentation tier/layer issue, not a middle tier/layer issue (which is where the entities/objects exist). By decorating your entities/objects with presentation-related attributes, you are creating a murky boundary between the two tiers/layers, which is against good design principles. Therefore, the DataForm control used this way is best suited to small applications and prototypes.

Creating a DataForm Control with Explicitly Defined Fields

Instead of having the fields in the data entry form dynamically generated at runtime as per the previous method, you can instead explicitly define the fields within the DataForm control in XAML instead. You'll then have complete control over the DataForm's fields, and will be able to lay out the fields exactly as required. However, the DataForm control can offer you a few benefits over laying out a data entry form manually without it, including

- The ability to navigate through each entity, if the control is bound to a collection, without needing to implement another means, such as a ListBox or a DataGrid, to select the current item. The header of the control contains some navigation buttons that you can use for this purpose.

- Built-in add and delete buttons, which will appear if the control is bound to a collection.

- Support for objects that implement the IEditableObject interface (discussed later in this chapter). A cancel button is displayed in the bottom-right corner of the control, enabling the user to cancel all their changes to the current item and will revert the bound properties back to their original values.

- The ability to display an icon next to the field, which will show a description for that field in a tooltip when the user hovers the mouse over it. This uses the DescriptionViewer control from the Silverlight Toolkit and can be used outside of the DataForm control if you wish.

- A built-in ValidationSummary control, displaying a summary of all the validation errors on the bound entity at the bottom of the control.

- A built-in ScrollViewer control that automatically displays a scroll bar if the fields extend past the area of the data entry form.

- The ability to define a different data template for each state that the DataForm control can be in. There are three data templates that you can define:

    - ReadOnlyTemplate: Used when the DataForm control is in read-only mode, this will be the default mode when the DataForm control's AutoEdit property is set to False, and it will also be used whenever the DataForm control's IsReadOnly property is set to True.

    - EditTemplate: Used when the DataForm control is in edit mode, this will be the mode when the DataForm control's AutoEdit property is set to True, assuming the user hasn't clicked the Edit button for the current item, and when its IsReadOnly property is set to False.

    - NewItemTemplate: Used when adding a new item to the bound collection.

You might notice some similarities between the structure of the DataForm control and the FormView and DetailsView controls in ASP.NET, such as that both support the ability to define different templates for different modes. With these controls, in ASP.NET, you could simply bind them to an ObjectDataSource control at design time, and the control would automatically generate the HTML for all the fields for you that you could then rearrange to create a custom layout.

Unfortunately, the DataForm control does not have this same feature. The XAML for the fields in a DataForm control is a little different than what we used earlier. For example, here is the XAML required for a simple DataForm, containing two explicitly defined fields:

```
<toolkit:DataForm AutoGenerateFields="False" Header="Product Data Entry"
        ItemsSource="{Binding ElementName=productDomainDataSource, Path=Data}">
    <toolkit:DataForm.EditTemplate>
        <DataTemplate>
            <Grid>
                <Grid.RowDefinitions>
                    <RowDefinition Height="Auto" />
                    <RowDefinition Height="Auto" />
                </Grid.RowDefinitions>

                <Grid.ColumnDefinitions>
                    <ColumnDefinition />
                </Grid.ColumnDefinitions>

                <toolkit:DataField Grid.Row="0" Grid.Column="0"
                            Label="Name:" LabelPosition="Auto">
                    <TextBox Text="{Binding Path=Name, Mode=TwoWay}"
```

```
                        Name="NameTextBox"
                        HorizontalAlignment="Stretch" VerticalAlignment="Top" />
            </toolkit:DataField>

            <toolkit:DataField Grid.Row="1" Grid.Column="0"
                                Label="Product Number:"
                                LabelPosition="Auto">
                <TextBox Text="{Binding Path=ProductNumber, Mode=TwoWay}"
                        HorizontalAlignment="Stretch" VerticalAlignment="Top" />
            </toolkit:DataField>
        </Grid>
    </DataTemplate>
  </toolkit:DataForm.EditTemplate>
</toolkit:DataForm>
```

Note the following from this XAML:

- The fields are defined within a data template, and assigned to the DataForm control's EditTemplate property.

- Each field is defined using a DataField control, to which you assign an input control (such as a TextBox control) as its content.

- There is no Label or TextBlock control defined for each field to display the field label. Instead, the text to be used as the field's label should be assigned to the DataField control's Label property.

- The DataField controls are laid out in a Grid, which contains only a single column. The DataForm control takes care of creating the labels and ensuring that the data input fields remain aligned regardless of the differing lengths of the labels.

The DataForm control in the preceding XAML results in the output shown in Figure 7-7 when it is bound to an entity or collection of entities.

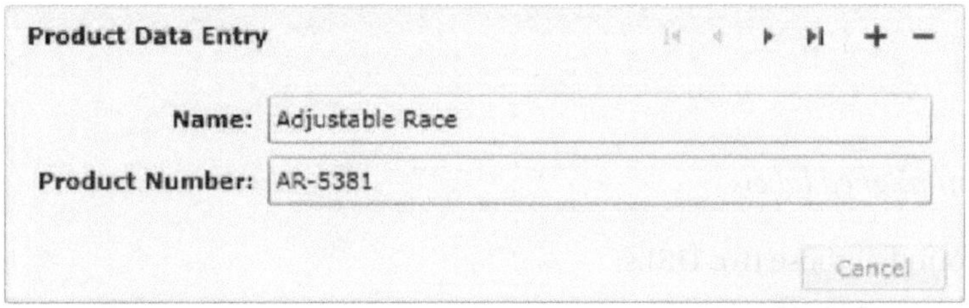

Figure 7-7. A DataForm control with a custom edit template

> ■ **Note** Optionally, you can assign a string to the DataField control's Description property. Doing so will display an icon next to the field that shows the description when the user hovers the mouse over it.

Unfortunately, the Data Sources window does not provide the ability to automatically generate a data entry form using the DataForm control. However, the XAML Power Toys add-in does have this ability, so you can use the method described in the previous section to create a data entry form, but with one difference. Instead of selecting Business Form from the Select Object To Create drop-down box at the top of the dialog, select Silverlight Data Form. This will create the XAML required for a data entry form using a DataForm control with explicitly defined fields and will save you a lot of time over building it manually.

Note When you paste the XAML for a DataForm control generated by the XAML Power Toys into your view, you'll need to change the `dataFormToolkit` namespace prefix that it uses to the `toolkit` namespace prefix we defined in the previous workshop. Alternatively, you can simply define the `dataFormToolkit` namespace prefix for your view.

Positioning the Labels

Although labels are, by default, positioned to the left of the fields, you can also position them above the fields by setting the DataForm control's `LabelPosition` property to `Top`. Top-aligned labels require less horizontal space, and some research has suggested that they enable users to complete forms faster because they can see both the label and the field together as they scan the form. In addition, you don't have to worry so much about how much room the label requires when a form is to be localized. Figure 7-8 demonstrates top-aligned labels.

Figure 7-8. A DataForm control with top-aligned labels

More information on this can be found at these two URLs:

- www.uxmatters.com/mt/archives/2006/07/label-placement-in-forms.php
- www.lukew.com/ff/entry.asp?504

Note The labels for the fields in Figure 7-8 are bolded, which indicates to the user that these fields require a value. This is because the bound properties are decorated with the `Required` validation attribute.

The Cancel Button

You may have noticed that a Cancel button has also been automatically been created at the bottom of the data entry form. When the DataForm is bound to an object that implements the IEditableObject interface, such as the entities and objects exposed by a domain service with RIA Services, this button will become enabled. The IEditableObject provides a mechanism with which any changes made to an object can be rolled back and the object restored to a previous state. If the bound object does not implement this interface, then the Cancel button will remain disabled. The IEditableObject interface will be discussed in more detail later in this chapter.

■ **Note** You can use the CancelButtonContent and CancelButtonStyle properties to customize the Cancel button if required.

The AutoEdit and AutoCommit Properties

By default, when the user navigates to a record, it will be immediately put into edit mode. In addition, the user will be able to navigate away from the record without saving their changes. You can make the editing of a record more explicit using the AutoEdit and AutoCommit properties on the DataForm control.

- Setting the DataForm control's AutoEdit property to False means that whenever the user navigates to a record, it will be in read-only mode, and will display the read-only template (if defined). A pencil icon will appear in the header of the DataForm control when it's in this read-only mode, which the user will need to click in order to be able to edit the record.

- Setting the DataForm control's AutoCommit property to False will result in an OK button appearing at the bottom of the DataForm control, next to the Cancel button. The user will need to click either the OK button or the Cancel button to navigate to a different record. However, note that any changes that the user makes to the data will still be immediately committed to the object as they are made.

■ **Note** You can use the CommitButtonContent and CommitButtonStyle properties to customize the OK button if required.

Customizing the Header

If the DataForm control's header doesn't suit the look of your application, you can retemplate it by assigning a new data template to its HeaderTemplate property, or remove it completely by changing its HeaderVisibility property to Collapsed. If you do hide the header, you can still invoke the functionality it provided using the DataForm control's methods. For example, the DataForm control has the following methods:

- AddNewItem: Adds a new item to the bound collection and navigates to it

- DeleteItem: Deletes the current item from the bound collection

- BeginEdit: Changes the mode to edit mode
- CommitEdit: Commits the current changes to the entity
- CancelEdit: Cancels the changes made since the editing began and restores the original property values of the control to what they were when BeginEdit was called

You may have noticed that there are no methods to navigate through the items in the bound collection. You can, however, use the CurrentIndex property for this purpose: increment and decrement it to move to the next and previous items; set it to 0 to move to the first item in the collection, or set it to the item count minus one to move to the last item in the collection.

■ **Note** Alternatively, if you've bound the DataForm control to a collection view, you can use the navigation methods provided by the collection view to navigate between records in code. This is particularly useful when you're following the MVVM design pattern and want to be able to navigate between records from a ViewModel class.

You can also choose which buttons you want to appear in the header. The DataForm control's CommandButtonsVisibility property can be used for this purpose, accepting any of the following values from the DataFormCommandButtonsVisibility enumeration:

- None: Don't show any buttons.
- Add: Show the Add button.
- Delete: Show the Delete button.
- Edit: Show the Edit button.
- Navigation: Show the first, previous, next, and last item buttons.
- Commit: Show the OK button (at the bottom of the DataForm control).
- Cancel: Show the Cancel button (at the bottom of the DataForm control).
- All: Show all the buttons (as appropriate).

You can combine multiple values if you wish. For example, you can configure the DataForm control in code to show only the Add and Delete buttons, like so:

```
ProductsDataForm.CommandButtonsVisibility = DataFormCommandButtonsVisibility.Add |
                                            DataFormCommandButtonsVisibility.Delete;
```

And here's how to do the same in XAML:

```
CommandButtonsVisibility="Add,Delete"
```

Refining the Data Entry Form's Functionality

It's extremely important that you create data entry forms in your applications that are easy to navigate and use. You want to minimize the amount of work that the user has to do to enter the data and preferably enable power users to keep their hands on the keyboard, increasing their productivity. In this section, we'll look at the most popular data input controls available in Silverlight and provide tips for making it easier for the user to enter data into the application.

Data Input Controls

Many data input controls are available in Silverlight and the Silverlight Toolkit that you can use in your data entry forms. Let's take a brief look at some of the more common ones.

The TextBox Control

The TextBox control enables users to enter free-form text, as shown in Figure 7-9.

Figure 7-9. *A TextBox control*

You can get/set the text in the TextBox via its Text property:

```
<TextBox Text="{Binding Name, Mode=TwoWay}" />
```

Sometimes, you need to format the bound value before displaying it—particularly when you're binding to a nonstring property such as a DateTime or a decimal. Use the StringFormat property on the binding to set the format, using the same types of formatting strings you would use if you were to format the value using its ToString method in code using either standard or custom formats. For example, the following binding displays the value formatted as currency, as shown in Figure 7-10:

```
<TextBox Text="{Binding TotalCost, Mode=TwoWay, StringFormat=C}" />
```

Figure 7-10. *A bound TextBox control with a custom string format*

■ **Note**   You will find more information about using the Binding object's StringFormat property in Chapter 11.

Unfortunately, the TextBox control doesn't have any masked edit functionality to restrict the input into the TextBox from the user. There are a number of third-party masked edit controls, as well as an open source one on CodePlex that you can get here: http://sivlerlightinputctrl.codeplex.com (note the misspelling of Silverlight in the URL name).

Alternatively, you can assign a behavior that adds masked edit functionality to a text box. For example, you will find one, written by Jim Fisher, in the Microsoft Expression Gallery, at http://gallery.expression.microsoft.com/en-us/CMEditMaskBehavior (using behaviors is discussed in Chapter 10.)

Here are some other miscellaneous features of Silverlight's TextBox control:

- You can set the maximum number of characters accepted by the TextBox control using its MaxLength property.

- If you want to stop the user from being able to enter text into the TextBox control, you can set its IsReadOnly property to True. Doing so still allows the user to select and copy text in the TextBox control, which can't be done when the TextBox control is disabled. The background of the TextBox control will change to a light gray color to indicate it cannot be edited.

- You can horizontally align the text in the TextBox control using its TextAlignment property. You can left-align the text (the default), right-align it, or center it. Note that although Justify appears in IntelliSense and the Properties window as an alignment option, it will throw an exception when used.

- By default, when more text is entered into the TextBox control than it can display, the text will remain on a single line and the beginning of the text will disappear off the TextBox's left edge. However, if you make your text box tall enough to display multiple lines, then you can get the text to wrap onto the next line by setting the TextBox control's TextWrapping property to Wrap (the default being NoWrap). If you want the user to be able to start new lines in the text box by pressing the Return/Enter key, you will need to set the TextBox control's AcceptsReturn property to True.

- By default, the vertical and horizontal scroll bars in the TextBox are hidden/disabled. You can enable them via the VerticalScrollBarVisibility and HorizontalScrollBarVisibility properties. Setting their values to Auto will cause the scroll bars to display only when the text exceeds the corresponding dimension of the text box, and setting them to Visible will cause them to display them regardless of whether they're required.

■ **Note** Setting the HorizontalScrollBarVisibility property to Visible will disable text wrapping.

The CheckBox Control

The CheckBox control enables the user to enter a True or False value, or a null value in the case of a three-state check box, as shown in Figure 7-11. You can get or set the value of the check box via its IsChecked property and set its label using its Content property:

```
<CheckBox IsChecked="{Binding FinishedGoodsFlag, Mode=TwoWay}"
          Content="Is Finished Goods" />
```

Figure 7-11. A bound CheckBox control

You can turn it into a three-state check box by setting its IsThreeState property to True. This enables an additional state, with a value of null, for the check box, which you may use to indicate that a value has not been set. Figure 7-12 shows what the third state looks like.

Figure 7-12. The third state in a three-state check box

The RadioButton Control

Radio buttons, also known as option buttons, enable the user to select one option from a number of options, as shown in Figure 7-13.

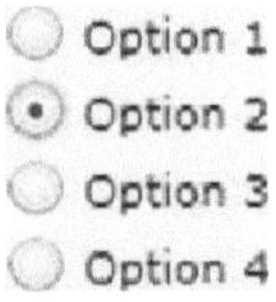

○ Option 1
⊙ Option 2
○ Option 3
○ Option 4

Figure 7-13. *Option buttons*

Much like the CheckBox control, you can get or set the value of a radio button via its IsChecked property and set its label using its Content property:

```
<RadioButton Content="Option 1" IsChecked="{Binding Option1, Mode=TwoWay}" />
<RadioButton Content="Option 2" IsChecked="{Binding Option2, Mode=TwoWay}" />
<RadioButton Content="Option 3" IsChecked="{Binding Option3, Mode=TwoWay}" />
<RadioButton Content="Option 4" IsChecked="{Binding Option4, Mode=TwoWay}" />
```

Often, you will want to bind a set of RadioButton controls to a single enumeration property on an object or entity, enabling the user to select the value it should have from a set of possible values. For example, say you want the RadioButton controls from the previous XAML to all be bound to the following property:

```
public enum Options
{
    Option1,
    Option2,
    Option3,
    Option4
}

public Options SelectedOption { get; set; }
```

To enable this, you will need to create a value converter and use it as part of the binding process. This value converter will need to compare the value of a property with a given value passed into the value converter as a parameter, returning True if the values match and False if they don't. We look at value converters further in Chapter 11, but you can find an example of a value converter that solves this problem in the sample code for this chapter, downloadable from the Apress web site.

All radio buttons are implicitly "linked," such that when you select one radio button, any currently selected radio button will be deselected. If you want to have multiple groups of radio buttons in your view that you don't want to interact, you can separate them by assigning each radio button to a group via its GroupName property. You can give each group whatever name you wish, and only the radio buttons with the same group name will interact. When you group radio buttons, ensure that the groups are visually separated in the view so that the user recognizes which options belong to which groups.

The ComboBox Control

The ComboBox control in Silverlight is not strictly a combo box as such, but a drop-down list (proper ComboBox controls accept free-form text entry, whereas the Silverlight ComboBox does not). You can bind its ItemsSource property to a collection of objects to display in much the same way as the ListBox control, or declare the items in XAML using the Items property. You can then get or set the selected item using its SelectedItem property.

The following XAML demonstrates creating a ComboBox in XAML, with the items to be displayed in the list also declared in XAML. This gives the output shown in Figure 7-14.

```
<ComboBox>
    <ComboBox.Items>
        <ComboBoxItem Content="Option 1" />
        <ComboBoxItem Content="Option 2" />
        <ComboBoxItem Content="Option 3" />
        <ComboBoxItem Content="Option 4" />
    </ComboBox.Items>
</ComboBox>
```

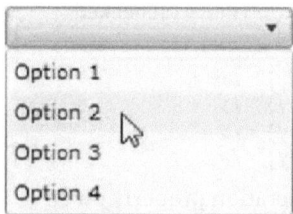

Figure 7-14. *A ComboBox control*

Let's now look at a real-world example. Say, for example, that you have a Product entity that has a property named ModelID, and a collection of Model objects, each with ID and Name properties. The ModelID property on the Product entity is a foreign key, representing an item in the collection of Model objects. You then want to enable the user to select a model for the product from a drop-down list, populated with Model objects, and displaying the name of the model for each item. When the user selects an item in the list, the ID of the selected Model needs to be assigned to the ModelID property of the Product entity. For this scenario, you need to

1.   Bind the collection of Model objects to the ComboBox's ItemsSource property.

2.   Set its SelectedValuePath to ID.

3.   Set its DisplayMemberPath to Name.

4.   Bind its SelectedValue property to the Product entity's ModelID property.

for example

```
<ComboBox ItemsSource="{StaticResource modelsResource}"
          SelectedValuePath="ID"
          SelectedValue="{Binding ModelID, Mode=TwoWay}"
          DisplayMemberPath="Name" />
```

The various properties that need to be set can be a little confusing, especially because the ComboBox control also has a SelectedItem property. Here's a summary:

•   The SelectedItem property gets or set the entire object that the selected item in the ComboBox is bound to. So in our previous example, the SelectedItem property will return the Model object currently selected in the ComboBox control. For binding purposes however, this property is rarely used, as it requires the Product entity to provide a property exposing an entire Model object that it can be bound to, whereas the Product entity will generally be able to provide only a property exposing the Model object's primary key value.

- The SelectedValuePath property is used to specify the name of the property on the objects in the bound collection that will be used to uniquely identify each object in that collection. In our example, this is assigned the ID property on the Model object.

- The SelectedValue property is used in conjunction with the SelectedValuePath property. Just like the SelectedItem property, it is used to get or set the selected item in the ComboBox control. However, you need to provide it with only the value of the property specified by the SelectedValuePath property to select that corresponding item. In our example, we just need to bind the ComboBox control's SelectedValue property to the ModelID property on the Product entity. The ComboBox control will then find the Model object in the collection that it's bound to whose ID property is equal to the value assigned to the Product entity's ModelID property and will select that item.

- The DisplayMemberPath property is used to designate a property on the objects in the bound collection whose value will displayed to represent each object. In our example, we've configured the ComboBox control to display the value of the Name property for each Model object in the collection.

One issue that you need to be aware of is that the collection of items to display in the ComboBox needs to be populated before you can bind its SelectedItem/SelectedValue property; otherwise, the ComboBox will not display the selected item. In other words, you need to populate the collection that the ComboBox control is bound to before you can bind the ComboBox control's selected item. This is something that you particularly need to be wary of when loading the contents of the ComboBox control from the server. A common pattern used when the data to populate a ComboBox control needs to be retrieved from the server is to bind the ComboBox control's ItemsSource property to an empty ObservableCollection and simply add items to that collection once the server has returned the data. However, if the items haven't been populated when a value is assigned to the ComboBox control's SelectedItem/SelectedValue property, it won't have an item available to select and will remain blank—even when the items are finally populated. Kyle McClellan has blogged about this problem and provided a solution that you can use if you're also experiencing it:
http://blogs.msdn.com/b/kylemc/archive/2010/06/18/combobox-sample-for-ria-services.aspx.

■ **Note** As with the ListBox control, you can customize the data template of each item by assigning a custom data template to the ComboBox's ItemTemplate property. This will allow you to show images, have multiple columns, and so on for your items.

The ListBox Control

You've already seen how to use the ListBox control to display a summary list and enable the user to drill down to a record in Chapter 6. You could also use it in a data entry scenario in much the same way as described for the ComboBox control—enabling the user to select an item from a collection. Another common use for the ListBox control in a data entry scenario is to have two lists, with the user able to move items from one list to another via dragging and dropping an item between lists or simply by selecting an item and clicking a button to move that item to the other list.

The Date Input Controls

There are two controls for entering and selecting dates in the Silverlight SDK: the Calendar control and the DatePicker control.

■ **Note** To use these controls, your project will need a reference to the `System.Windows.Controls.dll` assembly, and the `sdk` namespace prefix needs to be defined, like so:

`xmlns:sdk="http://schemas.microsoft.com/winfx/2006/xaml/presentation/sdk"`.

The Calendar Control

The Calendar control (shown in Figure 7-15) enables the user to select a date from a calendar. You can get this selected date from the Calendar control's `SelectedDate` property:

```
<sdk:Calendar SelectedDate="{Binding StartDate, Mode=TwoWay}"/>
```

You can also allow the user to select a range of dates by changing the control's `SelectionMode` property from `SingleDate` to `SingleRange` or `MultipleRange`. You can then get the selected dates from the control's `SelectedDates` property. Alternatively, you can use the Calendar control for display purposes only by setting its `SelectionMode` property to `None`.

Figure 7-15. *A Calendar control*

You can narrow the range of the date(s) that can be selected by assigning a start date for the range to the Calendar control's `DisplayDateStart` property and the end date for the range to the `DisplayDateEnd` property. All dates outside this range will be blanked out and nonselectable. You can also use the `BlackoutDates` property to set additional dates that the user cannot select. Instead of being blanked out, these dates will display a gray cross over them. This feature can be used to prevent a weekend or a public holiday from being selected. To assign dates to the `BlackoutDates` property, you will need to add `CalendarDateRange` objects to the collection, with a from and to date, or bind the property to a collection of these objects in XAML.

By default, the current date is always highlighted in the calendar. You can disable this by setting the `IsTodayHighlighted` property to `False`. You can change the first day of the week using the `FirstDayOfWeek` property.

The month view isn't the only type of view supported by the Calendar control. Using the control's `DisplayMode` property, you change the mode between `Month`, `Year`, and `Decade`.

The DatePicker Control

The DatePicker control has many features in common with the Calendar control, as shown in Figure 7-16. Clicking the button next to the text box or pressing Ctrl+down arrow when the text box has focus will pop up a calendar that the user can select the date from. Unlike the Calendar control, only a single date can be entered into or selected from the DatePicker control. However, you can still restrict the date entered to be within a range and black out various date ranges, like you can with the Calendar control. It does have one additional property: SelectedDateFormat. Instead of using the default short date format, you can change the date format to the long date format via that property.

```
<sdk:DatePicker SelectedDate="{Binding StartDate, Mode=TwoWay}" />
```

Figure 7-16. A DatePicker control

The Time Input Controls

In addition to the date data input controls in the Silverlight SDK, there are two controls for entering times in the Silverlight Toolkit: the TimeUpDown control and the TimePicker control.

■ **Note** To use these controls, your project will need a reference to the System.Windows.Controls.Data. Toolkit.dll assembly, and the toolkit namespace prefix will need to be defined, like so:

```
xmlns:toolkit="http://schemas.microsoft.com/winfx/2006/xaml/presentation/toolkit".
```

The TimeUpDown Control

The TimeUpDown control shown in Figure 7-17 lets the user either enter a time or select one using the up and down buttons. The control enables the user to enter a part of the time, and guesses the rest of it when the user tabs away. For example, the user can simply enter **9**, and the control will fill in **9:00 AM**. The user can also select a particular part of the time (hour, minute, etc.) and use the up and down buttons to change it accordingly.

| 6:55 AM |

Figure 7-17. A TimeUpDown control

You can get or set the time via its Value property:

```
<toolkit:TimeUpDown Value="{Binding StartTime, Mode=TwoWay}" />
```

You can change the format of the time's display in the control using the TimeUpDown control's Format property and assigning it either a standard or custom date formatting string. For example, you could specify HH:mm:ss as the format, which uses 24-hour time and includes the seconds.

You can force the user to enter the time only via the up and down buttons, by setting the control's IsEditable property to False. You can also stop the user from going past 11:59 p.m. or before 12:00 a.m. by setting the IsCyclic property to False.

The TimePicker Control

The TimePicker control is similar to the TimeUpDown control, except it also has a drop-down list that the user can select a time from, as shown in Figure 7-18.

```
<toolkit:TimePicker Value="{Binding StartTime, Mode=TwoWay}" />
```

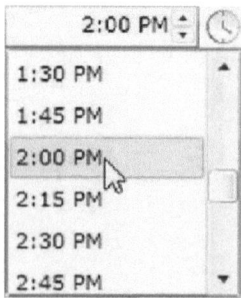

Figure 7-18. A TimePicker control

By default, the drop-down list contains an item for every half hour, but you could change this to every quarter of an hour, for example, by setting PopupMinutesInterval to 15.

The Up and Down Controls

You've seen how the TimeUpDown and TimePicker controls have up and down buttons to enable the user to modify the time using only the mouse. Two other controls in the Silverlight Toolkit also implement this same feature for other data types: the NumericUpDown control for numbers and the DomainUpDown control for selecting an item from a collection.

■ **Note** To use these controls, your project will need a reference to the System.Windows.Controls.Data.Toolkit.dll assembly, and the toolkit namespace prefix defined, like so:

xmlns:toolkit="http://schemas.microsoft.com/winfx/2006/xaml/presentation/toolkit".

The NumericUpDown Control

The NumericUpDown control allows only the entry of numbers—attempting to enter a nonnumeric value will result in the value being reverted to its original value when the field loses the focus. Its key features include

- The ability to set the number of decimal places that are displayed via the DecimalPlaces property

- The ability to set how much the value will increment or decrement when using the up or down buttons with the Increment property

- The ability to get or set the value via its Value property

The following code demonstrates creating a NumericUpDown control in XAML, and Figure 7-19 shows the result:

```
<toolkit:NumericUpDown DecimalPlaces="2" Increment="0.5"
                       Value="{Binding ListPrice, Mode=TwoWay}" />
```

Figure 7-19. A NumericUpDown control

The DomainUpDown Control

The DomainUpDown control is a bit like the ComboBox control in that it enables you use the up and down buttons to enter or select an item from a list of items. You bind a list of items to the ItemsSource property to select from, which could be an array of strings or a collection of objects. The user is constrained to entering values from only that collection.

You can choose from one of the following options as to what happens if the value entered by the user does not match an item in the list via the InvalidInputAction property:

- The UseFallbackItem option will result in the value being reverted to the value of the FallBackItem property when the field loses the focus. If a value for the FallBackItem property has not been specified, entering a value not in the list will result in the previous value being reinstated when the field loses the focus.

- The TextBoxCannotLoseFocus option forces the user to enter or select a valid item from the list before they can move on.

When binding the ItemsSource property to a collection of objects, you can use either the ValueMemberPath property or the ValueMemberBinding property on the DomainUpDown control to specify the property on the objects that will be displayed in the control:

- Generally, you will use the ValueMemberPath property, to which you simply assign the name of the property identifying that item.

- Alternatively, you can use the ValueMemberBinding property, to which you can assign a binding expression pointing to the property to use instead. This enables you to specify a value converter as a part of the binding if necessary.

For example, say you have a collection of objects representing U.S. states, each with two properties: one for the name of the state, and one for its short code (e.g., NY) You can display the name of the state in the control (we'll look at how to do this shortly) but set the ValueMemberPath property to the name of the short code property. If you do this, when editing the value of the field, the user can enter the short code for the state, and when the user tabs away from the field, the corresponding state name is displayed instead.

■ **Note** Unfortunately, unlike the ComboBox control, the DomainUpDown control has no `DisplayMemberPath` or `SelectedValuePath` property, nor does it have a `SelectedValue` property. When binding to a collection of objects (that aren't strings), the DomainUpDown control will simply call the `ToString` method on the object to get the text to display. Unless you have overridden the `ToString` method in your classes, you will therefore need to create a data template and assign it to the control's `ItemTemplate` property to customize what is displayed in the control. This also means that you can create a somewhat more complex custom layout to display in the control for each item if you wish.

The index of the currently selected item in the bound collection can be obtained via the `CurrentIndex` property. Much like the TimeUpDown control, this control also has `IsCyclic` and `IsEditable` properties.

The following code demonstrates creating a simple DomainUpDown control in XAML, and Figure 7-20 shows the result:

```
<toolkit:DomainUpDown ItemsSource="{StaticResource StatesResource}" />
```

Figure 7-20. *A DomainUpDown control*

The AutoCompleteBox Control

The AutoCompleteBox control can be used to enable the users to start typing a value that will be used to filter a list of items (appearing below the control when they begin to type), and select an item from the filtered list to complete that field's data input as shown in Figure 7-21. Under the covers, configuring the AutoCompleteBox control is similar to the DomainUpDown control. You bind its `ItemsSource` property to a collection that will used to populate the list of potential values. Usually this will be a collection of strings, but you can also bind it to a collection of objects and specify the property on these objects to be displayed using the control's `ValueMemberPath`/`ValueMemberBinding` property in the same way as previously described for the DomainUpDown control. You can also assign a data template to the AutoCompleteBox control's `ItemTemplate` property to customize how items appear in the list.

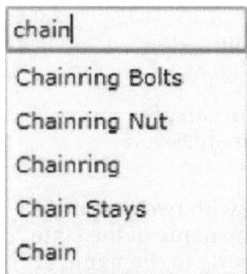

Figure 7-21. *The AutoCompleteBox control*

■ **Note** To speed up data input for power users, you may wish to use this control in some instances instead of a ComboBox control. However, this control does not restrict you from entering a value not in the bound collection.

By default, only items that start with the entered text appear in the list. However, you can alter this behavior using the Filter property. There are a number of different options, but the ones you will generally use are the StartsWith (the default) and Contains options. Alternatively, you could use the Custom option and create your own item or text filter, assigning it to the ItemFilter/TextFilter property accordingly (further discussion of custom filters is beyond the scope of this book).

You can have the text in the text box part of the control automatically complete with the first matching entry. Rather than having the user get partway through entering the value and then selecting an item from the list, which requires further effort, you can set the IsTextCompletionEnabled property to True to have the first matching item in the list already populate the text box, although the user can still keep typing to further refine the results. When the item within the text box is the one the user is after, simply pressing Tab will move to the next field.

The list of matches appears as soon as the user enters the first character, but if you have a very long list of items being filtered, it may be best to increase the MinimumPrefixLength property, which specifies the number of characters that the user has to enter in order for the drop-down list to appear with the matching filtered items. Alternatively (or in addition), you could assign a value to the MinimumPopulateDelay property, which specifies a period of time (in milliseconds) to wait before populating this list.

A very simple example of using the AutoCompleteBox control in XAML is provided here:

```
<sdk:AutoCompleteBox ItemsSource="{StaticResource StatesResource}"  />
```

The Label Control

Although it's not a data input control as such, the Label control has been designed for use alongside data input controls. You set some text to display (a label for a field) via its Content property, and then associate it with a data input control via its Target property, using ElementName binding (discussed in Chapter 11).

The benefit of using a Label control over a TextBlock control is that you can associate it with a particular data input control, using its Target property. By doing so, when the data entered into that control is invalid, the label will turn red to indicate that the field has an error. In addition, if the data input control is bound to a property marked as Required, using the validation attributes, the label will use bold text.

The following XAML demonstrates associating a Label control with a TextBox control named ProductNameTextBox:

```
<sdk:Label Content="Name:" Target="{Binding ElementName=ProductNameTextBox}" />
```

Setting the Tab Order

For the user to navigate between the data input controls using only the keyboard in a logical fashion, using the Tab key to move to the next control and Shift+Tab to move back to the previous control, you should set the tab order for each data input control in the user interface. You do this by assigning a numeric value to each control's TabIndex property. When the user tabs away from a control, the control with the same or next highest TabIndex value will receive the focus. The values do not have to be sequential, so it is a good idea to separate TabIndex values in increments of five or ten so that you can change the tab order of a control and insert it between two other controls without having to update the tab order of all the other controls.

You can prevent a control from getting the focus when the user is tabbing between controls by settings its IsTabStop property to False.

You can also customize the scope and behavior of tabbing using the TabNavigation property. The default value is Local, which tabs through all the data input fields and then through the controls outside the current view, the browser's address bar, and so on, before coming back to tab through the controls again. If you change this property at the container level (such as the view or page level) to Cycle, the focus will cycle between the controls in that container only, enabling you to restrict tab stops to only the data input controls in the data entry form. If you set this property to Once, the container and all its data input controls can be tabbed to only once.

Setting Focus

In addition to enabling the user to logically tab between the controls in your data entry form, you'll want to set the initial focus to a given data input control when a record is loaded. You can do so in the view's code behind by calling the control's Focus method (this requires you to give the control a name in the XAML), for example:

```
NameTextBox.Focus();
```

If you want to avoid writing code behind, you can use the control that Rocky Lhotka wrote and blogged about at www.lhotka.net/weblog/SettingFocusInXAMLWithNoCode.aspx. You just drop this control on a view and bind its TargetControl property to the control that should automatically receive the focus, using ElementName binding. Therefore, this control allows you to set the focus to a control without needing to write any code behind.

When the focus needs to be set to a field within a DataForm control, things become a little more complex. Let's first look at the instance where you have explicitly defined fields in your DataForm control—that is, the DataForm control's AutoGenerateFields property is set to False. Two problems arise here:

- The edit template is not instated in the DataForm control until the data is bound to it.

- If you give a data input control a name in XAML (within the DataForm control), it won't have a corresponding variable created in the code-behind that you could use to refer to it. This is because the control is within a data template. Because this template and its content can be repeated, to avoid possible name collisions, each data template is created in its own name scope (discussed in Chapter 2). If you were to refer to a control within a data template in code, it wouldn't know which instance to use.

You can overcome the first issue by waiting for the controls defined in the edit template to be loaded, which will be when the DataForm control's ContentLoaded event is raised. After this event is raised, you can set focus to a control, but first, you need to get a reference to that control. Since a variable is not created for the control in the code behind, you will need to search for it inside the data template. The DataForm control actually makes this procedure easier by providing a FindNameInContent method. Pass it the name of the control, and it will return you its current instance. You can then set the focus to this control, as demonstrated here:

```
private void dataForm_ContentLoaded(object sender, DataFormContentLoadEventArgs e)
{
    TextBox NameTextBox = ((DataForm)sender).FindNameInContent("NameTextBox")
                                                                    as TextBox;
    NameTextBox.Focus();
}
```

This works, but doing so interferes with the ability to navigate between records using the DataForm control's navigation buttons. Attempts to navigate between the objects in the collection will fail. The ContentLoaded event will be raised in response to the navigation, but for some reason, setting the focus to a control in the event handler for this event prevents the current item being changed, and the CurrentItemChanged event is consequently never raised. Instead, you will need to make use of the DispatcherTimer to delay setting focus to a control temporarily. The following code demonstrates delaying setting the focus to a control for 100 milliseconds, which solves the problem:

```
var timer = new DispatcherTimer();
timer.Interval = new TimeSpan(0, 0, 0, 0, 100);
timer.Tick +=
    (a, b) =>
    {
        timer.Stop();
        TextBox NameTextBox =
            ((DataForm)sender).FindNameInContent("NameTextBox") as TextBox;
        NameTextBox.Focus();
    };
timer.Start();
```

■ **Note** Rocky Lhotka's control can be used within the DataForm control's edit template to set the focus to a particular control. However, it also suffers this same drawback of preventing the user from navigating between records. You can modify that control to use a DispatcherTimer as just shown here, which will provide a code-free means of setting the focus to a control within the DataForm control.

When you configure the DataForm control to automatically generate data entry fields for you, you obviously won't be able to set the focus to a named control within it, because none of the controls will be named. Instead, the only solution is to search through the DataForm control's children for a data input control using the VisualTreeHelper class from the System.Windows.Media namespace. The following code provides a way for you to simply enumerate through all the children of a control, without the need to worry about recursion:

```
public IEnumerable<DependencyObject> Descendents(DependencyObject parent)
{
    int count = VisualTreeHelper.GetChildrenCount(parent);

    for (int index = 0; index < count; index++)
    {
        var child = VisualTreeHelper.GetChild(parent, index);
        yield return child;

        foreach (var descendent in Descendents(child))
```

```
            yield return descendent;
    }
}
```

You can then use this method to find the first TextBox control, which you can set focus to:

```
TextBox textBox =
    Descendents((DependencyObject)sender).FirstOrDefault(x => x is TextBox)
                                                       as TextBox;
```

Getting Focused Control

You can obtain a reference to the control that currently has the focus using the FocusManager object, which you can find in the System.Windows.Input namespace:

```
object element = FocusManager.GetFocusedElement();
```

Checking Whether Items Have Changed

It's generally a good idea to notify the user before navigating away from a data entry form where data has been entered or modified but has not been saved to prevent the accidental loss of changes to the data. This is often referred to as checking whether the data is "dirty." If the data is dirty, you can prompt the user to save or discard those changes.

If your bound object was retrieved from the server via RIA Services, you can cast the CurrentItem property of the DataForm control to a type of Entity and check its HasChanges property, like so:

```
bool hasChanges = ((Entity)ProductsDataForm.CurrentItem).HasChanges;
```

■ **Note** Although you should be able to check the DataForm control's IsItemChanged property to see whether any changes have been made to the current item, it doesn't seem to work (it only returns False).

If the user can edit multiple items in the data entry form, you will need to check whether the collection has changes. If the collection was returned from the server via RIA Services, you can simply use the HasChanges property of the domain context instance that returned the collection to find out whether unsaved changes have been made to the collection.

Using the DataGrid for Data Entry

In some scenarios, it may be appropriate to use the DataGrid control for data entry purposes instead of using a form-based layout. As described in the previous chapter, the DataGrid control is best suited for data entry purposes, rather than simply displaying data (in which a ListBox control would typically be more appropriate). It's best used when multiple objects in a collection need to be added or maintained, each of these objects relate to the parent entity, and there are few fields to be displayed or modified.

One good example of when you might like to use the DataGrid control is when you are creating a data entry form for editing an invoice. You could use the DataGrid control to display and modify the related invoice lines. In this scenario, there are multiple lines to be entered and displayed, all relating to the same invoice, and typically few fields involved (e.g., description, quantity, unit cost, tax, and line total). These features make this an ideal scenario for using a DataGrid control.

Configuring the Columns

Configuring and customizing the columns in a DataGrid control is discussed in Chapter 6, where you saw that there are three types of columns supported by the DataGrid control:

- `DataGridTextColumn`
- `DataGridCheckBoxColumn`
- `DataGridTemplateColumn`

You can specify the types of input control used for each field by using the appropriate column type, with the `DataGridTemplateColumn` type enabling you to insert any type of control into a cell.

■ **Note** When you assign bindings to the `DataGridTextColumn` and `DataGridCheckBoxColumn` types, the bindings for the corresponding input controls that the DataGrid creates when a row is in edit mode will automatically use the TwoWay binding mode, regardless of the mode assigned to a column's binding. Input controls in a `DataGridTemplateColumn` column will, however, need their binding mode explicitly set to TwoWay as usual.

Adding a Row

How you handle adding and deleting rows really depends on your requirements. Note that there are no AddRow or DeleteRow methods (or similar) on the DataGrid—instead, you will need to work directly with the underlying bound collection.

■ **Note** This bound collection will need to implement the `INotifyCollectionChanged` interface (such as the `ObservableCollection<T>` type) for the DataGrid control to recognize that a row has been added and show it accordingly.

The simplest way to implement this behavior is to simply add a button to your view that when clicked will add a new item to the collection that the DataGrid is bound to. If you have a reference to the bound collection or can cast the value of the DataGrid's ItemsSource property to that type, you should be able to simply call its Add method.

However, if the DataGrid control is bound to a DomainDataSource control, you will need to cast the value of the DataGrid's ItemsSource property to a DomainDataSourceView (one of the collection view types discussed in Chapter 6), for example:

```
DomainDataSourceView view = productDataGrid.ItemsSource as DomainDataSourceView;
Product newProduct = new Product();
view.Add(newProduct);
```

Once the row has been added, you will want to set focus to it, select it, make sure it's within the current view, and put it into edit mode:

```
// Scroll the first cell of the new row into view and start editing
productDataGrid.Focus();
productDataGrid.SelectedItem = newProduct;
productDataGrid.CurrentColumn = productDataGrid.Columns[0];
productDataGrid.ScrollIntoView(productDataGrid.SelectedItem,
                               productDataGrid.CurrentColumn);
productDataGrid.BeginEdit();
```

■ **Note** If any of the properties have default values that fail one or more validation rules, the validation summary will be automatically displayed at the bottom of the DataGrid as soon as the user starts editing a row, which isn't a particularly nice user experience. Unfortunately, this is the case with all the methods of adding items to the DataGrid described here. Rather annoyingly, the validation summary often covers the row being edited—hopefully this issue will be resolved in the near future. You can avoid this problem by assigning default values to the new object that will pass the validation rules.

Inserting a Row

You insert a row into a DataGrid control in much the same way as just described for adding a row. Instead of calling the Add method on the bound collection, simply call its Insert method, like so:

```
ObservableCollection<Product> collection =
    productDataGrid.ItemsSource as ObservableCollection<Product>;

int insertIndex = productDataGrid.SelectedIndex + 1;

// To counter some strange behavior by the DataGrid when the
// first row is selected, but not reported as such by the
// SelectedIndex property (right after the DataGrid is populated)
if (productDataGrid.SelectedIndex == -1 && collection.Count != 0)
    insertIndex = 1;

collection.Insert(insertIndex, new Product());

// Select and scroll the first cell of the new row into view and start editing
productDataGrid.SelectedIndex = insertIndex;
productDataGrid.CurrentColumn = productDataGrid.Columns[0];
productDataGrid.ScrollIntoView(productDataGrid.SelectedItem,
                               productDataGrid.CurrentColumn);
productDataGrid.BeginEdit();
```

■ **Note** If the DataGrid control is bound directly to a DomainDataSource control, you won't be able to insert row because the DomainDataSourceView class doesn't have an Insert method.

Spreadsheet-Like Editing

Another way to let the user enter multiple rows in a spreadsheet-like fashion is to populate the bound collection with items and remove the unused items from the collection before submitting the data back to the server. This is useful when you have a maximum number of rows that you will support. However, when the number of rows is undetermined, setting a fixed maximum number of rows isn't an ideal solution.

Maintaining an Empty Row for the Entry of New Records

The final and generally most user-friendly approach to let users add records using a DataGrid is to automatically maintain an empty row as the last row. Users can enter data for a new item in this row, and the DataGrid should automatically add a new empty row once they do. Sadly, there is no built-in feature like this in the core Silverlight DataGrid. You could add it yourself (the source code for the DataGrid control is available in the Silverlight Toolkit), but it's not a great idea, as you'd be tying yourself to that particular version of the DataGrid control and unable to easily take advantage of new features and bug fixes in future releases of Silverlight and the Silverlight Toolkit. You can, however, handle a number of events raised by the DataGrid control and manage this automatically. The steps are as follows:

1. Maintain a class-level variable that will reference the new item object:

```
private object addRowBoundItem = null;
```

2. Add a new item to the bound collection before or shortly after binding, and assign this item to the class-level variable. If binding the DataGrid directly to a DomainDataSource control, you would do this in the LoadedData event of the DomainDataSource control, like so:

```
DomainDataSourceView view = productDataGrid.ItemsSource as DomainDataSourceView;
addRowBoundItem = new Product();
view.Add(addRowBoundItem);
```

3. Handle the RowEditEnded event of the DataGrid control. If the row being committed is the empty row item that was edited (you can get the item in the collection that it is bound to from the DataContext property of the row), it's time to add a new item to the end of the bound collection, ensure it is visible, select it, and put it in edit mode, for example:

```
private void productDataGrid_RowEditEnded(object sender,
                                        DataGridRowEditEndedEventArgs e)
{
    if (e.EditAction == DataGridEditAction.Commit)
    {
        if (e.Row.DataContext == addRowBoundItem)
        {
            DomainDataSourceView view =
                productDataGrid.ItemsSource as DomainDataSourceView;

            addRowBoundItem = new Product();
            view.Add(addRowBoundItem);

            productDataGrid.SelectedItem = addRowBoundItem;
            productDataGrid.CurrentColumn = productDataGrid.Columns[0];

            productDataGrid.ScrollIntoView(addRowBoundItem,
```

```
                                                productDataGrid.CurrentColumn);
            productDataGrid.BeginEdit();
        }
    }
}
```

4. Remember to always delete the last item in the collection before submitting
    the changes back to the server, because it will always be the item representing
    the new row:

```
DomainDataSourceView view = productDataGrid.ItemsSource as DomainDataSourceView;
view.Remove(addRowBoundItem);
```

■ **Note** The Silverlight 4 GDR1 release did hold out some hope for a nicer way to implement this behavior, but that, unfortunately, has not come to fruition. Collection views have a NewItemPlaceholderPosition property, which supported only a value of None in the Silverlight 4 RTW release. The GDR1 release added an AtEnd value to this enumeration, which, when bound to a DataGrid control, should technically result in an empty row being displayed that would allow users to add new records. However, attempting to set the NewItemPlaceholderPosition property of any of Silverlight's collection view's to AtEnd results in an exception being raised, as none support this value. I've tried creating a collection view from scratch by creating a class that implements the ICollectionView and IEditableCollectionView interfaces, whose NewItemPlaceholderPosition property I could set to AtEnd to see whether this would work, but unfortunately, the DataGrid control does not seem to respond.

Deleting the Selected Rows

Deleting the selected row(s) in the DataGrid requires you to get the bound collection or collection view and enumerate through the SelectedItems property of the DataGrid, removing the corresponding item from the bound collection or collection view. This is can be a somewhat messy process due to removing items in an enumerated collection, but you can use LINQ to simplify the code somewhat:

```
ObservableCollection<Product> collection =
    productDataGrid.ItemsSource as ObservableCollection<Product>;

// Convert the SelectedItems property to an array so its enumerator won't be
// affected by deleting items from the source collection
// Note that this line requires the System.Linq namespace to be declared
var removeItems = productDataGrid.SelectedItems.Cast<Product>().ToArray();

foreach (Product product in removeItems)
    collection.Remove(product);
```

■ **Note** To use the Cast<T> method in this code, at the top of your file, you'll need to have a using directive to the System.Linq namespace.

Alternatively, you can force only one row to be selected at a time in the DataGrid by setting its SelectionMode property to Single rather than to the default value of Extended, meaning that you only need to worry about removing a single selected item. In this case, the following code would suffice:

```
ObservableCollection<Product> collection =
    productDataGrid.ItemsSource as ObservableCollection<Product>;

collection.Remove(productDataGrid.SelectedItem as Product);
```

Adding a Delete Button to Each Row

Adding a delete button to each row is reasonably easy. Simply use a template column, and define a data template for the cell containing a button:

```
<sdk:DataGridTemplateColumn Width="80">
    <sdk:DataGridTemplateColumn.CellTemplate>
        <DataTemplate>
            <Button Content="Delete" Click="DeleteButton_Click" />
        </DataTemplate>
    </sdk:DataGridTemplateColumn.CellTemplate>
</sdk:DataGridTemplateColumn>
```

Now, handle the Click event of the button in code to delete the corresponding item. The bound item in the collection is assigned to the data context of the row, and this is inherited down the hierarchy to the cell and then the button. Therefore, you can get the object or entity that the row is bound to from the Button control's DataContext property and remove it from the collection or view that the DataGrid is bound to:

```
private void DeleteButton_Click(object sender, RoutedEventArgs e)
{
    DomainDataSourceView view = productDataGrid.ItemsSource as DomainDataSourceView;
    view.Remove(((FrameworkElement)sender).DataContext);
}
```

■ **Note** This delete button is generally more attractive and less intrusive if you retemplate the button to simply contain an image. You may also prefer to show the button only when the row is selected.

Implementing DropDown Lists

Unfortunately, the DataGrid control doesn't have a column type that allows the user to pick a value for a cell from a set of values. You can, however, use a template column containing a ComboBox control to implement this behavior. Simply create a data template containing a ComboBox control, and bind its properties as normal, for example:

```
<sdk:DataGridTemplateColumn x:Name="classColumn" Header="Class" Width="100">
    <sdk:DataGridTemplateColumn.CellEditingTemplate>
        <DataTemplate>
            <ComboBox
                ItemsSource="{Binding Source={StaticResource productClasses}}"
```

```
                    DisplayMemberPath="Name" SelectedValuePath="ID"
                    SelectedValue="{Binding Class, Mode=TwoWay}" />
            </DataTemplate>
        </sdk:DataGridTemplateColumn.CellEditingTemplate>
    </sdk:DataGridTemplateColumn>
```

■ **Note**   As mentioned earlier, the collection of items to display in the ComboBox needs to be populated before you can bind its SelectedItem/SelectedValue property. Otherwise, the ComboBox will not display the selected item. That is, you need to populate the collection that the ComboBox control is bound to before you can bind the DataGrid to its collection of items.

If you don't want the ComboBox control to be visible unless the cell is in edit mode, you'll need to define another template and assign it to the template column's CellTemplate property, containing a TextBlock control with the description for the bound value. However, you'll face the issue of how to look up the description corresponding to the given value. One option is to use a value converter as part of the binding, which will look up the description for the value from a collection. The sample code accompanying this chapter demonstrates this solution. We'll look at value converters in detail in Chapter 11.

Structuring Objects for Use by Data Entry Forms

To create effective data entry forms, you should do a few things to make your objects friendlier to the user interface controls that will bind to them. RIA Services entities automatically implement these features by default, but if you are binding to objects whose classes are defined on the client, such as a ViewModel when using the MVVM design pattern discussed in Chapter 13, or you're simply not using RIA Services at all, you will need to implement these features manually. Let's take a look at the most important features you should add to your objects for the benefit of the user interface.

Implementing the INotifyPropertyChanged Interface

One of the key interfaces that your objects should implement is the INotifyPropertyChanged interface (found in the System.ComponentModel namespace). This is a simple interface, requiring your class to implement a single event named PropertyChanged. Bindings automatically listen for this event, and when it is raised, any binding associated with that property updates itself accordingly, and hence, the control associated with that binding is updated as well.

■ **Note**   Silverlight 5 has introduced the INotifyPropertyChanging interface, which you might like to implement in addition to the INotifyPropertyChanged interface on your classes. However, here we'll focus only on the INotifyPropertyChanged interface.

Basic Implementation (with "Magic Strings")

Once you've implemented the INotifyPropertyChanged interface on your class, you can notify listeners when a property's value has changed by raising the PropertyChanged event, passing it a PropertyChangedEventArgs object containing the name of the property being updated. The following example demonstrates the code that you would use to notify the user interface that the value of a property named Name has changed:

```
private string _name;

public string Name
{
    get { return _name; }
    set
    {
        _name = value;

        if (PropertyChanged != null)
            PropertyChanged(this, new PropertyChangedEventArgs("Name"));
    }
}
```

It's important to note that the PropertyChanged event is never raised when you use automatically implemented properties. For example, properties implemented in the following fashion do *not* raise the PropertyChanged event on the class, even when that class implements the INotifyPropertyChanged interface:

```
public string Name { get; set; }
```

Therefore, the user interface will not be aware of any changes to the value of that property that it did not make itself and will not be updated when the underlying property value is changed. Unfortunately, this means that you must implement the getter and setter for the property and maintain the property's value in a member variable. You can then raise the PropertyChanged event in the setter as required.

Note Some Visual Studio extensions enable you to easily turn an automatically implemented property into a property with a backing store (a member variable that maintains the property's value) and raise the PropertyChanged event for that property. Choosing this option saves you from having to hand-code the getters and setters. Alternatively, try searching the Web for "INotifyPropertyChanged snippets"—you will find a multitude of snippets to help you create your properties accordingly and that you can customize to suit your needs.

The INotifyPropertyChanged interface is very commonly used, and many developers add an OnPropertyChanged (or similarly named) method that raises the PropertyChanged event, rather than actually raising the event in the property setters. This simplifies the property setters, as you do not have to check that the PropertyChanged event is not null, which it will be if nothing is handling the event, before calling it.

```
protected void OnPropertyChanged(string propertyName)
{
    if (PropertyChanged != null)
        PropertyChanged(this, new PropertyChangedEventArgs(propertyName));
}
```

In the property setter now, you can simply use a single line of code to raise the event:

```
OnPropertyChanged("Name");
```

This makes your property setters somewhat neater, although there is still the unfortunate requirement to pass the method the name of the property as a string. This requirement can result in situations where the property name is different from the string. For example, the string may misspell the property name, or the property name may have been refactored but the string was not updated accordingly. These issues can lead to particularly difficult bugs to identify and track down. In the following sections, we'll look at some other alternatives that can avoid these issues. Which approach you choose will come down to personal taste.

Using Reflection Instead of Magic Strings

You can use reflection to get the name of the property in its setter (ignoring the first four characters, set_) and pass that to the OnPropertyChanged method:

```
OnPropertyChanged(MethodBase.GetCurrentMethod().Name.Substring(4));
```

■ **Note** For this code to compile, at the top of your file you will need a using directive to the System.Reflection namespace.

Using Reflection to Validate Magic Strings in Debug Mode

Alternatively, you may wish to continue with hard-coding the property name as a string and check in your OnPropertyChanged method that the property exists. The best idea is to perform this check in a separate method and call that method from the OnPropertyChanged method, as you can then decorate it with the Conditional attribute and have it run only when in debug mode:

```
[Conditional("DEBUG")]
private void EnsurePropertyExists(string propertyName)
{
    PropertyInfo propInfo = this.GetType().GetProperty(propertyName);
    Debug.Assert(propInfo != null, "The property " + propertyName + " does not " +
                                    "exist on this class");
}
```

■ **Note** For this method to work, you will need a using directive to both the System.Reflection namespace and the System.Diagnostics namespace.

Using Lambda Expressions Instead of Magic Strings

Yet another method is to use a lambda expression to specify the property name (instead of a string) and extract the name of the property from that. This popular method is faster than reflection and is refactoring safe (no magic strings). Start by adding the following using directive to the top of your class:

```
using System.Linq.Expressions;
```

Now, define the following method in your class (or a base class):

```
private string GetPropertyName<T>(Expression<Func<T>> property)
{
    MemberExpression expression = property.Body as MemberExpression;
    return expression.Member.Name;
}
```

■ **Note**   Generally, you would put the preceding method in the object's base class. Alternatively, you might like to define it as an extension method, as described by Jeremy Likeness at

http://csharperimage.jeremylikness.com/2010/06/tips-and-tricks-for-inotifypropertychan.html.

You can then call the OnPropertyChanged method from your property's setter using the following code, where Name is the name of the property:

```
OnPropertyChanged(GetPropertyName(() => Name));
```

Emiel Jongerius has written up some other alternatives, including another way of implementing this method that also sets the property's value, and how they compare performance-wise, at www.pochet.net/blog/2010/06/25/inotifypropertychanged-implementations-an-overview. Einar Ingebrigtsen also has a blog post with an extended version of this code that provides additional functionality at www.ingebrigtsen.info/post/2008/12/11/INotifyPropertyChanged-revisited.aspx.

Using Notify Property Weaver

Arguably the cleanest and simplest method of implementing property change notifications is using Notify Property Weaver. Notify Property Weaver is a Visual Studio extension created by Simon Cropp that removes the need for you to raise the PropertyChanged event in property setters. Your classes simply need to implement the INotifyPropertyChanged interface, and it handles the rest. It hooks into the compilation process, and "weaves" the required code into the application's IL code.

Benefits of this approach include the following:

- You get cleaner code. Without the need to raise property changed notifications in the property setters, you can now simply implement automatic properties, vastly reducing the amount of code you need to write.

- It doesn't require your classes to inherit from a base class.

- It's refactoring safe.

- There's no need for attributes on properties, which other IL weavers tend to require. However, you can use them to have more control over what is generated if you wish.

Let's look at how you can use this tool.

1. Get the Notify Property Weaver extension from the Visual Studio Extension Gallery (Tools ➤ Extension Manager). Do a search for it by its name.

2. With your Silverlight project as the active project, go to Project ➤ NotifyPropertyWeaver ➤ Configure.

3. A window will appear, allowing you to configure the IL weaving for the project. If you want to have more control over what is generated, select the IncludeAttributeAssembly check box on the Attribute Assembly tab.

4. Click OK. Your project will need to reload, but then it's all configured and you're ready to write code. The tool will now be configured as a build task. As long as your class implements the INotifyPropertyChanged interface, the tool will generate property changed notifications for each property in the class.

More information on Notify Property Weaver can be found at the project's web site: http://code.google.com/p/notifypropertyweaver/.

■ **Note** Various other solutions have been created to solve the property change notifications problem that we won't go into here, but you might like to investigate. Oren Eini has another interesting method of handling the INotifyPropertyChanged problem that you may like, where he has created an Observable<T> class. He has blogged about it at http://ayende.com/Blog/archive/2009/08/08/an-easier-way-to-manage-inotifypropertychanged.aspx. Justin Angel has yet another interesting method where he automatically implements INotifyPropertyChanged using Mono.Cecil and PostSharp at justinangel.net/AutomagicallyImplementingINotifyPropertyChanged.

Implementing the IEditableObject Interface

IEditableObject is another useful interface to implement in your objects (also found in the System.ComponentModel namespace). It is designed to enable you to cancel and roll back any changes made to an object (essentially an undo action). Any changes made to the object are tracked using a start/complete-type transaction that can be cancelled. When a transaction is cancelled, any changes made to the object since the beginning of the transaction are rolled back, and the object's original state is reinstated.

Implementing the IEditableObject interface requires your class to implement three methods: BeginEdit, EndEdit, and CancelEdit. The BeginEdit method should be called before any changes are made to the object, generally via a data entry form, and the EndEdit method should be called once those changes have been made and are to be committed.

Implementing the BeginEdit Method

In the BeginEdit method, you will need to write code to capture the state of the object at that time—that is, generally all the property values. The easiest way to implement this is using the MemberwiseClone method on the object to take a shallow copy of the state of the object:

```
private Product _originalState = null; // Member variable

public void BeginEdit()
{
    _originalState = this.MemberwiseClone() as Product;
}
```

Implementing the EndEdit Method

You can then discard this state in the EndEdit method, because any changes made to the object since the BeginEdit method was called will have been accepted (committed):

```
public void EndEdit()
{
    _originalState = null;
}
```

Implementing the CancelEdit Method

In the CancelEdit method, you need to restore the original state of the object as it was taken when the BeginEdit method was called, copying that state back to the current instance of the object. You can implement this method in one of two ways—either by manually assigning the values from the "backup" object or by using reflection.

■ **Note**   The reflection method is more reusable because it takes a more generic approach, but it is slower to execute.

Manually Assigning Property Values

You can have full control over what property values are reinstated by assigning the values back to the object's properties manually, either via the property setters or directly to each member variable backing the corresponding property being reinstated. Note that if you use the property setters, each will execute any code within itself, including the property-changed notifications and validation rules—behavior you may or may not want.

```
public void CancelEdit()
{
    if (_originalState != null)
    {
        Name = _originalState.Name;
        ProductNumber = _originalState.ProductNumber;
        // Etc...

        _originalState = null;
    }
}
```

> ■ **Note** If you choose to bypass the property setters, you may need to revalidate your object after reinstating the property values. (Validation is discussed later in this chapter.)

Assigning Property Values Using Reflection

Alternatively, you can use a generic method that copies the values of all the public properties on the originalState object back to the current instance using reflection:

```
public void CancelEdit()
{
    if (_originalState != null)
    {
        PropertyInfo[] objectProperties =
            this.GetType().GetProperties(BindingFlags.Public |
                                         BindingFlags.Instance);

        foreach (PropertyInfo propInfo in objectProperties)
        {
            object originalValue = propInfo.GetValue(_originalState, null);
            propInfo.SetValue(this, originalValue, null);
        }

        _originalState = null;
    }
}
```

> ■ **Note** The preceding method executes any code in the property setters.

Using the IEditableObject Methods

Both the DataForm and DataGrid controls have built-in support for calling the BeginEdit, EndEdit, and CancelEdit methods on bound objects that implement the IEditableObject interface.

The DataForm control will call the BeginEdit method when changes are first made to the bound object via the bound controls, and commit them by calling the EndEdit method either when the user navigates away from the current object, or when the user explicitly commits the changes by clicking the OK button when the DataForm's AutoCommit property is set to False. As discussed earlier in this chapter, when a DataForm control is bound to an object that implements the IEditableObject interface, a Cancel button will appear in the data entry form. Clicking this Cancel button will call the CancelEdit method on the object to return it to its original state.

The DataGrid also calls the BeginEdit method when changes are first made to a row and commits them by calling the EndEdit method when the user navigates away from the current row. Pressing the Esc key when editing a row will call the CancelEdit method on the object to return it to the state it was in prior to its being edited.

Adding Calculated Properties to Your Classes

Often, you may wish to display a calculated value in your user interface based upon the values of properties on an object. For example, you may have an object entity representing an invoice line and want to display the total amount of that line (quantity × unit price). Alternatively, you may wish to have a property that displays the full name of a person, built by concatenating their first name and surname, separated by a space.

If you have created the class on the client side (such as a ViewModel), you can simply add a new property to the class that performs the calculation. Your user interface controls can then bind to this property and display the calculated value.

```
public decimal LineTotal
{
    get
    {
        return Quantity * UnitPrice;
    }
}
```

If you are binding directly to entities exposed from the server via RIA Services, you can add calculated properties to these entities too. You should *never* modify the code generated by RIA Services, but each of the generated entities is a partial class, so you can simply create a corresponding partial of your own (in the client-side project) that extends the entity and adds the required calculated properties in the same way as was previously demonstrated.

You may be wondering how you can notify the user interface that the LineTotal property's value has changed, when the Quantity or UnitPrice properties are updated. If you shouldn't modify the code generated by RIA Services, where the Quantity or UnitPrice properties are defined, how can you notify the bindings that the value of the calculated property will have also changed? There are a number of options, but the best method is to extend one of the two partial methods that RIA Services has created for each property, which are called when their values are changing. For example, a UnitPrice property on an entity will have two corresponding methods: OnUnitPriceChanging (called before the value has changed) and OnUnitPriceChanged (called after the value has changed). You can extend the Changed method and notify the bindings of the property value change like so:

```
partial void OnListPriceChanged()
{
    OnPropertyChanged(new PropertyChangedEventArgs("LineTotal"));
}
```

Data Validation

One of the most important roles in a typical data entry form is to notify the user of any problems with the data that has been entered. Invalid data in a business system can have major consequences for the business, so effective validation of data is vital to reduce the number of data entry mistakes that make it into the system. It's impossible to catch all errors, but you want to minimize the number of them as much as possible, and ensure that almost all the data entered into the system is correct and accurate. In Chapter 4, we looked at how you can decorate entities and their properties exposed by RIA Services with validation attributes. These attributes are replicated by the RIA Services code generator on the corresponding client-side entities that it creates. These rules need to be executed as the data is being entered into the data entry form, notifying the user of any invalid data that's been entered and preventing any invalid data being submitted back to the server.

In this section, we'll look at how you can display validation errors to the user in your data entry forms. We'll also look at how you can implement validation behavior on your own objects via validation attributes and notify the user interface of the errors accordingly.

Displaying Validation Errors

Data entry forms require a friendly and nonintrusive way to notify users when they've entered invalid data and give them the reason why the data is invalid so that they can fix it accordingly. Silverlight has very strong support for displaying validation errors, with little work required on the part of the developer to implement them.

Data Entry Controls

Data entry controls can be notified by their bindings of any validation issues with their bound properties and will automatically restyle themselves accordingly to notify the user as such. A red border will appear around the control, and when the control has the focus, it will also display a red tooltip, showing the validation error message to explain the problem. If a Label control is associated with the control, it will also turn red. Figure 7-22 demonstrates what happens when the user enters invalid data into a TextBox control.

Figure 7-22. A TextBox control displaying a validation error

■ **Note** You can customize how a control displays validation errors by restyling the control's template. Customizing control templates is discussed in Chapter 9.

For the control to be notified of related validation errors by its bindings, the bindings need to be configured to listen for and handle validation errors. How you configure this depends on the method you are using to expose the validation errors to the user interface and will be discussed later in this chapter (in the "Exposing Validation Errors from Objects" section) as we detail these methods.

The ValidationSummary Control

The ValidationSummary control can be used to display a list of all the data validation errors for a data entry form. It listens for the BindingValidationError event raised by its container and maintains a collection of the validation errors that it reports. This means that you can simply place it in a view, like so:

```
<sdk:ValidationSummary />
```

Then it will automatically display any validation errors in your data entry form, as shown in Figure 7-23.

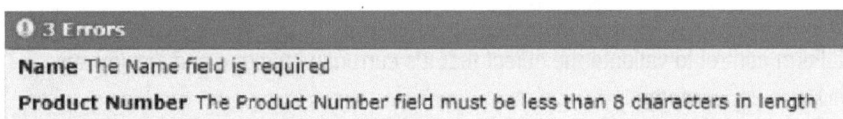

Figure 7-23. A ValidationSummary control

■ **Note** For their validation errors to appear in this control, data input controls in the data entry form need their bindings to have their NotifyOnValidationError property set to True. By default, its value is False.

The ValidationSummary control will remain hidden until it has validation errors to show and returns to the hidden state when the errors are fixed.

If you want to take a more manual approach to assigning errors for it to display, you can also manually assign errors to its Errors property in the code behind or bind this property to a collection of validation errors that you maintain, like so:

```
var error = new ValidationSummaryItem("The Name field is required", "Name",
                                   ValidationSummaryItemType.PropertyError,
                                   null, null);
validationSummary.Errors.Add(error);
```

The DataForm Control

The DataForm control has a built-in ValidationSummary control that will display validation errors, in addition to the validation error notification behavior exhibited by the data input controls within the form. The ValidationSummary control will automatically appear at the bottom of the DataForm control when the bound object reports any data validation errors, as shown in Figure 7-24.

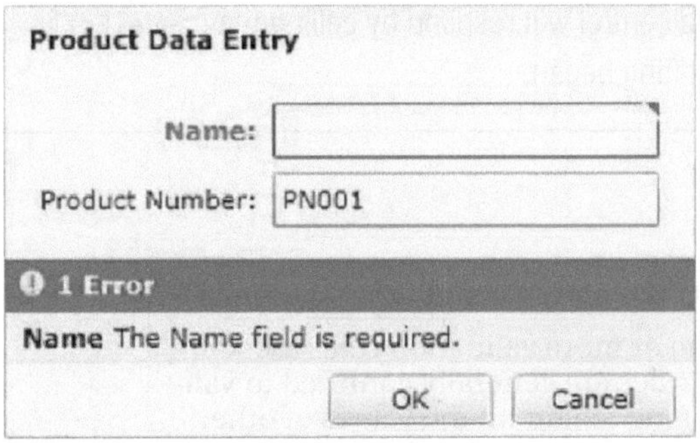

Figure 7-24. A DataForm control displaying a field in error and a validation summary

When its AutoCommit property is set to False, the DataForm control also ensures that the bound entity/object is valid before allowing the user to commit any changes. When its AutoCommit property is set to True, it prevents the user from moving away from the record until the validation errors have been resolved.

■ **Note** You can force the DataForm control to validate the object that it's currently bound to and display any validation errors by calling its `ValidateItem` method.

The DataGrid Control

Like the DataForm control, the DataGrid control also has a ValidationSummary control built in, which appears when the object/entity bound to the current row has validation errors. Validation errors will result in the background color of the row changing to a light red. Also, cells with associated validation errors will display a red border and a tooltip explaining the reason for the validation error when they have the focus, as shown in Figure 7-25.

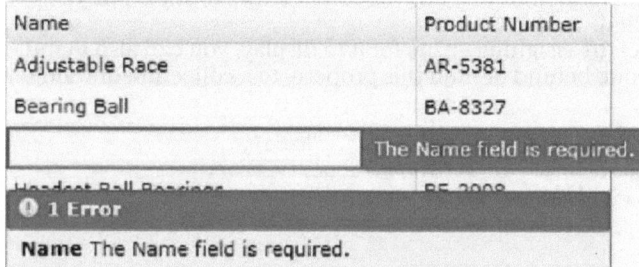

Figure 7-25. A DataGrid control displaying a cell in error and a validation summary

■ **Note** Until all validation errors are fixed on a row, the user cannot modify or add any other rows. If the bound object implements the `IEditableObject` interface, the user can press the Esc key (twice if a field is currently in edit mode; otherwise, once) to cancel the changes. The DataGrid control will respond by calling the `CancelEdit` method on that object and return the object to its state before editing began.

Types of Data Validation

There are three types of data validation that you usually need to perform in business applications:

- *Property-level validation*, in which there are one or more validation rules associated with a property. Property-level validation rules are generally confined to validating the value of a single property, without being reliant on the values of other properties on the object. For example, a typical property-level validation rule may ensure that a numeric value assigned to a property is within a given range. Property-level validation is performed whenever the value of a property is updated (in its setter) and when validating the object as a whole.

- *Object-level validation*, in which each validation rule generally relates to the values of multiple properties on a single object. For example, a typical object-level validation rule may ensure that the value of the EndDate property is greater than the value of the StartDate property. Object-level validation is performed when committing all the changes to the object, which is usually when the object's EndEdit method is called, assuming it implements the IEditableObject interface.

- *Domain-level validation*, in which a full object hierarchy is validated as a whole against a set of validation rules, with validation rules spanning across multiple objects. For example, a typical domain-level validation rule may ensure that when an order is placed enough items are in stock to fulfill the order. Domain-level validation is usually performed when committing changes back to the server, and often on the server itself.

In the following sections, we'll focus primarily on implementing property-level and object-level validation.

Defining Validation Rules

As described in Chapter 4, RIA Services enables you to define property-level and object-level validation rules by decorating your entities with validation attributes on the server, which are then replicated on the corresponding entities created on the client by the RIA Services code generator. This enables the validation rules to be run on the client as well as the server. Data can be validated on the client during data entry, and the rules will be run again on the server when the data is submitted.

When exposing entities from RIA Services, you will generally use validation attributes to specify property-level and object-level validation rules, but you can also use these attributes in your own client-side classes, such as your ViewModels, when using the MVVM design pattern (discussed in Chapter 13). Simply add a using directive to the System.ComponentModel.DataAnnotations namespace, and you can use the validation attributes described in Chapter 4 (e.g., Required, StringLength, Range, and RegularExpression) in exactly the same manner, for example:

```
[Required]
[StringLength(50)]
[RegularExpression(@"(?<user>[^@]+)@(?<host>.+)")]
public string EmailAddress;

[Range(0, 150)]
public int Age;
```

Note that the predefined validation attributes are all property-level rules. To define object-level validation rules, you will need to create a custom validation attribute that inherits from the base ValidationAttribute class demonstrated in Chapter 4. Repeating that same example, here is a custom validation rule for ensuring that the sell finish date on a product is later than the sell start date:

```
public class SellDatesValidationAttribute : ValidationAttribute
{
    protected override ValidationResult IsValid(object value,
                                    ValidationContext validationContext)
    {
        Product product = value as Product;
        return product.SellEndDate > product.SellStartDate ?
            ValidationResult.Success : new ValidationResult(
                "The sell end date must be greater than the sell start date");
    }
}
```

You can then apply the validation rule to your class like so:

```
[SellDatesValidation]
public class Product
```

Of course, you can also create custom property-level validation attributes in exactly the same way (also demonstrated in Chapter 4).

■ **Note** Using validation attributes is not the only way of implementing validation rules in Silverlight. Alternatively, you can manually implement property-level validation rules in the property setters and object-level validation rules in the object's EndEdit method, assuming you implement the IEditableObject interface. You can then expose them publicly using one of the approaches discussed in the next section. However, validation attributes tend to provide the most elegant means of implementing validation rules on your objects and allow the rules to be encapsulated and reused throughout your application.

Reporting Validation Errors from Objects

There are several means of reporting data validation errors from your entities/objects in Silverlight. Bindings can listen for validation errors reported by your objects using one of the following approaches:

- Throwing exceptions
- Implementing the IDataErrorInfo interface and its corresponding behavior
- Implementing the INotifyDataErrorInfo interface and its corresponding behavior

Let's look at each of these in turn.

■ **Note** Entities exposed from the server via RIA Services are automatically configured to report both property-level and object-level validation errors to the user interface. These entities inherit from the Entity class, which automatically implements the INotifyDataErrorInfo interface, and reports any data validation errors identified by the validation attributes when properties are updated to the bindings via the means provided by that interface. Therefore, the methods described here are primarily included to demonstrate the different methods that Silverlight provides to enable the user interface to be aware of data validation errors so that you can understand how data validation works behind the scenes and how to implement data validation in your own client-side classes.

Validation by Exception

Prior to Silverlight 4, the only means of notifying the user interface of property-level data validation errors was to throw an exception in the setter of the property. The ValidationException class (found in the System.ComponentModel.DataAnnotations namespace) was generally used for this purpose. An example of how you would validate a property value and notify the user interface of a data validation error using the exception approach is demonstrated here:

```
public string Name
{
    get { return _name; }
    set
    {
        _name = value;

        // Check validation rule
        if (string.IsNullOrEmpty(value))
            throw new ValidationException("You must enter a name for the product");
    }
}
```

When you bind the Text property of a TextBox control to this Name property, you need to set the binding's ValidatesOnExceptions property to True, like so:

```
<TextBox Text="{Binding Name, Mode=TwoWay, ValidatesOnExceptions=True}" />
```

Now if the user enters an "empty string" value into the text box and tabs away, the text box will display a validation error.

The process of throwing data validation errors as exceptions has never been popular with most developers, as conceptually data validation errors are not "exceptional" scenarios. Ideally, exceptions should be used only when an unexpected error occurs. Another problem with this method is that when you debug your application, every time an exception is thrown due to a data validation error, the execution of the application would break and throw you back into Visual Studio. You can still continue running the application, but it is a frustrating development experience.

■ **Note** You can stop Visual Studio breaking on these validation errors by opening the Exceptions window from the Debug menu in Visual Studio and configuring it to not break when a ValidationException exception is raised.

This validation by exception approach is also a problem when populating an entity with data, as assigning a value to a property that causes the object to temporarily become invalid, but will become valid as further properties are assigned their values, will raise an exception.

Although the exception approach of notifying bindings of validation errors has now been superseded by the approaches we'll discuss shortly, it can still be useful to turn on the ValidatesOnExceptions property of bindings, as it allows you to display validation errors due to type conversion errors. When a type converter fails to convert the user input to the destination type of the bound property, it will throw an exception. For example, the type converter behind the scenes will raise an exception when you try and enter a value of "asdf" into a text box that's bound to a property of type integer. Setting the ValidatesOnExceptions property to True will result in this exception being displayed to the user as a validation error.

■ **Note** It's not necessary to set the ValidatesOnExceptions property to True when the bindings are within a DataForm control—they will still be restyled and the validation summary will appear accordingly when there are validation errors on the bound object.

The IDataErrorInfo Interface

Silverlight 4 introduced support for the IDataErrorInfo interface, which was already being used in WPF to provide data validation support to objects. Implementing the IDataErrorInfo interface on an object enables you to expose validation errors for an entity/object, without requiring the use of exceptions. In addition, the big benefit of this approach is that it can report *all* the validation errors on an entity/object, instead of just that of the property being updated—a big advantage, especially when updating one property invalidates one or more other properties.

The IDataErrorInfo interface requires you to implement two properties on the object:

- The Error property exposes a string identifying the validation status of the entity/object as a whole (i.e., a single validation error message).

- The Item property accepts the name of a property as a parameter and returns any validation error as a string relating to that property.

The following code snippet demonstrates implementing the IDataErrorInfo interface in a simple class:

```
public class Product : IDataErrorInfo , INotifyPropertyChanged
{
    private string _name;
    private Dictionary<string, string> _validationErrors =
        new Dictionary<string, string>();

    public string Name
    {
        get { return _name; }
        set
        {
            _name = value;

            // Check validation rule
            if (string.IsNullOrEmpty(value))
            {
                _validationErrors["Name"] =
                    "You must enter a name for the product";
            }
            else
            {
                if (_validationErrors.ContainsKey("Name"))
                    _validationErrors.Remove("Name");
            }

            RaisePropertyChanged("Name");
        }
```

```
    }

    public string Error
    {
        get
        {
            string error = "";

            if (_validationErrors.Count != 0)
                error = "This object is invalid";

            return error;
        }
    }

    public string this[string columnName]
    {
        get
        {
            string error = "";

            if (_validationErrors.ContainsKey(columnName))
                error = _validationErrors[columnName];

            return error;
        }
    }

    private void RaisePropertyChanged(string propertyName)
    {
        if (PropertyChanged != null)
            PropertyChanged(this, new PropertyChangedEventArgs(propertyName));
    }

    public event PropertyChangedEventHandler PropertyChanged;
}
```

To configure bindings to look for validation errors reported by an object that implements the IDataErrorInfo interface, they have a property named ValidatesOnDataErrors which needs to be set to True (its default value is False.) You *must* set this to True on your bindings, even in the DataForm control; otherwise, the controls will not be notified of validation errors associated with their bound properties and thus won't restyle themselves accordingly.

```
<TextBox Text="{Binding Name, Mode=TwoWay, ValidatesOnDataErrors=True}" />
```

■ **Note** There is no event included in the IDataErrorInfo interface that can be raised when there is a data validation error, so you may be wondering how the user interface will be made aware of any data validation errors on a bound entity/object. You do so by implementing the INotifyPropertyChanged interface on your entity/object and raising the PropertyChanged event for the invalid property, as was demonstrated in the previous code snippet. Any bindings bound to the property will handle this event and be notified of the change accordingly. If a binding has its `ValidatesOnDataErrors` set to `True` and if the entity/object also implements the `IDataErrorInfo` interface, it will check the `Error` and `Item` properties for any data validation errors corresponding to its bound property. If validation errors are found, it will notify the control so that it can display them.

The INotifyDataErrorInfo Interface

In addition to the `IDataErrorInfo` interface, Silverlight 4 also introduced an interface named `INotifyDataErrorInfo`. This interface provides a number of benefits over the `IDataErrorInfo` interface and is generally the preferred approach for enabling your objects to publicly report data validation errors. Benefits of this approach include

- Unlike the `IDataErrorInfo` interface, `INotifyDataErrorInfo` requires the implementation of an `ErrorsChanged` event that can be used to notify bindings of validation errors, without relying on the `PropertyChanged` event from the `INotifyPropertyChanged` interface.

- You can report multiple validation errors per property.

- You can report multiple object-level validation errors.

- Bindings are automatically configured to listen for validation errors in this manner, without the need to explicitly configure them to do so.

- Data validation can be performed asynchronously. For example, you may wish to have a validation rule executed on the server and notify the user interface of the result when the call returns.

The `INotifyDataErrorInfo` interface requires your objects to implement the following members:

- `GetErrors`: This method returns a collection of all the errors related to a given property.

- `HasErrors`: This property returns a Boolean value indicating whether the entity or object has any errors.

- `ErrorsChanged`: This event should be raised when the collection of errors is changed—that is, when a validation rule fails and is added to the collection of errors, or when a validation error is resolved.

Bindings automatically listen for the `ErrorsChanged` event to be raised on the bound entity/object. When the `ErrorsChanged` event is raised for a property, corresponding bindings will call the `GetErrors` method to get the validation errors relating to that property.

■ **Note** The bindings treat this approach to implementing validation differently from the other approaches described. With those approaches, for the bound controls to be aware of validation errors, you have to explicitly set the value of the `ValidatesOnExceptions` and `ValidatesOnDataErrors` properties on the associated bindings to `True`. Bindings also have a `ValidatesOnNotifyDataErrors` property, but its default value is already `True`. This means that it's unnecessary to explicitly configure a binding for it to be aware of validation errors reported in this manner.

The following code snippet demonstrates implementing the INotifyDataErrorInfo interface in a simple class:

```
public class Product : INotifyDataErrorInfo
{
    private string _name;
    private Dictionary<string, List<string>> _validationErrors =
        new Dictionary<string, List<string>>();

    public string Name
    {
        get { return _name; }
        set
        {
            _name = value;

            // Check validation rule
            if (string.IsNullOrEmpty(value))
            {
                _validationErrors["Name"] = new List<string>();
                _validationErrors["Name"].Add(
                    "You must enter a name for the product");
            }
            else
            {
                if (_validationErrors.ContainsKey("Name"))
                    _validationErrors.Remove("Name");
            }

            RaiseErrorsChanged("Name");
        }
    }

    private void RaiseErrorsChanged(string propertyName)
    {
        if (ErrorsChanged != null)
            ErrorsChanged(this, new DataErrorsChangedEventArgs(propertyName));
    }

    public event EventHandler<DataErrorsChangedEventArgs> ErrorsChanged;

    public System.Collections.IEnumerable GetErrors(string propertyName)
    {
        List<string> errors = null;

        if (_validationErrors.ContainsKey(propertyName))
            errors = _validationErrors[propertyName];

        return errors;
    }

    public bool HasErrors
```

```
    {
        get { return _validationErrors.Count != 0; }
    }
}
```

Deciding Which Approach to Use

As you can see, three different approaches are available for exposing data validation errors from your entities/objects. Ultimately, the INotifyDataErrorInfo interface approach is the most flexible and provides the most benefits.

Exposing Object-Level Validation Errors

Sometimes, you need to define a validation rule that encompasses multiple properties on an object. You can implement this type of rule as an object-level validation rule, using similar techniques to how you implement property-level validation. However, instead of executing the validation rules in property setters as you do for property-level validation, you need to create a method in your class that will execute all the object-level validation rules and report any failures to the user interface. This logic is usually best implemented as part of the EndEdit method in your class, assuming the object implements the IEditableObject interface.

Both the DataForm and DataGrid controls automatically call the EndEdit method when attempting to commit the changes to the object, and you can use this opportunity to validate the object as a whole. You can execute the rules to validate the object, and then add any failures to the list of validation errors that you are maintaining and publicly reporting via the means provided when implementing the IDataErrorInfo or INotifyDataErrorInfo interface.

When publicly reporting these object-level validation errors, you still need to associate the validation errors with properties on the object; otherwise, the errors will not be displayed in the user interface. Therefore, you should associate object-level validation errors with each of the properties that the rule involves or, at the very least, assign the validation error to one of them instead.

Once you've done so, you will also have to notify the user interface of these validation errors. When implementing the IDataErrorInfo interface, you will need to raise the PropertyChanged event, available by implementing the INotifyPropertyChanged interface, for each property involved in the object-level validation rule. When implementing the INotifyDataErrorInfo interface, you will need to raise the ErrorsChanged event for each property involved in the object-level validation rule.

■ **Note**   Neither the DataForm nor the DataGrid controls will display validation errors associated with properties on a bound object that their fields/columns do not bind to. However, these controls *do* display validation errors for properties they do not bind to if the corresponding validation rules are implemented as validation attributes.

Handling Validation Errors in Your View's Code-Behind

Sometimes, you need to handle validation errors in your view's code behind. Bindings can raise an event when they detect a validation error associated with their bound property, which you can then handle in your code behind. The following steps are involved in this process:

1.   Set the binding's NotifyOnValidationError property to True.

2. Set the ValidatesOn property associated with the approach you've taken for reporting validation errors to True.

3. Handle the control's BindingValidationError event in the code behind.

A typical binding for this scenario is demonstrated here:

```
<TextBox Text="{Binding Name, Mode=TwoWay, NotifyOnValidationError=True,
                        ValidatesOnDataErrors=True}"
         BindingValidationError="NameTextBox_BindingValidationError" />
```

You can then handle the control's BindingValidationError event in the code behind, like so:

```
private void NameTextBox_BindingValidationError(object sender,
                                                ValidationErrorEventArgs e)
{
    if (e.Action == ValidationErrorEventAction.Added)
    {
        // Do something with the error
        string errorMessage = e.Error.ErrorContent.ToString();
    }
}
```

■ **Note** The NotifyOnValidationError property is used purely to specify whether the BindingValidationError event should be raised on the control and has no bearing on whether the control should display a validation error to the user, as its name might initially suggest.

Executing Validation Rules Implemented as Attributes

Chapter 4 shows how you can implement validation rules on an entity by decorating it with validation attributes. Entities exposed from the server via RIA Services inherit from the Entity class. This class automatically executes any validation rules corresponding to a property when it is updated (i.e., in its setter) and reports any validation errors to the bindings via the INotifyDataErrorInfo interface. However, when you decorate your own class's properties with validation attributes, you will need to perform this task yourself—simply decorating the properties with the validation rules is not enough. The reason is that the attributes are simply metadata, and you need to actually execute the validation rule(s) and notify the user interface yourself if any rules are broken.

To implement the same behavior as the RIA Services entities in your own client-side objects, you need to use the Validator class (found in the System.ComponentModel.DataAnnotations namespace). The Validator class is a static class and contains a number of methods that you can use to validate properties and objects decorated with validation attributes. You can use the methods on this class to validate property values as they are assigned (in the property setters) and to validate the object as a whole in its EndEdit method, assuming it implements the IEditableObject interface.

Validating Properties

To validate the new value for a property (in its setter), you can use either the ValidateProperty method or the TryValidateProperty method on the Validator class. When you call the ValidateProperty method, if the given value for a property fails a validation rule, it will raise a ValidationException exception. When you call the TryValidateProperty method, it will simply return a Boolean value, indicating whether the new value will be valid, and a collection of the failed rules. This is the preferred method because it allows you to avoid exceptions and handle the validation errors by using the means provided by implementing either the IDataErrorInfo or INotifyDataErrorInfo interface in your class.

Here's the process to use the property validation methods on the Validator object:

1. Create a ValidationContext object (to whose constructor you pass the object to validate, any services required by the validators, and any other validation state information that you want to pass to them).

```
ValidationContext validationContext = new ValidationContext(this, null, null);
```

2. Assign it the name of the property or member to be validated on the object to validate.

```
validationContext.MemberName = "Name";
```

3. Pass the ValidationContext object to the appropriate method (ValidateProperty or TryValidateProperty) on the Validator object, along with the value you are validating, plus an empty collection in which the method will put the results of the failed validation rules if you are calling the TryValidateProperty method.

```
bool isValid = Validator.TryValidateProperty(value, validationContext,
                                             validationResults);
```

■ **Note** As you may have noticed from the example of creating a custom validation attribute earlier in this chapter, the ValidationContext object is passed into each validation attribute on the property, which the validation attributes can then use as they see fit.

Typically, your classes will inherit from a base class that implements the INotifyDataErrorInfo interface and provides the validation functionality for your objects. The following code demonstrates a method that will validate a property based on its validation attributes and maintain the results in a class-level variable named _validationErrors.

```
private Dictionary<string, List<string>> _validationErrors =
                            new Dictionary<string, List<string>>();

protected bool ValidateProperty(string propertyName, object value)
{
    var validationResults = new List<ValidationResult>();

    var validationContext = new ValidationContext(this, null, null);
    validationContext.MemberName = propertyName;

    bool isValid = Validator.TryValidateProperty(value, validationContext,
                                                 validationResults);

    List<string> errors = new List<string>();

    foreach (ValidationResult result in validationResults)
        errors.Add(result.ErrorMessage);
```

```
    if (errors.Count == 0)
    {
        if (_validationErrors.ContainsKey(propertyName))
            _validationErrors.Remove(propertyName);
    }
    else
    {
        _validationErrors[propertyName] = errors;
    }

    if (ErrorsChanged != null)
        ErrorsChanged(this, new DataErrorsChangedEventArgs(propertyName));

    return isValid;
}
```

You can then implement the GetErrors method and HasErrors property required by the
INotifyPropertyChanged interface like so:

```
public IEnumerable GetErrors(string propertyName)
{
    List<string> errors = null;

    if (_validationErrors.ContainsKey(propertyName))
        errors = _validationErrors[propertyName];

    return errors;
}

public bool HasErrors
{
    get { return _validationErrors.Count != 0; }
}
```

You then call the ValidateProperty method in the property setters in your class to validate the properties as their values are set:

```
[Required]
public string Name
{
    get { return name; }
    set
    {
        name = value;

        if (PropertyChanged != null)
            PropertyChanged(this, new PropertyChangedEventArgs("Name"));

        ValidateProperty("Name", value);
    }
}
```

Validating Objects

You can also use the Validator class to validate the object as a whole, based on its validation attributes using the ValidateObject or TryValidateObject method. These methods behave similarly to their property validation counterparts, but validate the object using the validation attributes applied to the object itself and its properties. You'll generally validate the object in its EndEdit method when implementing the IEditableObject interface.

■ **Note** By default, the ValidateObject and TryValidateObject methods do not validate the object based on any of its property-level validation attributes other than the Required attribute (StringLength, Range, etc.). To include these property-level validations in the object-level validation, you will need to use the overload of the ValidateObject and TryValidateObject methods that includes the validateAllProperties parameter, which you should set to True, as demonstrated in the following example.

The following code can be used in conjunction with the code shown in the previous section. It will validate the current object and all its properties and add any validation errors to the _validationErrors class level variable.

```
public bool Validate()
{
    var validationContext = new ValidationContext(this, null, null);
    var validationResults = new List<ValidationResult>();

    bool isValid = Validator.TryValidateObject(this, validationContext,
                                        validationResults, true);

    _validationErrors.Clear();

    foreach (ValidationResult result in validationResults)
    {
        foreach (string propertyName in result.MemberNames)
        {
            List<string> errors = null;

            if (_validationErrors.ContainsKey(propertyName))
            {
                errors = _validationErrors[propertyName];
            }
            else
            {
                errors = new List<string>();
                _validationErrors[propertyName] = errors;
            }

            errors.Add(result.ErrorMessage);

            if (ErrorsChanged != null)
                ErrorsChanged(this,
```

```
                    new DataErrorsChangedEventArgs(propertyName));
        }
    }

    return isValid;
}
```

■ **Note** Although these examples have demonstrated validating an object or one of its properties from within the object itself, you can just as easily initiate the validation outside the object, in much the same way as the Data-Form and DataGrid controls automatically do, using exactly the same methods.

Customizing Validation Attribute Error Messages

Worth noting is that the default error messages provided by the validation attributes are not always particularly user friendly. By default, they reference the property that failed the validation rule by name, which will often be different from the label corresponding to that field in the user interface, especially if the application is localized. However, if you decorate the property with the Display attribute and assign a friendly name to its Name property, the validation error message will use the value of that property instead of the property name.

Alternatively, you can create a custom validation error message by assigning a value to the ErrorMessage property of the validation attribute, like so:

```
[Required(ErrorMessage="Please enter a name for the product")]
public string Name;
```

If you are storing your strings in resource files, you can use those instead by setting the ResourceType and ResourceName properties on the validation attributes instead, for example:

```
[Required(ResourceType=typeof(ProductResources), Name="ProductNameRequiredError")]
public string Name;
```

Complex Validation Rules

Sometimes, you need to implement complex validation rules on your properties or objects. For example, you may need to retrieve some data asynchronously from the server, or have the validation performed on the server itself. It may not have been immediately apparent when we looked at them earlier, but you can implement quite complex validation rules as custom validation attributes. The IsValid method on a custom validation attribute is passed in a ValidationContext object, which helps enable complex validation attributes to be implemented. For example, it contains an Items property that enables you to pass data into the validation attributes, and an ObjectInstance property that the validation attribute can use to reference the object being validated. (If a property is being validated, the ObjectInstance property will be assigned the property's parent object).

The best source for how to go about building complex validation attributes is Jeff Handley's blog at http://jeffhandley.com/tags/Validation/default.aspx. He has a series on validators and includes information on creating asynchronous validation rules, cross-entity validation rules, and more.

⚙ Workshop: Creating a Master/Details Screen

Let's create a very simple master/details screen to allow the user to edit product data.

1. Add a new view to your project, named EditProductsView.xaml.

2. Split the LayoutRoot Grid vertically into two rows.

```xml
<navigation:Page x:Class="AdventureWorks.Views.EditProductsView"
        xmlns="http://schemas.microsoft.com/winfx/2006/xaml/presentation"
        xmlns:x="http://schemas.microsoft.com/winfx/2006/xaml"
        xmlns:d="http://schemas.microsoft.com/expression/blend/2008"
        xmlns:mc="http://schemas.openxmlformats.org/markup-compatibility/2006"
        xmlns:navigation="clr-namespace:System.Windows.Controls;    ↵
                          assembly=System.Windows.Controls.Navigation"
        mc:Ignorable="d"
        d:DesignWidth="640" d:DesignHeight="480"
        Title="Edit Products">

    <Grid x:Name="LayoutRoot">
        <Grid.RowDefinitions>
            <RowDefinition Height="*" />
            <RowDefinition Height="*" />
        </Grid.RowDefinitions>
    </Grid>
</navigation:Page>
```

3. Define the following namespace prefixes on the root element in the file:

```xml
xmlns:riaControls="clr-namespace:System.Windows.Controls;    ↵
                   assembly=System.Windows.Controls.DomainServices"
xmlns:sdk="http://schemas.microsoft.com/winfx/2006/xaml/presentation/sdk"
xmlns:toolkit=
  "http://schemas.microsoft.com/winfx/2006/xaml/presentation/toolkit"
xmlns:my="clr-namespace:AdventureWorks.Web"
xmlns:my1="clr-namespace:AdventureWorks.Web.Services"
```

4. For simplicity's sake, we'll use the DomainDataSource control to handle loading the data from the server in this workshop. Add the DomainDataSource control to your view, as content of the LayoutRoot Grid control, and hook it up to the GetProducts domain operation exposed by the ProductService domain service that you created in Chapter 4.

```xml
<riaControls:DomainDataSource AutoLoad="True" Height="0" Width="0"
                d:DesignData="{d:DesignInstance my:Product, CreateList=true}"
                Name="productDDS" QueryName="GetProductsQuery">
    <riaControls:DomainDataSource.DomainContext>
        <my1:ProductContext />
    </riaControls:DomainDataSource.DomainContext>
</riaControls:DomainDataSource>
```

5. Add a DataGrid control to the top row of the LayoutRoot Grid, and bind its ItemsSource property to the DomainDataSource control.

```xml
<sdk:DataGrid ItemsSource="{Binding ElementName=productDDS, Path=Data}" />
```

6. Now, we need to create the data entry form. You've seen a couple of ways to generate this, including using the Data Sources window, using the XAML Power Toys, and using the DataForm control. However, for the purpose of this workshop we'll create it manually. We'll add a Grid to the bottom row of the LayoutRoot Grid, which we'll use to lay out our data entry form. The following XAML demonstrates a simple data entry form that allows you to edit five properties on a Product entity. It includes three text boxes (one which formats how the value should be displayed using the Binding object's StringFormat property), and two DatePicker controls. It also includes a ValidationSummary control to display the details of any data validation errors, hence the need for all the bindings to have their NotifyOnValidationError set to True so that the ValidationSummary control can be made aware of their validation errors.

```xaml
<Grid Grid.Row="1" DataContext="{Binding ElementName=productDDS, Path=Data}">
    <Grid.RowDefinitions>
        <RowDefinition Height="Auto" />
        <RowDefinition Height="Auto" />
        <RowDefinition Height="Auto" />
        <RowDefinition Height="Auto" />
        <RowDefinition Height="Auto" />
        <RowDefinition Height="*" />
    </Grid.RowDefinitions>

    <Grid.ColumnDefinitions>
        <ColumnDefinition Width="100" />
        <ColumnDefinition Width="250" />
    </Grid.ColumnDefinitions>

    <sdk:Label Grid.Row="0" Content="Name:"
               Target="{Binding ElementName=NameField}" />
    <sdk:Label Grid.Row="1" Content="Product Number:"
               Target="{Binding ElementName=ProductNumberField}" />
    <sdk:Label Grid.Row="2" Content="List Price:"
               Target="{Binding ElementName=ListPriceField}" />
    <sdk:Label Grid.Row="3" Content="Sell Start Date:"
               Target="{Binding ElementName=SellStartDate}" />
    <sdk:Label Grid.Row="4" Content="Sell End Date:"
               Target="{Binding ElementName=SellEndDate}" />

    <TextBox Name="NameField" Grid.Column="1" Grid.Row="0" Margin="2"
             Text="{Binding Name, Mode=TwoWay,
                     NotifyOnValidationError=True}" />

    <TextBox Name="ProductNumberField" Grid.Column="1" Grid.Row="1" Margin="2"
             Text="{Binding ProductNumber, Mode=TwoWay,
                     NotifyOnValidationError=True}" />

    <TextBox Name="ListPriceField"
             Grid.Column="1" Grid.Row="2" Margin="2"
             Text="{Binding ListPrice, Mode=TwoWay, StringFormat=C,
                     NotifyOnValidationError=True}" />

    <sdk:DatePicker Name="SellStartDateField"
                    Grid.Column="1" Grid.Row="3" Margin="2"
```

```
                    SelectedDate="{Binding SellStartDate, Mode=TwoWay,
                                   NotifyOnValidationError=True}" />

        <sdk:DatePicker Name="SellEndDateField"
                    Grid.Column="1" Grid.Row="4" Margin="2"
                    SelectedDate="{Binding SellEndDate, Mode=TwoWay,
                                   NotifyOnValidationError=True}" />

        <sdk:ValidationSummary Grid.Row="5" Grid.ColumnSpan="2"
                    VerticalAlignment="Bottom" />
</Grid>
```

■ **Note** As you can see, we're binding the top-level Grid control's DataContext property to the collection returned by the DomainDataSource control. The DomainDataSource control's Data property returns a collection view (a DomainDataSourceView), which maintains a CurrentItem property. Controls that expect to be bound to a single object instead of a collection see that they are bound to a collection view, automatically drill down to this property, and bind to the object that it exposes. The DataGrid control is also bound to this same collection view, and when a row is selected in the DataGrid, it will update the collection view's CurrentItem property accordingly. Therefore, when you select an item in the DataGrid, the details for that item will appear in the data entry form. This synchronization feature provided by collection views is very neat and makes it very easy to implement master/details views.

---

7. Now run your application. When you select an item in the DataGrid control, the details of that item will appear in the data entry form. When you enter some invalid data (such as clearing the value of the Name field), the control will change its appearance to indicate that the data is invalid, and a validation error will appear in the ValidationSummary control.

■ **Note** The next step is to provide a way to save the changes back to the server, which you can implement by binding a Button control to the DomainDataSource control's SubmitChangesCommand property, as described in Chapter 5.

Summary

We've now completed the round-trip of data—with data exposed by the server (covered in Chapter 4), consumed by the Silverlight client (covered in Chapter 5), displayed in a list (covered in Chapter 6), and modified with the changes submitted back to the server (covered in this chapter). We now have essentially developed an end-to-end Silverlight application. We will build on this core functionality and add supporting features in the upcoming chapters, including securing our application and styling it to make it more presentable.

CHAPTER 8

Securing Your Application

In any business application, securing data and operations appropriately so that only approved users have access should be a significant design factor. Not doing so effectively opens the business to threats from snooping competitors, breaches of privacy laws, and even sabotage. Therefore, designing effective security into your application is extremely important. This generally involves validating users' identities, tracking them and their assigned roles, and restricting their access to approved data and operations accordingly.

However, you should take into account some additional security-related considerations when designing your Silverlight application. For example, if the application is being run outside of the corporate network, you are at risk of your data being sniffed between the server and the client. Also, exposing your services publicly leaves you at risk of someone attempting to access them directly without going through the Silverlight client. Another concern is that your Silverlight application will be available publicly for download, enabling competitors to decompile it and obtain access to potentially sensitive intellectual property, such as algorithms and other assets.

In this chapter, we will take a look at these security-related issues, as well as how to implement restrictions based the users and their roles and the various preventative measures you can take to stop your data, applications, and business from being compromised.

Implementing Server-Side Security Using RIA Services

The following are different types of security functions that you generally need to consider as a part of your application design; these functions should be implemented in the services that expose data and operations from the server:

- Maintain a list of users, their authentication details, and their roles within the system.

- Validate that a user is permitted to access the application (known as user authentication). The most common technique for doing this is to require the user to enter a username and password in a login screen, although integration with the user's Windows profile is another method.

- Prevent users from calling specified operations until they are authenticated.

- Prevent users from calling operations that their roles do not permit them to call (known as *user authorization*), including create, read, update, delete (CRUD), invoke, and custom operations.

- Provide access to only a subset of the data in the database based on the user's role or ID—for example, users can view only the notes they've entered into the system, not those created by other users.

- Decide what part of a given set of data users are allowed to update and delete based on their IDs or roles. For example, a user may be able to view the notes entered into the system by all the users in the system, but not update or delete notes created by other users unless he or she is a manager (that is, in the Manager role).

- Enable users to view or edit only part of an entity based on their roles—for example, customer service personnel can only view the retail price of a product, not the markup amount or the price that the company paid for the product.

The preceding security options represent the most important security-related concepts to consider when designing a system, and RIA Services, in conjunction with the ASP.NET Membership API, helps provide an easy framework to implement most of them. RIA Services makes it very easy to design security into your system, and if you have used the Silverlight Business Application template as the base for your project, you will find that user authentication and registration functionality has already been included. Let's take a look at how to handle each of the preceding points on the server side with RIA Services.

Using the ASP.NET Membership API

As previously stated, if you've used the Silverlight Business Application project template as the base for your project, you will already have the basic infrastructure in place to handle authentication of users and registration of new users (the functionality can be disabled if not required or wanted). This template uses the ASP.NET Membership API to provide the user authentication and authorization features. You will probably be familiar with ASP.NET Membership if you have previously done any ASP.NET development, and the same infrastructure is leveraged by RIA Services to provide user authentication and authorization functionality in your Silverlight applications.

ASP.NET Membership's provider model is extremely flexible, with a number of extensibility points that allow you to either use the default provider or plug in your own, with the provider configuration managed through the web project's web.config file. This enables you to work with a single interface without worrying about the actual underlying implementation.

The default ASP.NET Membership authentication provider implemented in the Silverlight Business Application project template is the Forms Authentication provider. As in ASP.NET projects, this provider maintains your authentication status by storing a temporary cookie on the client (containing authentication information) after the user is authenticated, which is then passed back to the server with each request. The server automatically handles the processing of this cookie and populates the User identity for the current HTTP context with information about the users and their roles.

The other common approach is to use the Windows Authentication provider. This provider authenticates users using their Windows accounts and impersonates them on the server. This can be a good alternative to Forms Authentication if your Silverlight application will be run only within the corporate network, saving the user from needing to log into the application. However, if the application will be run outside the corporate network, Forms Authentication is the best choice.

■ **Note** To use Windows Authentication, you will need to use IIS to debug your application, as the Visual Studio development server does not support this mode. You will need to disable anonymous access on the application in IIS and enable one of the Windows-based authentication modes, such as Windows Integrated Authentication.

You can specify which authentication provider you wish to use in the web project's web.config file by setting the mode attribute of the authentication element to Forms or Windows:

```
<authentication mode="Forms" />
```

In addition to the authentication providers, there are membership, role, and profile providers. These providers are used to handle persisting the user, role, and profile data, generally in conjunction with the Forms Authentication provider. The default providers are as follows:

- *Membership*: The SQL membership provider (SqlMembershipProvider)
- *Role*: The SQL role provider (SqlRoleProvider)
- *Profile*: The SQL profile provider (SqlProfileProvider)

These providers store users, roles, and profile data in a SQL Server database. These providers and their default options are configured in the machine.config file found in the %WINDIR%\Microsoft.NET\Framework\<.NET Framework Version>\Config folder (change \Framework\ to \Framework64\ if your IIS server is running in 64-bit mode) but can be overridden in the web.config file in your web project. You will need to override the defaults when you want to specify a database to which the settings will be persisted, as will be demonstrated in the next section.

These default SQL Server providers write to their own database table structures. However, you may be working with an existing database with its own tables storing user, role, and profile data. Alternatively, you may be working with a database other than a SQL Server database, or you may not be using a database to store this data at all. In these cases, you will have to create your own custom user, role, and profile providers and plug them into the ASP.NET Membership model by configuring them in the web project's web.config file. This process won't be covered in this chapter, but creating a custom membership, role, or profile provider is easy—you simply create a class that inherits from the corresponding base provider class and override its methods and properties to add your own functionality.

This chapter will demonstrate using the Forms Authentication mode with the SQL membership, role and profile providers.

■ **Note** You can find further information on ASP.NET Membership at http://msdn.microsoft.com/en-us/ library/91f66yxt.aspx.

Configuring Your Database for Forms Authentication

Assuming your AdventureWorks application is still configured to use Forms Authentication (the default mode), you can simply run the project and register yourself as a new user. Silverlight's Business Application project template already implements the user interface that does this.

This all works because the template automatically creates a new SQL Server database called ASPNETDB.MDF for you in the App_Data folder of the web project and creates the required ASP.NET Membership tables. It then attaches this database to SQL Server or SQL Server Express as a user instance. However, you will most likely want to configure it to store the user data in your own database instead.

To do so, you will need to modify the web.config file, creating a connection string to the database and pointing the defaultProvider property of the authentication, roleManager, and profile sections to the name of that connection. Luckily, the Silverlight 5 version of the Silverlight Business Application project template already does these tasks for you; you just need to customize them to your needs. You simply need to update the existing ApplicationServices connection string and point it toward your database.

■ **Note** If you've implemented your own custom membership providers, targeting your own database schema for storing users, roles, and profile information, you will need to remove the existing provider references and add your own in their place.

Once you've got the providers pointing toward the database, you need to add the required ASP.NET Membership tables to the database's schema.

■ **Note** You can skip this step if you've implemented your own custom membership providers that target your own database schema for storing users, roles, and profile information.

Using the command line (or Run option in the Start menu), run `%WINDIR%\Microsoft.NET\Framework\v4.0.30319\aspnet_regsql.exe`. This will open a wizard that you can point toward your AdventureWorks database, and it will create the tables, views, and stored procedures that it requires.

You can now use the ASP.NET Configuration tool for the web application (the rightmost icon in the Solution Explorer window when the web project in your solution is selected) to set up users and roles for the application. Alternatively, simply run the project, and use the registration feature to add yourself as a user.

Setting Up Authentication

`AuthenticationService`, located in the `Services` folder, is a standard domain service that enables users to be logged in and out and their profiles to be retrieved and saved from the client. It inherits from the `AuthenticationBase` class, which contains a set of default authentication-related functions—including `Login`, `Logout`, `GetUser`, and `UpdateUser`, which make use of the corresponding functionality in the membership provider configured for the application. The `AuthenticationService` class is therefore very simple, because all the functionality is implemented in the base class, as shown in the following code:

```
[EnableClientAccess]
public class AuthenticationService : AuthenticationBase<User> { }
```

Nothing else needs to be added—simply defining this domain service in your web project allows user authentication to be enabled from the client, including returning the user details and roles to the client and maintains the user authentication status by creating a temporary Forms Authentication cookie to be passed between the client and the server with each server request.

■ **Note** The temporary Forms Authentication cookie has a default timeout of 2880 minutes (48 hours). That means that if there is no communication with the server for longer than 48 hours, the cookie will expire, and the user will be logged out. The actual implementation of how the expiry works is a little more complicated, but this is the simple version (you can find the more complicated behavior described at http://support.microsoft.com/ kb/910439). You can increase or decrease this value if required (in the web.config file), but it's not recommended to make it too long. The longer the lifetime of the cookie, the more opportunity someone has to steal it and impersonate the user. You may actually want to consider shortening this default lifespan of the cookie—especially if server communication is not being performed over an HTTPS connection. The forms element under the authentication element has a timeout attribute. Change its value (specified in minutes) to the new lifespan that the cookie should have.

Requiring Authentication

By default, the operations that you've created in your domain service can be called by any anonymous user who can get to your service. Ideally, as a first step, you'll want to limit access to these operations (perhaps some, perhaps all) to only authenticated users of your system.

■ **Note** Limiting access to the service calls on the client doesn't mean that those services are secure. Hackers— or more appropriately, crackers—who want to obtain your sensitive data will attempt to circumvent client limitations by directly connecting to the service on the server to see what they can obtain from it. Therefore, you shouldn't make any data available from the service unless the user is properly authenticated and authorized to access that data. In addition, you shouldn't permit the user to perform any operations on the data, such as insert/update/delete, without having the appropriate permissions.

To restrict access to all the operations in a domain service to only authenticated users, decorate the domain service class with the RequiresAuthentication attribute:

```
[EnableClientAccess]
[RequiresAuthentication]
public class ProductService :
    LinqToEntitiesDomainService<AdventureWorksEntities>
```

If the user is not authenticated and calls one of these operations, the service will raise a DomainOperationException on the client stating that access has been denied to the operation.

In some instances, you may want to select which operations in your domain service require authentication, leaving others available to anonymous users. This is possible by decorating only the operations that require the user to be authenticated with the RequiresAuthentication attribute.

Restricting Access to Operations by Role

Perhaps the user is authenticated, but you want to further restrict access to a domain service or an operation based on the user's role. In this case, you can simply decorate the domain service class or operation with the RequiresRole attribute and include which roles are permitted to call the operation. The following example shows how to limit access to the operation to only users who are in the Administrators role or the Managers role:

```
[RequiresRole("Administrators", "Managers")]
public IQueryable<Product> GetProducts()
```

■ **Note** By default, any users registering themselves through the Silverlight Business Application project will be added to the Registered Users role. To create additional roles you can use the ASP.NET Configuration tool for the web application (the rightmost icon in the Solution Explorer window). However, you will need to create the users through this same interface to assign them to those roles, or you need add the ability for roles to be specified when registering a user through the Silverlight project. See the "Registering Users" section for more information.

Including the role names as strings in multiple places is not ideal, so it's recommended that you define some constants with the role names and use these instead. Alternatively, you can create your own authorization attribute by creating a class in your project that inherits from AuthorizationAttribute, overriding its IsAuthorized method and inserting your own authorization logic, like so:

```
public class GTManagerRoleAttribute : AuthorizationAttribute
{
    protected override AuthorizationResult IsAuthorized(
                            System.Security.Principal.IPrincipal principal,
                            AuthorizationContext authorizationContext)
        if (principal.IsInRole("Administrators") || principal.IsInRole("Managers"))
            return AuthorizationResult.Allowed;
        else
            return new AuthorizationResult(
                "You do not have sufficient rights to perform this operation.");
    }
}
```

You can then decorate the operation with this attribute instead of the RequiresRole attribute:

```
[GTManagerRole]
public IQueryable<Product> GetProducts()
```

If you want to restrict access to all the domain operations in a domain service, you can simply decorate the domain service with the RequiresRole attribute, or with your own custom attribute, instead.

■ **Note** You may also need to implement per-user permission overrides, where users can be permitted access to certain functions that their roles do not allow without assigning an additional role with all its permissions—these permissions can be managed in the user object as properties, with the values stored in the user profile, as demonstrated in the "Exposing Custom User Profile Data" section later in this chapter. You will also need to create your own authorization attribute to handle this scenario.

For insert, update, and delete operations, you might need to reference the instance of the entity being passed into the operation in your authorization attribute. For example, you might want to ensure that the user is permitted to update the given entity. Note that there is an AuthorizationContext object being passed into the IsAuthorized method that you are overriding. The Instance property on that object will have the entity being inserted/updated/deleted assigned to it:

```
Product product = authorizationContext.Instance as Product;
```

If you need to pass additional data into the authorization attributes to use as part of the authorization process, you can override the Initialize method of the domain service class, create an instance of the AuthorizationContext class, and assign the data to its Items property, which is a Dictionary property to which you can assign any number of keyed values. Assign this to the AuthorizationContext property of the domain service, and this object will then be passed to any authorization attributes used in the domain service, for example:

```
public override void Initialize(DomainServiceContext context)
{
    base.Initialize(context);

    Dictionary<string, bool> customUserPermissions = new Dictionary<string, bool>();

    // Load user permissions
    AuthorizationContext = new AuthorizationContext(context);
    AuthorizationContext.Items["CustomUserPermissions"] = customUserPermissions;
}
```

You can then get this object from the AuthorizationContext object of your custom authorization attributes:

```
Dictionary<string, bool> customUserPermissions =
    authorizationContext.Items["CustomUserPermissions"] as Dictionary<string, bool>;
```

Returning a Subset of Data Based on the User's ID or Role

Returning a specific subset of data is more of an implementation issue than one that can be provided in the RIA Services framework. However, here is an example of how to obtain the user's credentials so that you can filter the data being queried accordingly.

The credentials you are likely to require are the user's ID, username, and/or roles. The identity of the user is exposed by the ServiceContext object on the DomainService base class. You will find a User principle object exposed as a property on the ServiceContext object. From here, you can get the user's username from the ServiceContext.User.Identity.Name property and determine whether the user is in a specific role using the ServiceContext.User.IsInRole method:

```
string userName = ServiceContext.User.Identity.Name;
bool isAdministrator = ServiceContext.User.IsInRole("Administrators");
```

To get additional details about the user, such as the user's ID and roles, you will need to turn to ASP.NET Membership's functions to get those details for the user from the database:

```
// You will need a using statement to System.Web.Security
MembershipUser user = Membership.GetUser();          // User object
Guid userID = (Guid)user.ProviderUserKey;            // User ID
string[] userRoles = Roles.GetRolesForUser();        // User roles
```

You can now use these details to filter the data being queried before returning the data to the client. In addition, you may have a requirement that entities can be passed back to users, but users may not be able to view or edit all the fields on that entity. For example, they may be allowed to view a customer entity but not be permitted to see the credit card number of that customer. This should be handled on the server so that the fields that the user can't access are not sent to the client. In this scenario, it is best to use plain-old CLR object (POCO) types when returning data and populate the fields of only each object that the user is permitted access to.

Permitting Update/Delete Operations According to Data

Sometimes, you may want to allow the user to retrieve a collection of entities from the server but enable that particular user to update or delete only some of them. This is also more of an implementation issue than one that the RIA Services framework can help with. Again, within the operation itself, you will need to obtain the list of the user's roles, and based on both the data that is passed into the operation and the user's roles, determine whether the user is permitted to perform that operation. Otherwise, raise an exception to notify the client that the call was unsuccessful.

Exposing Custom User Profile Data

As you may have noticed when we were defining the AuthenticationService class earlier in this chapter, in the "Setting Up Authentication" section, the AuthenticationBase class that it inherits from is a generic class, and you are specifying a type of User:

```
[EnableClientAccess]
public class AuthenticationService : AuthenticationBase<User> { }
```

The User class contains information about the user and is returned to the client when it attempts to authenticate with the server. This class can be found in the Models folder. It inherits from UserBase, which includes properties exposing the user name, the roles that the user is in, and whether the user has been authenticated. You can add additional properties to this class, and these properties will be returned with the object to the client. For example, you may wish to store additional information about the user (such as contact details), maintain a set of user preferences on the server, or provide some properties specifying additional permissions to those designated by the user's assigned roles. A corresponding User class will be created in the client project with the same properties that you defined on the User class in the web project, enabling the properties' values to be read and saved there too. You will find that the Silverlight Business Application project template has already created the FriendlyName property on the User object:

```
public string FriendlyName { get; set; }
```

The values of these custom user properties are stored in the profile membership table in the database, but you will need to define them in the web.config file before you can access them. You will already find the FriendlyName entry here, and you can add any additional properties below it:

```
<profile>
  <properties>
    <add name="FriendlyName" />
  </properties>
</profile>
```

You don't have to worry about populating the values of the properties you've created on the User object with the data from the profile, because the AuthenticationBase class does this automatically using reflection. However, when you add additional properties to the User object, be sure to add a corresponding entry to the web.config file, with a matching name. Otherwise, an exception will be raised when you attempt to use the authentication service. You will also need to populate each new profile property in the CreateUser method of the UserRegistrationService domain service.

Registering Users

To add users to the system, you can either use the ASP.NET Configuration tool for the web application or the registration facility already in the Silverlight project. This facility is enabled via the UserRegistrationService, located in the Services folder in the web project—a standard domain service simply exposing an AddUser domain operation enabling new users to be registered within the system via the Silverlight client. It's ready to create a user, with the details supplied, assigning that user to a default role called Registered Users, defined as a constant named DefaultRole within the service, enabling you to change it as required, and creating the profile for the user as described in the previous section.

However, in typical business applications, you don't allow users to register themselves. Generally, that's the role of another user who has permission to add users to the system. In this case, you want to prevent users from accessing this domain service unless they are authenticated and belong to a given role.

If you don't want to expose the ability to add users to the system publicly, you can simply delete the UserRegistrationService class, along with the corresponding functionality in the Silverlight client, preventing users from being created in the system though the application or directly via the domain service. Alternatively, you can restrict access to it such that only authenticated users with specific roles can register new users, using the methods discussed previously.

You can modify the UserRegistrationService domain service, adding additional functionality as you see fit. For example, you will generally need to enable the adding user to select what roles this new user will be assigned to. This will require the client to be able to access the full list of roles and pass the selected roles back to the server when the user is being created, functionality that unfortunately is not built into the Silverlight Business Application project template. To expose the full list of roles to the client, simply add the following Invoke operation to the UserRegistrationService domain service:

```
[Invoke]
public string[] GetAllRoles()
{
    return Roles.GetAllRoles();
}
```

You can then add a new property to the RegistrationData class (in the Models folder) to pass the selected roles back to the server and update the AddUser domain operation in the UserRegistrationService domain service to assign the user to those roles accordingly. Note that the RegistrationData class contains all the data about the user that you will use when registering the user. Therefore, if you have additional properties that you wish to add, such as data to populate any custom user profile properties that you've configured, you will need to add those properties to this class and update the AddUser domain operation in the UserRegistrationService domain service to save those property values as required. The registration form is generated at runtime by reflecting over the RegistrationData class, meaning that it will then automatically display data entry fields for any additional properties that you have added to this class.

■ **Note** If you want to remove the security question and answer properties from the user registration procedure, you can remove them from the RegistrationData class and update the AddUser domain operation in the UserRegistrationService domain service accordingly, but you will also need to update the ASP.NET Membership provider configuration in the web.config file in the web project to set its requiresQuestionAndAnswer property to false.

Avoiding SQL Injection Attacks

Throughout the history of application development, SQL injection has always been a relatively simple technique for hacking into the databases behind applications. This attack involves crafting a special query entered into a text box and submitting it to the web site. It exploits the fact that many developers simply concatenate the data entered into a form with their SQL database query. Therefore, if you enter the right text into the text box, you can effectively modify the query that is being run against the database!

This exploit can allow a user to gain access to all the tables and records in the database, including people's names, contact details, and credit card information, and even cause outright damage, such as enabling them to delete database tables. The latter issue, of course, can be prevented by ensuring that the database user account that the web application is running under has minimal privileges and cannot be used to delete tables.

The methods demonstrated throughout this book are not open to SQL injection, primarily because we're using the Entity Framework as our data access layer, which manages this issue; however, if you are using a different mechanism to query and persist changes to a database, such as building SQL statements manually, you should be aware of this issue and cater for it accordingly. Parameterized database queries are one of the best options for preventing SQL injection, but best practice is to also always validate any user input before using it in a database query or persisting data to the database. Also, never allow a query, such as a complex filter, to be dynamically created on the client and executed on the server—this makes it even easier for someone to gain complete control over your database than SQL injection does.

Sanitizing Errors Sent to the Client

To crackers, more knowledge makes it easier to find points of weakness that they can target. Therefore, it's always good practice to avoid sending error messages raised on the server directly to the client, because these generally include stack traces and other information detailing the inner workings of your application that crackers can find useful. Instead, any error messages should be sanitized before being sent to the client.

This can be configured in the customErrors element of your web.config file in the same manner as in a standard ASP.NET application/web site. By default, your ASP.NET application uses the RemoteOnly mode, meaning that full exception details will be passed to clients running on the local machine to the server but will be sanitized when clients are running on remote machines. Setting the mode property of the customErrors element to Off will disable exception sanitizing for all clients, remote or local, and setting it to On will enable it for all clients, which is useful when you want to test the client's experience when exceptions are thrown. For example, add the following element to the system.web section of your web.config file to sanitize server exceptions before exposing them to the client:

```
<customErrors mode="On" />
```

To identify the error such that you can fix the problem, log the error on the server, as described in the "Handling Server Errors" section of Chapter 4.

⚙ Workshop: Practicing with Server-Side Security

In Part 1 of this chapter's example, we'll add the required tables to the AdventureWorks database to maintain user membership and role information, point the membership providers to this database, and test this configuration using our project's existing functionality (generated by the Silverlight Business Application project template) to register a user and to log in as that user. In Part 2 of the workshop, we'll restrict access to the services to authenticated users only and restrict access to some domain operations to users with specific roles only.

Part 1: Configuring the Database

In Chapter 4, you installed the AdventureWorks database and hooked your AdventureWorks application up to work with it. We now need to add the ASP.NET Membership tables to the database. Use the following steps to configure the database:

1. Using the command line (or Run option in the Start menu), run the following to display the ASP.NET SQL Server Setup Wizard, as shown in Figure 8-1:

```
C:\Windows\Microsoft.NET\Framework\v4.0.30319\aspnet_regsql.exe
```

2. Click Next.

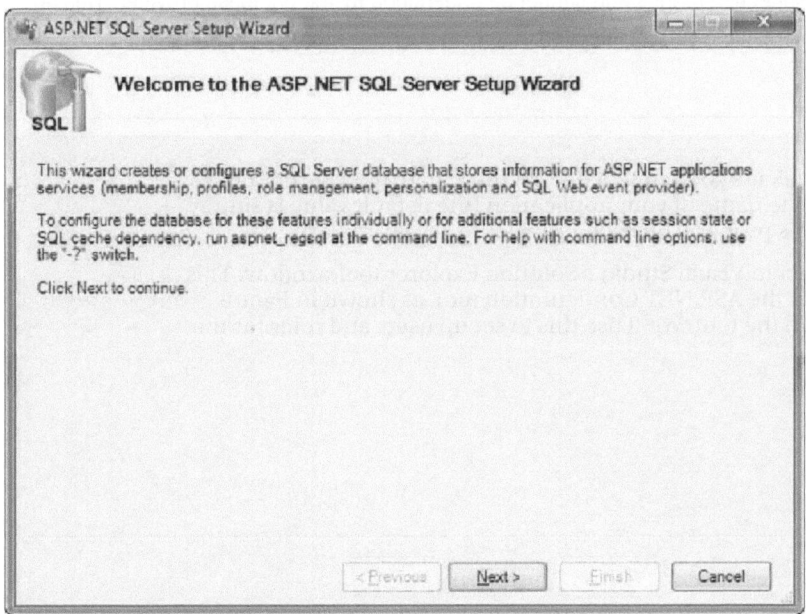

Figure 8-1. The ASP.NET SQL Server Setup Wizard

3. On the Setup Option step (page 2 of the wizard), select the "Configure SQL Server for application services" option. Then on the final step (Select the Server and Database), point it to your database. Click the Finish button, and the wizard will add the required tables, views, and stored procedures to the database. You can see these in your database using the SQL Server Management Studio or by adding the database to the Data Connections node in Visual Studio's Server Explorer.

4. We now need to point the ASP.NET Membership providers to this database. Open the web.config file in your Web project. You will find a connection string named ApplicationServices already defined and pointing to a database that's attached as a user instance. We need to modify this and point it to our AdventureWorks database instead. Your SQL Service instance may not be a local instance named SQLEXPRESS, as follows—you might need to alter this connection string accordingly:

```
<connectionStrings>
  <add name="ApplicationServices"
      connectionString="Data Source=.\SQLEXPRESS;Database=AdventureWorks;
                              Integrated Security=true"
      providerName="System.Data.SqlClient" />
</connectionStrings>
```

■ **Note** You cannot use the connection string used by your Entity Framework model, because it is formatted differently than normal database connection strings and cannot be understood by the database provider. This unfortunately means that you need to duplicate your connection strings in your web.config file and maintain them separately.

5. Although not essential, it's good practice to set the ApplicationName property on each provider to the name of your application (the default value is simply \). Set the value of this property on each provider to AdventureWorks.

6. Select the Web project in Visual Studio's Solution Explorer tool window. This will show the icon for the ASP.NET Configuration tool, as shown in Figure 8-2. Click this to open the tool. We'll use this to set up users and roles for the application.

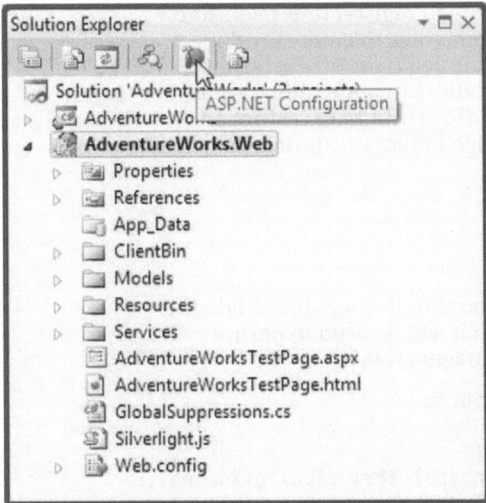

Figure 8-2. The ASP.NET Configuration tool's icon in the Solution Explorer tool window

7. The user interface for the ASP.NET Configuration tool is fairly straightforward, so we won't go through it step by step. Go to the Security section, and add three roles: Administrators, Managers, and Staff. Then add at least one user under each role, for example, AdminUser, ManagerUser, and StaffUser.

8. If you run your application now, you should be able to log in as each of those users, proving that it's all hooked up correctly.

Part 2: Implementing Security Restrictions

Let's use the following steps to restrict the UserRegistrationService and ProductService domain services to allow only authenticated users to access them:

1. Add the RequiresAuthentication attribute to their class definitions, like so:

```
[EnableClientAccess]
[RequiresAuthentication]
public class ProductService : LinqToEntitiesDomainService<AdventureWorksEntities>
```

and like so

```
[EnableClientAccess]
[RequiresAuthentication]
public class UserRegistrationService :
                        LinqToEntitiesDomainService<AdventureWorksEntities>
```

If you run your application now, you will find that you can view the list of products and register a user only if you're logged in. Otherwise, you should get a message stating that access is denied.

2. Let's now allow only users in the Administrators role to register new users and allow only users in the Administrators and Managers roles to delete products. We'll implement these both possible ways: using the RequiresRole attribute and (in step 10) creating our own custom authorization attribute. First, we'll use the RequiresRole attribute. Add the RequiresRole attribute to restrict access to the UserRegistrationService domain service's class to administrators:

```
[EnableClientAccess]
[RequiresAuthentication]
[RequiresRole("Administrators")]
public class UserRegistrationService : DomainService
```

3. Now, add a new class named GTManagerRoleAttribute to the Services folder in the project. It should have the following code, which will be used to permit access only to users in the Administrators and Managers roles:

```
public class GTManagerRoleAttribute : AuthorizationAttribute
{
    protected override AuthorizationResult IsAuthorized(
                            System.Security.Principal.IPrincipal principal,
                            AuthorizationContext authorizationContext)
        if (principal.IsInRole("Administrators") || principal.IsInRole("Managers"))
            return AuthorizationResult.Allowed;
        else
            return new AuthorizationResult(
                "You do not have sufficient rights to perform this operation.");
    }
}
```

4. Now, you can apply this attribute to the DeleteProduct domain operation in the ProductService domain service's class:

```
[GTManagerRole]
public void DeleteProduct(Product product)
```

5. Run the application. You will find that only if you are already logged in as AdminUser can you successfully register a new user, using the user registration functionality provided by the Silverlight Business Application project template (found by opening the Login window and clicking the "Register now" link on that window to show the user registration screen). Also, you can delete a product only if you're logged in as AdminUser or ManagerUser.

Implementing Client-Side Security

Now that the server has been configured to authenticate and register users and restrict access to data and operations accordingly, we should look at implementing the client-side security aspects of this functionality. In this section, we'll take a look at how to authenticate and register users on the client; get information about the user, such as their roles and profile; and restrict users from parts of the application based on their authentication status or assigned roles.

Authenticating and Registering Users

Let's take a look at what is already in the Silverlight project to support user authentication. When running the Silverlight project, you will find a login hyperlink at the top right of the window, below the About button. This will pop up a Login dialog, shown in Figure 8-3, that you can use to log into the system.

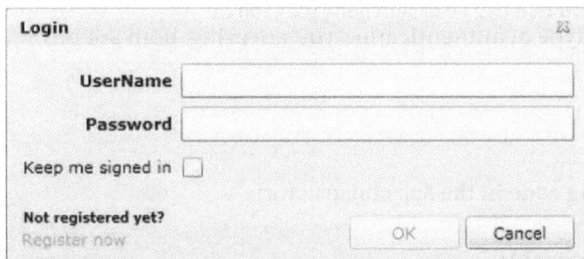

Figure 8-3. *The Login dialog from the Silverlight Business Application project template*

The first step you need to take is to actually register as a user, and you can do so by clicking the Register Now hyperlink in the bottom left of the Login dialog. This pops up a registration screen like the one shown in Figure 8-4.

Figure 8-4. *The Register dialog from the Silverlight Business Application project template*

■ **Note** You can modify the required password strength in the Web project's web.config file via the properties of the ASP.NET Membership provider, particularly its minRequiredPasswordLength and minRequiredNonalphanumericCharacters properties.

The Login and Registration screens communicate with the `AuthenticationService` and `UserRegistrationService`, respectively, on the server, as discussed earlier. Because these services are standard domain services, a corresponding context will be created for each service in the Silverlight client application (`AuthenticationContext` for the `AuthenticationService` service and `UserRegistrationContext` for the `UserRegistrationService` service).

However, although the `UserRegistrationContext` class is instantiated like all other domain contexts, the `AuthenticationContext` is rarely used. Instead, you use the `FormsAuthentication` or `WindowsAuthentication` classes, depending on what type of authentication you are using; both are provided by RIA Services.

Authenticating with the Server

Inside the `App.xaml.cs` file, you will find the following code in the `App` constructor:

```
WebContext webContext = new WebContext();
webContext.Authentication = new FormsAuthentication();
//webContext.Authentication = new WindowsAuthentication();
this.ApplicationLifetimeObjects.Add(webContext);
```

As you can see, the `WebContext` object is instantiated (its class generated by RIA Services); an instance of the authentication provider it should use is assigned to its `Authentication` property, and the `WebContext` object is then added to the application's `ApplicationLifetimeObjects` collection.

■ **Note** The `WebContext` object needs to be kept alive for the lifetime of the application, because it is used to maintain the current authentication status of the user and how the application authenticates with the server. It should be created when the application is started and not destroyed until the application is closed. Therefore, it is added to the `Application` object's `ApplicationLifetimeObjects` collection, ensuring it stays alive throughout the application's lifetime.

By default, the application uses Forms Authentication, but you can comment out the `FormsAuthentication` line and uncomment the `WindowsAuthentication` line to use Windows Authentication instead.

■ **Note** The authentication provider you select must match what you have configured in the `web.config` file in your Web project.

You will find a full example in the code behind the `LoginForm` view, but the following line demonstrates calling the `Login` method of the authentication object, configured in the application's constructor, passing it a username and password:

```
LoginOperation op = WebContext.Current.Authentication.Login(userName, password);
```

When the user has successfully been logged into the system, the `Completed` event will be raised on the `LoginOperation` object, which is returned when calling the authentication object's `Login` method. Alternatively, you can handle the `LoggedIn` event on the authentication object itself, which can be handled application-wide. There is also a `LoggedOut` event on the same object, which will be raised when the user logs out of the application.

Registering a New User

To register a new user, you need to populate a new `RegistrationData` entity with the user details and then pass it and the user's password to the `CreateUser` method of the `RegistrationContext` object, for example:

```
RegistrationData newUser = new RegistrationData();
newUser.UserName = userName;
newUser.FriendlyName = friendlyName;
// Populate any other properties on the RegistrationData object as required

UserRegistrationContext context = new UserRegistrationContext();
var op = context.CreateUser(newUser, password);
```

As with the login behavior, you will find the full example of the code required to register a user already implemented in the `RegistrationForm` view in the project.

■ **Note** The registration form registers the user and then immediately logs into the system as that user. If you are implementing the scenario described earlier in this chapter where an administrator creates users, rather than users registering themselves, you will want to disable this behavior. To do so, instead of calling the `Login` method once the user registration is complete, simply close the window.

Accessing and Updating User Information

Once the users are logged in, you may wish to customize the user interface to their needs (that is, target the user experience), read and save user preferences, display some information about a particular user, such as a name, or restrict access to certain functionality based on assigned roles. All of this is available to you from the `User` object that RIA Services exposes on the client through the static `Current` property on the `WebContext` class.

To start with, determining whether the current user has logged in and is authenticated simply requires you to check the `IsAuthenticated` property of the `User` object:

```
bool isUserAuthenticated = WebContext.Current.User.IsAuthenticated;
```

You can get an array of all the roles that the user is assigned to via the `Roles` property of the `User` object:

```
string[] userRoles = (string[])WebContext.Current.User.Roles;
```

Alternatively, you can simply check whether a user is in a given role using the `IsInRole` method of the `User` object:

```
bool isInAdminRole = WebContext.Current.User.IsInRole("Administrators");
```

■ **Note** Best practice is to always specify each of your roles as constants and to use those instead of hard-coding the role names when checking whether a user is in a given role.

Any properties that you defined on the User object in the Web project will automatically have corresponding properties created on the User object in the Silverlight project. These are automatically populated with the data from the database when the user is logged in, and this object is returned to the client. Therefore, as soon as the user is successfully logged in, you can start accessing profile settings via these properties. For example, the custom property FriendlyName that was created as a part of the Silverlight Business Application project template can be accessed from the client in the following manner:

```
string friendlyName = WebContext.Current.User.FriendlyName;
```

If you are storing user profile data, such as user preferences, that you have changed on the User object and you now want to update on the server, simply call the SaveUser method on the AuthenticationContext domain context:

```
WebContext.Current.User.FriendlyName = "Chris Anderson";
WebContext.Current.Authentication.SaveUser(true);
```

Implementing Client-Side Restrictions

Although securing access to data and operations should be handled on the server, it can also be useful to implement additional restrictions on the client side. For example, you might want to hide parts of the application while the user is not logged in, or hide parts that the user does not have permission to access. To do so, simply use the methods described in the previous section to determine whether the user is logged in and what roles that user is assigned. The strategies that you might choose for implementing client-side restrictions will generally be one of the following:

- All functions are visible, but when the user tries to access them, credentials will be checked, and users will be prevented from using the function if not allowed. This doesn't provide the best experience for the user, because using the application becomes somewhat of a hit-and-miss affair, where the user doesn't immediately know what can and can't be done within the application.

- Only functions that the user can access are enabled, while those that they can't are disabled (grayed out). This shows the users all the things that could be done in the application with the requisite privileges, but enables them to see that they can't actually use the disabled functionality.

- Only functions that the user can access are visible. This simplifies the application for the users and helps avoid overwhelming them with options, but they won't know when a function is actually implemented in the application and just not available to them so that they could ask for privilege elevation if they require it.

Which strategy you choose really depends on the nature and design of the application. The first option can be simply implemented in code using the methods described in the previous section before performing the requested function. However, there are a few different means to implement the other two options:

- If you name the controls that should be disabled/hidden depending on the user's privileges, you can disable/hide them in your code-behind when the view is loaded.

- If you are using the MVVM design pattern (covered in Chapter 13), you can expose properties representing the permissions from your ViewModel that the controls in the view can bind their IsEnabled/Visibility properties to.

- You can write some attached properties that can be applied to controls used in a view, controlling whether they are disabled or hidden depending on the user's privileges. A good example of this is in an article by Andrea Boschin on the Silver-lightShow.net web site: www.silverlightshow.net/items/A-RoleManager-to-apply-roles-declaratively-to-user-interface.aspx. The RIA Services team has also released a sample project implementing a similar method, which you can download from the WCF RIA Services Code Gallery, in the sample named "Authorization Based Dynamic UI and Navigation," found here: http://code.msdn.microsoft.com/RiaServices. Kyle McClellan has written instructions for using the library from this sample project here: http://blogs.msdn.com/b/kylemc/archive/2010/05/03/authorization-sample-101.aspx.

- You can declaratively bind to properties of the User and AuthenticationContext objects in XAML. If you open the code-behind for the App.xaml file, you will find that the current WebContext object is added to the application's resources when the application starts up. This means you can bind to it just as you would any other resource in XAML. If you want to bind to the Visibility property of a control, you will need to write a value converter to convert a Boolean value to a Visibility enumeration (value converters will be covered in Chapter 11). If you want to control whether the control is disabled or hidden based on the roles that the user is assigned, you can write a value converter to do that too. Here is a simple example of declaratively enabling a control only when the user is logged into the system:

```
<Button Content="Click Me!"
        IsEnabled="{Binding Path=User.IsAuthenticated,
                            Source={StaticResource WebContext}}" />
```

Ultimately, the best choice from the preceding options really depends on the structure of your project. If you are using the MVVM design pattern, the second option tends to give the cleanest and most easily maintained solution.

■ **Note** Simply preventing users from getting to a view by hiding or disabling the button that opens it won't stop them from opening that view. As described in Chapter 3, you can navigate directly to a view simply by entering the URI that opens it in the address bar of the web browser. This means that users can bypass your security measures based on what's available in the user interface and go directly to a view, if they know or can guess the URI. Therefore, you should always check that users have permission to access a view when they navigate to it and redirect them to a different view if they don't. Alternatively, you could implement a custom content loader for the navigation framework that provides this functionality, as detailed by David Poll his blog post at http://www.davidpoll.com/2010/01/01/opening-up-silverlight-4-navigation-authenticationauthorization-in-an-inavigationcontentloader/ and continued at http://www.davidpoll.com/2010/04/25/a-refreshing-authenticationauthorization-experience-with-silverlight-4/.

Storing Data Locally

It's worth noting that any data stored in isolated storage, which will be discussed in Chapter 16, should not be considered safe. Other Silverlight applications cannot access isolated storage for this application, but data is stored as files on disk and can be read like any other file. The data is usually stored somewhere in the %AppData%\LocalLow\Microsoft\Silverlight\is folder. The paths are not self-explanatory, but you could keep looking until you find what you are after. Therefore, it's recommended that you do not store sensitive data, passwords, and so on in isolated storage without encrypting them first.

Workshop: Practicing with Client-Side Security

In this workshop, we'll create an Administration view that allows you to manage users and their roles, and prevent users from accessing this page unless they are administrators. The majority of the steps in this example have already been covered in previous examples in this book, so I won't explain those steps in detail again.

1. Create a new view in the Views folder in your Silverlight application, named AdministrationView.

2. Create a menu item named AdministrationLink that, when clicked, will navigate to the new AdministrationView view. (See Part 1 of the example in Chapter 3 for more on how to do this.) Set its Visibility property to Collapsed.

3. For the purpose of this example, we'll implement the simplest method that we discussed earlier for implementing client-side restrictions: hiding this menu item for unauthenticated and nonadministrator users in the code behind. We'll handle the LoggedIn and LoggedOut events of the Authentication object, and hide/show this menu item based on the user's authentication status and assigned roles. In the MainPage.xaml.cs file, add event handlers for the Authentication object's LoggedIn and LoggedOut events, and register these event handlers in the MainPage constructor:

```
public MainPage()
{
    InitializeComponent();

    WebContext.Current.Authentication.LoggedIn += Authentication_LoggedIn;
    WebContext.Current.Authentication.LoggedOut += Authentication_LoggedOut;
}

private void Authentication_LoggedIn(object sender, AuthenticationEventArgs e)
{

}

private void Authentication_LoggedOut(object sender, AuthenticationEventArgs e)
{

}
```

4.   When the user logs in, we want to show the Administration menu item if the user is assigned the Administrators role, so add the following code to the LoggedIn event handler:

```
if (e.User.Identity.IsAuthenticated && e.User.IsInRole("Administrators"))
    AdministrationLink.Visibility = Visibility.Visible;
else
    AdministrationLink.Visibility = Visibility.Collapsed;
```

5.   When the user logs out, we want to hide the Administration menu item, so add the following line of code to the LoggedOut event handler:

```
AdministrationLink.Visibility = Visibility.Collapsed;
```

6.   Although the Administration menu item doesn't appear when you're not logged in or not an administrator, you will find that you can still access the view by tampering with the URI in the browser's address button. You, therefore, need to check that the user has permission to access the view when it is navigated to. Add an event handler for the AdministrationView view's Loaded event, and add the following code to it:

```
var user = WebContext.Current.User;

if (!user.IsAuthenticated || !user.IsInRole("Administrators"))
    NavigationService.Navigate(new Uri("Home", UriKind.Relative));
```

This will simply navigate back to the Home view if the user tries to access the AdministrationView view without being logged in or not being assigned the Administrators role.

7.   You can now go ahead and implement the administration view. This will be left as an exercise for you to undertake using the knowledge that you've gained so far from this book. Your view should display a list of users that can be maintained via the view. The user should then be able to add new users, including assigning them to roles; view/edit the details of existing users, including customizing what roles they are assigned to; and delete existing users. This exercise will require you to also modify the UserRegistrationService domain service in the Web project to add domain operations that return a list of all the registered users, return the details of a particular user, and delete a user. All this functionality is available on the ASP.NET membership provider, using the following methods:

```
Membership.GetAllUsers()
Membership.GetUser(string username)
Membership.DeleteUser(string username)
```

You might like to use the existing user registration view, found at Views\Login\RegistrationForm.xaml, in your AdministrationView view to provide the add user functionality. You will want to take out the logic where it logs into the application as the new user once it's created. You'll also want to remove the "Already registered? Back to Login" section from its user interface.

■ **Note**   You can remove the automatically generated Security Question and Security Answer fields from the registration form by deleting or commenting out the `Question` and `Answer` properties from the `UserRegistrationData` class in the Web project.

---

8. Because all user registration will be performed by the new `AdministrationView` view, you should now remove the register user functionality from the `LoginRegistrationWindow` view. You will also need to remove the "Not registered yet? Register now" section from the `LoginForm` control's user interface.

Encrypting Data Passed Between the Server and the Client

A common cracking technique is to sniff data as it travels over the network, capture this traffic, and extract any sensitive data to potentially be used for ulterior motives. You can try a form of this yourself by using a tool such as the Fiddler Web Debugger (a free tool that you can download from `http://www.fiddler2.com`) to sniff and capture network traffic on your machine. You may have also heard of a Firefox extension named Firesheep, which sniffs network traffic looking for cookies being passed between the machines on the network and certain web sites (such as Facebook) over unencrypted connections. Once a cookie is obtained, it allows you to impersonate that user on the web site and browse it as if you were them, demonstrating how vital it is to encrypt all traffic between the server and your application.

By default, RIA Services uses binary encoding when transferring data over the network, but it's still relatively easy to read with a Fiddler add-in, so it should not be considered encrypted traffic.

Ideally, if you are passing sensitive data between the server and the client, you want to encrypt this traffic by communicating over HTTPS, using SSL, to protect it from this sort of sniffing. This requires a server certificate to be purchased from a certification authority and installed on your IIS server (a full discussion on doing so is beyond the scope of this chapter). Alternatively, you can use a self-signed certificate for development and testing purposes. IIS 7.0 on Windows Vista/7 makes this easy to create, as described by Scott Guthrie in this blog post: `http://weblogs.asp.net/scottgu/archive/2007/04/06/tip-trick-enabling-ssl-on-iis7-using-self-signed-certificates.aspx`.

Assuming you have already installed a server certificate, let's look at what you need to do to get the service operating over HTTPS.

Enforcing that communication must be over HTTPS is specified at the service level and is simply a case of setting the `RequiresSecureEndpoint` property of the `EnableClientAccess` attribute to `true` for each domain service that must be accessed securely, including the `AuthenticationService`. Any requests to domain services over HTTP that have this property set to true will be denied access.

It's not necessary that the Silverlight application itself is accessed over HTTPS—you can access it over HTTP and then require server/client communication to be over HTTPS with this method:

```
[EnableClientAccess(RequiresSecureEndpoint=true)]
public class AuthenticationService : AuthenticationBase<User>
```

However, note that when you deliver the Silverlight application via HTTP but communicate with the domain services via HTTPS, you are effectively communicating with a different domain than the application's source. This means that you must implement a cross-domain access policy file that allows cross-scheme access, as will be described in the next section.

■ **Note** When debugging your application using this option, you will need to run it under IIS or IIS Express instead of the ASP.NET Development Server, because the ASP.NET Development Server (also known as Cassini) doesn't support HTTPS communication. You will also need to specify the machine name in the URL instead of ocalhost when navigating to the application. You can configure this in the project properties of the web project in your solution.

Restricting Access to Your Application

In some scenarios, you may want only certain users to be able access your application. Silverlight XAP files are easy to decompile, which may be a cause for concern if your application contains sensitive algorithms or assets. By letting anybody download your application, you are also allowing them to gain access to its contents.

As described in Chapter 1, a XAP file is simply a ZIP file with a different extension. Changing the extension to ZIP or simply opening the XAP file directly in a compression utility enables you to get access to all the assemblies and assets in your application. Then, using .NET Reflector from Red Gate Software, or a free alternative such as JustDecompile from Telerik or dotPeek from JetBrains, you can decompile the assemblies back into readable code.

Alternatively, Silverlight Spy, a commercial tool from First Floor Software, allows you to navigate to a URL hosting a Silverlight application, which it will display the contents of and run. It then allows you to browse to an assembly within the XAP file, decompile it by using .NET Reflector, and view its code.

Therefore, always assume everything within your application is accessible publicly. This includes the address and structure of your services, any encryption keys, any assemblies and algorithms contained therein, and any assets such as graphics and other resources. Anything that is sensitive (generally in the form of intellectual property) should not be used in a Silverlight project. While this is the simplest solution to this problem, it is not always viable. Therefore, you need to look for other alternatives.

Ideally, for best protection, sensitive algorithms should be placed on the server and called via service calls when required. Of course, depending on the nature of the application—for example, if it's being run in disconnected mode or is used to perform complex simulations—this solution is not always viable either. Therefore, you might consider using an obfuscator. Obfuscators modify your compiled binary, changing the names of variables, methods, classes, and so on, so they cannot be easily read and are no longer descriptive of their purpose. Generally, obfuscation doesn't stop your application from being decompiled, but it does make the results very difficult to read and follow. The strategy of obfuscators is "security through obscurity." They aren't perfect solutions for preventing reverse-engineering of your application, but they do provide a significant impediment to those attempting to do so. A number of free and commercial obfuscation tools are available that will obfuscate Silverlight XAP files, and a quick web search will turn up several of them. For example, Eazfuscator.NET (http://www.eazfuscator.net) is a free obfuscation tool, and CodeFort (http://codefort.org) has both free and commercial editions. When choosing an obfuscation tool, be sure to check that they support obfuscating Silverlight XAP files first, however, as not all obfuscation tools do.

■ **Note** To make obfuscation effective, you need to mark as many classes, methods, and properties as `internal` or `private` as possible within your project. The external (public) interface needs to remain the same so that the obfuscator can't change it. But the internal or private definitions can be safely changed; the obfuscator can modify all their references accordingly, knowing that nothing externally will be affected.

To protect assets used by your application, you may wish to consider downloading them on demand from the server rather than including them within your XAP file (a topic covered in Chapter 17). This means that you can restrict access to them by specifying the rules in a `web.config` file that you place into a folder where restricted assets are located. These rules can be used to restrict the assets in that folder from being downloaded unless the user is authenticated or assigned to a particular role, and you can even control access at the user-name level if you wish. This strategy integrates with the ASP.NET Membership security, meaning that all you need to do is to configure the access rules in the `web.config` file, with the authentication and authorization handled by the ASP.NET Membership providers. You can create the `web.config` files yourself—each folder requiring file restrictions needs to have a `web.config` file in it, containing the rules that apply to it—and manually configure the security settings, but the easiest way to configure the access rules is to use the ASP.NET Configuration tool for the Web project. Click the Security tab, and then click the "Create access rules" hyperlink in the Access Rules group on this page. You can use the user interface shown in Figure 8-5 to create the access rules, without needing to learn the syntax.

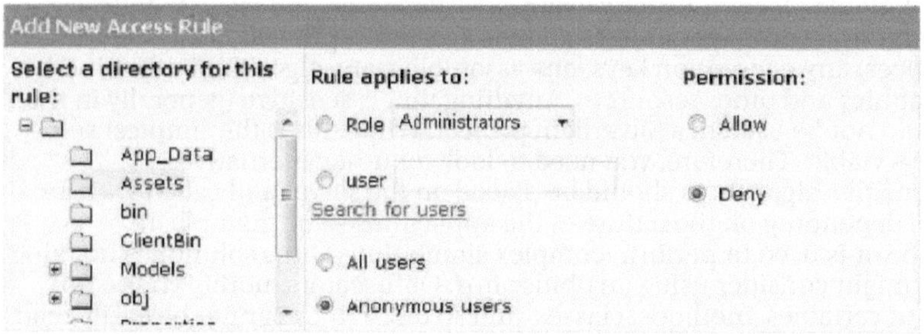

Figure 8-5. Configuring access rules in the ASP.NET Configuration tool

For example, limiting access to a folder in the Web project to authenticated users only will create a `web.config` file in that folder with the following contents:

```xml
<?xml version="1.0" encoding="utf-8"?>
<configuration>
    <system.web>
        <authorization>
            <deny users="?" />
        </authorization>
    </system.web>
</configuration>
```

You can download the assets from your Silverlight application once the user is logged in, using the techniques demonstrated in Chapter 5.

You may also wish to use this technique to restrict access to your Silverlight application itself. You can restrict access in the same manner to the ClientBin folder in your web project, so the users can't download the application unless they are already logged in. This can reduce the importance of protecting your application in the other ways described, but it does raise the issue of how the user will log into the application in the first place. There are a number of strategies that you might choose to implement:

- Because the authentication mechanism in RIA Services is exactly the same as the one used in ASP.NET projects, you could create an HTML–based login page that the user can use to log in to the system, which then loads the Silverlight application once the user has successfully been authenticated.

- Using some of the techniques described in Chapter 17, you could partition your application into a number of parts and load them on demand—protecting and loading the more sensitive parts only once the user is logged in.

- Implement a bootstrapper. Similar to the previous scenario, this will download and run a small Silverlight project—which you could use to provide a simple login screen and then continue to download the (protected) remainder of the application. The Silverlight Extensions project provides a bootstrapper that you can use to help you; it's available at http://slextensions.codeplex.com.

■ **Note** Dynamically loading parts of your application on demand isn't possible with applications that are being run in OOB mode.

You may even want to use this method to restrict access to any standard WCF web services that you use in your application. You can restrict access to their SVC files until the user is logged in, providing another degree of security. Note, however, that adding or updating these service references will not work if you have these restrictions in place while developing the application—implement these restrictions on the production server only.

Summary

Security should be designed into your application—not treated as an afterthought. Not all the issues discussed in this chapter will be of concern to you, but you can pick those that are and plan for them accordingly.

The best way to handle security issues is to try to think like a cracker: attempt to circumvent any security put in place, and look for weaknesses. It can often be worthwhile, depending on the sensitivity of the application, to get a security specialist to test it for you.

Alternatively, ask another developer to test it from a fresh perspective, without any preconceived knowledge of what security has been implemented in the system. The most important tip is to assume that the client will be compromised and design security elements into your domain services to always verify that the client has permission to perform every action immediately before executing it.

CHAPTER 9

Styling Your Application

One of the key features of XAML is that it enables exceptional user interfaces to be designed and implemented in Silverlight. When designing the look and feel of your application however, you don't want to have to customize each control and user interface element individually. This is where style resources come in—they enable you to maintain a core set of common styles to be used throughout your application.

Expression Blend has been designed to help you in the styling process, but in this chapter, we'll focus on the core fundamentals of styling in Silverlight, particularly how the styling model is structured and works, so that you can take advantage of it however you wish. This chapter won't discuss how to make your application more attractive, but it will take you through the various aspects of controlling the appearance of controls through XAML and maintaining these styles and templates as reusable resources.

Considering the Designer/Developer Workflow

The ability for XAML–based controls to be extensively styled and templated enables you to radically customize their appearance and permits the creation of visually pleasing applications. User interfaces can be designed that engage users and draw them into the application. However, simply using the Silverlight controls out of the box, on the default white canvas, can lead to a rather plain application, often followed by badly implemented attempts to make it more interesting by developers who may not have the skills to do so effectively. Unfortunately, this process results in many unsightly user interfaces. Silverlight projects can, therefore, greatly benefit from having a designer on board to create an attractive user interface.

Including designers as a part of the development process has, therefore, been a focus for Microsoft. That said, Visual Studio is not an application suited for use by designers, so Microsoft created the Expression Suite targeted toward designers' needs. From the Expression Suite, the Expression Blend and Expression Design tools are those that will be most useful to graphic designers when working on Silverlight projects.

Expression Blend is intended for designing XAML–based user interfaces for Silverlight and WPF. This includes extensive support for laying out controls, styling and templating them, and creating and applying animations to elements of the user interface. With Visual Studio 2010's new Silverlight designer, we now have a drag-and-drop design surface that we can view and interact with at design time, a feature not available in Visual Studio 2008. Therefore, developers who worked with XAML in addition to code now are less able to rely on Expression Blend than they may have previously. That said, Expression Blend still offers many design-related features that Visual Studio does not (without modifying the XAML directly, which can often be complex and inefficient). These features include

- Animations (including transition animations) can be designed for and applied to user interface elements. Animations can involve a lot of XAML, which would have to be hard-coded in Visual Studio. Not only does Expression Blend provide a friendly user interface for creating animations, but it also allows you preview the animation at design time without needing to compile and run your application first.

- Control templating is vastly easier in Expression Blend. Expression Blend also makes it much easier to create control templates for your own custom controls (discussed in Chapter 12).

- Sample data enables you to populate your user interface with data at design time, so you can see how the interface will look when you run your application.

These are just some of the areas in which Expression Blend provides guidance and makes those tasks much easier to implement. Therefore, for any nontrivial user interface design, it's generally recommended that you include Expression Blend as one of your tools.

Just as Visual Studio 2010 has some design-related features, Expression Blend has some code-related features too. Expression Blend can compile and run projects, and you can also modify code. However, Expression Blend's code-related features are as minimal as Visual Studio's design features. There are just enough code-related features in Expression Blend to do basic tasks but not enough for someone to solely use Expression Blend to create a Silverlight application in an efficient manner.

Microsoft has designed the Visual Studio and Expression Blend tools to enable developers and designers to work alongside each other on the same project in harmony. The two complement each other. Designers can work on the visual aspects of the application; developers work on the code aspects. This approach can be even more effective when using the Model-View-ViewModel (MVVM) design pattern discussed in Chapter 13, as it promotes a clear separation of the presentation of a view and its corresponding logic. This separation makes it much easier to enable both a designer and a developer to work on the same part of the project at the same time, with reduced numbers of collisions between them.

Expression Design is another tool for graphics designers focused toward working with vector graphics. Expression Blend has some support for working with vector graphics, but Expression Design is more targeted in that direction, and Expression Blend is more targeted toward designing user interfaces. Therefore, you could break up the graphics designer role further to a user interface designer, who would use Expression Blend, and a graphics designer, who would use Expression Design. However, these roles often blend into a single graphics designer role in practice.

Another role that is starting to become more popular in software projects is the user experience designer. A user experience designer typically takes the functional requirements of the software and creates a design for how the user will interact with the software that implements those requirements in the most efficient and user-friendly manner.

User experience design faces many misconceptions, and many people confuse it with the role of making the application attractive, believing that designing how users interact with the application is the role of the graphics designer. However, these should be treated as two completely separate skill sets: a user experience designer will determine the flow of the application based on the functional requirements, whereas a graphics designer will take this flow and implement it as an attractive user interface.

Another common misconception is that the graphic design or styling of the application should be one of the first tasks undertaken in the project. In fact, user experience design should be the main focus early on, with the styling performed later in the project. Support for the eventual styling should, of course, be included as a part of the user interface development process, but the interaction aspects are far more important to do up front. For this purpose, Microsoft added SketchFlow to Expression Blend. User experience designers can use SketchFlow to map the flow and rough layout of the application in order to generate prototypes.

As a summary, Visual Studio is targeted at developers; Expression Blend and Expression Design are targeted at user interface and graphics designers, and SketchFlow is targeted toward user experience designers.

Since this book is primarily targeted for developers, we are focusing primarily on what can be done in Visual Studio. Therefore, aspects such as how to use the Expression tools and how to create animations (which really requires Expression Blend to implement efficiently) will not be covered here.

■ **Note** In theory, the developer, graphics designer, and user experience designer should all be different people with dedicated roles and skill sets. However, in reality, this is not always the case. If your developer role includes design, you may need to become familiar with more than one of these products and switch between them, but promoting a clear separation between these roles generally leads to better software.

Defining Style Resources

The simplest form of styling your user interface is to assign values to properties exposed by controls, using attribute syntax. However, this will very soon lead to your XAML becoming an unmaintainable mess. Doing so will result in your XAML files becoming unwieldy, complex, and hard to read; and any necessary styling changes will often need to be made in numerous places within the application—essentially, you will have spaghetti XAML code.

The answer to this problem is to use style resources. Defining and using style resources has numerous advantages. If we want to change the styling of all our TextBox controls, we only need to set the value in one place, and it will automatically be applied to all the controls that reference that style. This simplifies the XAML by removing the need to repeatedly apply the same property values on each control. It also creates a clearer separation between your control definitions and their appearance.

You could consider style resources to be similar to CSS styles in traditional HTML–based web development. With CSS, you can define a style specifying various property values in your CSS file or in your HTML page header and apply that style to HTML elements by assigning the name of the style to their class property. Alternatively, you can define a style that specifies the values that the properties on all elements of a given type should automatically use. You can then override the property values defined in these styles by assigning different property values directly on the elements themselves.

Styling in Silverlight works in a similar fashion. Style resources can be defined in a resource dictionary or within a XAML file itself and applied to controls by pointing their Style properties to the style resource, using the StaticResource markup extension. Alternatively, you can exclude the key from a style resource definition, and all the controls of the given type will automatically use that style (known as implicit styling).

■ **Note** Unlike CSS, style resources are specific to their target control type, meaning you cannot create a style that defines a set of property values to be used by both TextBox controls and ComboBox controls, for example.

We have already discussed the concept of style resources in Chapter 2, which demonstrated how you could define a group of property values commonly assigned to a type of control as a style resource and then apply that to the Style property of any controls that use it. However, we will start with a quick overview and move on to discuss some more advanced styling features.

Defining a Style Resource

There are two types of style resources: explicit and implicit. Let's take a look at each of these in turn.

Explicit Styles

Let's say we have multiple TextBox controls in our project that use a common set of property values. Instead of assigning the same property values to each control, like this

```
<TextBox Name="FirstNameField" Margin="2" Background="LemonChiffon" Grid.Row="0" />
<TextBox Name="LastNameField" Margin="2" Background="LemonChiffon" Grid.Row="1" />
<TextBox Name="CompanyField" Margin="2" Background="LemonChiffon" Grid.Row="2" />
```

we can, instead, define these properties as a style resource:

```
<Style x:Key="UserFieldsStyle" TargetType="TextBox">
    <Setter Property="Margin" Value="2" />
    <Setter Property="Background" Value="LemonChiffon" />
</Style>
```

When defining our style resource, we are giving it a unique key to reference it using the x:Key attached property from the XAML namespace and specifying the type of control it can be applied to using the TargetType property. After that, it's a case of creating a Setter element for each property you want to specify a value for and providing it the name of the property and its corresponding value. We can now apply this style to the Style property on our controls, using the StaticResource XAML markup extension. The StaticResource markup extension is used to reference the style resource by using the key of the style resource to find it.

```
<TextBox Name="FirstNameField" Grid.Row="0" Style="{StaticResource UserFieldsStyle}" />
<TextBox Name="LastNameField" Grid.Row="1" Style="{StaticResource UserFieldsStyle}" />
<TextBox Name="CompanyField" Grid.Row="2" Style="{StaticResource UserFieldsStyle}" />
```

■ **Note** You can override the values from the style resource by simply applying alternate property values directly to the control itself, via inline styles.

This is a process of explicitly assigning a style to a control. We gave the style resource a key, and explicitly assigned that style to a control.

Implicit Styles

Alternatively, you may want to implicitly assign a style resource to all controls within a given scope. This is possible using the implicit styles functionality introduced in Silverlight 4. Simply omit the key when defining a style resource, and all controls of the control type that the style targets within the scope of the resource will automatically use that style. For example, if you define the previous style resource, without a key defined, at a view level—for example, in Page.Resources or UserControl.Resources—the style will be automatically applied to all of the TextBox controls within that view. If a style resource is defined at the application level, it will used by controls application-wide, which is a typical scenario when creating themes that will be discussed later in this chapter.

Let's revisit the example that was used to demonstrate explicit styles and convert it to use implicit styles now. Start by removing the key from the style definition:

```
<Style TargetType="TextBox">
    <Setter Property="Margin" Value="2" />
    <Setter Property="Background" Value="LemonChiffon" />
</Style>
```

Now, all your TextBox controls within the scope of this implicit style will automatically use the style without actually needing any reference to the style:

```
<TextBox Name="FirstNameField" Grid.Row="0" />
<TextBox Name="LastNameField" Grid.Row="1" />
<TextBox Name="CompanyField" Grid.Row="2" />
```

■ **Note** Microsoft recommends that you avoid assigning values to properties in style resources where the property is defining behavior (as opposed to appearance).

Defining Style Resources in the Object Hierarchy

Style resources can be defined at various levels of the object hierarchy, and the level at which a style is defined provides its scope. Let's look at the most common locations for defining style resources in your project.

At the Control Level

If you define a style resource in the Resources property of any element in the control hierarchy, it will be available for use by the descendents of that element. This isn't recommended however, due to potential maintainability issues—specifically because of confusion as to where a style resource definition can be found.

At the View Level

If style resources are defined at the view level in Page.Resources or UserControl.Resources in a XAML file, they will be available for use by all the controls in that view.

At the Application Level

You can define application-wide style resources on the Application.Resources property of the App.xaml file.

As a Resource Dictionary

Style resources defined at the application level are often defined in a resource dictionary and merged into the application's resources. This strategy has the following benefits:

- Keeps the style resource definitions from clogging up the App.xaml file

- Enables the style resources to be reused among projects

- Enables different style resources dictionaries to be easily swapped in and out

- Enables your application to be themed

The best example of this strategy is already implemented in the project you've generated from the Silverlight Business Application project template. All style resources are defined in a resource dictionary called Styles.xaml that is found in the Assets folder. This file is then merged into the application's resources, in the App.xaml file, like so:

```
<Application.Resources>
    <ResourceDictionary>
        <ResourceDictionary.MergedDictionaries>
            <ResourceDictionary Source="Assets/Styles.xaml"/>
        </ResourceDictionary.MergedDictionaries>
    </ResourceDictionary>
</Application.Resources>
```

■ **Note** Multiple resource dictionaries can be merged into a single Resources property. Therefore, you can maintain a logical separation between your various style resources, avoiding resource dictionaries becoming too large and complex and enabling multiple developers on the project to maintain styles at the same time. If a style is defined in more than one resource dictionary, the last one to be merged will used. If you have two implicit styles targeting the same control, the property setters won't be merged into a single style, but only the last style will be used.

Alternatively, if you have only a single resource dictionary to merge, you can simply assign the resource dictionary to Application.Resources:

```
<Application.Resources>
    <ResourceDictionary Source="Assets/Styles.xaml" />
</Application.Resources>
```

You can create a new resource dictionary by adding a new item to your project and selecting the Silverlight Resource Dictionary project template. This will leave you with an empty resource dictionary structure to which you can add your styles. For example, here is the UserFieldsStyle style resource we created earlier, defined in a resource dictionary:

```
<ResourceDictionary
    xmlns="http://schemas.microsoft.com/winfx/2006/xaml/presentation"
    xmlns:x="http://schemas.microsoft.com/winfx/2006/xaml">

    <Style x:Key="UserFieldsStyle" TargetType="TextBox">
        <Setter Property="Margin" Value="2" />
        <Setter Property="Background" Value="LemonChiffon" />
    </Style>
</ResourceDictionary>
```

As a Resource Dictionary in a Referenced Assembly

Themes are often defined in a resource dictionary, and defining this resource dictionary in its own assembly can be useful so that you can maintain the theme in a single location and use it in multiple projects.

Add a reference to the assembly containing the resource dictionary to use to your project. You can then merge the resource dictionary into your application's resources as previously demonstrated. However, the path to the view needs to be of the form "/[assembly];component/[viewpath]". For example, if the ThemeStyles.xaml view existed in a referenced assembly named MyTheme.dll, the path to navigate to it would be "/MyTheme;component/ThemeStyles.xaml".

```
<Application.Resources>
    <ResourceDictionary Source="/MyTheme;component/ThemeStyles.xaml" />
</Application.Resources>
```

In Generic.xaml

Custom controls generally have their styles and control templates defined in a resource dictionary named Generic.xaml, which does not need to be merged into any Resource property but must be placed under the Themes folder in the project where the corresponding controls are defined. This will be discussed in Chapter 12.

Storing Complex Property Values in Styles

It's worth noting that complex values can be stored in styles. For example, when defining a gradient on a property in a style, you use property element syntax to define the gradient the same way as you would if assigning the gradient directly on the control itself:

```
<Style x:Key="UserFieldsStyle" TargetType="Control">
    <Setter Property="Margin" Value="2" />
    <Setter Property="Background">
        <Setter.Value>
            <LinearGradientBrush EndPoint="1,0.5" StartPoint="0,0.5">
                <GradientStop Color="LemonChiffon" Offset="0" />
                <GradientStop Color="#FFFFFFCD" Offset="1" />
            </LinearGradientBrush>
        </Setter.Value>
    </Setter>
</Style>
```

Naming Style Resources

As a part of our design process, we need to look further than just how each control type will be styled and design and name styles based on their purpose within the application rather than what they consist of or the type of control they will be applied to. For example, you might have a TextBlock style resource that you want to use throughout your application to make the text bold, with a font size of 12 points, and colored navy. How should you name this style resource? Maybe TextBlockStyle, BoldNavy12ptStyle, PageHeaderStyle, or PageHeaderTextBlockStyle?

From both a management and a visual design perspective, PageHeaderStyle or PageHeaderTextBlockStyle would be the best way to name the style resource, because either of these names makes it easy to see what the purpose of each style is when navigating the style resource definitions. Also, if you are designing a new theme for the application or plan to support multiple themes, this naming scheme makes much more sense, because you are linking each style to a purpose rather than linking each style to how it is rendered on screen.

So even if two different definitions of a style resource have exactly the same property values, it is generally still better to define them as separate style resources. This may result in multiple styles containing the same property values but provides better support for future restyling.

Inheriting Style Resources

Only a single style resource can be applied to a control, which may initially seem somewhat limiting when you are designing your style resources. For example, you may wish to define some property values in a base style resource common to most or all controls of a given type and then define another style resource containing additional property values to be applied to only some controls of that type.

While you may not be able to apply both those style resources to a control, you can have your new style resource inherit the property value definitions from the base style resource, which will serve the same purpose. This is achieved using the BasedOn property of the Style, which you can point to another style resource that this style will inherit from. Because you are pointing to a resource, you need to use the StaticResource markup extension. For example, say we have this style resource that we want to use as our base:

```
<Style x:Key="UserFieldsStyleBase" TargetType="TextBox">
    <Setter Property="Margin" Value="2" />
    <Setter Property="Background" Value="LemonChiffon" />
</Style>
```

When defining a new style resource that should be based on this one, we can inherit from it using the BasedOn property, like so:

```
<Style x:Key="UserFieldsStyle" TargetType="TextBox"
    BasedOn="{StaticResource UserFieldsStyleBase}">
    <Setter Property="TextAlignment" Value="Right" />
</Style>
```

■ **Note** A style resource can only be based on a single style, but that style can be based on another style, and so on.

Not only can you inherit the property value definitions from a base style resource using this method but you can also override some of those property value definitions. For example, despite the Background property having a value of LemonChiffon in the base style, we've overridden that property in this style and assigned it a value of White instead:

```
<Style x:Key="UserFieldsStyle" TargetType="TextBox"
    BasedOn="{StaticResource UserFieldsStyleBase}">
    <Setter Property="Background" Value="White" />
</Style>
```

If you have a style resource that inherits a property value, but you want remove that property from the style, you can simply null its value like so:

```
<Setter Property="Background" Value="{x:Null}" />
```

■ **Note** The target control type from which you inherit a style must match that of the new style. For example, you cannot have a style targeting the TextBox control inherit from a style targeting the ComboBox control. You can, however, have a style that inherits from a style targeting one of its base classes. For example, a style targeting the TextBox control can inherit from a style targeting the Control class.

Styling Constraints

There are a few issues that you should be aware of when defining styles:

- Only a single style resource can be assigned to a control, and any further property values that need to be applied must be applied inline on the control itself.

- Styles cannot be applied to controls of different types. Each style has a single control type that it applies to, meaning that you cannot have a TextBox and a ComboBox control reference the same style. You can assign the target type to be a class common to both those controls, such as Control, but you will often find that the properties you wish to define values for will not exist on that base class, and therefore, the project will not compile. Note that attempting this with implicit styles will not work. The type of controls that will automatically use implicit styles must match the given target type of the style exactly; otherwise, the style will not be applied.

- Once you have assigned a style to a control, any implicit style that the control may have otherwise used will no longer be used by this control.

Applying Control Templates

You have now seen how we can define a style resource and apply it to controls, but what if we want to completely change the appearance of the control, including the appearance or function of its elements not exposed by the control as properties? In Silverlight, this is actually possible by applying an alternate control template to the control (in place of its default template). The structure of Silverlight custom controls encourages a separation between the control's presentation and behavior. The behavior of the control should be defined in the code, and its appearance should be defined in the control template. Between the two is a contract defining what the code needs access to from the presentation layer. With this clear separation of concerns, you can completely modify the appearance of a control without affecting its behavior, as long as you adhere to the control's behavior/presentation contract. This is an extremely powerful feature of XAML and really demonstrates its flexibility when defining user interfaces.

■ **Note** A *style* enables you to simply assign property values to a control, while a *control template* enables you to directly modify the core XAML of the control itself.

Using Default Control Templates

Default control templates and styles are defined in the Generic.xaml file in the Themes folder of the project or assembly containing the control. Each control template has its own resource dictionary within this file. When you want to apply your own alternate custom control template to a control, the easiest way to start is by making a copy of the default control template of that control and working from there. The easiest way to extract the default control template is using Expression Blend. It will allow you to copy the default control template for that control, from the Generic.xaml file in the control's assembly, into your project as a new resource. You can then customize this control template resource as you see fit—move elements around, add additional control elements, remove elements, and restyle elements—as long as you keep the template parts and states specified in the control's contract.

Unfortunately, without using Expression Blend, the only way to get the existing control template is to follow these steps:

1. Open the Generic.xaml file of the assembly that contains the control you want to modify. If you don't have the source code for the control, you will need to open the assembly using a decompilation tool (such as .NET Reflector) and extract the Generic.xaml file from there.

2. Find the style resource / control template pertaining to the control, and copy it into your project as a new style resource / control template.

3. Assign that new style resource / control template to your control.

As you can see, this is a somewhat messy and convoluted process when performed manually, but Expression Blend helps to automate it and make it easy.

Templating a Control

Using Expression Blend, you can make a copy of a control's default template by right-clicking the control in design view and selecting Edit Control Parts (Template) ➤ Edit a Copy from the context menu. This will open the window shown in Figure 9-1.

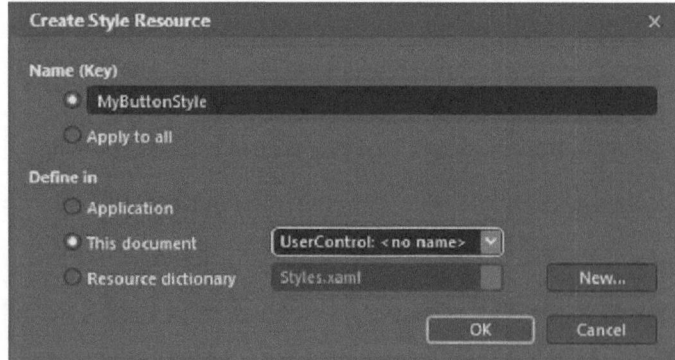

Figure 9-1. The Create Style Resource window in Expression Blend

Give the style resource a name or select the "Apply to all" option to make it an implicit style, and specify a location where it should be defined in your application. Once you've done so, Expression Blend will perform the previously mentioned process automatically and leave the file ready for you to make your customizations, which you can do visually using the Expression Blend design view or by modifying the XAML manually.

■ **Note** Despite the fact that you're making a copy of the control template, this process actually creates a style resource for the control, not a control template resource, although the style resource contains the control template. This style resource will then be assigned to the control's Style property. (A style can set property values, and Template is a property on the control.) However, if you already have a style assigned to this control, a control template resource will be created instead and assigned to the control's Template property.

You will find that creating a control template resource inserts a lot of XAML markup into your project. The amount will depend on the complexity of the control, and some controls like the DataGrid can be *very* complex. There is no way to minimize the amount of XAML generated without simplifying the visual structure of the control itself. For example, if you want to make only a slight adjustment to an existing element in the template, you're faced with an all-or-nothing approach. It's advisable to always maintain control templates in a separate resource file rather than inside a view, even if it is only used by that view, simply to ensure that your views are kept clean and tidy and without the burden of all the XAML that control templates generally impose.

■ **Note** Before customizing a control template, it's worth ensuring there isn't a style or template property on the control that will allow you to style or customize just a part of the control, without resorting to customizing the entire template.

Despite my advice against this, for the sake of completion, I'll demonstrate that you don't actually have to create styles and control templates as resources. They can also be defined inline to a control definition using property element syntax, and thus will apply to that control instance only, for example:

```
<TextBox>
    <TextBox.Template>
        <!-- Control template definition can go here -->
    </TextBox.Template>
</TextBox>
```

Structuring Control Templates

Let's now take a look at exactly what a control template is and how it is structured. Often, you will hear this structure referred to as the "parts and states model."

At its simplest, a control template simply defines the XAML that makes up the static presentation of the template that never changes, for example:

```
<ControlTemplate TargetType="Button">
    <Grid>
```

```
        <!-- etc -->
    </Grid>
</ControlTemplate>
```

■ **Note** We'll go through the structure of control templates in more detail in Chapter 12, as we look at how to build custom controls.

Visual States

Rarely will a control have a single static appearance, because almost all controls change their appearance in some way, such as when a control has focus or is disabled. In that case, we would define a base look for the control (its default state), and changes to the control's appearance would be made when appropriate. This default state should also include the elements that would be visible in the alternative states, even if they're not visible in the base state. If an element should not be visible in the control's base state, set its visibility to collapsed, or set its opacity to 0.

For example, a button looks a particular way when it is placed on a form (its default state). This appearance is updated when the control changes state, such as when it has the focus, is disabled, pressed, hovered over, and so on. This is where Visual States come in—each visual state defined describes how the base look of the control will be altered when that state is active to achieve the appearance of the control for that state. This involves altering the elements that make up the control's default state—for example, changing its color, visibility, opacity, and so on—to visually indicate that the control is in that state. In other words, we define each state in our control template, and each state defines the changes that need to be made to the default state in order to achieve its desired appearance. These changes are actually defined as animations and will be discussed in the next section of this chapter.

What triggers a state change on a control? Essentially, the control behavior (that is, the code for the control) manages its current state, based on the events it receives and/or the value assigned to one or more of its properties. For example, when the user clicks a button and holds the mouse button down, meaning the button is in the Pressed state, the button needs to change its visual state to visually indicate as such. Alternatively, the button may be disabled (IsEnabled="false"), in which case the button needs to visually indicate that by entering its Disabled state. The control's logic determines what state it should be in, but it then delegates updating the control's appearance to the Visual State Manager, which does so accordingly.

■ **Note** No changes should be made to the visual appearance of the control from the code. All presentation details should be defined within the control template as states.

You may also want to have a constant animation for the control while it is in a particular state, such as a button pulsing when the mouse is over it. This is known as in-state animation and is achieved using a storyboard containing various animations that change the property values of elements within the control over a given duration and that will generally be set to continually repeat while the control is in that state.

A simple example of animating a property on an element within the control is demonstrated in the following example. This animation is used to make the button appear to be pressed. It does so by changing the Opacity property of the PressedBorder element to 1, making that element visible.

```
<VisualState x:Name="Pressed">
    <Storyboard>
        <DoubleAnimationUsingKeyFrames
                    Storyboard.TargetProperty="(UIElement.Opacity)"
                    Storyboard.TargetName="PressedBorder">
            <EasingDoubleKeyFrame KeyTime="0" Value="1"/>
        </DoubleAnimationUsingKeyFrames>
    </Storyboard>
</VisualState>
```

■ **Note**   Each state must exist within a state group, as will be described shortly.

A full discussion of implementing animations is beyond the scope of this book, although you will find further examples in Chapter 12.

State Transitions

A control moves from state to state via a state transition. State transitions can be represented in the control template using the following:

• An explicitly defined animation, defined within a storyboard, in the same way as in-state animations, over a given duration, for example:

```
<VisualTransition GeneratedDuration="0:0:2" From="Inactive" To="Active">
    <Storyboard>
        <DoubleAnimation From="0" To="1" d:IsOptimized="True"
                    Storyboard.TargetProperty="(UIElement.Opacity)"
                    Storyboard.TargetName="LayoutRoot" />
    </Storyboard>
</VisualTransition>
```

• An automatic transition that smoothly animates each element in the control between its configuration in each state over a given duration, in a process managed by the Visual State Manager, for example:

```
<VisualTransition GeneratedDuration="0:0:2" From="Inactive" To="Active" />
```

■ **Note**   As a general rule, state transitions should have a very short duration (no more than half a second) so as to not slow the user's interaction with the application.

Visual State Groups

We need to take into account one more complexity, and that's when a control can be in more than one state at the one time. For example, a button may be in its Focused state, indicating the button has input focus, but it may also simultaneously be in its Pressed state, where the button has been clicked and the mouse button hasn't been released. How do we represent both states visually at the same time? Well, this is possible by having the states exist in different visual state groups. Visual state groups allow you to group related states together. Although only one state in each group can be active at a time, multiple states can be active across all the defined groups, and the control's appearance can combine each of these together. So as per the previous example, the base look is updated to indicate the button is pressed, and the focus rectangle will be drawn to indicate the button has focus.

```
<VisualStateManager.VisualStateGroups>
    <VisualStateGroup x:Name="CommonStates">
        <!-- Define common states here -->
    </VisualStateGroup>
    <VisualStateGroup x:Name="Focused">
        <!-- Define focused states here -->
    </VisualStateGroup>
    <VisualStateGroup x:Name="Pressed">
        <!-- Define pressed states here -->
    </VisualStateGroup>
</VisualStateManager.VisualStateGroups>
```

Template Parts

The final concept to understand is that of template parts. A control may need to reference certain visual elements that belong to it in the code for that control (that is, the behavior management code). Because of the strict separation between the control's behavior and presentation, and the ability for an alternative control template to be applied to the control, these elements need to be defined in the contract between its behavior and presentation as required elements in any control template that is applied. These elements are known as template parts. Template parts will be covered in more depth in Chapter 12.

Theming

Theming (sometimes also known as skinning) is essentially the process of either styling or retemplating control types to customize their appearance by overriding their default styles or control templates. Themes are generally designed as a way of maintaining the look of the controls in the application in a single location in your project, ensuring consistency across your application and simplifying mainte-nance. However, they are also particularly useful when creating packaged software that should make use of corporate colors and display the customer's branding.

The styles and control templates from a theme are automatically applied to their corresponding control instances wherever they may appear throughout the application.

Your application may also define a number of themes that the user can choose from. To do so, define each theme in a separate resource dictionary, and merge the selected theme file with the applica-tion's resources at runtime to apply it.

Creating a Custom Theme

You can create your own theme file by creating a resource dictionary, placing all of your style resources in it, and merging it with the application's resources, as detailed earlier in this chapter. You can also define this resource file in a separate assembly, which enables you to share in between projects.

You can define a new control template in a style resource to completely change the look of the target control type. Assign it to the control's `Template` property defined in the style, like so:

```
<Style TargetType="Button">
    <Setter Property="Template">
        <Setter.Value>
            <ControlTemplate TargetType="Button">
                <!-- Control template goes here -->
            </ControlTemplate>
        </Setter.Value>
    </Setter>
</Style>
```

If you make this style resource an implicit style, all controls of the specified target type for the style will automatically have the control template applied, thus resulting in a theme-like behavior.

Using Silverlight Toolkit Themes

The Silverlight Toolkit includes an array of predefined themes that you may like to use in your project to retemplate the standard Silverlight controls and the Silverlight Toolkit controls, providing a new distinct look to your application. You can use these as they are or modify them to suit your own tastes. More information can be found on the Silverlight Toolkit's CodePlex site at `http://silverlight.codeplex.com`.

Installing Silverlight Navigation and Business Application Themed Project Templates

Microsoft has started to release project templates that both restructure the visual layout of the application and retheme all the core Silverlight and Silverlight Toolkit controls—in other words, defining new control templates for all these controls.

You can download and install these from the Visual Studio Online Gallery, via Visual Studio's Extension Manager. From the Online Gallery, navigate to the Templates ➤ Silverlight category to find them. At the time of this writing, only the themes for the Silverlight Navigation Application project types are available for installing as project templates, but you can download Silverlight Business Application projects implementing these themes at `www.microsoft.com/downloads/details.aspx?FamilyID=e9da0eb8-f31b-4490-85b8-92c2f807df9e&displaylang=en`.

You will find a project template for each theme you install in the Silverlight category of Visual Studio's New Project dialog, which you can then use when creating a project.

New themes will be released over time, and at the time of this writing, the released themes include the following:

- Accent Color
- Cosmopolitan
- Windows 7
- JetPack

Effectively Using Icons and Images

Effective use of icons and images throughout your application can really enhance its visual appeal. Designing quality icons is really the job of a graphics designer, but if you don't have the budget for a graphics designer, there is still the viable and relatively inexpensive option of purchasing a stock icon library. Most libraries come as raster files, such as .png files, although some companies are starting to include, or sell separately, the original vector images.

■ **Note** While .png files work perfectly well in Silverlight, in some instances, you may prefer to use vector (XAML–based) images instead. Vector images are scalable without losing quality, can be modified easily, and often have a smaller file size than the equivalent raster image, depending on the complexity of the image. However, vector images are also more CPU intensive, so you need to choose the appropriate format for your particular requirements. As a general rule, for small images that don't need to be scaled, such as icons, raster images are a better choice. For large images, especially those that will change size, vector images may suit better.

Note that vector graphics often come as Adobe Photoshop (.psd), Adobe Illustrator (.ai), or Scalable Vector Graphics (.svg) files and need to be converted to XAML, possibly losing some definition along the way, to be used within a Silverlight application. A plug-in is available for Adobe Illustrator to export to XAML, or you can open these files from within Expression Blend, using the File ➤ Import Adobe Illustrator File menu option, or Expression Design, using File ➤ Open. Opening .ai files in Expression Design is a little more successful but often results in black shapes where Expression Design couldn't render the corresponding element correctly, most likely due to using rendering features not available in Silverlight. Ideally, you want the icons and images already converted to XAML files when you purchase them to save you these problems.

If you do buy icons or images formatted as XAML, ensure that they are formatted for Silverlight, not WPF. The file formats differ slightly, so if they are formatted for WPF, they will not be usable in Silverlight without modification. That said, if the Expression Design file type is also included, you can use that to export a new XAML file targeting Silverlight instead.

Applying Animation

You may wish to consider applying some animation effects to your user interface to give it a bit of additional flair. Animations, such as page transitions, can add pizzazz to your application and add to its "wow" factor.

However, you should use animations sparingly, so you do not distract users from their primary task when using your application. Animation can impress the user the first couple of times but can quickly become an annoyance. You must be particularly aware of this issue when developing business applications, as users will often spend considerable time in their working day with the application, and poorly implemented animations get old quickly. Transition animations should be fast and should not slow the user's interaction with the application.

Animations use storyboards to define the times at which various parts of the animation start and stop. Silverlight then handles the process of getting from one frame to another between the animation's start and stop times.

Creating animations is a huge topic and beyond the scope of this book, although we will take another brief look at them when we create a Wait Indicator custom control in Chapter 13. If you are creating animations, Expression Blend is an essential tool to help you with this task, as it provides a lot of functionality geared toward designing animations.

Applying Pixel Shaders and Effects

Pixel shaders enable you to add effects to Silverlight controls by modifying the pixels of their rendered output before displaying them on the screen. Typical effects include shadows, blurs, reflections, and color alteration, but the options are almost endless.

There are two pixel shaders included in the Silverlight 5 runtime:

- `DropShadowEffect`
- `BlurEffect`

Applying one of these effects is an easy as assigning the pixel shader to the `Effect` property of a control. The following example demonstrates assigning a drop shadow to a control, with the result shown in Figure 9-2:

```
<Button Content="Shadow" Width="75" Height="23">
    <Button.Effect>
        <DropShadowEffect Opacity="0.5" />
    </Button.Effect>
</Button>
```

Shadow

Figure 9-2. A button with a drop shadow effect

You can create your own pixel shaders using the High-Level Shader Language (HLSL), which you then need to compile into a `.ps` file, using the `fxc` command-line tool included with the DirectX SDK. An easy way to do this is using a free tool named Shazzam, by Walt Ritscher, which can be downloaded at `http://shazzam-tool.com`. This tool saves the need for downloading the large DirectX SDK and provides a user interface for editing, testing, and compiling pixel shaders. Writing pixel shaders is a complex topic and beyond the scope of this book. A good article by for learning how to write a pixel shader is the one by Rene Schulte available at `http://channel9.msdn.com/coding4fun/articles/SilverShader--Introduction-to-Silverlight-and-WPF-Pixel-Shaders`. However, it's rare to need to write your own pixel shaders, as a quick web search will probably turn up a pixel shader that provides the effect that you are after; many are available for download.

■ **Note** Pixel shader effects are rendered in software. Generally, they can be rather CPU-intensive to render, so you should use them sparingly to avoid negatively affecting the performance of your application.

Miscellaneous Styling Tips

Here are a few miscellaneous tips that you may find useful when designing your style resources.

Defining Constants in XAML

In instances where you want to maintain a set of constant values that can be used by multiple controls or style resources but that can be maintained in a single location, you can simply define those values as resources. For example, here we are defining a color constant that we can use:

```
<SolidColorBrush x:Key="BackgroundColorResource" Color="LemonChiffon "/>
```

You can then assign this resource directly to a control by using the `StaticResource` markup extension:

```
<TextBox Background="{StaticResource BackgroundColorResource}" />
```

Or you can use it in a style resource definition:

```
<Style x:Key="UserFieldsStyleBase" TargetType="TextBox">
    <Setter Property="Margin" Value="2" />
    <Setter Property="Background"
            Value="{StaticResource BackgroundColorResource}" />
</Style>
```

This tip can be particularly useful when defining theme files, where you may define a core color scheme using constants that you can maintain in one place and simply change their values between theme files.

Visual Studio provides a function that helps streamline the process of defining a value as a resource. Select a control in the XAML designer. In the property editor tool window, you'll note that there are little icons to the left of the property values. Clicking an icon will show a context menu, with functions you can perform on that property, as shown in Figure 9-3. Open the context menu for the property whose value you want to turn into a resource, and select the Extract Value to Resource item. This will show a dialog where you can enter the key for the resource and the location that it should be defined. Clicking the OK button will create the resource for you and wire the control's property to it.

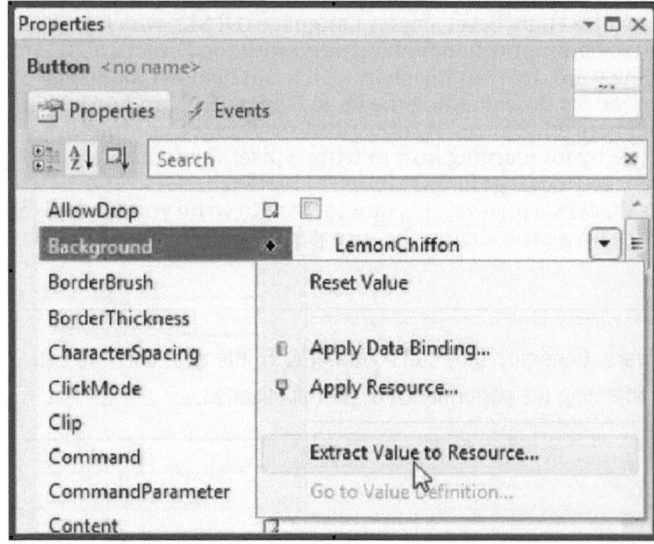

Figure 9-3. *Extracting a value to a resource, using Visual Studio's Properties tool window*

Finding a Control's Style Definition

When making extensive use of styles in your project, finding where a particular style is defined can become difficult. If a control is using the style, go to the Properties tool window, and show the context menu for the Style property, as detailed in the previous section. The "Go to Value Definition" menu item should be enabled, and clicking it will open the file where the style's defined and select it in the XAML editor.

■ **Note** This tip also applies to finding the definition of a resource that's applied to a property of a control.

Applying a Style to a Control Using the XAML Designer

When you have many styles defined in your project, you may not recall the name of the style that you want to use. You can select the control's Style property in the Properties tool window, show the context menu for the property, and select the Apply Resource menu item. This will display a list of resources matching the control type that you can select from and apply to the control.

■ **Note** This tip also applies to applying an existing resource to a property of a control.

Restoring a Control's Default Style

If you have an implicit style being applied to a control that you do not wish to have any styling applied, you can stop the style being applied by setting the Style property of the control to null, for example:

```
<TextBox Style="{x:Null}" />
```

This control will now use its default style instead of the implicit style.

Binding in Style Setters

A new feature in Silverlight 5 is the ability to apply a binding to a property setter in a style. Perhaps you want to bind the property to a resource string (such as when making your application multilingual), or to a property on an object that specifies global settings.

For example, say you have a class named GlobalSettings, containing a property named CompanyName:

```
public class GlobalSettings
{
    public GlobalSettings()
    {
        // Hardcode a default value to demonstrate the binding
        CompanyName = "Apress";
    }

    public string CompanyName { get; set; }
}
```

And it has been defined as a resource in your application's resources:

```
<app:GlobalSettings x:Key="settings" />
```

Say you also have TextBlock controls throughout your application in which you want to display the value of the CompanyName property. All these TextBlock controls use the CompanyNameTextBlockStyle style, like so:

```
<TextBlock Style="{StaticResource CompanyNameTextBlockStyle}" />
```

Therefore, ideally you'd add a setter to the style for the Text property and bind it to the CompanyName property on the GlobalSettings object to implement this requirement, rather than applying the binding to each individual TextBlock control. This was not possible in previous versions of Silverlight, as Silverlight didn't allow the use of bindings in styles. Silverlight 5 does allow this now, so we can implement the binding like so:

```
<Style x:Key="CompanyNameTextBlockStyle" TargetType="TextBlock">
    <Setter Property="Text"
            Value="{Binding CompanyName, Source={StaticResource settings}}" />
</Style>
```

Summary

In this chapter, you learned the fundamentals of styling and templating Silverlight controls. You also learned that styles shouldn't be randomly defined but designed with a view of how they fit into the overall look of your user interface. When styling an application, it is best to take a wholistic view of the process and actually design how the styles will be applied across the application, rather than taking a piecemeal approach. In Chapter 12, we'll look at actually building controls that can be styled and templated using this model.

CHAPTER 10

Advanced XAML

We covered the basics of XAML in Chapter 2 and expanded on most of those concepts through the chapters that followed. Let's now look at a few handy advanced features of XAML that you will find very useful when building your user interfaces.

Ignoring Elements and Attributes

Sometimes you want to insert some XAML into a view, but have it ignored at runtime. You can do so with the `Ignorable` attached property, from the markup compatibility namespace. You use this property to specify which namespace prefixes the XAML processor should ignore. You might have noticed that this is defined in all new XAML files, and is used to instruct the XAML processor to ignore the design-time properties from the Expression Blend namespace. Say you have the following XAML, which simply contains a `Label` control:

```
<UserControl x:Class="AdventureWorks.TestView"
    xmlns="http://schemas.microsoft.com/winfx/2006/xaml/presentation"
    xmlns:x="http://schemas.microsoft.com/winfx/2006/xaml"
    xmlns:d="http://schemas.microsoft.com/expression/blend/2008"
    xmlns:sdk="http://schemas.microsoft.com/winfx/2006/xaml/presentation/sdk"
    xmlns:mc="http://schemas.openxmlformats.org/markup-compatibility/2006"
    mc:Ignorable="d"
    d:DesignHeight="300" d:DesignWidth="400">

    <sdk:Label Content="A Label control from the sdk: namespace" />
</UserControl>
```

In this XAML, note how it has the `mc` namespace prefix defined. The `Ignorable` property from this namespace is attached to the `UserControl` element, and its value is set to `d`. This means that any element or attribute that uses the `d` prefix in the XAML will be ignored by the XAML processor at runtime. For example, the `DesignHeight` and `DesignWidth` attached properties used in the code, all using the `d` namespace prefix, are consequently ignored at runtime.

You can ignore additional namespaces by appending them to the `Ignorable` property's value, separated by a space. For example, if you wanted to also ignore elements using the `sdk` namespace at runtime, resulting in the `Label` control not appearing, you can set the `Ignorable` attribute's value like so:

```
mc:Ignorable="d sdk"
```

Comments in XAML

Just like code, often you want to add comments to your XAML to describe what it's for, and also comment out bits of XAML without having to delete it from the file. Let's look at some strategies for using comments in XAML.

Commenting Out Elements

You can use the standard XML tags, which are incidentally the same as HTML's, for inserting comments into your XAML. Begin the comment with `<!--`, and end it with `-->`, for example:

```
<!-- A XAML comment -->
```

At times, you might also want to comment out some XAML (instead of deleting it), for example:

```
<!-- <TextBlock Text="{Binding Name}" /> -->
```

■ **Note** As a shortcut, use the key chord Ctrl+K, C in Visual Studio to comment out the selected XAML, and use Ctrl+K, U to uncomment it again.

Commenting Out Attributes

Note that you can't insert comments in the middle of an element. For example, this is **not** valid XAML (or XML):

```
<TextBlock <!--Text="{Binding Name}"--> />
```

This inability to insert comments in the middle of an element unfortunately means that you can't comment out attributes within an element. However, there is an alternative way of achieving this outcome, by making use of the `mc:Ignorable` attached property from the markup compatibility namespace discussed earlier.

Start by declaring a namespace prefix—let's call it `ignore`—using a random namespace of your own choosing:

```
xmlns:ignore="http://schemas.microsoft.com/ignore"
```

and add this namespace prefix to the Ignorable attached property's value:

```
mc:Ignorable="d ignore"
```

You can now prepend any element or attribute with the ignore namespace prefix, and the XAML processor will ignore it. For example, say you have this simple `Button` control in your XAML:

```
<Button Content="Hello" />
```

To temporarily "comment out" the Content property—that is, request the XAML processor to ignore it—simply prepend it with the `ignore` namespace prefix:

```
<Button ignore:Content="Hello" />
```

Alternatively, you can prepend the entire `Button` element with the `ignore` namespace prefix so that the XAML processor will ignore the entire button:

```
<ignore:Button Content="Hello" />
```

Nesting Comments

One of the shortcomings of comments in XAML is that you can't nest comments. For example, attempting to comment out the following block of XAML, which already contains a comment, like so:

```
<!-- <Grid>
    <!-- <TextBlock Text="{Binding Name}" /> -->
</Grid> -->
```

will result in invalid XAML, as the end comment of the comment currently in the XAML will cause the outer comment to end too early. Therefore, you will first need to remove or comment out any comments currently in the XAML. MoXAML Power Toys (discussed later in the section "MoXAML Power Toys") has a solution for this.

Defining "Constants"

I briefly mentioned in Chapter 2 that strings and other simple BCL (Base Class Library) types could potentially be defined as resources in XAML, but we didn't investigate the topic further at the time. Let's take a look at how we can define strings and other BCL types as resources in XAML. (We'll refer to these as *constants*.) For example, uses for this technique include maintaining common values in a theme file, and supporting localization in your application by maintaining a set of strings in resource dictionaries, which you can merge when appropriate with your application's resources.

■ **Note** Only a limited number of types from the `System` namespace can actually be declared in XAML. For example, you cannot define a `DateTime` using this method.

The first step is to declare a namespace prefix to the `System` namespace in the root element of your XAML file where the constant is to be defined, like so:

```
xmlns:sys="clr-namespace:System;assembly=mscorlib"
```

You can then declare the constants (as resources) using the types in that namespace:

```
<sys:String x:Key="OKText">OK</sys:String>
```

■ **Note** You can declare these constants as you would any other resources, adding them to the `Resources` property of any element in the object hierarchy. A constant can then be used by any control below that element in the object hierarchy. Alternatively, you can define the constants in a resource dictionary, and merge it into the object hierarchy where required.

You can then use the StaticResource markup extension to make use of the constant:

```
<Button Content="{StaticResource OKText}" />
```

> **■ Note** When assigning the constant to a content property, such as in the preceding example, you must use attribute syntax rather than content element syntax, as discussed in Chapter 2.

Let's put it all together in a simple example:

```
<UserControl x:Class="Chapter10Sample.Views.ConstantsExample"
             xmlns="http://schemas.microsoft.com/winfx/2006/xaml/presentation"
             xmlns:x="http://schemas.microsoft.com/winfx/2006/xaml"
             xmlns:sys="clr-namespace:System;assembly=mscorlib">

    <UserControl.Resources>
        <sys:String x:Key="OKText">OK</sys:String>
    </UserControl.Resources>

    <Grid x:Name="LayoutRoot">
        <Button Content="{StaticResource OKText}" />
    </Grid>
</UserControl>
```

Using OR to Combine Enumerated Values in XAML

Sometimes, you find that you need to use the OR operator to join together a number of values from an enumeration, and assign the result to a property in XAML. The CommandButtonsVisibility property on the DataForm control is a perfect example of this. As you saw in Chapter 7, this property determines what command buttons should be displayed in the data form by using the OR operator to combine the corresponding values from the DataFormCommandButtonsVisibility enumeration. Whereas you might do the following in code:

```
ProductsDataForm.CommandButtonsVisibility =
                    DataFormCommandButtonsVisibility.Add |
                    DataFormCommandButtonsVisibility.Delete;
```

you can achieve the same result in XAML by simply concatenating the value names, separated by commas:

```
<toolkit:DataForm Name="ProductsDataForm"
                  CommandButtonsVisibility="Add,Delete" />
```

> **■ Note** This works only on control properties that accept a combination of enumeration values. Most control properties tend to accept only a single value from a set of enumerated values.

Triggers, Actions, and Behaviors

Ideally, we want as little code as necessary in a view's code-behind. Designers especially don't want to have to write and edit code to perform simple tasks. Instead, they want to define as much of the user interface's behavior as possible using simple drag, drop, and set property operations in the Expression Blend designer, with the behavior defined declaratively in XAML. However, you will often find that you need to turn to the code-behind to implement simple actions. What's more, most of these behaviors tend to be fairly generic, often following a common pattern, and are implemented often.

Take this scenario, for example: let's say you have a Save button, and you want to call the SubmitChanges method on a DomainDataSource control when the button is clicked. As discussed in Chapter 5, you can bind a Button control to a command provided by the DomainDataSource control, so that when the button is clicked the DomainDataSource control will submit any changes back to the server. However, let's look at an alternative approach to implementing this behavior. Let's implement a *trigger* that will listen for the Button control's Click event, and create an *action* that will call the DomainDataSource control's SubmitChanges method when the button is clicked.

Using Predefined Triggers and Actions

A trigger waits for something to happen, usually by listening for a control event to be raised, and when that event is raised, it invokes one or more actions that do something in response. For the most part, unlike WPF, Silverlight doesn't have the concept of triggers and actions. The EventTrigger is the only trigger available, and it will respond only to the Loaded event of a control and start an animation, meaning that it has limited use (and any use of it is generally discouraged). Because of this lack of triggers and actions in Silverlight and also the inability to extend WPF's triggers and actions, the Expression Blend team created its own triggers and actions implementation.

Although designed for use with Expression Blend, you can also use any of the predefined triggers and actions from the Expression Blend team's implementation in Visual Studio (but keep in mind that there is no designer support as there is in Expression Blend), and you can also write your own.

Adding the Required Assembly References

To use and create triggers and actions, you will need to start by adding a reference to the System.Windows.Interactivity.dll assembly to your project. You probably will want to also add a reference to the Microsoft.Expression.Interactions.dll assembly, as it provides a number of predefined triggers, actions, and behaviors that you probably will want to use. Note that these assemblies are not installed as part of the Silverlight SDK, but are installed as a part of Expression Blend instead.

■ **Note** If you don't have Expression Blend, you can get this assembly by downloading the Expression Blend SDK for free from the Microsoft web site at www.microsoft.com/downloads/details.aspx?displaylang= en&FamilyID=75e13d71-7c53-4382-9592-6c07c6a00207.

Depending on whether you have installed it as part of Expression Blend or its SDK, you should find it under the Silverlight\v5.0\Libraries path of the corresponding product.

Understanding How Triggers and Actions Interact

Let's consider the scenario previously described, where clicking a button calls the SubmitChanges method on a given DomainDataSource control, and how we can implement it using triggers and actions. Let's start by breaking down this scenario:

- The *trigger* will be the Click event of the button, so to capture this we'll need to use a trigger that can listen for an event raised by a control.

- In response to the trigger, the *action* will call the SubmitChanges method on a DomainDataSource control, so we'll need to use an action that can call a method on a given control.

Note that both the trigger and the action that we've extracted from this scenario are very generic. You can keep it at this very generic level if you wish, which has the advantage that you can simply use the predefined generic trigger and action that fill these requirements. However, being so generic has the disadvantage that each time you want to implement the scenario, you will need to configure both the trigger and the action to perform their tasks. That is, you need to assign the event that the trigger needs to listen for, and you need to assign the method to call on the target control for the action. Thus, you may wish to create a custom trigger and action to provide a more targeted solution to the problem and reduce the configuration burden on the developer/designer.

■ **Note** You can find a range of predefined generic triggers and actions in the Microsoft.Expression.Interactions.dll assembly. Like the System.Windows.Interactivity.dll assembly, this is installed with Expression Blend and the Expression Blend SDK, so you can reference it in your project and use the triggers/actions/behaviors that it provides. For example, in this assembly, you will find triggers such as KeyTrigger, DataTrigger, PropertyChangedTrigger, and TimerTrigger. (Note that EventTrigger is actually defined in System.Windows.Interactivity.dll.) In the Microsoft.Expression.Interactions.dll assembly, you will also find a number of actions, including HyperlinkAction, ChangePropertyAction, and CallMethodAction. There are also plenty of sources of triggers, actions, and behaviors available on the Web. The best places to start finding predefined triggers/actions/behaviors are http://expressionblend.codeplex.com and http://gallery.expression.microsoft.com.

Let's start by looking at how to implement the generic solution first, and then move on to writing and implementing a custom trigger and action to create a more targeted solution.

Configuring Triggers and Actions Using Expression Blend

The easiest way to configure triggers and actions is via Expression Blend. Triggers and actions (and behaviors) were specifically designed for use by designers so that they didn't need to write and edit code, and thus Expression Blend, a designer-focused product, has extensive support for them. In Expression Blend, you can simply drag an action from the asset library and drop it on a control. You'll find available actions in the Behaviors category, as shown in Figure 10-1.

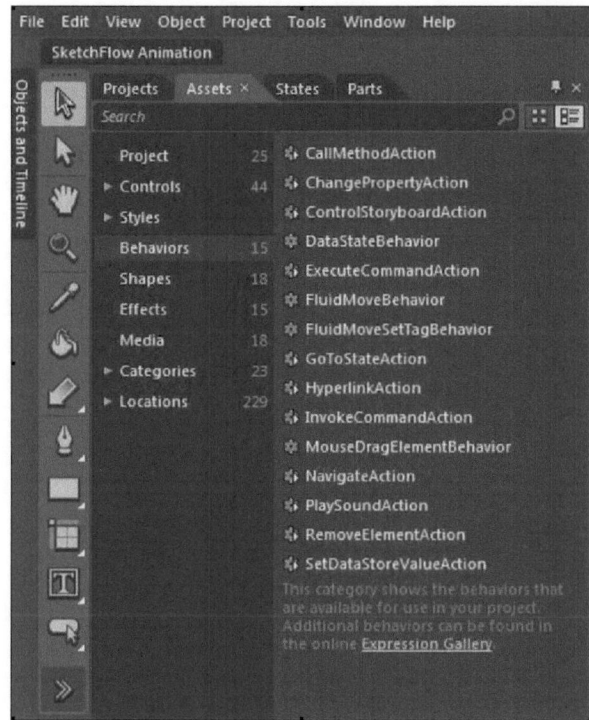

Figure 10-1. Behavior assets in Expression Blend

Blend will automatically create a trigger and assign the action to it. You can then configure the trigger and action via the Properties window. Visual Studio, unfortunately, doesn't have this level of support built in. Instead, you must manually define the trigger and action in XAML by hand. However, after you've created them, you can configure their properties via the Properties window.

If you plan to leverage triggers and actions extensively in your application, using the Expression Blend designer to implement them will make the whole process much easier and faster.

■ **Note** Coverage of Expression Blend is beyond the scope of this book. However, Kirupa Chinnathambi has a great blog post on using behaviors in Expression Blend at http://blog.kirupa.com/?p=351. You assign triggers and actions to controls in Expression Blend in much the same way as he demonstrates with behaviors. In addition, an article on the SilverlightShow.net web site by Andrej Tozon also walks you through using behaviors with Expression Blend; see www.silverlightshow.net/items/Exploring-Silverlight-behaviors-look-Ma-no-code.aspx.

Workshop: Implementing Triggers and Actions in XAML by Hand

Using the product details view you created in Chapter 7, let's implement a trigger and an action on the Save button to call the SubmitChanges method on the DomainDataSource control, instead of the code-behind currently being used.

1. Add references to the Microsoft.Expression.Interactions.dll and System.Windows.Interactivity.dll assemblies to your project as described earlier, if you haven't already done this.

2. Declare the interactivity and interactions namespace prefixes in your view:

```
xmlns:i="http://schemas.microsoft.com/expression/2010/interactivity"
xmlns:ei="http://schemas.microsoft.com/expression/2010/interactions"
```

■ **Note** The first namespace is for the core Expression Blend interactivity functions, from which you'll primarily use the EventTrigger, and the second is for the additional predefined interactions from the Microsoft. Expression.Interactions.dll assembly—for example, PropertyChangedTrigger, ChangePropertyAction, and so on.

---

3. Find the Save button in the XAML, attach the Interaction.Triggers property to the button, and add an EventTrigger trigger to it to listen for the button's Click event:

```
<Button Content="Save" Height="23" Width="75">
    <i:Interaction.Triggers>
        <i:EventTrigger EventName="Click">
            <!--Assign action(s) here-->
        </i:EventTrigger>
    </i:Interaction.Triggers>
</Button>
```

■ **Note** By default, triggers will listen for an event raised by the control on which they're attached. You can listen for an event raised by a different control instead by binding the SourceObject property of the trigger to that control, by using ElementName binding, as discussed in Chapter 11.

---

4. Now that you've configured your trigger, you need to assign one or more actions to it (in place of the "Assign action(s) here" comment) for it to invoke. We'll use CallMethodAction action to call the SubmitChanges method on our DomainDataSource control.

```
<Button Content="Save" Height="23" Width="75">
    <i:Interaction.Triggers>
```

```
      <i:EventTrigger EventName="Click">
         <ei:CallMethodAction
                  TargetObject="{Binding ElementName=productsDDS}"
                  MethodName="SubmitChanges"/>
      </i:EventTrigger>
   </i:Interaction.Triggers>
</Button>
```

> **Note** You use the `TargetObject` property of the action to specify the control upon which you want the action to act. If the action does not have this property set, the action will act upon the control that it is attached to.

5. Run your application. You will find that pressing the button will call the `SubmitChanges` method on the `DomainDataSource` control—all implemented declaratively, with no code necessary.

As you can see, this is a useful feature both for designers and for developers alike. However, implementing this solution required more steps than it would ideally, as both the trigger and the action were somewhat generic. That is, you needed to specify what event that the trigger needs to listen for, as well as the name of the method that the action needs to call. If implementing this scenario repeatedly, you'd benefit from having a custom and more targeted solution. Let's now try to reduce the number of steps required to implement this scenario by creating a custom trigger and action.

⚙ Workshop: Writing Custom Triggers

When writing custom triggers—this applies to actions and behaviors too—you are encapsulating a piece of logic in a reusable interaction component that you can attach to a control. Although you are writing these components in code, you are saving yourself the need to write code when it comes to using them. In this workshop, we'll create a custom trigger that will specifically listen for the `Click` event to be raised on the `Button` control it is attached to, and implement it in place of the generic `EventTrigger` trigger used in the previous workshop.

Part 1: Creating a Custom Trigger

1. Create a new folder in your AdventureWorks project named `Behaviors`, and add a new class to this folder named `ButtonClickTrigger`.

```
public class ButtonClickTrigger
{

}
```

> **Note** "Behaviors" tends to be a generic term covering triggers and actions, in addition to behaviors, which is why we're calling the folder `Behaviors` instead of `Triggers`.

2. Add the following using statements to the top of the file:

```
using System.Windows;
using System.Windows.Controls;
using System.Windows.Interactivity;
```

3. Custom triggers need to inherit from either TriggerBase or TriggerBase<T>, from the System.Windows.Interactivity namespace. By having it inherit from TriggerBase<T>, you can constrain the trigger to apply only to a given control type. Since we want this trigger to only appy to Button controls, it should inherit from TriggerBase<Button>.

```
public class ButtonClickTrigger : TriggerBase<Button>
{

}
```

4. Now you need to override the OnAttached and OnDetaching methods inherited from TriggerBase. In the OnAttached method, you need to add an event handler for the associated control's Click event (or whatever event the trigger should listen for). You get the reference to the control that the trigger should listen to events for from the AssociatedObject property on the base class. To prevent memory leaks, always remember to remove the event handler when the trigger is detaching (in the OnDetaching method).

```
protected override void OnAttached()
{
    base.OnAttached();

    AssociatedObject.Click += new RoutedEventHandler(AssociatedObject_Click);
}

protected override void OnDetaching()
{
    base.OnDetaching();

    AssociatedObject.Click -= new RoutedEventHandler(AssociatedObject_Click);
}

private void AssociatedObject_Click(object sender, RoutedEventArgs e)
{

}
```

5. The final step is to invoke the actions that have been associated with the trigger, by calling the InvokeActions method on the base class. This takes a parameter that allows an object to be passed to the actions, but we can assign it to null because we have nothing to pass.

```
private void AssociatedObject_Click(object sender, RoutedEventArgs e)
{
    InvokeActions(null);
}
```

The complete code for the trigger is as follows:

```
public class ButtonClickTrigger : TriggerBase<Button>
{
    protected override void OnAttached()
    {
        base.OnAttached();

        AssociatedObject.Click +=
                        new RoutedEventHandler(AssociatedObject_Click);
    }

    protected override void OnDetaching()
    {
        base.OnDetaching();

        AssociatedObject.Click -=
                        new RoutedEventHandler(AssociatedObject_Click);
    }

    private void AssociatedObject_Click(object sender, RoutedEventArgs e)
    {
        InvokeActions(null);
    }
}
```

Part 2: Using the Custom Trigger

We can now use this trigger in place of the more generic EventTrigger trigger in our application.

1. Start by declaring a prefix for the behavior's namespace in the view.

```
xmlns:b="clr-namespace:AdventureWorks.Behaviors"
```

2. Now you can replace the EventTrigger trigger with our custom ButtonClickTrigger trigger:

```
<Button Content="Save" Height="23" Width="75">
    <i:Interaction.Triggers>
        <b:ButtonClickTrigger>
            <ei:CallMethodAction
                        TargetObject="{Binding ElementName=productsDDS}"
                        MethodName="SubmitChanges"/>
        </b:ButtonClickTrigger >
    </i:Interaction.Triggers>
</Button>
```

■ **Note** For more complex triggers, you can add properties to the class to enable them to be configured when they are used, and use those values in your logic. This also applies to actions and behaviors. You can implement them as standard CLR properties, but note that they will need to be dependency properties, instead of standard properties, if you want to be able to bind them to something. I discuss implementing dependency properties in Chapter 12.

Workshop: Creating and Using Custom Actions

In this workshop, we'll create a custom action that we'll call the SubmitChanges event on the target DomainDataSource control, in response to a trigger, and implement it in place of the generic CallMethodAction action used in the previous workshop.

Part 1: Creating a Custom Action

1. Add a new class to the Behaviors folder in your project (created in the previous workshop), and name it SubmitChangesAction.

```
public class SubmitChangesAction
{

}
```

2. Add the following using statements to the top of the file:

```
using System.Windows.Controls;
using System.Windows.Interactivity;
```

3. Custom actions need to inherit from TriggerAction, TargetedTriggerAction, or their generic counterparts from the System.Windows.Interactivity namespace. The difference between TriggerAction and TargetedTriggerAction is that TriggerAction acts on the control to which the action is assigned, while the TargetedTriggerAction acts on a different control, as specified by the designer/developer. For this example, we are attaching the action to to a Button control, but we actually need the action to act on a DomainDataSource control. Therefore, our action needs to inherit from TargetedTriggerAction<DomainDataSource>.

```
public class SubmitChangesAction : TargetedTriggerAction<DomainDataSource>
{

}
```

■ **Note** Something to be aware of is that the generic parameter <T> for the TriggerAction<T> action is used to specify the type of control that it can *be attached to* and to designate the type of the AssociatedObject property on the base class. However, the generic parameter <T> for the TargetedTriggerAction<T> action is instead used to specify the type of control that it can *target,* and it will designate the type of the Target property on the base class. If you need to constrain what type of control that a TargetedTriggerAction action is attached to, you can decorate the class with the TypeConstraint attribute, passing this attribute the type of control it can be attached to as a parameter.

4. The next step is to override the Invoke method, and implement the action's logic in this method. Note that this method has a single parameter, which will pass into the method whatever object was passed to the parameter of the trigger's InvokeActions method, enabling triggers to pass data to actions. The following code calls the SubmitChanges method on the target control (i.e., the DomainDataSource) when it is invoked:

```
protected override void Invoke(object parameter)
{
    Target.SubmitChanges();
}
```

■ **Note** There are additional methods from the base class that you can override if you require. All the base trigger/action classes have OnAttached and OnDetaching methods that you can override. If your class inherits from TargetedTriggerAction or its generic counterpart, you can also override its OnTargetChanged method.

Part 2: Using the Custom Action

We can now use this trigger in place of the more generic EventTrigger trigger in our application.

1. If you haven't already done so, declare a prefix for the behavior's namespace in the view.

```
xmlns:b="clr-namespace:AdventureWorks.Behaviors"
```

2. Now you can replace the CallMethodAction action with our custom SubmitChangesAction action:

```
<Button Content="Save" Width="75">
    <i:Interaction.Triggers>
        <b:ButtonClickTrigger>
            <b:SubmitChangesAction
                    TargetObject="{Binding ElementName=productsDDS}" />
        </b:ButtonClickTrigger>
    </i:Interaction.Triggers>
</Button>
```

Additional Notes: Default Trigger

To make this trigger/action pair even easier to use in Expression Blend, you can specify a default trigger that the action will use when it is dropped onto a control. Our SubmitChangesAction action has been designed for use in conjunction with a ButtonClickTrigger trigger, so ideally a ButtonClickTrigger trigger should be created automatically when the action is dropped onto a control, and it used to invoke the SubmitChangesAction action. We can tell Expression Blend which trigger the action should create by decorating the action class with the DefaultTrigger attribute, like so:

```
[DefaultTrigger(typeof(Button), typeof(ButtonClickTrigger))]
public class SubmitChangesAction : TargetedTriggerAction<DomainDataSource>
```

The first parameter specifies the type of control that this action should use the default trigger for, and the second parameter specifies the type of trigger to use when attached to a control of that type. For example, in the preceding example, we are specifying that when the action is dropped onto a Button control, it should use the ButtonClickTrigger trigger by default. You can apply this attribute multiple times to the class if you wish, enabling you to specify a different default trigger for each type of control the action is attached to.

■ **Note** Generally, if a trigger and an action are tightly coupled, it's often better to use a behavior instead.

This is a very simple action that we've created, but you can create much more complex actions depending on the needs of your user interface. Note that they are discrete atomic blocks of interaction logic only; they do something and then exit. You can think of them as being much like a method in code. Actions cannot wait for another event to be raised, nor can they preserve their state between trigger invocations. If you need to provide a more persistent interaction, implementing behaviors may be a more suitable alternative instead.

Behaviors

Triggers and actions often come under the banner of behaviors, so when you read about behaviors, often you will find that the author is actually referring to triggers and actions rather than behaviors, which can make the concept somewhat confusing. Even Expression Blend includes actions in the Behaviors category in the Asset Library. Let's take a look at behaviors now.

What Is a Behavior?

Whereas triggers and actions are defined separately and can be mixed and matched, behaviors combine a trigger and an action into a single component, tightly coupling them. Behaviors are attached and detached from a control in the same way as triggers are and, thus, are alive for the lifetime of the control they are attached to. However, unlike a trigger, which expects to have one or more associated actions to perform the interaction logic, the behavior handles all the interaction logic internally.

At a conceptual level, you can think of a behavior as being designed to add additional functionality to the control that it is attached to. This may be a simple trigger/action combination, or may implement a more involved interaction such as a drag-and-drop operation.

Behaviors inherit from either the Behavior class or the generic Behavior<T> class, both of which are found in the System.Windows.Interactivity namespace.

One of the big advantages of combining triggers and actions into a single component is that it enables a preservation of state between the "trigger" events. A typical scenario in which you might want to maintain state between events is implementing a drag-and-drop operation. To implement this type of operation, you need to handle multiple events, including the MouseDown, MouseMove, and MouseUp events, and maintain the state of the drag-and-drop operation between them.

Behaviors typically define additional behavior and logic for the control that they are attached to, as opposed to interacting with other controls, unlike the SubmitChangesAction custom action we created earlier, which interacts with a DomainDataSource control when a button is clicked. For example, a typical behavior you might add to a text box might be one that automatically selects all the text when the text box gets the focus. This behavior entirely revolves around the text box it is attached to, without interacting with any other controls.

However, there's nothing stopping you from adding the ability to interact with other controls in a behavior; there's simply no built-in provision for it. That is, there's no TargetedBehavior base class provided.

Workshop: Creating and Using a Behavior

Let's revisit our previous example of calling the SubmitChanges method on a DomainDataSource control when a button is clicked, but this time, we will implement it as a behavior.

Part 1: Creating a Custom Behavior

1. Add a new class to the Behaviors folder in your project (created in the Custom Triggers workshop), and name it SubmitChangesBehavior.

```
public class SubmitChangesBehavior
{

}
```

2. Add the following using statements to the top of the file:

```
using System.Windows;
using System.Windows.Controls;
using System.Windows.Interactivity;
```

3. Custom triggers need to inherit from either Behavior or Behavior <T> from the System.Windows.Interactivity namespace. By having it inherit from Behavior<T>, you are able to constrain the behavior to only apply to a given control type. Since we want this behavior to only apply to Button controls, it should inherit from Behavior<Button>.

```
public class SubmitChangesBehavior : Behavior<Button>
{

}
```

4. Now you need to override the OnAttached and OnDetaching methods inherited from the Behavior class, and use them to add/remove an event handler for the associated control's Click event, in exactly the same way as you did when creating the custom trigger:

```csharp
protected override void OnAttached()
{
    base.OnAttached();

    AssociatedObject.Click += new RoutedEventHandler(AssociatedObject_Click);
}

protected override void OnDetaching()
{
    base.OnDetaching();

    AssociatedObject.Click -= new RoutedEventHandler(AssociatedObject_Click);
}

private void AssociatedObject_Click(object sender, RoutedEventArgs e)
{

}
```

5. Whereas our custom trigger called InvokeActions in its Click event handler, which invoked the trigger's associated actions, in a custom behavior we actually implement the logic we want executed when the button is clicked instead. However, we don't know which DomainDataSource control to call SubmitChanges on, as the Behavior class doesn't have a TargetObject property like actions that inherit from TargetedTriggerAction do. Therefore, we need to create our own property for this task. This needs to be a dependency property in order for it to accept a data binding expression for element name binding to the DomainDataSource control. (Dependency properties will be discussed in Chapter 12, so we won't go into depth here.) Note how, as a nicety, we're decorating the property with the CustomPropertyValueEditor attribute, which displays the element-binding picker to edit the property at design time:

```csharp
[CustomPropertyValueEditor(CustomPropertyValueEditor.ElementBinding)]
public DomainDataSource TargetObject
{
    get { return (DomainDataSource)GetValue(TargetObjectProperty); }
    set { SetValue(TargetObjectProperty, value); }
}

public static readonly DependencyProperty TargetObjectProperty =
    DependencyProperty.Register("TargetObject", typeof(DomainDataSource),
                        typeof(SubmitChangesBehavior), null);
```

6. You can now call the SubmitChanges method on the DomainDataSource control bound to the TargetObject property of the behavior:

```csharp
private void AssociatedObject_Click(object sender, RoutedEventArgs e)
{
    TargetObject.SubmitChanges();
}
```

The complete code for the behavior follows:

```csharp
public class SubmitChangesBehavior : Behavior<Button>
{
    [CustomPropertyValueEditor(CustomPropertyValueEditor.ElementBinding)]
```

```csharp
public DomainDataSource TargetObject
{
    get { return (DomainDataSource)GetValue(TargetObjectProperty); }
    set { SetValue(TargetObjectProperty, value); }
}

public static readonly DependencyProperty TargetObjectProperty =
    DependencyProperty.Register("TargetObject", typeof(DomainDataSource),
                            typeof(SubmitChangesBehavior), null);

protected override void OnAttached()
{
    base.OnAttached();

    AssociatedObject.Click +=
                        new RoutedEventHandler(AssociatedObject_Click);
}

protected override void OnDetaching()
{
    base.OnDetaching();

    AssociatedObject.Click -=
                        new RoutedEventHandler(AssociatedObject_Click);
}

private void AssociatedObject_Click(object sender, RoutedEventArgs e)
{
    TargetObject.SubmitChanges();
}
}
```

Part 2: Using the Custom Behavior

We can now use this trigger in place of the custom trigger and action in our application.

1. If you haven't already done so, declare a prefix for the behavior's namespace in the view.

```xml
xmlns:b="clr-namespace:AdventureWorks.Behaviors"
```

2. Now you can replace the ButtonClickTrigger trigger and SubmitChangesAction action with our custom SubmitChangesBehavior behavior instead:

```xml
<Button Content="Save" Width="75">
    <i:Interaction.Behaviors>
        <b:SubmitChangesBehavior Target="{Binding ElementName=productsDDS}" />
    </i:Interaction.Behaviors>
</Button>
```

■ **Note** We're assigning the behavior to the `Interaction.Behaviors` attached property on the button, rather than the `Interaction.Triggers` attached property, as we were before.

Which Should I Use?

So when should you use a behavior over a trigger/action combination? Ultimately, there are no fixed rules, and in some cases, there is a bit of overlap where either means is appropriate, as was demonstrated with our button click/submit changes example.

If the trigger and action are intrinsically tied together, and you want to minimize the amount of configuration necessary when using them, a behavior is probably the ideal candidate to implement the interaction logic. If you have complex interaction logic where state needs to be preserved between event handlers, such as a drag-and-drop operation, a behavior is essentially your only choice.

However, if you want to provide a more flexible use story and have interaction logic that could be triggered by different types of controls (and/or in different types of ways), implementing a separate trigger and action may be a better plan of action.

The possibilities are endless with triggers, actions, and behaviors, and going back through the examples provided throughout this book until now, you could replace almost all of the code-behind that we used with a trigger/action combination or a behavior. Now that you understand these concepts, every time you consider adding code to a view's code-behind, first consider whether encapsulating the logic in a trigger/action pair or a behavior might be a better alternative.

Triggers, actions, and behaviors are very powerful tools at your disposal, promoting both code reuse and interaction logic modularization and encapsulation. They are testable, and their biggest advantage is that they reduce and remove the need for designers to write interaction logic code.

Custom Markup Extensions

You were introduced to markup extensions in Chapter 2, and learned how a markup extension is essentially a class containing some logic that is evaluated at runtime. Examples of markup extensions built into Silverlight include `Binding`, `StaticResource`, and `x:Null`. However, Silverlight is missing a number of the handy markup extensions that are available in WPF, particularly the `x:Static` markup extension that enabled you to bind to a static property, field, constant, and so forth.

A new feature of Silverlight 5 is the ability to create your own custom markup extensions. This feature provides additional flexibility when writing XAML, and can enable you to implement solutions much more elegantly, with less XAML. Let's look at creating a custom markup extension now.

■ **Note** Although you will probably rarely need to write a custom markup extension, there are numerous scenarios where the ability to do so can be very useful. For example, you could implement a markup extension that returns localized text for labels according to the current (or a selected) culture, bind to XML, simplify binding to configuration settings, or use one to help implement role-based authorization in your application.

Creating a Custom Markup Extension

There are two means of creating custom markup extensions. One is by creating a class that inherits from the MarkupExtension class, and the other is by implementing the IMarkupExtension<T> interface. Both are found in the System.Windows.Markup namespace.

Inheriting from MarkupExtension

You can create a custom markup extension by simply creating a class that inherits from MarkupExtension, in the System.Windows.Markup namespace, and overrides its ProvideValue method, which returns the result. For example, here is a simple markup extension using this method, which returns TEST as a string:

```
using System;
using System.Windows.Markup;

public class SimpleMarkupExtension : MarkupExtension
{
    public override object ProvideValue(IServiceProvider serviceProvider)
    {
        return "TEST";
    }
}
```

This is hardly a very useful markup extension, but it demonstrates the concept. You can put your own logic in the ProvideValue method, and return that as the result instead. You can also add properties to the markup extension, and assign values to these in XAML when the markup extension is used. You can then use these values in the logic in the ProvideValue method.

Implementing IMarkupExtension<T>

Usually, you will inherit from the MarkupExtension class when creating a custom markup extension, but if you want your markup extension to inherit from another class—for example, the Binding markup extension inherits from BindingBase—you're out of luck because the .NET CLR doesn't support multiple inheritance. In addition, you'll have noticed that the ProvideValue method from the previous method returns an object, meaning that the value being returned is untyped.

You can solve both of these problems by having your custom markup extension class implement the IMarkupExtension<T> interface instead of inheriting from MarkupExtension. Here is the previous example, but implementing the IMarkupExtension<T> interface, returning the result typed as a string:

```
using System;
using System.Windows.Markup;

public class SimpleMarkupExtension : IMarkupExtension<string>
{
    public string ProvideValue(IServiceProvider serviceProvider)
    {
        return "TEST";
    }
}
```

■ **Note** The MarkupExtension class actually implements the IMarkupExtension<object> interface.

Although we won't discuss dependency properties until Chapter 12, implementing this interface allows your markup extension to inherit from DependencyObject, enabling it to host dependency properties—something you can't do when your markup extension inherits from the MarkupExtension class because it doesn't inherit from DependencyObject. If you want your markup extension to have properties that can accept a markup extension as their value, those properties need to be dependency properties and, thus, your markup extension needs to implement this interface.

■ **Note** A feature of custom markup extensions in WPF is that they can have a constructor that takes a single value, also known as a positional parameter. In Silverlight, you can see how the Binding markup extension uses this feature to allow you to pass it the path to bind to without needing to specify the Path property name—for example, {Binding FirstName} instead of {Binding Path=FirstName}. Unfortunately, there is no way to implement this same behavior for your custom markup extensions in Silverlight.

Extending the Binding Markup Extension

You can override the Binding markup extension and customize it to your needs, although there are a number of limitations when doing so. For example, if you set the same property values on bindings regularly, such as its Mode or Converter properties, you can override the Binding class and set property values in its constructor, reducing the verbosity of your XAML. For example, instead of setting the Mode property to TwoWay on each use, you can create a custom Binding class that has this value set by default:

```
public class TwoWayBinding : Binding
{
    public TwoWayBinding() : base()
    {
        Mode = BindingMode.TwoWay;
    }
}
```

There are limitations you'll face when doing this, however. You can't override the Binding class's ProvideValue method, nor will you be able to exclude the Path= when making use of the custom binding; its positional parameter will no longer work. However, it can make your XAML less verbose, especially if you use it to configure a value converter for the binding.

Services

You might have noticed that the ProvideValue method takes in an IServiceProvider parameter. A service provider is passed in via this parameter, which provides access to services available to the markup extension, giving it some context. You can call the GetService method on the service provider object, passing it the type of interface representing the service you want returned. Let's take a look at the key services you might want to get a reference to, and why.

IProvideValueTarget

Most commonly, you will use the GetService method on the service provider object to get the IProvideValueTarget service. This service returns details of the object/control and property that the markup extension is applied to.

Let's say you have the custom markup extension we created earlier, named SimpleMarkupExtension, and applied it to the Text property of a TextBox control:

```
<TextBox Text="{local:SimpleMarkupExtension}" />
```

You can get a reference to the TextBox control and the Text property that it's applied to from the TargetObject and TargetProperty properties on the IProvideValueTarget service:

```
IProvideValueTarget targetService =
    serviceProvider.GetService(typeof(IProvideValueTarget)) as
                                                IProvideValueTarget;

DependencyObject control = targetService.TargetObject as DependencyObject;
PropertyInfo property = targetService.TargetProperty as PropertyInfo;
```

So what uses could you have for this information? Well, most commonly, you would use this information to set the value of the property of the control at a later stage. An important point to note when creating custom markup extensions is that *the ProvideValue method is only ever called once on a markup extension*. Therefore, if you need to update the target property that the markup extension is applied to at a later stage, you'll need to cache this information to use then. For example, you might want to update the target property in response to something changing in the code-behind, such as an event being raised. Alternatively, the value that the target property should have might not be able to be determined at the time that the ProvideValue method is called. In that case, you can return a default/temporary value and update the target property when the value becomes available.

By providing a reference to the target object/control, you can also apply values to other properties on the object/control. For example, you might want to disable it by setting its IsEnabled property to false, hide it by setting its Visibility property to Collapsed, change its background in response to an invalid value, and so on.

You can assign a new value to the target property using the following line of code:

```
property.SetValue(control, value, null);
```

IRootObjectProvider

If you need to get a reference to the root control in your view, such as the UserControl or Page, you can use the IRootObjectProvider service to get this for you, like so:

```
IRootObjectProvider rootService =
    serviceProvider.GetService(typeof(IRootObjectProvider))
                                                as IRootObjectProvider;

object root = rootService.RootObject;
```

IXamlTypeResolver

The IXamlTypeResolver service resolves types referenced in XAML to CLR types. For example, say you add a property to your custom markup extension that takes in the name of a type as a string:

```
public string MyType { get; set; }
```

You also have a class named SomeCLRClass in your project—for this example, it will be in the same namespace as your custom markup extension:

```
public class SomeCLRClass
{

}
```

Now when using the custom markup extension in your XAML, you assign the name of the SomeCLRClass class to the MyType property on your markup extension:

```
<TextBox Text="{local:SimpleMarkupExtension MyType=local:SomeCLRClass}" />
```

In the ProvideValue method of your custom markup extension, you can now convert this type passed in from the XAML to an actual type that you can use in your logic:

```
IXamlTypeResolver typeResolverService =
    serviceProvider.GetService(typeof(IXamlTypeResolver))
                                            as IXamlTypeResolver;

Type type = typeResolverService.Resolve(MyType);
```

Advanced Markup Extension Behavior

On the surface, creating custom markup extensions seems like an easy process, and for the most part, that is indeed the case. However, you can use markup extensions in ways that might not seem immediately obvious. Let's take a bit of a deeper look at these advanced uses and behaviors.

Selecting Event Handlers Using Custom Markup Extensions

You might not have considered it initially, but you can actually assign a markup extension to an event and return an event handler. This can be useful to allow a handler to be chosen to handle the event at runtime. Another potential use is as a proxy that calls a method on a view model when the event is raised. As you'll see in Chapter 13, generally you will call a method on a view model, when using the MVVM design pattern, by using a command or behavior. You could also write a custom markup extension that performs the same task. Sergey Barskiy has a blog post covering a markup extension that he wrote to do just this, at http://dotnetspeak.com/index.php/2011/04/more-on-markup-extensions-in-silverlight-5/.

Custom Markup Extensions That Return Another Markup Extension

Your custom markup extension can actually return another markup extension as its value. This markup extension will then be evaluated to obtain the value to be assigned to the property that the custom markup extension is applied to. For example, you can have a custom markup extension that returns a binding:

```
public class ReturnBindingMarkupExtension : MarkupExtension
{
    public override object ProvideValue(IServiceProvider serviceProvider)
    {
        Binding binding = new Binding("FirstName");
        binding.Mode = BindingMode.TwoWay;
```

```
        return binding;
    }
}
```

Excluding "Extension" from a Markup Extension's Name When Using It

It's customary to suffix the name of a markup extension with "Extension"—for example, SimpleMarkup**Extension**. Note, however, that when using the custom markup extension, you don't have to include this Extension suffix when using it, in much the same way that you can exclude the Attribute suffix of an attribute's name when decorating classes, properties, etc. with it. If you name your custom markup extension SimpleMarkupExtension, you can actually reference it in your XAML like so:

```
<TextBox Text="{local:SimpleMarkup}" />
```

Workshop: Implementing the Custom Markup Extension

Let's implement a custom markup extension that returns the value of a static field/property, in much the same way x:Static does in WPF.

Part 1: Creating the Custom Markup Extension

1. Create a new folder named MarkupExtensions in your AdventureWorks project, and add a new class to it named StaticExtension.

2. Add the following using statements to the top of the file:

```
using System;
using System.Reflection;
using System.Windows.Markup;
```

3. Have your class inherit from MarkupExtension:

```
public class StaticExtension : MarkupExtension
{

}
```

4. Now you can override the ProvideValue method inherited from MarkupExtension, which contains the logic that needs to be performed, and returns the result:

```
public override object ProvideValue(IServiceProvider serviceProvider)
{

}
```

5. However, to implement our logic, we first need a property that provides the path of the static field/property that the markup extension will get the value of:

```
public string Path { get; set; };
```

6. Now we can actually implement our logic in the ProvideValue method:

```csharp
public override object ProvideValue(IServiceProvider serviceProvider)
{
    object result = null;

    if (Path != null && Path.IndexOf('.') != 0)
    {
        // Split into qualified type and property name
        string typeName = Path.Substring(0, Path.LastIndexOf('.'));
        string propertyName = Path.Substring(Path.LastIndexOf('.') + 1);

        Type type = Type.GetType(typeName, false, false);

        if (type != null)
        {
            FieldInfo field = type.GetField(propertyName,
                BindingFlags.Public | BindingFlags.Static);

            if (field != null)
            {
                result = field.GetValue(null);
            }
            else
            {
                PropertyInfo property = type.GetProperty(propertyName,
                    BindingFlags.Public | BindingFlags.Static);

                if (property != null)
                    result = property.GetValue(null, null);
            }
        }
    }

    return result;
}
```

7. The complete markup extension class should look like this:

```csharp
using System;
using System.Reflection;
using System.Windows.Markup;

namespace AdventureWorks.MarkupExtensions
{
    public class StaticExtension : MarkupExtension
    {
        object result = null;

        if (Path != null && Path.IndexOf('.') != 0)
        {
            // Split into qualified type and property name
            string typeName = Path.Substring(0, Path.LastIndexOf('.'));
```

```
        string propertyName = Path.Substring(Path.LastIndexOf('.') + 1);

        Type type = Type.GetType(typeName, false, false);

        if (type != null)
        {
            FieldInfo field = type.GetField(propertyName,
                BindingFlags.Public | BindingFlags.Static);

            if (field != null)
            {
                result = field.GetValue(null);
            }
            else
            {
                PropertyInfo property = type.GetProperty(propertyName,
                    BindingFlags.Public | BindingFlags.Static);

                if (property != null)
                    result = property.GetValue(null, null);
            }
        }
    }

    return result;
    }
}
```

■ **Note** This extension will get only the value of the static field/property; it won't update it. Nor will it respond to any changes in the value of the static field/property. As an exercise, try extending this markup extension to re-spond to changes in the value of the static field/property. Start by checking to see whether the "bound" type implements INotifyPropertyChanged, and if so, handle its PropertyChanged event to check for changes in the property value. Assuming you have cached the target object/control and target property, retrieved by using the IProvideValueTarget service, you can then update its value accordingly. Another exercise you can try is updat-ing the source field/property in response to changes to the target. For this case, the markup extension will need to add an event handler to the target control, handling the LostFocus, TextChanged, or other appropriate event, and update the value of the source field/property in response.

Part 2: Using the Custom Markup Extension

1. First, we need a static field/property that our markup extension will obtain the value of. Add a class to your project's root named GlobalSettings, and have it expose a static property (or field) named CompanyName:

```
namespace AdventureWorks
{
    public class GlobalSettings
    {
        public static string CompanyName
        {
            get
            {
                // Hardcoded value for demonstration purposes
                return "Apress";
            }
        }
    }
}
```

2. For testing purposes, add a new view named TestExtensionView to the Views folder in your application in order, and hook it up to the menu so that you can navigate to it, as was demonstrated in Chapter 3.

3. Add a namespace prefix declaration to the view, pointing to the AdventureWorks.MarkupExtensions namespace:

```
xmlns:me="clr-namespace:AdventureWorks.MarkupExtensions"
```

4. Add a TextBlock control to your view, and assign the markup extension to its Text property, pointing the Path of the markup extension to the static CompanyName property on the GlobalSettings class:

```
<TextBlock
    Text="{me:Static Path=AdventureWorks.GlobalSettings.CompanyName}" />
```

5. The full XAML for the view should look something like this:

```
<navigation:Page
  x:Class="AdventureWorks.Home"
  xmlns="http://schemas.microsoft.com/winfx/2006/xaml/presentation"
  xmlns:x="http://schemas.microsoft.com/winfx/2006/xaml"
  xmlns:d="http://schemas.microsoft.com/expression/blend/2008"
  xmlns:mc="http://schemas.openxmlformats.org/markup-compatibility/2006"
  xmlns:navigation="clr-namespace:System.Windows.Controls; ↵
                    assembly=System.Windows.Controls.Navigation"
  xmlns:me="clr-namespace:AdventureWorks.MarkupExtensions"
  mc:Ignorable="d" d:DesignWidth="640" d:DesignHeight="480"
  Style="{StaticResource PageStyle}">

    <Grid x:Name="LayoutRoot">
        <TextBlock
            Text="{me:Static Path=AdventureWorks.GlobalSettings.CompanyName}" />
    </Grid>
</navigation:Page>
```

Blendability

To be able to effectively design your application's user interface, designers often like to know the shape of the data that they are binding to, enabling them to take full advantage of the Expression Blend or Visual Studio XAML designer without resorting to editing the XAML directly. This allows them to see what fields are available in the data, and bind to them as required.

It can also be beneficial to be able to populate a view with data at design time in order to picture how it will appear to the user, and customize its appearance accordingly, instead of having to constantly compile and run the application to do so.

These features make the process of designing user interfaces more interactive, and are known as *blendability*. As you may have guessed from the name, this concept primarily relates to user interface design in Expression Blend, but we can also harness these design time features in the Visual Studio XAML designer via the same underlying mechanism (although with less support than provided by Expression Blend).

The Design-Time Data Mechanisms

As you might recall from Chapter 2, the design-time data mechanisms can be found in the Expression Blend 2008 namespace (http://schemas.microsoft.com/expression/blend/2008), which is automatically declared in your XAML files with a prefix of d. In this namespace, you will find the following data-related attached properties:

- DataContext
- DesignData
- DesignSource

You will also find the DesignData and DesignInstance markup extensions. We'll be using these to provide the blendability features in the XAML designer.

Defining the Shape of the Data

Let's start by defining the type of data that we will bind to, so that the data binding expression builder (discussed in Chapter 11) knows the structure of the data that you are binding to. In Chapter 5, you might have noticed that when you drag an entity returned from the server via RIA Services from the Data Sources window and drop it onto the design surface, the DomainDataSource control that's created for you has a design-time data property already applied:

```
<riaControls:DomainDataSource AutoLoad="True"
                    d:DesignData="{d:DesignInstance my1:ProductSummary,
                                    CreateList=true}"
                    Height="0" Width="0"
                    LoadedData="productSummaryDDS_LoadedData"
                    Name="productSummaryDDS"
                    QueryName="GetProductSummaryListQuery">
    <riaControls:DomainDataSource.DomainContext>
        <my:ProductsContext />
    </riaControls:DomainDataSource.DomainContext>
</riaControls:DomainDataSource>
```

The rather confusingly named d:DesignData design-time attached property—it has nothing to do with the d:DesignData markup extension, discussed shortly—is used to define the type of data that is served by a data source control via its Data property. Hence, this property can be applied only to data sources such as the DomainDataSource control. The key benefit of applying this design-time property to the DomainDataSource control is that you will now be able to see a list of available properties, from the type of data that it returns, and select a property to bind to when using the data binding expression builder (see Figure 11-3 in Chapter 11) on controls using it as a data source. For example, if the DomainDataSource control returns a collection of Product entities, you'll be able to bind a TextBox control's Text property to the Name property of a product by opening the data binding expression builder, and selecting the Name property from a list of the Product entity's fields.

To configure this property, we assign it a d:DesignInstance markup extension. This markup extension is primarily used to return an object of a given type or a collection of objects of that type. The default property on this markup extension is the Type property. You'll note from our example that it specifies that the DomainDataSource control will be returning ProductSummary entities. You will also note that the CreateList property of this markup extension is set to true. This is used to indicate whether the d:DesignInstance markup extension should return a *collection* of the given object type or a single instance of the object type.

By default, the d:DesignInstance markup extension reflects over the given object type, and creates and returns a corresponding substitute design-time type or an empty collection of that type if the CreateList property is set to true, which the XAML designer can use where required. However, it also has an IsDesignTimeCreatable property, which, when set to true, will actually instantiate and return an object of the given type, which is only of use when the CreateList property is set to false. Once you assign values to that object's properties in its constructor, these values will appear in the XAML designer—essentially populating it with data at design time.

You can also assign the d:DesignInstance markup extension to the d:DataContext design-time attached property. Whereas the d:DesignData property could be applied only to data source controls, the d:DataContext property is designed to be applied to controls that will bind to data via their DataContext property. Like data assigned to the DataContext property of a control, the value assigned to the d:DesignContext property will be inherited down the object hierarchy. For example, setting the d:DataContext property on a Grid, as demonstrated by the TextBlock control in the following example, will enable the data binding expression builder to display the available properties that the controls within the Grid can be bound to.

```
<Grid d:DataContext="{d:DesignInstance Type=my1:ProductSummary}">
    <TextBlock Text="{Binding Path=Name}" />
</Grid>
```

Using Sample Data

We've made the designer much friendlier for creating bindings, so let's now look at populating it with some sample data at design time. One way of doing this is to populate a single instance of an object with data in its constructor, and set the IsDesignTimeCreatable property on the d:DesignInstance markup extension to true. However, this is hardly an ideal solution for implementing design-time data. The design-time data has to be hard-coded in the class (not a good idea), and this method is suitable only when binding to a single object rather than to a collection of objects. There is another option however, and that's using the d:DesignData markup extension in place of the d:DesignInstance markup extension.

The d:DesignData markup extension has only a single property, named Source, which is, therefore, its default property. The design-time data needs to be defined in a separate XAML file, and you simply point the Source property to a XAML file containing the design-time data. That data will then be displayed in the XAML designer.

```
d:DataContext="{d:DesignData Source=/SampleData/ProductSampleData.xaml}"
```

The easiest way to create a sample data XAML file and populate it with data is from within Expression Blend. Expression Blend gives you the options of importing some data from XML, creating random data conforming to the structure of a given class, or simply creating your own structure before populating it with random data. Explaining how to create sample data files in Expression Blend is beyond the scope of this book, but you can find more information on doing so in the Expression Blend help, or on creating them manually in Visual Studio at this MSDN page: `http://msdn.microsoft.com/en-us/library/ff602279.aspx`.

Sample data XAML files should have a `Build Action` of either `DesignData`, where a substitute design-time type will be generated and used in place of the objects that the sample data is populating, or `DesignDataWithDesignTimeCreatableTypes`, where the actual objects the sample data is populating are instantiated and used at design time. You can then use the `d:DesignData` markup extension to point to the sample data XAML file and assign it to the `d:DataContext` attached property, as required.

Creating Consolidated Namespaces

In Chapter 2, we briefly discussed the concept of consolidated namespaces, where multiple namespaces could be combined into a single namespace declaration. This enables you to use a single namespace prefix covering multiple namespaces and/or assemblies, instead of declaring separate prefixes for each namespace/assembly combination individually. You can recognize a consolidated namespace, as it has a URI namespace instead of a CLR namespace. The default, and XAML namespaces that you find declared in all XAML files, are examples of consolidated namespaces, as is the SDK namespace:

```
xmlns:sdk="http://schemas.microsoft.com/winfx/2006/xaml/presentation/sdk"
```

These consolidated namespaces are predefined for you, but it is entirely possible for you to create your own if you wish, using the `XmlnsDefininition` attribute, as long as there is no overlap between the class names in the namespaces that you are consolidating.

There are a number of reasons why you might like to do so. One is to reduce the number of namespace prefix declarations you need to add to each XAML file. Another is to ensure consistency of the prefixes defined for each namespace across XAML files—different developers on a project using different prefixes will make maintaining the application a painful chore. An additional advantage is that the developers don't need to know or worry about which namespace a particular class or control is in to use it.

Let's take a look at creating a consolidated namespace to consolidate a number of namespaces in your Silverlight project. In the `AssemblyInfo.cs` file in your project, which you can find under the `Properties` folder, start by adding a `using` directive to the `System.Windows.Markup` namespace. Now, you need to come up with a URI to refer to the consolidated namespace you are about to create. A rough standard for doing so is something along these lines:

```
"http://schemas.yourbusinessurl.com/XAML"
```

Now, simply add attributes to your assembly that each attach a CLR namespace to this consolidated namespace URI:

```
[assembly: XmlnsDefinition("http://schemas.yourbusinessurl.com/XAML",
                           "AdventureWorks.Purchasing")]
[assembly: XmlnsDefinition("http://schemas.yourbusinessurl.com/XAML",
                           "AdventureWorks.ViewModels.Production")]
[assembly: XmlnsDefinition("http://schemas.yourbusinessurl.com/XAML",
                           "AdventureWorks.ViewModels.Sales")]
```

Next, you can declare a namespace prefix in a XAML file to this consolidated namespace URI, and then all the classes or controls across the combined CLR namespaces will be accessible via that prefix:

```
xmlns:vm="http://schemas.yourbusinessurl.com/XAML"
```

If you wish, you can also define a default prefix for that consolidated namespace using the `XmlnsPrefix` attribute:

```
[assembly: XmlnsPrefix("http://schemas.yourbusinessurl.com/XAML", "vm")]
```

This prefix will be used by Visual Studio and Expression Blend as the consolidated namespace's prefix when a control under that namespace is dragged from the toolbox onto the designer surface.

■ **Note** You will generally find this technique useful when creating custom control libraries, as discussed in Chapter 12, because you can define a consolidated namespace in a library that consolidates all the controls from different namespaces within that library into a single URI namespace.

MoXAML Power Toys

MoXAML Power Toys is a handy open source Visual Studio add-in by Pete O'Hanlon, providing a number of XAML and code helper functions for both Silverlight and WPF developers. You can download it from `http://peteohanlon.wordpress.com/moxaml-power-toys/`.

Some of the most useful features include the following:

- It includes a commenting helper. If you try to comment out XAML in the normal fashion, as described earlier in this chapter, and that XAML already contains comments, you will end up with invalid XAML. This function handles this scenario by first modifying the existing comment markers within the selected XAML, resulting in valid XAML instead.

- It contains a scrubber feature that cleans and formats the XAML in a file according to given options, such as converting tabs to spaces, putting attributes on their own line, and so on.

- You are able to create a user control from the selected XAML using the Extract User Control feature.

- As described in Chapter 2, by default all member variables created for controls are scoped as public. The Add `FieldModifier` function in MoXAML Power Toys goes through a XAML file and sets the `FieldModifier` property of each control with a name to "private".

- As discussed in Chapter 7, for bindings to be aware when the bound property's value has changed, the bound object needs to implement the `INotifyPropertyChanged` interface and raise its `PropertyChanged` event when each property's value is changed. This requires a backing member variable and additional code—automatically implemented properties do not implement this behavior. To simplify the task of creating properties that implement this behavior, the Notify Properties feature in MoXAML Power Toys enables you to right-click an automatically implemented property and select the Notify Property menu item from the MoXAML Power Toys submenu (in the context menu), and it will turn the property into a fully implemented property, with a backing member variable, and raise the `PropertyChanged` event.

- Creating dependency properties, discussed in depth in Chapter 12, can be a rather complex task. The Create Dependency Property feature pops up a window that will help you create a dependency property with the options that you specify.

You can get help for how to use these functions from the MoXAML Power Toys web site.

XAML Extensions for Visual Studio 2010

There are a number of XAML-related extensions on the Visual Studio Gallery, which you might find helpful when writing XAML by hand. This section references some that you might want to download, via the Extension Manager in Visual Studio.

■ **Note** A URL for each extension is provided, but you're probably best off simply searching for the extension by name at `http://visualstudiogallery.msdn.microsoft.com`.

XAML IntelliSense Presenter

Written by Karl Shifflet, who also wrote XAML Power Toys, the XAML IntelliSense Presenter extension extends IntelliSense in the XAML editor to provide additional features, such as Pascal case lookup, a narrowing list filter, filtering based on item type, and more.

More information is available here at `http://visualstudiogallery.msdn.microsoft.com/1a67eee3-fdd1-4745-b290-09d649d07ee0`.

XAML Regions

The XAML Regions extension enables you to define regions in your XAML, just like you can do in the code editor. This allows you to hide regions that are not important to you currently, and gets them out of the way. This is particularly useful when your XAML becomes complex, and hides away that complexity making your code easier to navigate.

More information is available at `http://visualstudiogallery.msdn.microsoft.com/3c534623-bb05-417f-afc0-c9e26bf0e177`.

XAML Styler

The XAML Styler extension sorts the attributes of elements in your XAML according to their importance. This can help make your XAML easier to read.

More information is available at `http://visualstudiogallery.msdn.microsoft.com/d6634d0e-38fb-48b6-829f-dadbc5c2fb62`. You can get the source at `http://xamlstyler.codeplex.com`.

Xaml Formatter

The Xaml Formatter extension reformats the indentation in your XAML, neatening it up for you, and making it easier to read.

More information is available at `http://visualstudiogallery.msdn.microsoft.com/a22d0202-2653-40e0-b29e-38eb5cd501ad`.

Summary

In this chapter, you've seen a number of advanced tips and techniques that you can use when writing XAML. Some of these you will use regularly, and others somewhat rarely, but either way, having them in your toolkit and at your disposal will greatly add to your ability to solve difficult problems in implementing your Silverlight business applications.

CHAPTER 11

Advanced Data Binding

So far in this book, you've learned how to bind your user interface controls to objects so that the user can view and edit data exposed by these objects. Instead of data being pushed into these controls, the extensive data binding support provided by XAML enables controls to pull the data into themselves. In other words, the controls are essentially controlling the process of consuming the data. You've learned that

- The object assigned to the DataContext property of a control is inherited down the object hierarchy.

- There are three different binding modes: OneTime, OneWay, and TwoWay (discussed in Chapter 2). You need to set the mode to TwoWay to update the bound object property via a control in the user interface.

- You can notify the bindings when bound property values on an object have changed, using the INotifyPropertyChanged interface, discussed in Chapter 7.

- You can notify the bindings when bound property values (or the bound object itself) are invalid by throwing exceptions, implementing the IDataErrorInfo interface, or by implementing the INotifyDataErrorInfo interface, as discussed in Chapter 7.

- The ObservableCollection<T> type can be used to maintain items in your collections, which will notify the bound user interface controls when items have been added or removed from the collection so they can update themselves accordingly (discussed in Chapter 6). Alternatively, you can implement the INotifyCollectionChanged interface in your own collection classes to enable them to exhibit the same behavior.

- You can create a view of a collection by wrapping it in a collection view, enabling the data in the collection to be manipulated (e.g., filtered, sorted, grouped, and paged) without actually modifying the underlying collection (discussed in Chapter 6). Collection views also provide a current record pointer that tracks the current item in the collection, enabling multiple controls bound to the same collection view to be kept synchronized. They also provide the ability to move this pointer and navigate through the items in the collection.

To develop business applications in Silverlight effectively, you need to have a thorough knowledge of the available data binding mechanisms at your disposal. In this chapter, we'll look at some of the advanced data binding features supported by Silverlight, and I'll provide you with tips, tricks, and techniques that you can use to harness the full power of Silverlight's data binding engine.

Assigning the Source of a Binding

When we first discussed data binding in Chapter 2, you learned that a binding has both a *source* and a *target*, with the binding source obtained from the bound control's DataContext property. The object assigned to the DataContext property is inherited down through the object hierarchy, so an object assigned to the DataContext property of a Grid control, for example, would automatically be available to all the controls contained within that Grid via their own DataContext properties.

However, what if you wanted a property on a control to bind to something *other* than the control's DataContext property, such as a resource, or a property on another control? Let's take a look at the different means available to achieve this in Silverlight.

Using the Binding's Source Property

If you set the Source property of the binding, it will use the given object as the binding source instead of the object assigned to the DataContext property of the control. If you're assigning this property in XAML, you will most likely be binding it to a resource, using the StaticResource markup extension.

For example, let's say you have a Product object that is defined as a resource, with productResource as its key, somewhere up the object hierarchy. (Defining and instantiating a class as a resource for binding to will be discussed in the "Binding to a Resource" section later in this chapter.) The standard way of binding to this resource is by assigning it to the DataContext property of the target control using the StaticResource markup extension. For example, you can bind the Text property of a TextBox control to the Name property on the Product object resource using the following XAML:

```
<TextBox DataContext="{StaticResource productResource}" Text="{Binding Name}" />
```

However, sometimes you want to bind a control's property to a given source, without altering the inherited data context for its child controls (where that data context has been set somewhere further up the hierarchy) or altering the binding source for its other properties. You can bind the Text property of the TextBox control directly to the resource without changing the value of the TextBox control's DataContext property to the resource by using the binding's Source property. The following binding expression demonstrates how you do this, with the same result as the previous example:

```
<TextBox Text="{Binding Name, Source={StaticResource productResource}}" />
```

■ **Note** Alternatively, if you are creating the data binding in code, which will be discussed later in this chapter, you can assign any object to this property to act as the source of the binding.

ElementName Binding

In Chapters 5 and 6, we looked at how you can bind the ItemsSource property of various controls to the Data property of a DomainDataSource control using ElementName binding, but we haven't yet looked at this type of binding in any depth. The DomainDataSource control was retrieving data from the server and exposing that data publicly via its Data property. We then consumed that data by binding the ItemsSource property of our ListBox, DataGrid, or DataForm control to the DomainDataSource control's Data property, essentially binding the property of one control to the property of another control. To bind a control's property to the property of another (named) control in the view like this, we needed to use a special kind of binding called ElementName binding. Using the ElementName property on a binding, you could provide it the name of a control, within the same name scope, that would act as the source for the binding (instead of the object assigned to the control's `DataContext` property). Let's take a look at some examples of employing ElementName binding to bind the properties of two controls together in XAML.

A very simple example is to link the Text property of two TextBox controls. When you modify the text in one text box, the second text box's text will update automatically:

```
<StackPanel>
    <TextBox Name="FirstTextBox" />
    <TextBox Name="SecondTextBox" Text="{Binding Text, ElementName=FirstTextBox}" />
</StackPanel>
```

■ **Note** If you change the mode of the second text box's binding to TwoWay, modifying the second text box's text will also update the first text box. That said, in this direction the first text box will be updated only when the second text box loses focus.

Similarly, we can display the current value of a Slider control in a text block by binding the Slider control's `Value` property to the TextBlock control's `Text` property:

```
<Slider Name="sourceSlider" />
<TextBlock Text="{Binding ElementName=sourceSlider, Path=Value}" />
```

The following XAML demonstrates taking the `ItemsSource` property of a ListBox control (acting as the target) and binding it to the `Data` property of a DomainDataSource control named `productSummaryDDS`:

```
<ListBox ItemsSource="{Binding ElementName=productSummaryDDS, Path=Data}" />
```

This example demonstrates binding the `IsBusy` property of the BusyIndicator control to the `IsBusy` property of a DomainDataSource control named `productSummaryDDS`. It will display the BusyIndicator control when the `IsBusy` property of the DomainDataSource control is true:

```
<controlsToolkit:BusyIndicator
    IsBusy="{Binding ElementName=productSummaryDDS, Path=IsBusy}" />
```

In this final example, we are binding the `Target` property of the Label control to a text box. Note that, by not specifying a path for the binding, we are binding the `Target` property to the text box itself, not a property on that text box:

```
<sdk:Label Content="Name:" Target="{Binding ElementName=ProductNameTextBox}" />
```

RelativeSource Binding

You may have noticed that there is a `RelativeSource` property on the `Binding` markup extension. This enables you to bind to a source relative to the target. You saw how ElementName binding enabled you to bind the property of one control to the property of another control. However, you can only use ElementName binding when the source control is named. RelativeSource binding allows you to bind to an unnamed source control *relative* to the target control.

You can obtain a reference to the source control using RelativeSource binding with the `RelativeSource` markup extension, whose return value can then be assigned to the binding's `RelativeSource` property. The `RelativeSource` markup extension has three modes: `Self`, `TemplatedParent`, and `FindAncestor`. Let's take a look at each of these in turn.

Self Mode

The Self mode returns the target control and is useful for binding two properties on the same control. This is generally most useful when you have attached properties on a control that you want to bind to properties on the control itself. For example, perhaps you want to display a tooltip when the user hovers over a text box, which will show all the text in the text box. Here, we'll use the ToolTipService.ToolTip attached property (demonstrated in Chapter 2) and bind it to the Text property of the text box using the Self mode of the RelativeSource markup extension:

```
<TextBox Text="{Binding Path=CurrentItem}"
                    ToolTipService.ToolTip="{Binding Text,
                                     RelativeSource={RelativeSource Self}}" />
```

TemplatedParent Mode

The TemplatedParent mode is applicable only when the control is contained within a control template or a data template. It returns the templated item and enables the target property to be bound to a property on that item. When used inside a data template, such as the data template for a ListBox item, the TemplatedParent mode will return the content presenter for that templated item. Note that it doesn't actually return the ListBoxItem control; the data template is actually being applied to the content presenter of the item, so it's the content presenter that will be returned, unlike when using a control template to template the ListBoxItem, where the TemplatedParent mode will return the ListBoxItem itself.

For example, the following binding expression in a data template will get the actual height of the content presenter:

```
"{Binding RelativeSource={RelativeSource TemplatedParent}, Path=ActualHeight}"
```

Another scenario where this binding may be useful in a data template is when you want to get the data context of the templated item. The data context is still inherited down the hierarchy in to data templates, but if you assign a different data context on a control in the data template, such as a Grid, you could use this method to obtain and bind to the original data context for the item again.

■ **Note** When used in a control template, the binding expression "{Binding RelativeSource= {RelativeSource TemplatedParent}}" is equivalent to the "{TemplateBinding}" markup extension. Unlike the TemplateBinding markup extension, which supports only a one-way binding, the RelativeSource markup extension can be used to enable a two-way binding, which can be very useful in some scenarios when creating control templates for custom controls. This will be discussed further in Chapter 12.

FindAncestor Mode

Silverlight 5 has introduced a new mode for RelativeSource binding—FindAncestor mode. FindAncestor mode allows you to search for a control of a given type higher up in the XAML hierarchy. For example, say you have the following XAML:

```
<Grid Background="Green" Width="200" Height="200">
    <Grid Background="Red" Margin="20">
        <Grid Background="Blue" Margin="20">
```

```
            <Grid Margin="20" />
        </Grid>
    </Grid>
</Grid>
```

As you can see, this XAML contains four nested Grid controls. Say that you now want to set the background color of the innermost Grid control to the same background color of one of the Grid controls further up the control hierarchy. We can use RelativeSource binding with the FindAncestor mode to do so. The RelativeSource markup extension has two properties that you use with this mode: AncestorType and AncestorLevel. The AncestorType property is used to specify the type of control that you are looking for up the control hierarchy, and the AncestorLevel property is used to specify how many times that control type should appear in the control hierarchy before that control is selected. The following XAML demonstrates binding the Background property of the innermost Grid control to the Background property of the top level Grid control, skipping two instances of the Grid control and taking the third:

```
<Grid Background="Green" Width="200" Height="200">
    <Grid Background="Red" Margin="20">
        <Grid Background="Blue" Margin="20">
            <Grid Background="{Binding Background,
                                RelativeSource={RelativeSource FindAncestor,
                                                AncestorType=Grid,
                                                AncestorLevel=3}}"
                Margin="20" />
        </Grid>
    </Grid>
</Grid>
```

If you change the value of the AncestorLevel property to 1 or 2, you'll find that the background of the innermost Grid control will change to that of the corresponding Grid control in the control hierarchy.

___

■ **Note** The FindAncestor mode of the RelativeSource binding has many potential uses. For example, if you assign a ViewModel object to the DataContext property of the view (i.e., on the Page or UserControl control), a control further down the control hierarchy whose DataContext is not set to that ViewModel object—which will be the case if the control is contained within a ListBox item, for example—may still need to bind to a property on that ViewModel object. RelativeSource binding with FindAncestor mode allows the binding to easily get a reference to the Page, UserControl, or other top level control, from which it can access its DataContext property to get to the ViewModel object. Another good use of FindAncestor is to enable controls within a list box item's data template to get a reference to the ListBoxItem control that they're contained within. This would enable the controls to access the ListBoxItem's IsSelected property, allowing them to change their states depending on whether the list box item is selected or not.

Binding a Control Property Directly to Its Data Context

You can bind a property of a control directly to the object assigned to its DataContext property, either assigned directly to the property on the control or inherited down the object hierarchy, by simply setting its value to "{Binding}". This scenario is common when binding a number of controls to the same inherited data context. For example, the data context of a Grid control is bound to a collection, and multiple controls within that Grid inherit that data context and use it as their binding source. Therefore, to bind the ItemsSource property of a ListBox control in the Grid to the collection, you can set its binding expression to "{Binding}".

As an example, the Text property of the TextBox control in the following XAML is bound to the TextBox control's DataContext property, resulting in the text box displaying "Hello" as its text:

```
<TextBox DataContext="Hello" Text="{Binding}" />
```

■ **Note** The "{Binding}" binding expression is equivalent to {Binding Path=.}, which is also the same as {Binding Path=}.

Detecting When the DataContext's Value Has Changed

Say that you have a view that handles events raised by the ViewModel object assigned to its DataContext property. If a new ViewModel object is assigned to the view's DataContext property, the view needs to unsubscribe from those events and handle the events on the new ViewModel object instead. In this scenario, the view needs to know when the value of its DataContext property has changed so it can respond accordingly.

In earlier versions of Silverlight, you had no easy way of determining when the value of a control's DataContext property had changed, making handling this scenario rather difficult. However, Silverlight 5 has introduced the DataContextChanged event, which is raised on a control when the value of its DataContext property is changed. You can handle this event and respond accordingly.

Let's take a look at an example demonstrating this event in action. The following XAML contains a Button control and a TextBox control. The Text property of the TextBox control is bound to its DataContext, and the TextBox control's DataContextChanged event is handled in the code behind. The Button control's Click event is also being handled in the code behind, as we'll use it to change the value of the TextBox control's DataContext property:

```
<StackPanel>
    <Button Name="ChangeContextButton" Content="Change Context"
            Height="33" Width="143" Click="ChangeContextButton_Click" />
    <TextBox Name="MyTextBox" Text="{Binding}"
            DataContextChanged="MyTextBox_DataContextChanged" />
</StackPanel>
```

In the code behind, we now need to handle the Button control's Click event, and the TextBox control's DataContextChanged event. In the Button control's Click event handler, change the value of the TextBox control's DataContext property. The following code assigns a new GUID to it:

```
private void ChangeContextButton_Click(object sender, RoutedEventArgs e)
{
    MyTextBox.DataContext = Guid.NewGuid();
}
```

In the TextBox control's DataContextChanged event handler, we'll simply show a message box indicating that the event has been fired:

```
private void MyTextBox_DataContextChanged(object sender, DependencyPropertyChangedEventArgs e)
{
    MessageBox.Show("My data context has changed!");
}
```

When you run this, you'll find that the message box is shown every time you click the button. As an exercise, assign the GUID to the view's DataContext property instead of the TextBox control's:

```
private void ChangeContextButton_Click(object sender, RoutedEventArgs e)
{
    this.DataContext = Guid.NewGuid();
}
```

The TextBox control will inherit this data context, and thus the value of its DataContext property will change when the value of the view's DataContext property is changed. Therefore, its DataContextChanged event will still be fired.

Binding to a Property in the View's Code Behind

You've seen how you can bind to a property on bound objects, resources, and other controls in the view, but what if the source of the property you want to bind to is actually the view's code-behind class? Let's say you have the following XAML for a view:

```
<UserControl x:Class="Chapter11Workshop.MainPage"
    xmlns="http://schemas.microsoft.com/winfx/2006/xaml/presentation"
    xmlns:x="http://schemas.microsoft.com/winfx/2006/xaml"
    xmlns:d="http://schemas.microsoft.com/expression/blend/2008"
    xmlns:mc="http://schemas.openxmlformats.org/markup-compatibility/2006"
    mc:Ignorable="d"
    d:DesignHeight="300" d:DesignWidth="400">

    <TextBlock Width="100" Height="20" />
</UserControl>
```

and the view's code behind defines a property named UserName, like so:

```
using System.Windows.Controls;

namespace Chapter11Workshop
{
    public partial class MainPage : UserControl
    {
        public MainPage()
        {
            InitializeComponent();
        }

        public string UserName
        {
```

```
        get { return "Chris Anderson"; }
      }
   }
}
```

The TextBlock control can use the FindAncestor mode of the RelativeSource binding to find the root element of the view and use it as the binding's source, like so:

```
<TextBlock Width="100" Height="20"
           Text="{Binding UserName,
                  RelativeSource={RelativeSource FindAncestor,
                                  AncestorType=UserControl}}" />
```

Alternatively, you can use ElementName binding to achieve the same result (though less elegantly) if you wish. Start by giving the root element in your XAML file a name, using its Name property. In this example we have named it Root. Now, you can simply use ElementName binding to assign that element as its binding source:

```
<TextBlock Width="100" Height="20" Text="{Binding UserName, ElementName=Root}" />
```

■ **Note** Usually, any properties that your view needs to bind to will be defined in a ViewModel class (part of the MVVM design pattern, discussed in Chapter 13). However, this technique is particularly useful when creating user controls that expose properties to the host. The properties are defined in the code behind; the host sets their values; and the XAML can consume those values directly via these bindings without requiring the intervention of the code behind apart from getting or setting the property values. Custom controls have a slightly different means of handling this type of scenario, as will be discussed in Chapter 12.

Instantiating a Class in XAML

You are able to instantiate classes in XAML, defining them as either a resource, or as the value of a control's property. Let's walk through how you can do this.

Creating a Class to Bind To

Let's start by creating the class that we will instantiate in XAML. Create a folder named ViewModels folder in your project. Add a new class to this folder, and name it ProductViewModel. Add some properties to it that we can bind to (Name, ProductNumber, etc.), and set some default values for them in the class's constructor:

```
public class ProductViewModel
{
    public string Name { get; set; }
    public string ProductNumber { get; set; }

    public ProductViewModel()
    {
```

```
        Name = "Helmet";
        ProductNumber = "H01";
    }
}
```

■ **Note** To instantiate a class in XAML, it must have a default constructor (a constructor without any parameters). If you do not define any constructors, a default constructor will be created for you, but otherwise, you will need to ensure that there is one added to the class.

Instantiating the Class as a Resource in XAML and Binding to It

The first step to instantiating a class in XAML is to declare a namespace prefix in your XAML file for the namespace where the class can be found:

```
xmlns:vm="clr-namespace:AdventureWorks.ViewModels"
```

The next step is to define and instantiate the class as a resource, remembering to give it a key:

```
<UserControl.Resources>
    <vm:ProductViewModel x:Key="productResource" />
</UserControl.Resources>
```

You can even assign values to the properties on the class at this stage if required (this will override their default values set in the class's constructor):

```
<vm:ProductViewModel x:Key="productResource" Name="Bike" ProductNumber="B001" />
```

■ **Note** You can assign values to only a few data types natively in XAML, such as `string`, `boolean`, `int`, and `double`. Other more complex types, such as `Decimal` and `DateTime`, require type converters to be applied to their properties to handle the conversion. Creating and using type converters will be discussed in Chapter 12.

The class has been instantiated and defined as a resource, allowing you to now bind to this object resource, using the `StaticResource` markup extension to reference it, in whatever way you wish:

```
<TextBox Text="{Binding Name, Source={StaticResource productResource}}" />
```

■ **Note** Any data that you've hard-coded in the class or assigned via the resource's properties will appear at design time in the bound controls.

Instantiating the Class as the Value of a Control's Property

You can also instantiate a class and assign the resulting object to the property of a control in XAML, without the need to define it as a resource first. For example, you might want to assign an instance of the ProductViewModel class to the view's DataContext property. You can achieve the same result as this code

```
this.DataContext = new ProductViewModel();
```

in XAML, like so, using property element syntax to do so:

```
<UserControl.DataContext>
    <vm:ProductViewModel />
</UserControl.DataContext>
```

This is a nice way to declaratively connect a view to its ViewModel, when using the MVVM design pattern.

You can also assign values to the properties on the object in the same manner as was demonstrated in the previous section for resources.

Defining Resources in the Code Behind

You've now seen how you can declaratively define resources in XAML, but sometimes, it can be useful to define resources using code instead. For example, you may have a factory class that instantiates objects for you, or the class may not have a parameterless constructor (as declarative instantiation in XAML requires). In these types of instances, you will need to take the object and add it as a resource in code.

You can see an example of this in projects generated by the Silverlight Business Application project template, such as the AdventureWorks application we've been building throughout this book. If you open the App.xaml.cs file in your AdventureWorks project and find the Application_Startup event handler method, you will find this line:

```
this.Resources.Add("WebContext", WebContext.Current);
```

This line adds a WebContext object as an applicationwide resource. As you can see, it simply gets a reference to a resource dictionary (in this case the Application object's resource dictionary) and calls the Add method on that dictionary—specifying a key for the resource (WebContext) and the object to be added as a resource (WebContext.Current). You can then bind to this resource in XAML as you would any other resource:

```
<Button Content="Click Me!"
        IsEnabled="{Binding Path=User.IsAuthenticated,
                    Source={StaticResource WebContext}}" />
```

Binding to Nested Properties

Generally, when creating a binding, you'll be binding to a single property on the source object. For example, the DataContext property of a TextBox control might be assigned a Person object, and you might want to bind to the FirstName property on that object, with the FirstName property returning a string:

```
<TextBox Text="{Binding FirstName, Source={StaticResource personResource}}" />
```

However, what if the Person object doesn't have a FirstName property but instead has a Name property that returns a PersonName object, and it's this object that has the FirstName property, meaning that you're effectively dealing with nested properties? How do you handle that sort of binding? This is possible by using the same style of dot notation you use in C# code to traverse down the object hierarchy:

```
<TextBox Text="{Binding Name.FirstName, Source={StaticResource personResource}}" />
```

You can traverse down multiple levels of the object hierarchy for as far as you need.

Binding to Indexed Properties

In addition to binding to nested properties, it's also possible to bind to indexed properties, with both integer and string indexes. The index selection syntax is much the same as it is in C#—simply append the index to the name of the property returning the collection surrounded by square brackets. For example, if a Person object had an Addresses property that returned a collection of Address objects, you could bind to the first Address object using the integer index syntax:

```
<TextBox DataContext="{StaticResource personResource}"
        Text="{Binding Address[0].AddressLine1}" />
```

If the collection has string indexes, such as a Dictionary<string, string>, you can refer to the item using the string index syntax, like so:

```
<TextBox DataContext="{StaticResource personResource}"
        Text="{Binding Address[HOME].AddressLine1}" />
```

In the preceding example, HOME is the string index of the Address object to return. If the given index is not found, the binding will silently fail, although an error will be written to the Output window in Visual Studio (discussed in the "Debugging Data Binding Issues" section later in this chapter).

Binding to Dynamic Properties

Sometimes, you need to bind to data that you don't know the structure of at design time, such as XML or JSON data. In this type of scenario, ideally, you'd be able to create an object at runtime that you could deserialize the data to and then bind to it. Silverlight 4 added support for dynamic types, which goes some way toward solving the issue. However, the downside to creating dynamic objects is that you can't actually bind to them, as Silverlight's binding engine doesn't recognize dynamic properties as real properties. Any attempt to bind directly to dynamic properties on objects will fail. To overcome this issue, Silverlight 5 introduced the ICustomTypeProvider interface that you can implement on a class to tell the binding engine what the structure of the object is.

The ICustomTypeProvider interface can be found in the System.Reflection namespace and simply requires the implementation of a single method: GetCustomType. However, the actual implementation of this method is unfortunately quite complex. You essentially need to create a type from scratch. The Type class is unsealed in Silverlight 5, enabling you to inherit from it and override its properties and methods.

Rather than writing this ICustomTypeProvider implementation yourself, Alexandra Rusina, a program manager in the Silverlight team at Microsoft, has created a helper class that will do the hard work for you, which you can download here: http://blogs.msdn.com/b/silverlight_sdk/archive/ 2011/04/26/binding-to-dynamic-properties-with-icustomtypeprovider-silverlight-5-beta.aspx. Using this helper class, you can then create a class that either inherits from this helper class (the easiest method) or implements the ICustomTypeProvider interface and delegates the GetCustomType method to the helper class. Use the latter method if your class already inherits from another class.

For example, let's create a Product class whose structure we'll define at runtime.

1. Start by creating the class, and inherit from the generic CustomTypeHelper class:

```
public class Product : CustomTypeHelper<Product> { }
```

2. Add properties to the class by calling the static AddProperty method that's been inherited from the CustomTypeHelper<T> class, giving each property a name and a type:

```
Product.AddProperty("ProductName", typeof(string));
Product.AddProperty("Category", typeof(string));
Product.AddProperty("QtyAvailable", typeof(int));
```

3. When you instantiate the class, you obviously won't be able to set the values for these properties in the way you would normally with properties defined at design time. Instead, you'll need to call the SetPropertyValue method on the Product class (again, inherited from the CustomTypeHelper<T> class), passing it the name of the property to set the value for, and its new value, like so:

```
Product product = new Product();
product.SetPropertyValue("ProductName", "Helmet");
product.SetPropertyValue("Category", "Accessories");
product.SetPropertyValue("QtyAvailable", 10);
```

4. You can now bind to this object and its properties in exactly the same way as you would any standard CLR object. Thanks to the helper class, the properties automatically implement the INotifyPropertyChanged interface, so you don't need to worry about that aspect. If necessary, you can get the property values in code using the GetPropertyValue method that the Product class has inherited from CustomTypeHelper<T>:

```
string productName = (string)product.GetPropertyValue("ProductName");
string category = (string)product.GetPropertyValue("Category");
int qtyAvailable = (int)product.GetPropertyValue("QtyAvailable");
```

■ **Note** Rather than write your own ICustomTypeProvider implementation to wrap XML or JSON data from scratch, Matt Duffield has provided ICustomTypeProvider implementations for these types of data that you may wish to try: http://mattduffield.wordpress.com/2011/09/16/using-icustomtypeprovider-in-silverlight-5-with-xml.

Enhancing Data Binding

The Binding class has a number of properties that you can use to further configure a data binding rather than simply connecting the value of the target property directly to the source property. These properties are the keys to enabling the power and flexibility of Silverlight's data binding capabilities, so let's take a look at them now.

String Formatting

Bindings have a StringFormat property that you can use to format a bound property's value before it is passed to the target control to be consumed. This can be a very useful feature when binding to a nonstring property, such as a DateTime or a decimal. You can use the StringFormat property on the binding to set the format, using the same types of formatting strings as you would use if you were to format the value using its ToString method in code, using either standard or custom formats. For example, the following binding uses a standard formatting string to display the bound property's value in the text box formatted as currency:

```
<TextBox Text="{Binding TotalCost, Mode=TwoWay, StringFormat=C}" />
```

Or you can format a date as a long date (e.g., Sunday, May 16, 2011) using a standard formatting string:

```
<TextBox Text="{Binding StartDate, Mode=TwoWay, StringFormat=D}" />
```

You can even format a date as a custom format (e.g., 2011-05-16) using a custom formatting string:

```
<TextBox Text="{Binding StartDate, Mode=TwoWay, StringFormat=yyyy-MM-dd}" />
```

You can also format a decimal, single, double, or float to a given number of decimal places (e.g., 3.14) using a custom formatting string:

```
<TextBox Text="{Binding PI, Mode=TwoWay, StringFormat=0.00}" />
```

If you want to include commas or other special characters in your string format, enclose the formatting string within apostrophes (not quotes, as they are used to delimit the whole property assignment):

```
<TextBox Text="{Binding StartDate, Mode=TwoWay, StringFormat='MMM dd, yyyy'}" />
```

Alternatively, you can simply escape them by inserting a backslash (\) prior to the special character:

```
<TextBox Text="{Binding StartDate, Mode=TwoWay, StringFormat=MMM dd\, yyyy}" />
```

■ **Note** The available standard formatting strings and custom format specifiers that can be used for formatting strings are detailed in the following MSDN topic (and its related topics): http://msdn.microsoft.com/en-us/library/26etazsy.aspx. Another source with examples can be found in the Visual Studio 2010 data binding expression builder (discussed later in this chapter).

Another neat data binding trick is to use the binding's StringFormat property to concatenate the bound value with other text. For example, you might want to show a label in front of the value. Say you bind to a property, which returns "Chris Anderson" as its value, and you want to display it in the view like so:

```
Name: Chris Anderson
```

You could use a StackPanel control to stack two TextBlock controls together to achieve this effect, like so:

```
<StackPanel Orientation="Horizontal">
    <TextBlock Text="Name: " />
    <TextBlock Text="{Binding Name}" />
</StackPanel>
```

Or make use of the TextBlock control's Inlines property:

```
<TextBlock>
    <TextBlock.Inlines>
        <Run Text="Name: " />
        <Run Text="{Binding Name}" />
    </TextBlock.Inlines>
</TextBlock>
```

You could even go so far as creating a value converter or custom markup extension to concatenate the strings for you. However, there's a much easier and more elegant way, by leveraging the StringFormat property of the Binding object to replace a token in a string with a value, in the same way as you do using the String class's StringFormat property in code:

```
<TextBlock Text="{Binding Name, StringFormat='Name: {0}'}" />
```

The {0} token in the format string is replaced with the bound value, effectively concatenating the two strings together.

Here's another example, where the bound value will be surrounded with brackets (i.e., the TextBlock control will display "(Chris Anderson)"):

```
<TextBlock Text="{Binding Name, StringFormat='({0})'}" />
```

Of course, you can only have one replacement value, as bindings only return a single value, but if that's all you need, this is a neat way of concatenating the bound value with some other text, without needing to resort more complicated to achieve the same effect.

Alternative Value When a Source Property Value Is Null

If the value of a property being bound to is null, you can specify an alternate value to use instead using the TargetNullValue property of the binding. This is a useful feature when you are binding to a nullable type and want to provide a default value when one isn't provided—for example:

```
<TextBlock Text="{Binding TotalAmount, TargetNullValue=0}" />
```

Fallback Values

If the source of the binding is null—that is, the value of both the DataContext property of the control and the Source property of the binding are null—or the property being bound to does not exist on the object assigned as the source of the binding, you can specify an alternative value to use instead using the FallbackValue property of the binding.For example, the following binding will display "Oops!" if the binding source is null:

```
<TextBox Text="{Binding Name, Mode=TwoWay, FallbackValue=Oops!}" />
```

UpdateSourceTrigger

The UpdateSourceTrigger property of the Binding object enables you to specify exactly when the source property of a two-way binding should be updated in response to changes in the target property. Most commonly used with bindings on the Text property of the TextBox control, the UpdateSourceTrigger property allows you to specify whether the control should be updated when the TextBox control loses focus, immediately whenever the text is changed, or only when the code explicitly says so. Let's look at each of these modes in turn.

Default Mode

When the UpdateSourceTrigger property is set to Default, the bound (source) property will usually only be updated when the TextBox control has lost focus, such as when the user tabs out of it. As its name suggests, this is the default UpdateSourceTrigger mode, so it is rarely explicitly set in XAML, but for the purpose of completion, you can set it like so:

```
<TextBox Text="{Binding Name, Mode=TwoWay, UpdateSourceTrigger=Default}" />
```

PropertyChanged Mode

Silverlight 5 now supports a new UpdateSourceTrigger mode named PropertyChanged. Setting the UpdateSourceTrigger property to PropertyChanged will result in the bound (source) property being updated immediately whenever a change is made to the text.

```
<TextBox Text="{Binding Name, Mode=TwoWay, UpdateSourceTrigger=PropertyChanged}" />
```

As demonstrated in Chapter 6, this mode is very useful when you want to implement a search text box that filters items in a list immediately as the user enters text into the text box, enabling you to create a user interface that is very reactive to user input.

Explicit Mode

In Chapter 7, we discussed implementing the IEditableObject interface to add transaction type behavior to our classes (begin, accept, and cancel changes). However, you may not have the luxury of implementing this interface in the classes that you bind to, so rather than rolling back unwanted changes (the behavior that the IEditableObject interface enables), you could alternatively prevent changes being made to the object until you explicitly commit them, such as when the user clicks the OK button. This behavior can be enabled by setting the UpdateSourceTrigger property of the Binding object to Explicit:

```
<TextBox Name="NameTextBox"
         Text="{Binding Name, Mode=TwoWay, UpdateSourceTrigger=Explicit}" />
```

Note how we have set the Name property of the TextBox control in this example. This is essential when using explicit update mode, as we'll need to reference the text box in our code behind.

If you run the application now, you will find that the source property will never be updated. For the source property of the binding to be updated, you must manually initiate the update in code. Say you have an OK button in the view, and you want to commit the changes made to the field back to the bound object when the button is clicked. To do so, you can handle the button's Click event in the code behind, and get the binding expression for the text box's Text property, using the GetBindingExpression method on the text box, which returns a BindingExpression object. You can then explicitly force the source property of the binding to be updated using the UpdateSource method on the BindingExpression object, like so:

```
BindingExpression expr = NameTextBox.GetBindingExpression(TextBox.TextProperty);
expr.UpdateSource();
```

Value Converters

You've seen how you can format the bound value, using the StringFormat property of a binding, before passing it onto the target control, but what if you want to *convert* the value to a completely different value instead? A perfect example is attempting to bind a Boolean value to the Visibility property of a control. This is not possible, because the Visibility property accepts values only from the Visibility enumeration (Visible or Collapsed). You could modify the property on the object that you are binding to in order to return a value from the Visibility enumeration instead, but this is not always possible or ideal. There is, however, a way we can transform the Boolean value to a Visibility enumeration as a part of the binding process, and that's using a *value converter*.

A value converter is a class that implements the IValueConverter interface, from the System.Windows.Data namespace, which has two methods:

- The Convert method is passed (as a parameter) the value of the property on the source object of the binding, and you can implement the required logic to convert it to the value to be assigned to the target property returned as the result of the method.

- The ConvertBack method is used in two-way bindings to convert the target value, modified in the user interface and passed into the method as a parameter, back to a value to be assigned to the bound property.

Creating a Simple Value Converter

Let's take a look at implementing a simple value converter to convert a Boolean value to a Visibility enumeration:

```
using System;
using System.Windows;
using System.Windows.Data;

public class BoolToVisibilityValueConverter : IValueConverter
{
    public object Convert(object value, Type targetType, object parameter,
                          System.Globalization.CultureInfo culture)
    {
        return (bool)value ? Visibility.Visible : Visibility.Collapsed;
    }

    public object ConvertBack(object value, Type targetType, object parameter,
                              System.Globalization.CultureInfo culture)
    {
        throw new NotImplementedException();
    }
}
```

Note that we didn't bother implementing any logic for the ConvertBack method, as bindings to the Visibility property of a control will only ever need to be one-time or one-way bindings (it doesn't expose user input). Therefore, this method will never be used and hence isn't worth implementing. However, for other types of conversions where you will want to convert the user's input back to something else, you will actually need to implement the logic to do so in this method.

■ **Note** If you used the Silverlight Business Application project template as the basis for your application, you will find that a couple of value converters are already in your project (in the Helpers folder) that you can take a look at, such as the NotOperatorValueConverter value converter that converts true values to false, and false values to true.

Using a Value Converter

Once you've created your value converter, you need to instantiate it in the resources somewhere in your object hierarchy. This will probably be in the resources of a page or user control, but you could also assign it to the resources of the Application object (in the App.xaml file) to use the value converter applicationwide. First, declare a namespace prefix to the namespace where your value converter can be found, for example:

```
xmlns:vc="clr-namespace:AdventureWorks.ValueConverters"
```

Next, instantiate the value converter as a resource in the object hierarchy:

```
<vc:BoolToVisibilityValueConverter x:Key="VisibilityConverter" />
```

Now, you can use this value converter by assigning it to the Converter property of the data binding, using the StaticResource markup extension to obtain a reference to it. The following example demonstrates hiding a Save button if the value of the IsDirty property of a bound object being edited (the object being inherited down the object hierarchy to the save button's DataContext property) is true:

```
<Button Content="Save" Height="23" Width="75"
    Visibility="{Binding IsDirty, Converter={StaticResource VisibilityConverter}}" />
```

Passing a Parameter to the Value Converter

Sometimes, you find that you need to pass additional information to the value converter to enable it to perform its task. You can pass the value converter an additional value, defined in XAML, using the ConverterParameter property of the binding.

In early versions of Silverlight, before support for the StringFormat property of the binding was added in Silverlight 4, value converters were commonly used to format the bound property value. The ConverterParameter property enabled generic formatting value converters to be created, with the actual string format to use passed to the converter using this property. Of course, this scenario is no longer necessary, but there are still plenty of other scenarios where this feature can be used.

A different scenario is one mentioned when discussing binding to RadioButton controls in Chapter 7, where you want to bind each of the RadioButton controls to a single property on the bound object exposing an enumeration type, with each RadioButton control representing a different enumeration value. As was discussed in that chapter, this is not a scenario that you can implement using standard data binding, but using a value converter in the binding and passing it a parameter makes this possible. The following value converter demonstrates creating a generic enumeration-to-Boolean value converter that compares the passed in value with the parameter passed in, returning true if they match, false if they don't:

```
using System;
using System.Windows.Data;
```

```
public class EnumEqualityValueConverter : IValueConverter
{
    public object Convert(object value, Type targetType, object parameter,
                          System.Globalization.CultureInfo culture)
    {
        return value.ToString() == parameter.ToString();
    }

    public object ConvertBack(object value, Type targetType, object parameter,
                              System.Globalization.CultureInfo culture)
    {
        return Enum.Parse(targetType, parameter.ToString(), true);
    }
}
```

■ **Note** In the preceding scenario, we have a TwoWay binding (the user can select an alternative age bracket via the radio buttons), so we need to be able to convert the selected radio button back to the enumeration value that it represents via the value converter. Therefore, you'll note that we needed to actually implement the ConvertBack method for this converter.

Now, to use this value converter, assuming you have already declared a namespace prefix and instantiated it as a resource, simply assign the value converter to the Converter property of the RadioButton control's bindings and assign the enumeration value that each RadioButton control represents to the ConverterParameter property of the binding, which will be compared to the bound property's value by the value converter and will return true if they match:

```
<RadioButton Content="&lt; 20" IsChecked="{Binding AgeBracket, Mode=TwoWay,
    Converter={StaticResource EnumConverter}, ConverterParameter=BelowTwenty}" />
<RadioButton Content="20 to 29" IsChecked="{Binding AgeBracket, Mode=TwoWay,
    Converter={StaticResource EnumConverter}, ConverterParameter=Twenties}" />
<RadioButton Content="30 to 39" IsChecked="{Binding AgeBracket, Mode=TwoWay,
    Converter={StaticResource EnumConverter}, ConverterParameter=Thirties}" />
<RadioButton Content="40 Plus" IsChecked="{Binding AgeBracket, Mode=TwoWay,
    Converter={StaticResource EnumConverter}, ConverterParameter=FourtyPlus}" />
```

Passing a Culture to a Value Converter

A CultureInfo object can also be passed into the value converter methods as a parameter. This can be used when displaying data that needs to be formatted according to a given culture.

By default, the language-culture passed into the value converter is obtained from the Language property assigned to the control, using the standard language-culture strings, such as en-US, which denotes English language with U.S. culture. This value is inherited down the object hierarchy, so if you assign a culture to this property on the root node in your XAML file, all the controls in that XAML file will also inherit that value. If a culture is not explicitly assigned via this property, it will default to U.S. English (en-US). You can explicitly pass a specific language-culture to a value converter using the ConverterCulture property on the binding. Any language-culture that you specify here will be passed into the value converter via the culture parameter.

Passing an Entire Object to a Value Converter

If you want to use multiple properties of the source object in the converter to produce a single output, such as combining the first name and surname properties into a single string for display, this is possible using a value converter too. Bind directly to the object itself in the binding, instead of a property on the object, and the entire object will be passed into the Convert method of the value converter via the value parameter. You can then cast it to the object type, get the first name and surname property values, combine them into a single string, and return that string as the result of the method, as demonstrated in the following code:

```
public class FullNameValueConverter : IValueConverter
{
    public object Convert(object value, Type targetType, object parameter,
                          System.Globalization.CultureInfo culture)
    {       Person person = value as Person;
        return person.FirstName + " " + person.Surname;
    }

    public object ConvertBack(object value, Type targetType, object parameter,
                              System.Globalization.CultureInfo culture)
    {
        throw new NotImplementedException();
    }
}
```

■ **Note** For this type of scenario, you would usually be better adding a FullName property to your ViewModel (when using the Model-View-ViewModel (MVVM) design pattern, as discussed in Chapter 13) and binding to that instead. However, if you are not implementing the MVVM pattern, value converters provide an alternative solution to modifying the objects you are binding to in order to suit the requirements of the user interface.

Binding Using Property Element Syntax

Although it's rare to want to do so, you can actually specify bindings using property element syntax. The following example demonstrates binding to a property named Name using property element syntax:

```
<TextBox>
    <TextBox.Text>
        <Binding Path="Name" />
    </TextBox.Text>
</TextBox>
```

MultiBinding

At times, you want to bind a control property to multiple properties on the binding source object, taking each of those property values and merging them into a single value to be consumed by the target. This is known in WPF as a *MultiBinding*, but this feature is not available in Silverlight. Earlier in this chapter, we discussed combining the values of multiple properties together while data binding using a value converter, which is a way to get around this omission. WPF's MultiBinding does have the advantage of being a slightly more generic solution, but you could make the value converter solution a little more generic by passing the names of the source properties to use in the converter parameter. Colin Eberhardt has created a means for implementing MultiBindings in Silverlight, which you can obtain at http://www.scottlogic.co.uk/blog/colin/2010/08/silverlight-multibinding-updated-adding-support-for-elementname-and-twoway-binding/.

■ **Note** If you are using the Model-View-ViewModel (MVVM) design pattern (discussed in Chapter 13), the need for a MultiBinding data binding is somewhat lessened, because you can simply add a new property to your View-Model which exposes the combined property values that should be displayed in the view.

Data Binding in Code

At times, you may find that you need to bind the property of a control in the code behind. This is possible using the GetBindingExpression and SetBinding methods on the control.

To create a new binding and assign it to a control property, simply instantiate a Binding object (found in the System.Windows.Data namespace),assign the binding configuration to its properties as required, and apply the binding to the target control property using the control's SetBinding method. The SetBinding method requires you to pass it the Binding object and the dependency property identifier associated with the property to bind to on the target control, remembering that you can assign data bindings only to dependency properties.

For example, let's bind the Name property of a Product entity to the Text property of a TextBox control named NameTextBox:

```
Binding binding = new Binding("Name");
binding.Mode = BindingMode.TwoWay;
NameTextBox.SetBinding(TextBox.TextProperty, binding);
```

This example of creating a binding in code is simple, but of course, you can assign values to all the other binding properties that we have previously discussed, such as StringFormat, TargetNullValue, FallbackValue, and Source.

You can obtain the binding assigned to a control's property using the GetBindingExpression method on the control.

```
BindingExpression expr = NameTextBox.GetBindingExpression(TextBox.TextProperty);
```

As its name suggests, this method does not actually return a Binding object but returns a BindingExpression object instead. The BindingExpression class has two properties: ParentBinding and DataItem, in addition to the UpdateSource method discussed earlier. The ParentBinding property provides the Binding object assigned to the control property, and the DataItem property provides the object acting as the source for the binding.

Getting and Setting Attached Property Values in Code

Although it's a somewhat different topic to data binding, getting and setting the value of an attached property on a control is similar to getting and setting bindings. Use the GetValue method of a control, passing it the dependency property corresponding to the attached property, to get the given attached property's value for that control. For example, use the following code to get which grid row a text box control named NameTextBox is in (hence, get the value of the `Grid.Row` attached property on the text box):

```
int row = (int)NameTextBox.GetValue(Grid.RowProperty);
```

You can then assign a different value to that attached property if you wish, using the `SetValue` method of the control, and passing it the corresponding dependency property and the new value to assign to it:

```
NameTextBox.SetValue(Grid.RowProperty, row);
```

Additional Tips

Let's take a look at some additional miscellaneous data binding tips that you may find useful when binding to data.

Visual Studio Data Binding Expression Builder

As mentioned in Chapter 2, Visual Studio 2010 provides a data binding expression builder (from the Properties window), which can be of help when learning how to write data binding expressions. This data binding expression builder will lead you through the process of creating a data binding expression.

To open the Visual Studio Data Binding Expression Builder, select the target control in the designer, find the target property that you want to bind to in the Properties window, and click the Advanced Properties icon next to its name. Select the Apply Data Binding menu item from the pop-up menu as shown in Figure 11-1.

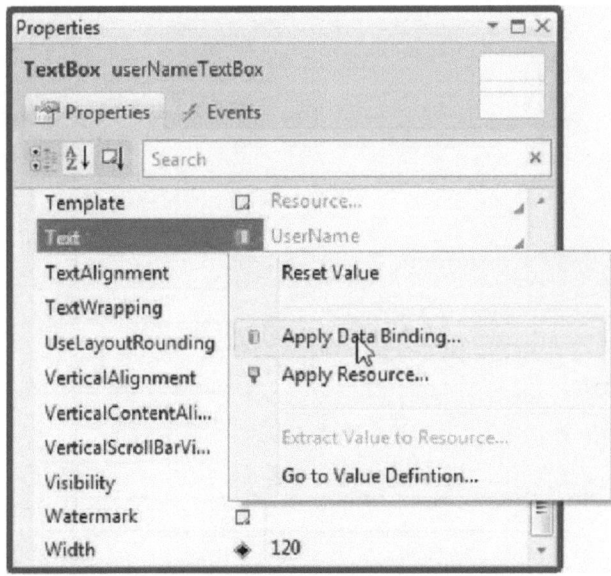

Figure 11-1. *Opening the data binding expression builder*

This will open the data binding expression builder as a pop-up window, as shown in Figure 11-2. Note that the builder has an accordion style layout, where you click each header to open the corresponding pane and select the options. The first step is to select a source for the binding.

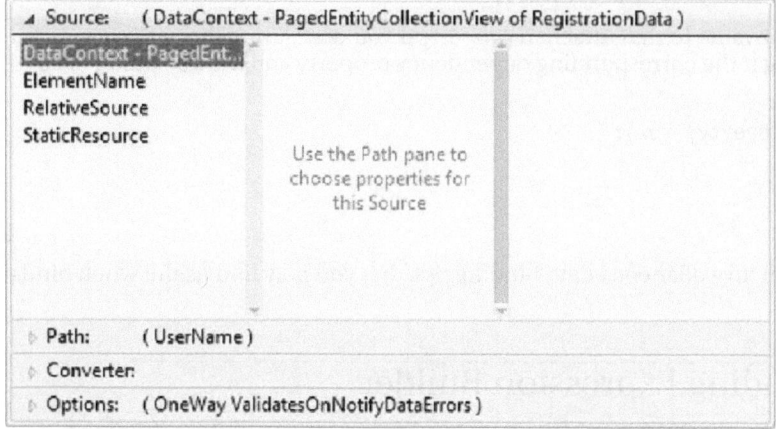

Figure 11-2. Selecting a data binding source

The next step is to select a path for the binding, as shown in Figure 11-3.

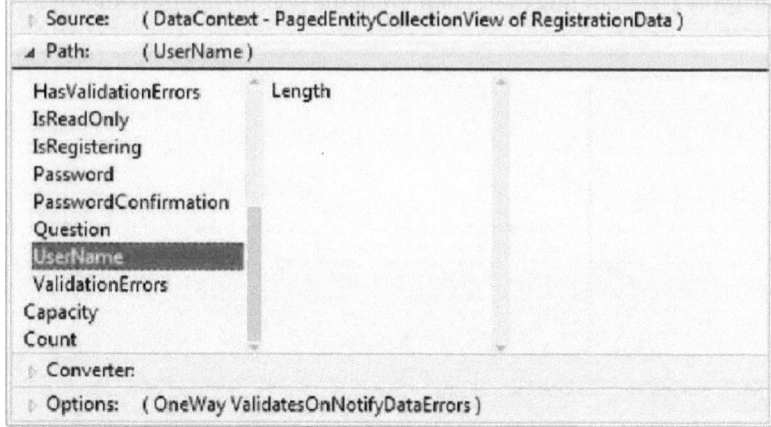

Figure 11-3. Selecting a path to bind to on the source

■ **Note** The properties of the binding source aren't displayed in the list shown in Figure 11-3 unless the builder actually knows what type of object is being bound to. As you can see from Figures 11-2 and 11-3, this builder knows that the binding source is a PagedEntityCollectionView that wraps a collection of RegistrationData objects. It knows this because the source of the data being inherited by the data context of the control being bound is the Data property of a DomainDataSource control, which uses the design-time data properties (discussed in Chapter 10) to define the type of data that the DomainDataSource control will return. Alternatively, if you are binding to a class that is defined and instantiated in the XAML file as a resource, the builder can also determine the properties available on the binding source to display here. If you are binding to another control in the view, again the builder will know what properties are available to bind to. However, in scenarios where it cannot determine what type of object the binding source is, which would be the case when you are assigning the data to bind to in the code behind but haven't used the design-time data properties to specify the type of the data that will be bound to, you won't be able to use the builder to select the source property to bind to unless you've provided design-time data definitions for the source data that will be bound to. The only alternative is to manually assign the data binding expression to the target property in the XAML.

If you wish, you can select a value converter for the binding to use, as shown in Figure 11-4.

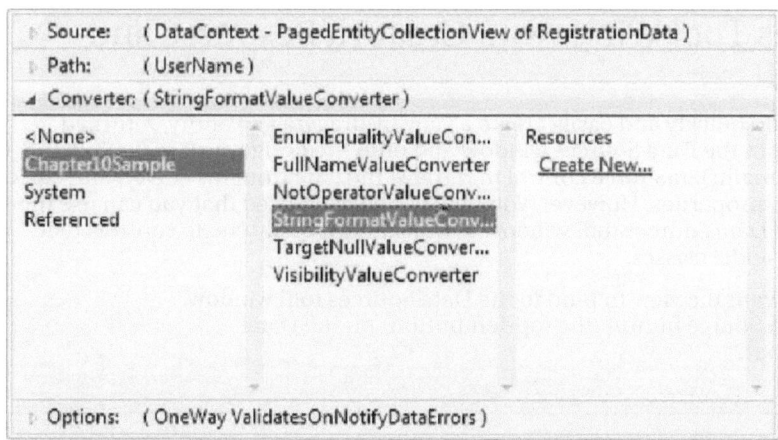

Figure 11-4. Selecting a value converter for the binding

■ **Note**   Once the converter has been created as a resource, which you can do by clicking the Create New button in the Resources list if there isn't one defined already, a parameter field will appear in the list where you can specify a parameter for the converter if you wish.

The final step is to select any additional options that should be applied to the binding, as shown in Figure 11-5.

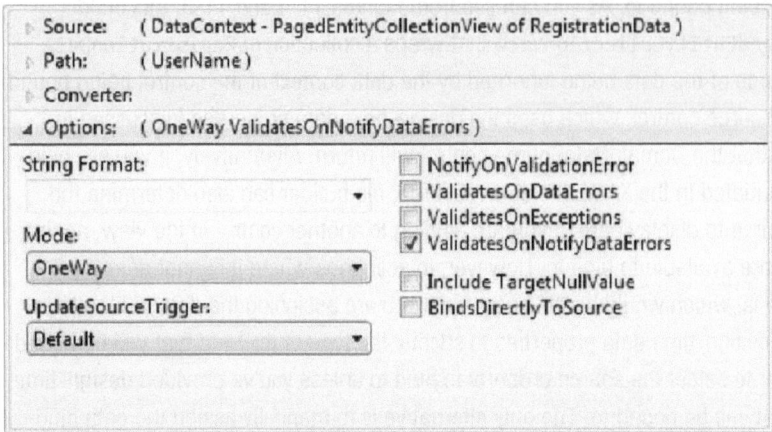

Figure 11-5. Selecting additional (miscellaneous) binding options

After selecting the options, simply clicking somewhere outside the data binding expression builder pop-up will close it and apply the generated binding string to the control property.

Using the Data Sources Tool Window to Create a Resource and Controls That Bind to It

In Chapter 5, you saw how you could quickly and easily create a view by dragging an entity, returned from the server via RIA Services, from the Data Sources window and onto the design surface, with that action automatically creating a DomainDataSource control to retrieve the data from the server, and controls to display and edit the entity's properties. However, you may not have realized that you can use the following steps to also leverage the Data Sources tool window to quickly and easily create controls that are bound to your ViewModels or model classes.

1. Add the class that you want the view to bind to the Data Sources tool window. Click the Add New Data Source button (the top-left button) on the Data Sources window's toolbar.

■ **Note** Ensure that your project is compiled first, as new classes don't appear in the list for selection.

---

2. In the dialog that appears, select Object as the data source type, and click Next.

3. Select the class that you want your view to bind to from the project tree, and click Finish. The class will now appear in the Data Sources tool window.

4. Select how you want the controls to be generated by clicking the little drop-down arrow that appears when you select the class in tree and selecting the type from the drop-down list. Usually, you will select either a DataGrid control or a Details layout. You can also change the types of controls generated by clicking the little drop-down arrow next to the fields (visible when the fields are selected), and selecting the control type from the drop-down list.

5. Now, drag the class from the Data Sources window, and drop it onto the view's design surface. Controls for each class property will be generated for you in the view and bound to a resource that has been defined in the view's resources.

You'll note that the resource that has been generated to which the controls are bound is actually a CollectionViewSource (discussed in detail in Chapter 6). For example, a class named TestData that's dropped onto the design surface will have the following resource created for it, which the controls then bind to:

```
<CollectionViewSource x:Key="testDataViewSource"
                      d:DesignSource="{d:DesignInstance my:TestData, CreateList=True}" />
```

As you learned in Chapter 6, a CollectionViewSource is used to create a collection view around a collection of objects. A design source has been assigned to it so that you can use the Visual Studio Data Binding Expression Builder to easily bind controls to it. You still need to set the source for the CollectionViewSource, and you'll find that the act of dragging the class from the Data Sources tool window onto the design surface has automatically added some commented out code to the view's Loaded event handler in the code behind, demonstrating how to do so:

```
private void UserControl_Loaded(object sender, RoutedEventArgs e)
{
    // Do not load your data at design time.
    // if (!System.ComponentModel.DesignerProperties.GetIsInDesignMode(this))
    // {
    //   //Load your data here and assign the result to the CollectionViewSource.
    //   System.Windows.Data.CollectionViewSource myCollectionViewSource =
    //           (System.Windows.Data.CollectionViewSource)
    //               this.Resources["Resource Key for CollectionViewSource"];
    //   myCollectionViewSource.Source = your data
    // }
}
```

Of course, the view may only bind to a single instance of your class (rather than a collection of objects), or you may want to bind your view to a collection of objects in some other way. If that's the case, you'll still find this technique very useful, because it allows you to create the controls in your view and set their bindings very quickly and easily. You simply need to change how the data context for these controls is assigned according to your needs.

Debugging Data Binding Issues

It is very easy to make a mistake when creating a binding, such as misspelling a property name in the path of the binding, or break a working binding when you refactor a class that acts as a binding source, such as renaming a property. At other times, bindings simply don't work in the way you would expect.

These types of data binding errors can be particularly hard to resolve at times, and it can be hard to even recognize that they exist because when bindings fail, they fail silently without throwing an exception in the application. There are, however, some techniques you can use to help you identify and track down data binding errors, which we'll take a look at here.

Viewing Data Binding Errors Logged to the Output Window

The first method you can use to see what data binding errors are occurring and why is to simply take a look at the Output window in Visual Studio. (Select View ➤ Output from the main menu if you can't find it.) Binding errors are automatically logged to the Output window when the application is being debugged, with a corresponding error message, the binding source object and property, and the binding target control and property. For example, setting the binding path to the Nam property (a misspelling, instead of Name) will result in the following error being logged to the Output window:

```
System.Windows.Data Error: BindingExpression path error: 'Nam' property not found on
'AdventureWorks.Models.Product' 'AdventureWorks.Models.Product' (HashCode=29083993).
BindingExpression: Path='Nam' DataItem='AdventureWorks.Models.Product' (HashCode=29083993);
target element is 'System.Windows.Controls.TextBox' (Name='NameTextBox'); target property is
'Text' (type 'System.String')..
```

This provides you with a fair amount of information about the error, which, in most cases, will help you track it down.

Unfortunately, in non-debugging scenarios, you cannot use this technique. An option is to assign a value to the FallbackValue property of the binding. Although it doesn't tell you *why* the binding failed, it can help prove that the binding *did* fail:

```
<TextBox Text="{Binding Name, Mode=TwoWay, FallbackValue=Binding failed!}" />
```

You could alternatively use the helper created by Karl Shifflett (creator of the XAML Power Toys, detailed in Chapter 7), called Glimpse. One of its features is displaying bindings that have no source. You can get more details about Glimpse and download it at
http://karlshifflett.wordpress.com/2009/06/08/glimpse-for-silverlight-viewing-exceptions-and-binding-errors/.

Putting Breakpoints on Data Bindings

The Silverlight 5 Tools introduce the ability to put breakpoints on bindings in your XAML, making it much easier to track down data binding issues. In Figure 11-6, you can see that a breakpoint has been applied to a binding that is failing, in the same way as you apply breakpoints in code, usually either by putting the cursor on the line and pressing F9, or by clicking in the left margin where the red breakpoint symbol is being shown.

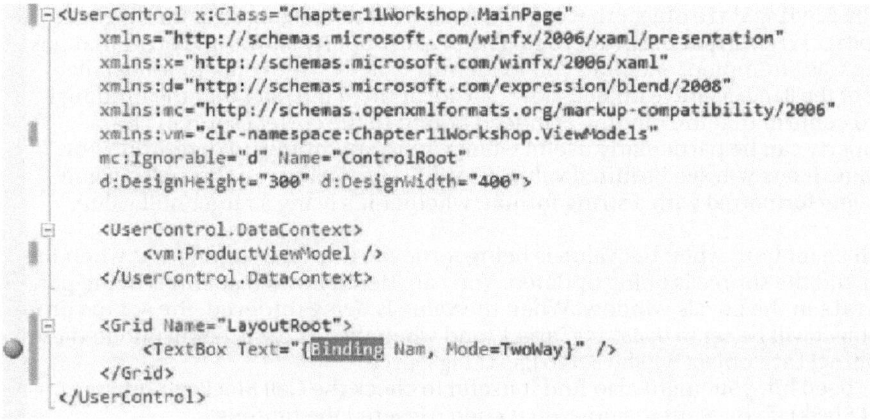

<UserControl x:Class="Chapter11Workshop.MainPage"
xmlns="http://schemas.microsoft.com/winfx/2006/xaml/presentation"
xmlns:x="http://schemas.microsoft.com/winfx/2006/xaml"
xmlns:d="http://schemas.microsoft.com/expression/blend/2008"
xmlns:mc="http://schemas.openxmlformats.org/markup-compatibility/2006"
xmlns:vm="clr-namespace:Chapter11Workshop.ViewModels"
mc:Ignorable="d" Name="ControlRoot"
d:DesignHeight="300" d:DesignWidth="400">
<UserControl.DataContext>
<vm:ProductViewModel />
</UserControl.DataContext>
<Grid Name="LayoutRoot">
<TextBox Text="{Binding Nam, Mode=TwoWay}" />
</Grid>
</UserControl>

Figure 11-6. Placing a breakpoint on a binding

■ **Note** You'll find that the XAML designer allows you to place breakpoints only on data bindings. It doesn't allow you to place them on any other type of XAML element. Note also that you can't have breakpoints on two bindings on the same line. If you have two bindings on the same element that you want to debug, put a line break between them so that each binding is on a different line.

When we now run the application, the breakpoint will be hit. Open up the Locals window (Debug ➤ Windows ➤ Locals) to interrogate the state of the binding. Figure 11-7 shows the Locals window when a breakpoint has been hit. As you can see, an error has occurred during the binding, with the `Nam` property not being found on the source object. We can use that information to determine that the binding path is misspelled and should instead be `Name`.

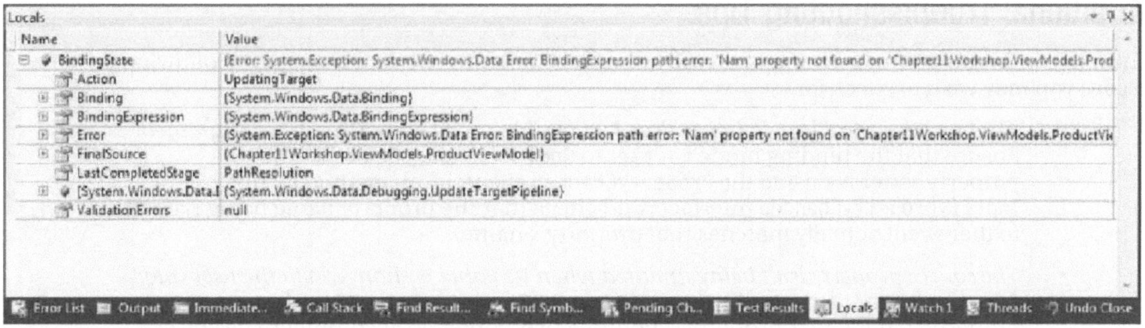

Locals
Name
Value
BindingState
Action
UpdatingTarget
Binding
{System.Windows.Data.Binding}
BindingExpression
{System.Windows.Data.BindingExpression}
Error
FinalSource
{Chapter11Workshop.ViewModels.ProductViewModel}
LastCompletedStage
PathResolution
{System.Windows.Data.Debugging.UpdateTargetPipeline}
ValidationErrors
null
Error List
Output
Immediate...
Call Stack
Find Result...
Find Symb...
Pending Ch...
Test Results
Locals
Watch 1
Threads
Undo Close

Figure 11-7. Interrogating the state of a binding

Three properties on the BindingState object that are very useful for debugging data bindings are the Error, FinalSource, and UpdateTargetPipeline properties. The Error property shows any error that has occurred when the binding was attempted, enabling you to identify exactly why a data binding failed. The FinalSource property of the BindingState object shows the location of the data that the binding is binding to, enabling you to confirm that the binding is indeed bound to the correct source. The UpdateTargetPipeline property can be particularly useful when you're attempting to determine how the binding got its final value. It lets you see its initial value, its value after being run through a value converter, its value after being formatted with a string format, whether it's using a target null value, and more.

Two-way bindings will be hit both when the value is being retrieved from the source, and when the target property is changed and the source is being updated. You can identify which action is being performed from the BindingState in the Locals window. When the value is being retrieved, the Action property of the BindingState object will be set to UpdatingTarget, and when the source is being updated the Action property of the BindingState object will be set to UpdatingSource.

After a breakpoint has been hit, you might also find it useful to check the Call Stack window (Debug ➤ Windows ➤ Call Stack) if you want to know what code triggered the binding.

It's also worth noting that breakpoints on bindings can have filters applied, conditions set, and other advanced configuration applied, just like standard breakpoints in code. Simply right-click the red breakpoint icon in the XAML editor's margin, and select the appropriate option from the context menu that appears.

You can disable binding breakpoints without removing them by setting the static IsDebuggingEnabled property on the Binding class to false:

```
Binding.IsDebuggingEnabled = false;
```

■ **Note** An alternative trick is to add a value converter to your binding and put a breakpoint in its Convert and ConvertBack methods. This was a common trick for debugging data bindings before the ability to put breakpoints on bindings was provided. Doing so will enable you to hook into the binding process and perhaps help you identify the issue that you are having with that binding.

Additional Troubleshooting Tips

Even if your bindings are hooked up correctly, they may fail for many other reasons. Following are a few issues you may wish to check for.

- *The bound control isn't being updated when the source property's value is updated.* Ensure that the binding mode isn't set to OneTime. Next, check that the property setter is raising the PropertyChanged event, implemented by the INotifyPropertyChanged interface, and check that the property name being passed to that event actually matches that property's name.

- *The source property isn't being updated when its value is changed via the user interface.* If you enter a new value into a control, such as a text box, but the source property that it's Text property is bound to isn't updated accordingly, start by ensuring that you've set the binding mode to TwoWay. Check that the setter for the property isn't set to private. Also, check that the UpdateSourceTrigger property of the binding isn't set to Explicit, and if it is, ensure that the UpdateSource method of the binding is called in the code behind.

- *Validation messages aren't appearing.* If a control isn't displaying any validation error messages, check that you've set the appropriate ValidatesOn property on the binding to true, where the ValidatesOn property that you need to set corresponds to the method your source object is using to publically report validation errors (i.e., ValidatesOnExceptions/ValidatesOnDataErrors/ValidatesOnNotifyData Errors). See the "Defining Validation Rules" section in Chapter 7 for more information.

- *Controls are not showing the right (or any) data.* Ensure that the data context for the binding is what you think it is and that a control further up the control hierarchy hasn't been assigned a different one, which is being inherited down the hierarchy instead.

Commands

Commands provide a means for encapsulating some logic, enabling that logic to be reused. One of the key benefits of commands, however, is that some controls allow you to bind to and execute them in XAML. In other words, not only can you bind to data in Silverlight but you can also bind to operations! For example, a ViewModel might expose a Save command, that a button in the View can bind to and execute when the button is clicked.

■ **Note** Commands are commonly used in conjunction with the MVVM design pattern to allow a ViewModel to expose operations to a View.

Creating a Command

To create a command class, it must implement the ICommand interface, as shown in Figure 13-6.

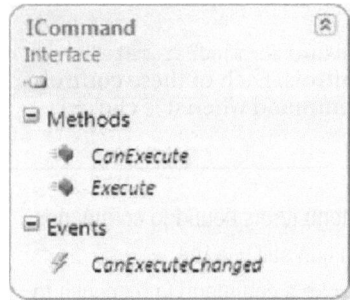

Figure 11-8. The ICommand interface

The CanExecute property specifies whether or not the command can be executed. When the command is bound to a button, the button will be enabled or disabled accordingly. In order for the button's enabled status to update when the property updates, the CanExecuteChanged event on the command should be raised. Any logic to be executed when the command is executed will go in the Execute method.

■ **Note** It's a common problem to forget to raise the CanExecuteChanged event after changing the value of the CanExecute property. If you find that your button is disabled despite having updated the value of the CanExecute property, this is most likely the source of the issue.

To create a command, create a new class and implement the ICommand interface. The following code demonstrates a simple command that will display a message box when it is executed:

```
using System;
using System.Windows;
using System.Windows.Input;

namespace Chapter11Sample
{
    public class TestCommand : ICommand
    {
        public bool CanExecute(object parameter)
        {
            return true;
        }

        public event EventHandler CanExecuteChanged;

        public void Execute(object parameter)
        {
            MessageBox.Show("Command executed!");
        }
    }
}
```

Binding to a Command

A number of controls in Silverlight have a pair of properties named Command and CommandParameter—namely the Button, HyperlinkButton, ToggleButton, and RepeatButton controls. Each of these controls can bind its Command property to a command and will execute the bound command when it is clicked.

■ **Note** The ContextMenu control from the Silverlight Toolkit can also have its menu items bound to commands. Unfortunately, no other controls have support for commands in Silverlight, but you can still use the InvokeCommandAction action from the Expression Blend Interactivity library to invoke a command in response to any event that a control raises (such as in response to an item in a ListBox control being selected).

The following code demonstrates creating the TestCommand command shown in the previous section as a resource and binding to it:

```
<UserControl x:Class="Chapter11Sample.MainPage"
    xmlns="http://schemas.microsoft.com/winfx/2006/xaml/presentation"
    xmlns:x="http://schemas.microsoft.com/winfx/2006/xaml"
    xmlns:local="clr-namespace:Chapter11Sample">

    <UserControl.Resources>
        <local:TestCommand x:Key="testCommand" />
    </UserControl.Resources>

    <Grid x:Name="LayoutRoot" Background="White">
        <Button Content="Test Command"
                Command="{Binding Source={StaticResource testCommand}}" />
    </Grid>
</UserControl>
```

Passing a Parameter to a Command

You may have noticed that the Execute method of the command has a parameter of type object. Any value that you assign or bind to the control's CommandParameter property will be passed into both the CanExecute method and the Execute method when the command is executed.

For example, you can bind this property to a property on another control (such as the SelectedItem property on a ListBox control), and the value of that control's property will be passed to the Execute method of the command as its parameter. The following XAML demonstrates this scenario:

```
<UserControl x:Class="Chapter11Sample.MainPage"
    xmlns="http://schemas.microsoft.com/winfx/2006/xaml/presentation"
    xmlns:x="http://schemas.microsoft.com/winfx/2006/xaml"
    xmlns:local="clr-namespace:Chapter11Sample">

    <UserControl.Resources>
        <local:TestCommand x:Key="testCommand" />
    </UserControl.Resources>

    <Grid x:Name="LayoutRoot" Background="White" Width="200" Height="300">
        <Grid.RowDefinitions>
            <RowDefinition Height="*" />
            <RowDefinition Height="40" />
        </Grid.RowDefinitions>

        <ListBox Name="ProductList" />

        <Button Content="Test Command" Grid.Row="1"
                Command="{Binding Source={StaticResource testCommand}}"
                CommandParameter="{Binding SelectedItem, ElementName=ProductList}" />
    </Grid>
</UserControl>
```

The DelegateCommand

You've seen how you can encapsulate a piece of logic within a command, but you may not always want to have to put commands in their own class. For example, you want to expose some logic from a View-Model class to a View as a command that can be bound to but retain the logic within the ViewModel class since it won't be used anywhere else in the application. In this scenario, you should consider implementing the command as a DelegateCommand. A DelegateCommand is an ICommand implementation that allows you to delegate the implementation of the command to a method in your ViewModel class. You can then expose the DelegateCommand object from your ViewModel class as a property, allowing you to easily expose operations from ViewModels as commands when using the MVVM design pattern. The following code is the source for the DelegateCommand class:

```
using System;
using System.Windows.Input;

namespace SimpleMVVM
{
    public class DelegateCommand : ICommand
    {
        private Func<object, bool> canExecute;
        private Action<object> executeAction;
        private bool canExecuteCache;

        public DelegateCommand(Action<object> executeAction, Func<object, bool> canExecute)
        {
            this.executeAction = executeAction;
            this.canExecute = canExecute;
        }

        #region ICommand Members
        public bool CanExecute(object parameter)
        {
            bool temp = canExecute(parameter);

            if (canExecuteCache != temp)
            {
                canExecuteCache = temp;
                if (CanExecuteChanged != null)
                {
                    CanExecuteChanged(this, new EventArgs());
                }
            }

            return canExecuteCache;
        }

        public event EventHandler CanExecuteChanged;

        public void Execute(object parameter)
        {
            executeAction(parameter);
        }
```

```
        #endregion
    }
}
```

In your ViewModel class, you will need to define two methods: one returning a Boolean value indicating whether the command can be executed, and the other that will be called when the command is actually executed. If we were to implement the TestCommand command demonstrated earlier as a DelegateCommand, you'd start by adding the following two methods to your ViewModel class:

```
private bool CanTest(object param)
{
    return true;
}

public void Test(object param)
{
    MessageBox.Show("Command executed!");
}
```

■ **Note** When you implement methods in a ViewModel class to be wrapped in a DelegateCommand like this, the methods must conform to the same signature demonstrated here (i.e., have the same parameters and return types).

The next step is to create an instance of the DelegateCommand class, passing the two methods to its constructor, and returning the resulting object as a property from your ViewModel class:

```
public ICommand TestCommand
{
  get { return new DelegateCommand(Test, CanTest); }
}
```

A Button control in the View can have its Command property bound to the TestCommand property on the ViewModel. When the button is clicked, the command will be executed, resulting in it calling the Test method in the ViewModel.

■ **Note** Another popular alternative to the DelegateCommand is the RelayCommand. An implementation of the RelayCommand command can be obtained from the MVVM Light Toolkit (one of the popular MVVM frameworks for Silverlight, which you will find listed in the "Frameworks section" in Chapter 13).

Summary

This chapter has provided several advanced tips and techniques that you can use when binding to data. One of Silverlight's greatest strengths when it comes to building business applications is its powerful data binding engine, and being aware of all its nooks and crannies, which we've probed in this chapter, can help you to get the most out of it. Some of these tips you will use regularly, and others somewhat rarely, but either way, having them in your toolkit will greatly add to your ability to solve difficult problems in implementing your Silverlight business applications.

CHAPTER 12

Creating User Controls and Custom Controls

When designing user interfaces in any technology, you ideally want to encapsulate the look and behavior of commonly used user interface elements into reusable components that you can use elsewhere in your application, or even in other applications. Creating custom controls also reduces the amount of code required in the code-behind, simplifies the XAML in your views, and helps maintain consistency in your user interface.

We already have a wide range of controls available to use from the core Silverlight control set, the Silverlight Toolkit, and open source controls on CodePlex. In addition, there are many more in the form of third-party controls from companies such as Telerik, ComponentOne, DevExpress, and Infragistics. Occasionally, however, you will find that you have specific requirements that no existing control currently provides. It's at this point that you should consider creating your own control.

There are two ways to create a reusable user interface component in Silverlight as a user control, or as a custom control. Generally, user controls simply combine multiple existing controls into a single component, while you will usually start from scratch with custom controls and provide the look and behavior yourself. In this chapter, we will look at creating and using both of these types of components. Some implementation details, such as exposing properties and events, are much the same between the two types of components, but other details and capabilities can differ greatly, particularly when it comes to styling and templating. However, let's start by simply extending an existing control to add additional behavior to it, before continuing on to focusing on how to create and use user controls and custom controls.

Adding Functionality to an Existing Control

If you simply want to add behavior to an existing control you can inherit from that control, rather than create a whole new control from scratch. For example, let's say you want the text in a TextBox control to automatically be selected when the control gains the focus, enabling the user to easily overwrite the existing text, instead of the default behavior in which the cursor is simply placed at the end of the existing text.

You have two main options you could use to achieve this behavior:

1. Create an action (as described in Chapter 10) that is triggered when the control gets the focus and selects the text as required. (Alternatively, you could create a behavior instead.) You can then apply that action to each control that should implement that behavior. However, this requires the designer/developer to remember to do so, and adds to the verbosity of the XAML in your views.

2. If the behavior is commonly implemented by the control throughout your pro-
    ject, you might like to create a class that inherits from the control, add the be-
    havior to it, and use the inherited control in its place.

Using our example of a TextBox that automatically selects all the text when it receives the focus, we can create a new class called CustomTextBox inherit from TextBox, and add the behavior:

```
public class CustomTextBox : TextBox
{
    protected override void OnGotFocus(RoutedEventArgs e)
    {
        base.OnGotFocus(e);
        this.SelectAll();
    }
}
```

By default, the new control (CustomTextBox) will continue to use the default control template that the control it inherits from uses (TextBox). So our CustomTextBox control will continue to use the TextBox's default control template. If you want to use a different default control template, simply assign the control's type to the DefaultStyleKey property in its constructor, as shown in the following code:

```
DefaultStyleKey = typeof(CustomTextBox);
```

You then need to define a corresponding style resource containing the control template in the Generic.xaml file, pointing both the style resource's TargetType property and the control template's TargetType property to the type assigned to the control's DefaultStyleKey property, like so:

```
<ResourceDictionary
    xmlns="http://schemas.microsoft.com/winfx/2006/xaml/presentation"
    xmlns:x="http://schemas.microsoft.com/winfx/2006/xaml"
    xmlns:local="clr-namespace:MyControlLibrary">

    <Style TargetType="local:CustomTextBox">
        <Setter Property="Template">
            <Setter.Value>
                <ControlTemplate TargetType="local:CustomTextBox">
                    <!-- Template goes here -->
                </ControlTemplate>
            </Setter.Value>
        </Setter>
    </Style>
</ResourceDictionary>
```

The control will automatically look for a style resource defined in the Generic.xaml file with a target type matching the type assigned to its DefaultStyleKey property, and use that as its default control
template.

■ **Note** A number of primitive controls don't appear in the Toolbox, but you might wish to inherit from them.
These primitive controls form the base of many other controls. For example, the Selector primitive control forms
the base for the ListBox and the ComboBox controls. You will find these primitive controls in the
System.Windows.Controls.Primitives namespace with controls including ButtonBase, Popup, RangeBase,
RepeatButton, ScrollBar, Selector, Thumb, and ToggleButton.

Creating User Controls

User controls enable you to build a user interface component that leverages one or more existing controls, combining them to form a single unit. Creating a user control is as simple as adding a new Silverlight User Control item to your project and adding controls to it using the XAML designer, designing it as you would a view. In fact, as you discovered back in Chapter 3, the MainPage class itself is a user control. Your user control then appears in the Toolbox, where you can drag and drop it into your views as required. You can write logic in the code-behind for the user control, and you can also define properties and events that can be used by the views that consume the user control.

✱ Workshop: Creating a Simple User Control

Let's create a simple user control that includes a label and a text box together as a single component.

1. Add a new item to the Controls folder in your AdventureWorks project, using the Silverlight User Control item template, and name it FormField.xaml

2. Declare the sdk namespace prefix in the root element of your XAML file:

```
xmlns:sdk="http://schemas.microsoft.com/winfx/2006/xaml/presentation/sdk"
```

3. Lay it out with a Label control and a TextBox control in a Grid, like so:

```
<Grid x:Name="LayoutRoot" Background="White">
    <Grid.ColumnDefinitions>
        <ColumnDefinition Width="Auto" />
        <ColumnDefinition Width="*" />
    </Grid.ColumnDefinitions>

    <sdk:Label Name="dataLabel" Padding="0,0,5,0" HorizontalAlignment="Right"
            Target="{Binding ElementName=dataField}" />

    <TextBox Name="dataField" Grid.Column="1"
            HorizontalAlignment="Stretch" VerticalAlignment="Center" />
</Grid>
```

4. If you set the design size of the user control to d:DesignWidth = 300, d:DesignHeight = 30, the control in the designer should be as shown in Figure 12-1.

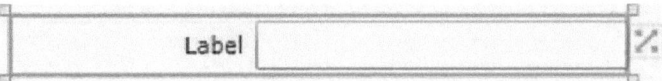

Figure 12-1. *The FormField control in the XAML designer*

The full XAML for the user control is as follows:

```
<UserControl x:Class="AdventureWorks.Controls.FormField"
    xmlns="http://schemas.microsoft.com/winfx/2006/xaml/presentation"
    xmlns:x="http://schemas.microsoft.com/winfx/2006/xaml"
    xmlns:d="http://schemas.microsoft.com/expression/blend/2008"
    xmlns:mc="http://schemas.openxmlformats.org/markup-compatibility/2006"
```

```
    xmlns:sdk="http://schemas.microsoft.com/winfx/2006/xaml/presentation/sdk"
    mc:Ignorable="d"
    d:DesignHeight="30" d:DesignWidth="300">

    <Grid x:Name="LayoutRoot" Background="White">
        <Grid.ColumnDefinitions>
            <ColumnDefinition Width="120" />
            <ColumnDefinition Width="*" />
        </Grid.ColumnDefinitions>

        <sdk:Label Name="dataLabel" Padding="0,0,5,0"
                   HorizontalAlignment="Right"
                   Target="{Binding ElementName=dataField}" />

        <TextBox Name="dataField" Grid.Column="1"
                 HorizontalAlignment="Stretch" VerticalAlignment="Center" />
    </Grid>
</UserControl>
```

5. Compile your project (this is necessary in order for your user control to appear in the Toolbox).

6. Add a new view to the Views folder in your project, named TestControlsView.xaml.

7. Open this view in the designer. You will find that your FormField user control appears in the Toolbox. You can now drag it from the Toolbox and onto the design surface of the TestControlsView view, just as you would any other control. Note that you can't set the label, nor get/set the text in the TextBox as yet, as we haven't exposed properties from the control enabling this as yet. We'll do that in the next workshop.

■ **Note** The MoXAML Power Toys described back in Chapter 10, provides a feature with which you can select some XAML from the XAML view in the designer and extract it to a user control. This can help you refactor elements of your views into a separate reusable user control. This functionality is built into Expression Blend; select the elements in the designer, right-click, and select Make Control from the context menu.

Exposing Properties Overview

For simple user controls that might simply display a static layout, such as some text, or consume and display some data via their DataContext property, you might not need to add any additional functionality to the control to allow the view consuming the control to interact with it. However, this sort of scenario will only apply to the simplest of controls, and your control will usually need to expose properties, methods, and events to the view that is consuming it.

When you dropped the FormField control (created in the previous workshop) onto the design surface of your view, there was no way to get/set the text in the label or text box. You can enable this by exposing some corresponding properties from the user control: Label and Value. The label will display the string assigned to the Label property, and the text box will display the value assigned to the Value property.

There are two ways to expose a property from a user control:

- As a standard property
- As a dependency property

Both of these are implemented quite differently, and you need to choose the right one based upon how you expect it to be used. Until now, we've avoided talking about dependency properties in depth, but you will find yourself needing them quite often when writing custom controls. We'll look at these in a bit, but first let's look at the somewhat simpler task of implementing standard properties.

Using Standard Properties

You know how to create standard CLR properties, and there's nothing difficult involved. However, when adding properties to a user control, you can choose whether their values will be "pushed" into the control's presentation layer, or whether the control's presentation layer will "pull" (consume) those property's values.

Throughout this book, we've discussed the push and pull mechanisms for populating views with data. Using the push-based model, the code supporting the views needs to know about and have access to the view and its contents. By implementing a pull-based model, taking advantage of XAML's powerful binding features, you enable the code to take a back seat, and simply act as a provider to the view. The view can then take charge of how it's populated, providing a cleaner model where the code-behind simply serves the needs of the view, without actually needing to know anything about the view itself. This concept also applies to creating controls, and is especially applicable to creating custom controls, as you'll discover later in this chapter, in which there is a wider separation between the XAML and the code than for user controls.

Let's take a look at implementing both the "push" and the "pull" methods in a user control.

■ **Note** Although your initial urge will probably be to push the data into the control from the code-behind, implementing the pull model will enable a cleaner separation of presentation from behavior and improve the testability of the control.

Properties That Push Their Values into the User Control's Presentation Layer

When creating a standard property on your user control, your initial urge might be to simply push the value into the control from the property's setter. With user controls, this approach probably makes sense, as user controls have little in the way of a clean separation of presentation from behavior. For example, you might implement the Label and Value properties for the FormField control like so:

```
public string Label
{
    get { return dataLabel.Content.ToString(); }
    set { dataLabel.Content = value; }
}

public string Value
```

```
{
    get { return dataField.Text; }
    set { dataField.Text = value; }
}
```

As you can see, the code-behind is in charge of getting/setting the appropriate control property values in the user control. This works quite satisfactorily, but tightly couples the control's presentation and logic. It may be acceptable to do this in user controls, but when it comes to creating custom controls, which we'll look at later in this chapter, doing so is not generally a good idea. Let's now look at the alternative method, in which the presentation layer consumes the property values instead.

Properties That Are Consumable from the Presentation Layer

We can turn things around, however, and put the presentation in charge of consuming the values of the properties. We simply need to maintain the values of the properties in the code-behind, and notify the presentation layer when their values have changed. The presentation layer will simply bind to these properties.

 Workshop: Implementing Standard Properties

In Chapter 7, we discussed how standard properties do not automatically notify bindings when their value has changed. Instead, you need to raise the PropertyChanged event when the property values are updated, which requires the entity/object to implement the INotifyPropertyChanged interface As you will recall, implementing the INotifyPropertyChanged interface enables control property bindings to be aware that the source property's value has changed, and to update the property on the control accordingly.

Likewise, when writing a user control whose presentation layer will bind to its properties, it should implement the INotifyPropertyChanged interface, and any standard property you create on your user control should raise the PropertyChanged event in its setter. Let's implement the Label and Value properties on our control now in this fashion:

1. Add the following using statement for the System.ComponentModel namespace to the FormField control's code-behind:

```
using System.ComponentModel;
```

2. Implement the INotifyPropertyChanged interface on the control:

```
public partial class FormField : UserControl, INotifyPropertyChanged
{
    public FormField()
    {
        InitializeComponent();
    }

    public event PropertyChangedEventHandler PropertyChanged;

    protected void OnPropertyChanged(string propertyName)
    {
        if (PropertyChanged != null)
            PropertyChanged(this,
```

```
                    new PropertyChangedEventArgs(propertyName));
    }
}
```

3. Create the properties, and raise the PropertyChanged event in their setters:

```
private string _label = "";
private string _value = "";

public string Label
{
    get { return _label; }
    set
    {
        _label = value;
        OnPropertyChanged("Label");
    }
}

public string Value
{
    get { return _value; }
    set
    {
        _value = value;
        OnPropertyChanged("Value");
    }
}
```

The code-behind for the FormField user control should now be as follows:

```
using System.ComponentModel;
using System.Windows.Controls;

namespace AdventureWorks.Controls
{
    public partial class FormField : UserControl, INotifyPropertyChanged
    {
        public FormField()
        {
            InitializeComponent();
        }

        private string _label = "";
        private string _value = "";

        public string Label
        {
            get { return _label; }
            set
            {
                _label = value;
                OnPropertyChanged("Label");
            }
        }
```

```
        public string Value
        {
            get { return _value; }
            set
            {
                _value = value;
                OnPropertyChanged("Value");
            }
        }

        public event PropertyChangedEventHandler PropertyChanged;

        protected void OnPropertyChanged(string propertyName)
        {
            if (PropertyChanged != null)
                PropertyChanged(this,
                            new PropertyChangedEventArgs(propertyName));
        }
    }
}
```

If you compile your project and return to the TestControlsView.xaml file, you will find that these two properties appear in the XAML IntelliSense and in the Properties window for the control, enabling you to get and set their values. Of course, they don't actually do anything as yet, because the presentation layer for the control isn't bound to them yet. Let's do that now.

 ## Workshop: Consuming the Properties in the Presentation Layer

We have a Label property and a Value property on our FormField control, enabling the view hosting the control to set the label of the control, and get or set the control's value (that is, the text in the text box). However, there is still a missing piece. We also need to connect the control's presentation layer to these properties, and consume their values. We need to bind the Content property of the Label control to the Label property, and the Text property of the TextBox control to the Value property. To do so, we need to use the techniques described in Chapter 11 (see the section "Binding to a Property in the View's Code-Behind").

1. In the XAML for the FormField control, bind the user control's DataContext property to the user control itself:

```
DataContext="{Binding RelativeSource={RelativeSource Self}}"
```

2. Bind the Content property of the Label control to the Label property you created on the user control:

```
<sdk:Label Name="dataLabel" Padding="0,0,5,0" HorizontalAlignment="Right"
        Content="{Binding Label}"
        Target="{Binding ElementName=dataField}" />
```

3. Next, bind the Text property of the TextBox control to the Value property you created on the user control:

```
<TextBox Name="dataField" Grid.Column="1"
        Text="{Binding Value, Mode=TwoWay}"
        HorizontalAlignment="Stretch" VerticalAlignment="Center" />
```

The complete XAML for the user control is now as follows:

```
<UserControl x:Class="AdventureWorks.Controls.FormField"
    xmlns="http://schemas.microsoft.com/winfx/2006/xaml/presentation"
    xmlns:x="http://schemas.microsoft.com/winfx/2006/xaml"
    xmlns:d="http://schemas.microsoft.com/expression/blend/2008"
    xmlns:mc="http://schemas.openxmlformats.org/markup-compatibility/2006"
    xmlns:sdk="http://schemas.microsoft.com/winfx/2006/xaml/presentation/sdk"
    mc:Ignorable="d"
    d:DesignHeight="30" d:DesignWidth="300"
    DataContext="{Binding RelativeSource={RelativeSource Self}}">

    <Grid x:Name="LayoutRoot" Background="White">
        <Grid.ColumnDefinitions>
            <ColumnDefinition Width="120" />
            <ColumnDefinition Width="*" />
        </Grid.ColumnDefinitions>

        <sdk:Label Name="dataLabel" Padding="0,0,5,0"
                HorizontalAlignment="Right"
                Content="{Binding Label}"
                Target="{Binding ElementName=dataField}" />

        <TextBox Name="dataField" Grid.Column="1"
                Text="{Binding Value, Mode=TwoWay}"
                HorizontalAlignment="Stretch" VerticalAlignment="Center" />
    </Grid>
</UserControl>
```

▦ **Note** The way you bind to the properties in the code for a user control is quite different than the way you do so with custom controls, as you will see later in this chapter.

Assigning the Properties Values in a View That Hosts the User Control

When you drop the FormField control onto a view, you can now assign values to its Label and Value properties, and the control will update its appearance in the XAML designer accordingly:

```
<my:FormField Label="First Name:" Value="Chris" Width="350" />
```

However, you're most likely going to want to bind the FormField control's Value property to some data:

```
<my:FormField Label="Test:" Value="{Binding FirstName}" Width="350" />
```

If you attempt to do so, though, you will find that an exception is thrown when you run the application. This is because standard properties cannot accept markup expressions, such as a binding, as their value. To accept a markup extension as its value, a property needs to be a *dependency property*. As this is a fairly normal requirement for properties on controls, it's probably time that we finally take a look at dependency properties in depth.

Using Dependency Properties

When WPF was in development, the team decided that standard CLR properties didn't fully meet the requirements for the new presentation technology they were developing. The standard properties didn't automatically notify any associated bindings when their value was changed, because you needed to implement the INotifyPropertyChanged interface to do so, and more importantly, they needed properties that could self-compute or resolve their value based on a number of external sources, such as a markup extension or value precedence criteria. To achieve these requirements, the WPF team came up with the concept of *dependency properties*, which have also been adapted to Silverlight, albeit in a slightly limited capacity.

■ **Note** They are named *dependency* properties because the property's value *depends* on external sources, such as a data binding or a resource.

Why We Need Dependency Properties

Dependency properties are possibly one of the most complex aspects of Silverlight to get your head around, but they are also a fundamental concept that you should understand, even if you aren't planning on creating your own custom controls.

Implementing standard properties on your controls may be acceptable for some properties, but as soon as you need to assign a markup expression to one, you will find that doing so throws an exception when you run your application. You might recall from Chapter 2 that any property you assign a markup extension, such as a data binding expression, *must* be a dependency property. Markup expressions are evaluated at runtime, so the property needs to recognize that it has been assigned a markup expression and evaluate it.

Assigning a markup extension to a standard property will result in an exception as the XAML engine tries but fails to convert the markup extension to the property's type, such as a string, integer, or Boolean. Dependency properties solve this problem by being able to accept markup extensions as values, and evaluate them at runtime to determine what value the property should use. This is one of the more common scenarios in which dependency properties are required. Another reason is that a property might have multiple sources of values that it should use, such as a style, animation, template, or binding, and it needs to be able to determine which value it should actually use. Dependency properties can accept all these values, and choose which value to use according to value precedence criteria.

■ **Note** Many Silverlight and WPF developers overuse dependency properties, mostly because they don't understand when they should and shouldn't be used. As a general rule, you will need to implement dependency properties only on custom controls. If you want to simply notify any bindings bound to a property that its value has changed, you are usually better off creating it as a standard property, implementing the INotifyPropertyChanged interface on the class and raising the PropertyChanged event in the property's setter instead.

Registering a Dependency Property

To declare a dependency property on a class, the first thing you need to ensure is that the class inherits from the `DependencyObject` class. The unique features of dependency properties are actually provided by this class and, thus, your control needs to inherit from it to enable them. As it is, the classes you will inherit from your control, such as `UserControl`, `Control`, and `ContentControl`, have already inherited from the `DependencyObject` class, usually a few generations back, and you should rarely need to inherit from the `DependencyObject` class directly.

The next step is to register your dependency property with the dependency system, using the `DependencyProperty.Register` method, as demonstrated here:

```
public static readonly DependencyProperty ValueProperty =
    DependencyProperty.Register("Value", typeof(string), typeof(FormField), null);
```

As you can see, this looks nothing like a standard CLR property definition. This syntax is rather complicated when you first look at it, so let's break it down into its component parts so that we can make some more sense of it. In this example, we are registering a dependency property named `Value` on the class. Let's look at the first part:

```
public static readonly DependencyProperty ValueProperty;
```

As you can see, we are declaring a field, known as a *dependency property identifier,* of type `DependencyProperty`, which we are naming `ValueProperty`. This field will be used to reference the property when getting and setting its value. The convention when declaring dependency properties is to suffix the dependency property identifier's name with "Property." So for a dependency property named `Value`, you should have a corresponding dependency property identifier named `ValueProperty`. Note that this field is marked `public`, `static`, and `readonly`, which is required for dependency property declarations.

Let's now take a look at what is being assigned to the `ValueProperty` dependency property identifier:

```
DependencyProperty.Register("Value", typeof(string), typeof(FormField), null);
```

The static `Register` method on the `DependencyProperty` class registers the dependency property with the dependency system, returning a `DependencyProperty` object that we then assign to `ValueProperty`. To this method we are passing (in order):

- *The name of the dependency property*: `"Value"`

- *The dependency property's type*: `typeof(string)`

- *The type of the class hosting the dependency property (i.e., the name of the user control)*: `typeof(FormField)`

- *Property metadata, in the form of a PropertyMetadata object*: In our example, we are simply passing that parameter a value of `null`. (Property metadata will be discussed further shortly.)

Getting and Setting a Dependency Property Value

You might be wondering how this property actually works, since it's declared as a `static readonly` field. It *doesn't* actually store the value of the property; the `DependencyObject` object stores and calculates it instead. When you register a dependency property with the dependency system, you pass the `Register` method the type of class to host it (the third parameter, `typeof(FormField)`). The dependency system registers the dependency property with the dependency object, which maintains the value of each dependency property in a `Dictionary`.

To actually get or set the value of the dependency property, you need to use the GetValue or SetValue method provided by the DependencyObject class passing it the dependency property identifier to get or set the corresponding value for.

For example, to get the value of the ValueProperty dependency property, you would use the following code:

```
string value = GetValue(ValueProperty).ToString();
```

■ **Note** The GetValue method returns the value as an object, and you therefore need to cast it to the required type.

And to set the value of the ValueProperty dependency property, you would use the following code, where value is a variable containing the value to assign to the dependency property:

```
SetValue(ValueProperty, value);
```

■ **Note** The GetValue and SetValue methods inherited from the DependencyObject class are public methods and, thus, can be called from both within and outside of the class.

Creating a Standard CLR Property Wrapper

Whether you want to get or set the value of a dependency property from inside or outside the confines of the class, calling the GetValue and SetValue methods on the class is hardly the friendliest means of accessing the property. They're certainly not as friendly as working with standard CLR properties. That's why you will generally see a corresponding (and somewhat friendlier) standard CLR property wrapping these methods for each dependency property on a class, like so:

```
public string Value
{
    get { return (string)GetValue(ValueProperty); }
    set { SetValue(ValueProperty, value); }
}
```

■ **Note** The XAML parser expects these CLR properties for dependency properties that you want to assign values to in XAML, even if it doesn't always use them, as will be explained shortly. You should use the same name for the standard CLR property as the name that you registered the dependency property with.

Therefore, to assign a value to the dependency property, you can use

```
valueField.Value = newValue;
```

instead of

```
valueField.SetValue(FormField.ValueProperty, newValue);
```

And to obtain the value of a dependency property, you can use

```
currentValue = valueField.Value;
```

instead of

```
currentValue = valueField.GetValue(FormField.ValueProperty).ToString();
```

■ **Note** There is no need to raise the `PropertyChanged` event from the `INotifyPropertyChanged` interface in your CLR property wrapper when the value of the dependency property is updated. As previously stated, one of the benefits of dependency properties is that they automatically support value change notifications, so there is no need to raise this event when the property is a dependency property.

There is a *very* important point to note when creating standard CLR property wrappers for your dependency properties: you should *never* add any logic to the getters or setters of these properties as there is no guarantee that this logic will be executed. For example, when you assign a markup extension to a dependency property in XAML, the CLR property wrapper getter and setter are not called. Instead, the runtime interacts directly with the dependency property, via the `GetValue` and `SetValue` methods on the class, without the involvement of the standard CLR property wrapper. If you need to perform some logic when the value of the property is modified, you should provide a method to call when the property's value is modified in the dependency property's metadata. You can then add your logic to that method, as described in the next section.

Dependency Property Metadata

In our earlier example, we kept things simple when demonstrating how to register a dependency property, and simply passed `null` to the `DependencyProperty.Register` method's `PropertyMetadata` parameter. In Silverlight, you can configure the following metadata for the dependency property:

- A default value for the property
- A callback method that will be called when the value of the dependency property is modified

These are assigned to a `PropertyMetadata` object which is then passed to the `DependencyProperty.Register` method. The constructor of the `PropertyMetadata` class has a number of overloads, enabling you to use either or both of these values. For the purpose of these examples, we'll just look at the overloads in which each metadata item is passed alone to the constructor.

As a general rule, you shouldn't set the default value of a dependency property in the control's constructor. Instead, you can provide a default value for a dependency property by assigning it in the property's metadata. The following code demonstrates setting a default value of `"default"` to the property via the `PropertyMetadata`'s constructor, as a parameter:

```
public static readonly DependencyProperty ValueProperty =
    DependencyProperty.Register("MyProperty", typeof(string), typeof(FormField),
                            new PropertyMetadata("default"));
```

■ **Note** When creating custom controls (discussed later in this chapter), another alternative means of setting the default value of the dependency property is to assign it a value in the style for the control in the Generic.xaml file.

To be notified when the value of the dependency property has changed, pass a callback method to the PropertyMetadata's constructor, like so:

```
public static readonly DependencyProperty ValueProperty =
    DependencyProperty.Register("Value", typeof(string), typeof(FormField),
            new PropertyMetadata(ValuePropertyChanged));
```

Also define a corresponding method to be called:

```
private static void ValuePropertyChanged(DependencyObject d,
                                        DependencyPropertyChangedEventArgs e)
{
    // Insert value changed logic here
}
```

As you can see, two parameters are passed into this method:

- d: The instance of the object for whom the property's value has changed

- e: A DependencyPropertyChangedEventArgs object containing additional information about the value modification

The DependencyPropertyChangedEventArgs object has three properties: NewValue, OldValue, and Property. The NewValue and OldValue properties are fairly self-explanatory, and the Property property passes the identifier of the dependency property whose value has changed.

■ **Note** You might have noticed that this method is static. Therefore, rather than executing the value changed logic in this method, where you have to qualify any member, property, or method access with the object instance passed into the method, it may be worthwhile to call a nonstatic method on the object instance from this method that implements the logic instead.

If you want to obtain the default value of a dependency property, you can get it from the metadata using the GetMetadata method on the dependency property identifier, and passing it the type of the control hosting it. For example:

```
PropertyMetadata metadata = ValueProperty.GetMetadata(typeof(FormField));
string defaultValue = metadata.DefaultValue.ToString();
```

Value Precedence

As discussed earlier, the core nature of a dependency property is that its value depends on a number of external sources, and these sources may each have a different value. Therefore, the dependency property needs to determine its value by placing an order of importance on each source, and using the one with the highest importance that also has a value. This order of importance is known as *value precedence* and is ordered as follows, from highest importance to lowest:

1. *Animation*: If an animation provides the dependency property with a value, it takes precedence over all sources.

2. *Local value*: A specific value has been assigned to a dependency property.

3. *Template*: A control template has been applied to the control and assigns the dependency property a value.

4. *Style*: A style has been applied to the control and assigns the dependency property a value.

5. *Default value*: If none of the preceding sources provide the dependency property with a value, its default value will prevail.

Simplifying Creation of Dependency Properties

As you can see from this discussion about dependency properties, a reasonable amount of code is required to create a dependency property, and initially, attempting to create them can be quite daunting. There is help at hand, however, in the form of property snippets. Visual Studio has the `propdp` snippet that you can use, although it was designed for use with WPF. The only difference is that you need to change the `PropertyMetadata` parameter of the `Register` method from `UIPropertyMetadata` to `PropertyMetadata`. If you're not comfortable with this, you can modify the snippet yourself, or you can download and use the Silverlight-specific snippets created by Robby Ingebretsen at `http://nerdplusart.com/silverlight-code-snippets`. You can use the `sldp` snippet or the `sldpc` snippet from his snippet library in place of the `propdp` snippet. A number of additional Silverlight-specific snippets are included in the library that you might also find useful, such as `slvc` for creating a value converter, and `slevent` for creating an event.

 Workshop: Creating a Dependency Property

You now know enough about dependency properties to try creating one yourself. Let's replace the standard properties on our `FormField` control from the previous workshop with dependency properties instead.

1. Remove the `INotifyPropertyChanged` implementation from the user control's code-behind, along with the `Label` and `Value` properties you previously created. You should be left with this code in the class:

```
using System.Windows.Controls;

namespace AdventureWorks.Controls
{
    public partial class FormField : UserControl
    {
        public FormField()
```

```
        {
            InitializeComponent();
        }
    }
}
```

2. Add the following using statement to the top of the file:

```
using System.Windows;
```

3. Let's re-create the Label property as a dependency property. Below the constructor, type propdp, and press TAB twice. The snippet of code shown in Figure 12-2 will be inserted in its place. This snippet provides the structure required for a dependency property, simply requiring you to fill in the "blanks."

```
public int MyProperty
{
    get { return (int)GetValue(MyPropertyProperty); }
    set { SetValue(MyPropertyProperty, value); }
}

// Using a DependencyProperty as the backing store for MyProperty.  This enables animation, styling, binding, etc...
public static readonly DependencyProperty MyPropertyProperty =
    DependencyProperty.Register("MyProperty", typeof(int), typeof(ownerclass), new UIPropertyMetadata(0));
```

Figure 12-2. The code inserted into a class using the propdp snippet

4. The Label property stores and returns a string, so type in string, overwriting the selected text of int, and press TAB.

5. Enter the name of the property (Label), and press TAB.

6. Enter the name of the class this dependency property is being added to. (In this case, enter FormField.)

7. Press ESC to leave the replacement mode for the snippet.

8. Remove the comment (it serves no value), and set the PropertyMetadata parameter of the Register method to null instead of new UIPropertyMetadata(0).

9. Now perform the same steps for the Value property. Your final code should look like this:

```
using System.Windows;
using System.Windows.Controls;

namespace AdventureWorks.Controls
{
    public partial class FormField : UserControl
    {
        public FormField()
        {
            InitializeComponent();
        }

        public string Label
        {
            get { return (string)GetValue(LabelProperty); }
```

```
        set { SetValue(LabelProperty, value); }
    }

    public static readonly DependencyProperty LabelProperty =
        DependencyProperty.Register("Label", typeof(string),
                                    typeof(FormField), null);

    public string Value
    {
        get { return (string)GetValue(ValueProperty); }
        set { SetValue(ValueProperty, value); }
    }

    public static readonly DependencyProperty ValueProperty =
        DependencyProperty.Register("Value", typeof(string),
                                    typeof(FormField), null);
    }
}
```

10. Recall that when we had only implemented standard properties, assigning
    binding expressions to the Label/Value properties values in the view that
    hosted the control threw an exception:

```
<my:FormField Label="Test:" Value="{Binding FirstName}" Width="350" />
```

However, now that the Value and Label properties are dependency properties,
you will now be able to successfully assign a binding expression to them when
consuming the FormField control.

Obtaining the Local Value

As per the value precedence order, a local value assigned to a dependency property has a high level
of importance in the determination of the dependency property's value. You can determine whether the
dependency property has a local value assigned by using the ReadLocalValue method on the dependency
object As opposed to the GetValue method, which gets the value of the dependency property based on all
its sources and the value precedence, the ReadLocalValue method returns a value only when a local value
has been assigned. If no local value is assigned, it will return a value of
DependencyProperty.UnsetValue:

```
object localValue = ReadLocalValue(ValueProperty);

if (localValue == DependencyProperty.UnsetValue)
{
    // No local value has been assigned to this dependency property
    // and it gets its value from other sources
}
else
{
    // This dependency property has a local value
}
```

Resetting a Dependency Property's Value

At times, you don't want to assign the dependency property a new value but simply want to clear the specific value that you have assigned to it—that is, its local value. This enables it to return to resolving its value from its other sources (template, style, or default) as per the value precedence order. You can use the ClearValue method provided by the DependencyObject class, to clear its value, passing it the dependency property identifier of the dependency property to clear, like so:

```
ClearValue(ValueProperty);
```

Dependency Properties in Summary

Dependency properties can be a difficult topic to grasp initially, so here are some of the most important points you need to remember about them:

- Dependency properties are just like other standard CLR properties that you declare on your classes, but they have additional features that extend their utility in the Silverlight environment (or more specifically cater to XAML's demands).

- Dependency properties are needed to support some of Silverlight's advanced features, such as data binding and animation.

- The most important features dependency properties support include evaluating markup extension expressions at runtime, and automatically notifying bound controls when their value changes.

- Although dependency properties are declared as static properties, their values are maintained per object instance, just like standard CLR properties. When you call the GetValue or SetValue methods, you are calling them on an object instance. Therefore, the dependency system knows which object instance the value relates to, and can get or set the corresponding value accordingly.

- Dependency properties and their values are managed by the dependency system. Therefore, the developer does not need to create a member variable to maintain the property value for the class. Instead, the dependency system maintains these values in a hash table, and you ask it to get or set a property value using the GetValue or SetValue methods.

- Even though it's not necessary to do so, dependency properties are generally wrapped in standard CLR properties, which call the GetValue and SetValue methods, making it easier to get or set their values in code.

- These standard CLR property wrappers should not have any logic in their getters and setters.

Type Converters

When you assign the value of a property in XAML, whatever value you give it, you are simply providing that value as a string. However, the XAML parser needs to convert the value from the string that you provided to the property's type before it can assign it to the property.

For a predefined subset of property types (string, integer, Boolean, and so on), this conversion is handled automatically by the XAML parser, and you will immediately be able to set the values of those properties in XAML when you consume the user control in a view. However, only a very limited number of types

are actually supported natively by the XAML parser. For example, say you have a control named
MyCustomControl, that exposes a property of type decimal:

```
public decimal TotalCost { get; set; }
```

and you want to be able to assign this property a value in XAML when you consume the control:

```
<my:MyCustomControl TotalCost="42" />
```

The XAML parser doesn't have built-in support for converting the string value of "42" set in XAML to
a decimal type that the control's property accepts. Assigning a value to a property whose type isn't supported by the XAML parser like this will result in an exception similar to the following:

```
Failed to create a 'System.Decimal' from the text '42'.
```

If you need to expose a property from your control as a type not supported by the XAML parser,
such as Decimal or DateTime, and you want to enable that value to be assigned in XAML, you will need to
implement a type converter. A *type converter* is used to provide the logic for converting one type to another.

To create a type converter, you will need to create a new class that inherits from TypeConverter,
from the System.ComponentModel namespace, and override its methods (CanConvertFrom, ConvertFrom,
CanConvertTo, and ConvertTo), providing them with the appropriate logic.

Note In the previous chapter, we discussed value converters. Value converters can be used as part of the data
binding process to completely change the source value to another for use by the target. Type converters are quite
similar in nature to value converters, but their role is (generally) only to translate the string values specified in
XAML to the type of the control/object properties they are being assigned to.

Let's take a look at the implementation of a simple type converter for the Decimal type:

```
public class DecimalTypeConverter : TypeConverter
{
    public override bool CanConvertFrom(ITypeDescriptorContext context,
                                        Type sourceType)
    {
        return sourceType == typeof(string);
    }

    public override bool CanConvertTo(ITypeDescriptorContext context,
                                      Type destinationType)
    {
        return destinationType == typeof(string);
    }

    public override object ConvertFrom(ITypeDescriptorContext context,
                    System.Globalization.CultureInfo culture, object value)
    {
        return Convert.ToDecimal(value);
    }
```

```
    public override object ConvertTo(ITypeDescriptorContext context,
                                    System.Globalization.CultureInfo culture,
                                    object value, Type destinationType)
    {
        return value.ToString();
    }
}
```

As you can see, very little logic is actually required, with each method requiring only a single line of code to implement. The CanConvertFrom and CanConvertTo methods determine whether this converter can actually convert between the type being represented (a decimal) and a given type. (Note that type converters don't actually check whether the value itself can be converted.) This given type will always be a string, when solving the problem of converting the value assigned in XAML, so we need to support only a source/destination type of string. Then, in the ConvertFrom and ConvertTo methods, you can perform the actual conversion of the given value to and from a string.

■ **Note** You can find a DateTimeTypeConverter and a TimeTypeConverter in the source code for the Silverlight Toolkit. Rather than creating a type converter for each type, another option is provided by Anthony Jones, who has an implementation of a generic type converter that you might wish to use, which you can obtain at

http://geekswithblogs.net/codingbloke/archive/2010/05/14/silverlight-iconvertible-typeconverter.aspx.

To use the DecimalTypeConverter type converter, you need to decorate a property in your user control with the TypeConverter attribute, passing it your converter as a parameter. For example:

```
[TypeConverter(typeof(DecimalTypeConverter))]
public decimal TotalCost { get; set; }
```

■ **Note** XAML has built-in support for enumeration types, so you don't need to implement a type converter for each of those types.

Implementing the ISupportInitialize Interface

If you have logic that is executed when the value of a property is changed, often you won't want this logic to actually be implemented on your user control until all the initial values of its properties have been assigned. This is particularly important when you have properties that are dependent on one another, or whose values need to be set in order.

This is where the ISupportInitialize interface, from the System.ComponentModel namespace, can help. It includes two methods, BeginInit and EndInit, which are called, respectively, before and after the initial values are assigned to the properties from the XAML. This enables you to set a flag, using a member variable, when the BeginInit method is called, and if that flag is set, you can skip any logic in your property setters. You can then reset the flag in the EndInit method, and execute any logic at that point, as required.

> ■ **Note** Markup extensions assigned to dependency properties often won't be evaluated until after the EndInit method is called, so you will not be able to use these values in the logic that you want to execute in the EndInit method.

Exposing Methods

You expose a method from your user control in exactly the same way as you would expose a method publicly from a class. For example:

```
public void DoSomething()
{
    // Do something here
}
```

Exposing Events

In Chapter 2, you learned about the concepts of direct events and routed events in Silverlight. In summary, direct events only raise the event on their source, whereas routed events bubble up the event along the object hierarchy until the root visual is reached or a control marks the event as handled.

> ■ **Note** There is no concept of tunneled events in Silverlight as there is in WPF.

You define a direct event on a Silverlight control in exactly the same way as you would in any standard C# application. Simply choose an existing delegate to use, such as the standard or generic EventHandler delegate, or create your own and define your event. The following example demonstrates creating an event named ValueChanged, which simply makes use of the standard EventHandler delegate:

```
public event EventHandler ValueChanged;
```

When implementing events in your custom controls, I recommend that you raise your events from a protected virtual method, enabling any controls that inherit from your control to suppress that event and handle it differently. The convention is to name the method with the same name as your event, but prefixed with On. For example:

```
protected virtual void OnValueChanged()
{
    if (ValueChanged != null)
        ValueChanged(this, new EventArgs());
}
```

When you want to raise the corresponding event, simply call this method.

■ **Note** Remember to always check for any listeners to your event before attempting to raise it, by checking whether it's null, as demonstrated. Otherwise, an exception will be thrown if you attempt to raise it but no one is listening for it.

Unfortunately, you cannot create your own routed events in Silverlight. If you want to provide a routed event on your control, you might wish to take a look at the custom implementation provided in the project, found here at http://sl3routedevents.codeplex.com.

Determining Whether a Control Is Executing in Design-Time or Runtime Mode

One thing that you might not have realized is that when you are viewing the control in the Visual Studio or Expression Blend designer, the control (including its code-behind), is actually being executed from the latest compiled version of your project. This is why you need to compile your project after creating the control for it to appear in the Toolbox. However, sometimes you need to implement a behavior in your control that should be executed at runtime, but not at design time—for example, when communicating with a web service to retrieve data for display.

To determine whether your control is being executed in a designer, you can simply check the value of the IsInDesignTool property of the DesignerProperties class, found in the System.ComponentModel namespace. When true, the control is executing in the Visual Studio or Expression Blend designer; when false, it is executing at runtime within your application.

```
if (DesignerProperties.IsInDesignTool)
    MessageBox.Show("Is in design-time mode");
else
    MessageBox.Show("Is in runtime mode");
```

Constraining the User Control's Size

If you want your user control to have a fixed size, handle its SizeChanged event, and set its width and height as required in the handler. For example:

```
private void UserControl_SizeChanged(object sender, SizeChangedEventArgs e)
{
    this.Width = 300;
    this.Height = 30;
}
```

Creating Custom Controls

An alternative way of creating a reusable control is to create a custom control. Custom controls are structured quite differently than user controls, imposing a much stricter separation of their look (defined in XAML), and their behavior (defined in code). This strict separation between the control's look and behavior enables the controls to be retemplated (have their look completely redefined) when they are used. To enable a custom control to be retemplated, you need to provide a formal contract between them using the parts and states model, as discussed back in Chapter 9.

When you should create a custom control instead of a user control is a difficult line to define. One of the advantages of a custom control is that they are templatable, unlike user controls. Typically, you would use user controls to bring a number of controls together into a single reusable component and, thus, they are not intended to be templated in the same way as custom controls are. Being less structured than custom controls, user controls are easier to create.

Essentially, if you are simply encapsulating some common functionality that is more or less specific to a single project, combining that functionality into a user control is the most appropriate strategy. However, if you want to create a very generic control that you could use in any project, then a custom control is your best choice.

■ **Note** As a general rule, third-party controls are always custom controls.

Let's take a look at creating a control named WaitIndicator, which you can use as an alternative to the BusyIndicator control discussed back in Chapter 6. This will display an animation while something is happening in the background. Figure 12-3 displays the animation.

Figure 12-3. *The WaitIndicator control*

■ **Note** The Silverlight Toolkit is a great resource for helping you understand how to write Silverlight custom controls. It can even provide a great starting point when creating your own controls.

⚙ Workshop: Creating the Base of a Custom Control

Let's create the base of a WaitIndicator custom control.

1. Generally, when you create custom controls, you will want to maintain them in a separate project from your main project, as a control library, making it easier to reuse the controls. Start by adding a new Silverlight Class Library project named MyControlLibrary to your solution.

2. Delete the default Class1.cs file so that the project is empty.

3. Add a new item to your project using the Silverlight Templated Control item template, as opposed to the Silverlight User Control we used earlier to create a user control, and name it WaitIndicator.

■ **Note** At the time of writing, this item template would crash when the PowerCommands extension was in-stalled for Visual Studio. If you experience this problem and have this extension installed, disable it, restart Visual Studio, and the item template should work correctly.

This will create a WaitIndicator.cs file, and it will also automatically create a Themes folder, con-taining a resource dictionary file named Generic.xaml, which you can see in Figure 12-4.

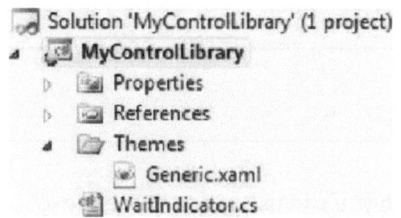

Figure 12-4. The solution structure for the class library

■ **Note** There is no XAML file corresponding to the custom control's code file as there is with user controls. In-stead, the default control template (that is, the XAML defining its default look) is defined in the Generic.xaml file.

The Control Structure

Let's take a closer look at the files that were created for us. First, we have the WaitIndicator.cs file, which defines the control and its associated behavior:

```
using System;
using System.Collections.Generic;
using System.Linq;
using System.Net;
using System.Windows;
using System.Windows.Controls;
using System.Windows.Documents;
using System.Windows.Input;
using System.Windows.Media;
using System.Windows.Media.Animation;
using System.Windows.Shapes;

namespace MyControlLibrary.Controls
{
    public class WaitIndicator : Control
    {
        public WaitIndicator()
        {
```

```
            this.DefaultStyleKey = typeof(WaitIndicator);
        }
    }
}
```

Note that the WaitIndicator class inherits from Control instead of from UserControl, as the user control did. In its constructor, it sets the DefaultStyleKey property in order to link the control's behavior, defined in this class, to its look. I will discuss how this works shortly.

Whereas user controls define their look in a .xaml file, which holds the presentation template for just that control, custom controls define their look in the Generic.xaml resource dictionary file, in the project's Themes folder, as a control template. This Generic.xaml file holds the control templates for all the custom controls in that assembly, each as a separate style resource.

The Silverlight Templated Control item template created this Generic.xaml file for us and defined an empty control template for our control:

```
<ResourceDictionary
    xmlns="http://schemas.microsoft.com/winfx/2006/xaml/presentation"
    xmlns:x="http://schemas.microsoft.com/winfx/2006/xaml"
    xmlns:local="clr-namespace:MyControlLibrary">

    <Style TargetType="local:WaitIndicator">
        <Setter Property="Template">
            <Setter.Value>
                <ControlTemplate TargetType="local:WaitIndicator">
                    <Border Background="{TemplateBinding Background}"
                            BorderBrush="{TemplateBinding BorderBrush}"
                            BorderThickness="{TemplateBinding BorderThickness}">
                    </Border>
                </ControlTemplate>
            </Setter.Value>
        </Setter>
    </Style>
</ResourceDictionary>
```

You can then define the look of your control in the control template defined in this style. By default, the control template simply incorporates a border around your control.

■ **Note** An important aspect to recognize and understand when designing custom controls is that the behavior *is* the control itself. The control template defines the visual characteristics of the control, but it can be replaced and switched, with alternative templates applied interchangeably as required. The structure of custom controls promotes a strict separation between its look and its behavior, with a contract on the control defining the interface that a control template must adhere to. The result of this structure is that the behavior will have no knowledge of the contents of the control template apart from what it expects to be available, as defined in its contract. The control templates, however, *will* know about the control, its contract, and the properties that it exposes. It's this structure that enables a custom control to be retemplated.

When you use a control in your project, it needs to determine what template to use. If one has not been explicitly specified when it is used, it will need to use its default template, if one has been defined. Custom controls know to always look in the Generic.xaml file under the Themes folder for their default control template, and find the correct control template by matching the type applied to the DefaultStyleKey property, which should be set in the control's constructor, as previously demonstrated, to the type assigned to a style resource's TargetType property.

Defining the Control's Default Template

In Chapter 9, we discussed how you can retemplate a custom control to give it a completely new look, and you learned about the parts and states model for controls in Silverlight with the VisualStateManager. You learned that the structure of a control template includes:

- States
- State transitions
- State groups
- Template parts

You use that same breakdown when creating your control template, except you won't have an existing template to work from as you did then because we are now creating the template from scratch. Therefore, you need to break up the visual aspects of your control in order to define each of these in its control template.

■ **Note** By structuring your control's default template properly, and keeping a strict separation between its look and behavior, you will make it possible for your control to be completely retemplated when it is being used, as was demonstrated in Chapter 9.

Creating/Editing the Control Template in Expression Blend

The easiest way to create a control template is in Expression Blend. Visual Studio doesn't enable you to modify or even view control templates defined in the Generic.xaml file in the designer, instead only displaying the message shown in Figure 12-5.

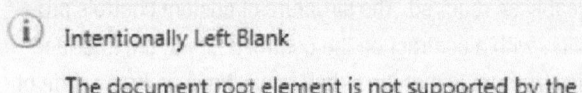

ⓘ Intentionally Left Blank

The document root element is not supported by the visual designer.

Figure 12-5. The message shown in the XAML designer when opening a ResourceDictionary

Therefore, unless you prefer writing all the XAML by hand, you are better off working in Blend. We won't be discussing how to use Expression Blend to create control templates in any depth here, but let's take a brief look at the basics of getting started doing so.

When you open the Generic.xaml file in Expression Blend, you will get a message stating that the file cannot be edited in design view. However, if you open the Resources tab and expand the Generic.xaml entry, you will see a list of the style resources in the file, and you can click the Edit Resource button next to one in order to view the control template defined in it. To modify this control template, right-click the control in the design view, and select Edit Template ➤ Edit Current from the context menu. You can now define the states, state groups, and state transitions in the States tab, and define the state animations and state transition animations in the Objects and Timeline tab.

Creating the Base State

The best place to start when creating a control template is to simply define the base state for the control, and work from there.

What Is a Base State?

The base state for a control is technically not a state at all, but defines all the visual elements of the control that will be used by each of the states. As a standard practice, the XAML you define here should define the layout and look of the control in its initial (Normal) state.

Any elements/controls that should not be visible in this initial state should have their Visibility property set to Collapsed, or their Opacity property set to 0 (which makes it invisible, but it will still consume its given area).

 Workshop: Specifying the Base State

Add the following XAML in bold to the control template that was created for the control in the Generic.xaml file:

```xml
<ControlTemplate TargetType="local:WaitIndicator">
    <Border Background="{TemplateBinding Background}"
            BorderBrush="{TemplateBinding BorderBrush}"
            BorderThickness="{TemplateBinding BorderThickness}">
        <Canvas x:Name="LayoutRoot" Opacity="0">
            <Ellipse x:Name="Ellipse1" Fill="#1E777777"
                    Canvas.Left="0" Canvas.Top="11" Height="8" Width="8"/>
            <Ellipse x:Name="Ellipse2" Fill="#1E777777"
                    Canvas.Left="3" Canvas.Top="3" Height="8" Width="8"/>
            <Ellipse x:Name="Ellipse3" Fill="#1E777777"
                    Canvas.Left="11" Canvas.Top="0" Height="8" Width="8"/>
            <Ellipse x:Name="Ellipse4" Fill="#2E777777"
                    Canvas.Left="19" Canvas.Top="3" Height="8" Width="8"/>
            <Ellipse x:Name="Ellipse5" Fill="#3E777777"
                    Canvas.Left="22" Canvas.Top="11" Height="8" Width="8"/>
            <Ellipse x:Name="Ellipse6" Fill="#6D777777"
                    Canvas.Left="19" Canvas.Top="19" Height="8" Width="8"/>
            <Ellipse x:Name="Ellipse7" Fill="#9C777777"
                    Canvas.Left="11" Canvas.Top="22" Height="8" Width="8"/>
            <Ellipse x:Name="Ellipse8" Fill="#CC777777"
                    Canvas.Left="3" Canvas.Top="19" Height="8" Width="8"/>
        </Canvas>
    </Border>
</ControlTemplate>
```

This XAML defines eight ellipses arranged in a circle, as was shown in Figure 12-3, each with a base color of #777777 (a gray color) but with varying degrees of alpha channel applied in the fill to lighten this color. It's the animation of this Fill property, specifically the alpha value, which will make the wait indicator "spin." Note that the Canvas in this XAML has its Opacity property set to 0 accordingly, as the control is to be invisible by default.

Identifying Visual States, and Organizing Them into Visual State Groups

As you learned in Chapter 9, each visual state defines how the control should look based on its current state, such as when it has the focus, is clicked, is disabled, and so on. To achieve this, a visual state defines the changes required, implemented as animations, to the base visual appearance of the control to visually indicate that the control is in that state.

For the simplest controls, you might only need to support a single state, in which case this will be your base visual state and no additional states or state groups need be defined in the control's default control template. However, in most cases, your custom control will need to support multiple states, and at times be in more than one state simultaneously.

Let's look at how you go about identifying and grouping these visual states.

Identifying Visual States

Once you've defined the base state for your control, the next step is to identify what states your control needs to support, and whether the control can exist in multiple states simultaneously. Let's use the CheckBox control as an example. A check box has the following states:

- Normal
- MouseOver
- Pressed
- Disabled
- Checked
- Unchecked
- Indeterminate
- Focused
- Unfocused
- Valid
- Invalid

As you may be able to tell, some of these states are mutually exclusive, such as the checked and unchecked states, whereas others, such as the checked state and the focused state, could simultaneously but independently coexist on the control.

Grouping Visual States into Visual State Groups

If you find there needs to be support for the control to be in more than one state simultaneously, you will need to group the states into named sets, in which the states in each set are mutually exclusive. For example, the CheckBox's states are grouped as follows:

- `CommonStates: Normal, MouseOver, Pressed, and Disabled`
- `CheckStates: Checked, Unchecked, and Indeterminate`
- `FocusStates: Focused and Unfocused`
- `ValidationStates: Valid and Invalid`

■ **Note** In the actual implementation of the `CheckBox` control, the `Invalid` state is actually split into `InvalidFocused` and `InvalidUnfocused`. However, we'll disregard this for the purposes of simplicity in this discussion.

Each group can have only a single active state at any one time. However, a control may have multiple states active simultaneously (one from each group). Hence, the control can be only in the `Focused` *or* the `Unfocused` state, never both at the same time, but it can, for example, be simultaneously in the `Normal`, `Checked`, `Focused`, and `Valid` states. These groups are known as *visual state groups*.

As the control can only have a single active state in a visual state group, when your control transitions to a new state, the visual state manager will first automatically transition the control away from any existing state that it is in within that same state group.

■ **Note** Even if you've determined that all the control's states are mutually exclusive, and the control does not need to exist in multiple states simultaneously, you still need to define one state group that will contain the various states you define. In other words, all states must exist within a state group.

⚙ Workshop: Defining Visual States and Visual State Groups

Our `WaitIndicator` control is actually very simple when it comes to its states. Our control will simply display an animation that can be turned on and off. Therefore, as no user interaction or input is involved, there is no need for focus states, mouse-over states, or validation states. This means that the control will need two primary states for use at runtime:

- `Inactive` (invisible and not animating)
- `Active` (visible and animated)

We'll also include an additional state named `Static`, which we'll use only when the control is being displayed in the designer so that the control is visible but not animated, to avoid distracting the designer.

Since each of these states is mutually exclusive, we need only a single state group, which we will call `CommonStates`. (The convention when defining custom control templates is to have the core control states in a state group with this name.) Let's define this state group and its related states in the control template now.

1. Add a VisualStateManager.VisualStateGroups element to your control template:

```
<ControlTemplate TargetType="local:WaitIndicator">
    <Border Background="{TemplateBinding Background}"
                    BorderBrush="{TemplateBinding BorderBrush}"
                    BorderThickness="{TemplateBinding BorderThickness}">
        <VisualStateManager.VisualStateGroups>
        </VisualStateManager.VisualStateGroups>
        <!--XAML for the default/base state of this control goes here-->
        <!--as defined earlier. Removed for brevity purposes-->
    </Border>
</ControlTemplate>
```

2. Add a VisualStateGroup to the VisualStateManager.VisualStateGroups element for each visual state group that you've identified. As already discussed, the WaitIndicator control will only have one visual state group—CommonStates:

```
<VisualStateManager.VisualStateGroups>
    <VisualStateGroup x:Name="CommonStates">
    </VisualStateGroup>
</VisualStateManager.VisualStateGroups>
```

3. Add a VisualState element to the group for each visual state that it should contain, giving each a name:

```
<VisualStateGroup x:Name="CommonStates">
    <VisualState x:Name="Inactive">
    </VisualState>

    <VisualState x:Name="Static" />
    </VisualState>

    <VisualState x:Name="Active" />
    </VisualState>
</VisualStateGroup>
```

The full XAML control template that you now have should be as follows:

```
<ControlTemplate TargetType="local:WaitIndicator">
    <Border Background="{TemplateBinding Background}"
            BorderBrush="{TemplateBinding BorderBrush}"
            BorderThickness="{TemplateBinding BorderThickness}">
        <VisualStateManager.VisualStateGroups>
            <VisualStateGroup x:Name="CommonStates">
                <VisualState x:Name="Inactive">
                </VisualState>

                <VisualState x:Name="Static">
                </VisualState>

                <VisualState x:Name="Active">
                </VisualState>
            </VisualStateGroup>
```

```
    </VisualStateManager.VisualStateGroups>

    <Canvas x:Name="LayoutRoot" Opacity="0">
        <Ellipse x:Name="Ellipse1" Fill="#1E777777"
                 Canvas.Left="0" Canvas.Top="11" Height="8" Width="8"/>
        <Ellipse x:Name="Ellipse2" Fill="#1E777777"
                 Canvas.Left="3" Canvas.Top="3" Height="8" Width="8"/>
        <Ellipse x:Name="Ellipse3" Fill="#1E777777"
                 Canvas.Left="11" Canvas.Top="0" Height="8" Width="8"/>
        <Ellipse x:Name="Ellipse4" Fill="#2E777777"
                 Canvas.Left="19" Canvas.Top="3" Height="8" Width="8"/>
        <Ellipse x:Name="Ellipse5" Fill="#3E777777"
                 Canvas.Left="22" Canvas.Top="11" Height="8" Width="8"/>
        <Ellipse x:Name="Ellipse6" Fill="#6D777777"
                 Canvas.Left="19" Canvas.Top="19" Height="8" Width="8"/>
        <Ellipse x:Name="Ellipse7" Fill="#9C777777"
                 Canvas.Left="11" Canvas.Top="22" Height="8" Width="8"/>
        <Ellipse x:Name="Ellipse8" Fill="#CC777777"
                 Canvas.Left="3" Canvas.Top="19" Height="8" Width="8"/>
    </Canvas>
  </Border>
</ControlTemplate>
```

Implementing the Visual States

We've now defined the visual states for the control, but they don't actually do anything yet. Each visual state now needs to define how the base state will be transformed to visually indicate that the custom control is in that state. This transformation is handled via an animation.

Implementing the "Inactive" Visual State

As a general rule, you should define an initial state in each state group, which will be empty—that is, it makes no modifications to the base state. This will provide a starting point for the control that you can then return to. The initial state for our WaitIndicator control should be the Inactive state, so the base state will be configured as per the requirements for the Inactive state. (Recall that we set the Opacity property of the LayoutRoot to 0 when defining the base state earlier, making the contents of the control invisible.) Therefore, we'll make no changes to the base state in the definition for the Inactive state, and leave it as it is (empty).

```
<VisualState x:Name="Inactive" />
```

Workshop: Implementing the "Static" Visual State

The next state we need to implement is the Static state. This will make the ellipses in the wait indicator visible, although we won't animate them in this state. In the base state, we had set the Opacity property of the LayoutRoot to 0, so we need to animate this property to change its value from 0 to 1 over a duration of 0 seconds, resulting in the ellipses immediately becoming visible when we transition to this state.

Add the following animation to the definition of the Static visual state:

```
<VisualState x:Name="Static">
    <Storyboard>
        <DoubleAnimation Duration="0" To="100"
                         Storyboard.TargetProperty="(UIElement.Opacity)"
                         Storyboard.TargetName="LayoutRoot" />
    </Storyboard>
</VisualState>
```

As you can see, we use an animation to change the value of the Opacity property of the element named LayoutRoot to 1, via a combination of the Storyboard.TargetName, Storyboard.TargetProperty, and the To property of a DoubleAnimation object. The Duration property for this animation is set to 0 (seconds), so the value of the LayoutRoot's Opacity property will immediately change from 0 (its base value) to 1 (as per the animation). Extending this duration will result in the LayoutRoot object fading into view, because the value of its Opacity property will change linearly from 0 to 1 over the given duration. You could even specify an easing function such that the value changes nonlinearly.

■ **Note**   As you can see from the XAML, all animations are defined within a Storyboard. Creating these animations and the corresponding XAML is a relatively simple and quick process using Expression Blend. However, coverage of animations in Silverlight is beyond the scope of this book.

 Workshop: Implementing the "Active" Visual State

The final state that we need to implement for our WaitIndicator control is the Active state. Like the Static state, we need to make the ellipses visible, but we also need to implement a repeating in-state animation.

While this in-state animation is running, it changes the alpha value of the ellipse's Fill property every 0.15 seconds, and repeats itself every 1.2 seconds. Each ellipse is 0.15 seconds out of phase, which gives the visual illusion of rotation. There are nine values for each ellipse's alpha value, with the first and the last alpha values being the same.

The XAML defining this animation is quite lengthy, so it won't be included here in its entirety, but here is a snippet of the animation for two of the ellipses:

```
<VisualState x:Name="Active">
    <Storyboard>
        <DoubleAnimation Duration="0" To="100"
                         Storyboard.TargetProperty="(UIElement.Opacity)"
                         Storyboard.TargetName="LayoutRoot" />

        <ColorAnimationUsingKeyFrames
                Storyboard.TargetName="Ellipse1"
                Storyboard.TargetProperty="(Fill).(Color)"
                BeginTime="0" RepeatBehavior="Forever">

            <LinearColorKeyFrame Value="#CC777777" KeyTime="00:00:00" />
            <LinearColorKeyFrame Value="#9C777777" KeyTime="00:00:00.15" />
```

```xml
        <LinearColorKeyFrame Value="#6D777777" KeyTime="00:00:00.3" />
        <LinearColorKeyFrame Value="#3E777777" KeyTime="00:00:00.45" />
        <LinearColorKeyFrame Value="#2E777777" KeyTime="00:00:00.60" />
        <LinearColorKeyFrame Value="#1E777777" KeyTime="00:00:00.75" />
        <LinearColorKeyFrame Value="#1E777777" KeyTime="00:00:00.90" />
        <LinearColorKeyFrame Value="#1E777777" KeyTime="00:00:01.05" />
        <LinearColorKeyFrame Value="#CC777777" KeyTime="00:00:01.20" />
    </ColorAnimationUsingKeyFrames>

    <ColorAnimationUsingKeyFrames
            Storyboard.TargetName="Ellipse2"
            Storyboard.TargetProperty="(Fill).(Color)"
            BeginTime="0" RepeatBehavior="Forever">

        <LinearColorKeyFrame Value="#1E777777" KeyTime="00:00:00" />
        <LinearColorKeyFrame Value="#CC777777" KeyTime="00:00:00.15" />
        <LinearColorKeyFrame Value="#9C777777" KeyTime="00:00:00.3" />
        <LinearColorKeyFrame Value="#6D777777" KeyTime="00:00:00.45" />
        <LinearColorKeyFrame Value="#3E777777" KeyTime="00:00:00.60" />
        <LinearColorKeyFrame Value="#2E777777" KeyTime="00:00:00.75" />
        <LinearColorKeyFrame Value="#1E777777" KeyTime="00:00:00.90" />
        <LinearColorKeyFrame Value="#1E777777" KeyTime="00:00:01.05" />
        <LinearColorKeyFrame Value="#1E777777" KeyTime="00:00:01.20" />
    </ColorAnimationUsingKeyFrames>

    <!--And so on for each ellipse.-->
    <!--Download the full animation from the Apress website-->

    </Storyboard>
</VisualState>
```

Note how the RepeatBehavior property of the ColorAnimationUsingKeyFrames object is set to Forever. This means that once complete, it will restart continually until the control transitions away from the Active state.

You can download the full code for this control from this book's web site.

■ **Note** When you run the control, it won't actually be in one of the states you have defined. Instead, it will be in its base state. Ideally, you want it to be in one of your defined states, so immediately after applying the control template to the control (in the OnApplyTemplate method, described shortly), you should tell the VisualStateManager to go to the initial state within each state group. We'll do this when we implement the code for this control.

Adding State Transition Animations

When you transition from one state to another, you might wish to ease the visual impact of jumping between the states by implementing a transition animation. Using the VisualTransition object, you can specify an animation for how the control should transition between two given states, from any state to a given state, or from a given state to any other state.

There are two ways that you can implement a transition. The first is to let the VisualStateManager determine how it should transition between the two states. You simply specify the duration for the transition and the states you want it to go to and from, and it will work out how to transition between those states smoothly—such as changing colors, opacity, and control positions—over the given duration. In the following example, I define a VisualTransition, specifying that the transition between the Inactive and Active states should be smoothly animated, over the duration of two seconds.

```
<VisualStateGroup x:Name="CommonStates">
    <VisualStateGroup.Transitions>
        <VisualTransition GeneratedDuration="0:0:2" From="Inactive" To="Active" />
    </VisualStateGroup.Transitions>

    <!--Visual State definitions removed for brevity-->
</VisualStateGroup>
```

■ **Note**   You can omit the From property if you want the transition to be applied whenever the control transitions to the state specified by the To property, regardless of what state the control was previously in. Alternatively, you can omit the To property if you want the transition to be applied whenever the control transitions away from the state specified by the From property, regardless of what state the control is changing to.

Alternatively, we can explicitly define our own animation for the transition by adding a Storyboard specifying the transition animation to the VisualTransition element. For example, the following transition consists of an animation that will fade in the control named LayoutRoot. It does so by changing the value of its Opacity property from 0 to 1 over a period of two seconds when transitioning from the Inactive to the Active state:

```
<VisualTransition GeneratedDuration="0:0:2" From="Inactive" To="Active">
    <Storyboard>
        <DoubleAnimation From="0" To="1"
                         Storyboard.TargetProperty="(UIElement.Opacity)"
                         Storyboard.TargetName="LayoutRoot" />
    </Storyboard>
</VisualTransition>
```

A state transition might seem like the best place to define the changes that should be made to the base state to get to a given visual state, but this is actually not the case. For example, when our WaitIndicator control transitions to the Static or Active states, the LayoutRoot element needs to become visible. That is, the value of its Opacity property needs to be set to 1. However, a transition is *not* the place to define the animation to do this, for a number of reasons. Transition animations can be skipped when moving from one state to another, so there's no guarantee that the animation will be executed. More importantly, however, is the fact that any changes made to the control's element's properties are applied only for the duration of the transition. If, for example, you define an animation as per the previous example, where we gradually made the LayoutRoot element visible, as soon as the transition animation is complete, the control will enter the destination state, and the VisualStateManager will apply that state's changes to the base state—not to the changes that were made during the transition. Therefore, unless you set the LayoutRoot element to be visible within the state itself, it will return to being invisible as soon as the transition has completed. Therefore, the rule is that all changes to the base state required by a state should be defined within the state itself.

Our WaitIndicator control has no need to transition between states, so we won't define any state transitions for it.

Binding to Properties in the Code

Earlier in this chapter, we discussed consuming properties defined in a user control's code-behind in XAML by binding to them. As mentioned at the time, custom controls do this in a different way than user controls. Rather than using a standard binding, you will usually use the TemplateBinding markup extension instead. In some cases, when you need a two-way binding, you will use a standard binding expression that makes use of the RelativeSource markup extension. Let's look at both of these methods now.

One-Way Binding Using the TemplateBinding Markup Extension

When binding a control property in your control template to a property on the control, you will usually use the TemplateBinding markup extension. This binding automatically finds the templated control and binds to the specified property on it. For example, if your custom control defines a property named HeaderText, you can bind the Text property of a TextBlock control to it, like so:

```
<TextBlock Text="{TemplateBinding HeaderText}" />
```

▮ **Note** This is where the pull-based model, discussed earlier in relation to user controls, comes in again, enabling the code to take a back seat, and simply act as a provider to the view. Although the code/behavior has no knowledge of the contents of the control template, apart from what it defines in its contract, the control template *does* know about the behavior. Hence, this scenario is ideal for implementing the pull-based model. To implement a push-based model, you would have to define the TextBlock control as a template part so that you could refer to it in the control's code; therefore, the pull-based model is a much better way.

Two-Way Binding Using the RelativeSource Markup Extension

The TemplateBinding markup extension is a OneWay binding only, and it has no Mode property to alter this like other binding types. This is fine in most scenarios, but if the control in the control template needs to update the property that it is bound to—that is, it requires a TwoWay binding—you will not be able to use the TemplateBinding markup extension for this purpose.

For example, say the TextBlock control from the previous example was actually a TextBox, where the user can modify the bound value. The TemplateBinding markup extension would be of no use here, as it would not enable the bound property to be updated according to the user's input.

To enable the bound property to be updated, you can use a combination of the `Binding` markup extension and the `RelativeSource` markup extension (detailed in Chapter 11) to bind to the property instead. The `Binding` markup extension will enable you to set up a `TwoWay` binding, and the `RelativeSource` markup extension will enable you to bind to the templated parent (that is, the control itself).

This binding is equivalent to the `TemplateBinding` example we used earlier, except this enables the binding to be `TwoWay`:

```
<TextBox Text="{Binding HeaderText, Mode=TwoWay,
                    RelativeSource={RelativeSource TemplatedParent}}" />
```

Splitting Your Generic.xaml File into Smaller Pieces

When you start adding many controls to your control library, you will begin to find that the `Generic.xaml` file becomes unwieldy and hard to navigate. Each control template can become quite large, compound-ing the problem even further. You might wish to consider defining your control templates in separate resource dictionary files, one control template per file, and merge those into the `Generic.xaml` file using the techniques described in Chapter 2. For example, you could create a new resource dictionary file named `WaitIndicator.xaml` under the `Themes` folder of the `MyControlLibrary` project, and define the `WaitIndicator` control's control template in that file instead of `Generic.xaml`. You then need to merge the contents of the `WaitIndicator.xaml` file into `Generic.xaml`, by adding the following XAML to `Generic.xaml`:

```
<ResourceDictionary.MergedDictionaries>
    <ResourceDictionary
        Source="/MyControlLibrary;component/Themes/WaitIndicator.xaml" />
</ResourceDictionary.MergedDictionaries>
```

■ **Note** You can't use a relative path when setting the `Source` property of the `ResourceDictionary` entry. Instead, you must use the full path to the XAML resource file, including the assembly name.

Each control can then define its control template in a separate file, which can then be merged into the `Generic.xaml` file. This will make your `Generic.xaml` file much more manageable and make it easier to modify the control templates for your custom controls when necessary.

Defining the Control's Behavior

In the control's behavior (code), you will define and expose properties (generally as dependency properties), methods, and events, just as you did with the user control. Where things differ, however, is when you actually need to interact with elements defined in the control's template. Because of the strict separation between the control's look and its behavior, and because the control knows nothing about the template that has been applied to it, this presents a problem.

This is where the control needs to identify the parts and states that it needs to reference and interact with in the control template, in the form of a contract. When a template part is defined in the control's contract, it essentially states that "a control/element of this type with this name must be present in the control template." Similarly, when a template visual state is defined in the control's contract, it expects a state with the given name to exist in the control template.

When the control is initialized, the Silverlight runtime will apply a control template to it, either one explicitly specified by the developer or its default control template, and notify the control when it has done so, by calling the OnApplyTemplate method on the control. It's up to the control in this method to get a reference to all the parts it requires from the control template, as defined by the contract, and store these references in member variables. It can then reference these controls in the control template via these member variables when required.

Let's take a deeper look at implementing the contract and behavior for a custom control.

Defining the Contract

If you want to interact with anything in the control template from the control's code, you should define a contract, by decorating the control's class with attributes. In this contract, you specify the parts and states that the control expects to exist in the control template.

■ **Note** It's not essential to define this contract on the control, but it is recommended as it formalizes the requirements of the control from its template, and provides benefits when retemplating the control in Expression Blend.

To specify that the control requires a given visual state, you decorate the class with the TemplateVisualState attribute, setting its Name and GroupName properties, using named parameters, to the name of the state that it expects to be defined in the control template, and the name of the visual state group that the state should be found in. For example, the following code demonstrates a contract that expects a visual state named Inactive to exist in the control template, within the CommonStates state group:

```
[TemplateVisualState(Name = "Inactive", GroupName = "CommonStates")]
public class WaitIndicator : Control
```

When you need to reference a named control/element from the control template in code, you should define a template part in the control's contract denoting that requirement, using the TemplatePart attribute. Using named parameters, you specify the name that you expect a control/element in the control template to have, and the type of control it should be. For example, this attribute defines that the control expects a template part named Ellipse1 to exist in the control template, of type Ellipse:

```
[TemplatePart(Name = "Ellipse1", Type = typeof(Ellipse))]
public class WaitIndicator : Control
```

Ideally, you should define as few template parts as possible, because each template part places additional restrictions and constraints on the freedom of the control template designer, and adds coupling points between the control and its template. Therefore, define a template part only if you really need access to it from the code, and see if you can expose a property that the control/element can bind to in order to implement the requirement instead. For example, instead of specifying a TextBlock as a template part so that you can set its Text property from the control's code, expose a property on the control that the Text property of the TextBlock can bind to.

You might have noticed that when defining the visual states and the template parts on the control, these were defined as strings. *Magic string* values are never a good idea, especially when they need to be used in multiple locations within the code, so it's generally best practice to define them as constants on the class. The name of each state, state group, and template part should be defined as a constant within the control's class, and you can then use them instead of the magic strings. For example, StateInactive, StateGroupCommon, and PartEllipse1 in the following example are all string constants that are defined in the control's class and used in place of the magic strings from the previous examples:

```
[TemplateVisualState(Name = StateInactive, GroupName = StateGroupCommon)]
[TemplatePart(Name = PartEllipse1, Type = typeof(Ellipse))]
public class WaitIndicator : Control
{
    private const string StateActive = "Active";
    private const string StateInactive = "Inactive";
    private const string StateStatic = "Static";
    private const string StateGroupCommon = "CommonStates";
    private const string PartEllipse1 = "Ellipse1";
```

Connecting the Code and the Default Control Template

When a control is initialized, the Silverlight runtime will automatically determine what template it should use, either its default template from the Generic.xaml file or the template provided by the consuming view, and apply it to the control. After it's done that, it will call the OnApplyTemplate method in the control's code. This method is defined in the base Control class, and you will need to override it to be notified that the template has been applied.

```
public override void OnApplyTemplate()
{
    base.OnApplyTemplate();
}
```

After the template has been applied, you are free to get a reference to all the elements required by the control, as defined as template parts in the contract, from the control template, and you can store these references in member variables that the control can use when it needs to interact with them. To get a reference to these elements, use the GetTemplateChild method, which is defined in the base Control class. Pass the GetTemplateChild method the name of the element that you want to get a reference to from the control template, and it will return the instance of that element (or null, if it's not found).

```
_ellipse1 = GetTemplateChild("Ellipse1") as Ellipse;
```

■ **Note** This code assumes a variable named _ellipse1, of type Ellipse, has been defined as a member variable on the control's class.

You can get a reference to each control/element defined in the control's contract using this method, but this can be a bit laborious when you have many template parts. Alternatively, you can use reflection to get these references automatically for you. Assuming you have defined all your required template parts in the control's contract, and have a corresponding member variable of the correct type and with a name matching that of the template part, you can use the following code to loop through each template part defined in the contract, get a reference to that control/element in the control template, and assign the reference to a member variable in the control's class with the same name:

```
public override void OnApplyTemplate()
{
    base.OnApplyTemplate();

    // Get all the attributes on this class that
    // are of type TemplatePartAttribute
    object[] templateParts =
        this.GetType().GetCustomAttributes(typeof(TemplatePartAttribute), true);

    // Loop through each of these attributes, get the member variable with the
    // same name as the template part, get the template part, and assign it to
    // the member variable
    foreach (TemplatePartAttribute attribute in templateParts)
    {
        FieldInfo field = this.GetType().GetField(attribute.Name,
            BindingFlags.Instance | BindingFlags.NonPublic |
            BindingFlags.Public);

        field.SetValue(this, GetTemplateChild(attribute.Name));
    }
}
```

After you've done this, you can interact with each of the elements via their corresponding member variable. For example:

```
Ellipse1.Fill = new SolidColorBrush(Colors.LightGray);
```

If a template part defined in the contract doesn't actually exist in the control template, the GetTemplateChild method will return null. You will need to decide how you want to handle this scenario. You can choose to continue without this part, or throw an exception. If you decide to continue without the template part, you will need to check if it's null each time before you try to use it in the code.

■ **Note** Be sure not to try interacting with any of the controls/elements defined as template parts before the control template has been applied, and references to the elements have been obtained. For example, let's say you want to set a property on a control/element in the control template when the value of a property on the control itself is changed. If the control's property is assigned a value in the XAML when it's being used, that property will actually be assigned the value *before* the OnApplyTemplate method is called. Therefore, you won't have a reference to the control/element as yet, which will cause problems. This is one of the reasons why you should use template parts as sparsely as possible, and where possible, look at binding the properties of the corresponding control/element to properties exposed by the control instead.

Handling Events for Elements Defined in the Control Template (in the Code)

If you need to handle events raised by controls/elements in your control's template, you will need to first ensure that those elements are defined as template parts, and that you get a reference to them in the control's OnApplyTemplate method. After you've gained a reference to the control/element, add the required event handlers that you need:

```
Ellipse1.MouseEnter += new MouseEventHandler(Ellipse1_MouseEnter);
```

You can then respond accordingly to the events in the event handlers that you've defined, which may involve accordingly raising an event on the control itself to notify the consuming view of that event.

Transitioning Between States

To transition from one state to another in your control, you can use the GoToState method of the VisualStateManager class, passing it the control to change the state for, the name of the state to transition to, and whether to display any transition animation defined between those states. The VisualStateManager will then handle the transition to that state accordingly. The following example demonstrates transitioning to the state named Active on the current custom control, with transition animations turned on:

```
VisualStateManager.GoToState(this, "Active", true);
```

■ **Note** If the state that you are attempting to transition to does not exist in the control template, this method will fail silently. It does, however, return a Boolean value that specifies whether or not it failed.

⚙ Workshop: Implementing the WaitIndicator's Behavior

The following code for the control will have been created for you by the item template:

```
using System;
using System.Collections.Generic;
using System.Linq;
using System.Net;
using System.Windows;
using System.Windows.Controls;
using System.Windows.Documents;
using System.Windows.Input;
using System.Windows.Media;
using System.Windows.Media.Animation;
using System.Windows.Shapes;

namespace MyControlLibrary
{
    public class WaitIndicator : Control
    {
        public WaitIndicator()
        {
            this.DefaultStyleKey = typeof(WaitIndicator);
        }
    }
}
```

As you can see, it doesn't actually do much yet. It simply sets the DefaultStyleKey property for the control, which tells the Silverlight runtime what control template it should use by default from the Generic.xaml file—that is, the template with a TargetType of WaitIndicator.

We now need to code the behavior of our control. For our WaitIndicator control, this behavior is actually very simple. We simply need a property on the control named IsBusy, which when toggled will show and hide the animation. That is, simply change the active visual state in the CommonStates visual state group.

1. Because we don't need to reference any controls/elements in the control template from the code-behind, there's no need to define template parts in the control's contract. We do need to control transitioning between visual states, so we do have to define our three states in the contract:

```
[TemplateVisualState(Name = StateInactive, GroupName = StateGroupCommon)]
[TemplateVisualState(Name = StateActive, GroupName = StateGroupCommon)]
[TemplateVisualState(Name = StateStatic, GroupName = StateGroupCommon)]
public class WaitIndicator : Control
```

2. So that we don't need to use magic strings in the contract's attributes, define the state names and state group name as constants:

```
private const string StateActive = "Active";
private const string StateInactive = "Inactive";
private const string StateStatic = "Static";
private const string StateGroupCommon = "CommonStates";
```

3. Now we need to override the OnApplyTemplate method. We have no template parts that we need to obtain a reference to, so this is quite minimal in its implementation. We do, however, need to set the default visual state for the control now that the control template has been applied. We'll tell it to transition from its base state at this point to the state that it should currently be in, by calling the SetVisualState method that we are about to define.

```
public override void OnApplyTemplate()
{
    base.OnApplyTemplate();
    SetVisualState();
}
```

4. We now need to create this SetVisualState method. This method defines the logic determining what state the control should be in, and tells the Visual State Manager to go to that state accordingly:

```
private void SetVisualState()
{
    if (DesignerProperties.IsInDesignTool)
        VisualStateManager.GoToState(this, StateStatic, true);
    else
        VisualStateManager.GoToState(this,
                                     IsBusy ? StateActive : StateInactive, true);
}
```

5. Finally, we need to define a dependency property that will be used to control what state the control should be in: busy (animated) or not busy (invisible). This is a simple Boolean property, and it will call the SetVisualState method when its value is changed to update its current state accordingly:

```
public static readonly DependencyProperty IsBusyProperty =
    DependencyProperty.Register("IsBusy", typeof(bool), typeof(WaitIndicator),
    new PropertyMetadata(false, IsBusyPropertyChanged));

public bool IsBusy
{
    get { return (bool)GetValue(IsBusyProperty); }
    set { SetValue(IsBusyProperty, value); }
}

private static void IsBusyPropertyChanged(DependencyObject d,
                                          DependencyPropertyChangedEventArgs e)
{
    ((WaitIndicator)d).SetVisualState();
}
```

Testing the Control

Now that the control is complete, you can test it. Start by compiling the MyControlLibrary project, as the control will actually be executing from the latest compiled version of it when displayed in the designer.

Assuming the MyControlLibrary project and the Silverlight test project are in the same solution, you will find that the control will automatically appear in your Toolbox, as shown in Figure 12-6, when you open a view in your Silverlight test project.

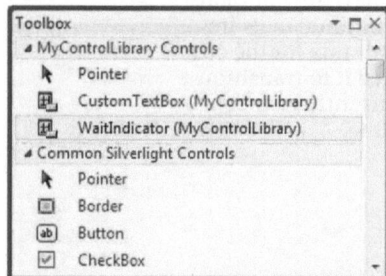

Figure 12-6. The WaitIndicator control in the Toolbox

> ■ **Note** If the MyControlLibrary project and the Silverlight test projects are not in the same solution, right-click the Toolbox, select Choose Items from the context menu, navigate to the compiled MyControlLibrary assembly, and add the control(s) from that assembly to the Toolbox.

Now, you can simply drag the control onto the design surface. Using the Properties window, set its IsBusy property to True. When you run your project, the control will be visible and animate. The custom control is complete!

Content Controls

Sometimes, you want to create a control that can contain some custom content. The Button control is a good example, enabling you to customize what is displayed within the button, such as an image, text, and so on. The Button control can contain only a single control as its content, but other content controls, such as the Grid control, can contain multiple controls as their content. Let's take a look at how you can create a custom content control that can contain either a single control as its content or multiple controls.

Containing a Single Control as Content

The Button control is a *content control*, and you can make your own control a content control by inheriting from ContentControl instead of Control. This will expose a Content property on your control, which can accept the content to be displayed within the control.

To display the content assigned to the control's Content property, you need to include a ContentPresenter in your control template. A ContentPresenter specifies where that content should be displayed within your control template. Think of a ContentPresenter as being a placeholder for the content of the control (the content being provided by the consumer).

Let's create a GroupBox control to demonstrate this concept. This control will be a content control that has a header and display some arbitrary content below it, as provided by the consuming view. Figure 12-7 demonstrates the final result.

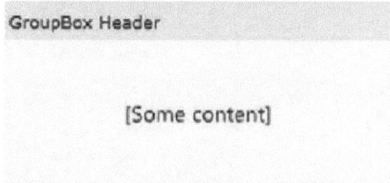

Figure 12-7. *The GroupBox control*

As you can see, we want the content to be displayed below the header. Therefore, we position the ContentPresenter in our control template in the location where the content should be displayed. In the control template's XAML, which follows, you can see that we are positioning the ContentPresenter in the second row of the Grid, with the header taking the first row:

```
<Style TargetType="local:GroupBox">
    <Setter Property="BorderThickness" Value="1" />
    <Setter Property="BorderBrush" Value="Gainsboro" />
    <Setter Property="Template">
        <Setter.Value>
            <ControlTemplate TargetType="local:GroupBox">
                <Border BorderBrush="{TemplateBinding BorderBrush}"
                        BorderThickness="{TemplateBinding BorderThickness}">
                    <Grid Background="{TemplateBinding Background}">
                        <Grid.RowDefinitions>
                            <RowDefinition Height="25" />
                            <RowDefinition />
                        </Grid.RowDefinitions>
```

```
                        <Rectangle Fill="{TemplateBinding BorderBrush}" />
                        <TextBlock Text="{TemplateBinding HeaderText}"
                                   Foreground="{TemplateBinding Foreground}"
                                   VerticalAlignment="Center" Margin="2" />

                        <ContentPresenter Grid.Row="1" Margin="2" />
                    </Grid>
                </Border>
            </ControlTemplate>
        </Setter.Value>
    </Setter>
</Style>
```

The ContentPresenter's default control template automatically binds its Content property to the control's Content property, and its ContentTemplate property to the control's ContentTemplate property. It will handle displaying whatever content is assigned to the control's Content property in its place in the control.

Very little code is required for this control. It simply needs the DefaultStyleKey property to be set for the control, and a HeaderText dependency property to be defined (which you might have noticed was bound to using the TemplateBinding markup extension in the control's template listed earlier):

```
public class GroupBox : ContentControl
{
    public GroupBox()
    {
        DefaultStyleKey = typeof(GroupBox);
    }

    public static readonly DependencyProperty HeaderTextProperty =
        DependencyProperty.Register("HeaderText", typeof(string),
                                    typeof(GroupBox), null);

    public string HeaderText
    {
        get { return (string)GetValue(HeaderTextProperty); }
        set { SetValue(HeaderTextProperty, value); }
    }
}
```

When using the control, you can now assign a control as content to this control using content element syntax, like so:

```
<my:GroupBox Height="120" Width="250" HeaderText="GroupBox Header">
    <TextBlock Text="[Some content]"
               VerticalAlignment="Center" HorizontalAlignment="Center" />
</my:GroupBox>
```

■ **Note** You might recall from Chapter 2 that to be able to assign a value to a property on a control using content element syntax, that property must be defined as the content property for the control. To specify which property is the content property, you need to decorate the control's class with the `ContentProperty` attribute, passing it the name of the property to automatically be assigned the control's content—that is, the XAML between the control's beginning and end tags. This enables you to avoid using property element syntax, which requires you to explicitly specify which property you are assigning the value to, and simplifies the XAML required when the control is being consumed in a view. When you inherit from `ContentControl`, the `ContentControl` class already has the `ContentProperty` attribute applied, specifying that any content provided to the control using content element syntax will be automatically assigned to the control's `Content` property. Therefore, you do not need to worry about decorating your control's class with this property, unless you want a property other than `Content` to be automatically assigned the control's content.

Containing Multiple Controls as Content

One of the limitations of our current `GroupBox` control is that it allows you to directly assign only a single control as its content. The `Content` property is of type `Object`, and attempting to assign multiple controls to the `Content` property in XAML will result in an error stating, "The property 'Content' is set more than once." For example, you can't currently do the following:

```
<my:GroupBox Height="120" Width="250" HeaderText="GroupBox Header">
    <TextBlock Text="[Some content]" />
    <TextBlock Text="[Some more content]" />
</my:GroupBox>
```

If you want to be able to assign multiple controls using content element syntax on a custom control, you will need to specify a different property as the control's content property (other than `Content`), and that property must be a collection type.

■ **Note** There are a number of examples of controls that accept more than one control, such as the `Grid`, `Canvas`, and `StackPanel` controls. These controls inherit from `Panel` (instead of `ContentControl`, as this control does), whose content property is its `Children` property. We'll create a similar property with the same name on our `GroupBox` custom control, and set it to be our content property for the control.

Start by defining a property on your control that will maintain a collection of the content controls. For this purpose, we'll create a property named `Children`, of type `ObservableCollection<UIElement>`.

```
public static readonly DependencyProperty ChildrenProperty =
    DependencyProperty.Register("Children",
            typeof(ObservableCollection<UIElement>), typeof(GroupBox),
            new PropertyMetadata(new ObservableCollection<UIElement>()));
```

```
public ObservableCollection<UIElement> Children
{
    get
    {
        return (ObservableCollection<UIElement>)GetValue(ChildrenProperty);
    }
    set
    {
        SetValue(ChildrenProperty, value);
    }
}
```

We now need to specify that the new Children property is our content property. We do so by decorating the control's class with the ContentProperty, like so:

```
[ContentProperty("Children")]
public class GroupBox : ContentControl
```

You will now be able to assign multiple controls to the Children property using content element syntax, like so:

```
<my:GroupBox HeaderText="GroupBox Header" Height="90" Width="200">
    <TextBlock Text="Child 1" />
    <TextBlock Text="Child 2" />
    <TextBlock Text="Child 3" />
    <TextBlock Text="Child 4" />
</my:GroupBox>
```

Note that none of the TextBlock controls will actually be displayed in the GroupBox's content area as yet. All we are doing is adding these controls to the collection exposed by the GroupBox control's Children property. The ContentPresenter in the control template is still bound to the control's Content property, so we'll need to change this to display the controls added to the Children collection instead.

How you will arrange these controls within the content area of the GroupBox control when you do display them is the next question. For the purpose of this example, let's divide the content area of the control into a two-by-two grid and display the first four controls assigned to the Children collection, one in each cell. There are a number of ways you could implement this, and we won't cover any of these ways in depth, but the basic concept is as follows. Each cell in the grid will contain a ContentPresenter. The Children property on the control is of type ObservableCollection, meaning that we can handle the CollectionChanged event that it exposes. This event will be raised when an item is added or removed from this collection. In an event handler for this event, you can then assign each item in the collection to a ContentPresenter in the control template. Code demonstrating this technique can be found in the code accompanying this book. This will result in the output shown in Figure 12-8.

Figure 12-8. *A content control with multiple controls as content*

Attached Properties

In Chapter 2, we discussed the concept of attached properties. In summary, these are properties that are registered on a control and can then be used by *any* control. For example, the Row property on the Grid control is an attached property that can be attached to a control within the Grid to tell the Grid what row that control should be positioned in. For example:

```
<Grid>
    <Grid.RowDefinitions>
        <RowDefinition />
        <RowDefinition />
        <RowDefinition />
    </Grid.RowDefinitions>

    <Button Content="OK" Grid.Row="2" />
</Grid>
```

You can define attached properties on your own custom controls, either with or without a backing dependency property. Let's say you want to define an attached property named ContentArea on your GroupBox control, enabling the controls assigned to the GroupBox control's Children property to specify which cell in the two-by-two grid they should appear in. Defining ContentArea as an attached property, of type integer, requires two static methods to be defined on the control, one named GetContentArea and the other named SetContentArea, each with the following signatures:

```
public static int GetContentArea(DependencyObject obj)
{

}

public static void SetContentArea(DependencyObject obj, int value)
{

}
```

By following this convention, of both the method names and their corresponding signatures, the Silverlight runtime will recognize these two methods combined as defining an attached property of type integer, named ContentArea. For example, you can now attach the ContentArea property to one of the GroupBox control's children, like so:

```
<TextBlock Text="Child 1" my:GroupBox.ContentArea="1" />
```

Whenever a control assigns a value to the ContentArea attached property, the SetContentArea method will be called. A reference to the control that assigned the value will be passed into the method as the first parameter (obj), and the value that has been assigned to the attached property will be passed in as the second parameter (value). You then need to store this value along with the corresponding control that the property was attached to. When you need to get the value for the attached property as attached to a given control, you can then call the GetContentArea method, passing a reference to the given control into the method as its parameter.

■ **Note** If you want to restrict the type of controls that the property can be attached to, change the type of the first parameter, as per the preceding example, from DependencyObject to the type of the control that it should be restricted to.

One of the issues of defining an attached property like this, without a backing dependency property, is that you'll need to maintain your own repository within the custom control that defines the attached property, to store the value assigned to this property for each control that it's attached to. Another issue is that you can't assign a binding to the attached property. Therefore, you will usually see attached properties defined with a corresponding dependency property that takes care of these issues.

When registering the backing dependency property, instead of calling the normal Register method to register the dependency property, you need to call the RegisterAttached method instead. For example:

```
public static readonly DependencyProperty ContentAreaProperty =
    DependencyProperty.RegisterAttached("ContentArea", typeof(int),
    typeof(GroupBox), null);
```

You will then be able to use this as the store for the values, like so:

```
public static int GetContentArea(DependencyObject obj)
{
    return (int)obj.GetValue(ContentAreaProperty);
}

public static void SetContentArea(DependencyObject obj, int value)
{
    obj.SetValue(ContentAreaProperty, value);
}
```

■ **Note** The propdp snippet was discussed earlier in this chapter as helping make defining dependency properties quick and easy. Visual Studio also has a built-in snippet, named propa, to help in creating attached properties.Like the propdp snippet, it too was designed for WPF and will require the reference to UIPropertyMetadata to be changed to PropertyMetadata when using it in Silverlight projects.

Summary

In this chapter, you learned about each of the methods available to you to create reusable controls for use in your applications. Which method you should use really depends on what you are trying to achieve:

- Inherit from an existing control if you simply want to add your own additional behavior to it.
- User controls are best for encapsulating some common functionality that is more or less specific to a single project, and is of limited complexity.
- Custom controls are best when you want to create a more generic control that might be used in other projects or needs to be templatable.
- Content controls enable your control to act as a container for other controls.

CHAPTER 13

The Model-View-ViewModel (MVVM) Design Pattern

Few topics surrounding Silverlight are so widely discussed as the Model-View-ViewModel (MVVM) design pattern. This pattern is used by many Silverlight, Windows Phone 7, and WPF developers, and even JavaScript libraries are starting to appear that enable HTML applications to make use of the pattern. The blogosphere is overflowing with posts on this topic, with so many differing and varied opinions on how it should be implemented that you might become a little overwhelmed. Adding to this confusion is the fact that the project templates in Visual Studio do not facilitate using the MVVM design pattern out of the box, and with no information on the amount of prerequisite Silverlight knowledge required to implement it effectively, many developers new to Silverlight shun the pattern until they become more experienced in the technology. However, there is general agreement in the development community that, regardless of how you implement the pattern, doing so is good practice. Developers who implement this pattern invariably say that their code is much better for it.

The MVVM design pattern has been mentioned frequently throughout this book, and some of the workshops in Chapters 6 and 7 even implemented it in its most primitive form. I've held off looking at the pattern in depth to avoid overloading you with too many new topics at the one time. However, now that we've covered the required data binding and XAML concepts that you will use when implementing the MVVM design pattern, this is the perfect time to learn about the MVVM and put those concepts into use implementing the design pattern.

Note There's a learning curve when getting up to speed on the MVVM design pattern, but once you get the hang of it, you won't look back. Using the MVVM design pattern when you're used to writing code-behind only for views is somewhat like learning an object-oriented programming language when you're familiar only with structured programming languages. It will feel a bit weird at first as you work out where things go and how they communicate, but once you get your head around it, it will feel completely natural.

In this chapter, we'll start by looking at the theory behind the MVVM design pattern, then move onto the practical aspects of implementing it, and finally, look at the more complex areas of working within the pattern and how you can approach these problems.

Benefits of Implementing the MVVM Design Pattern

You're no doubt familiar with projects whose views have a lot of code-behind, where that code-behind pushes data into the view. To behave in this fashion, the code needs to have intimate knowledge of the view itself. However, many benefits could be gained by having the view's logic extracted away from the view and into another class. It would then be totally ignorant of the view, and simply act as a provider of data and operations to it. In other words, a better design would result from having a clean separation of concerns between a view's look and its behavior. This is what the MVVM design pattern aims to achieve.

■ **Note** Although the implementation will be somewhat different, the MVVM design pattern does share a lot in common with the way that you design custom controls (discussed in Chapter 12). When looking at it from this perspective, a view is analogous to a control template, and a ViewModel is analogous to a control's logic.

One of the big issues with having all or much of the logic and behavior of a view written in its code-behind is that logic located there is simply not testable. Intertwining a view's look with its behavior means both have intimate knowledge of one another. This bidirectional tight coupling makes testing the view's behavior an incredibly difficult and messy, if not impossible, task.

Even if you do not write unit tests against your code (although you should strongly consider doing so) and don't consider testability a concern, implementing MVVM in your application still provides numerous other benefits:

- It allows you to create blendable projects, enabling you to easily populate your views with data at design time, so the designer can see what the user interface looks like populated with data without needing to compile and run the project.

- It enhances the designer/developer workflow, reducing the friction when both parties work simultaneously on the look, behavior, and logic of a view, without interfering with one another.

- It provides a step toward structuring your project to support the implementation of the inversion of control principle and dependency injection.

- It enables you to potentially reuse the view logic across multiple different view implementations.

- The loose coupling enables you to potentially apply different Views to the same ViewModel. For example, you could reuse your ViewModels from your Silverlight project in a Windows Phone 7 edition, with different views applied to suit the Windows Phone 7 controls and form factor.

- Even if you decide not to write unit tests against your project, having implemented MVVM in your project allows you to retrofit your project with unit tests at a later time without requiring too much (if any) restructuring.

As you can see, there are many potential benefits gained from implementing the MVVM design pattern in your Silverlight business applications.

MVVM Theory

At the heart of the MVVM design pattern is the separation of a view's logic from its look. Instead of having a mass of code in a View's code-behind, much of this code will be extracted out into a ViewModel class—separated from the View itself. This ViewModel class will then expose data and operations publicly for one or more Views to consume. The result of this will be that the view should have very little code-behind. You can then use data bindings and commands/behaviors as the glue to connect the View and the ViewModel together.

Let's take a look at the theory behind the MVVM design pattern and how you can put these principles in place in your Silverlight business applications.

The Layers

The MVVM design pattern consists of three core layers:

- Model
- View
- ViewModel

You could think of the pattern as being quite similar to the traditional three-tier pattern, which consists of a presentation tier, business logic tier, and data tier. Although they are quite different patterns and serve different needs, we can compare the layers in the MVVM design pattern to the tiers in the three-tier pattern in the following respects:

- The View layer corresponds to the presentation tier.
- The Model layer corresponds to the data tier.
- The ViewModel layer corresponds to the business logic tier.

However, all of the layers forming the MVVM design pattern actually exist within the presentation tier of the three-tier pattern (the Silverlight application acts as the entire tier), with each layer focused on serving the needs of the user interface. Figure 13-1 demonstrates how the layers within the MVVM design pattern relate to each other, with the arrows representing a "knows about" or "communicates with" interaction.

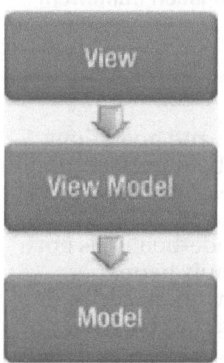

Figure 13-1. *The strict relationships between the View, ViewModel, and Model layers*

As Figure 13-1 shows, outside of its own layer, the View should technically know only about the ViewModel, and the ViewModel should know only about the Model(s). In practice, however, this is rarely the case, with the ViewModel often presenting the Model(s) to a View to consume directly; therefore, a View will typically have full knowledge of the structure of the Model(s), as demonstrated in Figure 13-2.

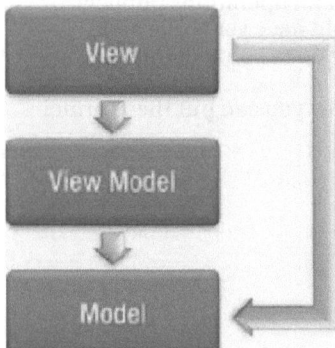

Figure 13-2. The more common relationships between the View, ViewModel, and Model layers

Let's now take a closer look at the purpose of each of these layers.

Views

You are already well versed in the purpose of Views by now. A View consists of both a XAML file and a code-behind class. Throughout this book, we have made extensive use of the navigation framework, and in this context, both the XAML file and the class inherit from Page (discussed in Chapter 3). How you choose to display Views within your application is of no consequence and has no impact on the implementation of the MVVM design pattern. You may choose use Prism, or perhaps no framework at all to display your Views.

■ **Note**   For the purpose of the examples in this chapter, I will assume you are using the navigation framework for structuring and composing your user interface.

In terms of the MVVM design pattern, think of views simply as consumers of data and operations provided by the ViewModel class. Theoretically, when using MVVM, the view's code-behind class should be considered essentially irrelevant, and little to no code should be written in it. Instead, the view's logic and behavior should be placed in the ViewModel class, leaving the code-behind class with just its bare-bones requirements, a goal often referred to as "zero code-behind." However, zero code-behind is not a requirement of the MVVM pattern and is often an unrealistic goal. Some tasks are simply better per-formed in the code-behind—especially when those tasks require directly interacting with the view. At-tempting to move these types of tasks into the ViewModel class will lead to increasing the complexity of your code and decreasing its maintainability, which all in all goes against the ultimate goal and primary focus of implementing the MVVM pattern.

■ **Note** When designing views in accordance to the MVVM design pattern, your focus should be on minimizing the use of code-behind but not on removing it all completely.

Models

A model is an object, usually containing data obtained from the server, that the view can display. When you are making use of RIA Services to communicate with the server, your model objects will be the entities returned by a domain service.

ViewModels

Although the view and the model both leverage existing components that you are already familiar with, the ViewModel is an entirely new piece to the puzzle. ViewModels are used to maintain the state of a view. In this, ViewModels have a dual purpose: to expose data and operations to the view and to handle the view's logic and behavior.

■ **Note** For the purposes of this explanation, we will focus on the case where each view has a single corresponding ViewModel (i.e., a one-to-one relationship). However, views and ViewModels can exist in multiple configurations: a ViewModel may have multiple views, or model objects may be wrapped in ViewModels before being exposed to the view. These configurations will be discussed further later in this chapter.

Although its name may indicate that the purpose of a ViewModel is to provide a view of a model, abstracting the model for consumption by the view, it's really the other way around. The real purpose of a ViewModel is to maintain the state of the view and, therefore, should be considered *a model of the view*. The view's state will be maintained within the ViewModel as data, exposed as properties, and operations, exposed as either methods or commands. The view can then bind to this ViewModel to consume the data and operations that it exposes, and you can then easily write unit tests around the ViewModel.

■ **Note** Good ViewModel design dictates that a ViewModel should expose state-related data, rather than view-specific data—both naming-wise and data type–wise. For example, instead of exposing a property named `SaveButtonEnabled`, a better name would be the more generic `CanSave`. As another example, say you have a details panel on your view that you want displayed only once the data has been retrieved from the server. Instead of exposing a property named `DetailsPanelVisibility` of type `Visibility` from your ViewModel, expose a property named `AreDetailsLoaded` of type `boolean`. The details panel in the view can then bind its `Visibility` property to the `AreDetailsLoaded` property on the ViewModel, using a value converter to convert the value from a `boolean` to a `Visibility` enumeration value. It may seem like more work, but following a less view-specific naming and data type strategy enables the ViewModel to be much more generic and reusable.

Connecting the Layers

We now have three independent layers, with a reasonably clean boundary defined between each. Let's take a look now at how the layers can be connected together and communicate with one another.

Connecting the Models to the ViewModels

There's nothing special about the way that the model objects are connected to the ViewModel. Often, the ViewModel will hand off the task of retrieving data from the server to a service agent that will return them to the ViewModel when it's done. The ViewModel can then retain a reference to these models and expose them to the view.

Let's consider the scenario where you are using RIA Services to retrieve data from the server and use that data to populate the view. As discussed in Chapter 5, you can use two methods to communicate with the domain services on the server: the DomainDataSource control or the domain context object directly. The DomainDataSource control is designed to be used declaratively in XAML and thus would completely bypass the ViewModel, making it unsuitable for use in conjunction with the MVVM design pattern. However, the ViewModel class can request data from the server using a domain context and then expose the data it returns to the view.

■ **Note** When retrieving data from the server using RIA Services in conjunction with the MVVM design pattern, you will usually make use of the `DomainCollectionView` collection view (discussed in Chapter 6) when querying and exposing data from your ViewModel.

Connecting the ViewModel to the View

To connect a ViewModel to a view, you generally assign an instance of the ViewModel to the view's `DataContext` property. This enables properties of the controls in the view to bind directly to properties on the ViewModel, or the models that it exposes.

There are numerous approaches to instantiating a ViewModel object and assigning it to a view's `DataContext` property, including these:

- Instantiating the ViewModel directly in the view's XAML

- Instantiating the ViewModel directly in the view's code-behind

- Instantiating the ViewModel elsewhere and passing it as a parameter to the view's constructor

- Using a ViewModel locator (a common utility included with various MVVM frameworks that follows the service locator pattern)

For example, you can instantiate a ViewModel in XAML and assign it to the `DataContext` property of the view like so:

```
<navigation:Page x:Class="Chapter13Sample.Views.LoginView"
    xmlns="http://schemas.microsoft.com/winfx/2006/xaml/presentation"
    xmlns:x="http://schemas.microsoft.com/winfx/2006/xaml"
    xmlns:d="http://schemas.microsoft.com/expression/blend/2008"
```

```
        xmlns:mc="http://schemas.openxmlformats.org/markup-compatibility/2006"
        xmlns:navigation="clr-namespace:System.Windows.Controls;  ↵
               assembly=System.Windows.Controls.Navigation"
        xmlns:vm="clr-namespace:Chapter13Sample.ViewModels"
        mc:Ignorable="d" Title="Login">

  <navigation:Page.DataContext>
    <vm:LoginViewModel />
  </navigation:Page.DataContext>

  <Grid x:Name="LayoutRoot">
    <!-- Removed for the purpose of brevity -->
  </Grid>
</navigation:Page>
```

> ■ **Note** To instantiate a ViewModel in XAML like this, the XAML parser requires the ViewModel to have a para-meterless constructor. If this is not possible (for example, the view needs to pass the ViewModel the ID of an entity to load), you will have to instantiate it from the code-behind instead.

The previous XAML is the equivalent of the following line of code:

```
this.DataContext = new LoginViewModel();
```

Consuming a ViewModel's Data and Operations in a View

Connecting a view to its ViewModel is only a small part of the story. Once a view is bound to a View-Model, it needs the ability to consume the data and operations that the ViewModel exposes. Let's look at how it can do this now.

Data

If the ViewModel exposes data as public properties, the view can then use data bindings to bind to those properties and consume the data. This effectively provides a two-way connection, bridging the boundary between the view and the ViewModel. The view can consume the data exposed by the ViewModel and update the ViewModel again with any changes that the user makes to the data in the view, via the two-way data binding connection demonstrated in Figure 13-3.

Figure 13-3. The interaction between the view and the ViewModel using bindings

■ **Note** When you bind the control properties to the ViewModel's properties, the bindings also listen for the PropertyChanged and the ErrorsChanged events raised by the ViewModel, assuming that the ViewModel implements the INotifyPropertyChanged and INotifyDataErrorInfo interfaces. This means that the view will be aware of ViewModel property values changing and of validation errors and will be able to respond accordingly. When list controls, such as the ListBox, DataGrid, and ComboBox controls, are bound to a collection that implements the ICollectionChanged interface (such as the ObservableCollection<T> type), those controls will automatically update themselves when items are added to or removed from the collection. Hence, Silverlight's binding engine provides additional, hidden interaction between the layers, which the MVVM design pattern takes advantage of to keep a clean separation of concerns between the view and the ViewModel.

Operations

Operations that expose logic and behavior from a ViewModel to a view can be implemented as either public methods or as commands. For example, say you want the user to be able to click a Save button in the view and have the view call the ViewModel to handle the save logic. You might choose to expose the save operation as either a save command that the view can bind to and execute or as a save method that an action/behavior can call, as shown in Figure 13-4.

Let's look at these approaches and compare them.

Figure 13-4. The interactions of the View invoking an operation on a ViewModel

Commands

As discussed in Chapter 11, commands are used to encapsulate a piece of logic, which various Silverlight controls can bind to and execute in response to an event, such as a button being clicked. You can expose a command from a ViewModel as a property and bind the Command property of a control in the View to it. When the control is clicked, the command will be executed.

Methods

Methods are the general means of exposing operations from a class according to object-oriented design principles. Methods can be called from XAML using an action/behavior (discussed in Chapter 10). Actions/behaviors aren't native functionality available in Silverlight but are available using the Expression Blend Interactivity library.You can leverage the CallMethodAction action from this library to call a method on the ViewModel in response to a control's event. That is, when something happens in the user interface, the CallMethodAction action can call a method in the ViewModel.

Method vs. Commands

Whether you use methods or commands to expose operations on a ViewModel comes down to personal taste. A command can encapsulate a piece of logic and decouple it from your ViewModel so that it can be reused, but commands do require more code to implement than methods. Methods are an easy way of exposing operations from a ViewModel, but you need to use an action or a behavior, such as the CallMethodAction action, to invoke them from XAML—adding additional XAML and complexity to your view. That said, this is not usually an issue if you use Expression Blend to wire your view and ViewModel up, because it provides a point-and-click approach for applying actions and behaviors to controls. Unfortunately, however, Visual Studio doesn't have the same ability built in, and the action/behavior XAML will need to be hand coded. Ultimately, both methods are equally acceptable and can be mixed and matched according to your needs.

Notifying the View of an Event from a ViewModel

Looking at the other side of the coin now, how does the ViewModel notify the view that something has happened that it might want to respond to? Silverlight's binding engine is intelligent enough to respond to changes in bound data from the ViewModel (property value changes, validation errors, collection changes, etc.), but what if you need the view to respond to a notification from the ViewModel, such as when it raises an event? This is particularly important in Silverlight, where all calls to the server are asynchronous. For example, perhaps the view needs to navigate to another view once a save operation is complete. We can implement this behavior by raising an event from the ViewModel that the view can listen for by doing either of the following:

- Wiring up an event handler in the view's code-behind and writing some code to respond to the event

- Implementing a trigger in the view that listens for the event and responds accordingly, as shown in Figure 13-5

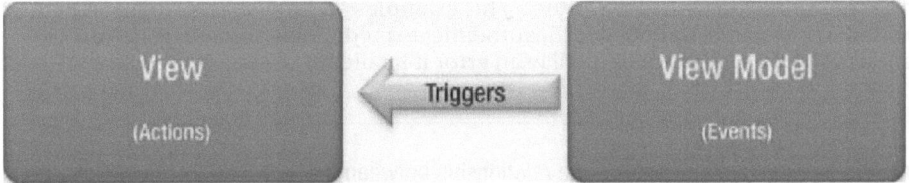

Figure 13-5. The interaction of the View handling notifications from the ViewModel

Layer Interaction Summary

Now that we've discussed the core concepts of the MVVM pattern, let's put them together in a single diagram, shown in Figure 13-6, so that you can get a complete overall perspective on how the layers can communicate with one another.

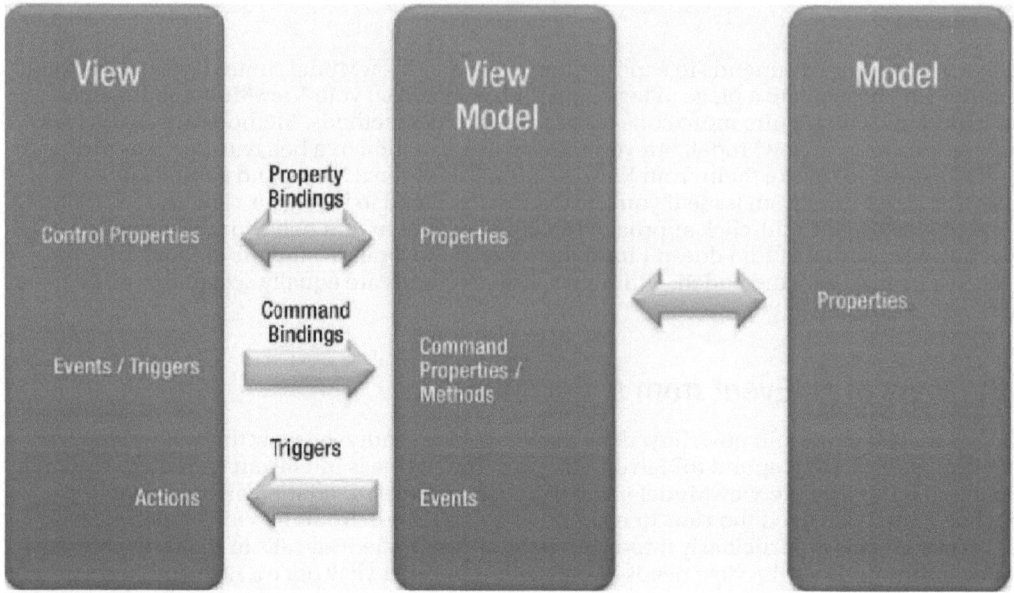

Figure 13-6. *An overview of the interactions between the MVVM layers*

MVVM in Practice

Now that you've seen the theory, it's time to learn how you can apply the MVVM design pattern to a simple example that will demonstrate the key concepts covered in the theory of how to structure the layers, and allow them to communicate with one another. This example will implement a login screen that allows the user to enter a user name and password, authenticate credentials, and navigate to another view if the authentication was successful or display an error if it failed.

■ **Note** For this scenario, we'll be assuming a one-to-one relationship between the view and the ViewModel to keep the implementation of this example simple.

Creating the Layers

To implement our simple scenario, let's start by creating the objects in the layers independently, before bringing them together.

 **Workshop: Creating the LoginView View**

By now, you will be familiar with creating new views using the navigation framework. We'll create a simple view for this example consisting of two text boxes, with corresponding labels, for the user to enter a user name and password into and a button that will initiate the user authentication check on the server.

1. Add a new view named LoginView to your project, using the SilverlightPage item template.

2. Add the following code in bold to the view:

```
<navigation:Page x:Class="Chapter13Sample.Views.LoginView"
    xmlns="http://schemas.microsoft.com/winfx/2006/xaml/presentation"
    xmlns:x="http://schemas.microsoft.com/winfx/2006/xaml"
    xmlns:d="http://schemas.microsoft.com/expression/blend/2008"
    xmlns:mc="http://schemas.openxmlformats.org/markup-compatibility/2006"
    xmlns:navigation="clr-namespace:System.Windows.Controls; ↵
            assembly=System.Windows.Controls.Navigation"
    xmlns:sdk="http://schemas.microsoft.com/winfx/2006/xaml/presentation/sdk"
    mc:Ignorable="d" Title="Login">

    <Grid x:Name="LayoutRoot" Background="White" Width="300" Height="110">
        <Grid.ColumnDefinitions>
            <ColumnDefinition Width="90" />
            <ColumnDefinition Width="*" />
        </Grid.ColumnDefinitions>

        <Grid.RowDefinitions>
            <RowDefinition Height="35" />
            <RowDefinition Height="35" />
            <RowDefinition Height="*" />
        </Grid.RowDefinitions>

        <sdk:Label Content="User Name:" Margin="5,0"
                HorizontalContentAlignment="Right" />
        <sdk:Label Content="Password:" Margin="5,0"
                HorizontalContentAlignment="Right" Grid.Row="1" />

        <TextBox Name="UserNameField" Grid.Column="1" Height="25" />
        <PasswordBox Name="PasswordField" Grid.Column="1" Grid.Row="1" Height="25" />

        <Button Name="LoginButton" Content="Log In" Margin="0,5,0,0"
                Grid.Column="1" Grid.Row="2" Height="30" Width="90"
                HorizontalAlignment="Right" VerticalAlignment="Top" />
    </Grid>
</navigation:Page>
```

This will give you the View layout shown in Figure 13-7.

Figure 13-7. *The login View*

Creating the Model

For the purposes of this example, where we are primarily concerned with the interaction of the view and the ViewModel, we'll be disregarding the model from the equation to keep things simple. However, as an exercise for when you have completed this workshop, use the authentication service provided by RIA Services to validate the user's credentials. In that scenario, the User entity returned from RIA Services will act as the model.

⚙ Workshop: Creating the LoginViewModel ViewModel Class

The next step is to create a ViewModel class that will serve the needs of the view.

1. Add a new class to your project, named LoginViewModel.

2. Implement the INotifyPropertyChanged interface on the class:

```
using System;
using System.ComponentModel;
using System.Windows.Input;

namespace Chapter13Sample
{
    public class LoginViewModel : INotifyPropertyChanged
    {
        public event PropertyChangedEventHandler PropertyChanged;
    }
}
```

■ **Note** Usually, your ViewModels will inherit from a base class that provides common functionality required by all the ViewModels in your project. At a minimum, this base class will implement the INotifyPropertyChanged interface, and it will commonly also implement either the INotifyDataErrorInfo or the IDataErrorInfo interface. If you make use of a MVVM framework, this base class will generally be provided as a key part of the framework. However, to demonstrate the simplicity of implementing the MVVM design pattern, we'll avoid hiding details away in base classes in this workshop and implement all the requirements directly in the ViewModel class.

---

3. The ViewModel class needs to expose two properties—UserName and Password:

```
private string _userName;
private string _password;

public string UserName
{
    get { return _userName; }
    set
    {
        _userName = value;

        if (PropertyChanged != null)
            PropertyChanged(this, new PropertyChangedEventArgs("UserName"));
    }
}

public string Password
{
    get { return _password; }
    set
    {
        _password = value;

        if (PropertyChanged != null)
            PropertyChanged(this, new PropertyChangedEventArgs("Password"));
    }
}
```

■ **Note** As demonstrated, all properties exposed by the ViewModel should raise the PropertyChanged event when their value changes. This will notify the view of the change so that it can update itself accordingly. However, rather than raising these events manually, you are better off having this behavior implemented automatically, using a tool such as NotifyPropertyWeaver (discussed in Chapter 7).

4. The ViewModel class also needs to expose a Login operation to the view. As discussed earlier in this chapter, you can implement this operation either as a command that the View can bind to or simply as a method. For this workshop, we'll do use a command. So we can keep the operation's logic inside our ViewModel class, we'll implement the command as a DelegateCommand. Add the code for the DelegateCommand to your project (the code can be found in Chapter 11 and in the source code for this chapter, downloadable from the Apress web site). Now define the Execute and CanExecute methods for the command in your ViewModel class, and create a property that will expose the command to the view:

```
public ICommand LoginCommand
{
    get
    {
```

```
        return new DelegateCommand(BeginLogin, CanLogin);
    }
}

private void BeginLogin(object param)
{
    // Logic to validate the user's login goes here
}

private bool CanLogin(object param)
{
    return true;
}
```

5. In a scenario like this, the login logic would generally have to make an asynchronous call to the server to validate the user's credentials. Once that call returns, the ViewModel needs to notify the View of the result, which it can do by raising one of the following events defined on the ViewModel:

```
public event EventHandler LoginSuccessful;
public event EventHandler LoginFailed;
public event EventHandler LoginError;
```

6. To keep this workshop simple, we'll avoid making the asynchronous call and simply raise the LoginSuccessful event as soon as the Login command is executed. Update the BeginLogin method like so:

```
private void BeginLogin(object param)
{
    // Logic to validate the user's login goes here.  We'll assume the
    // credentials are immediately valid (you'd normally go back to the
    // server first), and raise the LoginSuccessful event
    if (LoginSuccessful != null)
        LoginSuccessful(this, new EventArgs());
}
```

⚙ Workshop: Connecting the ViewModel to the View

Now that you have both the View and the ViewModel, it's time to connect them.

1. Declare a namespace prefix named vm, pointing to the namespace where the ViewModel class can be found, and assign an instance of the ViewModel to the View's DataContext property:

```
<navigation:Page x:Class="Chapter13Sample.Views.LoginView"
    xmlns="http://schemas.microsoft.com/winfx/2006/xaml/presentation"
    xmlns:x="http://schemas.microsoft.com/winfx/2006/xaml"
    xmlns:d="http://schemas.microsoft.com/expression/blend/2008"
    xmlns:mc="http://schemas.openxmlformats.org/markup-compatibility/2006"
    xmlns:navigation="clr-namespace:System.Windows.Controls; ↵
            assembly=System.Windows.Controls.Navigation"
    xmlns:sdk="http://schemas.microsoft.com/winfx/2006/xaml/presentation/sdk"
    xmlns:vm="clr-namespace:Chapter13Sample"
```

```
    mc:Ignorable="d" Title="Login">

  <navigation:Page.DataContext>
      <vm:LoginViewModel />
  </navigation:Page.DataContext>

  <!-- View contents removed for brevity -->
</navigation:Page>
```

■ **Note** When you declaratively connect the ViewModel to the view in this fashion, the Visual Studio XAML designer actually creates an instance of your ViewModel class. Be careful when doing so because any logic in the ViewModel's constructor will be executed at design time each time the View is opened in the designer. For example, you generally won't want to make calls to the server at design time. If you have logic in the ViewModel's constructor that you don't want to be executed at design time, you can put it in an `if` block that checks whether it's in design-time mode. The `System.ComponentModel.DesignerProperties.IsInDesignTool` static property can be used for this purpose.

Alternatively, you can simply assign an instance of the ViewModel class to the View's `DataContext` property in the View's constructor in the code-behind:

```
this.DataContext = new LoginViewModel();
```

Communicating Between the View and the ViewModel

Let's now look at how you can implement the three core interactions between a View and a ViewModel:

- Consuming data from the ViewModel in the view (data binding)

- Enabling the view to invoke an operation on the ViewModel (binding to a command)

- Enabling the view to respond to an event in the ViewModel (implementing a trigger)

⚙ Workshop: Consuming Data from the ViewModel in the View

The Text properties of both text fields in our view now need to be bound to their corresponding properties on the ViewModel using two-way binding.

1. Bind the Text property of the `UserNameField` control in the View to the `UserName` property on the ViewModel:

```
<TextBox Name="UserNameField" Grid.Column="1" Height="25"
        Text="{Binding UserName, Mode=TwoWay}" />
```

2. Bind the Text property of the PasswordField control in the View to the Password
property on the ViewModel, like so:

```
<PasswordBox Name="PasswordField" Grid.Column="1" Grid.Row="1" Height="25"
        Password="{Binding Password, Mode=TwoWay}" />
```

⚙ Workshop: Invoking the Login Operation (Command) on the ViewModel

We now need the Log In button in the view to execute the LoginCommand property exposed by the
ViewModel.

1. Bind the Command property of the Button control in the View to the
LoginCommand property exposed by the ViewModel class.

```
<Button Name="LoginButton" Content="Log In" Margin="0,5,0,0"
        Grid.Column="1" Grid.Row="2" Height="30" Width="90"
        HorizontalAlignment="Right" VerticalAlignment="Top"
        Command="{Binding LoginCommand}" />
```

When the button is clicked, the LoginCommand command will call the
BeginLogin method in the ViewModel class.

⚙ Workshop: Invoking the Login Operation (Method) on the ViewModel

Instead of a command, if you were to simply expose a parameterless method named Login (for example)
from the ViewModel class, you can use the CallMethodAction action from the Expression Blend Interactivity Library to wire up the Button control to call that method when it's clicked. Let's look at how you
can invoke an operation exposed from the ViewModel class as a method instead of as a command, as the
previous workshop demonstrated.

1. Add a public method named Login to the LoginViewModel class. This will be the
method that will be called when the Log In button in the View is clicked. We'll
simply add the same logic to it that we used for the command:

```
public void Login()
{
    // Logic to validate the user's login goes here.  We'll assume the
    // credentials are immediately valid (you'd normally go back to the
    // server first), and raise the LoginSuccessful event
    if (LoginSuccessful != null)
        LoginSuccessful(this, new EventArgs());
}
```

2. Add a reference to the System.Windows.Interactivity.dll and
Microsoft.Expression.Interactions.dll assemblies to your project. As discussed in Chapter 10, these assemblies are installed along with Express Blend,
or the Expression Blend SDK, and can be found under the
Silverlight\v5.0\Libraries path of the corresponding product.

3. Declare the following namespace prefixes in the XAML file:

```
xmlns:i="http://schemas.microsoft.com/expression/2010/interactivity"
xmlns:ei="http://schemas.microsoft.com/expression/2010/interactions"
```

4. Add the following XAML in bold to the Log In button:

```
<Button Name="LoginButton" Content="Log In"
        Grid.Column="1" Grid.Row="2" Height="30" Width="90"
        HorizontalAlignment="Right" VerticalAlignment="Top">
    <i:Interaction.Triggers>
        <i:EventTrigger EventName="Click">
            <ei:CallMethodAction TargetObject="{Binding}" MethodName="Login" />
        </i:EventTrigger>
    </i:Interaction.Triggers>
</Button>
```

5. Now when you click the button, the Login method on the ViewModel class will be called.

⚙ Workshop: Responding to the ViewModel's LoginSuccessful Event in the View

Our ViewModel raises a LoginSuccessful event to simulate the successful authentication of the user's credentials. We now need to configure the View to listen for this event and respond accordingly. One way of doing so is by simply handling the event in the View's code-behind. For example, the XAML that instantiates the LoginViewModel class and assigns it to the View's DataContext property can wire up an event handler to handle the event in the code-behind, like so:

```
<navigation:Page.DataContext>
    <vm:LoginViewModel LoginSuccessful="LoginViewModel_LoginSuccessful" />
</navigation:Page.DataContext>
```

You can then write the logic for how the View should respond to that event in the event handler in the code-behind.

In this workshop, we're going to focus on a more declarative approach to the problem. We'll use the EventTrigger trigger and listen for the LoginSuccessful event to be raised on the ViewModel. The trigger can then invoke an action in response to the event.

1. To start, we need an action to call once the event is raised. Typically, in a scenario like this, once the user has logged in successfully, you'd navigate to a new view. The section titled "How Do I Navigate to a Different View?" later in this chapter includes the source for a custom action named NavigateAction that you can used for this purpose, but to keep this workshop simple, we'll just create a simple action that displays a message box when it is invoked. Add a new class named LoginSuccessAction to your project, and add the following code to it:

```
using System;
using System.Windows;
using System.Windows.Interactivity;

namespace Chapter13Sample.Actions
{
    public class LoginSuccessAction : TriggerAction<UIElement>
    {
        protected override void Invoke(object parameter)
        {
```

```
            MessageBox.Show("Login successful!");
        }
    }
}
```

2. Define a namespace prefix in the XAML file to let us use the action:

```
xmlns:actions="clr-namespace:Chapter13Sample.Actions"
```

■ **Note**   You'll also need the i and ei namespace prefixes declared, as in the previous workshop.

---

3. You can now make use of the Interaction.Triggers attached property to han-
    dle the LoginSuccessful event and invoke the action when the event is raised.
    You can use this attached property anywhere in your XAML. Since it can be
    considered a View-level trigger, let's define it immediately after setting the
    view's DataContext property. We'll use an EventTrigger to bind to the View-
    Model and listen for the LoginSuccessful event. When the event is raised, the
    trigger will invoke the LoginSuccessAction action that we created in step 1:

```
<navigation:Page x:Class="Chapter13Sample.Views.LoginView"
    xmlns="http://schemas.microsoft.com/winfx/2006/xaml/presentation"
    xmlns:x="http://schemas.microsoft.com/winfx/2006/xaml"
    xmlns:d="http://schemas.microsoft.com/expression/blend/2008"
    xmlns:mc="http://schemas.openxmlformats.org/markup-compatibility/2006"
    xmlns:navigation="clr-namespace:System.Windows.Controls; ↵
            assembly=System.Windows.Controls.Navigation"
    xmlns:sdk="http://schemas.microsoft.com/winfx/2006/xaml/presentation/sdk"
    xmlns:vm="clr-namespace:Chapter13Sample"
    xmlns:i="http://schemas.microsoft.com/expression/2010/interactivity"
    xmlns:ei="http://schemas.microsoft.com/expression/2010/interactions"
    xmlns:actions="clr-namespace:Chapter13Sample.Actions"
    mc:Ignorable="d" Title="Login">

    <navigation:Page.DataContext>
        <vm:LoginViewModel />
    </navigation:Page.DataContext>

    <i:Interaction.Triggers>
        <i:EventTrigger SourceObject="{Binding Mode=OneWay}"
                        EventName="LoginSuccessful">
            <actions:LoginSuccessAction />
        </i:EventTrigger>
    </i:Interaction.Triggers>

    <!-- View contents removed for brevity -->
</navigation:Page>
```

4. When you click the button, the login operation exposed by the ViewModel will be called, via one of the methods described in the previous workshops. That operation will then raise the `LoginSuccessful` event. The trigger we just defined is now listening for that event and will invoke the `LoginSuccessAction` action when the event is raised, showing the message box.

MVVM Frameworks

Although the core principles of the MVVM design pattern are reasonably straightforward, in practice, maintaining a clean separation between the View and its corresponding ViewModel can be a difficult task at times. However, a number of frameworks have developed solutions for the most common hurdles that you will face (displaying dialogs, navigation, View and ViewModel composition, etc.) and are well worth looking into.

Popular MVVM Frameworks

Here are some of the most popular frameworks that provide support for the MVVM design pattern (and often a host of additional other features) that you may wish to consider:

- *MVVM Light Toolkit*: http://mvvmlight.codeplex.com
- *Prism*: http://compositewpf.codeplex.com
- *Caliburn Micro*: http://caliburnmicro.codeplex.com
- *Silverlight.FX*: http://projects.nikhilk.net/SilverlightFX
- *nRoute*: http://nroute.codeplex.com
- *Cinch:* http://cinch.codeplex.com
- *Jounce:* http://jounce.codeplex.com
- *Simple MVVM Toolkit:* http://simplemvvmtoolkit.codeplex.com

Should I Use a MVVM Framework?

A number of frameworks are available that can provide additional support for structuring your application using the MVVM design pattern (as discussed later in this chapter). However, some developers believe that you are better off rolling your own and that it's not necessary or worthwhile to implement a major framework. To properly grasp the principles of MVVM and identify if and where a framework can help you, without becoming too overwhelmed by all their features, it's probably best that you start off without using a framework, but investigate the available options when implementing a major project. However, many of the popular frameworks go beyond simply supporting the MVVM design pattern and add a lot of helpful infrastructure to your project, so they are well worth looking into.

Creating a Simple MVVM Framework

At its simplest, an MVVM framework will just provide a base ViewModel class. Typically, this base ViewModel class would implement the `INotifyPropertyChanged` interface, and perhaps `INotifyDataErrorInfo`. The sample code for this chapter, downloadable from the Apress web site, provides a simple base ViewModel class named `ViewModelBase` that you can use to get you started if you don't want to jump into using a full-fledged MVVM framework.

As you can see from the class shown in Figure 13-8, the `ViewModelBase` class implements the `INotifyPropertyChanged` and `INotifyDataErrorInfo` interfaces and predominantly focuses on implementing property changed and error notifications.

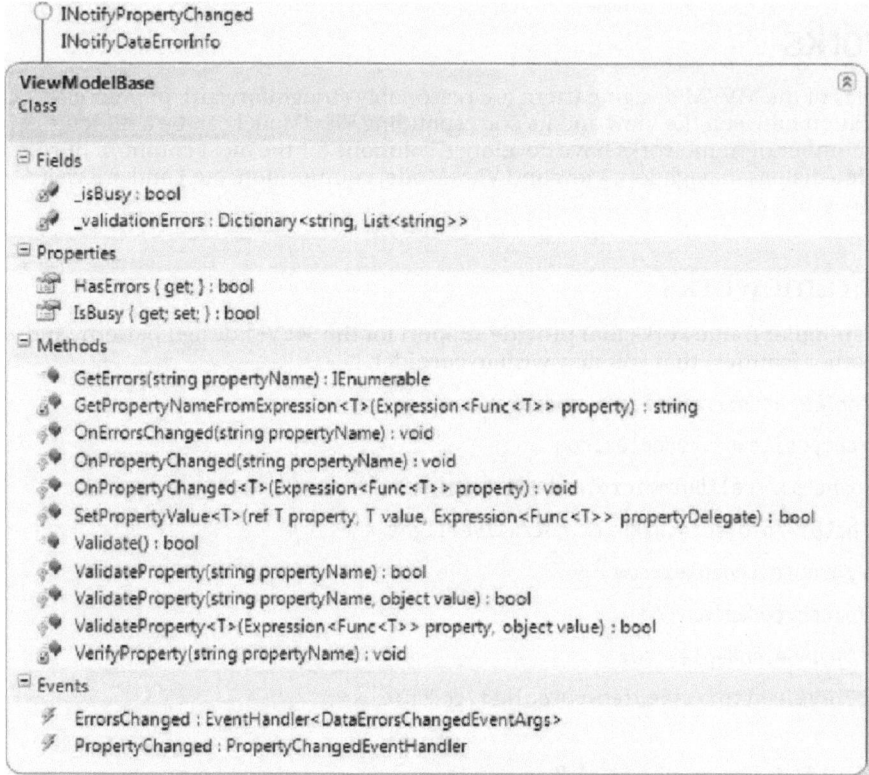

Figure 13-8. Class diagram for a simple base ViewModel class

The benefit of having your ViewModel inherit from this class is that you can call the `ViewModelBase` class's `SetPropertyValue` method in a property setter, which will validate the property against any validation attributes applied to it and raise the `PropertyChanged` event for the property. This saves you having to write all that logic in each and every property setter in your ViewModel. The following code demonstrates how you would implement a property when your ViewModel class inherits from the `ViewModelBase` class. Note how the `SetPropertyValue` method is being called in the property's setter. The method handles assigning the new value to the property's backing field (`_userName`), validates the property (in this case, it handles the `Required` validation rule applied to the property), and raises the `PropertyChanged` event for the property.

```
private string _userName;

[Required]
public string UserName
```

```
{
    get { return _userName; }
    set { SetPropertyValue(ref _userName, value, () => UserName); }
}
```

■ **Note** The SetPropertyValue method accepts a strongly typed reference to the property, using the syntax ()
=> UserName, as described in Chapter 7. This provides a refactoring-safe way of letting the method know what
property this is and avoids the use of "magic strings" in your code.

Implementing Common Scenarios with MVVM

Many common scenarios are easy to implement when writing your View's logic in its code-behind, because you have full control over the View. However, once you start using the MVVM design pattern and have a clean separation of concerns between the View's look and its logic/behavior, implementing these scenarios requires a bit more thought. Let's look at how you can "control" the View from the ViewModel and solve some of the implementation issues commonly faced when using the MVVM design pattern.

How Do I Assign a Value to a Control's Property?

When writing code-behind, you would typically assign a control's property like so:

```
NameTextBox.Text = "Chris Anderson";
```

When using the MVVM design pattern, instead of setting the control's property in code, the ViewModel class should expose a property, like so:

```
private string _name;

public string Name
{
    get { return _name; }
    set
    {
        _name = value;

        if (PropertyChanged != null)
            PropertyChanged(this, new PropertyChangedEventArgs("Name"));
    }
}
```

And the control in the View can bind to it:

```
<TextBox Name="NameTextBox" Text="{Binding Name, Mode=TwoWay}" />
```

Of course, it's vital that your ViewModel class implements the INotifyPropertyChanged interface and raises the PropertyChanged event when the value of the property changes. Otherwise, the View won't be aware of the change in the property's value, and consequently, the control's property value won't update.

How Do I Enable/Disable Controls?

Simply expose a Boolean property from your ViewModel class, and bind the control's IsEnabled property to it. As discussed earlier in this chapter, try not to name the property according to its purpose—it's best to name it according to what its value represents, rather than how it is to be used. Therefore, instead of naming your exposed property SaveButtonEnabled, for example, a better name would be the more generic CanSave.

How Do I Show/Hide Controls?

You can control whether controls are hidden or displayed by binding their Visibility property to a property exposed by your ViewModel class. The Visibility property on controls is an enumeration of type Visibility. However, best practice is to not expose View-specific data types like this from your View-Model. As has been discussed earlier in this chapter, you should try to make your ViewModel classes as generic as possible. Value converters are the key to allowing your ViewModels to expose properties that don't necessarily match the control properties that will bind to them. Instead of exposing a property named DetailsPanelVisibility of type Visibility from your ViewModel, it's best to expose a property named AreDetailsLoaded of type boolean. Despite being two different data types, the details panel in the View can still bind its Visibility property to the AreDetailsLoaded property on the ViewModel, but use a value converter to convert the value from a Boolean to a Visibility enumeration value.

How Do I Display a Validation Error in the View?

Implement either the INotifyDataErrorInfo or IDataErrorInfo interface on your ViewModel class, as described in Chapter 7. This will provide a means for the View to be aware of validation errors and display them accordingly. You can even apply validation attributes to properties on your ViewModel, defining validation rules for the properties.

■ **Note** When applying validation attributes to properties on your ViewModel class, you will need to write code in the property's setter to invoke the validation using the Validator class. Most of this code will generally reside in a base ViewModel class. See Chapter 7 for more information.

How Do I Add/Remove Items from a List?

As discussed in Chapter 6, the best way to populate a list, such as a ListBox or a DataGrid control, is to assign a collection of type ObservableCollection<T> to the control's ItemsSource property. These controls listen for the CollectionChanged event that an ObservableCollection (or any collection that implements the INotifyCollectionChanged interface) raises when items are added or removed from it and update themselves accordingly. Therefore, if you expose a collection as an ObservableCollection from your ViewModel class for a ListBox, DataGrid, ComboBox, or similar control to bind to, you can then simply add or remove items to/from the collection, and the control will update itself accordingly.

■ **Note** The ObservableCollection<T> type can be extremely useful when you need to asynchronously retrieve data from the server and populate a control in the view with it. When the initial binding takes place and the data is not available yet, you can simply expose an empty collection of type ObservableCollection<T> from the ViewModel for the control to bind to. Then, when the asynchronous call has completed and the data has been retrieved from the server, you can update the collection with new items, and the bound control will update itself accordingly.

How Do I Select an Item in a List or Get the Currently Selected Item?

One way is to expose a property from your ViewModel class that the control's SelectedItem property can bind to. For example, your ViewModel class might expose two properties: a collection used to populate the control in the View (Products) and an object maintaining the currently selected item (CurrentProduct):

```
private ObservableCollection<Product> _products;
private Product _currentProduct;

public ObservableCollection<Product> Products
{
    get { return _products; }
    set
    {
        _products = value;

        if (PropertyChanged != null)
            PropertyChanged(this, new PropertyChangedEventArgs("Products"));
    }
}

public Product CurrentProduct
{
    get { return _currentProduct; }
    set
    {
        _currentProduct = value;

        if (PropertyChanged != null)
            PropertyChanged(this, new PropertyChangedEventArgs("CurrentProduct"));
    }
}
```

The control can then bind its ItemsSource and SelectedItem properties to these properties, like so:

```
<ListBox ItemsSource="{Binding Products}"
        SelectedItem="{Binding CurrentProduct, Mode=TwoWay}" />
```

■ **Note** Remember to set the binding mode to TwoWay when binding the control's SelectedItem property to the property on the ViewModel. Otherwise, you'll be able to set the selected item for the control but the ViewModel's property won't be updated when the user selects a different item.

When the user selects an item in the ListBox control, the selected item will be assigned to the CurrentProduct property on the ViewModel. If you assign a Product object to the CurrentProduct property in the ViewModel, the ListBox will automatically change its selected item to the one for that Product. If you need to perform additional actions when the selected item is changed, you can do so in the CurrentProduct property's setter.

■ **Note** The ListBox and ComboBox controls have a pair of properties named SelectedValuePath and SelectedValue properties, which we looked at in Chapter 7. You can use these together to select an item or get the selected item using a unique key property to identify the selected object, instead of the whole object. This is particularly useful when you need to select an item in a ComboBox control but have only a foreign key value to identify that item. See Chapter 7 for more details on using these properties.

Another approach to the problem is to expose the collection as a collection view, rather than as an ObservableCollection. As discussed in Chapter 6, collection views maintain a current record pointer, which tracks the current item in the collection. When you bind a DataGrid, ListBox, ComboBox, or similar control to a collection view, such as a PagedCollectionView, these controls will update the collection view's CurrentItem property according to the item that is currently selected.

■ **Note** Although most of the time this is the behavior that you will want, sometimes, you may wish to have more control over the process. You will find that some of these controls, such as the ListBox control, have an IsSynchronizedWithCurrentItem property, whose default value is null. You can't actually set this property to true (it will throw an exception if you try), as it depends on whether or not the binding source is a collection view to determine whether synchronization with the current item is possible. If the binding source is a collection view, current item synchronization will automatically be turned on, although you can explicitly turn it off by setting the property to false.

To select an item in the view from the ViewModel, you can't assign a value to the collection view's CurrentItem property, but you can call its MoveCurrentTo method and pass it an object as its parameter. The control in the View will automatically select the item corresponding to that object.

As a general rule, the collection view approach is the more elegant of the two, but both are suitable ways of selecting items in list controls.

■ **Note** Both ways are suitable for implementing a master/details–style View, containing a list on one side of the screen and a details view (such as a DataForm control) on the other side. Let's say that when the user selects an item in the list, you want the selected item's details to appear in the DataForm control. When implementing the first approach described, bind the list control to the `Products` property on the ViewModel and the DataForm control to the `CurrentProduct` property. Using the collection view approach, both controls can simply be bound to the collection view exposed by the ViewModel, and they will automatically stay synchronized and exhibit the required behavior.

How Do I Control the Filtering, Sorting, Grouping, and Paging of Items Displayed in a List?

Expose the collection from the ViewModel as a collection view, such as a `PagedCollectionView`, as detailed in Chapter 6. This will permit you to control the filtering, sorting, grouping, and paging of the data from the ViewModel by configuring these requirements on the collection view.

How Can I Handle Control Events?

Sometimes, you need to handle events in your ViewModel class raised by controls in the view. Technically, this should be a rare occurrence, as it's often more appropriate to handle control events in the view itself. However, when you need to do so, there are two main methods you can use:

- A simple (albeit not particularly elegant) way is to handle the event in the code-behind and call a method on the ViewModel.

- Alternatively, use an event trigger and the `CallMethodAction` action in the View's XAML to listen for the event and call a method on the ViewModel. We did this earlier in this chapter, in the section titled "Workshop: Invoking the Login Operation (Method) on the ViewModel."

How Do I Revert a ViewModel to a Previous State?

Implement the `IEditableObject` interface on your ViewModel, as described in Chapter 7. When the `BeginEdit` method on the ViewModel is called, you can capture the ViewModel's state and cache it somewhere. When the `EndEdit` method is called, that cache can be discarded. However, if the `CancelEdit` method is called, the ViewModel's state can be reinstated from the cache.

This allows you to implement a "cancel changes" type behavior on your ViewModel and revert to the ViewModel state before the `BeginEdit` method was called.

How Do I Prevent the User from Doing Anything While an Asynchronous Operation is in Progress?

Generally, you will expose a property from the ViewModel named `IsBusy`. This is a `Boolean` value that your ViewModel can set to true when an asynchronous operation is in progress. You can then bind this

IsBusy property to the `IsBusy` property on a BusyIndicator control in your View, which results in the BusyIndicator control appearing in the View when the ViewModel's `IsBusy` property is set to true. The BusyIndicator control serves two purposes: to inform the user that something is happening and to block the user from interacting with the View until the operation is complete. See Chapter 6 for more details on the BusyIndicator control.

How Do I Notify the View When an Asynchronous Operation Is Complete?

You can notify the view of the completion of an asynchronous operation, such as a save operation, by simply raising an event in the ViewModel. The view can then listen for this event using a trigger or code-behind and respond accordingly.

How Do I Set Focus to a Control?

What control should have focus is more often than not a View issue and is not something a ViewModel should typically be particularly concerned about. Instead, the ViewModel should expose information about a change in its state, generally by raising an event, which the View can respond to and set focus to a control accordingly.

For example, say you have a data entry form that allows users to enter data for a product, and you click a button to save the data and create a new (empty) record. In this scenario, the ViewModel can raise an event, named `NewRecordStarted`, for example, which the View can respond to and set the focus to the first control in the form accordingly. You can respond to the event and set focus to the control in the code-behind, or you can take a more declarative approach and define an event trigger in the XAML that listens for the event and invokes an action that sets the control's focus.

Here's the code for an example action that can be used to set the focus on a control:

```
using System.Windows.Controls;
using System.Windows.Interactivity;

namespace Chapter13Sample.Actions
{
    public class SetFocusAction : TargetedTriggerAction<Control>
    {
        protected override void Invoke(object parameter)
        {
            if (Target != null)
                Target.Focus();
        }
    }
}
```

You can easily test this action by updating the code you have from the workshop titled "Workshop: Responding to the ViewModel's LoginSuccessful Event in the View" to set the focus on the text box named `UserNameField` when the ViewModel raises the `LoginSuccessful` event. Simply replace the use of the `LoginSuccessAction` action with this `SetFocusAction` action instead, like so:

```
<i:Interaction.Triggers>
    <i:EventTrigger SourceObject="{Binding Mode=OneWay}"
                    EventName="LoginSuccessful">
        <actions:SetFocusAction TargetName="UserNameField" />
```

```
        </i:EventTrigger>
    </i:Interaction.Triggers>
```

As you can see, we just need to set the `TargetName` property on the action, which our `SetFocusAction` action inherited from the `TargetedTriggerAction<T>` class, specifying the control (`UserNameField`) that should receive the focus when the action is invoked. Now when the Login button is clicked, which invokes the login operation on the ViewModel, which in turn raises the `LoginSuccessful` event, the `SetFocusAction` action will be invoked, and the control named `UserNameField` will receive the focus.

■ **Note**   You don't have to rely on the ViewModel raising an event to use this action. Instead, if you prefer, you can configure the event trigger to listen for an event raised by another control in the view, such as the `Click` event raised by a Button control.

How Do I Display a Message Box to the User?

ViewModels should rarely concern themselves with displaying message boxes to the users, as these are primarily a view-related issue. Common reasons for displaying message boxes include:

- *Notifying the user of an error, such as when an error occurs saving data to the server*: As no response from the user is required, consider displaying the error in another way in the view. For example, reserve an area at the top or bottom of the view for displaying errors, add a property to your ViewModel exposing the last error message, and bind a control (such as a TextBox) to that property in the view. Alternatively, make use of Silverlight's validation functionality, and implement either the `INotifyDataErrorInfo` or `IDataErrorInfo` interface to expose the error as an object level error that the view can display. Displaying error messages in this manner can often provide a better user experience for your users than implementing message boxes.

- *Miscellaneous notifications*: Sometimes, you want to notify the user of something that has just happened, such as the completion of a long-running process. Like the previous point, as no response is required from the user, consider implementing this notification in a more user-friendly manner than via a message box.

- *Notifying the user of invalid data*: Instead of using message boxes, you should take advantage of Silverlight's rich data validation framework. See Chapter 7 for more details on making use of this built-in data validation behavior.

- *Confirmation dialogs*: This is a valid use for displaying message boxes, but the question is whether your ViewModel should actually control this behavior. If you want to confirm a delete operation, for example, perhaps the View should display the dialog when a delete button is clicked, *before* invoking the delete operation on the ViewModel. In some cases, some logic needs to be performed before the dialog can be shown, in which case the ViewModel will need to invoke the confirmation dialog. In this scenario, controlling the display of a message box from a ViewModel is probably a valid requirement.

- *Asking questions*: Sometimes, the ViewModel needs to ask the user a question to determine how its logic should proceed. Assuming there is no better way of implementing the logic to obtain all the information needed from the user up front, controlling the display of a message box from a ViewModel is probably a valid requirement.

As you can see, you will generally display message boxes to the user only when a response is required. One way of implementing this behavior is to raise an event from the ViewModel that has custom argument object containing a property in which the result of the user's input can be returned to the ViewModel. You can then handle that event in the View's code-behind, display the message box to the user, and assign the result to the property on the arguments object that was passed into the event handler method as a parameter. This is a workable solution, although not a particularly elegant one.

More elegant solutions can be found in various MVVM frameworks, such as MVVM Light and Prism. For example, MVVM Light provides a Messenger class that can be used for this purpose, which you can find out more about at http://blog.galasoft.ch/archive/2009/09/27/mvvm-light-toolkit-messenger-v2-beta.aspx. Prism also contains some guidance in the section titled "User Interaction Patterns" in Chapter 6 of the *Prism Guidance* documentation at http://msdn.microsoft.com/en-us/library/gg405494.aspx.

If you're not using a MVVM framework, you might like to try one of the following alternative solutions:

- Alexandr Vitenberg has a "Bindable event-driven MessageBox" solution that you can find at www.yumasoft.com/node/47.

- Jeremy Likness has a Simple Dialog Service solution that he has documented at http://csharperimage.jeremylikness.com/2010/01/simple-dialog-service-in-silverlight.html.

- Josh Smith has a solution that uses the service locator pattern and has documented it at www.codeproject.com/KB/WPF/MessageBoxInMVVM.aspx. Despite the article being focused on WPF, the concepts are still transferrable to Silverlight.

How Do I Start a State Transition or Control an Animation?

Raise an event from your ViewModel indicating a change in its state that can be used to invoke a state transition or change to an animation in the View. You can then handle this event in the View's XAML using an event trigger and use one of the following actions in response to it:

- GoToStateAction: This will activate a given state in the View, as defined using the VisualStateManger. Kirupa Chinnathambi has more information on using this action at www.kirupa.com/blend_silverlight/gotoStateAction.htm.

- ControlStoryboardAction: This will change the state of a given storyboard in the View. Kirupa Chinnathambi has more information on using this action at http://blogs.msdn.com/b/expression/archive/2010/05/25/control-storyboards-easily-using-behaviors.aspx.

How Can I Pass Complex Objects Between Views?

As discussed in Chapter 3, the navigation framework doesn't allow you to pass complex objects between Views. For example, you can't pass a Product object from a product list view to a product details view when navigating between them. However, in scenarios like the one just described, it may be valid to use the same ViewModel to manage the logic for both views. If you maintain the same instance of the

ViewModel object for use by both views, there's no need to pass data between the views, as this data will be maintained within the same ViewModel instance. This requires you to take more of a View-Model-first approach, as opposed to the view-first approach demonstrated so far in this chapter. We'll compare and contrast these two approaches in the "Alternative View / ViewModel Configurations" section later in this chapter.

How Do I Navigate to a Different View?

If you're using the navigation framework in your application, you will often need to control the navigation between views from your ViewModels. You can solve this problem in numerous ways. A simple way, following the pattern for most of the solutions for MVVM issues described so far, is to raise an event from your ViewModel and handle that event either in the View's code-behind or using an event trigger in XAML. If you do so in the code-behind, you can simply navigate to a view using the view's Navigation-Service object, as covered in Chapter 3. If you choose to use the event trigger method, you can write an action that will perform the navigation for you. The following code demonstrates an action named NavigateAction, which you can use to navigate to a different view when the action is invoked:

```
using System;
using System.Windows;
using System.Windows.Controls;
using System.Windows.Interactivity;
using System.Windows.Media;

namespace Chapter13Sample.Actions
{
    public class NavigateAction : TriggerAction<UIElement>
    {
        public String Url
        {
            get { return (String)GetValue(UrlProperty); }
            set { SetValue(UrlProperty, value); }
        }

        public static readonly DependencyProperty UrlProperty =
            DependencyProperty.Register("Url", typeof(String),
                                typeof(NavigateAction), null);

        protected override void Invoke(object parameter)
        {
            Frame frame = FindAncestorOfType(this.AssociatedObject,
                                        typeof(Frame)) as Frame;

            if (frame != null)
                frame.Navigate(new Uri(Url, UriKind.Relative));
        }

        public static DependencyObject FindAncestorOfType(DependencyObject element,
                                                    Type locateType)
        {
            DependencyObject parent = element;

            do
```

```
        {
            parent = VisualTreeHelper.GetParent(parent);

            if (parent != null && parent.GetType() == locateType)
                return parent;
        }
        while (parent != null);

        return null;
    }
  }
}
```

You can easily test this action by updating the code you have from the workshop titled "Workshop: Responding to the ViewModel's LoginSuccessful Event in the View" to navigate to a new view when the ViewModel raises the LoginSuccessful event. Simply replace the use of the LoginSuccessAction action with this NavigateAction action instead, like so:

```
<i:Interaction.Triggers>
    <i:EventTrigger SourceObject="{Binding Mode=OneWay}"
                    EventName="LoginSuccessful">
        <actions:NavigateAction Url="/Dashboard" />
    </i:EventTrigger>
</i:Interaction.Triggers>
```

As you can see, we're setting the Url property on the action, designating what view should be navigated to. You could alternatively bind the Url property to a property exposed by your ViewModel, enabling the ViewModel to actually control what view should be navigated to in response to the event.

Other ways you might like to consider include:

- Have an application-wide UIController object that controls the navigation between views. The view containing the Frame control can register the Frame with the UIController object. ViewModels can then tell the UIController object to navigate to the view. To enable ViewModels to communicate with the UIController object, rather than having a direct dependency on it, you might want to consider implementing an event aggregator in your application, which we'll discuss in the section titled "How Can my ViewModels Communicate with One Another?"

- Use Rob Garfoot's solution that allows a ViewModel to directly control the navigation. He enables this by wrapping the NavigationService object and using a behavior in the View to assign it to the ViewModel, requiring the ViewModel to implement an interface containing a property that can accept the NavigationService object. The ViewModel can then use this NavigationService object to control the navigation. You can find more details at http://garfoot.com/blog/2010/09/silverlight-navigation-with-the-mvvm-pattern.

How Do I Show a ChildWindow/Dialog?

Showing a ChildWindow from your ViewModel is a similar type of problem to that of navigating between Views. Likewise, there are a number of approaches you can take to solve this problem.

■ **Note** The ViewModel should *not* create an instance of the ChildWindow and show it. This would violate the separation of concerns principle and tightly couple the source ViewModel to the ChildWindow View.

- If the ChildWindow should be shown in response to a user's action in a view, per- haps your best option would be to simply handle the instantiation and showing of the ChildWindow in the view's code-behind. For example, say you have a product list view and want to display the details of a given product in a ChildWindow when the user clicks a button to select an item in the list. You can leave the ViewModel out of this interaction and simply handle the Button control's Click event in the code-behind. In this event handler, you can then instantiate and show the Child- Window, passing it a reference to the selected product as a parameter to its con- structor. This approach is particularly relevant in scenarios such as displaying an OpenFileDialog or SaveFileDialog, which for security reasons can be displayed only in response to a user-initiated action, unless the application is running with elevated trust privileges.

- If the dialog is specific to the View, you could take the approach of raising an event from the ViewModel and using code or an action in the View to instantiate and show the ChildWindow. This is not a particularly viable solution in most cases, especially when data needs to be passed to the ChildWindow instance.

- The previous section recommended a UIController object as a possible solution to controlling navigation from a ViewModel. You can have this class handle the in- stantiation and display of ChildWindows as well. The ViewModel can then request that this UIController object display a ChildWindow.

■ **Note** If the ChildWindow needs to return a result to the ViewModel that requested it, you will probably need to provide a way for the ChildWindow's ViewModel to communicate with the source View's ViewModel. See the sec- tion titled "How Can my ViewModels Communicate with One Another?" for information on how you can enable this.

How Do I Close a ChildWindow?

Raise an event from your ViewModel and handle that event either in the View's code-behind or using an event trigger in XAML. If you do so in the code-behind, you can simply call the Close method on the ChildWindow object. If you choose to use the event trigger method, you can write an action that will close the ChildWindow for you. The following code demonstrates an action named CloseChildWindowAction, which you can use to close the ChildWindow when the action is invoked:

```
using System.Windows;
using System.Windows.Controls;
using System.Windows.Interactivity;

namespace Chapter13Sample.Actions
{
    public class CloseChildWindowAction : TriggerAction<ChildWindow>
```

```
    {
        public bool? Result
        {
            get { return (bool?)GetValue(ResultProperty); }
            set { SetValue(ResultProperty, value); }
        }

        public static readonly DependencyProperty ResultProperty =
            DependencyProperty.Register("Result", typeof(bool?),
                                    typeof(CloseChildWindowAction), null);

        protected override void Invoke(object parameter)
        {
            AssociatedObject.DialogResult = Result ?? true;
        }
    }
}
```

You can then use this action in your XAML to respond to an event raised by the ViewModel, like so:

```
<i:Interaction.Triggers>
    <i:EventTrigger SourceObject="{Binding Mode=OneWay}"
                    EventName="LoginSuccessful">
        <actions:CloseChildWindowAction />
    </i:EventTrigger>
</i:Interaction.Triggers>
```

You can bind the CloseChildWindowAction action's Result property to a property on your ViewModel if you want to control the ChildWindow's result. Otherwise, it will simply return a result of true.

■ **Note** You might be wondering why we don't simply bind the ChildWindow's DialogResult property to a property on the ViewModel since ChildWindow will close when its DialogResult property is assigned a value. However, the DialogResult property is not a dependency property; hence, you cannot bind it to a property on your ViewModel, and therefore cannot use it to close the ChildWindow.

How Can My ViewModels Communicate with One Another?

At times, you need to provide the ability for your ViewModels or other loosely coupled parts of your application to communicate with one another. For example, say you have a product list view hosted as a Page in a Frame control, which has spawned a product details view as a ChildWindow. This would result in both views being open simultaneously and possibly needing to communicate with one another, such as if the product details view needed to return a result to the product list ViewModel. Assuming that both views have their own individual ViewModels, you would need to provide a channel over which both those ViewModels can communicate.

In this type of scenario, using an MVVM framework in your project can be very handy, as MVVM frameworks typically come with this ability built in. Most solutions follow the Mediator design pattern, where an object is used as an intermediary for the publishing of messages and subscribing to them, enabling the publishers and subscribers to be loosely coupled from one another. For example, Prism provides an EventAggregator class that can be used for this purpose, and MVVM Light provides the Messenger class.

Since the implementation of this inter-ViewModel communication will depend on what MVVM framework you choose to use, let's just focus on the theory. A ViewModel can subscribe to the mediator object and listen for any messages that concern it. Another ViewModel can then publish messages to the mediator object, which broadcasts the message to all message subscribers. When the second ViewModel publishes a message, the first ViewModel can then be notified of it and respond accordingly. With this solution, you have a way for your ViewModels to communicate in a loosely coupled fashion.

How Can I Use My ViewModels at Design Time?

Earlier in this chapter, you connected the ViewModel to the View in a declarative manner (in the workshop titled "Workshop: Connecting the ViewModel to the View"). To jog your memory, you did the following (in bold):

```
<navigation:Page x:Class="Chapter13Sample.Views.LoginView"
    xmlns="http://schemas.microsoft.com/winfx/2006/xaml/presentation"
    xmlns:x="http://schemas.microsoft.com/winfx/2006/xaml"
    xmlns:d="http://schemas.microsoft.com/expression/blend/2008"
    xmlns:mc="http://schemas.openxmlformats.org/markup-compatibility/2006"
    xmlns:navigation="clr-namespace:System.Windows.Controls;↵
            assembly=System.Windows.Controls.Navigation"
    xmlns:vm="clr-namespace:Chapter13Sample.ViewModels"
    mc:Ignorable="d" Title="Login">

  <navigation:Page.DataContext>
    <vm:LoginViewModel />
  </navigation:Page.DataContext>

  <Grid x:Name="LayoutRoot">
    <!-- Removed for the purpose of brevity -->
  </Grid>
</navigation:Page>
```

One of the benefits of hooking up your ViewModel to your view in this way is that the Visual Studio XAML designer now knows the shape of your ViewModel class, which can make it easier to bind your view to the ViewModel. You can then use Visual Studio's Data Binding Expression Builder (covered in Chapter 11) to help you easily bind the properties of controls in the view to properties on your ViewModel class, in a point-and-click fashion. If you're not connecting your ViewModel to the view in this way, you can still make use of Visual Studio's design-time data mechanisms (covered in Chapter 10) to create a design-time connection between the two. This will enable you to still make full use of Visual Studio's Data Binding Expression Builder. Try this by changing the code in bold from the previous XAML to the following XAML:

```
<d:DesignProperties.DataContext>
    <vm:LoginViewModel LoginSuccessful="LoginViewModel_LoginSuccessful" />
</d:DesignProperties.DataContext>
```

You will find that you can still make full use of Visual Studio's Data Binding Expression Builder against the ViewModel class. Alternatively, you can use the d:DataContext attached property in place of the syntax used in the previous example to set the design-time data context, like so:

```
d:DataContext="{d:DesignInstance Type=vm:LoginViewModel, IsDesignTimeCreatable=True}"
```

Attach this property to an element in your XAML file, and it will also assign a ViewModel as the de-sign-time data context for a View, with the same result as the previously demonstrated syntax.

As was discussed earlier in this chapter, in the section titled "Workshop: Connecting the View and the ViewModel," when you declaratively connect the ViewModel to the view in either of these fashions, the Visual Studio XAML designer actually creates an instance of your ViewModel class. You can prove this by assigning one of the ViewModel's properties a value in the ViewModel's constructor. Say that you then bind the Text property of a TextBox control to that ViewModel property. When you next compile the project, the value will appear in the control at design time. This provides a way of providing design-time data to your view. If the ViewModel sees that it's in design-time mode, it can assign some hard-coded data to its properties, enabling the designer to see what the view will look like when it's running, without having to actually compile and run the application.

■ **Note** As was mentioned earlier, because of this instantiation at design-time behavior, be careful of what logic you have in the ViewModel's parameterless constructor, as that logic will be executed at design time. Always per-form a check for whether it's design time or runtime before executing runtime specific logic (such as calls to the server). The `System.ComponentModel.DesignerProperties.IsInDesignTool` static property can be used for this purpose. Alternatively, you might want to have different ViewModels for use at design time to those used at run-time and implement a ViewModel locator that swaps between them accordingly. We'll discuss ViewModel locators later in this chapter.

How Can I Use RIA Services in a MVVM-Friendly Manner?

In Chapter 6, we discussed how some aspects of RIA Services aren't particularly MVVM-friendly. The DomainDataSource control results in the coupling of your Views to the service layer, violating the sepa-ration of concerns principle. Instead, your ViewModel should handle retrieving/persisting data from a domain service via its corresponding domain context.

This gets you most of the way toward enabling you to work with RIA Services in an MVVM-friendly manner, but you still face issues when it comes to consuming a collection in the View and paging that data. When you have paged data in the view and wire the view to the domain service using the DomainDataSource control, the DomainDataSource control automatically takes care of the retrieval of new pages of data as the user navigates between them and automatically requires the server when the user changes the filtering or sorting of the list. Things are somewhat more complicated, however, when you need to handle all of this behavior manually in the ViewModel.

For this reason, the RIA Services team created a collection view named DomainCollectionView, which you can use to expose server data from your ViewModel to the View. It monitors for scenarios where the server needs to be required, such as when the user navigates to a new page of data, and lets the View-Model know what data the view needs so that it can make the call to the server accordingly. The DomainCollectionView isn't a part of RIA Services itself but can be found in the WCF RIA Services Toolkit. Chapter 6 covers the DomainCollectionView in depth and actually demonstrates using the DomainCollectionView in an MVVM-compliant manner, even though we hadn't broached the topic of MVVM at that point.

Here are some tips for exposing data obtained from the server using RIA Services in a ViewModel:

- The entities returned from the server will act as the models in the MVVM design pattern.

- Expose collections of data from your ViewModels wrapped in a
  DomainCollectionView.

- You will generally query the server for data in the constructor of the ViewModel
  class. When doing so, always check for if the ViewModel is being created at design
  time, and skip the server request if so.

- When the data exposed by a ViewModel is editable, also expose a command that
  will call the data context's SaveChanges method when it is executed. The View can
  then bind a Save button to this command to persist any changes back to the server
  when it is clicked.

- Have your ViewModels expose an IsBusy property that they can set to true when
  they're waiting for a response from the server (i.e., when querying/submitting
  data). You can then bind the IsBusy property of a BusyIndicator in your View to
  this property, which will let the user know that an operation is happening in the
  background.

■ **Note** The sample code for this chapter, downloadable from the Apress web site, contains a project demonstrating the use of RIA Services in an MVVM-friendly manner.

Common MVVM Questions

As has been indicated throughout this chapter, there are many ways of implementing the MVVM design pattern, and with no clear single best practice, the decision of how to do so will come down to what suits your project and development process best. Let's look at a few questions you might have on how you should implement the MVVM design pattern.

Should I Implement Dependency Properties or Standard Properties on My ViewModel Class?

Generally, you need to implement only standard properties on your ViewModel class. Because you are binding *to* the properties on the ViewModel class, which act as the *source* of the data, there's no need for them to be dependency properties. Therefore,as a general rule, standard properties that raise the PropertyChanged event from the INotifyPropertyChanged interface are the best choice for implementing properties in ViewModels.

Should Model Objects Really Be Exposed Directly to the View?

Some developers like to keep a clean separation between the View and the Model layers, wrapping the Model layer's objects in ViewModels before exposing them to the View layer. From a pure design perspective, ideally the view should know nothing about the model objects, and interact only with the ViewModel objects, keeping the View and the Model layers completely decoupled.

However, from a practical perspective, wrapping your model objects in ViewModels adds additional overhead, increases the amount of code and the complexity, and reduces maintainability. Ultimately, depending on the scenario, it's generally best to simply expose your model objects (or collections of model objects) directly to the view via a property on the ViewModel.

Should ViewModels Copy Data to and from the Models?

If you have chosen to not expose your model objects directly to the view (exposing the data via a View-Model instead), you will need to decide between the following options:

- You will simply create property setters and getters in your ViewModel that expose the corresponding property values from the model, with the ViewModel maintaining the original model objects, like so:

```
// The ViewModel class holds a reference to a Model,
// and just wraps its properties in its own
public string ProductName
{
    get { return _product.Name; }
    set { _product.Name = value; }
}
```

- Alternatively, you should copy all the data from a model object into the View-Model and rehydrate (or update) the model object with the data from the View-Model when you want to persist it back to the server/store again, for example:

```
// Model data is stored locally in member variables
public string ProductName
{
    get { return _productName; }
    set { _productName = value; }
}
```

What Should Come First, the View or the ViewModel?

This question can be asked in regard both to the design and to the instantiation of the view and View-Model. Whether you design the view or the ViewModel first will really depend on your development practices.

However, how the view and the ViewModel are instantiated is a more important question. The examples throughout this chapter have demonstrated the view creating the ViewModel, and hence, the view maintains ownership over the ViewModel, with the ViewModel simply serving the view's needs. Let's look at the alternatives for View/ViewModel instantiation.

View First

When implementing view-first–style MVVM, the view may handle instantiating the ViewModel either declaratively in XAML or in the code-behind, as demonstrated earlier in this chapter. Alternatively, it may pass this job off to a ViewModel locator, which will handle the instantiation of the correct View-Model for the view to bind to.

■ **Note** A ViewModel locator is an implementation of the service locator design pattern, used to help views to "locate" their ViewModel, often from a dependency injection container. This enables the views to be completely decoupled from their ViewModels, which allows you to swap in different ViewModels for use in different scenarios (design time, etc.). The MVVM Light Toolkit provides a ViewModel locator implementation that you can use if you wish, as do most other MVVM frameworks. Alternatively, John Papa has created a simple ViewModel locator, which he has blogged about and made available at `http://johnpapa.net/simple-viewmodel-locator-for-mvvm-the-patients-have-left-the-asylum`.

The view-first approach tends to be the most common way of marrying views and ViewModels when using the MVVM design pattern.

ViewModel First

Some schools of thought prefer that the ViewModel should come first and handle instantiating the view. This may suit scenarios where you have multiple views being served by a single ViewModel.

■ **Note** The ViewModel-first approach does not mean that the ViewModel has intimate knowledge of the view; it simply knows that the view exists.

Completely Decoupled

Yet another school of thought prefers that both the view and the ViewModel be completely decoupled from each other and instantiated independently. This method is generally preferred by those using inversion of control principles.

Alternative View / ViewModel Configurations

Throughout this chapter, we've demonstrated the scenario where we have a one-to-one relationship between the views and the ViewModels, with each ViewModel representing its corresponding view as a whole. This is an ideal scenario for learning the pattern (and reasonably common in practice), but it isn't a fixed requirement. Let's take a look at some additional configurations you may come across or want to use yourself.

One ViewModel Serving Multiple Views

In some scenarios, you may have one ViewModel that serves multiple views, such as a wizard. In this case, the ViewModel-first approach might be best.

One View Interacting with Multiple ViewModels

Alternatively, a single view may interact with multiple ViewModels. Instead of having the ViewModel exposing model objects directly to the view, some developers choose to wrap their model objects in ViewModels, abstracting the model from the view. Instead of the view binding directly to the data (i.e., the models), it will bind to a ViewModel instead.

For example, a view may populate a list box with a collection of `ProductViewModel` objects, with each wrapping a `Product` model object. These ViewModels could essentially be considered a "view of the model." Additional properties, calculations, logic, and so on, could be added to these ViewModel objects, serving the needs of the view while saving the model from being polluted with view-related requirements.

■ **Note**   Another potential benefit of this practice is that it can save needing to implement value converters in your bindings to convert the property values of the model to suit the needs of the view. Instead, these conversions can be performed within the ViewModel and exposed as properties that the view can directly bind to and consume. For example, rather than implementing a value converter to convert a Boolean value exposed by a property on the ViewModel to a `Visibility` value, you could expose the `Visibility` value directly from the ViewModel. That said, doing this tends to make your ViewModel a little too coupled to the needs of the view, which some developers consider to be a bad practice. Therefore, if you choose to do this, do so sparingly.

The big issue with the practice of wrapping all your model objects in ViewModels is the amount of overhead and additional code required to wrap each of the model objects in a ViewModel—often resulting in properties on the ViewModel that purely exist to relay property values from the model objects. Most of the time, the outcome of this practice is simply an unnecessary duplication of code. Therefore, whether you undertake this practice will generally be on a case-by-case basis.

■ **Note**   The XAML Power Toys add-in (discussed in Chapter 7) has a Create ViewModel For Class option that you can use to take a lot of the manual work out of the task of wrapping model objects in ViewModels.

Summary

The MVVM design pattern is one that all Silverlight developers should learn and understand, even if they don't use it in their projects. There are competing design patterns that you may wish to look into (such as the Model-View-Presenter design pattern, also known as MVP), but MVVM lends itself particularly well to applications developed in Silverlight.

However, this pattern is one with no fixed, agreed upon, or uniform standard. Therefore, don't become too concerned with whether you are doing it the right way—*there isn't one*. Rather than jumping in at the deep end, try to ease into MVVM instead, preferably by starting with a small project.

You will get overwhelmed if you try to read everything written about the pattern and understand it completely before actually putting the pattern into practice. You can easily fall into analysis paralysis by doing so; don't overthink it. The best approach is to take what's written here, start implementing the core concepts in a small test project, and expand on them as the project grows. It's often best to do this before jumping headfirst into using a complex framework.

Don't be too pedantic and go overboard in trying to put all the view's logic in the ViewModel and having zero code-behind, because often, this goal is unachievable, and attempts to do so will potentially result in messier and more complicated code than you would have when not following the pattern.

Do what's right for your project at the time. If a task takes more work than it should, requires messy workarounds, or requires you to fight the pattern to implement simple application requirements, you're taking the wrong approach. You will hit walls along the way, but do persist—it's worth the effort.

CHAPTER 14

The Managed Extensibility Framework

The Managed Extensibility Framework (MEF) is designed to help you create extensible applications. It can discover loosely coupled components (known as parts) at runtime, and "composes" them together. MEF can provide the following two key benefits to your application:

- As a simple dependency injection framework, MEF allows parts of your application to be decoupled, with the dependencies resolved at runtime.

- MEF provides a plug-in framework, helping you to modularize your application and make it extensible.

One of the common uses of MEF in Silverlight applications is to provide a way for you to modularize your application, and have the modules download separately from the "shell application." This allows the shell application to download quickly, saving the user from having to wait for the entire application to be downloaded before they can start using it.

Although MEF's key focus is on extensibility, it's also often used as a dependency injection framework. MEF is installed with Silverlight as a part of the Silverlight SDK, so it is an obvious choice when there is no need for a more fully fledged dependency injection framework.

Note Discussion of the concept of dependency injection and the dependency inversion principle is beyond the scope of this book, but in summary, the dependency inversion principle states the following:

- High-level modules should not depend on low-level modules. Both should depend on abstractions.

- Abstractions should not depend upon details. Details should depend upon abstractions.

MEF provides a way for us to decouple parts of our applications to remove dependencies between them, and have the dependencies resolved at runtime.

In this chapter, we'll look at what MEF is, show you how you can get started with using MEF in your Silverlight applications, and get you to the point where you can use MEF to help you modularize your applications.

Terminology

Let's start by explaining the terminology that we will use throughout this chapter.

- *Parts*: Parts are components of your application that MEF can compose together. For example, say that you have a shell application that hosts modules, where the shell application and the modules are loosely coupled, with MEF providing the modules to the shell application at runtime. In this scenario, both the shell application and the modules can be considered parts. Parts are the classes that provide services to other parts, which we'll refer to as *exports*, and/or consume services from other parts, which we'll refer to as *imports*. In doing so, they enable MEF to discover them and compose them together.

- *Exports and imports*: A part provides services to other parts by *exporting* them. A service may be the part itself (the class), its properties, and/or its methods. By doing so, it makes itself known to MEF, enabling other parts to consume those services. These parts consume those exports by *importing* them, with MEF *composing* them together. In this chapter, we'll reference exported services as *exports*, and imported services as *imports*.

■ **Note**   Parts can export their properties and methods but are often exported themselves (i.e., the class representing the part is itself exported). This chapter will focus only on exporting classes, and because a part is a class, you'll therefore see references to exporting/importing *parts* throughout this chapter, rather than the more correct, but somewhat vague, term "services."

- *Contract*: A contract is used to identify an export so that it can be found and used by an import, with the contract essentially acting as a bridge between the two. As a result of using a contract to bridge the exports and the imports, the parts will be loosely coupled. Exports declare a contract. When MEF encounters an import, it searches for an export with a matching contract. This contract may be the class's type, an interface that it implements, or simply a string used to name the contract. When a corresponding export is found, it will instantiate the part, if MEF does not already have a reference to an instance of the part, and "inject" it where it is needed.

- *Catalog*: A catalog is responsible for discovering parts and providing them to the composition container.

- *Composition container*: The composition container composes parts together. The parts are obtained from the catalog that the composition container is configured to use. When the composition container encounters a part containing an import request, it will look for a corresponding export with a matching contract to inject into the part.

Using MEF

To use MEF, you need to add the following two assemblies to your project:

- `System.ComponentModel.Composition.dll`
- `System.ComponentModel.Composition.Initialization.dll`

The first assembly is the key MEF assembly, and the second adds additional Silverlight-specific features to MEF. Let's look at how you go about using MEF in your Silverlight application.

Key Steps in the Composition Process

The following three steps are key in the composition process with MEF:

- Export parts
- Import parts
- Compose the parts together

You export parts, import them, and then compose them. When you think of MEF in these terms, you can really start to see how simple it is. Let's look at each of these steps in more depth.

Exporting Parts

You can export a class by decorating it with the `Export` attribute, found in the `System.ComponentModel.Composition` namespace of the assembly by the same name. This turns it into a part that MEF can compose with other parts. For example:

```
[Export]
public class MyExportedPart
```

By exporting a class in this manner, with no contract supplied to the `Export` attribute, the export will create a default contract using the class's type (i.e., `MyExportedPart`). However, for this part to be imported, the import will need to reference the part by its type, which tightly couples the two together. Ideally, you should specify a contract that will decouple them from one another. You can do so by providing the `Export` attribute's constructor with a contract for it to be discovered by. This may be a base class that the class being exported derives from, an interface that it implements, or simply a string that can be used to identify the export. For example, you can tell the `Export` attribute to use an interface as the contract, like so:

```
[Export(typeof(IExamplePart))]
public class MyExportedPart : IExamplePart
```

Alternatively, you can simply give the export a name as a string, as follows:

```
[Export("ExamplePart")]
public class MyExportedPart : IExamplePart
```

By simply providing a name for the contract in this manner, the class will be exported as an object, so you will usually want to give the contract a type, like so:

```
[Export("ExamplePart", typeof(IExamplePart))]
public class MyExportedPart : IExamplePart
```

■ **Note** Mostly, you will use an interface as the contract, but using a string to name the contract is useful when you have multiple exports that implement the same contract but want to be able to differentiate between them and choose which one should be used in a given scenario.

Importing Parts

When you want to consume a part, you *import* it. Any class that imports other parts becomes a part itself. In other words, MEF will then see this class as a part, and compose it together with the part that it's importing.

When you import a part, MEF will provide an instance of that class for you, without the need for you to "new up" an instance of the class. "Newing up" an instance of a part requires the consumer to know what the concrete type of the import will be. MEF enables the consumer to be completely unaware of the concrete type that will be imported, and leaves MEF to handle the details of discovering the concrete type and injecting it where it is required. This allows for the parts to be loosely coupled.

Importing a Single Part

After you've exported a part, another part can consume it by importing it. The easiest way to get a reference to an instance of a part is by creating a public property on your class that the instance can be assigned to, and decorate it with the `Import` attribute, found in the `System.ComponentModel.Composition` namespace of the assembly by the same name. For example:

```
[Import]
public IExamplePart MyImportedPart { get; set; }
```

■ **Note** You can decorate only `public` fields and properties with the `Import` attribute. Attempting to do so for `private`/`protected`/`internal` fields or properties will result in an exception.

When MEF composes the parts, it will see that a part is required, search for a corresponding part matching the contract specified by the import among the exports, and assign an instance of the part that it finds to the property. In this case, no contract was explicitly passed to the Import attribute, so MEF will infer the contract from the property's type—that is, it will look for an export using the IExamplePart interface as its contract. For example, MEF will match the following export to the previous import:

```
[Export(typeof(IExamplePart))]
public class MyExportedPart : IExamplePart
```

■ **Note** If no part is found matching the import's contract, an exception will be thrown.

You can explicitly specify a contract to be used when you import a part. This is particularly necessary when you've named the contract using a string. For example, when you've exported a class, like so:

```
[Export("ExamplePart", typeof(IExamplePart))]
public class MyExportedPart : IExamplePart
```

you can import it as follows:

```
[Import("ExamplePart")]
public IExamplePart MyImportedPart { get; set; }
```

■ **Note** When you import a part, by default that instance will be shared wherever it is imported in your application. You can change this behavior by using a few different techniques, which we'll discuss in the section "Managing the Lifetime of Parts."

Importing Multiple Parts

The previous section demonstrated importing a part into a property on another part. However, if you create another class that is exported using the same contract and run your application, MEF will generate a composition error. This is because there are two parts matching the import's contract, and it doesn't know which one it should import. When you want to import multiple parts exported using the same contract, you need to change the property to an array/collection, and decorate it with the ImportMany attribute instead of the Import attribute. This is particularly useful when implementing a plug-in architecture, where you have multiple plug-ins that implement the same interface that MEF can discover and import for you.

The following code demonstrates a property that multiple parts can be imported into.

```
[ImportMany]
public IExamplePart[] MyImportedParts { get; set; }
```

■ **Note** You can specify what contract an ImportMany attribute should use in the same way you do with the Import attribute.

Composing the Parts

After you've marked your exports and imports, you need to tell MEF to compose them together. In other words, you need to tell MEF to fulfill the demands of the imports. Usually, you would do this in the constructor of the class containing the imports.

Approach 1: Manually Configuring the Catalogs and Composition Container

As previously mentioned, MEF uses a catalog to discover the parts, and a composition container to compose them. The following code demonstrates how you can create a catalog and a composition container, providing the composition container with the catalog for it to use:

```
var catalog = new DeploymentCatalog();
var container = new CompositionContainer(catalog);
```

■ **Note** We'll take a look at the available catalog types and when to use each later in this chapter. The
DeploymentCatalog catalog used here looks for all the exports in the current XAP file.

A consumer of parts can then ask the composition container to fulfill its imports, like so:

```
container.ComposeParts(this);
```

When this method is called, the composition container will reflect over the class passed into the ComposeParts method as its parameter looking for imports. When it finds one, it will find an export in the catalog with a matching contract, and inject it into the import.

Approach 2: Using the CompositionInitializer Class

Silverlight's edition of MEF provides a simpler way to initiate the composition process, by providing a static class named CompositionInitializer, which contains a SatisfyImports method. You can find this class in the System.ComponentModel.Composition namespace of the System.ComponentModel.Composition .Initialization.dll assembly. Instead of manually initializing the composition container and configuring the catalogs for it to use, as demonstrated in the previous section, you can simply use the following line of code:

```
CompositionInitializer.SatisfyImports(this);
```

The CompositionInitializer creates a default container that uses a catalog containing all the parts in the current XAP file. This default container will be maintained for the duration of the application's lifetime, and is used throughout the application.

You can take control over the container that the CompositionInitializer uses if you wish, using the static CompositionHost class to configure it. For example, you can provide a catalog for the default container to use by calling the Initialize method on the CompositionHost class, and passing it the catalog to be used, like so:

```
var catalog = new DeploymentCatalog();
CompositionHost.Initialize(catalog);
```

You can even provide it a container for it to use, as follows:

```
var catalog = new DeploymentCatalog();
var container = new CompositionContainer(catalog);
CompositionHost.Initialize(container);
```

Now whenever you call the CompositionInitializer.SatisfyImports method, the catalog/container that you configured in this manner will be used to compose the parts.

> ■ **Note** When a container instantiates a part, it retains that part and reuses it for future imports. This means that when you take this approach, any parts that the container instantiates will be kept alive for the duration of the application's lifetime. We'll look at how you can deal with this behavior in the section "Managing the Lifetime of Parts."

Choosing an Approach

Using the `CompositionInitializer.SatisfyImports` method is the approach generally taken when using MEF in Silverlight applications. However, it does have one major downside, in that it only works when the consumer does not itself contain exports. If you attempt to satisfy the imports of a class that also contains exports, such as the following class:

```
[Export]
public class PartImporterAndExporter
{
    [Import]
    public IExamplePart MyImportedPart { get; set; }

    public PartImporterAndExporter()
    {
        CompositionInitializer.SatisfyImports(this);
    }
}
```

you will find that the following composition exception will be thrown:

```
Cannot call SatisfyImports on a object of type 'XXX' because it is marked with one or more
ExportAttributes.
```

Therefore, in the scenario where the consumer does contain exports, you will need to take the first approach instead—that is, you will need to manually configure the catalogs and composition container.

Managing the Lifetime of Parts

By default, a composition container creates singleton objects. That is, it creates an instance of a part once, and reuses that instance wherever that part is imported in your application. However, this is not always the behavior that you want. Often, you will want to have a new instance of the part each time it is imported. For example, say that you export a `ViewModel` class, which is then imported by a view. Each time the view is opened, it will generally want to use a new instance of the `ViewModel` class. MEF allows you to configure this behavior either when the `ViewModel` class is exported, or when the `ViewModel` class is imported.

You can configure that a new instance of a class should be created each time it is imported by decorating it with the `PartCreationPolicy` attribute. This attribute's constructor accepts a `CreationPolicy` enumeration parameter, containing the following values:

- Any: This will default the policy to `Shared`, unless the import requests a `NonShared` instance. This is the default behavior when a creation policy isn't provided for an export.

- • NonShared: A new instance of this class will be created each time it is imported.

- • Shared: A single instance will be shared between all imports of this part.

The following code demonstrates decorating a class with the PartCreationPolicy attribute, telling the composition container to create a new instance of the class each time it is imported:

```
[Export]
[PartCreationPolicy(CreationPolicy.NonShared)]
public class ProductListViewModel
```

Alternatively, an import can tell the composition container that it wants a new instance of the class that it is importing by assigning the NonShared value of the CreationPolicy enumeration to the Import attribute's RequiredCreationPolicy property, as the following code demonstrates:

```
[Import(RequiredCreationPolicy = CreationPolicy.NonShared)]
public IExamplePart MyImportedPart { get; set; }
```

■ **Note**   When you set a part's creation policy to NonShared, the composition container will not maintain a reference to the part, enabling it to be garbage collected.

Lazy Imports

When you designate an import, you don't necessary want an instance of the part to be instantiated during the composition process. Sometimes, you want the part to be instantiated only when you first use it. This saves unnecessary instantiations when a part might not even actually end up being used.

MEF supports this scenario, by enabling you to turn an import into a "lazy import." Say you have the following import:

```
[Import(RequiredCreationPolicy = CreationPolicy.NonShared)]
public IExamplePart MyImportedPart { get; set; }
```

The composition container will create an instance of the concrete type to be imported when the part containing the import is composed. That is, when the following method is called in the class's constructor:

```
CompositionInitializer.SatisfyImports(this);
```

You can change the import to be lazy, like so:

```
[Import(RequiredCreationPolicy = CreationPolicy.NonShared)]
public Lazy<IExamplePart> MyImportedPart { get; set; }
```

The Lazy<T> type was introduced with Silverlight 4, and allows you to delay the instantiation of a type until you need it. The concrete type that MEF imports will be instantiated only when you get the value of the property's Value property, like so:

```
IExamplePart myImportedPartInstance = MyImportedPart.Value;
```

Obtaining New Export Instances on Demand

The previous section demonstrated how a part can be instantiated only when it is first used, but sometimes the consumer will want to make use of multiple instances of an export, and create those instances on demand. You can use an export factory for this purpose. The following code demonstrates the declaration of an export factory:

```
[Import]
public ExportFactory<IExamplePart> MyExportFactory { get; set; }
```

As you can see, we have a property designated as an import, of type ExportFactory<T>, where T is the type contract of the export. Each time you need a new instance of the part that the factory provides, you can simply call the property's CreateExport method, like so:

```
IExamplePart examplePartInstance = MyExportFactory.CreateExport().Value;
```

Catalogs

Catalogs discover parts and make them available to the composition container to use. MEF provides a number of catalogs that discover parts in different ways from one another. Let's look at the different types of catalogs that MEF provides.

■ **Note** All of these catalogs reside under the System.ComponentModel.Composition.Hosting namespace.

AssemblyCatalog

The AssemblyCatalog catalog discovers all the exports within a given assembly. You simply pass the assembly for it to discover exports in to its constructor. For example, the following code demonstrates configuring an AssemblyCatalog catalog to search for all exports in the current assembly:

```
var catalog =
    new AssemblyCatalog(System.Reflection.Assembly.GetExecutingAssembly());
```

TypeCatalog

The TypeCatalog catalog discovers all the exports within a given set of parts. You pass the catalog the types for it to discover exports in to its constructor. For example, the following code demonstrates configuring a TypeCatalog catalog to search for all the exports defined in three classes: MyExportedPart, MyExportedPart1, and MyExportedPart2.

```
var catalog = new TypeCatalog(typeof(MyExportedPart),
                              typeof(MyExportedPart1),
                              typeof(MyExportedPart2));
```

DeploymentCatalog

The DeploymentCatalog catalog discovers all the exports within a given XAP file. The following code demonstrates configuring a DeploymentCatalog catalog to search for all exports in the current XAP file:

```
var catalog = new DeploymentCatalog();
```

You can also use the DeploymentCatalog catalog to download other XAP files, and discover their parts. Simply pass the DeploymentCatalog class's constructor the URI to a XAP file, and then call its DownloadAsync method, like so:

```
var catalog = new DeploymentCatalog(new Uri("Module1.xap", UriKind.Relative));
catalog.DownloadAsync();
```

While the XAP file is downloading, the composition container will often continue to be used in the meantime to compose parts using the exports that it currently has available to it. When the XAP file has finished loading, the DeploymentCatalog will notify the composition container that new parts are available. The composition container will then update the imports of any previously composed parts as a result of new exports becoming available—a process known as *recomposition*. For imports to be successfully updated, however, you need to explicitly set the AllowRecomposition property of the Import/ImportMany attribute to true, like so:

```
[ImportMany(AllowRecomposition=true)]
public ObservableCollection<IExamplePart> MyImportedParts { get; set; }
```

You *must* set this property to true on any imports that may be recomposed as a result of new exports being found in the downloaded XAP file; otherwise, it will result in an exception being thrown during the recomposition process.

You can detect for any errors in downloading the XAP file or errors that occurred during the composition process by handling the DeploymentCatalog object's DownloadCompleted event. This event is raised after the XAP file has finish downloading, and the composition container has recomposed it with the existing imports. The AsyncCompletedEventArgs object passed into the event handler as a parameter has an Error property that you can use to check for any errors.

■ **Note** You can even use the DeploymentCatalog catalog to download modules on demand. We look at how you can implement this "on demand" behavior in the "Downloading Modules on Demand Using MEF" section of Chapter 17.

AggregateCatalog

The AggregateCatalog catalog enables you to aggregate multiple catalogs, potentially of different types. In other words, it's a catalog that contains other catalogs. For example, say you want to provide discovery of parts across several specific assemblies. You can create multiple AssemblyCatalog instances (each referencing an assembly), and add them to an AggregateCatalog catalog. You can then pass this
AggregateCatalog catalog to the composition container to enable it to use all the parts across those catalogs. Start by creating an AggregateCatalog object, as follows:

```
var aggregateCatalog = new AggregateCatalog();
```

You can then add catalogs to its Catalogs collection, like so:

```
var catalog = new AssemblyCatalog(Assembly.GetExecutingAssembly());
aggregateCatalog.Catalogs.Add(catalog);
```

Usually, you will make use of an AggregateCatalog catalog to aggregate DeploymentCatalog catalogs. For example, the following code demonstrates aggregating the current XAP file and another that it downloads on demand:

```
var aggregateCatalog = new AggregateCatalog();

var catalog1 = new DeploymentCatalog();
aggregateCatalog.Catalogs.Add(catalog1);

var catalog2 = new DeploymentCatalog(new Uri("Module1.xap", UriKind.Relative));
catalog2.DownloadAsync();
aggregateCatalog.Catalogs.Add(catalog2);
```

■ **Note** You can also add parts to an aggregate catalog, adding them to the collection provided by its Parts property.

⚙ Workshop: Getting Started with MEF

Let's look at a very simple scenario in which MEF can be used to "inject" an instance of a class into another class, without the need to explicitly "new up" the class instance. We'll make the class known to MEF by "exporting" it, and "import" it into the view's code-behind class so that it can use it.

1. Create a new project using the Silverlight Application project template, named Chapter14Sample.

2. Add a reference to the following MEF assemblies:

   • System.ComponentModel.Composition.dll

   • System.ComponentModel.Composition.Initialization.dll

3. Add a new class to the project, named PersonPart.cs, containing the following code:

```
namespace Chapter14Sample
{
    public class PersonPart
    {
        public string Name { get; set; }

        public PersonPart()
        {
            Name = "Homer Simpson";
        }
    }
}
```

Essentially, we've just added a property named Name to the class, and assigned it a value in the class's constructor. We'll use that value to demonstrate that an instance of this class has been successfully imported shortly.

4. We now want to make this class known to MEF. Start by adding the following using statement to the top of the class's file:

```
using System.ComponentModel.Composition;
```

5. We can now "export" this class to announce to MEF that this is a composable part. Decorate the class with MEF's Export attribute, like so:

```
[Export]
public class PersonPart
```

The completed code for the PersonPart class that you should now have is as follows:

```
using System.ComponentModel.Composition;

namespace Chapter14Sample
{
    [Export]
    public class PersonPart
    {
        public string Name { get; set; }

        public PersonPart()
        {
            Name = "Homer Simpson";
        }
    }
}
```

6. Open the code-behind file for the MainPage.xaml view. Let's "import" the PersonPart class that we just exported into this view, and display the value assigned to its Name property. Start by adding the following using statement to the top of the MainPage.xaml.cs file:

```
using System.ComponentModel.Composition;
```

7. Add a public property to the MainPage class that MEF will inject a PersonPart object into, like so:

```
public PersonPart MyImportedPersonPart { get; set; }
```

8. We can now get MEF to assign an instance of the PersonPart class to this property for us by decorating the property with MEF's Import attribute, as follows:

```
[Import]
public PersonPart MyImportedPersonPart { get; set; }
```

9. We now need to tell MEF to go ahead and "new up" an instance of the PersonPart class and assign it to this property. You do so using the SatisfyImports method on the CompositionInitializer class. Add the following line of code to the MainPage class's constructor:

```
CompositionInitializer.SatisfyImports(this);
```

This will result in the parts being "composed" by MEF when the MainPage class is initialized, with an instance of the PersonPart class being assigned to the MyImportedPersonPart property.

10. Finally, to prove that the PersonPart part has been successfully imported, let's display the value that we assigned to its Name property in its constructor in the view. Add the following code in bold to the MainPage class's constructor:

```
public MainPage()
{
    InitializeComponent();

    CompositionInitializer.SatisfyImports(this);

    var nameTextBlock = new TextBlock();
    nameTextBlock.Text = MyImportedPersonPart.Name;
    LayoutRoot.Children.Add(nameTextBlock);
}
```

This code adds a TextBlock control to the view, and displays the value assigned to the PersonPart part's Name property in the view. The complete code that you should now have for the MainPage class is as follows:

```
using System.ComponentModel.Composition;
using System.Windows.Controls;

namespace Chapter14Sample
{
    public partial class MainPage : UserControl
    {
        [Import]
        public PersonPart MyImportedPersonPart { get; set; }

        public MainPage()
        {
            InitializeComponent();

            CompositionInitializer.SatisfyImports(this);

            var nameTextBlock = new TextBlock();
            nameTextBlock.Text = MyImportedPersonPart.Name;
            LayoutRoot.Children.Add(nameTextBlock);
        }
    }
}
```

11. Run the application. The text "Homer Simpson" should appear in the top-left corner of the view.

⚙ Workshop: Specifying a Contract

The previous workshop demonstrated how you could make use of a "part" without the need to "new it up." However, it provided no benefit over simply "newing it up." You may as well have simply done this in the MainPage class's constructor, like this:

```
MyImportedPersonPart = new PersonPart();
```

The MainPage class is still tightly coupled to the PersonPart class. The benefits of MEF are realized only when you make use of a contract to decouple them, exporting the part according to an interface instead of its concrete implementation. By taking a contract-based approach, you can then swap in alternative parts to the PersonPart part, depending on the current scenario. This is particularly useful for improving the testability of your application, allowing you to import "mock" parts that help you to test a component in isolation from the rest of the application. It's also useful for creating a plug-in architecture, where plug-ins simply need to conform to a given interface in order for the application to be able to consume them, with MEF handling the discovering of the plug-ins.

A contract is just an interface that a part implements. A class tells MEF to import a part that implements that interface, and MEF will discover it and compose the two together. In this workshop, we'll refactor the code from the previous workshop and implement a contract to decouple the MainPage and PersonPart classes.

1. The first step is to create the contract. This contract will simply be an interface that requires classes to implement a property named Name. Add a new file to your project named IPersonPart.cs, using the Code File item template. Add the following code to it:

```
namespace Chapter14Sample
{
    public interface IPersonPart
    {
        string Name { get;set; }
    }
}
```

■ **Note** An easier way to create this file is to right-click somewhere in the code for the PersonPart class, and select Refactor ➤ Extract Interface from the context menu. The dialog that appears will help create the interface for you.

---

2. Now have the PersonPart class implement this interface.

```
[Export]
public class PersonPart : IPersonPart
```

3. You now need to change the Export attribute to export the part by its interface rather than its concrete implementation. You do this by passing the interface's type to the Export attributes constructor, like so:

```
[Export(typeof(IPersonPart))]
public class PersonPart : IPersonPart
```

4.   Now change the `MyImportedPersonPart` property's type to `IPersonPart`, as follows:

```
[Import]
public IPersonPart MyImportedPersonPart { get; set; }
```

The `MainPage` class and `PersonPart` class are now decoupled, with the `MainPage` class now knowing nothing about the `PersonPart` class, except the interface that it implements. MEF handles the discovery of the concrete implementation of the `IPersonPart` interface, and injects it into the `MainPage` class. If you now run your application, it will work exactly the same way as it did before.

⚙ Workshop: Importing Multiple Parts

If you have multiple classes that export the `IPersonPart` interface that we created in the previous workshop, MEF won't know which part to import into the `MyImportedPersonPart` property, and will throw an exception when you call `CompositionInitializer.SatisfyImports`. However, by turning the `MyImportedPersonPart` property into an array/collection, and using the `ImportMany` attribute instead of `Import`, multiple parts can be imported into the `MyImportedPersonPart` property.

In this workshop, we'll modify what we have from the previous two workshops, and make multiple parts available to the `MainPage` class.

1.   Add a new class to the `Chapter14Sample` project, named `AnotherPersonPart.cs`, and add the following code to it:

```
using System.ComponentModel.Composition;

namespace Chapter14Sample
{
    [Export(typeof(IPersonPart))]
    public class AnotherPersonPart : IPersonPart
    {
        public string Name { get; set; }

        public AnotherPersonPart()
        {
            Name = "Marge Simpson";
        }
    }
}
```

As you can see, it's simply another implementation of the `IPersonPart` interface, essentially identical to the `PersonPart` class, but with a different value assigned to its `Name` property in its constructor.

2.   If you try and run the application now, an exception will be raised because MEF doesn't know which class (`PersonPart` or `AnotherPersonPart`) it should import into the `MyImportedPersonPart` property on the `MainPage` class. We can make the `MyImportedPersonPart` property accept multiple parts by turning it into an array, and decorating it with the `ImportMany` attribute instead of the `Import` attribute, like so:

```
[ImportMany]
public IPersonPart[] MyImportedPersonParts { get; set; }
```

3. In the first workshop, we created a TextBlock to display the value of the imported part's Name property. We now need to modify this code to display the value of the Name property for all of the imported parts. Instead of the TextBlock, let's display the names in a ListBox control. The full code for the MainPage class follows, with the required changes in bold:

```
using System.ComponentModel.Composition;
using System.Windows.Controls;

namespace Chapter14Sample
{
    public partial class MainPage : UserControl
    {
        [ImportMany]
        public IPersonPart[] MyImportedPersonParts { get; set; }

        public MainPage()
        {
            InitializeComponent();

            CompositionInitializer.SatisfyImports(this);

            var list = new ListBox();
            list.ItemsSource = MyImportedPersonParts;
            list.DisplayMemberPath = "Name";
            LayoutRoot.Children.Add(list);
        }
    }
}
```

4. Run your application. Both parts will show up in the ListBox that has been added to the view. Go ahead and add additional classes to your project that implement the IPersonPart interface and export themselves. They too will automatically appear in the list.

⚙ Workshop: Configuring Catalogs and Downloading Modules

So far, we've been using the default composition container and the default catalog that it uses. In this workshop, we're going to take control of the catalogs being used by the default composition container. We'll configure two DeploymentCatalog catalogs to use parts from—one to find parts in the current XAP file, and another that will download another XAP file and find parts in it. We'll then tie these together using an AggregateCatalog catalog, and associate them with the default container.

1. This workshop will extend the previous workshop to allow the discovery of parts that export themselves using the IPersonPart interface as their contract across multiple XAP files. The first step is to create a new "common" assembly that will contain the interface, which both XAP files can reference. Add a new project to the solution named Chapter14Sample.Common, using the Silverlight Class Library project template.

2. Move the IPersonPart interface from the Chapter14Sample project to this new Chapter14Sample.Common project.

3. The Chapter14Sample project needs a reference to the Chapter14Sample.Common project. Add this now. If you compile and run your project, it should run as per the previous workshop.

4. Let's now configure the catalogs that the default composition container should use. Start by adding the following using statement to the top of the MainPage.xaml.cs file:

```
using System.ComponentModel.Composition.Hosting;
```

5. Add the following code in bold to the MainPage class's constructor:

```
public MainPage()
{
    InitializeComponent();

    var aggregateCatalog = new AggregateCatalog();

    var catalog1 = new DeploymentCatalog();
    aggregateCatalog.Catalogs.Add(catalog1);

    CompositionHost.Initialize(aggregateCatalog);
    CompositionInitializer.SatisfyImports(this);

    var list = new ListBox();
    list.ItemsSource = MyImportedPersonParts;
    list.DisplayMemberPath = "Name";
    LayoutRoot.Children.Add(list);
}
```

In this code, we've added a DeploymentCatalog instance to an AggregateCatalog catalog, and passed the AggregateCatalog catalog to the CompositionHost to use. The DeploymentCatalog catalog is configured to simply look in the current XAP file for any exports. Once again, if you compile and run your project, it should run as per the previous workshop.

6. Now we'll create a new "module" that will be compiled into its own XAP file, and downloaded by another DeploymentCatalog catalog. Add a new project to the solution named Module1, using the Silverlight Application project template. Deselect the "Add a test page that references the application" check box in the wizard that appears, and click OK.

7. Add the following references to the project:

- System.ComponentModel.Composition.dll

- Chapter14Sample.Common.dll (as a project reference)

8. Add a new class to the module project, named YetAnotherPersonPart.cs.

9. This class will be just like the PersonPart and AnotherPersonPart classes that you created in the previous workshops. Simply assign another name to the Name property in its constructor to differentiate it from the other classes.

```
using System.ComponentModel.Composition;

namespace Module1
{
    [Export(typeof(IPersonPart))]
    public class YetAnotherPersonPart : IPersonPart
    {
        public string Name { get; set; }

        public YetAnotherPersonPart()
        {
            Name = "Bart Simpson";
        }
    }
}
```

10. Open the MainPage class in the Chapter14Sample project. We now need to create a new DeploymentCatalog instance that points to the XAP file of the module that we just created, and add it to the AggregateCatalog catalog. Add the following code in bold to the MainPage class's constructor:

```
public MainPage()
{
    InitializeComponent();

    var aggregateCatalog = new AggregateCatalog();

    var catalog1 = new DeploymentCatalog();
    aggregateCatalog.Catalogs.Add(catalog1);

    var catalog2 =
        new DeploymentCatalog(new Uri("Module1.xap", UriKind.Relative));
    catalog2.DownloadAsync();
    aggregateCatalog.Catalogs.Add(catalog2);

    CompositionHost.Initialize(aggregateCatalog);
    CompositionInitializer.SatisfyImports(this);

    var list = new ListBox();
    list.ItemsSource = MyImportedPersonParts;
    list.DisplayMemberPath = "Name";
    LayoutRoot.Children.Add(list);
}
```

11. The final step is to allow the MyImportedPersonParts property to support re-composition. This will allow it to be updated with new parts as they become available (i.e., after the module XAP file has been downloaded).

```
[ImportMany(AllowRecomposition=true)]
public ObservableCollection<IPersonPart> MyImportedPersonParts { get; set; }
```

Note how the type was changed from an array to an observable collection. MEF will update this collection as parts become available, and being an observable collection means that the ListBox control will be aware of the changes

and update itself accordingly. This will require the following using statement
to be added to the top of the file:

```
using System.Collections.ObjectModel;
```

The final code that you should have for the MainPage class is as follows:

```
using System;
using System.Collections.ObjectModel;
using System.ComponentModel.Composition;
using System.ComponentModel.Composition.Hosting;
using System.Windows.Controls;

namespace Chapter14Sample
{
    public partial class MainPage : UserControl
    {
        [ImportMany(AllowRecomposition=true)]
        public ObservableCollection<IPersonPart> MyImportedPersonParts
            { get; set; }

        public MainPage()
        {
            InitializeComponent();

            var aggregateCatalog = new AggregateCatalog();

            var catalog1 = new DeploymentCatalog();
            aggregateCatalog.Catalogs.Add(catalog1);

            var catalog2 =
                new DeploymentCatalog(new Uri("Module1.xap", UriKind.Relative));
            catalog2.DownloadAsync();
            aggregateCatalog.Catalogs.Add(catalog2);

            CompositionHost.Initialize(aggregateCatalog);
            CompositionInitializer.SatisfyImports(this);

            var list = new ListBox();
            list.ItemsSource = MyImportedPersonParts;
            list.DisplayMemberPath = "Name";
            LayoutRoot.Children.Add(list);
        }
    }
}
```

12. Now run your application. You should see three names appear in the list:
    Homer Simpson and Marge Simpson (from the main application's XAP file),
    and Bart Simpson (from the module).

■ **Note** The `Chapter14Sample.Common.dll` assembly will be compiled into both the `Chapter14Sample.xap` and `Module1.xap` files. You can use Silverlight's assembly caching feature, covered in Chapter 17, to download the assembly independently from both XAP files, resulting in only one copy needing to be downloaded to the client. This is rather important when you have many shared libraries between the "shell application" and the modules, especially when the shared libraries are sizable.

Summary

The focus for this chapter was on getting you to a point where you could use MEF to modularize your application, and download the modules separately from the "shell application." This provides a much better loading experience for the user, as they won't need to wait for the entire application to be downloaded before they can start using it. As modules are downloaded, MEF will make them available to the shell application, and the user can then start using the functionality that they provide. (Note: We'll take this a step further in the "Downloading Modules on Demand Using MEF" section of Chapter 17, and enable these modules to be downloaded on demand. We'll look at using MEF in tandem with the Navigation Framework, such that when the user navigates to a view in a module not previously downloaded, MEF will go ahead and download the module, and then display the requested view to the user.)

We've really only just touched the surface of MEF's capabilities here, but you can find more information in the documentation section of MEF's CodePlex site: `http://mef.codeplex.com/wikipage?title=Guide`.

CHAPTER 15

Printing and Reporting

Prior to Silverlight 4, much was made of the fact that Silverlight didn't have any native printing abilities, and this excuse was often used to back the common belief that Silverlight was not ready for business applications, because printing/reporting is a vital requirement in most business applications. Alternative solutions to work around this omission were implemented that could provide reporting and printing support in Silverlight applications in the meantime, but finally, Silverlight 4 introduced the long-awaited printing functionality developers wanted. Silverlight 5 has gone on to improve this functionality greatly. That said, some of the alternative solutions created before Silverlight implemented printing are still often very viable options for implementing reporting.

In this chapter, we will look at a number of methods of displaying and printing reports in your Silverlight application. We'll also look at how you can use Silverlight's native printing capability, and finally, we'll look at the PivotViewer control, which you might like to leverage to make your data more interactive for the application's users.

The Importance of Implementing Reporting

Businesses need to be able to store their data, but they also want to obtain information from the system to track and monitor various aspects of the business, such as performance, cash flow, forecasts, sales vs. targets, and so on. An ideal means of achieving this is by implementing reporting functionality in the application.

A report generally consists of data retrieved from one or more databases inserted into a predefined template—often with some sort of intermediate processing to turn the data into useful information. Reports can range from the extremely simple to the extremely complex, but both follow the same workflow from an application perspective. At runtime, data is

- Extracted from the database

- Passed through to the report generator/writer, which processes the data and formats the results in a human-readable form suitable for printing

The complexity of processing the data, populating the report, and formatting the results is handled by the reporting engine using the rules defined in the template.

■ **Note** Users won't always want to have to produce reports for information that they regularly monitor but don't print—this functionality is probably better implemented within an application dashboard. Therefore, reports are most appropriately used when printing is required (which it is in most line-of-business applications). This means that whatever your solution for displaying reports in Silverlight, it must also include the ability to print them.

Examples of simple reports include invoices and data printouts, which require minimal processing and generally just insert data from a database directly into the report. More complex reporting may involve mining the data in the database to determine patterns or relationships (correlations) between various data points or to create predictive models on which management can base its ongoing tactics and help determine future strategies. Some reports may take some time to produce when a lot of processing is required, and if generating reports places a high load on the web server, you should consider offloading the processing to a separate dedicated server, such as SQL Server Reporting Services. In summary, reporting helps enable business intelligence and knowledge management from within your line-of-business application.

Potential Solutions for Implementing Reporting

There are a number of ways to implement reporting in Silverlight applications, each with its pros and cons, including the following:

- Using Silverlight printing functionality
- Generating a PDF
- Generating HTML
- Generating Office documents

The following sections explore each of the preceding possibilities.

Using Silverlight's Printing Functionality

The introduction of printing in Silverlight 4 allowed you to print an object hierarchy, such as what's displayed on a screen. Unfortunately, it only supported sending the output to the printer as a bitmap, rather than using a vector-based output, resulting in low print quality and large files being sent to the printer. This made it suitable only for printing screens, instead of reports.

Silverlight 5 has fixed this limitation by providing support for vector printing, making Silverlight's native printing capability much more viable for printing reports. That said, Silverlight 5's printing support is still somewhat primitive, requiring you to manually handle the entire printing process, including page breaks and so on. If you want to use Silverlight's printing functionality to print reports, you are probably best off using a third-party report viewer, which we'll look at in the "Third-Party Report Viewers" section.

■ **Note** Pete Brown and David Poll have a simple report writer project on CodePlex that you may want to look into if you want to generate reports using Silverlight's built-in print functionality. This project includes handling page headers and footers, page numbering, pagination, and the report footer, among other features. You can get more information and download it at `http://silverlightreporting.codeplex.com`.

Generating a PDF

You are probably used to generating reports using a reporting tool, such as the local report designer in Visual Studio or Crystal Reports, and then displaying the report in the provided viewers. Unfortunately, neither of these tools has a viewer for Silverlight, but an alternative solution is to output the reports they generate to a PDF file, stream that through to the client, and display the PDF using one of the following techniques:

- In a new window
- In an IFrame overlaid on the application, when running inside the browser
- In a WebBrowser control to display the PDF, when running outside the browser or inside the browser with elevated trust

When the PDF is displayed in the window, it will be displayed in the Adobe Reader plug-in. This provides the ability to print the PDF, enabling you to both display and print the report in the application, provided that the user has the Adobe Reader plug-in installed.

■ **Note** Generating a PDF was the preferred solution when printing was not available in Silverlight, and it tends to still provide an excellent solution for printing complex reports.

Generating HTML

You can use the same techniques for displaying plain HTML in a Silverlight application as described for displaying a PDF; the HTML can then be printed by a browser. If you generate your reports as HTML, this provides another potential solution for printing reports.

Generating Office Documents

Once again, you can use the same techniques for displaying Word and Excel documents in a Silverlight application as described for displaying a PDF. These documents will be loaded in their corresponding viewers within the IFrame/WebBrowser control, which will provide the ability to print the documents. If you have your reports generating as Word or Excel documents, this provides another potential solution for printing reports.

■ **Note** One of the advantages of generating Word and Excel documents is that it gives the user the opportunity to modify the generated report before printing it. Most users have Word installed, and when using the Open XML standard (DOCX) format introduced in Microsoft Word 2007 (with the Office Compatibility Pack downloadable from Microsoft to open these files in earlier versions of Word), it can be easy to populate a Word document template with data on the server without requiring messy automation. In some cases, it may be better to move to a reporting engine that can generate DOC or DOCX files as their output—for example, scaling up to SQL Server Reporting Services.

Third-Party Report Viewers

A number of third-party reporting solutions have viewers for Silverlight. Let's take a look at some of them.

Perpetuum Software's Report Sharp-Shooter for Silverlight

Perpetuum Software (`www.perpetuumsoft.com`) has a Silverlight viewer control named Silverlight Viewer for Reporting Services, which displays reports generated by SQL Server Reporting Services directly within Silverlight and enables you to print them. If you use SQL Server Reporting Services to generate reports, this may be a viable option. Perpetuum also has its own report designer/engine with a Silverlight Viewer control called Report Sharp-Shooter for Silverlight that you may want to use.

At the time of this writing, a single license for Perpetuum's Silverlight Viewer for Reporting Services is $500.

Telerik Reporting

Telerik (`www.telerik.com`) has a Silverlight report viewer for its Telerik Reporting, which enables you to view and print reports generated by its reporting engine in your Silverlight application.

At the time of this writing, a single license for Telerik Reporting is $399, or $599 with source code and major version updates.

DevExpress XtraReports Suite

DevExpress (`www.devexpress.com`) has a Silverlight report viewer named DocumentPreview, for its XtraReports Suite; it enables you to view and print reports generated by its reporting engine in your Silverlight application.

At the time of this writing, a single license for DevExpress's XtraReports Suite is $349.99, or $499.99 with source code.

Infragistics NetAdvantage Reporting

Infragistics (`www.infragistics.com`) has a Silverlight report viewer as part of its NetAdvantage Reporting product; it enables you to view and print reports generated by its reporting engine in your Silverlight application.

At the time of this writing, a single license for Infragistics NetAdvantage Reporting is $995 and includes full source code.

ComponentOne C1ReportViewer

ComponentOne (www.componentone.com) has a Silverlight report viewer named C1ReportViewer as part of its Studio for Silverlight. This viewer enables you to view and print reports generated by various reporting engines in your Silverlight application.

At the time of this writing, a single license for ComponentOne's Studio for Silverlight starts at $895.

Stimulsoft Reports.Silverlight and Reports Designer.Silverlight

Stimulsoft (www.stimulsoft.com) has a Silverlight report viewer, which enables you to view and print reports generated by its reporting engine in your Silverlight application. It also has a Silverlight report designer, which enables your users to design a report within your application.

At the time of this writing, a single license for Stimulsoft's Reports.Silverlight is $599.95, or $999.95 with source code. Stimulsoft's Reports Designer.Silverlight is $299.95, or $499.95 with source code.

MindFusion.Reporting

MindFusion (www.mindfusion.eu) has a Silverlight report viewer as part of its Silverlight Pack, which enables you to view and print reports. At the time of this writing, a single license for MindFusion's Silverlight Pack is $300, or $650 with source code.

GrapeCity ActiveReports

GrapeCity (www.pcpowertools.com) has a Silverlight report viewer as part of the a generated by the ActiveReports reporting engine.

At the time of this writing, a single license for the Professional edition of ActiveReports is $1599, or $2159 with maintenance.

First Floor Software's Document Toolkit + Aspose Converter

First Floor Software (www.firstfloorsoftware.com) has a Document Toolkit that enables XML Paper Specification (XPS) documents to be displayed in a Silverlight application. XPS is a XAML-based document format from Microsoft, which makes it perfect for displaying documents such as reports within a Silverlight application. Therefore, if you can output your reports to XPS, you can display them in your application using the Document Toolkit.

To create an XPS file, you can simply print a document to the Microsoft XPS Document Writer. XPS documents are ZIP files, and you can inspect their contents by changing their extension to .zip and expanding them. You'll note that the core document contents are stored as XAML, so you could potentially harness this to generate reports on the server using a template XPS document, populating it on the fly when a user requests a report, and serving it up to the Silverlight client for display. This is a very crude solution, but it would work. For example, you could parse these files (such as using regular expressions to replace predefined tokens in the document with actual values), zip up the document (with an .xps extension), and serve this to the Silverlight client for display.

A somewhat better solution is to automatically generate the XPS document, which you can do using Aspose.Words for .NET (another commercial product, available at www.aspose.com). You can find an example of implementing this in the Document Toolkit Extensions project on CodePlex at http://documenttoolkit.codeplex.com.

■ **Note**   Some sample code is available in a number of places on the Internet that demonstrates displaying XPS documents in Silverlight (with source code) but is incomplete and done purely as proof of concept. You may want to look at these too, but the Document Toolkit is currently the only full-fledged XPS viewer available for Silverlight without creating your own. At the time of this writing, there is experimental support for displaying PDFs in addition to XPS documents.

At the time of this writing, a single license for First Floor Software's Document Toolkit is €299. A single license for Aspose.Words for .NET starts at $999.

Office Integration Using COM

In Chapter 16, we will discuss running the application outside the browser with elevated trust. This scenario gives you access to COM, through which you can interact with the various Office applications installed on the user's machine (Word, Excel, and so on).

You can use this technique to enable your Silverlight application to generate a report directly in Word or Excel, which the user can then print. We won't be looking at this option in this chapter, but Beth Massi has an in-depth blog post demonstrating how you can use the technique here: http://blogs.msdn.com/b/bethmassi/archive/2010/09/10/using-microsoft-word-to-create-reports-for-lightswitch-or-silverlight.aspx. Although the blog post is geared toward generating reports in Word using LightSwitch, you should be able to easily adapt it to Silverlight.

Choosing a Reporting Strategy

We've looked at the potential solutions for implementing reporting in Silverlight, and which option is the most appropriate will depend on the nature of your project. In the remainder of this chapter, we will look at the two most common scenarios:

- Using Silverlight's printing features

- Generating a PDF report on the server using a reporting tool/engine and displaying it on the client, where it can be printed using the Adobe Reader plug-in's printing capabilities

Using Silverlight's Native Printing Functionality

Silverlight's printing functionality revolves around the PrintDocument class. This class provides a very primitive means of sending content to the printer, but it's quite easy to use for simple tasks. Let's look at how you can use it to send some output to the printer.

■ **Note** For simple printing tasks such as printing a screen, the PrintDocument class provides a nice, easy means of doing so. However, when it comes to printing reports and other more complex printing jobs, it can become quite unwieldy to implement printing at such a low level. Therefore, generating and displaying PDF reports may be a solution better suited to those needs. We'll look at this alternative shortly.

Starting a Print Job

Silverlight's printing mechanism works using an event-based model, where you do the work required in response to its events. The PrintDocument class has three events to which you can respond:

- BeginPrint: You can take this opportunity to initialize the content you want to print.

- PrintPage: You use this event to provide the content for a page to the printer. This event is fired for each page that is printed.

- EndPrint: This event will be raised when printing is complete or an error has occurred.

The only event you need to handle is the PrintPage event, although it's also useful to handle the EndPrint event so that you can determine whether an error has occurred during the printing process.

To start a print job, create an instance of the PrintDocument class, add event handlers for the events you want to handle on this object, and then call the Print method, to which you pass a name for the document, to start printing. Note that at this stage you haven't specified what content is to be printed; you actually do this in response to the PrintPage event.

```
PrintDocument pd = new PrintDocument();
pd.PrintPage += Document_PrintPage;
pd.Print("Chapter 15 - Printing Workshop");
```

■ **Note** By default, the Print method of the PrintDocument class uses the vector printing mode in Silverlight 5 (assuming the printer is PostScript-enabled). The PrintDocument class also has a PrintBitmap method that you can use to force bitmap printing if you wish. This method behaves exactly the same as the PrintDocument class's Print method did in Silverlight 4 when vector printing was not supported. Vector printing is generally your best option, because it results in higher quality print output and smaller files being sent to the printer. However, the Print method will automatically fall back to bitmap printing if the object tree to be printed contains non-PostScript-compatible objects. In this scenario, you can still force vector printing using the PrinterFallbackSettings class, which we'll look at shortly.

Providing the Content for a Printed Page

When you call the PrintDocument class's Print/PrintBitmap method, the standard Windows print dialog will be displayed. Assuming the user goes ahead with the printing, the BeginPrint event of the PrintDocument object will be raised, after which the PrintPage event will be raised. This is where you can now send some content to the printer.

```
private void Document_PrintPage(object sender, PrintPageEventArgs e)
{
}
```

The event handler method is passed a PrintPageEventArgs object, which has four properties:

- HasMorePages
- PageMargins
- PageVisual
- PrintableArea

You assign an object hierarchy to the PageVisual property, representing the content to send to the printer for that page. This can be a control in a view or an object hierarchy that you create in code. For example, if you have a DataForm control named ProductDataForm that you want to print, your event handler for the PrintPage event will be as follows:

```
private void Document_PrintPage(object sender, PrintPageEventArgs e)
{
    e.PageVisual = ProductDataForm;
    e.HasMorePages = false;
}
```

Note that this code sets the HasMorePages property of the PrintPageEventArgs object to false. To print additional pages, you need to set this property to true. When the property is set to true, the event will be raised again, and you can send the next page's content to the printer (and so on). When you have reached the last page to be printed, set this property to false. The EndPrint event will then be raised, and the print job will complete.

Advanced Print Settings

As demonstrated earlier, the Print method of the PrintDocument class takes a document name as its parameter. This method also has an overload, enabling you to pass in an instance of the terFallbackSettings class. This class has two properties: ForceVector and OpacityThreshold.

- The ForceVector property enables you to force vector printing, even if the object tree to be printed contains non-PostScript-compatible objects.

- The OpacityThreshold property is used to set the opacity value that objects in the object hierarchy need be above in order to be printed. Vector printing does not support opacity, so you need to designate an opacity value where all objects whose opacity is below that value will not be printed, and those above it will be (with full opacity). Its default value is 0, meaning that all objects in the object hierarchy will be printed (with full opacity).

The overload of the Print method that takes an instance of the PrinterFallbackSettings class also has an optional parameter that allows you to skip displaying the Windows print dialog and automatically print to the default printer. This is only possible when the application is running with elevated privileges, which we'll discuss in Chapter 16. Attempting to do so without having elevated privileges will result in an exception being raised.

The following code demonstrates specifying fallback settings and skips displaying the Windows print dialog by setting the useDefaultPrinter parameter of the Print method to true:

```
PrintDocument pd = new PrintDocument();
pd.PrintPage += new EventHandler<PrintPageEventArgs>(pd_PrintPage);

var fallbackSettings = new PrinterFallbackSettings();
fallbackSettings.ForceVector = true;
fallbackSettings.OpacityThreshold = 0.5;
pd.Print("Chapter 15 - Printing Workshop", fallbackSettings, true);
```

⚙ Workshop: Printing a Screen

In this workshop, we're simply going to print a view.

1. Create a view, and place various controls on it to be printed. Also add a button named PrintButton on the view, and handle its Click event in the code behind, like so:

```
<Button Name="Printbutton" Content="Print" Height="25" Width="80"
    Click="PrintButton_Click" />
```

2. Open the code behind for the view. Add the following using statement:

```
using System.Windows.Printing;
```

3. In the PrintButton control's Click event, add the following code:

```
private void PrintButton_Click(object sender, System.Windows.RoutedEventArgs e)
{
    PrintDocument pd = new PrintDocument();
    pd.PrintPage += Document_PrintPage;
    pd.Print("Chapter 15 - Printing Workshop");
}
```

4. Now, you need to handle the PrintDocument class's PrintPage event, like so:

```
private void Document_PrintPage(object sender, PrintPageEventArgs e)
{

}
```

5. Add the following code in bold. This simply tells the PrintDocument object to print this view, and then tells it that there are no more pages to print.

```
private void Document_PrintPage(object sender, PrintPageEventArgs e)
{
    e.PageVisual = this;
    e.HasMorePages = false;
}
```

6. Run your application. When you click the Print button, the Windows printer dialog will appear, and then go on to print the current view to the selected printer.

■ **Note** When testing printing, you're best off printing to a virtual print driver (such as PrimoPDF, www.primopdf.com), rather than to an actual printer. This will save paper and allow you to quickly see the result on the screen. Of course, you should complete your testing against a real printer once you're happy with the output.

⚙ Workshop: Printing a Report Created in Code

Sometimes, you want to print content that isn't being displayed to the user. In this case, you need to build an object hierarchy in code and assign the top-level object to the PrintPageEventArg's PageVisual property.

In Chapter 4, we created a ProductSummary presentation model object on the server and exposed a collection of ProductSummary objects to the client. In Chapters 5 and 6, you learned how to consume that data in your Silverlight application. In this workshop, we're going to print this data as a tabular report. We could simply create a DataGrid control via code, populate it with the collection of ProductSummary objects, and print the DataGrid, but instead, we'll take a slightly finer grained approach and lay out the page using TextBlock controls within a Grid control.

For the purpose of this workshop, we'll assume that the collection of ProductSummary objects has already been retrieved from the server and has been stored in a class-level variable named _productCollection of type List<T>. We'll print the Name, Number, QuantityAvailable, ListPrice, and Model properties for each ProductSummary object in the collection.

1. Implement the previous workshop first, because we'll use that as a base and modify it to print the report that we'll generate instead of the view.

2. Add a class level constant named rowsPerPage. We're going to implement a primitive form of paging, displaying a fixed number of rows on each page (65 in this example). In a real-world scenario, you should calculate this based on the page margins and printable area, but we'll keep things simple for this workshop.

```
private const int rowsPerPage = 65;
```

3. Change the Document_PrintPage event handler as follows (changes in bold):

```
private void Document_PrintPage(object sender, PrintPageEventArgs e)
{
    PrintDocument pd = sender as PrintDocument;
    e.PageVisual = GenerateReportPage(pd.PrintedPageCount, e);
    e.HasMorePages = ((pd.PrintedPageCount + 1) * rowsPerPage < _productCollection.Count);
}
```

Here, we are passing off the generation of the page to a method named GenerateReportPage and determining whether further pages should be printed based on the current page number, the number of rows to be displayed on each page, and the size of the collection being printed.

4.   The remainder of the code is included here in full. In summary, we configure a Grid control to hold all the data for the page, with columns and a header row. Then, for each item in the collection that appears in the current page, we add a TextBox control to the appropriate cell in the Grid control, which displays the value of the item's property. We then return the Grid control back to the caller (Document_PrintPage), which outputs it to the printer.

```
private UIElement GenerateReportPage(int pageNumber, PrintPageEventArgs printPage)
{
    Grid pageLayoutGrid = CreatePageLayout(printPage);

    int startIndex = pageNumber * rowsPerPage;

    for (int rowIndex = 0; rowIndex < rowsPerPage; rowIndex++)
    {
        if (startIndex + rowIndex < _productCollection.Count)
        {
            // Create the row
            RowDefinition row = new RowDefinition();
            row.Height = new GridLength(1, GridUnitType.Auto);
            pageLayoutGrid.RowDefinitions.Add(row);

            // Populate it with data from the current item in the collection
            ProductSummary product = _productCollection[startIndex + rowIndex];
            AddGridCell(pageLayoutGrid, rowIndex + 1, 0, product.Name);
            AddGridCell(pageLayoutGrid, rowIndex + 1, 1, product.Number);
            AddGridCell(pageLayoutGrid, rowIndex + 1, 2,
                        product.QuantityAvailable.ToString());
            AddGridCell(pageLayoutGrid, rowIndex + 1, 3, product.ListPrice.ToString("C"));
            AddGridCell(pageLayoutGrid, rowIndex + 1, 4, product.Model);
        }
    }

    return pageLayoutGrid;
}

private Grid CreatePageLayout(PrintPageEventArgs printPage)
{
    Grid pageLayoutGrid = new Grid();
    pageLayoutGrid.MaxWidth = printPage.PrintableArea.Width;

    // Create the columns
    for (int colIndex = 0; colIndex < 5; colIndex++ )
    {
        var column = new ColumnDefinition();
        column.Width = new GridLength(1, GridUnitType.Auto);
        pageLayoutGrid.ColumnDefinitions.Add(column);
    }

    // Create the header row
    RowDefinition headerRow = new RowDefinition();
    headerRow.Height = new GridLength(1, GridUnitType.Auto);
    pageLayoutGrid.RowDefinitions.Add(headerRow);
```

```
    AddGridCell(pageLayoutGrid, 0, 0, "Name", true);
    AddGridCell(pageLayoutGrid, 0, 1, "Number", true);
    AddGridCell(pageLayoutGrid, 0, 2, "Quantity Available", true);
    AddGridCell(pageLayoutGrid, 0, 3, "List Price", true);
    AddGridCell(pageLayoutGrid, 0, 4, "Model", true);

    // Show a line underneath the header
    Line line = new Line();
    line.Stretch = Stretch.Fill;
    line.VerticalAlignment = VerticalAlignment.Bottom;
    line.Stroke = new SolidColorBrush(Colors.Black);
    line.X2 = pageLayoutGrid.MaxWidth;
    line.SetValue(Grid.RowProperty, 0);
    line.SetValue(Grid.ColumnProperty, 0);
    line.SetValue(Grid.ColumnSpanProperty, 5);
    pageLayoutGrid.Children.Add(line);

    return pageLayoutGrid;
}

private void AddGridCell(Grid pageLayoutGrid, int row, int col,
                         string text, bool isBold = false)
{
    TextBlock cellText = new TextBlock();
    cellText.Text = text;
    cellText.Margin = new Thickness(3, 0, 3, 0);

    if (isBold)
        cellText.FontWeight = FontWeights.Bold;

    cellText.SetValue(Grid.RowProperty, row);
    cellText.SetValue(Grid.ColumnProperty, col);

    pageLayoutGrid.Children.Add(cellText);
}
```

- Now, run your application, and click the Print button. The Windows print dialog will appear, and you can print all the data in the collection to the report, as shown in Figure 15-1.

Name	Number	Quantity Available	List Price	Model
HL Road Frame – Black, 58	FR-R92B-58		$1,431.50	HL Road Frame
HL Road Frame – Red, 58	FR-R92R-58		$1,431.50	HL Road Frame
Sport-100 Helmet, Red	HL-U509-R	288	$34.99	Sport-100
Sport-100 Helmet, Black	HL-U509	324	$34.99	Sport-100
Mountain Bike Socks, M	SO-B909-M	180	$9.50	Mountain Bike Socks
Mountain Bike Socks, L	SO-B909-L	216	$9.50	Mountain Bike Socks
Sport-100 Helmet, Blue	HL-U509-B	216	$34.99	Sport-100
AWC Logo Cap	CA-1098	288	$8.99	Cycling Cap
Long-Sleeve Logo Jersey, S	LJ-0192-S	144	$49.99	Long-Sleeve Logo Jersey

Figure 15-1. A subset of the output from printing a report created in code

Generating and Displaying a PDF Report

Let's now look at how you can use a common reporting tool to generate the reports as PDF files and display them within the application. We will use a reporting tool to generate the PDF and then display the report in the application, by overlaying an IFrame on the application when running inside the browser and using the WebBrowser control when running outside the browser.

Generating a Report on the Server

The first step is to generate the PDF reports on the server and make them available to the Silverlight client. Let's look at how you can go about implementing this.

Choosing a Reporting Tool/Engine

When implementing reports, you could take the path of manually creating the reports yourself, which is a time-consuming and mostly unnecessary meta-problem that diverts focus away from actually solving the business problem at hand, or you can use one of the many reporting tools available on the market to manage the reporting component of your system.

There are three major components to a reporting tool:

- The report designer
- The reporting engine
- The report viewer

The report designer enables you to create the structure of the report, its formatting, and its rules (filter/sorting/grouping logic, database queries, calculations, and so on)—effectively, it's used to create a report template. The reporting engine then uses these templates to create and populate the reports when they are requested. When reports are served up to the client, the client needs some means of displaying the report to the user. This is where the report viewer component comes in; the reporting engine may generate the reports in a proprietary format in which a custom viewer is required, or it may generate the report in an open or common format (such as PDF, DOC, XLS, and so on) in which that format may have its own viewer.

When choosing a reporting tool, you need to ensure all three components are compatible with the technologies used in your system. Since the report designer is used only to create the templates, it's not really dependent on the system; however, since each report designer works in different way, you will need to ensure it has the ability to cater for the complexity of your reports. You need to have programmatic access to the reporting engine so you can ask it to generate a report, using the parameters and data you pass to it, and then capture this output and stream it back to the client, unless the engine can expose the reports on the Web that your application can directly access. Finally, the reporting tool needs to contain a report viewer control that can display the report in your Silverlight application.

There are reporting solutions for Windows Forms and ASP.NET provided with each copy of Visual Studio (Crystal Reports for Visual Studio in the Professional or higher editions, and the Visual Studio Report Designer, also known as Report Viewer in the Standard or higher editions and in the Visual Web Developer 2010 Express Edition after installing an add-in). While the report designer and reporting engine components of each are suitable for our system, neither of these generates reports in a format that can be viewed or printed within a Silverlight application, and neither has a Silverlight-enabled report viewer control. This is a problem since you need to display the report within your application to users and then give them the ability to send it to their printers. However, the reports can be generated as PDF files, which, using the method described shortly, can be displayed in your Silverlight application and printed.

In most cases, you are by far best off using a commercial reporting tool; otherwise, reports become difficult to maintain and modify, and maintaining the reporting tool tends to become a never-ending project on its own. Some of the third-party reporting tools discussed earlier in this chapter come with source code, so there is little reason to create your own tool for fear of vendor lock-in.

■ **Note** You may have to try various reporting tools to find one with the flexibility you require, but in the vast majority of cases, you are better off using an off-the-shelf reporting tool. Many developers have created a black hole in the cost and time budget of a project while attempting to write their own reporting tool, and the project/client ends up suffering greatly for this decision. There are many reporting tool packages out there, and although none of them is perfect, one will tend to satisfy most client requirements at a reasonable cost.

In the following workshops, we will focus on generating the reports using the Visual Studio Report Designer along with the Local Report Engine here, because it's a reasonably capable reporting tool (it uses the same template format as used by SQL Server Reporting Services). Also, it's a reporting tool that all Silverlight developers will have available, since it's provided with the Standard and higher editions of Visual Studio. Many third-party reporting tools are available—most of which can export reports to PDF and be used in the manner described in this chapter. If you have a preferred reporting tool, it should be fairly easy to substitute the one used here with your own.

■ **Note** A report designer is built into Visual Studio 2010 Standard edition and higher, but this is omitted from the Visual Web Developer 2010 Express edition. At the time of this writing, Microsoft has chosen not to release an add-in to provide the Visual Web Developer 2010 Express edition with a report builder (as it did for the 2008 version), so this will be an issue if you are using this for developing your Silverlight applications. One option is to download the Visual Web Developer 2008 Express edition and download the add-in from `www.microsoft.com/download/en/details.aspx?id=16682` to design your reports. Another is to download SQL Server Express 2008 with Advanced Services and use the Business Intelligence Development Studio 2008 tool that it contains to design your reports. Alternatively, you can try using the open source fyiReporting designer, which you can get from `www.fyireporting.com`. When using any of these options, you will need to download and install the Microsoft Report Viewer 2010 Redistributable Package to generate the reports at runtime; it's at `www.microsoft.com/download/en/details.aspx?id=6442`.

Unfortunately, the reporting tool we are using doesn't have a particular name that we can use to refer to it as a whole. It's particularly hard to find help on it on the Web because of this (`www.gotreportviewer.com` is probably the best place to start if you want more information). It's often referred to as Report Viewer, which apart from not being particularly unique is also a bit confusing, because the tool is not just used for viewing reports. You may want to try searching for RDLC (the file extension of the report templates). Throughout this chapter, I will refer to the report designer as the Visual Studio Report Designer, the reporting engine as the Local Report Engine, and the report viewer control as the Report Viewer.

Choosing an Output Format

The Local Report Engine can render to a number of different formats, including the following:

- HTML (when hosted within the ASP.NET Report Viewer control)

- A Word document

- An Excel document

- An image

- A PDF document

Each of these can be displayed within a browser (HTML and images natively, Excel and PDF documents by browser plug-ins).

Only the image output can be displayed directly within a Silverlight application, but this option is not a particularly suitable because of the large file size of the images and because the quality of the printouts would be low. Therefore, we need to look at other means of rendering the report outside the Silverlight application, using the capabilities of the browser instead.

Of the four remaining options, we can exclude rendering to Excel because it would generally be appropriate to do so only when generating matrix- or table-based reports.

Although we can now (using the 2008 or higher version) print directly from ASP.NET's Report Viewer control, doing so requires the installation of an ActiveX control, which will work only in Internet Explorer running on Windows (not Mac) machines and will not work within Firefox. You want your Silverlight application to run cross-browser and cross-platform, so this could be considered an unnecessary restriction to put on your application in most scenarios, and printing is a vital feature for implementing reporting.

This leaves PDF or Word documents as the only viable options, and both provide the functionality we require. They both do the following:

- Display on the screen exactly as they appear on the printed page

- Can be printed directly from within the browser where they are being viewed (assuming the users have the Adobe Reader or FoxIt Reader plug-in installed, which is not an unrealistic expectation, or otherwise are using Google Chrome as their browser, which has a PDF reader built in)

- Can be saved to the user's hard disk (or a network drive) for archiving purposes

- Can be easily e-mailed to colleagues

- Can be published to content management/collaboration/document management systems such as Microsoft SharePoint

For the purpose of this chapter, we will be generating reports as PDFs.

Serving Reports to the Client

To serve reports to your Silverlight application, you need to create a mechanism that enables the application to request a report from the server, have the server generate the report (using the Local Report Engine and rendered as a PDF), and finally stream this back to the application for display.

To handle report requests on the server, we'll create an *HTTP handler* in our web project. The Silverlight application will make a web request to the HTTP handler (which is a simple HTTP request, via a URL). The HTTP handler will then do the following:

- Ensure the user is authenticated

- Find the corresponding report renderer for the report requested
- Let it handle the logic for generating the report

■ **Note** A *report renderer* is a class created by the author and used to simplify the generation of reports.

The report renderer will return the report to the HTTP handler, which will then stream it back to the client as a PDF.

You'll also create report renderers. Each report will have a corresponding report renderer that handles the following:

- The logic behind generating that report (such as specifying the location of the report template)
- Ensuring the user has permission to generate the report based on the roles to which they are assigned
- Obtaining the data from the database to populate the report with

---

■ **Note** You will need to add a reference to `Microsoft.Reporting.WebForms.dll` to your web project to enable reports to be generated using the Local Report Engine.

⚙ Workshop: Obtaining Data to Populate the Report

The first step that we need to do when generating a report is to provide a way to populate it with data. The Local Report Engine will accept either DataTables or collections of objects as a data source. In this set of workshops, we'll be using an existing product catalog report that we'll populate with data from our Entity Framework model, and we'll do so using a collection of objects.

1. Being a predefined report, our objects will need to conform to the data that is expected, meaning that it must have properties with names that match the fields used in the report. For this, we'll create a class named `ProductCatalogReportData`, like so:

```
using System.Collections.Generic;
using System.Linq;

namespace Chapter15Sample.Web.Reports.Products
{
    public class ProductCatalogReportData
    {
        public string ProdSubCat { get; set; }
        public string ProdModel { get; set; }
        public string ProdCat { get; set; }
        public string Description { get; set; }
        public byte[] LargePhoto { get; set; }
        public string ProdName { get; set; }
        public string ProductNumber { get; set; }
        public string Color { get; set; }
```

```
        public string Size { get; set; }
        public decimal? Weight { get; set; }
        public decimal StandardCost { get; set; }
        public string Style { get; set; }
        public string Class { get; set; }
        public decimal ListPrice { get; set; }
    }
}
```

2. We now need to create a collection of ProductCatalogReportData objects, populated with data from our Entity Framework model. For a class to appear as a project data source in the report designer, it needs to have a static method that returns a collection (such as a List<T> or array) of itself. You'll find that you can't simply select entities from the Entity Framework model when building a report because of this requirement for a static method. In any case, reports often require data combined from multiple entities, so you will generally need to create your own data source class to populate the report with anyway. Therefore, we'll follow this pattern to populate a collection with data from our Entity Framework model. Add the following static method to the ProductCatalogReportData class:

```
public static List<ProductCatalogReportData> GetCatalogProductReportData()
{
    using (AdventureWorksEntities context = new AdventureWorksEntities())
    {
        var reportData = from p in context.Products
                         where p.ProductModel != null && p.ProductSubcategory != null
                         select new ProductCatalogReportData()
                         {
                             ProdName = p.Name,
                             ProductNumber = p.ProductNumber,
                             ListPrice = p.ListPrice,
                             Class = p.Class.TrimEnd(),
                             Color = p.Color,
                             Size = p.Size,
                             StandardCost = p.StandardCost,
                             Style = p.Style.TrimEnd(),
                             Weight = p.Weight,
                             ProdCat = p.ProductSubcategory.ProductCategory.Name,
                             ProdSubCat = p.ProductSubcategory.Name,
                             ProdModel = p.ProductModel.Name,
                             LargePhoto = p.ProductProductPhotoes
                                         .FirstOrDefault().ProductPhoto.LargePhoto,
                             Description = p.ProductModel
                                         .ProductModelProductDescriptionCultures
                                         .Where(x => x.CultureID == "en")
                                         .FirstOrDefault()
                                         .ProductDescription.Description
                         };

        return reportData.ToList();
    }
}
```

⚙ Workshop: Creating the Report Template

The next step is to create your report template using the Local Report Designer that comes with Visual Studio 2010. Creating reports is beyond the scope of this book, but you can find some good tutorials to help you at http://gotreportviewer.com. In summary, the class created in the previous workshop will show up as a data source that the report can use, and you can then lay out the report, mapping fields to the data source class's properties, as required.

For the purpose of this set of workshops, we'll use a predefined report named ProductCatalog.rdlc as our report template. This report shipped as part of the SQL Server Reporting Services examples on CodePlex (www.codeplex.com/MSFTRSProdSamples) and has been included as part of the code accompanying this book, available from the Apress web site. Simply create a Reports folder in your Web project, and put the report template file into it.

Creating a Report Renderer

We now need to provide a way to populate a report template with data. Instead of doing this in the HTTP handler, which can get very complicated very quickly, we'll create a report renderer class that will handle the generation of the report. Often, there are a few processes in generating a report—such as populating the report with data, populating subreports with data, and so on—and properties to set—such as the report path, name, authorization rights, orientation, size, and so on—that are specific to that report. A report renderer essentially handles this whole process.

To simplify the creation of a report renderer, a base report renderer class providing much of the required functionality can be found in the code accompanying this book. Let's take a quick look at this class and then look at implementing a functional report renderer.

About the Base Report Renderer Class

The sample project accompanying this chapter contains a base report renderer class, named BaseReportRenderer. Its class diagram is shown in Figure 15-2.

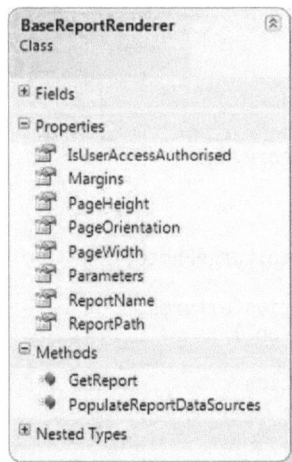

Figure 15-2. The BaseReportRenderer class diagram

Each report should have a dedicated renderer class that inherits from BaseReportRenderer and overrides the appropriate methods and properties that will be called when generating the report.

Your report renderer class basically needs to inherit from this base class and override the ReportPath property and the PopulateReportDataSources function in the report renderer (the minimum requirements for any report to be rendered).

The GetReport method in the base class handles the generation of the report, and its workflow is as follows:

- Create a LocalReport instance.
- Set the location to the report template.
- Populate the report data sources.
- Return this LocalReport instance back to the HTTP handler.

If you have the need to implement a different workflow, you can override the GetReport function to have full control over this workflow.

 Workshop: Creating a Report Renderer

Let's create a report renderer that will handle generating the Product Catalog report:

1. Add the BaseReportRenderer.cs class from the sample code for this chapter (available from the Apress web site) to your project.

2. Create a new class in your project, named ProductCatalogReportRenderer, that inherits from the BaseReportRenderer class:

```
using SilverlightLOBFramework.Reports;

namespace Chapter15Sample.Web.Reports.Products
{
    public class ProductCatalogReportRenderer : BaseReportRenderer
    {

    }
}
```

3. Add the following using statements to the top of the class's file:

```
using System.Collections.Generic;
using Microsoft.Reporting.WebForms;
```

4. You now need to override some of the base class's methods and properties. Start by overriding the ReportPath property, and return the path to the report template (.rdlc) file.

```
public override string ReportPath
{
    get { return @"Reports\Product Catalog.rdlc"; }
}
```

5. Override the ReportName property, and return a name for the report.

```
public override string ReportName
{
    get { return "Product Catalog"; }
}
```

6. Finally, you need to override the PopulateReportDataSources method. This method essentially gets a collection of objects to populate the report with and adds the collection to the collection of data sources used by the report. In the following code, we get a collection of ProductCatalogReportData objects by calling the ProductCatalogReportData class's static GetCatalogProductReportData method that we created earlier in the workshop titled "Obtaining Data to Populate the Report."

```
public override void PopulateReportDataSources(ReportDataSourceCollection dataSources)
{
    List<ProductCatalogReportData> productCatalogReportData =
                        ProductCatalogReportData.GetCatalogProductReportData();
    dataSources.Add(new ReportDataSource("ProductCatalog", productCatalogReportData));
}
```

The report renderer class is now complete. The base report render class takes care of actually generating the report using the report template and the data that you provided in this class.

Creating the Report HTTP Handler

HTTP handlers execute in response to an HTTP request and return custom output to the client. We need to create a HTTP handler that will generate and serve up reports to the client. To make creating HTTP handlers that generate reports easier, the sample code accompanying this chapter has a class named BaseReportHandler that your HTTP handler can inherit from, providing much of the base functionality required by your handler. Let's take a quick look at this class and then look at implementing a functional report HTTP handler.

About the Base Report HTTP Handler

The sample project accompanying this chapter contains a base report renderer class, named BaseReportHandler. Figure 15-3 shows the class diagram for this class.

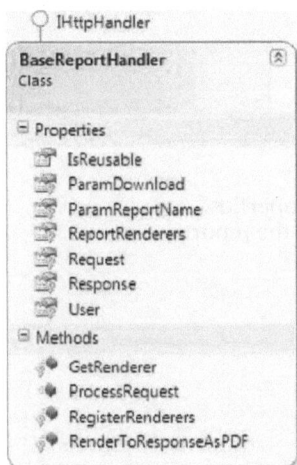

Figure 15-3. The BaseReportHandler class diagram

The BaseReportHandler class has been designed to permit reusability of the HTTP handler code that handles report requests in a generic fashion. This class handles the following:

- Ensuring the user is authenticated

- Finding the renderer for the report they have requested and checking whether the user is authorized to view that report

- Requesting that the renderer handle the report generation

- Streaming it back to the client as a PDF file

⚙ Workshop: Creating the Report HTTP Handler

Creating a report HTTP handler that will serve up reports to your Silverlight application is very easy when you use the BaseReportHandler class provided in the code accompanying this book. Let's create one that serves up the Product Catalog report:

1. Add the BaseReportHandler.cs class from the sample code for this chapter (available from the Apress web site) to your project.

2. Create a new HTTP handler in your project named Report.ashx, using the Generic Handler item template (found under the Web category in the Add New Item dialog) as its base.

3. Instead of implementing IHttpHandler, change the class definition to inherit from the BaseReportHandler class:

```
public class Report : BaseReportHandler
```

4. Remove the content of the class that was created by the Generic Handler item template, so that the class is empty.

```
public class Report : BaseReportHandler
{

}
```

5. Add the following using statements to the top of the file:

```
using System;
using System.Collections.Generic;
using Chapter15Sample.Web.Reports.Products;
using SilverlightLOBFramework.Reports;
```

6. Override the base class's RegisterRenderers method. The purpose of this method is to populate the ReportRenderers dictionary in the base class, which defines all the supported renderers, providing each with a unique name that will be used to reference the renderer and the renderer object's type. The following code demonstrates registering the ProductCatalogReportRenderer report renderer that we created in the previous workshop and naming it ProductCatalog. The client will use this name when requesting the report that the corresponding report renderer generated.

```
public class Report : BaseReportHandler
{
    protected override void RegisterRenderers(Dictionary<string, Type> reportRenderers)
```

```
    {
        reportRenderers.Add("ProductCatalog", typeof(ProductCatalogReportRenderer));
    }
}
```

When a report is requested, the base class will then find the entry matching the ReportName query parameter from the HTTP request and instantiate the associated report renderer from the specified type. The report renderer will then generate the report, and the report HTTP handler will stream the report back to the client. This entire process is handled for you by the base classes. You need to worry only about configuring the report in the report renderer class and registering the report renderer with the report HTTP handler; the rest is taken care of for you.

■ **Note** You might like to put each of the report renderers in a separate assembly, reference these assemblies in the web.config file, and have the report HTTP handler load them dynamically for even more generic code, enabling you to add reports to the server without needing to recompile the core server code. However, for the purposes of this example, we'll keep the implementation as simple as possible.

Passing Parameters to the Report

The workshops that we've just worked through demonstrate a simple scenario that requires no parameters (i.e., the report is being populated with all the data from the database). However, often you will want to pass parameters to the report renderer to be used in the database query. For example, you may have a Product Details report and want to pass a ProductID parameter from the client to the server such that the report displays the details for only the given product. The base HTTP handler and report renderer classes help you with this task. The base report renderer class contains a Parameters property (of type NameValueCollection) that the base HTTP handler will assign all the HTTP request query parameters to. The report renderer can then find the required parameters and their values from this collection and pass the values through to the static Get function of the data class to be included as part of the where clause when querying the database.

To see how this is done, the sample code that accompanies this chapter demonstrates a Product Details report that accepts a ProductID parameter, and displays the data in the report for that product only. Look at the ProductDetailsReportRenderer and ProductDetailsReportData classes for the details.

Securing Access to the Report

To limit the users who are permitted access to a report, you can override the IsUserAccessAuthorised property in the report renderer and determine, based on the user's role, whether that person should be permitted access to the report, as was demonstrated in the ProductDetailsReportRenderer code. For example, the following code demonstrates overriding the BaseReportRenderer class's IsUserAccessAuthorised property and providing permission only for user's with the Managers role to view the report.

```
public override bool IsUserAccessAuthorised
{
    get
    {
        // Sample role check - user must be a manager
```

```
        return HttpContext.Current.User.IsInRole("Managers");
    }
}
```

You may also want to limit what data users are permitted to view by their user IDs or roles, such as allowing salespeople to view only lists of their own sales. This should be implemented in the PopulateReportDataSources function as part of the where clause in your LINQ to Entities query.

■ **Note** It's important to implement security on your reports because they may contain the most sensitive business data that you would not want anyone to obtain access to. Another function security can provide is to filter the data in a report to contain only the data that a specific user has the rights to view, while still using a common report template.

Deploying the Report Viewer/Engine

When deploying the application to the server, you will need to install the runtime for the report engine, which isn't installed as part of the .NET Framework. If you don't have the Microsoft Report Viewer Redistributable 2010 setup file, you can download it from www.microsoft.com/downloads/details.aspx ?FamilyID=a941c6b2-64dd-4d03-9ca7-4017a0d164fd. Alternatively, you can simply copy the referenced reporting DLLs to your Bin directory on the server.

Displaying the Report on the Client

Unfortunately, you cannot view a PDF document from within a Silverlight application. However, you can take advantage of the browser's ability to host the Adobe Reader or FoxIt Reader plug-in, which will host your PDF report, and that is what we'll be looking at next

Creating the HtmlViewer Control

You now need to display the PDF that you generated on the server in your Silverlight application. Doing so requires a little bit of work. When you navigate to a PDF file in your web browser, it will be displayed within the browser using the Adobe Reader or FoxIt Reader plug-in, assuming you have one of those installed. Google Chrome is an exception, in that it provides its own built-in PDF reader and will display the PDF file using that instead. Ideally, we'd like to implement the same sort of behavior in our application, and we'll look at doing that now.

Solution Overview

Silverlight 4 introduced a WebBrowser control that you could display the PDF within; however, when you run your application inside the browser, you will get the output shown in Figure 15-4.

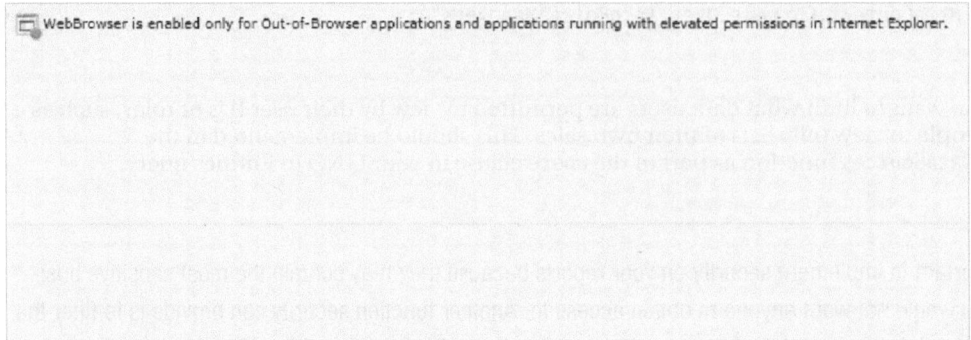

WebBrowser is enabled only for Out-of-Browser applications and applications running with elevated permissions in Internet Explorer.

Figure 15-4. The WebBrowser control when used in an application running inside the browser

For security purposes, the WebBrowser control will work only when the application is running outside the browser (as will be discussed in Chapter 16) or in the browser with elevated trust in Internet Explorer (also discussed in Chapter 16). If your application is running in one of these modes, you can use this control in your application and navigate to the URL for your report, and the report will be displayed within the control. However, if your application isn't running in one of these modes, another solution is required.

Simply opening the report in another browser window is a possible solution but is not ideal because it separates the display of the report from the application.

Ultimately, the best solution, although a little complex to implement, is to manipulate the underlying HTML page, using the HTML Bridge, and overlay an IFrame onto your application. You can then display the PDF in this IFrame to achieve the effect you want. This solution won't work when the application is running outside the browser because the HTML Bridge would not be available in this mode, but you can use the WebBrowser control instead.

To support displaying an IFrame within the application, the sample code accompanying this book contains a control that wraps this functionality into a reusable component. It handles creating and destroying the IFrame when running inside the browser and uses the WebBrowser control when running outside the browser. This way, wherever support is required in this or other applications for displaying HTML content within the application itself, you can easily drop it in.

The HTML Bridge

The HTML Bridge provides the means to interact with the underlying browser and Document Object Model (DOM) from a Silverlight application. You may also see this referenced as HTML DOM Interoperability. Throughout this chapter, you will see how you can use the HTML Bridge to provide various features such as opening a pop-up window, creating elements in the DOM (such as an IFrame), inspecting the DOM (checking properties of the Silverlight plug-in), and handling JavaScript events.

To access the HTML Bridge, add a reference to the System.Windows.Browser namespace, and then, you can access the DOM of the underlying HTML document that is hosting the plug-in via the static HtmlPage class.

■ **Note** The HTML Bridge is not available when the application is running outside the browser, because it's not (technically) being hosted by an HTML page. It is, however, being hosted by a browser control (Internet Explorer on Windows and Safari on Mac), which then hosts your Silverlight application. If you're interested in finding out more, try using Microsoft Spy++ to inspect the window and its structure.

Overlaying an IFrame on Your Application

Now that you know a bit about the HTML Bridge, let's look at some of the issues that you will face in displaying an IFrame over the top of your Silverlight plug-in.

Setting Windowless Mode

The primary issue that you face is that, by default, the Silverlight plug-in is in windowed mode, where the plug-in handles rendering the Silverlight content in its own window, on top of any HTML content in the underlying HTML document. Therefore, even though you are able to create the IFrame in the underlying HTML document, it won't be visible because the Silverlight plug-in occupies the entire browser area, rendering on top of any HTML content in the DOM of the page, regardless of the z-index of the plug-in or the IFrame. Therefore, you need to ensure windowed mode is turned off so that the browser is in charge of the rendering instead of the Silverlight plug-in; then, your Silverlight content will be rendered alongside the underlying HTML content.

■ **Note** There are performance issues in placing the browser in charge of the rendering, so the decision to use windowless mode needs to be carefully considered. Silverlight is optimized for rendering complex animations and video, and using windowless mode will cause a significant performance loss in these two areas. Considering that we are building a line-of-business application here, the loss in rendering performance is unlikely to affect us in most cases, so the benefits in this case should outweigh the costs.

To enable windowless mode, you need to open the HTML page hosting the Silverlight plug-in, find the object tag, and add a param node to its children that specifies a value for the Windowless property—setting its value to true as follows:

```
<param name="Windowless" value="True" />
```

Creating the IFrame

The next step is to create the IFrame in the underlying HTML page. The IFrame is contained within a DIV element so that you can set its position properly. This DIV should have its z-index set to 99 so that it displays on top of other controls, assuming each of their z-index values is less than 99, and its positioning mode should be set to absolute. This means you can set its position by its coordinates in the browser window. You can then append this DIV as a child of the FORM tag in the DOM and append the IFrame element as a child of the DIV tag.

```
divElement = HtmlPage.Document.CreateElement("div");
divElement.Id = "HtmlFrameDiv";
divElement.SetStyleAttribute("position", "absolute");
divElement.SetStyleAttribute("z-index", "99");

iframeElement = HtmlPage.Document.CreateElement("iframe");
iframeElement.Id = "HtmlFrame";
iframeElement.SetAttribute("scrolling", "no");
iframeElement.SetAttribute("frameborder", "0");

HtmlElement formElement =
    HtmlPage.Document.GetElementsByTagName("form")[0] as HtmlElement;

formElement.AppendChild(divElement);
divElement.AppendChild(iframeElement);
```

Positioning and Sizing the IFrame

Once the required elements have been created in the DOM, you need to position and size them. As previously mentioned, this involves setting the coordinates and size of the DIV. The height and width of the IFrame also need to be set to support multiple browsers. In some browsers, the IFrame fills the area of the DIV, and in others, it doesn't.

Because the content being displayed is not being rendered by Silverlight, you need to take resizing of the IFrame into account yourself. If the control is resized (such as if the browser window was resized or a grid splitter was implemented that enabled the user to resize or move the location of the control), you need to handle the LayoutChanged event of the control and adjust the size and location of the IFrame accordingly.

■ **Note** We're deliberately not handling the SizeChanged event for detecting any repositioning or resizing of the IFrame control—the reason being that if the control location was simply moved, the SizeChanged event is not raised. Therefore, although the LayoutChanged event is raised even when the control hasn't been moved or resized (and can be raised many times for many reasons because it is raised when anything occurs in the visual tree), it's the only event that will handle all situations—even if it isn't ideal. It is best to never handle this event if an alternative is available, because of the high frequency at which it can be raised.

Additional Features and Functionality

The HtmlViewer control is already created and available for download as part of the sample code accompanying this chapter. However, let's take a look at some of the more important aspects of how it was built.

Ensuring That the Windowless Property Is Set

For the control to work properly, you must have turned on the Windowless property for the Silverlight plug-in. Since we are creating a reusable control, it's worth checking to make sure this Windowless property is turned on and raise an exception if not in order to save confusion as to why the IFrame isn't being displayed.

Using the HTML Bridge, the HtmlViewer control can navigate through the DOM of the page and ensure this property is turned on. First, it needs to get a reference to the plug-in element, which is rendered as an object tag. Rather than searching for the object tag in the page, we can simply get a reference to it using the HtmlPage.Plugin property. Then, the control enumerates through its children looking for param tags that have a name attribute of Windowless. If the tag isn't found or its value is set to false, the control throws an exception.

```
HtmlElement silverlightObject = HtmlPage.Plugin;
bool isWindowless = false;

foreach (HtmlElement param in silverlightObject.Children)
{
    if (param.TagName == "param")
    {
        string name = param.GetAttribute("name");
        string value = param.GetAttribute("value");

        if (name == "Windowless")
        {
            isWindowless = Convert.ToBoolean(value);
            break;
        }
    }
}

if (!isWindowless)
    throw new Exception("The Silverlight plugin needs to be in windowless mode!");
```

Positioning and Sizing the IFrame

This involves working out the location of the control with reference to the application root visual element—in other words, the whole area occupied by the Silverlight plug-in—by creating a transform object to transform the coordinates of the two and relating (0, 0) on the control to (0, 0) on the application root visual element. This gives you the coordinates of the control with reference to the application root visual element but not necessarily with reference to the browser window itself, if the Silverlight control is not located at (0, 0) to the browser window. Therefore, for completeness, you should calculate the offset of the Silverlight plug-in in the underlying page, moving up the DOM and adding offsets of each parent element, and add that to your calculations.

Because the Silverlight application is filling the entire browser window, it will be located at (0, 0), making this calculation unnecessary, so the HtmlViewer control makes this an assumption and forgoes these additional calculations. Therefore, it can now use these coordinates to set the left and top properties of the DIV, and the width and height properties are simply the width and height of the control.

```
if (iframeElement != null && this.ActualHeight != 0)
{
    GeneralTransform gt = this.TransformToVisual(Application.Current.RootVisual);
    Point pos = gt.Transform(new Point(0, 0));
    divElement.SetStyleAttribute("left", pos.X.ToString() + "px");
    divElement.SetStyleAttribute("top", pos.Y.ToString() + "px");
    divElement.SetStyleAttribute("width", this.ActualWidth.ToString() + "px");
    divElement.SetStyleAttribute("height", this.ActualHeight.ToString() + "px");

    iframeElement.SetStyleAttribute("width", this.ActualWidth.ToString() + "px");
```

```
    iframeElement.SetStyleAttribute("height", this.ActualHeight.ToString() + "px");
}
```

Determining When Content Is Loaded

Ideally, the HtmlViewer control would monitor when the content has loaded, handling the JavaScript onLoad event raised by the IFrame via the HTML Bridge, and raise an event to notify the application as such. This could potentially be useful in showing an animation and/or indicating that the application is communicating with the server.

Capturing this DOM event in Silverlight is actually quite easy—when creating the IFrame, you can use the AttachEvent method on the HTML element, specifying the JavaScript event to capture and the .NET method to handle the event. However, you run into a problem in loading a PDF in the IFrame, because for some reason, the onLoad event is never raised, presumably it is because a separate plug-in takes over loading the page, although it is raised correctly for HTML pages.

Therefore, because the reports will be PDF files, you won't be able to use this feature in your application to indicate that server communication is in progress, although the functionality has still been included in this control for reuse purposes when displaying HTML pages. It is preferable to show something to the user rather than a blank area while the report loads, such as a "Please wait—loading . . ." message in the control area. If you set some HTML locally to display immediately in the IFrame before navigating to the report URL on the server, this will continue to display until the report has been retrieved from the server (and the PDF reader plug-in has loaded itself and the report). Figure 15-5 demonstrates a simple example of doing so.

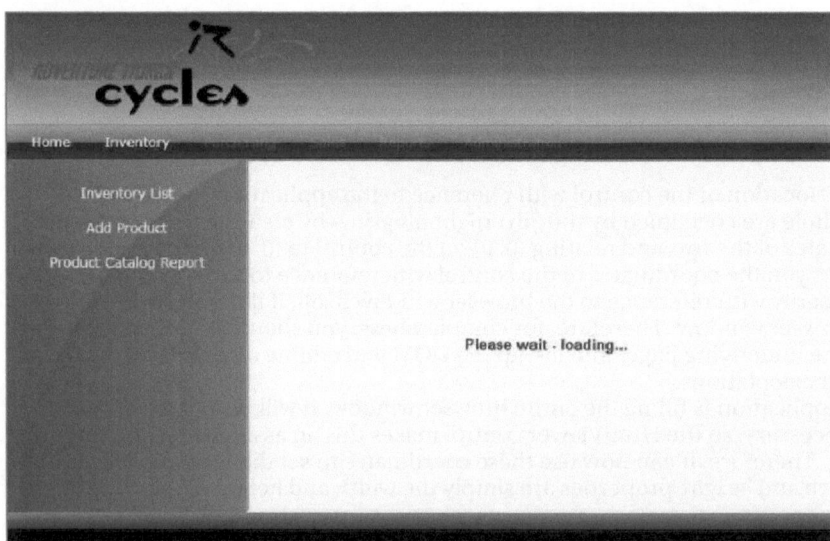

Figure 15-5. *The "Please wait" message*

If you attempt to build up the page to display using the DOM object available via the HTML Bridge, you will find that it is displayed differently in Internet Explorer (IE) than in Firefox. IE will display the content in quirks mode, and there is no way to set the DOCTYPE for the loading page via the DOM. Therefore, you need to use an alternative means of creating and loading this page locally. Another method is to get a reference to the empty document created in the IFrame automatically when it is created and use it instead to set the content to display. You can then open it for direct HTML content writing, write the entire

HTML document to be displayed (including the DOCTYPE, html, head, and body tags), and then close it. This document would then be displayed in the IFrame. The open, write, and close functions are not available via the HTML Bridge but can be called using the Invoke method on the document object.

```
// Add some HTML to the iframe before requesting the document
HtmlWindow contentWindow = iframeElement.GetProperty("contentWindow") as HtmlWindow;
HtmlDocument document = contentWindow.GetProperty("document") as HtmlDocument;

// Write the html to display to the document
document.Invoke("open", null);
document.Invoke("write", "<HTML to display goes here>");
document.Invoke("close", null);
```

■ **Note** There appears to be a bug in Internet Explorer 8 and below, for which there doesn't seem to be a work-around. Even after the report has loaded, the progress bar in the status bar continues to show. This appears to be because of a combination of writing directly to the document in the IFrame and then navigating to a different page—if you comment out one or the other, the progress bar is hidden correctly, but using both together leaves it visible. This problem does not appear to occur in Firefox or Chrome.

Destroying the IFrame

The final issue is how to know when to remove the IFrame from the underlying DOM. Silverlight user controls don't have a Closing or Closed event, the Dispose event when implementing IDisposable isn't automatically called, and the destructor/finalize method being called is unreliable because it relies on the idiosyncrasies of the garbage collector as to when the control is cleaned up.

The HtmlViewer control still implements the IDisposable interface and uses the Dispose method to remove the IFrame from the DOM, but you need to know when to call this method. When it's created, the control will walk its way up the visual tree and see whether it can find a Page object that is hosting it. If so, the application is using the navigation framework, and the Page object exposes a NavigationService object whose Navigating event the HtmlViewer control hooks into to determine when the page is being navigated away from. When this event is raised, it will call the Dispose method to remove the IFrame.

If the application isn't using the navigation framework, the HtmlViewer control won't know when the IFrame should be removed, and the application hosting it will need to call its Dispose method at the appropriate time.

Using the WebBrowser Control When Running Outside the Browser

As previously mentioned, the HTML Bridge isn't available when running outside the browser, so you can't create an IFrame in this scenario. However, Silverlight 4 introduced the WebBrowser control that you can use instead in out-of-browser scenarios. The HtmlViewer control determines whether the application is running inside or outside of the browser and will create an IFrame or a WebBrowser control accordingly, providing a seamless solution to this problem.

■ **Note** Silverlight 5 introduces the ability for the WebBrowser control to be used when running inside the browser, but the Silverlight application must be running with elevated privileges inside the browser (discussed in Chapter 16), and it will work only in Internet Explorer. Due to these restrictions, the HtmlViewer control will simply use the IFrame method whenever the host Silverlight application is running inside the browser.

⚙ Workshop: Using the HtmlViewer Control

Now that you have seen how the HtmlViewer control works, it's time to use it to display a report in our application. In this workshop, we're going to use the HtmlViewer control to display the Product Catalog report generated by the server.

1. The first task is to ensure that your Silverlight application object is set to run in windowless mode. Without this, the HtmlViewer control will raise an exception when it loads. Open the HTML page hosting the Silverlight plug-in, find the object tag, and add a param node to its children that sets the Silverlight plug-in's Windowless property to true:

```
<param name="Windowless" value="True" />
```

2. If the HtmlViewer control is near the right or bottom edge of the application, Internet Explorer 9 tries to show scroll bars on the page (this behavior has not been detected in other browsers or earlier versions of Internet Explorer). This starts a battle between the HtmlViewer control and the browser resizing, causing the browser to go crazy. If this is happening for you, or simply to prevent it from happening, find the html, body style in the HTML page that hosts the Silverlight plug-in, and set its overflow property to hidden, instead of its default of auto. This prevents the browser from showing scroll bars and stops the problem from occurring.

```
html, body {
    height: 100%;
    overflow: hidden;
}
```

3. Add the HtmlViewer control and the ReportRequest class to your project, and compile the project. The HtmlViewer control and the ReportRequest class can both be found in the sample code accompanying this chapter on the Apress web site.

4. Create a new view in your project, using the Page item template, and declare the layout namespace prefix, like so:

```
xmlns:my="clr-namespace:SilverlightLOBFramework.Controls.Layout"
```

5. Now, add the HtmlViewer control to the view:

```
<layout:HtmlViewer Name="htmlViewer" />
```

6.   You now need to set the HtmlViewer control's Url property to the URL of the
     report HTTP handler on the server, passing it the report name and any report
     parameters in its query string. Although you set this property in XAML, doing
     so would result in you hard-coding the URL, when you will usually want it to
     be dynamic—pointing to the server from which the Silverlight application was
     downloaded and passing it some parameters. Therefore, you're best off bind-
     ing the Url property to a view model or setting its value in the code behind. For
     the purpose of simplicity, we'll simply set this value in the code behind.

```
htmlViewer.Url = ReportRequest.GetReportUrl("ProductCatalog");
```

     As you can see, we're using the ReportRequest class that we added to the pro-
     ject earlier, which contains a helper function for building up this URL when
     requesting reports. This class determines the location of the Report.ashx HTTP
     handler on the same server that's hosting the Silverlight application and
     passes it the report name as a query string parameter. An overload of the
     GetReportUrl method also takes in key/value pairs as parameters and includes
     them as part of the URL's query string, enabling you to easily pass parameters
     to the report.

■ **Note**   The ReportRequest also contains another helper function for requesting reports. Instead of using
the HtmlViewer control to display the report "within" the application, you might want to use the
OpenReportInNewWindow method, which will open the report in a new browser window. This is a simple process
that uses the HTML Bridge—the HtmlPage.PopupWindow function will pop up a new window with the specified
options, such as the size of the window, whether the menu bar or scroll bars should be shown, and so on, and will
navigate to the specified URL. Of course, this requires the browser to permit the opening of pop-up windows, so
the IFrame option will generally be your best option.

---

7.   When you run the application and navigate to this view, you will see a "please
     wait" message while the PDF report downloads, and the report will then ap-
     pear, seemingly within your application. Figure 15-6 demonstrates the final re-
     sult of displaying the Product Catalog report in the HtmlViewer control.

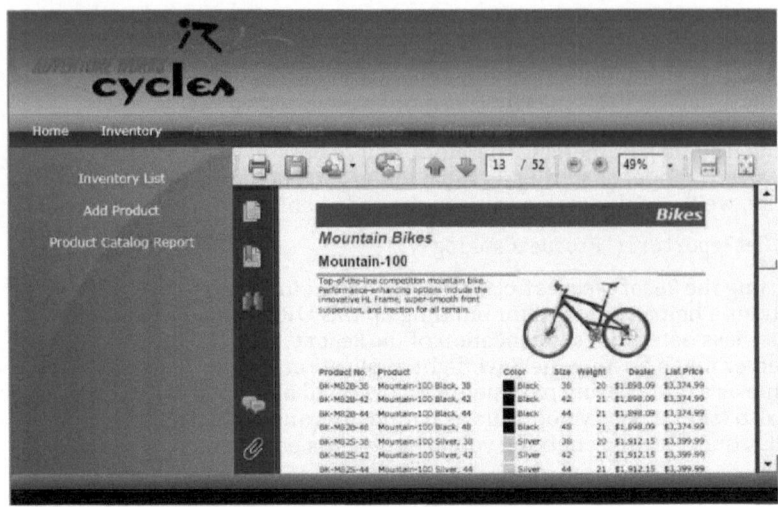

***Figure 15-6.** The Product Catalog report*

■ **Note** An issue worth mentioning (because it can create confusion and frustration) is that the Adobe Acrobat Reader plug-in occasionally fails to load, leaving you with just a white screen where the report should be. You can fix this by opening Task Manager and ending the AcroRd32.exe process. When you then attempt to view the report again, the plug-in should load correctly.

The PivotViewer Control

The PivotViewer control is a neat control that you can use to display data in an innovative and interactive manner, and in some cases, you can even use it in place of reports, letting users pivot and mine data for information. Let's take a look at its features and how you can make use of it in your Silverlight business application.

Key Features of the PivotViewer Control

To understand the control, it's best to look at and play with it in action. The sample code accompanying this chapter (available from the Apress web site) provides a working example that's worth opening if you have it available, but for now, I'll point out its key features in screenshots. Figure 15-7 shows the control displaying product data retrieved from the server.

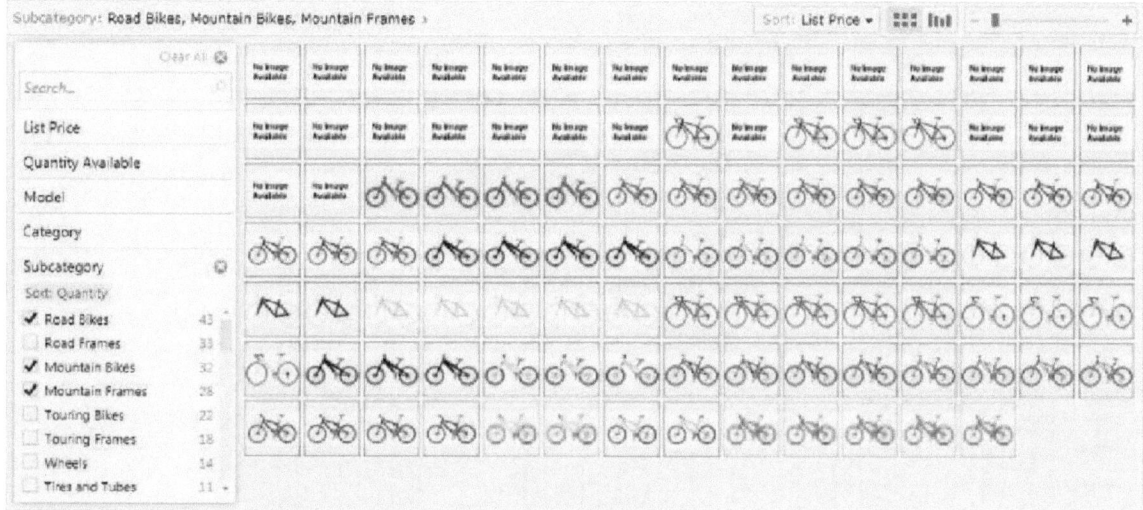

Figure 15-7. The PivotViewer control displaying filtered data

Each data item, in this case, each product, is shown as a trading card within the control. A *trading card* is a visual representation of a data item and often consists of a related image. For example, each trading card in the figures demonstrating the PivotViewer control throughout this section display an image of the product that it represents. The control essentially allows you to filter, sort, and group data freely, with the trading cards rearranging and stacking themselves according to how you've filtered, sorted, and grouped the data.

Filtering Data

Note the filter pane on the left side of the control, shown in Figure 15-6. This allows users to filter the data items displayed in the control according to their needs. They can search for items using the search text box at the top of the pane, and they can also filter for items with specific property values for the different filter categories that have been defined. Figure 15-7 demonstrates filtering the items to just those that have a value of Road Bikes, Mountain Bikes, or Mountain Frames for their Subcategory property. The users can filter values across categories if they wish. For numeric and date properties, the user can also filter by range. The trading cards will fly in and out of the control as they are included in or out of the filtered data set.

Sorting Data

Data items can be sorted by selecting a property to sort by from the Sort dropdown menu at the top of the control. Figure 15-8 demonstrates sorting the data items by their List Price property.

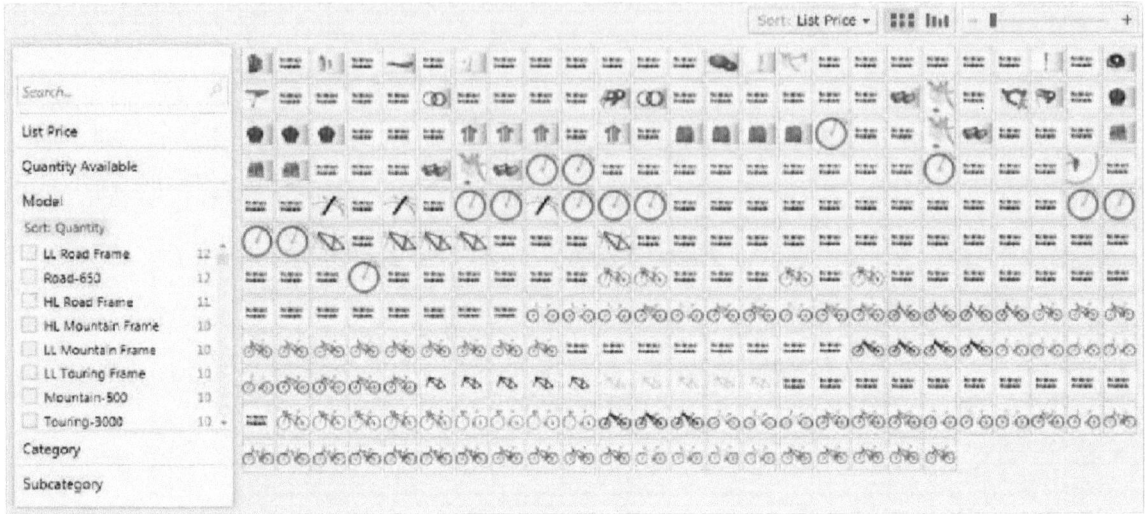

Figure 15-8. *The PivotViewer control displaying sorted data*

Grouping the Data

Figure 15-9 demonstrates grouping of the data items by their List Price property. Seeing that this was a numeric property, the PivotViewer control automatically divided up the list prices into discrete ranges and stacked the product cards into their corresponding range, with the result looking just like a bar chart. As you can see, the list price of the majority of products that the AdventureWorks store sells is within the range of $0 to $500. You can change the grouping of the data using the Sort drop-down menu at the top of the control (grouping is effectively a form of sorting).

■ **Note**   The PivotViewer control also supports grouping by date range and by string values.

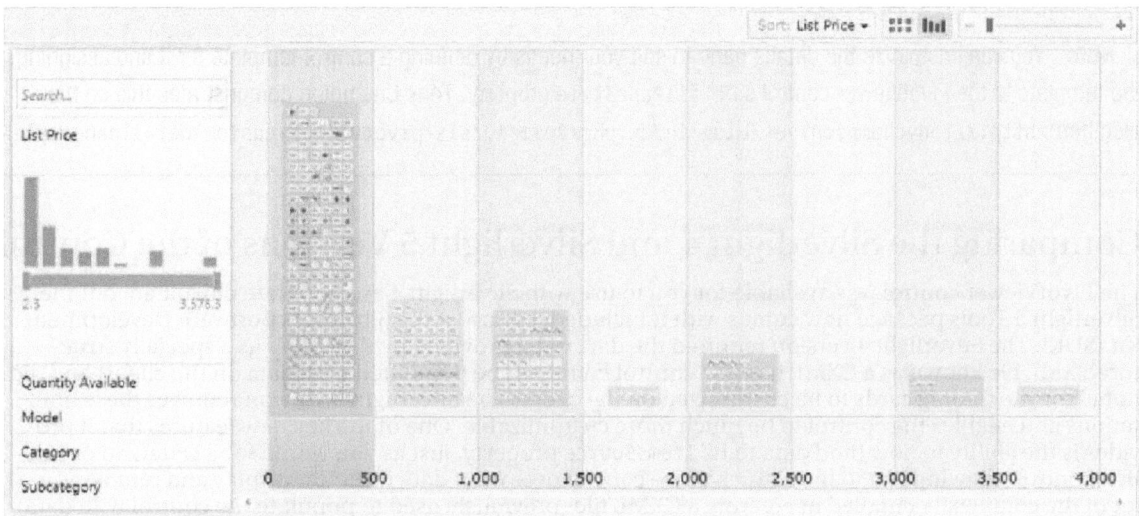

Figure 15-9. The PivotViewer control displaying grouped/stacked data

Viewing Details of a Data Item

The PivotViewer control allows you to zoom in and out on the data items. You can zoom using the scroll wheel on your mouse, or by using the zoom slider at the top-right corner of the control. When you zoom in close enough on a data item or select one, the details pane will be shown on the right side of the control, showing details of the item, as shown in Figure 15-10.

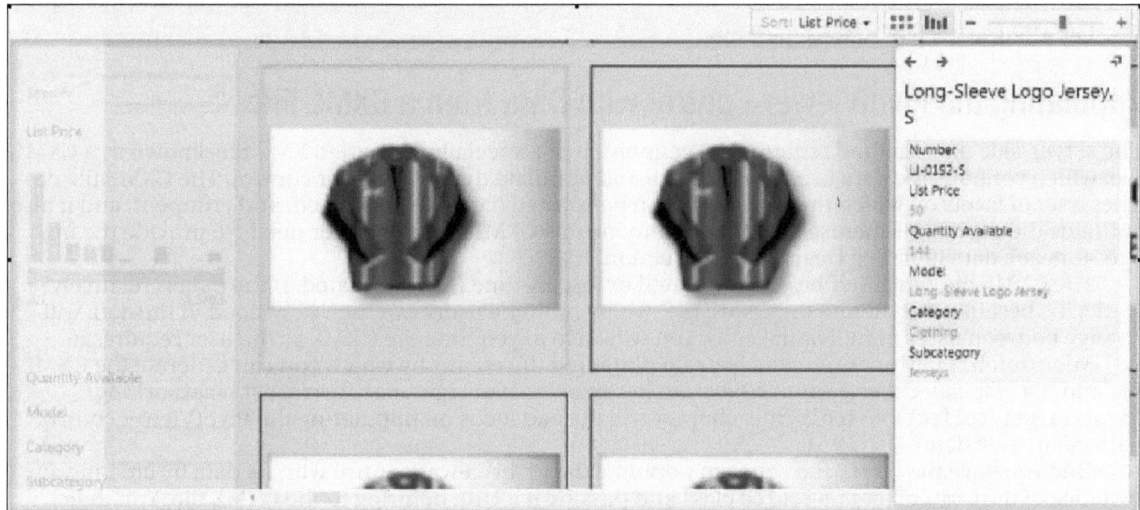

Figure 15-10. The PivotViewer control displaying details of a selected data item

---

■ **Note** You can customize the details pane to suit your needs by defining a control template for it and assigning the template to the PivotViewer control's `DetailPaneStyle` property. Tony Champion demonstrates this on his blog here: `http://tonychampion.net/blog/index.php/2011/10/sl5-pivotviewer-custom-detailpanestyle`.

Comparing the Silverlight 4 and Silverlight 5 Versions of the Control

The PivotViewer control was available for you to use with Silverlight 4 as a separate download, but the Silverlight 5 Tools package now comes with it included, as part of the Silverlight Software Development Kit (SDK). The Silverlight 4 version required the data to be provided by the server as a specially structured XML file known as a CXML file (the control could not be populated with data on the client) and did not allow the trading cards to be customized on the client. The Silverlight 5 version removes these limitations and enables the control to be much more customizable. One of the key new features that it provides is the ability to now bind data to its `ItemsSource` property, just as you would for a DataGrid or ListBox control, allowing you to have much more control over what data it should display and removing a lot of the complexity entailed in creating a CXML file (previously used to populate the control with data) on the server. In addition, the PivotViewer control originally used Deep Zoom to display images downloaded from the server, but the Silverlight 5 version of the control has introduced the ability to use XAML templates to define the trading cards.

Configuring the PivotViewer Control for Use

There are two different means of populating the PivotViewer control with data:

- Server-side data, using a CXML file
- Client-side data, using a collection of objects

Let's look at each of these separately.

Populating the PivotViewer Control with Data from a CXML File

The server-side data method requires the generation of a specially formatted XML file, known as a CXML file, which contains the data used to configure and populate the PivotViewer control. The CXML file defines a set of facets on which the data items can be pivoted (i.e., filtered, sorted, and grouped), and it also contains the data items themselves. Accompanying this CXML file, the server needs to provide the images for each data item as a Deep Zoom collection.

The CXML file can either be pre-generated or just-in-time (JIT) generated. If the data is relatively static, it's best to pre-generate the CXML file, which multiple users can then download. If the data will change between users or individual calls, you will have to generate the CXML as the user requires it.

Microsoft has fairly comprehensively documented the means by which you can generate the CXML file and the associated Deep Zoom collection here: `www.silverlight.net/learn/data-networking/pivot-viewer/collection-tools` (this chapter will instead focus on populating the PivotViewer control with client-side data).

One you have the CXML file, you can populate the PivotViewer control with its data by creating an instance of the `CxmlCollectionSource` class and passing it a URL pointing to the CXML file. You then assign the properties exposed by this object (`ItemProperties`, `ItemTemplates`, and `Items`) to their corresponding properties on the PivotViewer control (`PivotProperties`, `ItemTemplates`, and `ItemsSource`). This will display the data from the CXML file in the control.

Populating the PivotViewer Control with a Collection of Objects

The other way to populate a PivotViewer control is to define pivot properties on the control and bind a collection of objects to the controls' ItemsSource property. The latter option was introduced with the Silverlight 5 version of the PivotViewer control and is an easier and more flexible means of populating the control with data than using a CXML file.

There are three key steps involved in configuring the PivotViewer control for use with client-side data:

1. Configure its pivot properties.

2. Define the trading cards for each data item.

3. Bind its ItemsSource property to a collection of objects, which will be used as the data items displayed within the PivotViewer control.

Let's look at these steps in a bit more depth.

Defining Pivot Properties

Pivot properties are points that the user can use to "pivot" the data items in the PivotViewer control around (i.e., filter, sort, and group them). Each pivot property has a type, which will determine how it can be pivoted. The following pivot property types are available:

- PivotViewerStringProperty

- PivotViewerNumericProperty

- PivotViewerDateTimeProperty

- PivotViewerLinkProperty

The following code demonstrates the definition of a string pivot property in XAML. As you can see, you give it a unique ID, a display name, options specifying how the data can be pivoted around this property, and a binding expression that binds the pivot property to a property on the objects in the collection used to populate the control with data.

```
<sdk:PivotViewerStringProperty Id="Model" DisplayName="Model" Options="CanFilter"
                               Binding="{Binding Model}" />
```

You then need to assign these pivot properties to the collection exposed by the PivotViewer control's PivotProperties properties:

```
<sdk:PivotViewer>
    <sdk:PivotViewer.PivotProperties>
        <sdk:PivotViewerStringProperty Id="Category" DisplayName="Category"
                                       Options="CanFilter" Binding="{Binding Category}" />
    </sdk:PivotViewer.PivotProperties>
</sdk:PivotViewer>
```

■ **Note** CXML files use the term "facets" instead of "pivot properties."

Customizing the Trading Cards

You define the layout of the trading cards using one or more XAML templates. The PivotViewer control has an ItemTemplates property, to which you can assign one or more PivotViewerItemTemplate templates. The PivotViewerItemTemplate class has a DataType property that enables you to display different trading card templates based on the type of object that the data item is bound to. It also has a MaxWidth property, which allows you to display different templates at different zoom levels. When the width of a trading card exceeds the value assigned to its template's MaxWidth property, the PivotViewer control will then change the item's template to one supporting a larger sized trading card. This capability allows to you completely change the layout and look of the trading card as the user zooms into it if you wish.

The following code demonstrates a very simple item template, simply displaying a text block bound to the data item's Name property:

```
<sdk:PivotViewer>
    <sdk:PivotViewer.ItemTemplates>
        <sdk:PivotViewerItemTemplate>
            <Border Height="100" Width="100" BorderBrush="Black" BorderThickness="1">
                <TextBlock Text="{Binding Name}" />
            </Border>
        </sdk:PivotViewerItemTemplate>
    </sdk:PivotViewer.ItemTemplates>
</sdk:PivotViewer>
```

■ **Note** Trading cards must have a fixed height and width. Otherwise, the control will crash when attempting to display the items. If you are only defining a single item template to be displayed at all resolutions, it's best to define it at a high resolution so that when users zoom in, the item will still have a crisp and clean appearance.

You might expect that by defining the trading cards' templates in XAML you would be able to make them interactive by adding various controls, such as buttons, to them. However, this is not the case. The PivotViewer control is still a Deep Zoom viewer, and thus the trading cards are rendered to images for use by the control. Therefore, although the controls will appear in the trading card, they will not provide interactivity because they are just part of the trading card's image. If you want the user to be able to interact with a trading card—for example, selecting an item and adding it to a shopping cart—you will need to provide *item adorners*, which replace *custom actions* in the Silverlight 4 version of the control. Item adorners are XAML overlays that display on a data item when the mouse is over it, enabling the user to interact with that item. For example, an item adorner might display a button that, when clicked, will execute some logic. To define an item adorner for the trading cards, you simply need to define the XAML for it as a control template and assign it to the PivotViewer control's ItemAdornerStyle. We'll look at how you do this in a workshop shortly.

Populating the PivotViewer Control with Data

Once you have configured the PivotViewer control with pivot properties and trading card templates, you can simply populate the PivotViewer control with data by binding a collection of objects to the control's ItemsSource property.

```
<sdk:PivotViewer ItemsSource="{Binding ProductCollectionView}" />
```

Populating the PivotViewer Control with a CXML File or a Collection of Objects

The ability added to the Silverlight 5 version of the PivotViewer control that enables you to populate it with a collection of objects makes the control much easier to implement than generating a CXML file and corresponding Deep Zoom collection on the server. Therefore, you will most likely choose this approach when implementing the PivotViewer control in your Silverlight application. However, the CXML file approach does provide one key benefit that you should consider before automatically taking the collection-based approach. When you want to display large images for data items' trading cards in the PivotViewer control that are located on the server, each of those images would need to be downloaded to the client at their full resolution before the PivotViewer control can display the data when using the collection-based approach. By providing the images as a Deep Zoom collection on the server, the PivotViewer control can progressively download the images at higher resolutions as it requires them, improving the performance of the control greatly. Therefore, take this point into consideration before automatically choosing the collection-based approach by default.

Saving and Restoring the PivotViewer Control's State

You can save the user's filter options, sort options, and zoom state using the PivotViewer control's SerializeViewerState method, like so:

```
string viewerState = pv.SerializeViewerState();
```

You can then restore this state (or set a predefined state) using the PivotViewer control's SetViewerState method, like so:

```
pv.SetViewerState(viewerState);
```

Uses for the PivotViewer Control

You might want to use the PivotViewer control myriad ways in your Silverlight business application. For example, you might use it to allow users to mine the data in the database in a very flexible manner without resorting to predefined reports. Another possibility is to implement interactive summary lists – giving your users a cool, fun, and flexible way of navigating through the data in the application and drilling down to records.

Finding More Information on the PivotViewer Control

The PivotViewer control can be quite a complex control, and you'll no doubt want some more information about certain aspects of it. Some good additional information can be found at the following web sites and blogs:

- www.silverlight.net/learn/data-networking/pivot-viewer/
- http://xpert360.wordpress.com/2011/05/17/xpert360-pivotviewer-blog-article-index/
- http://tonychampion.net/blog/index.php/category/silverlight/pivotviewer-silverlight/
- www.jasonrshaver.com/?tag=/PivotViewer
- www.rogernoble.com/tag/pivotviewer/

⚙ Workshop: Implementing the PivotViewer Control

In this workshop, we'll walk through how you can populate the PivotViewer control with a collection of objects.

1. Add a new view to your application, and make sure that you can navigate to it (as detailed in Chapter 3).

2. Add a reference to the `System.Windows.Controls.Pivot.dll` assembly to your Silverlight project.

3. Add the following namespace prefix declaration to your view:

```
xmlns:sdk="http://schemas.microsoft.com/winfx/2006/xaml/presentation/sdk"
```

4. You need to provide a source of data for the control. Let's populate the control with a collection of `ProductSummary` objects that we exposed from the server via RIA Services in Chapter 4 and learned how to consume in our Silverlight application in Chapters 5 and 6. We'll use the DomainDataSource control to do so in this workshop:

```
<riaControls:DomainDataSource Name="productSummaryDDS"
                    AutoLoad="True"
                    QueryName="GetProductSummaryList"
                    LoadedData="productSummaryDDS_LoadedData">
    <riaControls:DomainDataSource.DomainContext>
        <my:ProductSummaryContext />
    </riaControls:DomainDataSource.DomainContext>
</riaControls:DomainDataSource>
```

5. Define the PivotViewer control in your view and bind its `ItemsSource` property to the DomainDataSource control's `Data` property:

```
<sdk:PivotViewer ItemsSource="{Binding Data, ElementName=productSummaryDDS}">

</sdk:PivotViewer>
```

6. Define some pivot properties on the control, and bind them to properties on the `ProductSummary` objects being returned from the server. Note that the type of pivot property being defined depends on the type of data that it is binding to:

```
<sdk:PivotViewer ItemsSource="{Binding Data, ElementName=productSummaryDDS}">
    <sdk:PivotViewer.PivotProperties>
        <sdk:PivotViewerStringProperty Id="Name" Options="CanSearchText"
                            DisplayName="Name" Binding="{Binding Name}" />
        <sdk:PivotViewerStringProperty Id="Number" Options="CanSearchText"
                            DisplayName="Number" Binding="{Binding Number}" />
        <sdk:PivotViewerNumericProperty Id="ListPrice" Options="CanFilter"
                            DisplayName="List Price"
                            Binding="{Binding ListPrice}" />
        <sdk:PivotViewerNumericProperty Id="QuantityAvailable" Options="CanFilter"
                            DisplayName="Quantity Available"
                            Binding="{Binding QuantityAvailable}" />
        <sdk:PivotViewerStringProperty Id="Model" Options="CanFilter"
                            DisplayName="Model" Binding="{Binding Model}" />
```

```
    <sdk:PivotViewerStringProperty Id="Category" Options="CanFilter"
                                   DisplayName="Category"
                                   Binding="{Binding Category}" />
    <sdk:PivotViewerStringProperty Id="Subcategory" Options="CanFilter"
                                   DisplayName="Subcategory"
                                   Binding="{Binding Subcategory}" />
  </sdk:PivotViewer.PivotProperties>
</sdk:PivotViewer>
```

7. Define one or more item templates for the data items' trading cards. To keep this workshop simple, we'll simply display a TextBlock control bound to the Name property on the source data item object.

```
<sdk:PivotViewer ItemsSource="{Binding Data, ElementName=productSummaryDDS}">
    <!--Pivot property definitions excluded for brevity-->

    <sdk:PivotViewer.ItemTemplates>
        <sdk:PivotViewerItemTemplate>
            <Border Height="100" Width="100" BorderBrush="Black" BorderThickness="1">
                <TextBlock Text="{Binding Name}" />
            </Border>
        </sdk:PivotViewerItemTemplate>
    </sdk:PivotViewer.ItemTemplates>
</sdk:PivotViewer>
```

■ **Note** The code accompanying this chapter, downloadable from the Apress web site, displays an image of each product. However, due to the complexity of the data being returned from the server as GIFs that need to be translated to a format that Silverlight can understand, we'll stick to simply displaying the name of the product here instead.

---

8. Run your application. The collection of ProductSummary objects will be retrieved from the server and used to populate the PivotViewer control. You can then pivot the data around the defined pivot properties.

⚙ Workshop: Applying an Item Adorner to Trading Cards

In this workshop, we'll define an item adorner to be applied to each trading card, allowing the user to interact with the data in the PivotViewer control. The item adorner will display a button that, when clicked, will simply show a message box displaying the name of the corresponding product.

1. The first step is to assign a control template to the PivotViewer control's ItemAdornerStyle property. The following code demonstrates displaying a Button control in the top-right corner of the trading card. You'll also note the use of the Rectangle control. This will highlight the trading card under the mouse by overlaying it with the rectangle filled with a color but containing some opacity so that you can still see through to the trading card underneath.

```xml
<sdk:PivotViewer ItemsSource="{Binding Data, ElementName=productSummaryDDS}">
    <!--Pivot property and item template definitions excluded for brevity-->

    <sdk:PivotViewer.ItemAdornerStyle>
        <Style TargetType="sdk:PivotViewerItemAdorner">
            <Setter Property="Template">
                <Setter.Value>
                    <ControlTemplate TargetType="sdk:PivotViewerItemAdorner">
                        <Grid>
                            <Grid.RowDefinitions>
                                <RowDefinition MaxHeight="40" />
                                <RowDefinition />
                            </Grid.RowDefinitions>

                            <Grid.ColumnDefinitions>
                                <ColumnDefinition />
                                <ColumnDefinition Width="2*" MaxWidth="100" />
                            </Grid.ColumnDefinitions>

                            <Rectangle Fill="Navy" Opacity="0.5"
                                       Grid.ColumnSpan="2" Grid.RowSpan="2" />

                            <Button Content="Details" Click="ItemAdornerButton_Click"
                                    Grid.Column="1" Margin="3" />
                        </Grid>
                    </ControlTemplate>
                </Setter.Value>
            </Setter>
        </Style>
    </sdk:PivotViewer.ItemAdornerStyle>
</sdk:PivotViewer>
```

2. We now need to handle the Button control's Click event in the code behind, to which we assigned an event handler in the previous XAML. In this event handler, we'll get a reference to the bound object, and display the product's name in a message box:

```csharp
private void ItemAdornerButton_Click(object sender, System.Windows.RoutedEventArgs e)
{
    Button button = sender as Button;
    ProductSummary product = button.DataContext as ProductSummary;

    MessageBox.Show("Item adorner clicked for the " + product.Name + " product!");
}
```

3. Run your application. When you put your mouse over a data item in the PivotViewer control, the item adorner will appear at the top left of the data item. When you click the button, the associated command will be executed, and a message box will display the name of the selected product.

Summary

You now have implemented a means for printing screens using Silverlight's printing functionality and displaying PDF reports (generated on the server) "within" the application. These both provide viable solutions for this important business application task without requiring a lot of code to be written or resorting to third-party solutions. You've also seen the PivotViewer control and learned how you can use it to display data to your users in an innovative and interactive manner.

CHAPTER 16

Interacting with the Host Operating System

Although Silverlight started as a sandboxed platform that ran only within a web browser window, it's grown to become a mature platform for building applications that inevitably required a certain level of integration and interaction with the host operating system.

With the introduction of Silverlight 3, we gained the ability to run a Silverlight application outside the browser in its own window, launching it from an icon on the desktop or the start menu, and using it in much the same way as a standard (native) application. Silverlight 4 enabled developers to request elevated trust permissions to gain direct access to the file system and COM for applications that ran outside the browser, permitting applications to have a closer relationship with the host operating system and enabling a whole range of new capabilities and possibilities for your applications. Silverlight 5 took things one step further by enabling Silverlight applications to run inside the browser with elevated trust and added support for P/Invoke calls and multiple out-of-browser windows. These features enable you to build more powerful and functional applications in Silverlight.

In this chapter, we'll look at how you can configure your Silverlight application to run outside the browser and interact with the host operating system.

Running Silverlight Applications Out of the Browser

Initially, Silverlight was designed to run inside a browser window, either as a widget on a web page or filling the whole browser window as an application. However, Silverlight 3 introduced a major new feature that enabled Silverlight applications to be installed locally on the user's machine. The process of installing a Silverlight application places the .xap file in a permanent location within the user's profile (that is, outside of the user's browser cache) and creates shortcuts on the user's desktop and/or start menu to enable them to run it locally. When the user clicks or double-clicks the shortcut, the application opens in its own window as if it were a standard, native application. This is known as out-of-browser (OOB) mode, and we'll be referring to it throughout this chapter as such.

Note A key benefit of installing the application within the user's profile is that there is no need for the user installing it to have administrative privileges, which greatly simplifies the deployment of your application and allows updates to be easily installed.

One of the biggest benefits of OOB mode is that it works cross platform—specifically working on both Windows and OSX, making Silverlight now a great way of building cross-platform applications.

Configuring OOB Mode

By default, your application is not configured to be installable and run in OOB mode. You need to explicitly turn on this feature via the project's properties. Start by selecting the "Enable running application out of the browser" check box as shown in Figure 16-1.

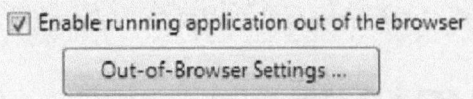

Figure 16-1. The "Enable running application out of the browser" option

You will now be able to click the Out-of-Browser Settings button below the check box, which will open the window shown in Figure 16-2.

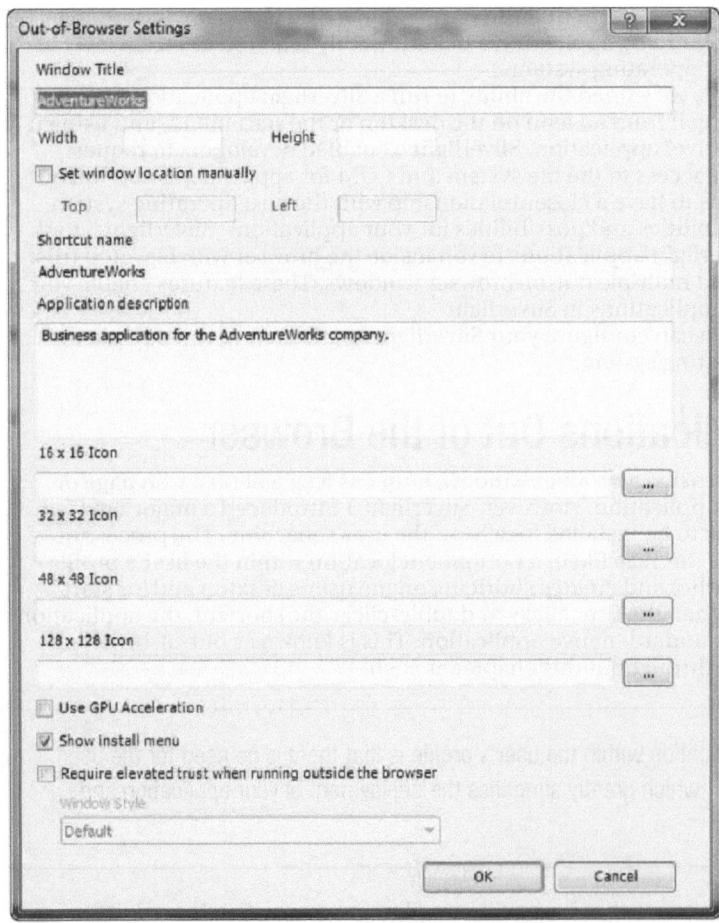

Figure 16-2. The Out-Of-Browser Settings window

This dialog provides you with a variety of options that apply when the application is running in OOB mode. These options can be broken up into three primary areas: window options, install options, and miscellaneous options.

Window Options

The window options enable you to specify the text that should appear in the title bar of the OOB window and the window's initial width and height. Without these options set, the window will default to a size of 800 × 600 and will be resizable unless you turn off the default window chrome by using custom chrome. By default, the application will center itself in the screen, but by selecting the "Set window location manually" check box, you can specify exactly where on the screen you want your application to appear.

Install Options

The install options enable you to specify the name of the shortcut that will be created on the user's desktop and/or start menu, a description that will appear in the tooltip on the application's shortcuts, and a number of icons of varying sizes. These icons will be used for the application's shortcuts and will be displayed in the install dialog, the title bar of the window, and as the taskbar icon. If no image files are assigned to these settings, default Silverlight icons will be used instead.

░ **Note** These icon options should be assigned image files, not .ico files. (.ico is an image format specific to Windows). The Silverlight runtime will automatically create icons native to the host operating system from the image files as required.

Miscellaneous Options

The various miscellaneous options include the following:

- Enabling GPU acceleration for cached compositions via the "Use GPU Acceleration" check box
- Deciding whether an install option should appear in the context menu when the user right-clicks the application via the "Show install menu" check box
- Determining whether the application requires elevated trust when running outside the browser via the "Require elevated trust when running outside the browser" check box
- Specifying whether the application should use custom chrome via the "Window style" drop-down list, which is available only when "Require elevated trust when running outside the browser" is selected

---

░ **Note** You can read the options that were set in the Out-of-Browser Settings dialog for the application at runtime in code using the `Deployment.Current.OutOfBrowserSettings` object. However, you cannot modify them at runtime.

Installing the Application to Run Out of the Browser

The user can install your application to run outside the browser in two ways. One is by simply right-clicking anywhere in the application and selecting the "Install *XXX* application on this computer..." option from the context menu, assuming this menu is enabled in the Out-of-Browser Settings dialog, which it is by default when the application is configured to be installed and run outside the browser. The context menu is shown in Figure 16-3.

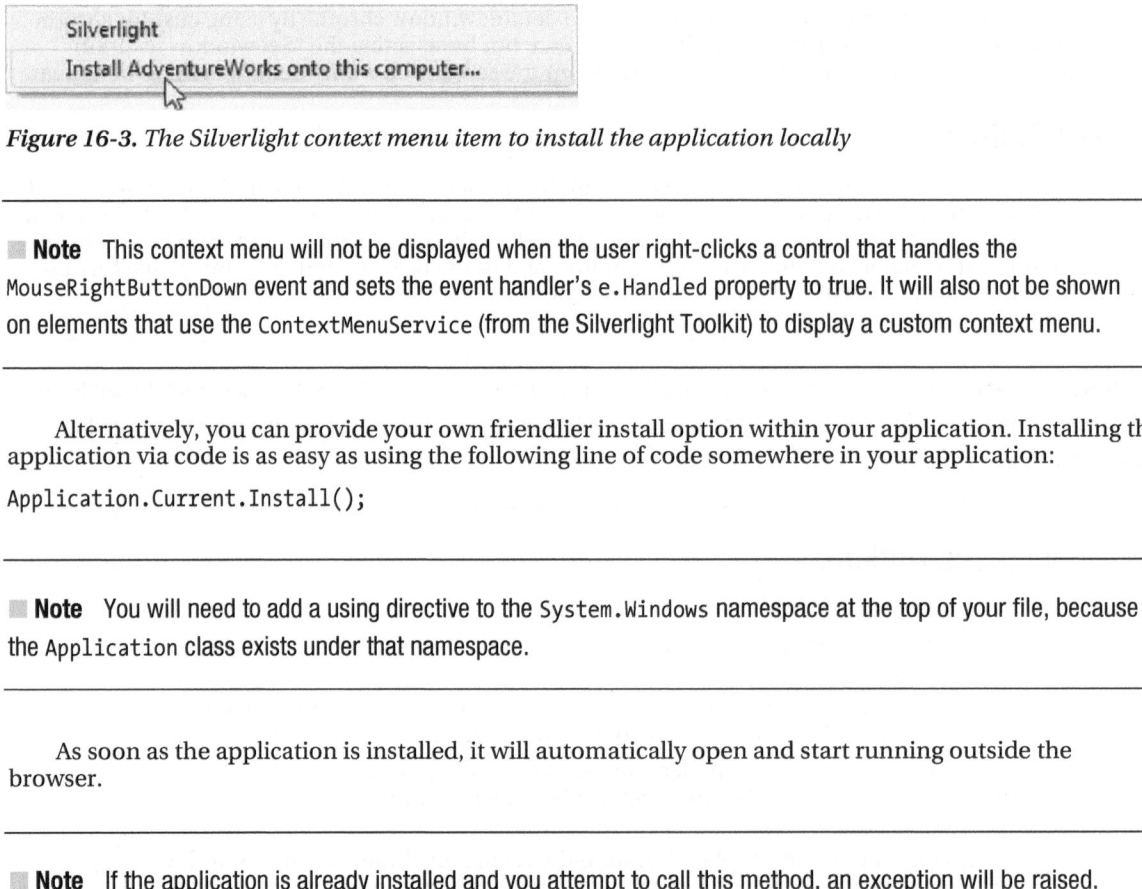

Figure 16-3. *The Silverlight context menu item to install the application locally*

■ **Note**   This context menu will not be displayed when the user right-clicks a control that handles the MouseRightButtonDown event and sets the event handler's e.Handled property to true. It will also not be shown on elements that use the ContextMenuService (from the Silverlight Toolkit) to display a custom context menu.

Alternatively, you can provide your own friendlier install option within your application. Installing the application via code is as easy as using the following line of code somewhere in your application:

```
Application.Current.Install();
```

■ **Note**   You will need to add a using directive to the System.Windows namespace at the top of your file, because the Application class exists under that namespace.

As soon as the application is installed, it will automatically open and start running outside the browser.

■ **Note**   If the application is already installed and you attempt to call this method, an exception will be raised. Therefore, you should always check whether the application is installed first before calling this method. How you can do so will be covered in the next section.

One thing you need to be aware of is that, for the purposes of security, a call to the Install method must be in response to a user-initiated event. In other words, you can call this method only in an event raised by some sort of user input, such as a button's Click event. Any attempt to call the Install method in an event handler not raised as a result of user input, such as in response to the Loaded event for a control, will be ignored.

Note You can also create a desktop installer and install the application that way too. This method is discussed in Chapter 17.

Once the user has initiated the install action, the install dialog shown in Figure 16-4 will appear, requiring the user to confirm the installation and specify what icons to create.

Figure 16-4. The "Install application" dialog

Note If an icon was specified in the Out-of-Browser Settings dialog, it will be displayed in the dialog in place of the generic Silverlight application icon displayed in Figure 16-4.

A different dialog will be displayed when elevated trust permissions are being requested. This dialog will be discussed later in this chapter.

Determining Installation Status

You can determine whether or not the application is already installed by interrogating the InstallState property of the Application.Current object. This property returns an enumeration, with the following values:

- NotInstalled
- Installed
- Installing
- InstallFailed

For example, the following code can be used to determine whether or not the application is installed:

```
bool isInstalled = (Application.Current.InstallState == InstallState.Installed);
```

You can determine when the installation status of the application changes by handling the InstallStateChanged event of the Application.Current object. Start by adding an event handler for the event:

```
Application.Current.InstallStateChanged += Application_InstallStateChanged;
```

Then, implement the event handler like so:

```
private void Application_InstallStateChanged(object sender, EventArgs e)
{
    // Handle the state change as required here
}
```

Within this event handler, you can interrogate the InstallState property of the Application.Current object to determine the new installation status of the application.

Determining Whether Running Inside or Outside the Browser

You can determine whether the application is running inside or outside the browser by interrogating the IsRunningOutOfBrowser property of the Application.Current object, for example:

```
bool isRunningOutOfBrowser = Application.Current.IsRunningOutOfBrowser;
```

If your application isn't designed to run inside the browser, you should use this property to detect whether the application is running inside the browser when it starts, and if so, display a view to the users from which they can install the application.

■ **Note** Unfortunately, there is no way to launch the application in OOB mode from within the browser if it's already installed. Therefore, you will need to ask the user to do so manually if this is necessary.

Where/How Is the Application's .xap File Stored and Run?

When a Silverlight application is installed, a folder is created inside the user's profile folders to permanently store the application (outside of the browser's cache). This path will differ across operating systems, but on Windows Vista or 7 you can view the installed Silverlight applications by typing the following path into the Windows Explorer address bar: %userprofile%\AppData\LocalLow\Microsoft\ Silverlight\OutOfBrowser. Each installed application has its own folder under this, containing the .xap file for that application, along with a number of associated files—such as an HTML page to host it, an icon, and some metadata files.

The sllauncher.exe executable is used to host the Silverlight application when it is running in OOB mode. It is passed the ID of an application to launch like so:

```
sllauncher.exe appid
```

The application ID will match the name of the folder in the OOB store for that application. For example, the following command line demonstrates an example shortcut path to launch the application:

```
"C:\Program Files\Microsoft Silverlight\sllauncher.exe" 1990526816.localhost
```

Interacting with the OOB Window

When your application is running in OOB mode, you can get a reference to the application's main window like so:

```
Window window = Application.Current.MainWindow;
```

This window object provides you with a number of properties, methods, and events that enable you to interact with and manipulate it.

■ **Note** Many of these properties and methods are needed particularly when you have turned on custom chrome. Custom chrome is discussed in detail later in this chapter.

Closing the Window

Using the reference to the window, you can close it using its Close method:

```
Application.Current.MainWindow.Close();
```

You can detect when the window is being closed and prevent it from closing by handling its Closing event. Start by adding an event handler to the event:

```
Application.Current.MainWindow.Closing += MainWindow_Closing;
```

And then you can handle the event (and cancel the window being closed) like so:

```
private void MainWindow_Closing(object sender, ClosingEventArgs e)
{
    if (e.IsCancelable)
    {
        MessageBoxResult result = MessageBox.Show("Are you sure you wish to quit?",
                                "AdventureWorks", MessageBoxButton.OKCancel);
        e.Cancel = (result != MessageBoxResult.OK);
    }
}
```

Window State, Position, and Dimensions

You can use the WindowState property of the window to maximize it, minimize it, or return it to its normal state. It accepts and returns an enumeration of type WindowState, which has the possible values Maximized, Minimized, and Normal. Here's an example:

```
Application.Current.MainWindow.WindowState = WindowState.Maximized;
```

You can set the size of the window using its Width and Height properties:

```
Application.Current.MainWindow.Width = 600;
Application.Current.MainWindow.Height = 800;
```

You can set the position of the window using its Top and Left properties. However, at runtime, you can set these properties only if the "Set window location manually" check box was selected in the

Out-Of-Browser Settings window shown in Figure 16-2, and the properties must be set before the end of the application's Startup event. After this, any changes to their values will be ignored.

Other Window Settings

You can set the window to be a topmost window, so it always appears on top of other windows whether or not it has the focus, by setting its TopMost property to true:

```
Application.Current.MainWindow.TopMost = true;
```

You can determine whether a window is active by interrogating its IsActive property, and you can activate it (i.e., bring it to the forefront of the various open windows and give it the focus) using its Activate method:

```
Application.Current.MainWindow.Activate();
```

■ **Note** You do not have access to the HTML DOM using the HtmlPage object when running outside the browser as you do when running inside the browser.

Checking for Updates

One of the issues with running a Silverlight application outside the browser is that users are no longer requesting the application from the server. Normally, when browsing to a Silverlight application using a web browser, the browser will check if it has previously downloaded the .xap file by checking for it in its cache. If it doesn't find it, it will automatically download the .xap file from the server. If it does find it, it will check with the server as to whether the cached version matches the version on the server. That is, it will check to see whether it has the latest version already. If it does, it will just use the cached version, saving the need to download it again. Otherwise, it will download the new version, overwriting the now out-of-date cached version before running it.

■ **Note** You can see this caching behavior by using the free Fiddler tool, which you can download from www.fiddler2.com.

However, when running in OOB mode, the .xap file is simply loaded from its installation location on disk, meaning that it will not be updated as new versions become available on the server. Therefore, a strategy needs to be implemented to ensure that the installed application is kept up to date. Luckily, Silverlight has some functionality built-in to help you do that. You can determine whether an update is available by using the following line of code:

```
Application.Current.CheckAndDownloadUpdateAsync();
```

With this method call, the application will go back to the URL that it originated from and see whether a new version of the application is available. If an update is found, it will be automatically downloaded and installed just prior to when the application is next run. This action is performed asynchronously, and thus does not have a return value.

You can determine whether or not an update was found by handling the
CheckAndDownloadUpdateCompleted event. Start by assigning an event handler to the event:

```
Application.Current.CheckAndDownloadUpdateCompleted +=
    Application_CheckAndDownloadUpdateCompleted;
```

You can then handle the event like so:

```
private void Application_CheckAndDownloadUpdateCompleted(object sender,
                                    CheckAndDownloadUpdateCompletedEventArgs e)
{
    if (e.UpdateAvailable)
    {
        // Logic can go here
    }
}
```

■ **Note** You can determine whether an error occurred when checking for an update by interrogating the Error
property of the CheckAndDownloadUpdateCompletedEventArgs object passed into the event handler as a
parameter.

If an update is found, it won't be installed until the application is next restarted. It's your decision as
to whether to force the user to restart the application, perhaps by preventing the users from using the
application until it is restarted, or allow the users to continue working with the existing version.

You may choose to automatically perform a check for updates each time the application is started,
or alternatively, you can simply provide a feature that enables the users to check for updates at their
leisure.

■ **Note** When running the application in OOB mode *with elevated trust* (described later in this chapter), the application will automatically update itself only if the application is signed. You won't see this behavior when the source
of the update is localhost, because updates are permitted in this scenario for development purposes. However,
once you deploy the application to production, it must be signed to be able to update itself. Application signing is
covered in Chapter 17.

Debugging in OOB Mode

When you run your Silverlight project in debugging mode in Visual Studio, the application is run within
a browser window. However, at times, you want to debug your application while it is running in OOB
mode—especially when you want to debug features that aren't available when the application is running
inside the browser.

To configure the application to launch in OOB mode from Visual Studio, you need to

1. Enable OOB support for your Silverlight application, as previously detailed.

2.   Set the Silverlight project as the startup project for the solution (instead of the Web project).

The Silverlight application will start in OOB mode with the debugger attached, enabling you to debug the application as required.

■ **Note**   Without OOB support configured for the application, simply setting the Silverlight project as the startup project will run it within the browser instead, using a file path. If you find that this is the case, and that the application is still running within the browser, check to ensure that you've configured to application to support OOB mode.

You can also attach the Visual Studio debugger to an already running instance of the application running in OOB mode, and debug it in that manner, like so:

3.   In Visual Studio, start by going to Tools ➤ Attach To Process.

4.   In the dialog window that appears, scroll down the list of available processes until you find the sllauncher.exe process (the Silverlight launcher process discussed earlier in this chapter). If there is more than one listed, look for the one with the title that matches that of the Silverlight application that you want to debug.

5.   Click the Attach button. The Visual Studio debugger will attach to the application and enable you to debug it as required.

Uninstalling the Application

When you no longer want a Silverlight application installed on your machine, you can remove it in one of two ways. The first is by simply right-clicking anywhere within the application's window and selecting "Remove this application" from the context menu. The other method is to use the operating system's uninstall application tool (such as Windows Vista or 7's Programs and Features tool). The application will appear as an entry in that tool, and you will be able to uninstall it as you would any other application.

■ **Note**   You cannot uninstall the application through code.

Toast Notifications

Silverlight 4 introduced the ability to display toast notifications; these are the little windows that pop up for a couple of seconds, usually in the bottom-right corner of your screen, to notify you of something that has happened in the application.

For example, Microsoft Outlook displays a toast notification when a new e-mail is received, and TweetDeck (a popular Twitter client) displays a toast notification when a new tweet appears in your Twitter feed. Toast notifications in Silverlight enable you to implement this same sort of notification in your Silverlight applications. For example, you might like to display a notification when an order is placed in the system or when a product is getting low in stock. An example of a simple notification window is shown in Figure 16-5.

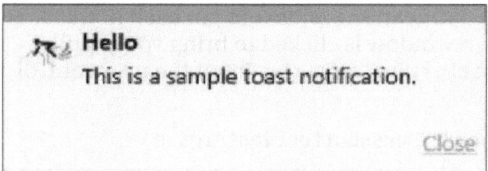

Figure 16-5. *A simple toast notification window*

■ **Note** You can display toast notifications only when the application is running in OOB mode or when it's running with elevated trust permissions inside the browser. Attempting to do so otherwise will throw an exception, so you should always check to ensure that the application meets these criteria before attempting to show a toast notification, like so:

```
if (App.Current.IsRunningOutOfBrowser || App.Current.HasElevatedPermissions)
{
    // Show toast notification
}
```

To display a toast notification, you create an instance of the NotificationWindow class and assign it some content. Unfortunately, you cannot create a XAML file that inherits from the NotificationWindow class as it is sealed. You can, however, create a user control and assign an instance of that to the NotificationWindow class's Content property, which is the strategy that will be demonstrated here. Before we do, however, let's start by simply displaying an empty notification. To do so, you simply create a new instance of the NotificationWindow class, set the size of the toast notification window, and call its Show method, passing it the amount of time in milliseconds to display the notification, like so:

```
NotificationWindow toastWindow = new NotificationWindow();
toastWindow.Width = 280;
toastWindow.Height = 100;
toastWindow.Show(4000);
```

Running this code will result in a small window appearing in the bottom right-hand side of the screen and automatically disappearing after 4 seconds.

■ **Note** Toast notifications can be displayed for a maximum of 30 seconds (30,000 milliseconds) and are limited to a maximum width of 400 pixels and a maximum height of 100 pixels.

An empty notification window is of little use, so let's display some content in it. You do so by assigning a control to its Content property. The easiest way to implement the content of a toast notification is to create a user control in your project, design the content in its XAML file, and then assign an instance of the user control to the NotificationWindow object's Content property, for example:

```
toastWindow.Content = new MessageArrivedNotification();
```

If your application is in the background and showing the notification window to get itself noticed, a good idea is to activate the main window when the notification window is clicked to bring your application to the front. You can implement this by handling the MouseLeftButtonDown event of the user control and activating the main window in the event handler:

```
private void UserControl_MouseLeftButtonDown(object sender, MouseButtonEventArgs e)
{
    Application.Current.MainWindow.Activate();
}
```

It can also be a good idea to provide a way to close the notification window so that the user can dismiss the notification and continue working. The NotificationWindow object has a Close method, but you need that object to call the method on, which you don't have in the user control unless you want to trawl through the visual tree hierarchy to get it. The simple solution to this is to accept a NotificationWindow object in the user control's constructor, which it can then stash away as a member variable for later use, and pass this through when the object is being created.

```
toastWindow.Content = new MessageArrivedNotification(toastWindow);
```

You can then call the Close method on this object from within the user control as required.

■ **Note** You may also wish to pass the constructor an object containing data that the notification window can display if required.

Caching Data Locally

As you saw from some of the chapters earlier in this book, RIA Services provides an easy and elegant means for obtaining data from and persisting data to a server. However, what if a connection to the server is suddenly not available? Do you want all the users of your application to be forced to wait until they are (or the server is) back online again? Or do you want them to be able to continue working (as much as possible) in the meantime until a connection to the server is restored?

This type of scenario is known as "occasionally connected applications" and is generally handled by downloading and caching commonly used data from the server locally that the users may require when they are offline. This cache will need to be regularly updated and hold enough data to enable the users to continue working until they get back online again. While the application is offline, it will need to cache the changes, additions, and deletions the user has made to the data and synchronize these back to the server when the application is next online.

■ **Note** In addition, you may wish to cache data on the client that rarely or never changes to reduce the amount of network traffic that passes between the server and the client.

Let's take a look at some strategies for caching data on the client and catering for scenarios where the application may be going back and forth between connected and disconnected modes.

Caching to Isolated Storage

As a part of its sandbox, to protect your computer from rogue Silverlight applications, Silverlight doesn't allow you direct access to the user's file system unless you are running with elevated trust—discussed later in this chapter. However, it does provide you with a virtual file system known as isolated storage that enables you to cache data and files locally. As its name suggests, isolated storage is a virtual file system that is stored on disk but isolated from the computer's main file system and that of other applications. Files can be maintained in this store within directories in the same way as you normally organize files in a file system.

■ **Note** An isolated storage store is not specific to the browser that the user is running the application within. The same store is used across browsers and when running outside the browser. However, each Windows user on the computer will have their own isolated storage store.

Isolated storage is partitioned into two sections: an application store and a site store. The application store can be used to store files available to your application only, while the site store can be used to store files available across Silverlight applications originating from the same domain. Each isolated storage store is given a size quota that can be increased, with the permission of the user, if required.

Let's take a look at the various ways you can persist and retrieve data from an isolated storage store.

Storing Settings in Isolated Storage

The easiest way to persist and retrieve data from an isolated storage store is by using the IsolatedStorageSettings class, which can be found under the System.IO.IsolatedStorage namespace. This class enables you to easily maintain a collection of settings in isolated storage as key/value pairs that can be maintained as a file in either of the two stores (application and site) discussed earlier. Instead of having to manage serializing and deserializing the settings to and from a file, this class abstracts that away from you so that you need to maintain the settings only as a collection of key/value pairs, and it will handle persisting and retrieving the collection to/from isolated storage for you.

The IsolatedStorageSettings.ApplicationSettings property provides a means to maintain settings in the application store, and the IsolatedStorageSetting.SiteSettings property provides a means to maintain settings in the site store. Both of these properties return an object of type IsolatedStorageSettings that is a wrapper around a Dictionary of type <string, object>. Both are used in exactly the same manner as a Dictionary (and hence each other), so we will focus on demonstrating maintaining application settings here.

■ **Note** Apart from application settings, another perfect use for storing as settings is dictionary data (used to populate drop-down lists, etc). For dictionaries that rarely or never change, caching them in isolated storage will result in less network traffic needing to pass between the server and the client and a much more responsive application that doesn't need to wait to load these from the server.

Persisting a Value to Isolated Storage

Each setting is a key/value pair; the key needs to be a string, but the value can be any type of object. To persist a value to isolated storage, you simply need to assign it to the indexer of this class, using the key as its index:

```
IsolatedStorageSettings.ApplicationSettings["Key"] = "Value";
```

■ **Note** You don't need to use the Add method when adding a new setting to the dictionary. Simply assigning the value as demonstrated will take care of this and save you the trouble of needing to determine whether the key exists in the dictionary and add/update it accordingly.

As mentioned, the IsolatedStorageSettings class is a Dictionary of type <string, object>, meaning that any type of object (not just strings) can be persisted as an isolated storage setting and that object will be automatically serialized to and deserialized from isolated storage.

The changes to the settings are maintained in memory and will be automatically saved to isolated storage when the application is closed. However, if the application were to crash before this time, the changes made would be lost. Therefore, it's recommended that you call the Save method of the IsolatedStorageSettings object to explicitly save the current settings collection to isolated storage after modifying the collection:

```
IsolatedStorageSettings.ApplicationSettings.Save();
```

■ **Note** When you first try to access the settings, all the settings data will be loaded from isolated storage into memory and deserialized. The more data that your store in the settings, the longer this will take, and the more memory it will use. Therefore, store an excessive amount of data as settings in isolated storage is not recommended, because this will have an adverse effect on the performance of your application and potentially of the user's computer. An alternative is to serialize large collections/objects and persist them as individual files within the isolated storage store. This will enable them to be loaded only when required and disposed of (removing them from memory) once you no longer need them. We'll look at this idea later in this chapter.

Retrieving a Value from Isolated Storage

When you want to retrieve a setting from isolated storage, you will need to check that it exists first. You can use the Contains method to do this and then retrieve its value, if it exists, using its key as the index, like so:

```
if (IsolatedStorageSettings.ApplicationSettings.Contains("Key"))
{
    string value = IsolatedStorageSettings.ApplicationSettings["Value"].ToString();
    // Do something with the value
}
```

Alternatively, you can use the TryGetValue method that bundles checking that the setting exists and retrieving its value if it does into a single task. With the out parameter being a generic type, it will also save the need for casting the returned object:

```
string value;
bool settingExists =
    IsolatedStorageSettings.ApplicationSettings.TryGetValue("Key", out value);
```

Binding to Settings

You can bind to isolated storage settings using indexed property binding, as demonstrated in Chapter 11. The following XAML demonstrates binding to a setting named Setting1:

```
<TextBox Name="Setting1TextBox" Text="{Binding [Setting1], Mode=TwoWay}" />
```

Due to the non-creatable nature of the IsolatedStorageSettings class, as it has a private constructor, you will need to assign the DataContext of the control or of a control further up in the object hierarchy in the code behind, as follows:

```
Setting1TextBox.DataContext = IsolatedStorageSettings.ApplicationSettings;
```

■ **Note** As a general rule, you are better off wrapping the settings in properties and exposing them from a class instead of attempting to bind to them directly.

Enumerating the Settings

If you want to enumerate through the existing settings, the Keys property will expose what keys exist in the store, and you can then get their values as required:

```
foreach (string key in IsolatedStorageSettings.ApplicationSettings.Keys)
{
    object value = IsolatedStorageSettings.ApplicationSettings[key];
    // Do something with the value
}
```

Removing Settings

You can remove a setting using the Remove method of the dictionary, passing it the key of the setting to remove:

```
IsolatedStorageSettings.ApplicationSettings.Remove("Key");
```

You can remove all the settings in a dictionary by calling its Clear method:

```
IsolatedStorageSettings.ApplicationSettings.Clear();
```

Storing Files in Isolated Storage

Isolated storage is a virtual file system, meaning that you can create directories and files within isolated storage in much the same way as you would with the operating system's file system. For example, you may wish to store images, documents, and even .xap files downloaded from the server (providing dynamically loaded content, discussed in Chapter 17) in isolated storage. Let's look at how to perform some of these tasks in an isolated storage store.

Opening an Isolated Storage Store

The first step is to open the store that you want to work with. To open the application store, you use the GetUserStoreForApplication method of the IsolatedStorageFile class. Alternatively, you will need to use the IsolatedStorageFile class's GetUserStoreForSite method to open the site store.

■ **Note** For the purposes of this demonstration, you will be working with the application store, but working with the site store is performed in exactly the same manner after opening the site store instead.

The following code demonstrates opening the application store:

```
using (IsolatedStorageFile store = IsolatedStorageFile.GetUserStoreForApplication())
{
    // Work with the files and directories in the store here
}
```

■ **Note** As a general rule, you should use a using block, as demonstrated previously, to ensure that the store instance is disposed of properly once you are finished working with it.

Working with Directories

Once you have opened a store you can create, move, and delete directories using the methods on the object instance you have of the IsolatedStorageFile class. For example, you can create a directory named "Images" like so:

```
store.CreateDirectory("Images");
```

If you want to create a subdirectory named "Icons" within the "Images" directory, you will need to include the full path to create, as follows:

```
store.CreateDirectory(@"Images\Icons");
```

You can determine whether a directory exists using the DirectoryExists method:

```
bool dirExists = store.DirectoryExists("Images");
```

■ **Note** You should attempt to keep the paths to your files as short as possible. The full path to the file, including the path to the isolated storage store on the disk, must be less than 260 characters. Exceeding this length will result in an exception being thrown. The number of characters available for your directory and file names will depend on what operating system the user is running, so as a general rule, it's best to keep the paths of the files within the isolated storage store to a maximum of 70 characters in length.

Enumerating Through Files and Directories

The IsolatedStorageFile class provides a method to enable you to enumerate through the files and directories within an isolated storage store. For example, you can obtain a string array containing the names of the directories using the GetDirectoryNames method, like so:

```
string[] directories = store.GetDirectoryNames();
```

Note that only the directories within the root of the store are returned in this example. To get a list of the subdirectories within a given directory, you need to pass in the path to that directory as a search pattern followed by a wildcard. The following example demonstrates getting the names of the directories within the "Images" folder:

```
string[] directories = store.GetDirectoryNames(@"Images\*");
```

Similarly, you can get a list of the files in the isolated storage store using the GetFileNames method:

```
string[] fileNames = store.GetFileNames();
```

As with getting the subdirectories within a directory, to get the files within a directory, you will need to pass in the path to that directory as a search pattern followed by a wildcard:

```
string[] fileNames = store.GetFileNames(@"Images\*");
```

Working with Files

Various methods are provided to work with files, such as creating, copying, moving, deleting, and opening a file. For example, you can determine whether a file exists using the FileExists method:

```
bool fileExists = store.FileExists("Test.txt");
```

Writing a Text File

The following code demonstrates writing a string to a text file in isolated storage:

```
using (IsolatedStorageFileStream fileStream =
    store.OpenFile("Test.txt", FileMode.Create))
{
    using (StreamWriter writer = new StreamWriter(fileStream))
    {
        writer.WriteLine("Text written from Silverlight");
        writer.Close();
```

```
    }
    fileStream.Close();
}
```

■ **Note** You will need to add a using directive to the System.IO namespace for this and the following examples to work.

Writing a Binary File

The following code demonstrates writing a byte array (named fileContents) to a file in isolated storage:

```
using (IsolatedStorageFileStream fileStream =
    store.OpenFile("Test.jpg", FileMode.Create))
{
    fileStream.Write(fileContents, 0, fileContents.Length);
    fileStream.Close();
}
```

Reading a Text File

The following code demonstrates reading the contents of a text file from isolated storage into a string:

```
string fileContents = null;

using (IsolatedStorageFileStream fileStream =
    store.OpenFile("Test.txt", FileMode.Open))
{
    using (StreamReader reader = new StreamReader(fileStream))
    {
        fileContents = reader.ReadToEnd();
        reader.Close();
    }

    fileStream.Close();
}

// Do something with the file contents
```

Reading a Binary File

The following code demonstrates reading the contents of a binary file from isolated storage into a byte array:

```
byte[] fileContents = null;

using (IsolatedStorageFileStream fileStream =
    store.OpenFile("Test.jpg", FileMode.Open))
{
```

```
    fileContents = new byte[fileStream.Length];
    fileStream.Read(fileContents, 0, (int)fileStream.Length);
    fileStream.Close();
}

// Do something with the file contents
```

Serializing an Object to a File

Generally, you will be maintaining data in objects and collections within your application, and you may wish to persist this data to isolated storage. Rather than writing the data to a file using a custom format and then needing to parse it and rehydrate the corresponding objects or collections when you want to load the data again, you can simply serialize or deserialize the data to or from XML, using the DataContractSerializer class to help you.

Let's say you have a collection of Product objects that you want to serialize to a file within an isolated storage store. The following code demonstrates serializing and writing a collection of Product objects to isolated storage:

```
using (IsolatedStorageFileStream fileStream =
    store.OpenFile("ProductCollection.xml", FileMode.Create))
{
    DataContractSerializer serializer =
        new DataContractSerializer(typeof(List<Product>));
    serializer.WriteObject(fileStream, productCollection);
}
```

■ **Note** You will need to add a using directive to the System.Runtime.Serialization namespace for this and the following example to work.

Deserializing and Rehydrating an Object from File

The following code demonstrates deserializing a collection of Product objects read from a file in isolated storage, and rehydrating the collection:

```
using (IsolatedStorageFileStream fileStream =
    store.OpenFile("ProductCollection.xml", FileMode.Open))
{
    DataContractSerializer serializer =
        new DataContractSerializer(typeof(List<Product>));
    List<Product> productCollection =
        serializer.ReadObject(fileStream) as List<Product>;

    // Do something with the collection

    fileStream.Close();
}
```

Disk Space Quota

When a Silverlight application is first run, it is given a quota of 1MB of space to use in its isolated storage store. This quota is assigned on a per-domain basis, meaning that the quota is shared between all the Silverlight applications originating from the same domain, even though each application has its own separate isolated storage store. Attempting to exceed this quota will result in an exception being raised.

■ **Note** Whenever you work with isolated storage, you should place the code within a try . . . catch block to handle this possibility. Even if your application only expects to use a very small amount of isolated storage space, it can still exceed the quota, as the quota is shared among all applications originating from the same domain. Another application from the same domain may have used most of or the entire quota already, which will affect the amount of space your application has left to use.

You can determine how much quota you have free by checking the AvailableFreeSpace property of the IsolatedStorageFile object. This value returns the number of bytes still available for use in the isolated storage store:

```
long freeSpace = store.AvailableFreeSpace;
```

You can also retrieve the total quota assigned to the domain via the store's Quota property, and retrieve the amount of quote already used via the store's UsedSize property.

When a Silverlight application is installed to run outside the browser, its quota will be automatically increased from the initial 1MB to 25MB. However, you can request additional space at any time if it is required. This request requires that the user provide permission for the domain to be assigned further quota by displaying a dialog, as shown in Figure 16-6.

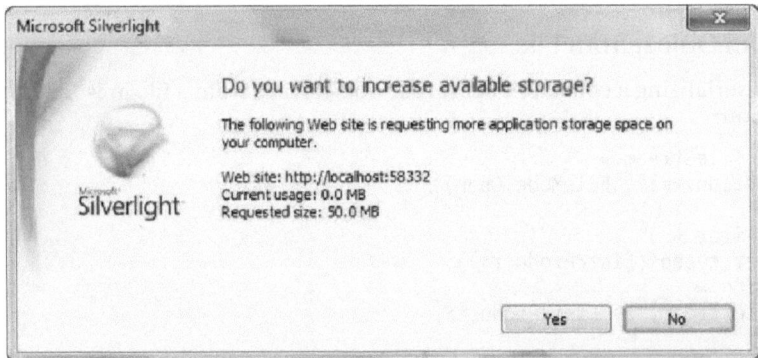

Figure 16-6. *The dialog for the application requesting increased isolated storage quota*

To request additional quota, you can simply call the IncreaseQuotaTo method of the IsolatedStorageFile object, passing it the amount of space that you want (in bytes). For example, you can use the following code to request your quota to be increased to 50MB of isolated storage space:

```
bool increasePermitted = store.IncreaseQuotaTo(50 * 1024 * 1024);
```

The method returns a Boolean value indicating whether permission for the additional space has been granted or denied by the user. Requesting a smaller quota than that already granted will throw an ArgumentException exception stating that "The new quota must be larger than the old quota," so be prepared for this scenario and put the call in a try . . . catch block, or make sure the value you are setting is greater than that of the store's Quota property.

■ **Note** The call to the IncreaseQuotaTo method must originate from a user-initiated event. In other words, you can request additional isolated storage quota only in an event raised by some sort of user input, such as the Click event. Any attempt to request additional isolated storage quota in an event handler not initiated by user input, such as in response to the Loaded event of a control, will simply be denied. This rule applies only when the application is running in sandboxed mode. When the application is running with elevated trust permissions (described later in this chapter), this limitation is lifted.

Encrypting Data

Something to be aware of when writing data to isolated storage is that it is easily accessible by burrowing into the user's profile folders. The isolated storage store is maintained in a hidden folder with the exact same file/directory structure as the folders were created in the store, as demonstrated in Figure 16-7.

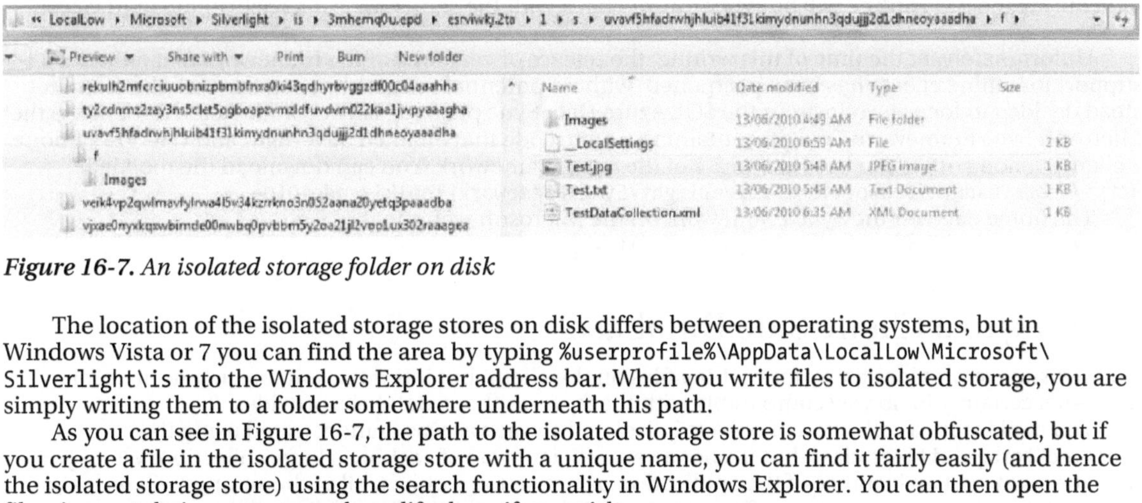

Figure 16-7. An isolated storage folder on disk

The location of the isolated storage stores on disk differs between operating systems, but in Windows Vista or 7 you can find the area by typing %userprofile%\AppData\LocalLow\Microsoft\Silverlight\is into the Windows Explorer address bar. When you write files to isolated storage, you are simply writing them to a folder somewhere underneath this path.

As you can see in Figure 16-7, the path to the isolated storage store is somewhat obfuscated, but if you create a file in the isolated storage store with a unique name, you can find it fairly easily (and hence the isolated storage store) using the search functionality in Windows Explorer. You can then open the files, inspect their contents, and modify them if you wish.

The point you need to note from this example is that nothing you write to isolated storage should be considered secure, and thus you should not write sensitive data to isolated storage or assume that it can't be modified outside your application.

You may wish to consider encrypting your files to help prevent these sorts of issues if they are of concern to you. The following MSDN article should point you in the right direction for doing so: http://msdn.microsoft.com/en-au/library/dd153755.aspx.

Compressing Data

With a default quota of 1MB, depending on the type and number of files you want to cache in isolated storage, you may wish to consider attempting to make the most efficient use of the available space within isolated storage by compressing the files, saving the need to request additional quota from the user soon after creating the store.

Silverlight doesn't have any built-in compression routines, but you can use an open source library that provides this functionality instead. Two of the best options available to you are Silverlight ports of the SharpZipLib and DotNetZip projects. SharpZipLib has a GPL license, and DotNetZip has a less-restrictive Ms-PL license.

You can download the Silverlight port of the SharpZipLib project from http://slsharpziplib.codeplex.com. However, the DotNetZip project has no official port attempt (the original project can be found at http://dotnetzip.codeplex.com). If you download the Document Toolkit Extensions project however, you will find a Silverlight port of both projects in it that is available at http://documenttoolkit.codeplex.com.

Refer to the documentation of the project that you choose to use for details of how to use it.

The Microsoft Sync Framework

The Microsoft Sync Framework web site describes the framework as "a comprehensive synchronization platform that enables collaboration and offline access for applications, services, and devices with support for any data type, any data store, any transfer protocol, and any network topology." In simpler terms, you can use it as a framework for synchronizing data between a Silverlight application and the server, providing a range of new possibilities for occasionally connected Silverlight applications. Data is maintained in a local store for use by the Silverlight application while it is offline, and changes in the data during the time offline will be synchronized back with the server once it's back online (and vice versa).

Unfortunately, at the time of this writing, the release of version 4 of the framework that enhanced support for offline clients has been postponed, with no potential release date set, because the team instead decided to focus its efforts on the SQL Azure Data Sync product. However, the team did release the Microsoft Sync Framework Toolkit, containing source code that enabled Silverlight and Windows Phone 7 clients, among others, to use version 2.1 of the Sync Framework. You can download the toolkit at http://code.msdn.microsoft.com/silverlight/Sync-Framework-Toolkit-4dc10f0e.

The home page for the Sync Framework on the Microsoft web site is http://msdn.microsoft.com/en-us/sync/default.aspx.

Caching to a Client-Side Database

Isolated storage provides a way for caching files on the client, but it is not a suitable means of caching data—it's certainly in no way comparable with the features that a database provides.

You could store a collection of objects in isolated storage as was demonstrated using the IsolatedStorageSettings class, but it's not a very efficient way of caching a large collection. When you first attempt to get an instance of the application or site settings object, all of the settings will be loaded from isolated storage into memory. To get a single object would require loading all the settings into memory, and to simply insert, update, or delete a setting would require all the settings to be loaded and then persisted back to isolated storage.

We also discussed and demonstrated serializing objects as files to isolated storage as well, but for large sets of data, this can be an inefficient means of maintaining the data also.

Unfortunately, Silverlight has no built-in client-side database engine to solve these problems, which can be an issue when it comes to implementing occasionally connected applications. There are a number of potential solutions however (of differing degrees of suitability), discussed briefly in the following sections.

Sterling

Sterling is a free, lightweight NoSQL object-oriented database engine, written by Jeremy Likness. This is probably your best option if your Silverlight application needs a client-side database. It stores the database in isolated storage but can use the local file system instead if the application is running with elevated trust. It supports keys and table indexes for fast querying of data and allows you to write queries using LINQ and can be used by Windows Phone 7 and .NET applications, in addition to Silverlight applications. The home page for the Sterling database is at www.sterlingdatabase.com, and you can download it (including its source code) from http://sterling.codeplex.com. Both sites have links to articles and documentation on how you can use the Sterling database engine in your application.

Silverlight Database

The Silverlight Database (SilverDB) engine also serializes the tables and their data to a file in isolated storage, but without the key and index support that Sterling provides. It is worth investigating if you want to provide a simple predefined means to persisting and retrieving data in isolated storage. You can get this library at http://silverdb.codeplex.com.

SQLite

SQLite is a popular database engine with a small footprint and an extremely permissive license that has been around for quite some time now. It is written in C and ported to many environments (the original project is here: www.sqlite.org). If you need a relational database, unlike the object-oriented database Sterling implements, you might like to consider using one of its Silverlight ports.

Noah Hart ported SQLite to C#. He named the engine C#-SQLite (http://code.google.com/p/csharp-sqlite), and it runs against the full .NET Framework but not Silverlight. This project was ported to Silverlight by Tim Anderson as a proof of concept (not in a production-ready state) and can be downloaded from www.itwriting.com/blog/1695-proof-of-concept-c-sqlite-running-in-silverlight.html.

A separate, more recent attempt has been made at porting SQLite to Windows Phone 7 and Silverlight, which you might like to also investigate (http://wp7sqlite.codeplex.com).

SQLite was a part of the now-deprecated Google Gears, and this provides another possibility for use as a database engine and store. You can create and store data in a SQLite database using the JavaScript API provided by Google Gears. An example of doing so is demonstrated at www.mojoportal.com/silverlight-google-gears-awesome-at-least-in-firefox.aspx. Note that since JavaScript is required to communicate with the database, it can be used only within the browser (that is, it will not be accessible to applications running outside the browser).

Sharp HSql

Craig Dunn produced a proof-of-concept port of the Sharp HSql database engine to Silverlight (that was itself a port of the HSQLDB database engine written for Java) and has made it available at http://conceptdev.blogspot.com/2009/07/sql-in-silverlight.html.

Commercial Options

As you can see from the descriptions of the previous database engines, apart from Sterling, none of the free database engines listed is considered production ready. However, you may wish to consider the following commercial offerings:

- *Perst* is an open source database engine released under the GPL license, so it's not a commercial offering per se. However, for use in closed-source applications, you will need to buy a license, in which case it becomes a commercial offering. A single developer license for its Silverlight edition (at the time of this writing) is $495. You can purchase and download it from www.mcobject.com/perst.

- *Siaqodb* is a database engine targeting a number of platforms. One of its key features is its Sync Framework provider, enabling client-side databases to be easily synchronized with a server-side database. A single developer license for its Silverlight edition (at the time of this writing) is $186. You can purchase and download it from http://siaqodb.com.

- *EffiProz Embedded C# Database* is a database engine targeting both Silverlight and Windows Phone 7. A single developer license for its Silverlight edition (at the time of this writing) is $490. You can purchase and download it from www.effiproz.com/product_sl.aspx.

Communicating with Local Database Engines

When your application is running with elevated trust on Windows systems, you will have access to COM. You can take advantage of the ADO COM objects to interact with the various database engines installed on the user's machine, such as SQL Server, SQL Compact, and Microsoft Access. We'll look at how you can use the ADO COM objects from Silverlight later in this chapter.

Detecting Network Connection Availability

To effectively support occasionally connected scenarios, you need the ability to detect whether the application is online or offline and cater for the current state accordingly. You also need the ability to detect when this state changes (from offline to online) and start synchronizing cached data back with the server.

Silverlight has the built-in ability to detect network availability and any changes in it, and you can find the classes to help you do so under the System.Net.NetworkInformation namespace. You can use the NetworkInterface class to help determine whether a network connection is available, and you can use the NetworkChange class to notify you when this state changes.

For example, the following code determines if a network connection is available:

```
bool isNetworkAvailable = NetworkInterface.GetIsNetworkAvailable();
```

■ **Note** The NetworkInterface.GetIsNetworkAvailable method may report that you have a connection available, but there's no guarantee that you actually have a connection to the Internet or that the server you want to communicate with is accessible. It simply reports whether or not there is a network adapter available that currently has an IP address; it won't if it has no network connection.

You can monitor for changes in network availability by handling the NetworkAddressChanged event of the NetworkChange class like so:

```
NetworkChange.NetworkAddressChanged += NetworkChange_NetworkAddressChanged;

private void NetworkChange_NetworkAddressChanged(object sender, EventArgs e)
{
    // Handle network state changed as required
}
```

■ **Note** The NetworkAddressChanged event doesn't tell you whether or not a network connection is now available—merely that the IP address of a network adapter has changed. You will need to use it in conjunction with the NetworkInterface.GetIsNetworkAvailable method to determine the new network connection state.

File System Open and Save Dialogs

Isolated storage is the primary means Silverlight provides to store and retrieve data locally on the user's machine, but sometimes you need to read and write to actual files within the user's file system. For example, you may want to save a file that was downloaded from the server or upload a file to the server from the user's machine.

As part of the Silverlight sandbox, you can't read or write files directly from or to disk without user interaction, unless you have elevated permissions (discussed later in this chapter). Instead, you need to display an open/save dialog first to gain explicit permission from the user to read or write a file. Let's take a look at how you use these dialogs, and the file based operations that they enable.

■ **Note** Attempting to display an open or save file dialog must be the result of a user initiated action. In other words, you can show an open or save file dialog only in response to an event raised by some sort of user input, such as the Click event. Any attempt to display the open or save file dialog in an event not initiated by user input, as in response to the Loaded event of a control, would raise an exception. This rule applies only when the application is running in sandboxed mode. When the application is running with elevated trust permissions (described later in this chapter), this limitation is lifted.

The Open File Dialog

You can use the OpenFileDialog class to display a dialog that enables the user to select a file to open, as shown in Figure 16-8. This will provide you with the permission to access the selected file by returning one or more FileInfo objects (from the System.IO namespace) that enable you to open the file and read the data from it.

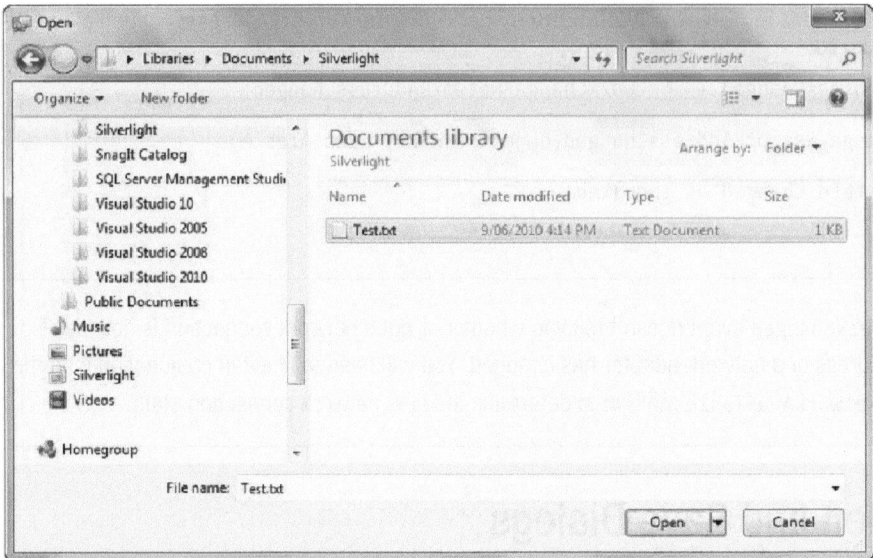

Figure 16-8. The Open File dialog

Displaying the Dialog

The code to display the open file dialog is as follows:

```
OpenFileDialog dialog = new OpenFileDialog();
bool? fileSelected = dialog.ShowDialog();

if (fileSelected.HasValue && fileSelected.Value)
{
    // Code to open and read the file goes here
}
```

The ShowDialog method is the code that actually displays the dialog and returns a nullable Boolean indicating whether the user selected a file or cancelled the operation. This variable will be set to true if the user selected a file and then clicked the Open button.

■ **Note** This method may throw an InvalidOperationException or SecurityException exception. Ensure that your code catches this exception and handles it accordingly.

Filtering the Files

You can limit the dialog to displaying files of only a given type (or types) by specifying one or more file filters using the Filter property of the dialog object. Unfortunately, the way to assign these filters is somewhat archaic, but it aligns to what you may be used to when configuring file filters for dialogs in other technologies, such as Windows Forms. For example, to limit files to just text files (files with a .txt extension), you can use the following syntax before opening the dialog:

```
dialog.Filter = "Text Files|*.txt";
```

This string is split into two sections, separated by a pipe character. The first section denotes the text to display representing the filter in the drop-down list, and the second section denotes the actual filter to apply to limit the files displayed.

You can extend this filter to include a number of file types and extensions by separating the file extensions in the second section of the filter string with a semicolon, as follows:

```
dialog.Filter = "Documents|*.doc;*.docx;*.rtf";
```

Alternatively, you can have multiple filters that the user can select from in the dialog like so:

```
dialog.Filter = "Word 2002/2003 Documents|*.doc|Word 2007/2010 Documents|*.docx";
```

As you can see, another pipe character is used to separate each entry. If the first entry is not the one you want to use as the default selection, you can specify a different one using the FilterIndex property. This is a one-based index, so you would set this property to 2 to select the Word 2007 and 2010 Documents filter (that is, the second filter) from the preceding example.

Opening and Reading a Selected File

Once the user has selected a file, you can retrieve the FileInfo object that it has created. When running in sandbox mode, you can view only limited information about the selected file. Attempting to access file properties such as its directory or its attributes will be denied, resulting in a SecurityException being thrown. You can get its name from the FileInfo's Name property and its size from its Length property.

▦ **Note** You can't create an instance of the FileInfo class unless you are running with elevated trust, as discussed later in this chapter. Attempting to do so will result in a SecurityException, stating that access to the file has been denied.

The FileInfo object is assigned only limited permissions for the actions you can perform on it, but it does allow you to open the file and read its contents. There are two methods on the object that you can use to do so: OpenText and OpenRead.

Opening and Reading Text Files

If you know (or expect) the selected file to be a text file, you can use the OpenText method to read its contents. This method allows you to read the file by retrieving:

- A given number of characters at a time
- The contents line by line
- The entire contents of the file in a single step

The latter two methods are the most common when dealing with text files and are demonstrated in the following sections.

Reading the File Line by Line

To read the file one line at a time, use the ReadLine method:

```
string fileContents = null;

using (StreamReader fileStream = dialog.File.OpenText())
{
    while (!fileStream.EndOfStream)
    {
        fileContents = fileStream.ReadLine();
        // Do something with the line contents
    }

    fileStream.Close();
}

// Do something with the file contents
```

Reading the Whole File in a Single Step

To read the whole file in a single step, use the ReadToEnd method:

```
string fileContents = null;

using (StreamReader fileStream = dialog.File.OpenText())
{
    fileContents = fileStream.ReadToEnd();
    fileStream.Close();
}

// Do something with the file contents
```

Opening and Reading Binary Files

When working with other non-text file types, such as images and documents, you will need to use the OpenRead method to read their contents as a byte array.

Reading the Whole File in a Single Step

The following code demonstrates reading the entire contents of a file into a byte array using the Read method:

```
byte[] fileContents = null;

using (FileStream fileStream = dialog.File.OpenRead())
{
    fileContents = new byte[dialog.File.Length];
    fileStream.Read(fileContents, 0, (int)dialog.File.Length);
    fileStream.Close();
}

// Do something with the file contents
```

Reading the File in a Chunks

You can read the file in chunks, also using the Read method like so (especially useful when the file is large):

```
const int chunkSize = 4096; // 4kb blocks

using (FileStream fileStream = dialog.File.OpenRead())
{
    byte[] chunk = new byte[chunkSize];
    int bytesRead = 0;
    int position = 0;

    do
    {
        bytesRead = fileStream.Read(chunk, 0, chunkSize);

        // Do something with the chunk

        position += bytesRead;
    } while (bytesRead > 0);

    fileStream.Close();
}
```

Reading and Dislaying an Image File

If you want to load an image to display in an Image control, the code is even simpler. The following code demonstrates populating a BitmapImage object with the contents of a file and assigning it to the Source property of an Image control (named imageControl in the code):

```
using (FileStream fileStream = dialog.File.OpenRead())
{
    BitmapImage image = new BitmapImage();
    image.SetSource(fileStream);

    // Assign the BitmapImage object to the Source property of an Image control
    imageControl.Source = image;

    fileStream.Close();
}
```

Enabling Multiple File Selection

By default, the user can select only a single file from the open file dialog. However, you can set its Multiselect property to true to enable the user to select multiple files at the same time. The File property will return only the first file selected, but you can use the Files property instead. That returns an array of FileInfo objects that you can loop through and read as required.

The Save File Dialog

You can use the SaveFileDialog class, as shown in Figure 16-9, to display a dialog that enables the user to specify the name and location of a file to save or select a file to overwrite. This will provide you with the permission to write to the selected file, by returning a `FileInfo` object that enables you to create the file and write data to it.

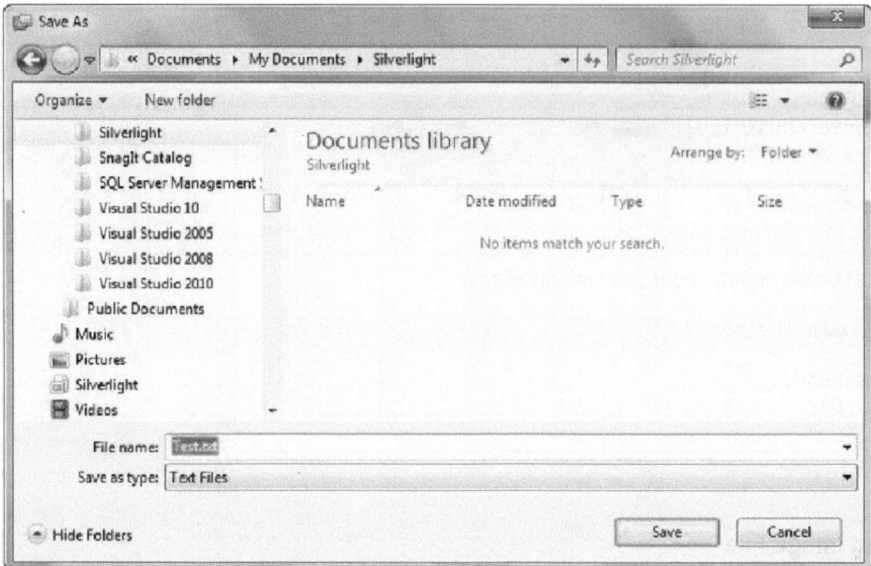

Figure 16-9. The Save File dialog

Displaying the Dialog

The code to display the open file dialog is as follows:

```
SaveFileDialog dialog = new SaveFileDialog();
bool? fileEntered = dialog.ShowDialog();

if (fileEntered.HasValue && fileEntered.Value)
{
    // Code to open and write the file goes here
}
```

You'll note that this is very similar to how the `OpenFileDialog` class is used.

■ **Note** If the user enters invalid characters as the file name, this will raise a message box notifying the user as such, and the dialog won't accept a file name with these characters. However, on a Mac, the dialog will accept these characters but will consequently throw an `ArgumentException`. Ensure that your code catches this exception and handles it accordingly.

Setting a Default File Name

Silverlight 5 introduced the ability for you now to specify a default file name when opening the save file dialog. Simply assign the default name that the file should have to the SaveFileDialog object's DefaultFileName property.

Setting a Default Extension

Like the OpenFileDialog class, you can set various filters to limit the files displayed in the dialog. If you specify one or more filters and the user does not enter an extension with the file name, the extension associated with the selected filter will be automatically appended to the file name. If no filter is specified or if it is an All Files (*.*) type filter, the value assigned to the DefaultExt property of the OpenFileDialog class will be appended to the file name instead (if provided).

Writing to the File

Once the user has specified a name and path for the file, you can create it and open it for writing to by calling the SaveFileDialog object's OpenFile method You will note that unlike the OpenFileDialog class, which has separate methods for reading files as text or binary, the SaveFileDialog class has only this single method.

■ **Note** You can get the name of the file as provided by the user, excluding path information, from the dialog class's SafeFileName property.

Writing a Text File

To write text to the file, you need to create a StreamWriter from the stream returned from the OpenFile method. You can then use the Write or the WriteLine methods of the StreamWriter object to write text to the file as required.

```
using (Stream stream = dialog.OpenFile())
{
    using (StreamWriter writer = new StreamWriter(stream))
    {
        writer.WriteLine("Text written from Silverlight");
        writer.Close();
    }

    stream.Close();
}
```

Writing a Binary File

Writing binary data to a file is actually easier than writing text because there's no need for a StreamWriter (or similar) to help you in doing so. You can simply use the Write method of the stream that's returned when opening the file to write the contents of a byte array to the file. The following code demonstrates writing the contents of a byte array named `fileContents` to the file:

```
using (Stream stream = dialog.OpenFile())
{
    stream.Write(fileContents, 0, fileContents.Length);
    stream.Close();
}
```

Drag-and-Drop Target

Silverlight 4 introduced the ability for your application to act as a drop target for files that have been dragged from the desktop or Windows Explorer. This feature is even available when the application is running within the browser. This provides an alternative means for reading a file from the user's file system, without the user having to go via the open file dialog. For example, you might want to create a file uploader, where users can drag files onto your application and have them automatically uploaded to the server.

The first step when implementing this feature is to decide where you want files to be able to be dropped within your application. For this simple demonstration, let's enable the user to drop a file on an Image control and have that control display that file if it is an image file. Unfortunately, despite supporting the required events, the Image control won't raise the drag-and-drop events when a file is dragged over and dropped on the control, but you can place it inside a Border control, which will raise these events for us.

■ **Note** The Border control requires its `Background` property to be assigned a value, or its drag-and-drop events won't be raised either.

Therefore, the Border control in your view will be a drop target, and to enable it to accept dropped files, you need to set its `AllowDrop` property to true and handle the drag-and-drop events that you require:

```
<Border Name="imageBorder" Height="300" Width="300" AllowDrop="True"
        BorderThickness="1" BorderBrush="Black" Background="White"
        Drop="imageBorder_Drop">
    <Image Name="droppedImage" Stretch="Uniform" />
</Border>
```

Now, when the user drags a file from the file system over this control, the `DragEnter` event will be raised when the file is dragged within the bounds of the control, the `DragOver` event will be raised as the dragged file is moved over the control, and the `DragLeave` event will be raised when the file is dragged outside of the bounds of the control again. However, the event you are most interested in is the `Drop` event, which is raised when a file is dropped onto the control.

```
private void imageBorder_Drop(object sender, DragEventArgs e)
{
    // Code to open/read the dropped files goes here
}
```

The DragEventArgs object passed through to this event handler enables you to get the details of the files dropped on the control, using the GetData method of the IDataObject object that it exposes:

```
FileInfo[] files = e.Data.GetData(DataFormats.FileDrop) as FileInfo[];
```

Now you can loop through these files, opening them and reading their contents as required, in the same manner as demonstrated when discussing the open file dialog. The following code demonstrates opening a dropped file, ensuring it is an image file, reading its contents, and displaying it in the Image control in your view:

```
if (files.Length != 0)
{
    // Ensure that the file is an image (by validating the extension)
    string[] validExtensions = new string[] { ".jpg", ".png" };

    // NOTE: Multiple files can be dropped on the application, but we are
    // displaying only the first file.
    if (validExtensions.Contains(files[0].Extension.ToLower()))
    {
        try
        {
            // Open the file, read it into a BitmapImage object, and
            // display it in the Image control.
            using (FileStream fileStream = files[0].OpenRead())
            {
                BitmapImage bitmap = new BitmapImage();
                bitmap.SetSource(fileStream);
                fileStream.Close();

                droppedImage.Source = bitmap;
            }
        }
        catch { }
    }
}
```

Note that you will need to add using directives to the following namespaces to the top of your code file:

```
using System.IO;
using System.Linq;
using System.Windows.Media.Imaging;
```

■ **Note** Unfortunately, dropping files on a Silverlight application when it's running on a Mac requires some workarounds to support the feature and will work only in Safari. These workarounds are documented in the MSDN article found at http://msdn.microsoft.com/en-us/library/ee670998.aspx.

Clipboard

The user can use the standard cut, copy, and paste shortcut keys (Ctrl+X, Ctrl+C, and Ctrl+V on Windows) from within controls such as the TextBox and the RichTextBox to cut, copy, and paste the selected text in the control to and from the host operating system's clipboard. However, prior to Silverlight 4, you could not cut, copy, or paste text to and from the clipboard programmatically.

Silverlight 4 finally introduced the Clipboard class (found in the System.Windows namespace) to enable you to do so. This class enables you to get the text currently on the clipboard by using its GetText method, set the text on the clipboard by using its SetText method, and query whether there is any text on the clipboard by using its ContainsText method.

You can get the text currently on the clipboard like so:

```
string clipboardText = Clipboard.GetText();
```

And you can set the text on the clipboard like this:

```
Clipboard.SetText("Some text");
```

You can check whether there is any text available on the clipboard using:

```
bool clipboardHasText = Clipboard.ContainsText();
```

However, you should be aware of a few limitations and issues. The first is that a dialog will appear, asking the user for permission to allow the application access to the clipboard, as shown in Figure 16-10. This permission dialog will appear only once and will not appear again until the next time the application is run, although you can select the check box that says to remember your answer.

■ **Note**　If the user refuses the application permission to access the clipboard, an exception will be thrown. Therefore, always remember to wrap your calls to the clipboard in a try . . . catch block.

Figure 16-10. The dialog requesting permission to access the clipboard

Another issue to be aware of is that, like displaying the open or save dialogs, the clipboard interaction must be user initiated. Any attempt to interact with the clipboard in an event handler that isn't user input initiated (such as in response to the Loaded event of a control) will immediately raise an exception. That is, the dialog asking for permission will not be displayed; permission will automatically be refused. This limitation is lifted, however, when the application is running with elevated trust permissions (described later in this chapter).

The other major limitation of the Clipboard class is that it supports copying and pasting only text to and from the clipboard. Other types of data, such as images, are not supported. The only way to copy an image to the clipboard would be to encode it as Base64, an encoding commonly used to convert binary data to a text representation. However, no other application is likely to be able to recognize this, and thus doing so has very limited uses and benefits.

■ **Note** Worth noting is that the DataGrid control has a built-in copy feature where you can select a number of rows and press Ctrl+C to copy them to the clipboard (in tab-delimited form). You can then paste them into another application, such as Microsoft Excel.

Three copy modes are available, and you can select which mode you want to support by setting the ClipboardCopyMode property on the DataGrid control. The modes are None (the user can't copy row data to the clipboard), ExcludeHeader (don't include the column headers as the first line of data), and IncludeHeader (do include the column headers as the first line of data).

Additionally, you can specify what data is copied for a column, if it should be different from what is displayed, using the ClipboardContentBinding property on the DataGridColumn. You can also handle the CopyingRowClipboardContent event on the DataGrid, which is raised as each row is copied so that you can see what content is being copied to the clipboard, although you can't modify that content, which limits its use.

Running in Full-Screen Mode

You can set your Silverlight application to run in full-screen mode if you wish, even when it is running inside the browser. This feature was designed to enable streaming video to be played on the full screen and for games, but you may find some uses for it in your business applications too, such as for kiosk applications. Let's take a look at how to do this.

Initiating Full-Screen Mode

The following code sets the application to run in full-screen mode:

```
Application.Current.Host.Content.IsFullScreen = true;
```

Once the application is in full-screen mode, the user can press the Escape key to go back to running normally. When the application enters full-screen mode, it will briefly flash a message telling the user of how to exit, as shown in Figure 16-11.

Figure 16-11. The message that briefly appears when entering full-screen mode

Alternatively, you can set the IsFullScreen property to false to return to normal mode program-matically. You will need to implement this when enabling full-screen mode when running with elevated trust, as the Escape key does not automatically exit full-screen in that scenario.

As with opening an open or save dialog or interacting with the clipboard, setting the application to display full screen must be a user-initiated action. That is, you can do so only from a Click event handler or similar, where the event is raised in response to user input. Attempting to do so otherwise, such as in the Loaded event of a page or view, will simply result in the action being ignored.

If the application is running with elevated trust, this limitation is lifted. In this scenario, you can set the application to run in full-screen mode from the application's Startup event or from the Loaded event or constructor of a page or view (for example) if you wish. However, when doing so from the application's Startup event or the constructor of the RootVisual, you must use the BeginInvoke com-mand when setting the IsFullScreen property to true so that it does so on the user interface thread. Oth-erwise, it won't work. The following code demonstrates how to do this:

```
Deployment.Current.Dispatcher.BeginInvoke(() =>
    {
        Application.Current.Host.Content.IsFullScreen = true;
    });
```

Detecting the Switch to and from Full-Screen Mode

You can detect when the application has entered or left full-screen mode by handling the FullScreenChanged event on the Application.Current.Host.Content object, like so:

```
Application.Current.Host.Content.FullScreenChanged += Application_FullScreenChanged;

private void Application_FullScreenChanged(object sender, EventArgs e)
{
    // Full screen changed logic goes here
}
```

Retaining Full-Screen Mode When Unfocused

While the application is running in full-screen mode, attempting to switch to another application will take it back out to running in normal mode, either to its browser window or out-of-browser window. You can prevent this behavior so that it remains in full-screen mode, but with the other window in front of it, using the following code:

```
Application.Current.Host.Content.FullScreenOptions =
    System.Windows.Interop.FullScreenOptions.StaysFullScreenWhenUnfocused;
```

After setting this option, when you next attempt to go into full-screen mode, the user will be asked for permission to enable the application to remain in full-screen mode, regardless of other applications obtaining the focus, as shown in Figure 16-12.

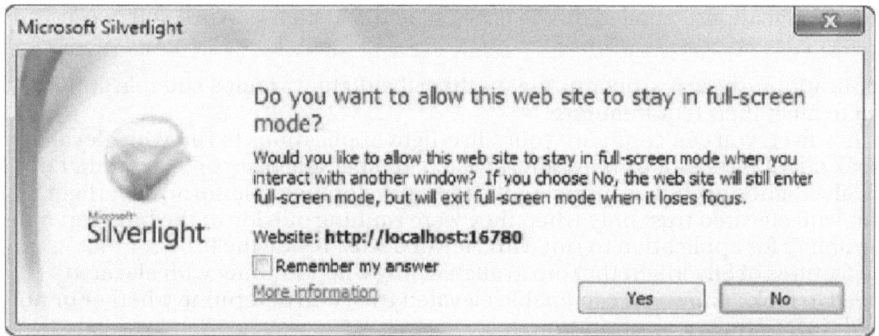

Figure 16-12. The dialog asking whether it should be able to stay in full-screen mode

This message won't be displayed when the application is running in OOB mode with elevated trust.

■ **Note** Unfortunately, unless the application is running with elevated trust, attempting to display an open or save dialog box will return the application to normal mode, even if the FullScreenOptions property is set to StaysFullScreenWhenUnfocused.

Keyboard Access

One of the primary limitations of full-screen mode is that the majority of keyboard input is disabled. This behavior is intended to prevent a rogue Silverlight application from impersonating the Windows lock screen (for example), where you may unintentionally enter your user credentials and have someone steal them from you. Mouse input will still work as normal in full-screen mode, as will the following keyboard keys: the arrow keys, space bar, and Tab, Page Up, Page Down, Home, End, and Enter keys. As mentioned earlier, the Escape key is captured by the Silverlight runtime and exits the full-screen mode.
Running with elevated trust lifts this restriction.

Configuring Elevated Trust

Prior to Silverlight 4, Silverlight applications could run only in a sandboxed mode, with partial trust. This protective measure prevented rogue Silverlight applications from damaging the user's machine. This was an essential security measure but vastly limited the possibilities available to Silverlight applications. By restricting you to the sandbox, you couldn't interact with the host operating system. For example, you couldn't

- Read or write files from the users' file systems without their interaction via the open or save file dialogs.

- Interact with hardware attached to the users' machines, such as printers, scanners, and biometric devices.

- Query a local database engine, such as SQL Server.

- Interact with oter applications installed on the users' machines, such as Word and Excel.

For some business applications, these restrictions meant that Silverlight was not a suitable application development platform to meet their requirements.

From Silverlight 4 on, however, you can configure your Silverlight applications to run with elevated trust, enabling them to break out of the sandbox (partially, at least) and helping overcome a number of the prevailing concerns of Silverlight's usefulness as an application development platform. Silverlight 4 enabled applications to run with elevated trust only when they were running outside of the browser, but Silverlight 5 introduces the ability for application to run with elevated trust inside the browser too.

Let's go through some features of Silverlight that are available only when running with elevated trust. First, however, we need to look at how you can enable elevated trust and determine whether or not the application has elevated trust permissions at runtime.

■ **Note** Despite having elevated trust, the application will not exceed the user's Windows privileges. Therefore, having elevated trust will not enable users to read or write to file paths that they have no access to, nor will they be able to perform actions via COM that their Windows privileges do not permit.

Enabling Elevated Trust in OOB Mode

Enabling your Silverlight application to run with elevated trust when it is running outside the browser is a very simple process. In the Out-Of-Browser Settings window properties (shown previously in Figure 16-2), which you can get to via the project's properties, select the "Require elevated trust when running outside the browser" check box. You'll note that with this option set, the install dialog for the application is quite different from the one displayed without the option set (as was shown in Figure 16-4). Instead, the user will get a more severe-looking dialog, as shown in Figure 16-13.

Figure 16-13. *The install dialog for unsigned applications requesting elevated trust permissions*

This dialog can be made a little friendlier by signing your XAP file. Doing so will change the warning at the top of the dialog to a simple question asking whether you want to install the application and will also display the application's icon (XAP signing is discussed in Chapter 17).

Before invoking any functionality that requires elevated trust, you should ensure that the application is actually running with elevated trust permissions. Despite having set the option that it should do so, while it is running within the browser, it won't have these privileges. Only when the application is installed and actually running in OOB mode will it have the elevated trust permissions.

You can determine whether the application has elevated trust permissions when it's running by checking the HasElevatedPermissions property of the current Application object, like so:

```
bool hasElevatedTrust = Application.Current.HasElevatedPermissions;
```

Whenever your application attempts to use features that require elevated trust, it should check this property first to ensure that it has permission to use them.

■ **Note** Often, when an application makes extensive use of features that require elevated trust, it will insist that it be installed and run in OOB mode when accessed by displaying an install button only when it runs inside the browser. The means for implementing this was discussed earlier in this chapter.

Enabling Elevated Trust Inside the Browser

Although Silverlight 4 allowed your applications to request and run with elevated trust privileges, they could do so only when running outside the browser. Not all Silverlight applications are suited to being run outside the browser, so forcing them to do so to gain elevated trust privileges posed quite a limitation on those applications. However, Silverlight 5 now permits applications requiring elevated trust privileges to run inside the browser as well, although there are a few hoops you need to jump through to enable this on client machines.

■ **Note** In addition to gaining elevated trust privileges inside the browser, enabling you to use COM and P/Invoke and directly access files, turning on in-browser elevated trust enables you to display toast notifications and use the WebBrowser control when your Silverlight applications are running within the browser. However, the WebBrowser control will work only for Silverlight applications running inside Internet Explorer; it will not work in other web browsers. You also cannot open additional windows inside the browser using the Window class.

To configure your application to request elevated trust privileges when running inside the browser, open the Silverlight tab of the Silverlight application's project properties, and select the "Require elevated trust when running in-browser" option, as shown in Figure 16-14.

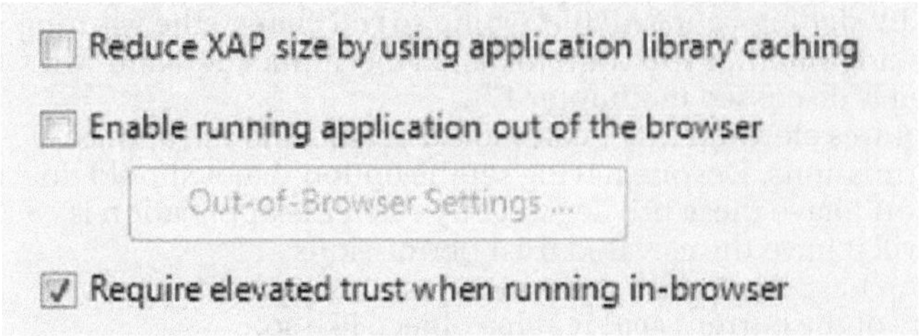

Figure 16-14. Turning on elevated trust for Silverlight applications running inside the browser

If you were to run your Silverlight application now from localhost, you will find that it is successfully running with elevated trust privileges inside the browser. You can confirm this by checking the value of the Application.Current.HasElevatedPermissions property. However, when you deploy your application to a server and run it, you will find that it won't run with elevated trust privileges. You can easily test this by replacing localhost in the browser's address bar with the name of your machine instead. For example, change

http://**localhost**/AventureWorksTestPage.aspx

to

http://**chrispc**/AventureWorksTestPage.aspx

You'll find that when the Silverlight application is downloaded from the second URL, the application will not have elevated trust privileges, despite it having them when it's downloaded from the first URL. The reason the application runs with elevated trust privileges under localhost is because localhost is a white-listed domain, which enables you to debug and test applications without needing the application to be signed and so on. Unfortunately, this behavior can be rather confusing if you're not aware of it, with the application working successfully on your local machine but not when you deploy it to a server.

For Silverlight applications to run inside the browser with elevated trust when the application is hosted on a server, the XAP file needs to be signed, the client machines need to permit them to do so by having a special registry key set, and the client machines also need to have the certificate used to sign the XAP file installed.

Follow these steps to enable your Silverlight application to run with elevated trust inside the browser once it is deployed:

1. Select the "Require elevated trust when running in-browser" option in the project properties, as previously described.

2. Sign your XAP file. The application will not run with elevated trust privileges inside the browser without being signed, unless it's run from localhost. This can be a self-signed certificate if you don't have a real certificate available. See Chapter 17 for details on how to sign XAP files. Your application is now properly configured to run with elevated trust privileges inside the browser, but you need to configure your clients to permit the application to run with elevated trust privileges inside the browser.

3. The certificate that you used to sign the application needs to be installed on the client machines. Usually, you will do this throughout an organization using Active Directory Domain Services and a group policy. Steps for doing so can be found at http://technet.microsoft.com/en-us/library/cc770315.aspx. The certificate will need to be installed to the Trusted Publishers certificate store. If

it is a self-signed certificate, it will also need to be installed to the Trusted Root Certification Authorities certificate store.

4. The client machines also require a registry key to be set, explicitly permitting Silverlight applications to run with elevated trust privileges inside the browser. Your best option again is using a group policy to configure this registry key. You need to add a value named AllowElevatedTrustAppsInBrowser of type DWORD under the following keys:

   • HKEY_LOCAL_MACHINE\Software\Microsoft\Silverlight\ for 32-bit Windows

   • HKEY_LOCAL_MACHINE\Software\Wow6432Node\Microsoft\Silverlight\ for 64-bit Windows

   Set its value to 1 to enable Silverlight applications run with elevated trust privileges inside the browser or 0 to disable them from doing so.

With both your Silverlight application and the client machines configured accordingly, your Silverlight application will successfully run with elevated trust privileges when it is deployed and run on those machines. Be aware, however, that the privileges of the Silverlight application are still subject to the browser's security settings. For example, Internet Explorer's protected mode, turned on by default for the Internet zone, will affect your application's privileges.

■ **Note** You can determine whether the application has been configured to run with elevated trust privileges inside the browser at runtime in code using the Deployment.Current.InBrowserSettings object. However, you cannot modify the settings at runtime, and this does not indicate that the application actually has elevated trust privileges.

Accessing the File System

Having elevated trust permissions opens the user's file system to direct reading and writing, without the need to go via the open or save file dialogs. Silverlight 4 limited users to accessing only the folders within their profile, but Silverlight 5 has lifted this restriction, enabling reading and writing of files anywhere that the user has privileges to do so.

The classes that enable you to read from and write to the file system can be found under the System.IO namespace and closely mirror those available in the full .NET Framework. For example, you will find the Directory, DirectoryInfo, File, FileInfo, and Path classes in this namespace that you can use when running with elevated trust. Despite many of these classes having methods that appear to allow you certain functionality, not all of these methods are actually implemented.

Let's take a look at some of the tasks you can perform on the file system when running with elevated trust permissions.

Getting the Path of a Special Folder

To access a file for reading or writing, you first have to determine the location of the file, a task performed by the user via the open or save file dialogs in the examples detailed earlier in this chapter. To do so, you can use the GetFolderPath method of the Environment class, passing it a value from the

Environment.SpecialFolder enumeration that denotes the folder you are after. The following code demonstrates obtaining the path to the user's Documents folder:

```
string docPath = Environment.GetFolderPath(Environment.SpecialFolder.MyDocuments);
```

Enumerating Files and Directories Within a Folder

Once you've obtained a folder's path, you can enumerate through the files and directories within the folder.

To enumerate through the files within a folder, you can create a DirectoryInfo object, passing in the path to its constructor, and use the methods that it exposes. For example, you can enumerate through the files within the user's Documents folder like so:

```
string docPath = Environment.GetFolderPath(Environment.SpecialFolder.MyDocuments);
DirectoryInfo docPathInfo = new DirectoryInfo(docPath);

IEnumerable<FileInfo> docPathFiles = docPathInfo.EnumerateFiles();

foreach (FileInfo file in docPathFiles)
{
    // Work with the FileInfo object here as required
}
```

■ **Note** When calling the EnumerateFiles method, you can make use of one of its overloads to provide a pattern to filter the files that should be returned. Another overload allows you to specify whether files from all the subdirectories below the folder should be returned as well.

Likewise, you can enumerate through the directories within the folder like so:

```
string docPath = Environment.GetFolderPath(Environment.SpecialFolder.MyDocuments);
DirectoryInfo docPathInfo = new DirectoryInfo(docPath);

IEnumerable<DirectoryInfo> docPathSubdirectories =
    docPathInfo.EnumerateDirectories();

foreach (DirectoryInfo directory in docPathSubdirectories)
{
    // Work with the DirectoryInfo object here as required
}
```

■ **Note** Like the EnumerateFiles method, the EnumerateDirectories method also provides some overloads. One enables you to supply a pattern filtering what directories should be returned, and another enables you to specify whether it should also return directories from all the subdirectories below the folder.

You can return both files and directories within a folder in a single method call using the EnumerateFileSystemInfos method, in the same manner as described for the other two methods, but this method returns a collection of FileSystemInfo objects.

■ **Note** You can also access corresponding methods from the Directory class without the need to create a DirectoryInfo object first. Both means are completely valid, and the one you use will depend on your personal preference.

Determining Whether a File or Folder Exists

You can determine whether a file exists by using the Exists method on the File class. For example, the following code determines whether a file named Test.txt exists under the user's Documents folder:

```
string docPath = Environment.GetFolderPath(Environment.SpecialFolder.MyDocuments);
bool fileExists = File.Exists(Path.Combine(docPath, "Test.txt"));
```

In a similar fashion, you can determine whether a folder exists by using the Exists method on the Directory class. For example, the following code determines whether a folder named Test exists under the user's Documents folder:

```
string docPath = Environment.GetFolderPath(Environment.SpecialFolder.MyDocuments);
bool folderExists = Directory.Exists(Path.Combine(docPath, "Test"));
```

■ **Note** Alternatively, you can create a FileInfo or DirectoryInfo object, passing in the name of the file/directory to its constructor, and check the Exists property on that instead.

Reading Data from a File

You can read text or binary data from a file in the same manner as was demonstrated previously when discussing the open file dialog, after obtaining or creating a FileInfo object pointing to the file.

Elevating trust permissions opens a number of other methods of reading data from a file that are somewhat easier to use than the previously described methods. From the File class, you now have access to the ReadAllText, ReadLines, ReadAllBytes, OpenText, and OpenRead methods. Each of these reduces the amount of code required to read data from a file. For example, the following code demonstrates reading the entire contents of a text file into a string:

```
string fileContents = File.ReadAllText(filePath);
```

Saving Data to a File

As with reading data from a file, having elevated trust permissions opens a number of other easier methods of writing data to a file. From the File class, you now have access to the WriteAllText,

WriteAllLines, WriteAllBytes, OpenWrite, OpenText, CreateText, and Create methods. For example, the following code demonstrates writing "Hello" to a text file:

```
File.WriteAllText(filePath, "Hello");
```

Appending Text to a File

The File class also exposes the AppendText, AppendAllLines, AppendAllText methods that enable you to append text to a file. If the given file doesn't exist, these methods will create it for you. For example, you may wish to keep a log file containing all of the errors experienced on the client for later analysis. These methods will enable you to implement that behavior. For example, the following code demonstrates appending "Hello" to a file:

```
File.AppendAllText(filePath, "Hello");
```

Creating a New Folder

You can create a new folder within the user's profile via the CreateDirectory method of the Directory class. For example, to create a folder named Test under the user's Documents folder, you would use the following code:

```
string docPath = Environment.GetFolderPath(Environment.SpecialFolder.MyDocuments);
Directory.CreateDirectory(Path.Combine(docPath, "Test"));
```

■ **Note** Alternatively, you can use the CreateSubdirectory method of a DirectoryInfo object to achieve the same outcome.

Deleting a File

You can delete a file either via the Delete method of either a FileInfo object or the File class, for example:

```
File.Delete(filePath);
```

Copying or Moving a File

You can copy a file to a folder using either the CopyTo method of a FileInfo object or the Copy method of the File class, for example:

```
File.Copy(sourceFilePath, destinationFilePath);
```

Moving a file is a very similar process, using either the MoveTo method of a FileInfo object or the Move method of the File class:

```
File.Move(sourceFilePath, destinationFilePath);
```

■ **Note** The Copy method has an overload with an additional overwrite parameter that enables you to specify that any existing file in the destination folder with the same name can be overwritten.

Accessing File/Folder Attributes

It's worth noting that once you are running with elevated trust permissions, you can access the file at-tributes, such as creation time and directory, that you were unable to access from the FileInfo objects returned from the OpenFileDialog class when your application is running in the normal sandboxed mode. However, even with elevated trust, selecting a file located outside the user's profile folders via the OpenFileDialog class will still deny access to its file attributes–file attributes will be accessible only if the file resides in the user's profile folders, regardless of trust level.

COM Automation

A somewhat controversial feature added to Silverlight 4 was support for enabling COM automation. Most people have an overwhelmingly negative memory of dealing with COM, and they generally prefer that it remains just that—a memory. A more important argument against support for COM is that it is a Windows-only feature, so using it deviates from Silverlight's cross-platform nature.

However, COM does underpin many of Windows features and those of a number of high-profile Windows applications, such as the Office suite. Therefore, Silverlight's COM support opens a wide range of new possibilities for applications running with elevated trust, some of which will be discussed here.

Determining Whether COM Automation Is Available

Before attempting to call COM, you should perform a basic check to ensure that you can actually do so. To access a COM component, you must be running with elevated trust and on a Windows operating system. The IsAvailable property of the AutomationFactory class (found under the System.Runtime.InteropServices.Automation namespace) will return a Boolean value indicating whether these conditions are satisfied, denoting that the application can access COM automation.

```
bool canAccessCOM = AutomationFactory.IsAvailable;
```

Accessing COM Components

Once you know that you have access to COM automation, you need to create or obtain an instance of the COM component you wish to automate. You can do so using either the CreateObject or the GetObject methods of the AutomationFactory class. You can use the CreateObject method to create a new instance of the COM object, and you can use the GetObject to obtain an existing instance of the COM object. For example, if you wanted to interact with a running instance of Word, you could use the GetObject method to get that existing instance, returning the most recent instance if there are multiple instances running, or you could use the CreateObject method to start a new instance.

■ **Note** The preceding behavior can differ between COM components.

To create or obtain a COM object instance, you need to know its programmatic identifier, most commonly known as its progID. Every COM component has a Globally Unique Identifier (GUID) that uniquely identifies that component, known as a CLSID. This is a unique identifier that the COM component is registered in Windows with. However, this CLSID is not particularly human friendly, so each COM component has a corresponding meaningful string that can be used to access it—its progID. For example, the progID to automate Word is Word.Application.

■ **Note** To find the progID for a specific COM component, refer to its associated documentation.

Once you have obtained an instance of a COM object, you need to assign it to a variable. However, you have no assembly reference providing the types that you can cast the instance to because you can't add any sort of reference to those types in Silverlight, which creates a problem. Therefore, if you assign the instance to a variable of type object, the only way to call methods on the COM object and access properties is via reflection. Help is at hand, however, with the dynamic keyword.

The dynamic keyword enables you to assign an object instance to a variable and call methods or access properties on that object—without needing to cast it to a particular type first. This is particularly useful when interacting with a COM component, as you don't know its type and cannot cast an object instance to one. Essentially, a variable's type is resolved at runtime, as opposed to the var keyword that resolves a variable's type at compile time—a concept known as late binding.

■ **Note** To use the dynamic keyword, you first need to reference the Microsoft.CSharp.dll assembly in your project.

Putting it all together now, let's create a new instance of a Word application (which has a progID of Word.Application):

```
using (dynamic word = AutomationFactory.CreateObject("Word.Application"))
{
    // Put code to interact with Word here
}
```

■ **Note** As a general rule, you should use a using block as demonstrated in the preceding example, to ensure that the instance is disposed of properly once you are finished interacting with it.

Obtaining an existing instance of Word is almost identical to the previous example; simply replace the CreateObject method with GetObject instead:

```
using (dynamic word = AutomationFactory.GetObject("Word.Application"))
{
    // Put code to interact with Word here
}
```

■ **Note** Attempting to obtain an existing instance of a COM object using the GetObject method will raise a generic Exception exception if no instance is currently running, stating that it failed to get an object instance for the specified progID.

One of the downsides of defining a variable as a dynamic type is that you don't get any help from IntelliSense in the Visual Studio code editor. Therefore, it may be worth writing the code somewhere where you do, such as creating an application using the full .NET Framework and the Visual Studio Tools for Office to write the initial code and then translating it to run in Silverlight instead, making the code-writing process much easier and involving less trial and error.

Determining Whether a COM Component Is Available

There's no way to tell if a COM component is registered on the system without attempting to create or get an instance of the component. For example, you may want to interact with Word, but the users may not have Word installed on their machines or may not have the right version of Word.

When attempting to create or get an instance of a COM component, a generic Exception exception will be raised, stating that no object was found registered with the specified progID. Therefore, always wrap your calls to COM components in a try . . . catch block, as there's no guarantee that the COM component will actually be available on the users' machines.

Using the Windows Script Host Object

The Windows Script Host is a COM component built into Windows that is generally used to script and automate administrative tasks. It contains a number of COM objects that you can use to perform tasks, such as running applications, reading from and writing to the registry, and creating shortcuts to name a few.

For example, you can launch an application using the Run method of the WScript.Shell COM object. The following code demonstrates launching the Windows Calculator application:

```
using (dynamic shell = AutomationFactory.CreateObject("WScript.Shell"))
{
    shell.Run("calc.exe");
}
```

■ **Note** A full breakdown of the variety of tasks you can perform with the Windows Script Host component can be found in the MSDN article at http://msdn.microsoft.com/en-us/library/9y04zt1a.aspx.

Reading and Writing Files

A complete range of file system access functions are available via the Scripting.FileSystemObject COM component built into Windows, including functionality that isn't provided to you by the Silverlight run-time. For example, the following code demonstrates enumerating all the drives on the host machine and displaying the list in a message box:

```
using (dynamic fso = AutomationFactory.CreateObject("Scripting.FileSystemObject"))
{
    StringBuilder driveInfo = new StringBuilder();

    foreach (dynamic drive in fso.Drives)
    {
        driveInfo.AppendLine("Drive path: " + drive.Path);
    }

    MessageBox.Show(driveInfo.ToString());
}
```

■ **Note** More information on how to use the FileSystemObject component can be found in the MSDN article at http://msdn.microsoft.com/en-us/library/6kxy1a51.aspx.

Automating Office Applications

As discussed earlier, you can automate Word by creating or obtaining an instance of it using its progID of Word.Application. The following example demonstrates creating a new instance of Word, adding a document, and inserting some text into it:

```
using (dynamic word = AutomationFactory.CreateObject("Word.Application"))
{
    dynamic document = word.Documents.Add();
    document.Content = "This was inserted by Silverlight";
    word.Visible = true;
}
```

You can automate Excel in a very similar fashion, by creating or obtaining an instance of it using its progID of Excel.Application. The following example demonstrates creating a new instance of Excel, adding a worksheet, and inserting some text into its first cell:

```
using (dynamic excel = AutomationFactory.CreateObject("Excel.Application"))
{
    dynamic workbook = excel.Workbooks.Add();
    dynamic cell = workbook.ActiveSheet.Cells[1, 1];
    cell.Value = "This was inserted by Silverlight";
    excel.Visible = true;
}
```

Integrating with the Office applications is one of the more common uses that you will have for COM in your Silverlight business applications. This will allow the users to extract data from the system and manipulate it for their own uses, such as producing reports and letters in Word and charts in Excel.

■ **Note** When automating the Office applications, always remember to set their Visible property to true, as demonstrated, because they are hidden by default until you do so.

Handling COM Events

You can handle events raised by COM components using the GetEvent method of the AutomationFactory class. You pass the object and the name of the event to handle to this method, and it will return an AutomationEvent object, whose EventRaised event will be raised in turn when the COM object's event is raised.

For example, following on from the previous example of opening Excel and creating a new workbook, you could handle the BeforeClose event of the Workbook object returned from the excel.Workbooks.Add method, like so:

```
AutomationEvent beforeClosingEvent =
    AutomationFactory.GetEvent(workbook, "BeforeClose");

beforeClosingEvent.EventRaised += (s1, e1) =>
    {
        System.Diagnostics.Debug.WriteLine("The workbook is closing!");
    };
```

This will write a line to the output window in Visual Studio when the workbook is about to be closed in Excel.

Communicating with Local Databases

As discussed earlier in this chapter, there's no built-in client-side database that can be used by Silverlight to store data locally on the user's machine. However, COM automation enables you to read and write data to an existing database on the user's machine. For example, the following code demonstrates reading data from a local SQL Server database using ADO:

```
using (dynamic connection = AutomationFactory.CreateObject("ADODB.Connection"))
{
    using (dynamic rs = AutomationFactory.CreateObject("ADODB.RecordSet"))
    {

        string connectionString = @"Provider=SQLNCLI10.1;Data Source=.\SQL2008;" +
                            "Database=AdventureWorks;Integrated Security=SSPI";
        connection.Open(connectionString);

        rs.Open("SELECT TOP 5 ProductID, Name FROM Production.Product", connection);

        while (!rs.EOF)
        {
            int productID = (int)rs.Fields.Item("ProductID").Value;
            string name = rs.Fields.Item("Name").Value;

            // Write out the data to Visual Studio's Output window
            System.Diagnostics.Debug.WriteLine("{0} - {1}", productID, name);
            rs.MoveNext();
        }

        rs.Close();
    }

    connection.Close();
}
```

And the following code demonstrates inserting a row into the database:

```
using (dynamic connection = AutomationFactory.CreateObject("ADODB.Connection"))
{
    using (dynamic command = AutomationFactory.CreateObject("ADODB.Command"))
    {
        string connectionString = @"Provider=SQLNCLI10.1;Data Source=.\SQL2008;" +
                            "Database=AdventureWorks;Integrated Security=SSPI";
        connection.Open(connectionString);
        command.ActiveConnection = connection;
        command.CommandText = "INSERT INTO ErrorLog(ErrorTime, UserName, " +
            "ErrorNumber, ErrorSeverity, ErrorState, ErrorProcedure, ErrorLine, " +
            "ErrorMessage)" +
            "VALUES (GETDATE(), 'UserName', 0, 0, 0, 'None', 0, 'Test Insert!')";
    }

    connection.Close();
}
```

Accessing Local Hardware Devices

Silverlight 4 introduced support for accessing the webcam, microphone, and printer attached to the user's machine, but what if you have other hardware devices attached locally? If these hardware devices are accessible via a COM component, accessing them is entirely possible. Windows also provides a generic automation layer for some device types that you can take advantage of to gain access to devices. For example, Windows includes an automation layer that enables access to the Windows Image Acquisition (WIA) platform, which provides access to imaging hardware such as cameras and scanners. Features of its associated COM component include enabling you to enumerate the connected cameras and scanners, take pictures, and scan images.

For example, the following code demonstrates displaying the Acquire Image dialog and saving the acquired image to the user's Pictures folder:

```
using (dynamic acquireDialog = AutomationFactory.CreateObject("WIA.CommonDialog"))
{
    dynamic image = acquireDialog.ShowAcquireImage();

    if (image != null)
    {
        string path =
            Environment.GetFolderPath(Environment.SpecialFolder.MyPictures);

        image.SaveFile(Path.Combine(path, "ScannedImage.jpg"));
    }
}
```

■ **Note** You can get more information about the WIA automation layer from the MSDN article at http://msdn.microsoft.com/en-us/library/ms630827.aspx.

Creating and Installing Your Own COM Component

The built-in COM components demonstrated in the preceding sections provide a wide array of additional functionality that you can access from your Silverlight application, but you can also create your own COM component, providing further native functionality, and have that downloaded and registered by your application if the available Windows privileges allow it (or have it preinstalled by an administrator).

You can expose classes from projects targeting the full .NET Framework by making their corresponding assemblies COM-visible. Doing so enables you to implement features not possible in Silverlight and make them available to Silverlight applications. An excellent article written by Elton Saulsberry on doing so is published here: www.codeproject.com/KB/silverlight/Silverlight4COM.aspx.

The downsides of this particular method is that it requires the user to have the full .NET Framework installed on their machine, in which case the application may as well have been completely implemented in WPF. Alternatively, you may wish to develop the component using Visual C++ and ATL to avoid this requirement. You can find an old (but helpful) article written by C. Lung in 1999 on doing so at www.codeguru.com/cpp/com-tech/atl/tutorials/article.php/c17.

P/Invoke

Platform Invoke, better known as P/Invoke, provides a means for calling functions in the Win32 API and other unmanaged DLLs that export functions. This feature, introduced with Silverlight 5, is applicable only to Silverlight applications running under Windows, and it essentially provides a way to access functionality under Windows that's not available via COM. You can now access the full Windows API and potentially access hardware that you cannot access via any other means.

The following example demonstrates how you can use P/Invoke to get the user name and computer name and display them in a message box:

1. Add the following using statements to the top of a code-behind file:

```
using System.Runtime.InteropServices;
using System.Text;
```

2. Within the class (but not within a method), declare the following external methods:

```
[DllImport("Kernel32")]
public static extern bool GetComputerName(StringBuilder buffer, ref int size);

[DllImport("Advapi32.dll")]
private static extern bool GetUserName(StringBuilder buffer, ref int Size);
```

3. Now, you can call these methods. For example, add the following code to the Click event handler of a Button control, passing in a StringBuilder object with a predefined capacity that will be populated with the result and the size of the buffer (that is, the StringBuilder object's capacity).

```
int size = 64;
StringBuilder computerName = new StringBuilder(size);
GetComputerName(computerName, ref size);

size = 64;
StringBuilder userName = new StringBuilder(size);
GetUserName(userName, ref size);

MessageBox.Show("You are " + userName.ToString() + " on " + computerName.ToString());
```

4. Run your application. When the code is executed, it will display the name of the current user and the computer's name in the message box.

■ **Note** Making P/Invoke calls can become very complicated. To find information on the signature of various method declarations and their use, www.pinvoke.net can be a very helpful source, with information and examples for many popular P/Invoke calls. Alexandra Rusina, a member of the Silverlight team at Microsoft, has some advanced examples of using P/Invoke in Silverlight 5 on her blog at http://blogs.msdn.com/b/silverlight_sdk/archive/2011/09/27/pinvoke-in-silverlight5-and-net-framework.aspx.

Creating Additional OOB Windows

Since Silverlight 3, we've had the ability to run Silverlight applications in a window, outside the browser. However, the applications have been limited to operating in just that one window. However, Silverlight 5 lifts this restriction and enables you to create additional windows when your application is running outside the browser with elevated trust.

■ **Note** You cannot create windows in this manner when your Silverlight application is running inside the browser, even if it has elevated trust privileges.

Unlike WPF, you can't create a window using an item template. Instead, like the `NotificationWindow` class for toast notifications, you need to create an instance of the `Window` class and assign content to its `Content` property. Your best option is to create a user control containing the window's contents. Let's say you have a user control named `MyWindowContents`. To open a new window with this user control as its contents, use the following code:

```
Window window = new Window();
window.Content = new MyWindowContents();
window.Title = "My Window";
window.Width = 640;
window.Height = 480;
window.Show();
```

As you can see, you simply need to create a `Window` object, set its content and title, set its width and height, and then show it.

You can also set the state of the window: `WindowState.Normal`, `WindowState.Minimized`, or `WindowState.Maximized`, for example:

```
window.WindowState = WindowState.Maximized;
```

For windows whose window state is set to normal, the window will be positioned randomly on the screen, unless you set its `Top` and `Left` properties before you show it:

```
window.Top = 300;
window.Left = 700;
```

These windows can have custom chrome, just like the main window. Simply set their `WindowStyle` property to `WindowStyle.SingleBorderWindow`, `WindowStyle.None`, or `WindowStyle.BorderlessRoundCornersWindow`, for example:

```
window.WindowStyle = WindowStyle.BorderlessRoundCornersWindow;
```

You can enumerate all the open windows using the `Application.Current.Windows` collection.

■ **Note** If you close the main window, the other windows that it spawned will be closed too.

Custom Chrome

When your application is running in OOB mode it will have the standard window chrome as determined by your operating system's display theme. However, this standard chrome can look quite out of place in comparison to the design of your application's user interface, and it would be nice to be able to implement your own custom chrome that is more integrated with your application's design instead. This is possible when the application has elevated trust permissions.

When your application is configured to run with elevated trust, you can select the Window Style option that you want to use from the Out-Of-Browser Settings window (shown in Figure 16-2). The default option is Default, where your application is contained within the standard window chrome, as shown in Figure 16-15, but the other options available include No Border and Borderless Round Corners.

With the default chrome, a very basic Silverlight application running out of browser might look like the example shown in Figure 16-14.

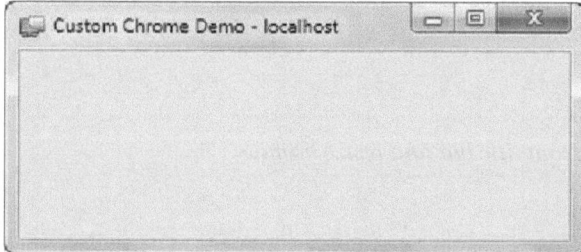

Figure 16-15. An OOB application window with the default window chrome

By setting the Window Style option to No Border, you will get the output shown in Figure 16-16.

Figure 16-16 An OOB application window with no chrome

This is a very square window shape, whereas most windows these days have rounded corners. You can implement a borderless window with rounded corners by setting the Window Style option to Borderless Round Corners. This will give you the output shown in Figure 16-17.

Figure 16-17. An OOB application window with no chrome and rounded corners

One of the issues that you will find when turning on custom chrome is that your application will not only have no border but will have no title bar either. This means that the user can't move the application around the screen, minimize or maximize it, close it, or resize it. You will now have to implement each of these features manually.

Minimizing and maximizing your application's window (setting its state) is easy, as is closing it. Similarly, the ability to move and resize the window is also surprisingly easy to implement. Let's implement a custom title bar that enables the user to move the window around the screen and a resize handle to enable the user to resize the window, as shown in Figure 16-18.

Figure 16-18. An OOB application window with a custom title bar and resize handle

Moving the Window

To enable the window to be moved, let's create a custom title bar using the following XAML:

```
<Rectangle Name="TitleBar" Height="15" Fill="#D8727272" VerticalAlignment="Top"
        MouseLeftButtonDown="TitleBar_MouseLeftButtonDown" />
```

Note that you are handling the MouseLeftButtonDown event on the Rectangle. You will use this event to initiate the window move, as per the following code:

```
private void TitleBar_MouseLeftButtonDown(object sender, MouseButtonEventArgs e)
{
    Application.Current.MainWindow.DragMove();
}
```

That's all there is to it. The DragMove method on the window will tell the window to move based on the position of the mouse, relative to its current position, and it will automatically continue to do so until the left mouse button is released.

Resizing the Window

To enable the window to be resized, let's create a handle that will appear in the bottom-right corner of the window that the user can click and drag to resize it, using the following XAML:

```
<Path Name="ResizeGlyph" Data="M20,0 L20,20 L0,20 z" Fill="#D8727272"
      Grid.Row="2" HorizontalAlignment="Right" VerticalAlignment="Bottom"
      Height="20" Width="20" Cursor="SizeNWSE"
      MouseLeftButtonDown="ResizeGlyph_MouseLeftButtonDown" />
```

Note that you are handling the MouseLeftButtonDown event of the Path. You will use this event to initiate the window resizing, as follows:

```
private void ResizeGlyph_MouseLeftButtonDown(object sender, MouseButtonEventArgs e)
{
    Application.Current.MainWindow.DragResize(WindowResizeEdge.BottomRight);
}
```

This works in exactly the same way as moving the window, where the DragResize method on the window will tell the window to resize based on the position of the mouse, relative to its current position, and it will automatically continue to do so until the left mouse button is released. Note that you need to provide what edge of the window the user is resizing to the DragResize method as a parameter, so that the resizing can be handled accordingly.

Other Restrictions Lifted by Elevated Trust

Running with elevated trust lifts a number of other restrictions imposed by the sandbox, including the following:

- When attempting to communicate with a server that isn't the site of origin for the application (that is, communicating cross-domain), you no longer require a cross-domain policy file to be located in the root of that server in order to do so (detailed in Chapter 8).

- Attempting to communicate with a server via sockets no longer requires a cross-domain policy file. Also, the application is not limited to only communicating over ports within the range 4502–4534 (detailed in Chapter 8).

- As described earlier, most keyboard input was disabled while the application was in full-screen mode. This will no longer be the case.

- Consent messages will no longer be displayed when the application attempts to access the clipboard, switch to full-screen mode, and so on. However, the user will have to provide permission for the application to access the video and audio streams.

- Copying to and pasting from the clipboard, displaying open and save file dialogs, and initiating full-screen mode no longer need to be user-initiated actions.

Restrictions Imposed by Elevated Trust

Although elevated trust lifts a number of the restrictions placed on Silverlight applications, having elevated trust does impose one restriction on the application that is not placed on standard OOB applications. Earlier in this chapter, we discussed having your OOB Silverlight application check the server for an update, download it, and automatically apply it the update the next time it is started. However, this poses a potential security risk to machines if the application has elevated trust permissions, simply because of the additional access to the user's machine granted to the application. A rogue application update could potentially be put in place that is designed to harm the user's machine. With the application having elevated trust, it could potentially do so.

Therefore, Silverlight applications having elevated trust can automatically update only if the application is signed. This confirms that the update is sourced from the original application developer and should therefore be safe to install. When the update has been downloaded, Silverlight will check that the signature of the original application matches that of the update and will only install the update if they do.

Rather confusingly, however, Silverlight applications with elevated trust *will* update if sourced from localhost, even if they aren't signed. This feature was implemented to make testing easier in a development environment but can lead to frustration when developers deploy their applications to a production environment and find out that it won't update (and don't know why).

Therefore, Silverlight applications with elevated trust should always be signed. Application signing is discussed in Chapter 17.

Enabling/Disabling Elevated Trust Applications with a Windows Group Policy

System administrators may want to install the Silverlight runtime but not permit Silverlight applications that request elevated trust permissions to be installed on the machine. This can be implemented via a Windows group policy setting, as detailed here:

```
www.microsoft.com/GetSilverlight/resources/documentation/grouppolicysettings
.aspx#TrustedApplications
```

Summary

Silverlight provides a number of ways to interact with the host operating system, providing read and write access to isolated storage, files, and the clipboard; installing on the machine and running in a similar fashion to a standard, native application, and even breaking out of its sandbox to run with elevated trust permissions.

By enabling Silverlight applications to break out of the sandbox, particularly with COM support, a wide range of new possibilities is opened up to applications. These possibilities narrow the gap between what is and isn't possible to achieve in Silverlight and WPF and enable Silverlight to be considered for a wider range of development projects.

CHAPTER 17

Application Deployment

After you have developed your application in Silverlight, you then need to ensure that you deliver it in an effective manner to your users. One of Silverlight's advantages is that it makes it very easy to install and run applications on your end-user's computer. All that the user needs is a browser and a web connection. With just those two things you can have a "clean" PC up and running with a Silverlight application in a matter of minutes, with both the Silverlight runtime and the application deployed to the user's machine automatically (with their permission), and with no machine restarts necessary.

As we all know, first impressions are important. The first impression that the user will have of your application is waiting for it to download, and very possibly requiring the installation of Silverlight itself. Therefore, you need to ensure that they have the best experience possible, as their experience here can greatly shape their opinion and acceptance of the application.

This chapter will take you through how to deploy your Silverlight applications to both the server and the clients, and we will also take a look at how you can improve on the default installation experience to help entice users to make the leap and install Silverlight in order to run your application.

Deploying the Application to the Server

Depending on the nature of your Silverlight application, it might simply involve a client component (the Silverlight application itself), or it could include both server and client components (both a Silverlight application running on the client, and services running on the server). Both the server and the client components are deployed to the server, and it's the server that then deploys the client components to the clients.

To deploy a Silverlight application to the server, you actually deploy the Web project, as it contains both the server and the client components. The process is essentially identical to deploying a traditional ASP.NET web application/web site to a server.

You have the following three primary options of deploying your application to the server:

- Simply copy the files to the server and configure the web server manually.
- Use Visual Studio's built-in publishing functionality.
- Create a setup program.

We'll take a look at these methods shortly, but let's first discuss the requirements for the server.

Server Requirements

As a general rule, Silverlight applications are downloaded from a server, and therefore, the server must be able to serve up the application to the client via web server software. In addition, depending on the various needs of your Silverlight application, the application could place additional demands on the server to serve it up data. Let's look at the requirements that your Silverlight application might place on the server, and what it needs installed to meet these needs.

Server Operating System and Web Server

One of the things that many people do not realize is that you *do not* need a Windows-based server, running Internet Information Services (IIS), to host your Silverlight application. Silverlight is a client-based technology, and hence, is executed on the client, not the server. Therefore, Silverlight applications simply need to be downloadable from a server, and will be run entirely by the Silverlight runtime on the client, requiring no special handling on the host server. This means that you could potentially host a Silverlight application on a Linux box running an Apache HTTP Server or Apache Tomcat server, or even on cloud-based platforms such as Windows Azure. Essentially, any web server that can serve files over HTTP can be used to deploy Silverlight applications.

That said, Silverlight applications that need to communicate with ASP.NET-based services on the server, such as RIA Services, will obviously require those services to be hosted by a Windows-based server running IIS. However, the Silverlight application still does not place any requirements on the server.

■ **Note** If you don't have custom web services accompanying your Silverlight business application, but use existing services hosted elsewhere, such as on Windows Azure, the application does not need to be deployed from a Windows-based server.

RIA Services

As a core focus of this book has been around creating end-to-end business applications that make use of RIA Services, we will assume here that you are also deploying these services as a part of your server deployment. Hence, the server must adhere to the following rules:

- It must be a Windows-based server.
- It must be running IIS.
- It must have the .NET Framework 4 installed (full profile).

Installing RIA Services Assemblies to the GAC

You can choose to deploy RIA Services to the Global Assembly Cache (GAC) so that it's accessible to all web applications, or you can distribute these as a part of your deployment. By default, the RIA Services assemblies referenced by your Web project are not copied to your Bin folder, and hence, are not deployed with your application when you publish your web site to the server.

To deploy RIA Services to the GAC, start by downloading the RIA Services installer from www.silverlight.net/learn/advanced-techniques/wcf-ria-services/get-started-with-wcf-ria-services. If you tried running this installer, you will probably find that it complains about requiring both Visual Studio 2010 and Silverlight to be installed on the machine, neither of which the server will generally have. However, you can type the following line at the command prompt to perform a server install, which will install only the components required by a server:

```
msiexec /i RIAServices.msi SERVER=true
```

Installing RIA Services Assemblies to the Bin Directory

On a hosted server, you most likely will not be able to deploy the RIA Services assemblies to the GAC, but you can deploy the RIA Services assemblies required by your application along with it to its Bin directory. Simply select all the assemblies starting with System.ServiceModel.DomainServices in the Solution Explorer window for your Web project, and set their "Copy Local" property (in the Properties window) to True. They will be copied into the Bin directory in your project, and deployed when you publish the Web project to the server.

▪ **Note** If you encounter RIA Services–related issues when attempting to run your Silverlight application, Saurabh Pant, a member of the RIA Services team, has a detailed blog post on troubleshooting these, which should be your first port of call. You can access it at http://blogs.msdn.com/b/saurabh/archive/2010/03/16/ria-services-application-deployment.aspx.

Cross-Domain Policy File

If your services are deployed to a different location from where your Silverlight application will be downloaded from, you will need to place a cross-domain policy file in the *root* of the web site containing the services in order for the Silverlight application to be permitted to access them. See Chapter 5 for more information on the required contents of this file and where it needs to be placed on the server.

Using Xcopy

The most primitive means of deploying your application to a server is by copying the required files to the required location (a process often referred to as xcopy, from the old DOS command), and configuring an application in IIS to point to the folder that these files were copied to.

Copy all the noncode-related files from the Web project—the HTML file hosting the Silverlight plug-in, any JavaScript files, the web.config file, the ClientBin folder, the Bin folder, and so on—to a folder on the server. This may be a new folder, or you can add to/update a folder containing an existing web site.

▪ **Note** The quickest way to determine what files must be copied to the server is to publish your project to a folder on your local hard drive (using the procedure detailed in the next section), and then copy all the contents of that folder to your server. When doing this, ensure that the "Items to deploy" option in the Package/Publish Web tab in the project properties has been set to "Only files required to run this application."

If you are creating a new web site, you need to configure an "application" in IIS. How you go about doing so will largely depend on the version of IIS that it will be running under, and the type of user interface available to you—that is, either the Internet Information Services Manager or a web-based user interface. Therefore, we will not go through a step-by-step process for this in detail, but it follows the same process as for configuring an ASP.NET 4 web site. A guide for creating an application in IIS 7 can be found at http://technet.microsoft.com/en-us/library/cc772042.aspx.

⚙ Workshop: Publishing from Visual Studio

Visual Studio 2010 provides a feature enabling you to publish a web site in a myriad of ways to a server—both local and remote. Depending on the settings you are using, publishing a web site using Visual Studio will both copy the required files to a server and create the application for you in IIS if it's not already configured. This feature makes it easy to deploy your project from right within Visual Studio.

1. Start by right-clicking on your Web project in the Solution Explorer window, and select the "Package/Publish Settings" item from the context menu. This will open the Package/Publish Web tab in the project properties, and enable you to configure what will be deployed to the server as a part of the publishing process, and where on the server it will be published.

2. After you have configured the settings appropriately, right-click on the Web project in the Solution Explorer window again, and select the Publish item from the context menu. This will display the Publish Web dialog shown in Figure 17-1.

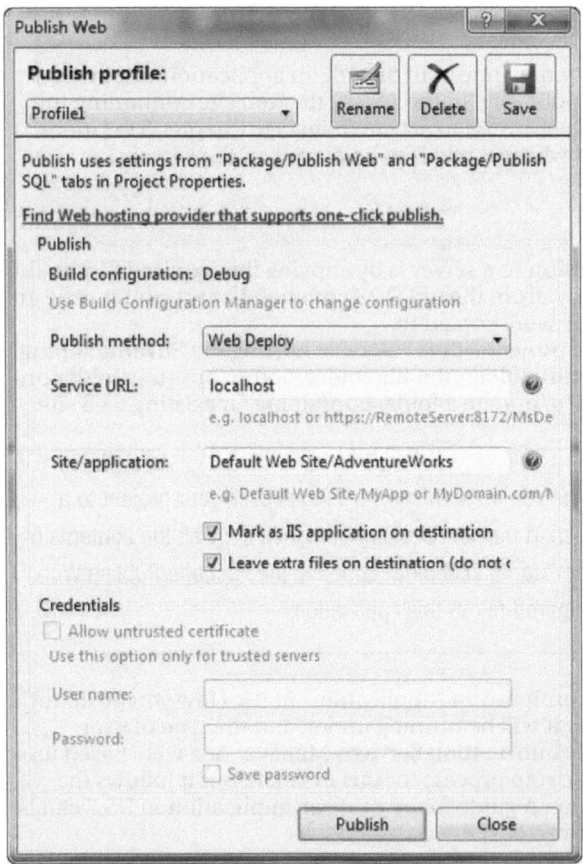

Figure 17-1. The Publish Web dialog

3. Using this dialog, configure how you want to publish your web site, and click the Publish button to start the publishing process. It will copy the files used in your Web project (that will include your Silverlight application), and will create the application in IIS if you have selected the "Mark as IIS application on destination" option in the Publish Web dialog.

■ **Note** You can publish your project to the file system, and then xcopy these files to the server if required.

Workshop: Creating a Web Package

Instead of publishing the web site directly to the server, you can instead create a web package, which is essentially a .zip file containing your web site and configuration files dictating how the web site should be created under IIS on the server. You can then take this package and import it into IIS either using the Internet Information Services Manager or via the command line using the msdeploy tool.

■ **Note** You can get more information about the msdeploy tool from `http://blogs.iis.net/msdeploy/default.aspx`.

To create a package, follow these steps:

1. Right-click your Web project in the Solution Explorer window, and select the "Build Deployment Package" item from the context menu. This will immediately compile the web site into a package, using the settings configured in the Package/Publish Web tab in the project properties for the Web project.

2. Open up the Internet Information Services Manager and import the package. This will install the files on the server, and create the application in IIS. Alternatively, if you want to import the package via the command line, you can find instructions on doing so in a text file created in the same folder as the package.

Workshop: Creating a Setup Program

If your application is to be a packaged product sold to companies who then install it on their own server, the best way to provide it to your customers to install it is as a setup program.

1. Add a new project to your solution, and use the Web Setup Project template. (You will find this under the Other Project Types ➤ Setup and Deployment ➤ Visual Studio Installer category.)

2. In the Solution Explorer window, right-click the setup project, and select Add ➤ Project Output.

3. When the dialog that appears, select the Web project from the Project drop-down, and select both the "Primary Output" and the "Content Files" outputs from the list. Click OK.

4. Select the setup project in the Solution Explorer window again, then go to the Properties window and assign values to the properties, as you require. After you are done, you can compile the project.

You can test the setup program locally by compiling your project and then right-clicking on the setup project in the Solution Explorer window and selecting the Install item from the context menu.

Deploying the Application to the Client

One of the great features of Silverlight is that you can go from a "clean PC" (a machine without Silverlight installed or the application downloaded) to being up and running with the application in a matter of minutes. This makes Silverlight a very effective means of deploying applications to client machines. By default, the HTML page that hosts the Silverlight plug-in notifies the user if they don't have Silverlight installed, and points them to a link where they can download the Silverlight runtime and install it. After the Silverlight runtime is installed, the HTML page will be automatically refreshed and the download of the application will begin, running it after the download is complete.

As you can see, deploying a Silverlight application to the client is a two-step process. The process involves the following:

- Downloading and installing the Silverlight runtime if it's not already installed

- Downloading the application if it's not already downloaded or is not up to date

Let's take a closer look at how this process works, how to customize it to create a more streamlined user experience, and other methods you could use to deploy the Silverlight runtime and your application to the users.

The Default Silverlight Installation Process

Let's start by taking a look at what happens when the user attempts to run your Silverlight application but doesn't have Silverlight installed. Let's assume that no version of Silverlight is currently installed on the user's machine, and that they have navigated to the URL for your application. The user will be presented with a blank page, containing the image shown in Figure 17-2.

Figure 17-2. The default image displayed in the browser when Silverlight is not installed

If you view the source of the HTML page that's used in your application to host the Silverlight plug-in (detailed in Chapter 1), you will find the following lines of HTML in its body:

```
<object data="data:application/x-silverlight-2," type="application/x-silverlight-2"
        width="100%" height="100%">
    <param name="source" value="ClientBin/AdventureWorks.xap"/>
    <param name="onError" value="onSilverlightError" />
    <param name="background" value="white" />
    <param name="minRuntimeVersion" value="5.0.61118.0" />
    <param name="autoUpgrade" value="true" />
    <a href="http://go.microsoft.com/fwlink/?LinkID=149156&v=5.0.61118.0"
                                        style="text-decoration:none">
        <img src="http://go.microsoft.com/fwlink/?LinkId=161376"
            alt="Get Microsoft Silverlight" style="border-style:none"/>
    </a>
</object>
```

If the browser does not know what the object is supposed to be because the Silverlight plug-in hasn't been installed, it will ignore the object tag and simply display the content between the opening and closing object tags instead. The default HTML between the tags (in bold) simply displays the image you see in Figure 17-2, and when it is clicked, it will download the Silverlight plug-in from the Microsoft web site.

■ **Note** We'll look at improving this default Silverlight installation experience to make it somewhat friendlier and more enticing by swapping out this default "install Silverlight" HTML with your own content later in this chapter.

You will also note the following line in the head section of the HTML file:

```
<script type="text/javascript" src="Silverlight.js"></script>
```

This script file contains a number of helper functions, including one that automatically reloads the page when it recognizes that the Silverlight plug-in is installed, and various additional functions that enable you to create a Silverlight object in a web page via JavaScript.

After the Silverlight runtime has been installed, the page will be automatically refreshed, and the application will begin to download from the server (and be displayed after the download is complete).

■ **Note** If an earlier version of Silverlight has been installed on the user's machine but your application is targeting a more recent version, the new version will be downloaded and installed automatically. However, the user will have to restart their browser. The Silverlight plug-in is backward compatible, meaning that any Silverlight application written in a previous version of Silverlight will run without issues in a more recent version of the plug-in. Additional Silverlight versioning information can be found at http://msdn.microsoft.com/en-us/library/cc265156.aspx.

Customizing the Silverlight Installation Experience

You saw in the previous section how easy it was to get set up and running with Silverlight on a clean PC. However, despite the ease with which you can deploy your applications using Silverlight, the default experience isn't particularly ideal. Let's take a look at why you should customize the Silverlight installation experience, and how you can do so.

Why You Should Customize the Silverlight Installation Experience

When a user navigates to your application, the last thing they want is something blocking their way, like the installation of a plug-in. Depending on their level of commitment to running your application, it opens up a barrier for the user, providing a decision point that may lead to them deciding to abandon the attempt and turn away. You really want to avoid this possibility at all costs.

■ **Note** This is not such an issue with standard business applications that are running in corporate environments. The IT department will have bought into Silverlight as the technology running one or more of their applications, they will likely automatically deploy the Silverlight runtime to users' PCs, and the use of the application will have been mandated by the company management. However, there are many other scenarios in which this issue should be considered. If you are providing your application as software as a service (SAAS) or a packaged product, this will be an issue. Alternatively, if you have users working from home, it's important that you provide a low-friction install experience for getting them up and running with your application.

Unfortunately, the default "Silverlight requires installation" experience does nothing to help the issue of getting user buy-in. The simple image and link, shown previously in Figure 17-2, fails at the following points:

- It tells the user nothing about
    - Your application or your business
    - Why your application needs Silverlight
    - Why they should install Silverlight
    - What value installing Silverlight provides
    - Instructions for timid users to walk them through how to complete the installation
- It does not
    - Provide any preview that demonstrates what the user will get on the other side of the installation process
    - Attempt to engage and entice the user by explaining why it's worth going through the process of installing Silverlight to run your application
    - Maintain consistency with the rest of your web site or the Silverlight application, and by not providing any visual consistency, its appearance will be jarring to the user, thus leading to a suboptimal user experience

- Make any attempt to ease any fears that the user might have

- It does not provide any background information on Silverlight, such as

  - A link to the Microsoft Silverlight site

  - What it will (or will not) do to the user's computer

  - What Silverlight is

  - Whether Silverlight can be easily uninstalled

  - How many major web sites use Silverlight, and how the user will now gain access to these sites as well

  - Why the plug-in can be trusted, apart from the Microsoft logo. For all the user knows, this could be an advertisement designed to trick them into installing something malicious, or that they don't need or want.

  - Why the user might not be able to install Silverlight on their machine. For example, they might be running an unsupported operating system or browser. In addition, that the user will need administrative rights on their machine to be allowed to complete the installation.

You should personalize the installation experience, tailoring it to your business and the application, and entice the user to work through the minor impediment of not having Silverlight in order to run your application. Ideally, if you had a designer work on the design of your application, you should also have them design the Silverlight installation and application deployment process too, to maintain consistency in all three phases: Silverlight installation, application deployment, and application execution.

It's important to think like a user, and try to identify with them and their psychology when they first use your application. There are many classes of users, including those who will

- Click on and install anything that gets them where they want to go

- Be fearful of using computers and what they install on them

- Have short attention spans and give up quickly if they come to any sort of barrier

Take these behaviors into account and design your Silverlight installation experience accordingly.

■ **Note** As the popularity of Silverlight grows, these initial installation issues will become less of a problem. However, you will still need to support users with a freshly installed operating system who will not yet have Silverlight installed. Also, with the number of Silverlight versions that have been released, it's always likely that the user will be running an older version of Silverlight than what you are targeting. As discussed in the introduction of this book, you can get a rough idea of the reach of a particular version of Silverlight at a site such as www.riastats.com. At the time of this writing, this site is reporting that a little over 75 percent of Internet-connected devices already have a version of Silverlight installed.

Seeing What the User Sees Without Silverlight Installed

The first step in customizing the Silverlight installation experience is to see what the user sees in the browser if they don't have Silverlight installed. You could always uninstall Silverlight from your machine using the operating system's uninstall application tool, such as Windows Vista/7's Programs and Features tool, but there is a simpler way: you can simply disable the Silverlight plug-in in your browser of choice. For example, in Internet Explorer go to Tools ➤ Manage Add-ons, select the Microsoft Silverlight plug-in, and then click the Disable button. Now when you navigate to the URL hosting your application, it won't be able to load the Silverlight plug-in, and thus, will enable you to test what will happen when users don't have Silverlight installed.

If you then open the Manage Add-ons dialog again and re-enable the Silverlight plug-in and close the dialog again, you will notice that within a second or two the page will be automatically refreshed and your application will be loaded. This is thanks to the Silverlight.js file that is referenced in the HTML/ASPX page hosting your application and distributed with your application. When it detects that the Silverlight plug-in isn't installed, it will continually monitor the browser for it until it is found, which will be when the user has successfully installed the Silverlight plug-in. At this point, it will automatically refresh the page in order to load your application. Therefore, all you really need to focus on is designing an effective landing page.

Implementing a Custom Landing Page

To implement a custom landing page, in the page that is hosting your Silverlight application, replace the following lines of HTML between the opening and closing object tags with your own custom HTML:

```
<a href="http://go.microsoft.com/fwlink/?LinkID=149156&v=5.0.60818.0"
                              style="text-decoration:none">
     <img src="http://go.microsoft.com/fwlink/?LinkId=161376"
        alt="Get Microsoft Silverlight" style="border-style:none"/>
</a>
```

Ideally, you would replace this HTML with some that will help address each of the issues listed in the previous section detailing why you should customize the Silverlight installation experience, but still retain the link to download the Silverlight runtime from the default HTML. Try to retain as much consistency as possible with the rest of your web site structure and style, make sure the user knows what is happening and what they need to do, and brand it with your company and/or application.

Note that if you want to provide the users with step-by-step instructions on installing Silverlight, each browser requires slightly different steps to be taken, and each displays different dialogs. Ideally, you would recognize the browser type on the server, and provide the corresponding instructions accordingly. For this purpose, you might want to host the Silverlight object in the .aspx page instead of the .html page, which would let you determine the browser type and version on the server (using the following article as a guide: http://msdn.microsoft.com/en-us/library/3yekbd5b.aspx), and output your instructions to the page, between the opening and closing object tags, accordingly.

■ **Note** It can be a good exercise to disable the Silverlight plug-in using the method described earlier and investigate how other Silverlight applications have customized their landing page to handle users that need to install Silverlight. You will note how much of a difference it can make to the Silverlight installation experience just by properly customizing this page. Good examples of custom Silverlight install experiences that are well executed include the www.silverlight.net web site and the Netflix Watch Instantly web site (www.netflix.com/BrowseGenres/Watch_Instantly/gev).

Further Customization Guidance

A great source of information regarding creating custom Silverlight installation experiences, and a must-read when creating your own, is the Silverlight Installation Experience Guidance whitepaper, which you can find a link to at www.microsoft.com/download/en/details.aspx?id=15072. This is an extremely detailed document that can be used to guide you in creating a functional and effective custom Silverlight installation experience, and also has a template (in the accompanying download) that you can use.

Pushing the Silverlight Runtime to Users in the Enterprise

One of the issues in deploying the Silverlight runtime, particularly in enterprise environments, is that the user will need to be a local administrator on their machine in order to install the Silverlight plug-in, as is the case with any plug-in. If the user doesn't already have the Silverlight runtime installed on their machine and does not have local administration rights, they won't be able to install the Silverlight plug-in.

■ **Note** It's worth clarifying that the user *does* need to be a local administrator on their machine in order to install the Silverlight *runtime/plug-in*. However, they *don't* need to be a local administrator on their machine in order to install a Silverlight *application* to run outside the browser.

The Silverlight runtime can be pushed out to users using the Microsoft Systems Management Server automated installation, or by setting up a group policy. Despite being for Silverlight 2.0, the Silverlight Enterprise Deployment whitepaper available from www.microsoft.com/silverlight/whitepapers/ is a very thorough and detailed guide for methods of deploying Silverlight in enterprise environments.

Building a Client Desktop Installer

In Chapter 16, we discuss how to install your Silverlight application to run outside the browser, in much the same way as a standard (native) desktop application. In some scenarios, you might find that web deployment of your application is not always suitable or even possible. In this case, you will need to have a more traditional setup program that can be run on the client and install the Silverlight application as an out-of-browser application. You can do this using the silent install feature of the Silverlight launcher (sllauncher.exe).

■ **Note** Unfortunately, the Silverlight runtime has not been packaged into a merge module, so it can't be included as a part of your setup program and will need to be installed separately. This method therefore assumes the client already has the Silverlight runtime installed. You can download the Silverlight runtime installer from the www.silverlight.net web site.

The sllauncher.exe application accepts various command-line parameters, which can be used to install/uninstall/run a Silverlight application.

If you type the following line on the command line:

```
"%ProgramFiles%\Microsoft Silverlight\sllauncher.exe"
```

it will display the message box shown in Figure 17-3.

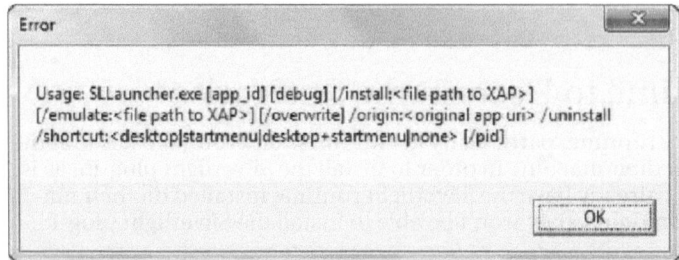

Figure 17-3. The SLLauncher command-line parameters dialog

■ **Note** These examples will work only under Windows, and you will need to change %ProgramFiles% to %ProgramFiles(x86)% when running under the 64-bit edition of Windows in this and the following examples.

This tells you what command-line parameters you can take advantage of to enable you to install the application on the machine. Of particular interest are the following options:

- /install: the path to the XAP file (required)

- /origin: the URI specifying the site-of-origin for the application (that is, where it was downloaded from). Even though the application was not downloaded from the Web, this is a required parameter and must be assigned a URI.

- /shortcut: what shortcuts should be created—start menu, desktop, both, or none (optional)

- /overwrite: when used will overwrite any existing version already installed (optional)

The following is an example of installing an application using these options:

```
"%ProgramFiles%\Microsoft Silverlight\sllauncher.exe" /install:"AdventureWorks.xap" ↵
/origin:"http://localhost/AdventureWorks.xap" /shortcut:desktop+startmenu /overwrite
```

You can take advantage of this silent install feature in your own setup programs by adding the .xap file from your Silverlight project to your setup project, and creating a custom action to extract your .xap file to a temporary location and running sllauncher.exe with the appropriate command-line parameters to install it. A full explanation of this procedure is beyond the scope of this book; however, Anoop Madhusudanan has a prebuilt NSIS script that you can use to create a setup package, which can also install the Silverlight runtime, at http://amazedsaint.blogspot.com/2010/05/how-to-create-offline-installer-no.html. Alternatively, a somewhat simpler option would be to deploy a batch file along with the application, which when executed will install the application using the method described here.

Forcing an Update of the Cached XAP File for New Versions

A common issue experienced when deploying a new version of a Silverlight application is that the new version is not always downloaded by the clients, with their browser simply loading its cached version of the application instead. Different browsers behave in different ways, complicating the issue. The generally accepted best solution is to append a query string to the URL pointing to the .xap file, and change this query string whenever a new version of the application is deployed. So in the definition of the Silverlight object in the HTML/ASPX page, we need to change the bolded line in the following HTML:

```
<object data="data:application/x-silverlight-2," type="application/x-silverlight-2"
        width="100%" height="100%">
    <param name="source" value="ClientBin/AdventureWorks.xap"/>
    <param name="onError" value="onSilverlightError" />
    <param name="background" value="white" />
    <param name="minRuntimeVersion" value="5.0.60818.0" />
    <param name="autoUpgrade" value="true" />
    <a href="http://go.microsoft.com/fwlink/?LinkID=149156&v=5.0.60818.0"
                                            style="text-decoration:none">
        <img src="http://go.microsoft.com/fwlink/?LinkId=161376"
            alt="Get Microsoft Silverlight" style="border-style:none"/>
    </a>
</object>
```

to something like:

```
<param name="source" value="ClientBin/AdventureWorks.xap?XAPDate=111125041735"/>
```

The portion in bold is a query string that we append to the .xap file's URL, containing a value generated from the date that the .xap file was last modified. When this value changes, the browser will not match it to an entry in its cache, so it will go back to the server and get the latest version of the .xap file. To generate this query string automatically, you'll need to use the ASPX page instead of the HTML page to host the Silverlight object. Doing so will allow you to write some server-side code into the page, which will run each time the page is requested from the server, and append a dynamically generated query string to the .xap file's URL. Replace the source param line to the code in bold in the following example:

```
<object data="data:application/x-silverlight-2," type="application/x-silverlight-2"
        width="100%" height="100%">
    <%
    string source = @"ClientBin/AdventureWorks.xap";

    string xapFullPath = HttpContext.Current.Server.MapPath(@"") + @"\" + source;
    DateTime xapDate = System.IO.File.GetLastWriteTime(xapFullPath);
    source += "?XAPDate=" + xapDate.ToString("yyMMddHHmmss");

    string paramLine = "<param name=\"source\" value=\"" + source + "\"/>";
    Response.Write(paramLine);
    %>
    <param name="onError" value="onSilverlightError" />
    <param name="background" value="white" />
    <param name="minRuntimeVersion" value="5.0.60818.0" />
    <param name="autoUpgrade" value="true" />
    <a href="http://go.microsoft.com/fwlink/?LinkID=149156&v=5.0.60818.0"
                                            style="text-decoration:none">
        <img src="http://go.microsoft.com/fwlink/?LinkId=161376"
```

```
                     alt="Get Microsoft Silverlight" style="border-style:none"/>
    </a>
</object>
```

Now, the URL to the .xap file will change each time the application is updated, which will result in the clients redownloading the application from the server again, and resolving your caching issues.

Improving on the Default Application Loading Screen

After improving the Silverlight installation experience, the next step is to improve the experience for your users while your Silverlight application is being downloaded from the server. You are no doubt familiar with the blue spinning balls animation that is displayed while your application is being downloaded, as shown in Figure 17-4, which provides a generic indicator that something is currently happening. If after half a second the application is still downloading, Silverlight will automatically display this default loading animation until the application has finished downloading.

Figure 17-4. The default "Downloading Application" animation

However, as with the default Silverlight installation experience, this simple wait indicator with no associated branding or personalization is not an ideal user experience. Instead, you should replace this animation with your own custom one, commonly referred to as either a preloader or a splash screen.

An application preloader is essentially a XAML page that is requested from the server by the Silverlight plug-in prior to the application itself. Designed to be very small (much smaller than the application), it will be downloaded first and be displayed while the main application continues to download. Whereas the main application will be compiled and compressed into an .xap file, the preloader is not a part of the Silverlight project. Instead, it is a standalone XAML file added to your Web project, and is, therefore, not compiled into an .xap file. This also means that you can't write any code-behind against the CLR; however, you can make use of the JavaScript API (as was used back in Silverlight 1.0) to control the user interface, which can be written in a .js file and downloaded along with the XAML file.

In the following workshops, we're going to create and test a simple application preloader. Figure 17-5 demonstrates what the preloader you will be creating will look like.

Figure 17-5. The custom preloader

As you can see, it displays an image with the company logo, tells the user what it's doing, and displays a progress bar and the progress as a percentage.

⚙️ Workshop: Creating the Application Preloader Files

In this workshop, we'll create the files required for the simple application preloader, and get them to a point where the project compiles, although the preloader will be blank.

■ **Note** Follow through these instructions step by step, without jumping around, trying to compile, and so on. This is very important. Unfortunately, the process isn't particularly straightforward, and not going through each step in order, one at a time, is likely to lead to confusion and frustration.

---

1. Start by adding a new item to your Web project, using the Silverlight 1.0 JScript Page item template (found in the Silverlight category), and name it `AppPreloader.xaml`. This template will actually create two files: a XAML file with the name you specified in the Add New Item window, and a JavaScript file with the same name as the XAML file but with a `.js` extension.

2. After the file has been created and opened, you'll note that there is no XAML designer support. However, if you close the file and open it again, the designer will appear but will display an error due to it not supporting the referenced default namespace used by Silverlight 1.0.

3. Delete the contents of both the XAML file and the JavaScript file, as it's just the files you need, not their contents. You will be using a different default namespace than that used in the XAML file created for us, and trying to use the default namespace from the item template will end up just creating problems and confusion for you. Likewise, none of the contents of the JavaScript file are required; you'll add your own code shortly.

4. Now add the following XAML to the XAML file:

```
<Grid xmlns="http://schemas.microsoft.com/winfx/2006/xaml/presentation"
      xmlns:x="http://schemas.microsoft.com/winfx/2006/xaml">

</Grid>
```

■ **Note** There is no IntelliSense in the XAML editor as yet. This will come after the next step has been performed.

---

5. Click the "Reload the designer" button in the designer. The error that was being displayed will disappear.

6. Attempting to compile the solution now will result in the following error:

```
Project file must include the .NET Framework assembly 'WindowsBase, PresentationCore,
PresentationFramework' in the reference list.
```

With the designer open now, you can have these references automatically added to your project by simply dragging a TextBox from the Toolbox into the designer. Alternatively you can simply type an open angle bracket (<) in the XAML editor, with the designer open, which will have the same effect. You should now be able to successfully compile the project.

⚙ Workshop: Designing the Application Preloader's Appearance

Now that you have the required files properly configured, you can start adding the content you want to display in the preloader. One of the most important points when creating a preloader is to try to keep it very small. As a general rule, try to keep it less than 5 percent of your application's total size, and no more than 10 KB so that it can download and be displayed to the user as quickly as possible, even on slow connections.

Almost all preloaders display an indicator to the user showing the current progress of the application download. This enables the user to be aware that something is actually happening, and how much longer it might take. The Silverlight plug-in raises an event at a regular interval that you can handle in the JavaScript file, reporting the current progress of the application download. The preloader should also display some branding for both the company and the application.

■ **Note** When implementing preloaders, you will need to stick to using only the controls in the *core* Silverlight runtime. Essentially, you are limited to using Silverlight 1.0 controls only. Controls available for you to use include the Canvas, Grid, StackPanel, InkPresenter, MediaElement, TextBlock, Image, Rectangle, Line, Ellipse, Path, Polygon, and Polyline. However, other controls such as the ProgressBar (which would be very useful in a preloader), Button, and so on are unfortunately not available.

---

1. Add the following XAML to the XAML file that you created in the previous workshop:

```xml
<Grid xmlns="http://schemas.microsoft.com/winfx/2006/xaml/presentation"
      xmlns:x="http://schemas.microsoft.com/winfx/2006/xaml">
    <StackPanel VerticalAlignment="Center">
        <Image Width="352" Height="111" Source="../Logo.png" />
        <TextBlock HorizontalAlignment="Center" Margin="0,10,0,5"
                   Text="Please wait - downloading..." />
        <Grid HorizontalAlignment="Center">
            <Rectangle Stroke="#FF5F91B4" Height="7" Width="454" />
            <Rectangle Fill="#FF5F91B4" Margin="2,0,0,0"
                       Height="3" Width="450" HorizontalAlignment="Left">
                <Rectangle.RenderTransform>
                    <TransformGroup>
                        <ScaleTransform x:Name="ProgressBarTransform" ScaleX="1"/>
```

```
                </TransformGroup>
              </Rectangle.RenderTransform>
          </Rectangle>
      </Grid>

      <TextBlock Name="ProgressText" Text="0%"
                 HorizontalAlignment="Center" Margin="0,0,0,5" />
    </StackPanel>
</Grid>
```

You'll note that instead of using a ProgressBar control in the preloader, we're creating our own "poor man's version" of a progress bar using two Rectangle controls instead. Unfortunately, the ProgressBar control isn't available for us, as it's not in the core Silverlight runtime. Therefore, we need to create our own using only the primitive controls available to us. One rectangle forms the outer border of the progress bar, and an inner rectangle is used as the progress indicator. The trick for this is that you create the progress indicator rectangle, setting its width as it will be when displaying a value of 100 percent, but apply a scale transform that will be used to scale its width in proportion to the progress value it is indicating. By altering the transform's ScaleX property with values between 0 and 1 (in JavaScript code), you will be able to display the progress from 0 percent to 100 percent accordingly. This provides an elegant way to implement the progress bar without needing to worry about calculating the required width in pixels in the JavaScript code. The transform has a name, enabling us to refer to it in the code and adjust the scale accordingly, as you will see in the next workshop.

You will also note the use of the Image control. The Logo.png file it refers to is a file in the Web project, and you are using a relative path to specify its location. Don't be concerned about the fact that the image doesn't appear in the XAML designer; it may not appear there, but it will appear when the preloader is being displayed at runtime.

■ **Note** As with the advice given earlier, you should ensure that any images used are as small as possible, and keep the entire preloader and its resources under 10 KB if you can. You might try running the image through a tool that shrinks the size of images, as these can result in a drastic size reduction. Some of these tools are online tools and, therefore, easy to try. One such tool is available at www.imageoptimizer.net.

⚙ Workshop: Updating the Application Download Progress

Now that you have the visual aspects of your application preloader in place, you need to update the progress being displayed. This involves updating both the progress bar indicator's scale transform, and the text displaying the progress as a percentage.

The Silverlight plug-in has the following two events it raises that you can handle:

- OnSourceDownloadProgressChanged

- OnSourceDownloadComplete

The OnSourceDownloadProgressChanged event will be raised on a regular basis, and you can use the progress property of the EventArgs object passed into the handler as a parameter to determine the progress. This will be a value between 0 and 1, so you can assign this value directly to the ScaleX property of the progress bar indicator's scale transform, and multiply it by 100 to display the value as a percentage.

637

Add the following code to the JavaScript file in order to update the preloader when the onSourceDownloadProgressChanged event is raised:

```
function onSourceDownloadProgressChanged(sender, eventArgs) {
    var progress = Math.round((eventArgs.progress * 100));
    var ProgressBarTransform = sender.findName("ProgressBarTransform");
    var ProgressText = sender.findName("ProgressText");

    if (ProgressBarTransform != null)
        ProgressBarTransform.ScaleX = eventArgs.progress;

    if (ProgressText != null)
        ProgressText.Text = progress + "%";
}
```

■ **Note** This event handler will be wired up in the next section.

The OnSourceDownloadComplete event is called after the application has completed downloading, but is rarely used, as the application will load immediately after it's raised.

⚙ Workshop: Configuring the Preloader in the HTML File

You now have your application preloader's design in place, and the code to update it when the application's download progress changes. However, you now need to actually wire both of these things up so that the Silverlight plug-in knows about them.

1. Start by opening up the HTML page that hosts the Silverlight plug-in. In the head tag, add the following reference to the JavaScript file:

```
<script type="text/javascript" src="AppPreloader.js"></script>
```

2. Now locate the Silverlight plug-in, and add the following two parameters to it:

```
<param name="splashscreensource" value="AppPreloader.xaml"/>
<param name="onSourceDownloadProgressChanged"
       value="onSourceDownloadProgressChanged" />
```

These two parameters connect everything together, and you're now ready to test it all.

■ **Note** Ensure that the HTML or ASPX page you are modifying is actually the file set as the start page for your Web project. Better yet, delete the page you're not using. Otherwise, you might face some confusion wondering why the preloader isn't being displayed, when you are simply browsing the wrong file when you run your application.

Testing the Application Preloader

Testing the application preloader may initially seem like a simple enough task, but it's actually a deceptively complex process. The issue is that when running your application locally, the download process will generally be extremely fast and the preloader will not have time to actually be displayed, or will be displayed only momentarily. This obviously makes it difficult to test and debug. However, there are some tricks you can use to slow down its display. Let's take a look at some of these.

Note You might often get errors such as "Failed to download the splash screen" or "Could not download the Silverlight application. Check web server settings." when debugging your application locally. Alternatively, you could get a blank screen, with neither the preloader nor the application itself loading. This appears to be an issue with the application download in this scenario being faster than it takes to download and display the preloader. This should not be a problem in production environments, however.

Adding a Large File to the Silverlight Project

The easiest thing you can do to try to slow the downloading process and give your application preloader some time to be displayed is to add one or more large files to your Silverlight project in order to increase its size. The larger the project, the longer it will take to download. Simply add a large file to your project, and set its Build Action property to Content by selecting the file in Solution Explorer and then setting the property value in the Properties window. This is a simple way of slowing the download process, but not particularly effective.

Not Assigning the Application's RootVisual

The application preloader is displayed until the RootVisual property of the Application object is assigned. Therefore, if you don't assign a value to this property, the preloader will continue to be displayed indefinitely.

In your Silverlight project, open up the code-behind for the App.xaml file, find the Application_Startup event handler method, and comment out the following line of code:

```
this.InitializeRootVisual();
```

Now when you run your project, the preloader will continue to be displayed, without displaying your main application. This trick won't help you in testing your progress bar, but will help in testing the look and feel of your preloader.

Note Another option is to sleep the thread, using the System.Threading.Thread.Sleep method, for a fixed period immediately prior to initializing the RootVisual.

Using Fiddler

Fiddler is a web debugging proxy that intercepts all incoming and outgoing HTTP/HTTPS connections, enabling you to log and modify the traffic. You can use Fiddler to slow down the downloading of the application, giving you time to view and test the preloader.

■ **Note**   You can download Fiddler for free from `www.fiddler2.com`.

When you open Fiddler, it will immediately start capturing the traffic. Select both the Simulate Modem Speeds and the Disable Caching options from the Rules ➤ Performance menu. This slows down the traffic to simulate 56k modems speeds, and also disables caching such that when you refresh the page, the application will need to be downloaded from the server again, enabling you to test your preloader again without the application being immediately loaded from the browser cache.

Unfortunately, simply running your application is not enough for this all to work. Fiddler bypasses capturing local traffic, but there is a trick that you can use to ensure that it intercepts your application. Change the use of "`localhost`" in the URL in your browser's address bar to "`127.0.0.1.`" (the localhost loopback IP address, followed by another period). This will trick Fiddler into capturing the traffic, and you will find that the application now downloads slowly enough for you to adequately test your preloader. After the application has loaded, you can simply refresh the page to have it downloaded again, because it will not be cached.

Partitioning Your Application

The next issue that you should target is the size of your application. As soon as you start referencing various assemblies and adding assets to your application, it can rapidly increase in size. It will depend on the nature of your application as to whether this is an issue you should be concerned about. In an internal corporate environment where the application will be downloaded from a server located on the local network, this is generally not a particularly big issue. However, if your application is being deployed over the Internet, it becomes something that you should pay closer attention to. The larger the application, the longer it will take for the user to download it and get it up and running, and the more bandwidth it will require (for both you and the user). It provides more of a barrier for the user to use your application and gives them another reason to abandon the attempt. Let's take a look at some strategies you can implement to reduce the size of your application, or partition it into modules that can be downloaded on demand.

Initial Steps

The first step you should take is to look at the size of your `.xap` file and decide on how acceptable its size is. You might want to use the feature of Fiddler, discussed previously, to simulate modem speeds in order to determine how acceptable the time it takes to download might be to various users.

The next step is to ensure you aren't referencing any assemblies or assets not actually being used by your application. If your `.xap` file is still large, then it might be worth analyzing its contents, by changing its extension to `.zip` and unzipping it, as discussed in Chapter 1. Look for the largest files, and determine whether you can remove them or replace them with a suitable alternative.

Assembly Caching

One thing that you can do to partition you application into smaller pieces is to turn on assembly caching for your application. You will find a "Reduce XAP size by using application library caching" option that you can turn on in the project properties for your Silverlight project. Instead of creating a single large .xap file containing all the assemblies required by your application not part of the core Silverlight runtime, using this option will move all the assemblies with an accompanying extension mapping configuration file out of this file and into separate .zip files, as you can see in Figure 17-6.

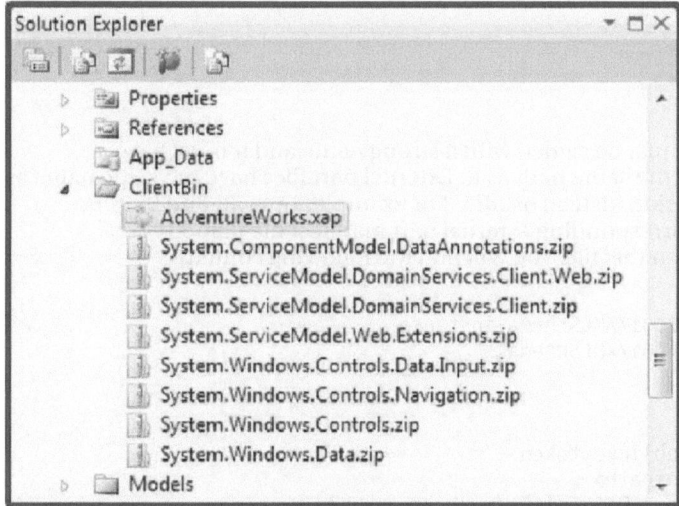

Figure 17-6. *The ClientBin folder when using assembly caching*

Why Use Assembly Caching

Assembly caching will result in the size of the .xap file shrinking. It won't actually reduce the total size of your application when it's initially downloaded, but it provides a big advantage when it comes to deploying updates to your application. Without assembly caching turned on, each time you deploy a new version of your application, the user needs to download the entire application from the server again—including the assemblies referenced by your application that haven't changed.

By turning assembly caching on, when you deploy an application update to the users, only the .xap file containing the application itself will need to be downloaded again. The assemblies referenced by your application that remained unchanged will not need to be downloaded again because they will remain cached in the user's browser cache.

Some of the assemblies, such as System.Windows.Controls.Data.dll, which contains the DataGrid control, are quite large, so requiring these assemblies to be downloaded only when the application is initially deployed will result in much smaller updates.

■ **Note**   One of the big downsides of turning this option on is that it can't be used with applications configured to be installable and run outside the browser. Out-of-browser applications require all of their assemblies to be located in the .xap file, excluding those assemblies downloaded on demand, as described in the next section. If your application is configured to run outside the browser, trying to turn this option on will result in a dialog appearing, requiring you to decide on one option or the other. However, if your application is designed to run solely within the browser, you should take advantage of this option.

How Assembly Caching Works

For an assembly to be able to be cached, it must be signed with a strong name and it must have a corresponding external part manifest file in the same path as it. External part files have the same name as the assembly but have an .extmap.xml extension instead of .dll. For example, you will find that the System.Windows.Data.dll assembly has a corresponding external part manifest file named System.Windows.Data.extmap.xml. If you open this file, you will find the following contents:

```
<?xml version="1.0"?>
<manifest xmlns:xsi="http://www.w3.org/2001/XMLSchema-instance"
          xmlns:xsd="http://www.w3.org/2001/XMLSchema">
  <assembly>
    <name>System.Windows.Data</name>
    <version>2.0.5.0</version>
    <publickeytoken>31bf3856ad364e35</publickeytoken>
    <relpath>System.Windows.Data.dll</relpath>
    <extension downloadUri="System.Windows.Data.zip" />
  </assembly>
</manifest>
```

This essentially defines the path where the assembly can be found, and where it can download the package containing it. When an external part manifest file is found for an assembly, and assembly caching is turned on, the assembly will be excluded from the .xap file, and packaged into its own .zip file, having the name as the download URI specified in the external part file.

■ **Note**   If the external part manifest file specifies an absolute URI, the assembly won't be packaged into a .zip file. Instead, it will be downloaded from the specified URI rather than from the site from where the application is being downloaded. However, this is a cross-domain operation and, hence, requires a cross-domain policy file put in place in the root of the site from where the package is to be downloaded. See Chapter 5 for more information on implementing cross-domain policy files.

The assembly will then be referenced in the Deployment.ExternalParts section of the AppManifest.xaml file in the .xap file, enabling the Silverlight plug-in to know what additional packages it needs to download before it can run the application.

Enabling Your Own Assemblies to Be Cached

If you inspect your .xap file's contents, by changing its extension to .zip and unzipping it, as discussed in Chapter 1, you might find that not all the referenced assemblies have been packaged as external parts and are still packaged in your .xap file—particularly assemblies that you created yourself. For an assembly to be cached, it must be signed with a strong name and have an external part manifest file.

⚙ Workshop: Signing an Assembly

In this workshop, you'll learn how to sign an assembly with a strong name.

1. Open up the project properties for the project, and open the Signing tab.

2. Select the "Sign the assembly" check box as shown in Figure 17-7.

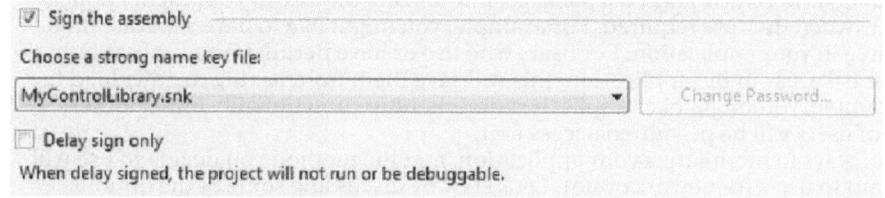

Figure 17-7. *Configuring the strong name for the assembly*

3. Select <New...> from the drop-down list, and enter a name and password for the strong name key file in the dialog that appears.

    The next time your application is compiled, it will then be signed.

⚙ Workshop: Creating an External Part Manifest File

The next step is to create the external part manifest file. The easiest way to create this is to use the DevCorner ExtMap Maker Utility tool created by Alex Golesh, which you can download from http://blogs.microsoft.co.il/blogs/alex_golesh/archive/2011/11/24/utility-extmap-maker-v1-1.aspx. This is a command-line utility, named Emm.exe, that you can point to your assembly, passing the path to the assembly as its command-line parameter, and it will create a corresponding external part manifest file for you in the same path as the assembly is located.

   In this workshop, we'll demonstrate configuring a class library project to generate the .extmap.xml file each time you compile it. This assumes the class library project already exists, and is referenced by your main application.

1. Add a folder named Libs to your class library project.

2. Download the ExtMap Maker tool, and put the Emm.exe file in the Libs folder.

3. Open the class library's project properties window, and open the Build Events tab.

4. Add the following line to the post-build command line:

```
"$(ProjectDir)Libs\Emm" "$(TargetPath)"
```

5. Compile the project. You'll note that when you next compile the main application, a `.zip` file will be created for the assembly, and it will no longer be packaged into the `.xap` file.

■ **Note** You won't be able to perform the preceding procedure for third-party assemblies, but you can still run the ExtMap Maker tool to generate an `.extmap.xml` file for the assembly using the command line and store that file in the same location from where the `.dll` file is being referenced.

Downloading Modules on Demand

Another way you can partition your application is by breaking it up into modules, each in their own assembly. These can be excluded from the main `.xap` package, minimizing the size of your main application, and downloaded only when they are required. For example, you might like to have separate modules for each functional area in your application. For users who use or have permission to access only one or two of those functional areas in the application, this will save them from having to download the entire application. For example, you might like to split the administrative functionality into another module, as only a subset of users will be permitted access to it.

There are a number of ways to modularize your application, and the method you decide to use will often depend on if you want to use a framework or not. Let's start by discussing some of the options available to you, and then look at implementing a simple means of modularizing your application.

One of the key decisions will be whether you are prepared to use an existing framework to modularize your application, or whether you'd rather create your own custom solution. Incorporating a framework can provide many benefits in addition to the modularization; however, it may also impose on the structure and design of your application—which, depending on the stage you are at in your development process, may or may not be an issue. Frameworks can also introduce additional complexity into your application and incur a significant learning curve. It will depend on the nature of both your application and your team as to whether you are prepared to undertake this process.

The most popular frameworks for implementing modularization in Silverlight applications include Prism and the Managed Extensibility Framework (MEF).

Downloading Modules on Demand Using the Navigation Framework

An option that doesn't rely on a framework such as Prism or MEF is to create a custom content loader for the Navigation Framework, which we briefly discussed in Chapter 3. This technique allows you to split your application's views up into separate assemblies. When the user navigates to a view in another assembly, the custom content loader needs to check whether that assembly is in the cache and, if not, download it. After it is downloaded, the requested view within that assembly can then be displayed within the frame.

David Poll has an excellent method for doing this that he has documented on his blog at `www.davidpoll.com/2010/02/01/on-demand-loading-of-assemblies-with-silverlight-navigation-revisited-for-silverlight-4-beta/`. He provides an easy way of implementing this behavior, which you can take advantage of in your Silverlight project by referencing some assemblies he's created, and following the instructions he has provided in his blog post.

Jeff Prosise also has an excellent article on implementing a content loader that dynamically downloads content, using a different method than David's, at `www.wintellect.com/CS/blogs/jprosise/archive/2010/06/27/dynamic-page-loading-in-silverlight-navigation-apps.aspx`.

Downloading Modules on Demand Using Prism

We discussed Prism in Chapter 14, and if you're using Prism within your Silverlight application, your best option is to use Prism's built-in on-demand module loading behavior. One of the key benefits of designing Silverlight applications according to the Prism guidance is how it encourages you to modularize your application's structure. Therefore, your application should already be in a state where you can identify modules than can be downloaded on demand. To make a module load on demand, you essentially need to set its InitializationMode to OnDemand. You can do so in code, in XAML, or in the application's configuration. More information on this topic can be found in Chapter 4 of the Prism guide at http://msdn.microsoft.com/en-us/library/gg405479.aspx. You might also find the Prism Navigation Framework project on CodePlex useful (http://prismnavigation.codeplex.com), created by Slobodan Pavkov.

Downloading Modules on Demand Using MEF

We discussed MEF in Chapter 14, but one of its features not mentioned there was its DeploymentCatalog feature. This feature allows you to break down your application into multiple XAP files, which can be downloaded on demand, and stitch the pieces back together.

■ **Note** An in-depth discussion of MEF's DeploymentCatalog feature is beyond the scope of this book, but you can find out more information about it from http://mef.codeplex.com/wikipage?title=DeploymentCatalog.

 Workshop: Modularizing Your Application

In this workshop, we're going to modularize a Silverlight application, breaking it up into multiple XAP files, and make use of a prebuilt assembly (MEFModuleLoader) to help us download and display the content from the modules on demand. The MEFModuleLoader assembly provides a custom content loader for the Navigation Framework, which will automatically download a module when the user navigates to a view in it. After the module has downloaded, the requested view will be displayed within the shell application's Frame control. By wrapping all this functionality, you just need to focus on modularizing your application, and the MEFModuleLoader assembly will take care of the rest.

■ **Note** The MEFModuleLoader assembly is based upon a project on CodePlex named Silverlight MEF (http://silverlightmef.codeplex.com), by Michael Albaladejo, but with some slight modifications to make it easier for you to drop into a Silverlight project and start using it. You can find this assembly and its source code in the sample code for this chapter (downloadable from the Source Code/Download area of the Apress web site [www.apress.com]).

---

1. Create a solution folder named Modules in your solution, and create a solution folder under it for each module. Create a corresponding folder structure on disk.

2. Add a new project to the solution folder for each module, using the Silverlight Application project template to create it. The code in this workshop will use a module named AdventureWorks.ProductionModule. When the project wizard dialog appears, have the module hosted by the Web project, but deselect the "Add a test page that references the application" check box. Leave the "Enable WCF RIA Services" check box unchecked.

3. Turn on assembly caching for the shell project and each of the module projects, by selecting the "Reduce XAP size by using application library caching" option in its project properties.

■ **Note** The "shell" project is the main Silverlight application that will host the modules. This workshop will assume that your shell project is named AdventureWorks.

---

4. Create a solution folder named Libs. Get the MEFModuleLoader assembly, which you can find in the sample code for this chapter (downloadable from the Apress web site [www.apress.com]), and put it in this Libs solution folder. You're solution structure should now look something like that shown in Figure 17-8.

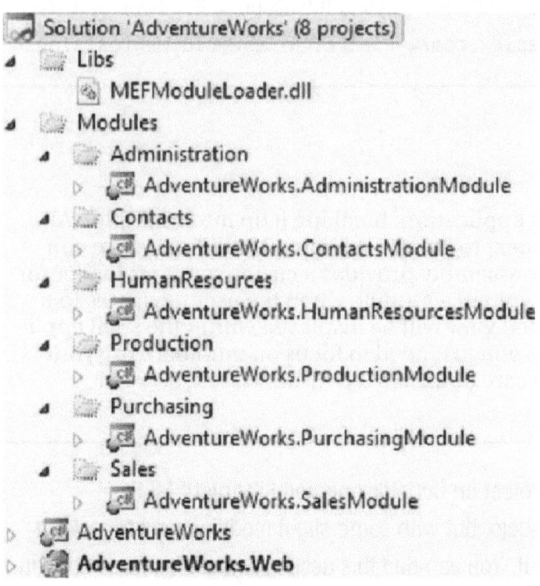

Figure 17-8. *The modularlized solution structure*

5. Add a reference to the MEFModuleLoader assembly to the shell project and each of the module projects.

6. Each view in a module must have the ExportModulePage attribute (found in the MEFModuleLoader.Attributes namespace) from the MEFModuleLoader assembly applied to its class in the code-behind.

```
[ExportModulePage(NavigateUri="MainPage")]
public partial class MainPage : Page
```

7. Each module needs a reference to the following assemblies, as does the shell:

```
System.ComponentModel.Composition.dll
System.ComponentModel.Composition.Initialization.dll
System.Windows.Controls.Navigation.dll
```

8. Open the MainPage.xaml file in the shell project. Define the contentLoader namespace prefix in this file, like so:

```
xmlns:contentLoader="clr-namespace:MEFModuleLoader.ContentLoader;assembly=MEFModuleLoader"
```

9. Set the ContentLoader property on the Frame control, as follows:

```
<navigation:Frame.ContentLoader>
    <contentLoader:MEFContentLoader />
</navigation:Frame.ContentLoader>
```

10. Define a resource at the view level, instantiating a ModulesLoadingStatusModel object provided by the MEFModuleLoader assembly. This has a property named IsBusy, which will be set to true when a module is downloading.

```
<UserControl.Resources>
    <contentLoader:ModulesLoadingStatusModel x:Key="loadingStatus" />
</UserControl.Resources>
```

11. We now want to show a message to the user when a module is downloading. Define the controls namespace prefix as follows. (Note that this namespace will depend on your project's name and assumes that you've used the Silverlight Business Application project template when creating the shell project.)

```
xmlns:controls="clr-namespace:AdventureWorks.Controls"
```

Then wrap the MainPage user control's existing content in a BusyIndicator control, like so:

```
<controls:BusyIndicator IsBusy="{Binding IsBusy, Source={StaticResource loadingStatus}}"
                        BusyContent="Please wait - downloading module...">
    <Grid x:Name="LayoutRoot" Style="{StaticResource LayoutRootGridStyle}">
        <!--Remainder of content excluded for brevity-->
    </Grid>
</controls:BusyIndicator>
```

12. You now need to provide a way for users to navigate to the content in the modules. Start by adding a URI mapping for each module, that you want the application to be able to download and use.

```
<uriMapper:UriMapping Uri="Production/{pageName}"
                      MappedUri="AdventureWorks.ProductionModule.xap;{pageName}"/>
```

■ **Note** These module URI mappings will need to be positioned between the blank URI mapping and the generic /{pageName} URI mapping.

---

13. You can then create links that navigate to pages in each module. For example:

```
<HyperlinkButton NavigateUri="/Production/ProductListView" Content="Products" />
```

14. Now run your application. When you click on a link to a view in a module, you'll see the BusyIndicator control briefly appear as the module is being downloaded, and after the download is complete, the view that you've requested will be displayed in the Frame control in the shell application. If you navigate away from this view and then back again, you'll find that the view immediately loads, as the module has been cached so that it does not need to be downloaded again during this session.

⚙ Workshop: Communication Between the Shell Application and the Modules

You will often find that your shell application and the modules need to communicate with each other. The shell project should have no direct reference to any of the module projects, and the module projects should have no direct reference to each other either. Instead, any communication should be via objects in a "Common" assembly that all these projects reference. In this workshop, we'll look at how you can create this assembly, and use it to enable the projects to communicate with each other.

1. Create a class library project named AdventureWorks.Common, using the Silverlight Class Library project template.

2. Configure it to permit it to participate in assembly caching, as detailed in the "Assembly Caching" section of this chapter. In summary, sign the assembly, and create an .extmap.xml file for it.

3. The shell project and each of the module projects should each add a reference to this common assembly.

4. There are a number of ways you can enable the shell and the modules to communicate with each other using this assembly. One way is to have commands in this file that a listener can define and that others can execute. Let's look at how you can enable the modules to request that the shell display the login window using this method. Start by creating a static class named GlobalCommands in the common assembly, containing a public field named ShowLoginWindow of type ICommand, like so:

```
public static class GlobalCommands
{
    public static ICommand ShowLoginWindow = null;
}
```

5. Define a ShowLoginWindow command implementation in the shell project. For example:

```
public class ShowLoginWindowCommand : ICommand
{
    public bool CanExecute(object parameter)
```

```
    {
        return !WebContext.Current.User.IsAuthenticated;
    }

    public event EventHandler CanExecuteChanged;

    public void Execute(object parameter)
    {
        if (CanExecute(parameter))
        {
            LoginRegistrationWindow loginWindow = new LoginRegistrationWindow();
            loginWindow.Show();
        }
    }
}
```

6. Assign an instance of this command to the ShowLoginWindow field in the GlobalCommands class. This can be done at any time by the shell project, including just as the application starts up, in the Application object's Startup event handler, as follows:

```
GlobalCommands.ShowLoginWindow = new ShowLoginWindowCommand();
```

7. Modules can now execute this command, and the shell project will display the login window:

```
GlobalCommands.ShowLoginWindow.Execute(null);
```

■ **Note** You can also use this common assembly to share resources and data between the shell project and the modules. For example, you can extract the resource files defining the application's theme/styling into this assembly, from which both the shell project and the modules can then reference them.

Using RIA Services with Modular Applications

One of the issues you'll face with modularizing your application is how to work RIA Services into this structure. By default, RIA Services generates code directly into the shell project, which the modules will not be able to access. So how can you modularize your application but still take advantage of RIA Services? There are two solutions, and both require use of the RIA Services class library feature.

In Chapter 4, we looked at how you could extract your domain services and the code generated by the RIA Services code generator from your Web project and Silverlight project, respectively, into class libraries (see the section "Encapsulating Logic in a Separate WCF RIA Services Class Library"). If you follow the workshop that leads you through this process in that chapter, and configure the client class library project to support application caching, you will have an assembly that your shell project and all the modules can reference and share. The downside of this approach is that you will end up with one monolithic assembly, containing all the domain contexts, models, and shared code required by your application.

A better approach is to create a pair of RIA Services class library projects for each individual module in your application. The result of this structure is that each module can have its own dedicated set of domain services and corresponding domain contexts, and can include the client RIA Services class library in its

XAP file, where the domain contexts, models, and shared code that it uses will only be downloaded to the client when the module is downloaded.

Creating RIA Services class library projects was also covered in Chapter 4, but you don't need to go through all the steps that the workshop walked you through for each module. To create these projects for a module, simply add a new project to the solution folder for the module, using the RIA Services Class Library project template. This will create pair of class library projects: one for the server and one for the client. Add a reference to the client class library project to the module project, and add a reference to the server class library project to the Web project. You can then start adding domain services to the server class library project for the module to consume. You can find an example of this structure in the sample code accompanying this chapter, downloadable from the Source Code/Download area of the Apress web site (www.apress.com).

■ **Note** Domain services/contexts that are shared by multiple modules can be maintained in a common pair of RIA Services class library projects, which they all can share and reference in addition to their own dedicated pair of RIA Services class library projects.

Digitally Signing Your Application

In some scenarios, you should sign your XAP file before deploying it to the users. Let's look at when you would want to do so, and how you do so.

Why Sign Your Application

Following are three key reasons why you might want to sign your application:

- If you want your Silverlight application to be able to run inside the browser with elevated trust privileges, your application can only do so when the XAP file is signed.

- When the user tries to install an unsigned Silverlight application to run outside the browser with elevated trust privileges, it will display a rather stern warning in the install dialog, as shown in Figure 17-9, stating that the publisher could not be verified. When you see this warning, it means that the application has not been signed. Signing your application will still show a dialog, but it will be a much friendlier one.

- You might want to sign your application if it is configured to run in OOB mode with elevated trust privileges. For an application that has elevated trust privileges to be updatable, the XAP file must be signed. Application updates will work when the site of origin for the application is localhost, but they will fail once the application goes into production if it isn't signed.

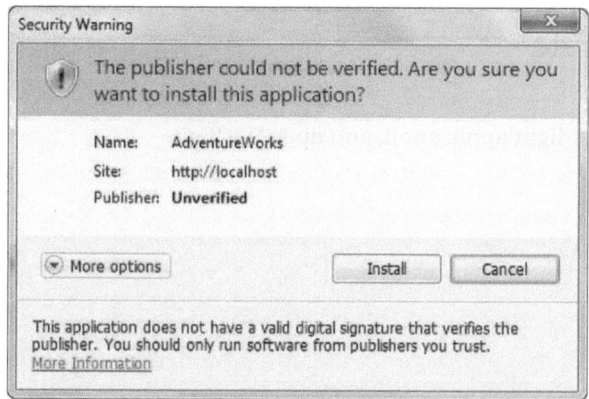

Figure 17-9. The installation dialog for unsigned applications that request elevated trust privileges

■ **Note** When the application is being updated, the certificate of the existing application must match that of the update, and the certificate must still not have expired. Otherwise, the update will fail.

If your Silverlight application does not meet any of these criteria, you can still sign your XAP file if you wish, but doing so will have no impact on its execution.

Obtaining a Code-Signing Certificate

Signing an XAP file involves obtaining a verified Authenticode code-signing certificate from a trusted certificate authority (CA). The process of obtaining a certificate is beyond the scope of this book, but you can find a thorough walkthrough written by Jeff Wilcox on his blog, available at www.jeff.wilcox.name/2010/02/codesigning101/.

■ **Note** A code-signing certificate is not the same as an SSL certificate.

In summary, you purchase a certificate from a CA, they will verify your identity, and (generally) within a couple of days they will issue you with a valid certificate. You can then export the certificate from your certificate store as a .pfx file, which you can then use to sign your XAP file.

■ **Note** If you don't have a code-signing certificate but still want to sign your application for testing purposes, you can create a self-signed certificate. We'll look at how you can do this in the following workshop.

⚙️ Workshop: Signing Your XAP File

Let's look at how you go about signing the XAP file.

1. Open the Project Properties for your Silverlight application, and open the Signing tab, as shown in Figure 17-10.

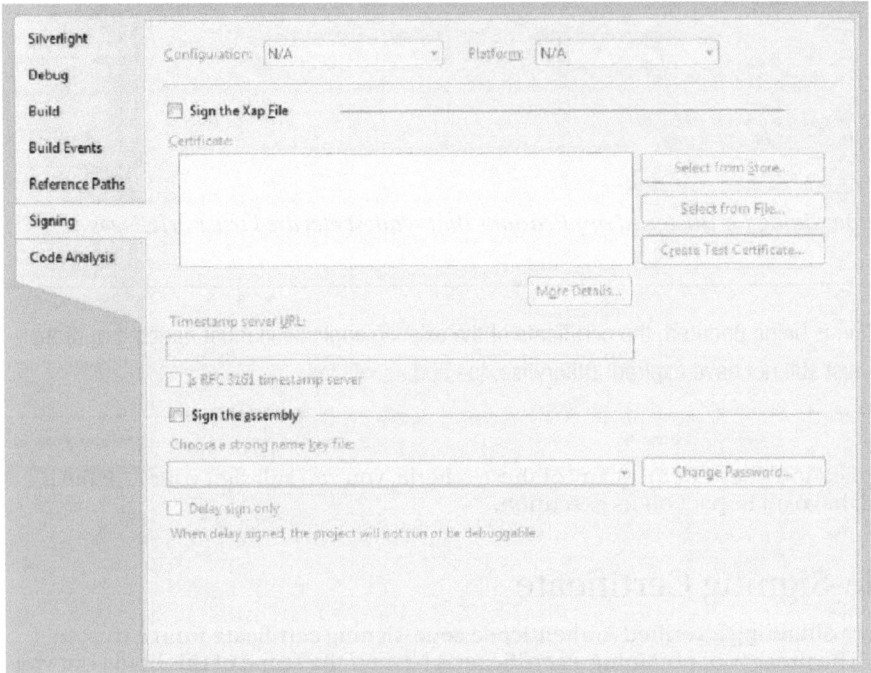

Figure 17-10. The Signing tab in the Project Properties

2. Select the "Sign the Xap File" check box, and click the Select from File button. Find your .pfx file and select it. Its details will appear in the Certificate box.

■ **Note** Alternatively, if you don't have a certificate from a CA, you can create your own temporary certificate for use while you are testing the application. Click the Create Test Certificate button, and enter a password in the two text boxes in the dialog that appears. This simple process will create a .pfx file for you and add it to your project for use during the compilation process.

---

3. You now need to install the certificate as a Trusted Root certificate on your machine. Click the More Details button, which will display the dialog shown in Figure 17-11.

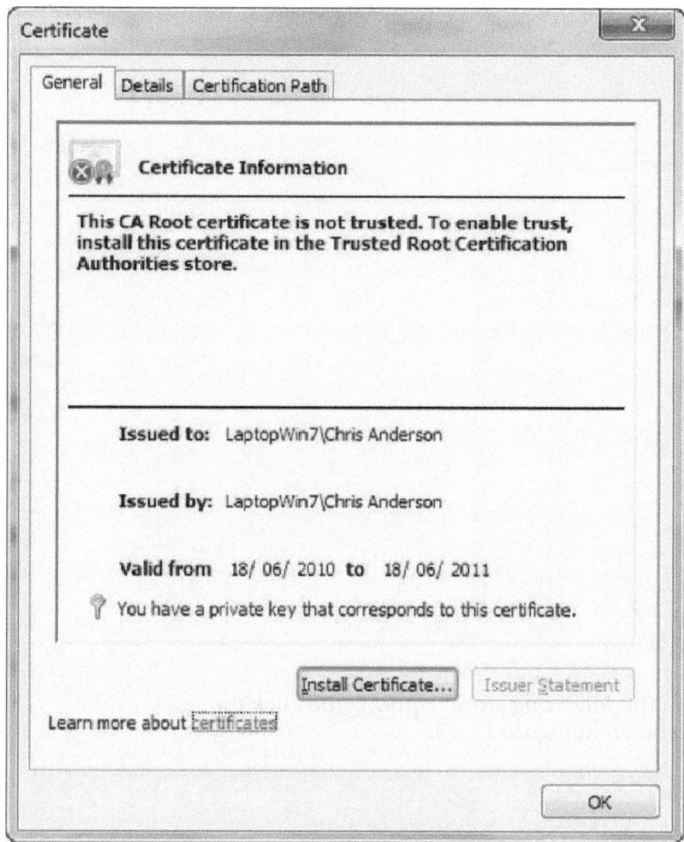

Figure 17-11. The Certificate Information dialog

4.   If this dialog says that this CA root certificate is not trusted, you will need to install it. Click the Install Certificate button, and click through the wizard to the screen shown in Figure 17-12.

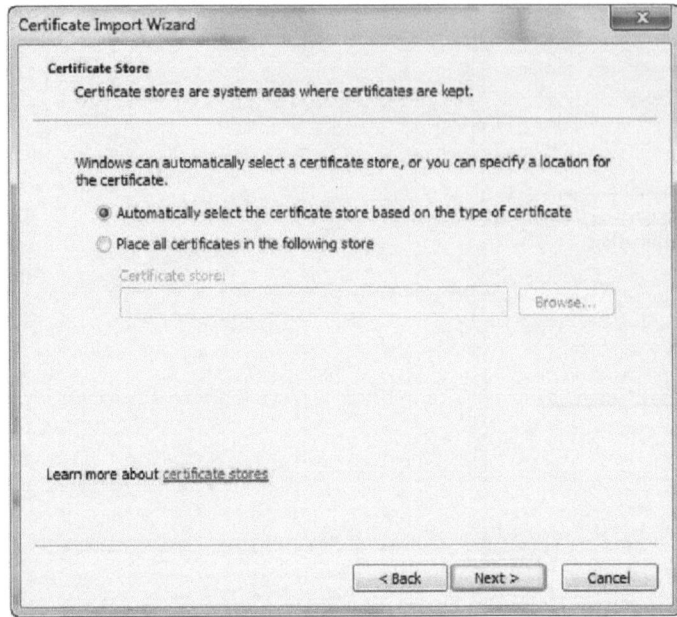

Figure 17-12. The Certificate Import Wizard dialog

    5.   Select the "Place all certificates in the following store" option, and click the
Browse button to see the dialog shown in Figure 17-13.

Figure 17-13. Selecting a certificate store

    6.   Select the Trusted Root Certification Authorities store, and press OK. Finish
the wizard, and the certificate will be successfully installed.

    7.   Now when you compile and run your application, you will get the much
friendlier install dialog, as displayed in Figure 17-14.

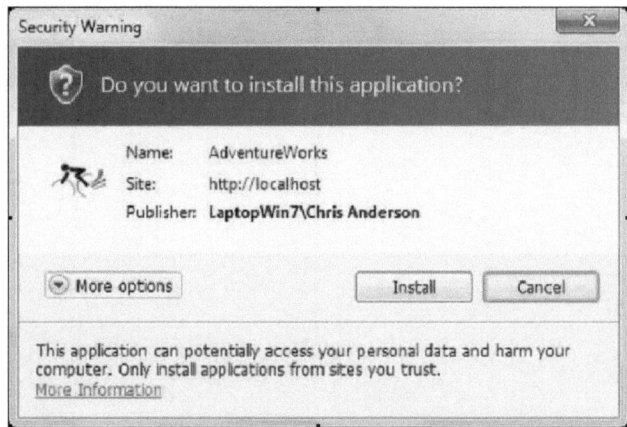

Figure 17-14. The installation dialog for signed applications that request elevated trust

Summary

In this chapter, you've seen how to deploy your application to both the server and the client, and how you can improve the Silverlight install and application download user experience. Despite being fairly easy, adding personalization and branding to the application deployment is often overlooked by Silverlight developers. However, doing so can create a more positive experience for the user and avoid confusion. Finally, you saw how you can partition your application into small modules, streamlining the entire application deployment experience to the user, reducing both waiting times and user frustration.

Index

A

X, Y, Z